EASY CAR CARE 4th Edition

W9-AXC-327

CHILTON'S CHILTON'S

President	Dean F. Morgantini, S.A.E.
Vice President–Finance	Barry L. Beck
Vice President–Sales	Glenn D. Potere
Executive Editor	Kevin M. G. Maher
Production Manager	Ben Greisler, S.A.E.
Production Assistant	Melinda Possinger
Project Managers	George B. Heinrich III, S.A.E., Will Kessler, A.S.E., S.A.E., James R. Marotta, S.T.S., Richard Schwartz, Todd W. Stidham
Schematics Editor	Christopher G. Ritchie
Editor	W. Calvin Settle, Jr.

CHILTON™ Automotive Books

PUBLISHED BY **W. G. NICHOLS, INC.**

Manufactured in USA
© 1998 W. G. Nichols
1020 Andrew Drive
West Chester, PA 19380
ISBN 0-8019-8852-7
Library of Congress Catalog Card No. 98-71219
1234567890 7654321098

Contents

Contents

Contents

Contents

TRAILER TOWING **27**

BODY CARE AND REPAIR **28**

ANTI-THEFT SYSTEMS **29**

BUYING AND OWNING A VEHICLE **30**

HOW TO DEAL WITH MOTOR VEHICLE EMERGENCIES **31**

WAYS TO SAVE FUEL **32**

GLOSSARY **33**

MASTER INDEX

SAFETY NOTICE

Proper service and repair procedures are vital to the safe, reliable operation of all motor vehicles, as well as the personal safety of those performing repairs. This manual outlines procedures for servicing and repairing vehicles using safe, effective methods. The procedures contain many NOTES, CAUTIONS and WARNINGS which should be followed, along with standard procedures, to eliminate the possibility of personal injury or improper service which could damage the vehicle or compromise its safety.

It is important to note that repair procedures and techniques, tools and parts for servicing motor vehicles, as well as the skill and experience of the individual performing the work, vary widely. It is not possible to anticipate all of the conceivable ways or conditions under which vehicles may be serviced, or to provide cautions as to all possible hazards that may result. Standard and accepted safety precautions and equipment should be used during cutting, grinding, chiseling, prying, or any other process that can cause material removal or projectiles.

Some procedures require the use of tools specially designed for a specific purpose. Before substituting another tool or procedure, you must be completely satisfied that neither your personal safety, nor the performance of the vehicle, will be endangered.

Although information in this manual is based on industry sources and is complete as possible at the time of publication, the possibility exists that some vehicle manufacturers made later changes which could not be included here. While striving for total accuracy, NP/Chilton cannot assume responsibility for any errors, changes or omissions that may occur in the compilation of this data.

PART NUMBERS

Part numbers listed in this reference are not recommendations by Chilton for any product brand name. They are references that can be used with interchange manuals and aftermarket supplier catalogs to locate each brand supplier's discrete part number.

SPECIAL TOOLS

Special tools are recommended by the vehicle manufacturer to perform their specific job. Use has been kept to a minimum, but, where absolutely necessary, they are referred to in the text by the part number of the tool manufacturer. These tools can be purchased, under the appropriate part number, from your local dealer or regional distributor, or an equivalent tool can be purchased locally from a tool supplier or parts outlet. Before substituting any tool for the one recommended, read the SAFETY NOTICE at the top of this page.

ACKNOWLEDGMENTS

A special thanks to the fine companies who supported the production of this book. Hand tools, supplied by Craftsman, were used during all phases of vehicle teardown and photography. Many of the fine specialty tools used in procedures were provided courtesy of Lisle Corporation. Lincoln Automotive Products has provided their industrial shop equipment including jacks, engine stands and shop presses. A Rotary lift, the largest automobile lift manufacturer in the world offering the biggest variety of surface and inground lifts available, was also used.

The editors express appreciation to the following manufacturers for their cooperation and technical assistance:

- 303 Products, Inc. — Palo Cedro, CA
- Bayco Products, Inc — Dallas, Texas
- B-Seen Products — Cinnaminson, NJ
- Cal-Van Tools — Fremont, OH
- CMI Inc. — Lake Bluff, IL
- Cooper Automotive — Chesterfield, MO
- Critzas Industries, Inc. "GOOP" — Saint Louis, MO
- Double Duty Container Co. — St. George, UT
- Eagle One Industries — Carlsbad, CA
- Enviro Motive — Lake Park, FL
- Gas-O-Haul — Lamar, CO
- Gent-l-kleen® Products, Inc. — York, PA
- HC Protek — Northvale, NJ
- Liquid Glass Enterprises, Inc. — Teaneck, NJ
- Lisle Corp. — Clarinda, IA
- MAAS Polishing Systemes® — Willowbrook, IL
- Mothers® Polishes, Waxes, Cleaners — Huntington Beach, CA
- Nupla Corp. — Sun Valley, CA
- Pressure, Inc. — Telford, PA
- Star brite — Ft. Lauderdale, FL
- Stoner, Inc. — Quarryville, PA
- Syon Corp. — Ashland, MA
- Treatment Products Ltd. — Chicago, IL
- Tru-Cut Automotive — Salem, OH
- Unelko Corp. "Rain-X" — Scottsdale, AZ
- Valco Cincinnati, Inc. — Cincinnati, OH
- Versa Chem® — West Palm Beach, FL
- WEN Products, Inc. — Bensenville, IL

1

TOOLS
& SUPPLIES

TOOLS AND SUPPLIES

Analyze Your Needs

Nearly everybody needs some tools, whether they're just for fixing the kitchen sink, or overhauling the engine in the family vehicle. As far as vehicle repairs go, pliers and a can of oil aren't going to get you very far down the path of do-it-yourself service. However, you don't have to equip your garage like the local service station either. Somewhere between these two extremes, there's a level that suits the average do-it-yourselfer. Just where that point is depends on your needs, your ability and your interest. The trick is to match your tools and equipment to the jobs you're willing and able to tackle.

Choose Your Own Level

To sort things out in an orderly manner, think about your repair work in three levels: basic, average and advanced. Before you purchase any tools, sit down and determine your present level of mechanical expertise. After you have determined that (be honest), determine just how far you intend to progress as an amateur mechanic. Knowing what you can and/or will do in the way of automotive repairs is the most important step you can take. Obviously, if all you ever intend to do is to change the oil and the plugs now and then, you won't need very many tools. If, however, you plan some extensive repair work, you're going to end up with a complete collection of tools.

Once you have determined your level of mechanical involvement, evaluate your tool purchases on a "must have" and a "nice-to-have" basis.

BASIC LEVEL

At a basic level of involvement, you'll probably do such things as check the coolant, oil and other fluid levels, and change the oil and filter. You also might perform basic maintenance, keep an eye on the tire pressures, keep the vehicle waxed and polished, and perhaps perform some minor body touch-up.

AVERAGE LEVEL

The average level involvement will probably include replacing belts and hoses, replacing shocks, and engine tune-up.

ADVANCED LEVEL

At the advanced level, you might dig deeply enough to re-line the brakes, check compression, install a trailer hitch, replace a bad muffler, or repair body damage.

➡ **The advanced level would be a good choice for someone getting into the automotive service profession.**

Basic Tools

▶ **See Figures 1 and 2**

After you've determined your level of mechanical expertise, and how far you want to progress as an amateur mechanic, you have to buy some tools. No matter what level you have decided on, there are some tools you must have. These include pliers, open and box end wrenches, a ratchet and sockets, various types of screwdrivers, some punches and chisels, a hammer and hacksaw.

It will be worth your while to buy quality hand tools. You can buy tools in supermarkets but they'll probably only cause you grief. Stick to the name-brand tools and you won't go wrong. Manufacturers like Craftsman, Mac, Snap-On, SK etc. make top-quality tools that will last a lifetime. Many name-brand tools are also sold with a "no questions" guarantee. If you break it, just take it back and it will be replaced, no questions asked. So, buy your tools from a reputable tool manufacturer. You'll pay a little more, but it's worth it to avoid skinned knuckles and rounded-off bolts.

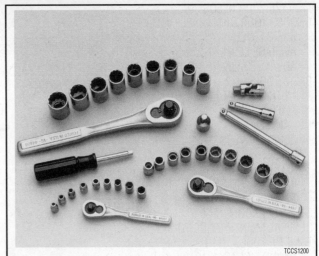

TCCS1200

Fig. 1 All but the most basic procedures will require an assortment of ratchets

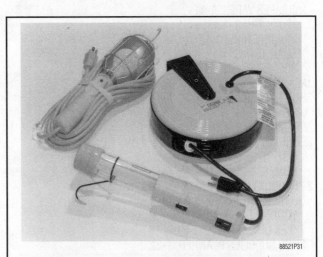

88521P31

Fig. 2 Trouble lights come in a variety of configurations. The Incandescent model on the left is the old stand-by, however the florescent work light remains cool with use and is excellent for working in close quarters.

METRIC OR SAE?

▶ **See Figures 3 and 4**

There are two different types of fasteners used on vehicles today, metric and SAE. While SAE is actually the abbreviation for Society of Automotive Engineers, it is the common term frequently used to describe U.S. standard or fractional fasteners.

Deciding whether you needed metric or SAE tools did not use to be a problem. Years ago, American made vehicles used SAE fasteners, and import vehicles used metric. These days with components for American vehicles being engineered in various places using both SAE and Metric measurements you may find your domestic vehicle has both types of fasteners used. If you own an import vehicle, more than likely you'll need metric tools. Likewise, if you have a late-model American vehicle, you might need some, or all metric tools.

Common metric fasteners and the wrench size required are listed in the following chart.

SAE/METRIC WRENCH SIZES

Many import cars and a few American cars use metric wrench sizes. In a few cases, an SAE wrench or socket may appear to fit a metric bolt, but a chewed up bolt and skinned knuckles will be the only result. It's always best to use the right size wrench. The following chart compares common SAE and metric wrench sizes.

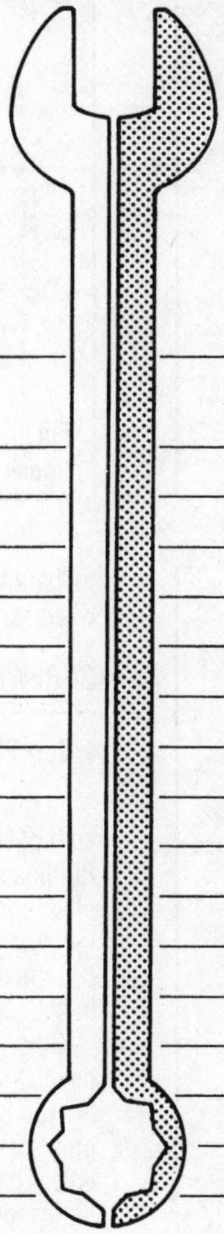

SAE Wrench Sizes

Metric Wrench Sizes

INCHES	DECIMAL		DECIMAL	MILLIMETERS
1/8"	.125		.118	3mm
3/16"	.187		.157	4mm
1/4"	.250		.236	6mm
5/16"	.312		.354	9mm
3/8"	.375		.394	10mm
7/16"	.437		.472	12mm
1/2"	.500		.512	13mm
9/16"	.562		.590	15mm
5/8"	.625		.630	16mm
11/16"	.687		.709	18mm
3/4"	.750		.748	19mm
13/16"	.812		.787	20mm
7/8"	.875		.866	22mm
15/16"	.937		.945	24mm
1"	1.00		.984	25mm

88521G02

Fig. 3 SAE and Metric wrench sizes

Fastener Size (Millimeters)	Required Wrench
4 × .7	7 mm
5 × .8	8 mm
6.3 × 1	10 mm
8 × 1.25	13 mm
10 × 1.5	15 mm
12 × 1.75	18 mm
14 × 2	21 mm
16 × 2	24 mm

88521G03

Fig. 4 Metric fastener to wrench sizes

Before you buy any tools, check with your dealer to determine just what kind of fasteners your vehicle has. Some American vehicles are metric, while some are part metric and part SAE. Also, keep in mind that some import vehicles (such as Volvo) utilize some SAE fasteners.

While there are some points of interchange between the metric and inch sizes, it's not a good idea to use metric wrenches on SAE fasteners and vice versa. In an emergency, you can use anything that will fit, but prolonged use will only ruin the fastener.

PLIERS

▶ See Figures 5 and 6

Pliers come in a variety of shapes and sizes and you'll probably need at least three different kinds for a beginning tool kit. The regular slip-joint kind that everyone is familiar with is an absolute necessity. Long-nosed or needle-nosed pliers should be in everyone's tool kit also. The number of jobs these two tools are good for is endless. Locking pliers (commonly called Vise Grips®) are so useful; you'll wonder how you ever got along without them. A good pair of cutting pliers is necessary for any kind of wiring job.

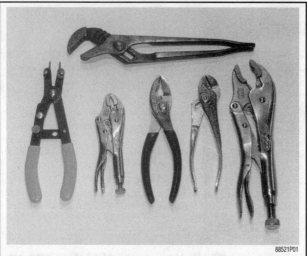

Fig. 5 Pliers come in all shapes and sizes. Locking pliers are handy for removing old rusted parts.

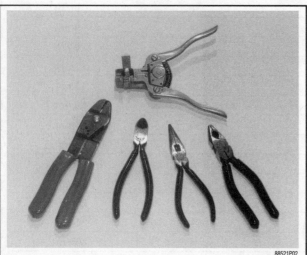

Fig. 6 Wire strippers and cutting pliers are handy for doing electrical work

Eventually, you may want to add specialized pliers. There are pointed-tip pliers for spreading lock rings and hooked pliers for removing brake springs. Some pliers have a groove in the end to compress the wire hose clamps used on many radiator hoses, although these can be made from a pair of old pliers by filing a groove in the end.

Wire strippers are also handy for electrical work. Most have special grooves for stripping various gauges of wire without cutting the wire inside.

HAMMERS

▶ See Figure 7

Hammers come in four basic types—machinist's (ball peen), plastic (soft faced), sledge, and dead blow. The basic hammer for a mechanic is the ball peen. If you already have a good claw hammer, keep it with your carpentry tools, it won't do for automotive use.

If you are going to buy a hammer, get one with an 8- or 12-ounce head that is drop forged and heat-treated. The handle of a quality hammer will be hickory, ash or fiberglass.

A soft faced mallet is useful in situations where less force is required,

Fig. 7 A variety of hammers are useful for different applications—Ball peen, soft faced, sledges, and dead blow.

rubber mallets are good for installing snap-on hubcaps, and other jobs where you don't want to mar the surface.

SCREWDRIVERS

▶ See Figures 8, 9, 10 and 11

Screwdrivers are another must for anyone planning to do any sort of automobile repair work. There are two general types of screwdrivers—Phillips head and slot head screwdrivers. Keep in mind that these types of screwdrivers come in various sizes, so just because you have a slotted head screwdriver, and a Phillips head doesn't mean you're going to be able to fit every screw you come across. Screwdrivers are often sold in sets containing all the common types.

Other specialized screwdrivers (Torx® and Reed Prince tips, clutch head, butterfly) are only useful if your vehicle uses screws that they will fit. The best practice is to acquire them as necessary. If you are working on a screw in an awkward location, a magnetic screwdriver is indispensable. There are also locking screwdrivers known as screw starters that are handy for this operation. Many of the magnetic screwdrivers have interchangeable bits for various types of screw heads.

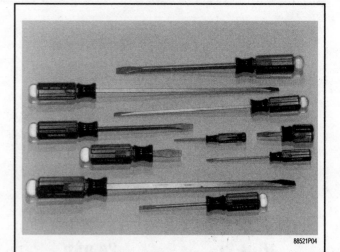

Fig. 8 Slot head screwdrivers come in assorted sizes and lengths

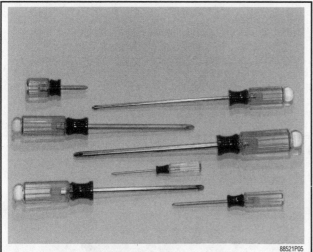

Fig. 9 Phillips screwdrivers also come in assorted sizes and lengths, these are more common in automotive use

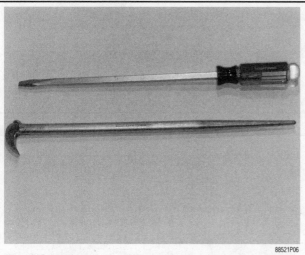

Fig. 10 Screwdrivers are NOT made for prying! Use only a pry-bar for prying.

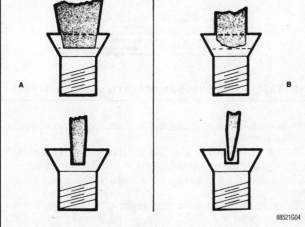

Fig. 11 Keep your screwdriver tips in good shape. They should fit in the screw slot as shown in "A". If they look like the ones in "B" they need to be ground or replaced.

WRENCHES

▶ **See Figures 12 and 13**

Wrenches come in two kinds—open end and box end. Both kinds are necessary for any sort of tool kit. The box end wrenches are ordinarily of the twelve-point type, and offer a better grip than the open-end type, although obviously they cannot be used for some jobs.

Wrench offset is a consideration when buying wrenches. The head may be angled to make access to some bolts or nuts easier. Standard offset is 15°–30°, but most wrenches are available from straight (0°) to right angle (90°) offsets. Many tool manufacturers offer combination wrenches, which are an open-end wrench on one end and a box end on the other. Box end wrenches are also available in ratcheting models, although their usefulness is limited for the amateur mechanic.

For fuel and brake line work, a special type of wrench known as a line wrench is available. It is nothing more than a box end wrench with one of the flats cut out so that it can be slipped over the line.

Adjustable open wrenches are also very handy, but the cheap kinds are no good at all, since they won't hold they're setting. Good quality adjustable wrenches are available in various lengths, and you should have at least one.

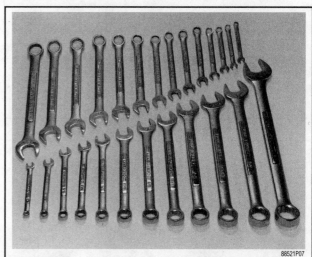

Fig. 12 Combination wrenches come in both metric and SAE sizes

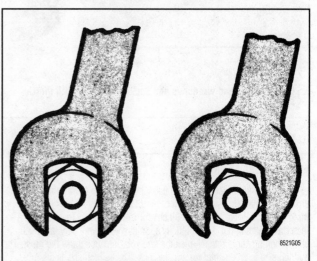

Fig. 13 When you are using an open end wrench, use the correct size and position it properly on the flats of the nut or bolt

ALLEN AND STAR WRENCHES

▶ **See Figures 14 and 15**

Allen and star (Torx®) wrenches are required more and more to work on vehicles. Allen wrenches are hexagonal and Torx® bits are multi-serrated inserts that fit inside a bolt or screw head rather than lining around the outside of the head. They can be L-shaped tools with their own handles or are available to fit a ratchet handle.

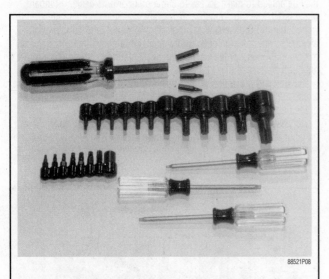

Fig. 14 Torx® drivers come in both ratchet and screwdriver type

Fig. 15 Allen head wrenches and sockets come in both metric and SAE

RATCHET AND SOCKETS

▶ **See Figures 16 and 17**

A ratchet and socket set will probably be one of the most expensive purchases you make in assembling a basic tool kit. Ratchet drives come in three common sizes, ½ inch, ⅜ inch and ¼ inch drive. (There is also a ¾ inch drive ratchet, but it is of little use, unless you own a very large vehicle.) When buying a ratchet, pick the size you think you'll use the most. The ¼ inch size is only useful for smaller jobs. The ⅜ inch size is the most popular and useful. Sockets come in six- or twelve-point faces, and in standard and deep lengths.

There are plenty of specialty tools for socket sets. Universal joints allow you to get into tight places, but are frequently hard to maneuver. Adapters let you use different size drive sockets on other ratchet handles. Crowfoot wrenches are simply open-end wrench heads that fit a ratchet drive. Speeder handles; super-deep sockets, magnetic inserts, and screwdriver bits are all nice to have, if you have a use for them. If not, don't bother cluttering up your toolbox. Spark plugs require a deep socket, while the standard length is suitable for most of the other jobs you will encounter. The six-point sockets are heavier and give a better

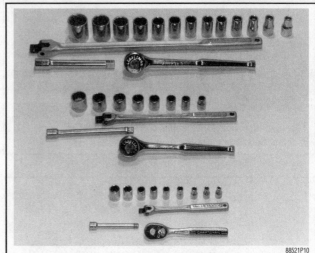

Fig. 16 Common ratchet sets come in ½ inch, ⅜ inch, and ¼ inch sizes

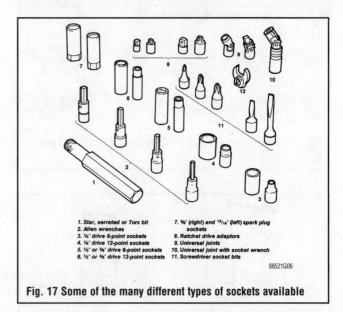

1. Star, serrated or Torx bit
2. Allen wrenches
3. ¼" drive 6-point sockets
4. ¼" drive 12-point sockets
5. ½" or ⅜" drive 6-point sockets
6. ½" or ⅜" drive 12-point sockets
7. ⅝" (right) and ¹³/₁₆" (left) spark plug sockets
8. Ratchet drive adaptors
9. Universal joints
10. Universal joint with socket wrench
11. Screwdriver socket bits

Fig. 17 Some of the many different types of sockets available

grip, but the twelve-point sockets offer more turning positions for working in tight places.

You can also do yourself a big favor and choose a flexible head ratchet over a regular ratchet. A flex head ⅜ inch drive ratchet with a 6 inch extension will enable you to do most any job you want to do.

The ratchet handle comes in various lengths with a varying number of teeth on the ratchet. If you have a choice, pick the shorter ratchet handle and the one with the most teeth on the ratchet mechanism (most clicks per turn of the handle). This will give you the greatest flexibility to reach tight places and the fewest bruised knuckles.

TORQUE WRENCH

▶ **See Figures 18 and 19**

If you plan to do anything more involved than changing the oil, you'll need a torque wrench. The beam-type models are perfectly adequate, although the click-type models are much more precise. Keep in mind that if you're tightening a part that has a torque value given, it's there for a reason. So, use the torque wrench.

Click-type (or breakaway) torque wrenches can be dialed to any desired setting and will automatically release once the setting is reached. These are used mostly by professionals, and are not necessary for the backyard mechanic. The beam-type torque wrench, while not quite as accurate or as fast to use as the click-type, is adequate for most everyday use, and is usually quite inexpensive. When using a torque wrench on any fasteners, keep the socket as straight as possible on the fastener. Trying to torque something on an angle just won't work. Using the wrench on an angle will create increased resistance and the result will be an inaccurate reading.

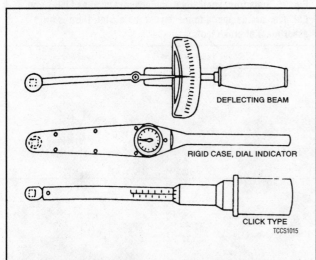

Fig. 18 Various styles of torque wrenches are available at your local automotive store

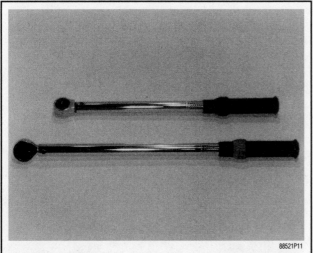

Fig. 19 Common click type torque wrenches are the most popular

Specialty Tools

▶ **See Figures 20 thru 28**

In addition to basic tools, you'll find a number of small specialty tools that will make your life as a do-it-yourselfer much easier. A battery terminal puller (for top terminal batteries) costs only a few bucks, and will save you a lot of trouble when you remove your battery cables. A combination cable and terminal cleaner is also handy. A tire pressure gauge is an absolute must if you plan to get the most wear out of your tires. Buy a good one, since tire pressure is critical to tire life. An antifreeze hydrometer is necessary to keep an eye on the state of your coolant.

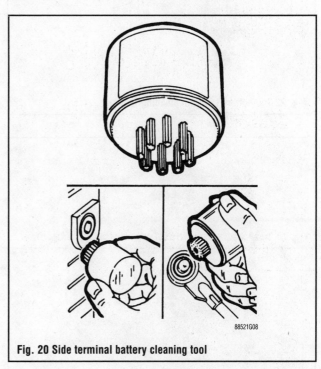

Fig. 20 Side terminal battery cleaning tool

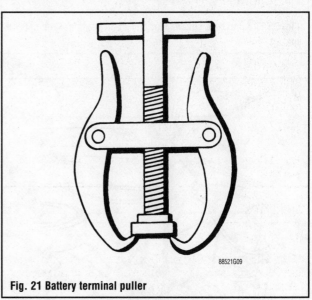

Fig. 21 Battery terminal puller

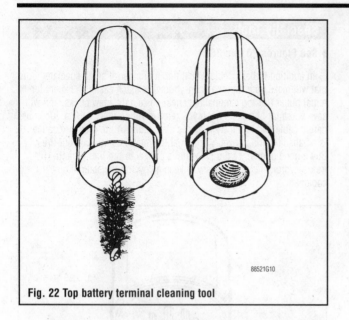

88521G10

Fig. 22 Top battery terminal cleaning tool

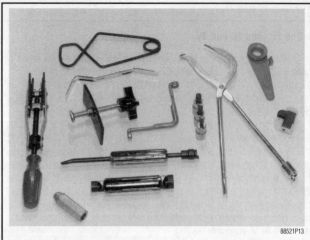

88521P13

Fig. 25 Tools from specialty manufacturers such as Lisle® and Cal-Van® are designed to make your job easier. Here is an assortment of brake tools.

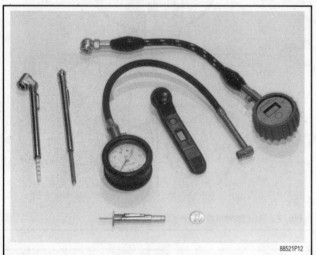

88521P12

Fig. 23 Tire pressure gauges top, and tread depth gauges bottom

88521P14

Fig. 26 Specialty sockets are required for many sensors and axle nuts. Acquire these as the job calls for it.

88521G11

Fig. 24 A hydrometer is necessary to check antifreeze protection

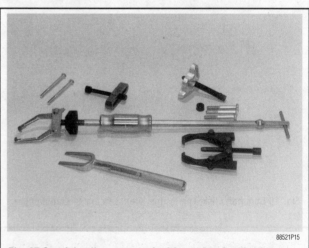

88521P15

Fig. 27 Special pullers are required for various applications. Often these tools can be rented from a tool rental or auto parts store.

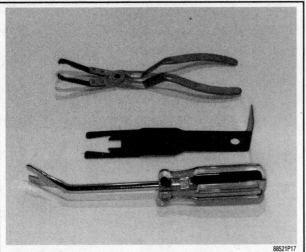

Fig. 28 Interior door panels and handles often require special clip removers

Fig. 30 Lubrication tools—suction gun, grease gun, and bearing packers

General Maintenance Tools

▶ **See Figures 29, 30 and 31**

The list of general maintenance tools is practically endless, depending on the degree of your involvement. However, a basic list for the average do-it-yourself mechanic would include:

- An oil filter wrench,
- A grease gun,
- A container for draining oil,
- A suction gun,
- Battery terminal cleaners, and
- Many rags for cleaning up the inevitable mess.

Oil filter wrenches come in various types. The strap wrench is the most common and will handle most filters. A more sophisticated filter wrench combines a strap or band wrench with a ratchet drive. This type is useful when the filter is located in an out-of-the-way place. Many oil filters on front wheel drive vehicles, can only be removed with this type of wrench. The other types of filter wrenches are applied to the end of the oil filter, and both are designed for use with a ratchet drive.

Fig. 31 This type of oil drain pan enables you to take your waste oil to a recycling station. Remember to drain the filter into the pan.

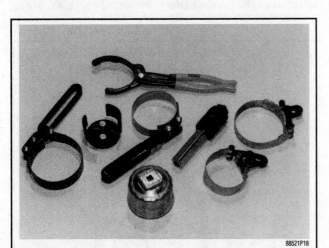

Fig. 29 Oil filter wrenches come in a number of styles. You will have to experiment to find the correct combination for your vehicle.

A funnel is the best way to get oil from the bottle into the engine with a minimum of mess. Any other way will surely result in oil spilled on the engine, which will turn to smoke when the engine gets hot. Other types of fillers have flexible spouts for filling automatic transmissions and other hard-to-reach filler tubes.

A grease gun is also the only way to lubricate the vehicle's chassis. The grease gun comes in various sizes that accept cartridges of different kinds of grease and a variety of flexible and odd-shaped fittings to reach hard-to-get-at grease nipples.

A fluid suction gun is almost a necessity to add (or remove) oil from a differential. The filler plugs on differentials and manual transmissions are frequently in a spot that you cannot fill directly from the container. You will probably have to transfer the fluid from the container into a suction gun first. The fluid is also frequently heavy oil, which does not flow easily, which further complicates the problem. To remove fluid from a unit without a drain plug, a suction gun is invaluable.

Battery cleaning tools are inexpensive and make battery terminal cleaning easier and quicker. They generally come in two styles, one for top terminals and one for side terminals. The one for side terminals is nothing more than a miniature wire brush, which you can easily substitute.

Tune-Up Tools

▶ See Figures 32, 33 and 34

➡The word "tune-up" actually applies only to older vehicles, on which you can perform the traditional work associated with "tune-up"—spark plug replacement, ignition contact point replacement, dwell adjustment, ignition timing adjustment and carburetor idle and mixture adjustment.

For today's vehicles, engine performance maintenance is a more accurate term. Modern vehicles are equipped with electronic ignition (no points) and an on-board computer that automatically adjusts the ignition timing fuel mixture and idle speed. In fact, on modern computer-controlled vehicles, it's usually impossible to adjust these yourself:

If you plan to do your own engine performance maintenance, there are some specialized tools you are going to need. You'll need a round wire gauge to check and set the plug gap, a timing light (if your ignition timing is adjustable), a dwell-tach or just a tach (to set idle speed if it is adjustable). A compression gauge is also handy, though not necessary.

An important element in checking the overall condition of your engine is to check compression. This becomes increasingly more important on high

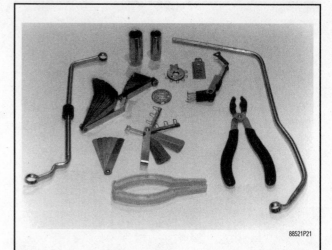
88521P21

Fig. 34 A variety of tools used for spark plug installation and timing adjustment

mileage vehicles. Compression gauges are available as screw-in types and hold-in types. The screw-in type is slower to use, but eliminates the possibility of a faulty reading due to escaping pressure. A compression reading will uncover many problems that can cause rough running. Normally, these are not the sort of problems that can be cured by a tune-up. Vacuum gauges are also handy for discovering air leaks, late ignition or valve timing, and a number of other problems.

TIMING LIGHTS

▶ See Figure 35

There are two basic kinds of timing lights—DC powered timing lights, which operate from your vehicle's battery, and AC powered timing lights, which operate on 110 volt house current. Of the two, the DC light is preferable because it produces more light to see the timing marks in bright daylight.

Regardless of what kind is used, the light normally connects in series with the No. 1 spark plug using an adapter. Models that are more expensive sometimes use an inductive pickup, which simply clamps around the plug wire and senses firing impulses. Inexpensive models use alligator clips; one clamps onto the connection between the plug and the plug wire, and the others clamp onto the vehicle battery terminals.

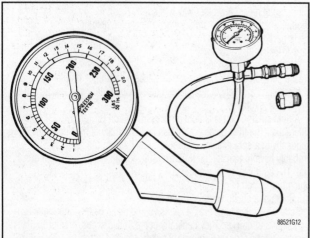
TCCS1213

Fig. 32 Proper information is vital, so always have a Chilton Total-Car Care manual handy

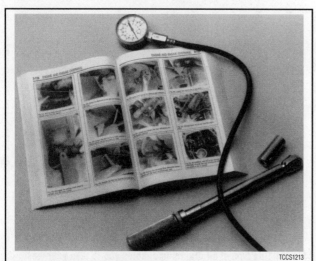
88521G12

Fig. 33 Two styles of compression gauges. The screw-in type on top is more accurate and is easier to use, but is more expensive.

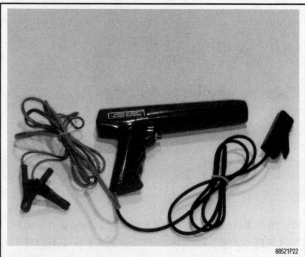
88521P22

Fig. 35 A modern electronic timing light. Note the inductive pick-up clamp.

➡**Some timing lights will not work on electronic ignition systems, so unless you still own a vehicle equipped with points, check to make sure the timing light you buy will work.**

The biggest problem you will probably have when using a timing light is trying to see the timing marks on the crankshaft pulley. Before you time the engine, mark the appropriate timing indicators with fluorescent paint or chalk. Stay out of direct sunlight when you time the engine and buy a timing light with a xenon light, not a neon light. Timing lights that use a xenon tube provide a much brighter flash than those that use a neon tube do.

TACHOMETER

♦ See Figure 36

You're not going to have much use for the dwell function of a dwell tachometer on late-model vehicles as it is controlled by the computer and is not adjustable. However, if you need to set the base idle speed, and it is adjustable, the tachometer will provide more accuracy than one on your instrument cluster. You don't need one of those gigantic analyzers to set the rpm on your vehicle. Prices range from less than $50–$100 and more. Make sure you get a dwell-tach or tach that is compatible with your vehicle's ignition system.

Dwell-tachs are simple to hook up. Some dwell-tachs are powered by the circuit being tested, some operate off the vehicle battery, and some have their own power source. Electronic ignition systems have specific connection procedures and you'll have to check with your dealer to determine the tach hook-up.

There are several Multi-Meter/Engine Analyzers on the market which provide the functions of a Multi Meter and a Engine Analyzers (Dwell & Tach).

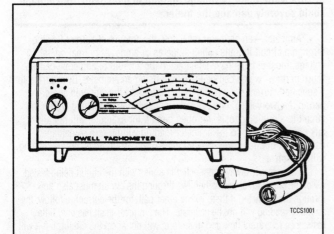

TCCS1001

Fig. 36 Typical aftermarket dwell tachometer—used to check dwell on old point type ignition, and RPM on point and electronic ignition systems.

Electrical and Diagnostic Tools

JUMPER WIRES

✳✳ CAUTION

Never use jumper wires made from a thinner gauge wire than the circuit being tested. If the jumper wire is of too small a gauge, it may overheat and possibly melt. Never use jumpers to bypass high resistance loads in a circuit. Bypassing resistances, in effect, creates a short circuit. This may, in turn, cause damage and fire. Jumper wires should only be used to bypass lengths of wire.

Jumper wires are simple, yet extremely valuable, pieces of test equipment. They are basically test wires which are used to bypass sections of a circuit. Although jumper wires can be purchased, they are usually fabricated from lengths of standard automotive wire and whatever type of connector (alligator clip, spade connector or pin connector) that is required for the particular application being tested. In cramped, hard-to-reach areas, it is advisable to have insulated boots over the jumper wire terminals in order to prevent accidental grounding. It is also advisable to include a standard automotive fuse in any jumper wire. This is commonly referred to as a "fused jumper". By inserting an in-line fuse holder between a set of test leads, a fused jumper wire can be used for bypassing open circuits. Use a 5 amp fuse to provide protection against voltage spikes.

Jumper wires are used primarily to locate open electrical circuits, on either the ground (-) side of the circuit or on the power (+) side. If an electrical component fails to operate, connect the jumper wire between the component and a good ground. If the component operates only with the jumper installed, the ground circuit is open. If the ground circuit is good, but the component does not operate, the circuit between the power feed and component may be open. By moving the jumper wire successively back from the component toward the power source, you can isolate the area of the circuit where the open is located. When the component stops functioning, or the power is cut off, the open is in the segment of wire between the jumper and the point previously tested.

You can sometimes connect the jumper wire directly from the battery to the "hot" terminal of the component, but first make sure the component uses 12 volts in operation. Some electrical components, such as fuel injectors, are designed to operate on about 4 volts, and running 12 volts directly to these components will cause damage.

TEST LIGHTS

♦ See Figure 37

The test light is used to check circuits and components while electrical current is flowing through them. It is used for voltage and ground tests. To use a 12 volt test light, connect the ground clip to a good ground and probe wherever necessary with the pick. The test light will illuminate when voltage is detected. This does not necessarily mean that 12 volts (or any particular amount of voltage) is present; it only means that some voltage is present. It is advisable before using the test light to touch its ground clip and probe across the battery posts or terminals to make sure the light is operating properly.

✳✳ WARNING

Do not use a test light to probe ignition spark plug or coil wires. Never use a pick-type test light to probe wiring on computer controlled systems unless specifically instructed to do so. Any wire insulation that is pierced by the test light probe is a good candidate for failure. Most vehicle manufactures recommend against this, some also recommend against back-probing. Back-probing is where the tip of the probe is forced into the back of the connector. Refer to the specific vehicle manufacturers for recommendations.

Like the jumper wire, the 12 volt test light is used to isolate opens in circuits. But, whereas the jumper wire is used to bypass the open to operate the load, the 12 volt test light is used to locate the presence of voltage in a circuit. If the test light illuminates, there is power up to that point in the circuit; if the test light does not illuminate, there is an open circuit (no power). Move the test light in successive steps back toward the power source until the light in the handle illuminates. The open is then between the probe and a point which was previously probed.

The self-powered test light is similar in design to the 12 volt test light, but contains a battery in the handle. It is most often used in place of a multimeter to check for open or short circuits when power is isolated from the circuit (continuity test).

The battery in a self-powered test light does not provide much current. A weak battery may not provide enough power to illuminate the test light even

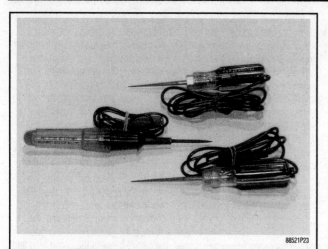

Fig. 37 Test lights are simple to use, however check manufacturers recommendations before probing any wires or connectors.

when a complete circuit is made (especially if there is high resistance in the circuit). Always make sure that the test battery is strong. To check the battery, briefly touch the ground clip to the probe; if the light glows brightly, the battery is strong enough for testing.

➡**A self-powered test light should not be used on any computer controlled system or component. Even the small amount of electricity transmitted by the test light is enough to damage many electronic automotive components.**

MULTIMETERS

▸ **See Figure 38**

Multimeters are an extremely useful tool for troubleshooting electrical problems. They can be purchased in either analog or digital form and have a price range to suit any budget. A multimeter is a voltmeter, ammeter and ohmmeter (along with other features) combined into one instrument. It is often used when testing solid state circuits because of its high input impedance (usually 10 megaohms or more). A brief description of the multimeter main test functions follows:

• Voltmeter—the voltmeter is used to measure voltage at any point in a circuit, or to measure the voltage drop across any part of a circuit. Voltmeters usually have various scales and a selector switch to allow the read-

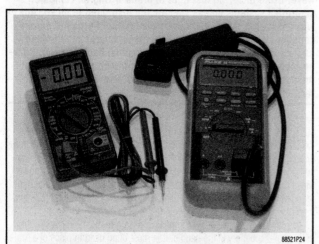

Fig. 38 Combination Multi-Meter and Engine Analyzer makes these the most important diagnostic tools you own. Pro model on right has inductive pick-up

ing of different voltage ranges. The voltmeter has a positive and a negative lead. To avoid damage to the meter, always connect the negative lead to the negative (-) side of the circuit (to ground or nearest the ground side of the circuit) and connect the positive lead to the positive (+) side of the circuit (to the power source or the nearest power source). Note that the negative voltmeter lead will always be black and that the positive voltmeter will always be some color other than black (usually red).

• Ohmmeter—the ohmmeter is designed to read resistance (measured in ohms) in a circuit or component. All ohmmeters will have a selector switch which permits the measurement of different ranges of resistance (usually the selector switch allows the multiplication of the meter reading by 10, 100, 1,000 and 10,000). Since the meters are powered by an internal battery, the ohmmeter can be used as a self-powered test light. When the ohmmeter is connected, current from the ohmmeter flows through the circuit or component being tested. Since the ohmmeter's internal resistance and voltage are known values, the amount of current flow through the meter depends on the resistance of the circuit or component being tested.

The ohmmeter can also be used to perform a continuity test for suspected open circuits. In using the meter for making continuity checks, do not be concerned with the actual resistance readings. Zero resistance, or any ohm reading, indicates continuity in the circuit. Infinite resistance indicates an opening in the circuit. A high resistance reading where there should be none indicates a problem in the circuit. Checks for short circuits are made in the same manner as checks for open circuits, except that the circuit must be isolated from both power and normal ground. Infinite resistance indicates no continuity to ground, while zero resistance indicates a dead short to ground.

✳✳ WARNING

Never use an ohmmeter to check the resistance of a component or wire while there is voltage applied to the circuit. The voltage could severely damage the meter.

• Ammeter—an ammeter measures the amount of current flowing through a circuit in units called amperes or amps. At normal operating voltage, most circuits have a characteristic amount of amperes, called "current draw" which can be measured using an ammeter. By referring to a specified current draw rating, then measuring the amperes and comparing the two values, one can determine what is happening within the circuit to aid in diagnosis. An open circuit, for example, will not allow any current to flow, so the ammeter reading will be zero. A damaged component or circuit will have an increased current draw, so the reading will be high.

The ammeter is always connected in series with the circuit being tested. All of the current that normally flows through the circuit must also flow through the ammeter; if there is any other path for the current to follow, the ammeter reading will not be accurate. The ammeter itself has very little resistance to current flow and, therefore, will not affect the circuit, but it will measure current draw only when the circuit is closed and electricity is flowing. Excessive current draw can blow fuses and drain the battery, while a reduced current draw can cause motors to run slowly, lights to dim and other components to not operate properly.

SCAN TOOLS

▸ **See Figures 39 and 40**

All late-model vehicles utilize computer modules to monitor and control the functions of on-board systems. These modules are known by many names such as Engine Control Unit (ECU), Engine Control Module (ECM), Powertrain Control Module (PCM) and Vehicle Control Module (VCM) just to name a few. When problems occur in control circuits, these modules record a diagnostic trouble code which can be used to help solve the problem. Over the years, there have been many different types of systems, each with their own unique way of retrieving these codes. On a good number of the older systems, the stored codes were flashed on various trouble lights (found in the dashboard) once a small jumper wire was placed across the proper diagnostic terminals. However the use of a hand-held scan tool was still preferred for these systems.

Fig. 39 Typical aftermarket scan tool used to access diagnostic codes from the Electronic Control Module.

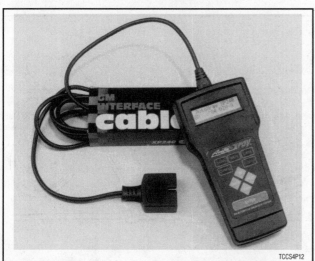

Fig. 40 This Auto Xray® scan tool uses manufacturer specific cables to interface with the various connectors.

For some models produced during the 1995 model year and on almost every single 1996 and later model, a new form of trouble codes was developed which required the use of a scan tool. On Board Diagnostic-II (OBD-II) compliant vehicles use a 5 digit, alpha-numeric code which would be difficult or impossible to read using a flashing light, therefore trouble code reading on an OBD-II compliant requires a scan tool.

There are many manufacturers of these tools, but a purchaser must be certain that the tool is proper for the intended use. If you own a scan type tool, it probably came with comprehensive instructions on proper use. Be sure to follow the instructions that came with your unit

The scan tool allows any stored codes to be read from the computer module memory. The tool also allows the operator to view the data being sent to the computer control module while the engine is running. This ability has obvious diagnostic advantages; the use of the scan tool is frequently required for component testing. The scan tool makes collecting information easier; the data must be correctly interpreted by an operator familiar with the system.

An example of the usefulness of the scan tool may be seen in the case of a temperature sensor which has changed its electrical characteristics. The computer module is reacting to an apparently warmer engine (causing a driveability problem), but the sensor's voltage has not changed enough to set a fault code. Connecting the scan tool, the voltage signal being sent to the module may be viewed; comparison to normal values or a known good vehicle reveals the problem quickly.

SOLDERING GUN

Soldering is a quick, efficient method of joining metals permanently. Everyone who has the occasion to make electrical repairs should know how to solder. Electrical connections that are soldered are far less likely to come apart and will conduct electricity far better than connections that are only "pig-tailed" together.

The most popular (and preferred) method of soldering is with an electric soldering gun. Soldering irons are available in many sizes and wattage ratings. Irons with high wattage ratings deliver higher temperatures and recover lost heat faster. A small soldering iron rated for no more than 40 watts is recommended for home use, especially on electrical projects where excess heat can damage the components being soldered.

There are three ingredients necessary for successful soldering—proper flux, good solder and sufficient heat.

Flux

A soldering flux is necessary to clean the metal of tarnish, prepare it for soldering and to enable the solder to spread into tiny crevices. When soldering electrical work, always use a resin flux or resin core solder, which is non-corrosive and will not attract moisture once the job is finished. Other types of flux (acid-core) will leave a residue that will attract moisture, causing the wires to corrode.

Good Solder

Tin is a unique metal with a low melting point. In a molten state, it dissolves and alloys easily with many metals. Solder is made by mixing tin (which is very expensive) with lead (which is very inexpensive). The most common proportions are 40/60, 50/50 and 60/40, the percentage of tin always being listed first.

Low-priced solders often contain less tin, making them very difficult for a beginner to use because more heat is required to melt the solder. A common solder is 40/60 which is well suited for all-around general use, but 60/40 melts easier, has more tin for a better joint and is preferred for electrical work.

Sufficient Heat

♦ See Figure 41

Successful soldering requires that the metals to be joined be heated to a temperature that will melt the solder, usually somewhere around 360–460°F (182–237°C), depending on the tin content of the solder. Contrary to popular belief, the purpose of the soldering iron is not to melt the solder itself, but to

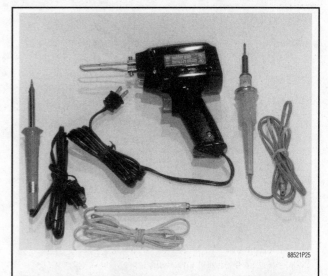

Fig. 41 These are several types of soldering guns and irons

heat the parts being soldered to a temperature high enough to melt solder when it is touched to the work. Melting flux-cored solder on the soldering iron will usually destroy the effectiveness of the flux.

How to Solder

▶ See Figures 42, 43, 44 and 45

1. Soldering tips are made of copper for good heat conductance, but must be "tinned" regularly for quick transference of heat to the project and to prevent the solder from sticking to the iron. To "tin" the iron, simply heat it and touch flux-cored solder to the tip; the solder will flow over the tip. Wipe the excess off with a rag.

2. After some use, the tip may become pitted. If so, dress the tip smooth with a fine file and "tin" the tip again.

3. An old saying holds that "metals well-cleaned are half soldered." Flux-cored solder will remove oxides, but rust, bits of insulation and oil or grease must be removed with a wire brush or emery cloth.

4. For maximum strength in soldered parts, the joint must start off clean and tight. Weak joints will result in gaps too wide for the solder to bridge.

5. If a separate soldering flux is used, it should be brushed or swabbed on only those areas that are to be soldered. Most solder contains a core of flux and separate fluxing is unnecessary.

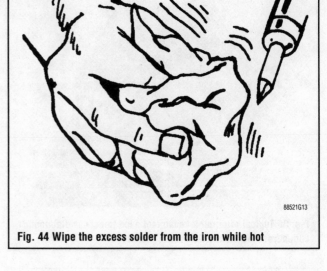

Fig. 44 Wipe the excess solder from the iron while hot

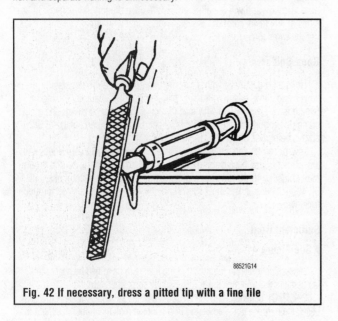

Fig. 42 If necessary, dress a pitted tip with a fine file

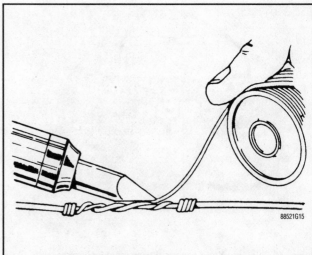

Fig. 45 The correct method of soldering. Let the heat transferred to the work melt the solder

6. Hold the work to be soldered firmly. It is best to solder on a wooden board, because a metal vise will only rob the piece to be soldered of heat and make it difficult to melt solder. Hold the soldering tip with the broadest face against the work to be soldered. Apply solder under the tip close to the work. Apply enough solder to give a heavy film between the iron and piece being soldered, moving slowly and making sure the solder melts properly. Keep the work level or the solder will run to the lowest part, and favor the thicker parts, because these require more heat to melt the solder. If the soldering tip overheats, (the solder coating on the face of the tip burns up). The tip should be re-tinned.

7. Once the soldering is completed, let the soldered joint stand until cool.

Jacks and Jackstands

▶ See Figures 46, 47, 48 and 49

A vehicle must be raised in order to lubricate the chassis, change the oil and gain access to various parts under the vehicle. Above all, a vehicle must be raised and supported safely. Never attempt to work under a vehicle supported only by a jack.

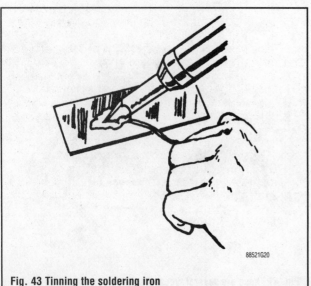

Fig. 43 Tinning the soldering iron

Fig. 46 A hydraulic floor jack and a set of jackstands are essential for lifting and supporting the vehicle

Fig. 48 . . . new style ramps have angle adapters to allow clearance for front spoilers on many of today's vehicles.

Fig. 47 Car ramps may substitute for a jack and jackstands, however, old style ramps don't provide adequate clearance for late-model vehicles . . .

Fig. 49 When using ramps or jackstands, always block the wheels on the opposite end of the vehicle

The jack that comes with the vehicle is suitable for raising the vehicle, but is not suitable for supporting the vehicle while you work under it. Once the vehicle is raised, place safety stands under it before attempting any work.

Scissors jacks are the least expensive types of jacks. These are mechanically operated by a threaded rod that is turned inside a diamond-shaped frame. Cranking the screw causes the diamond-shaped frame to expand or contract, raising or lowering the vehicle.

Hydraulic jacks are the best and quickest means of lifting a vehicle off the ground. Hydraulic jacks run anywhere from $30–$300, depending on the size and quality of the jack. They are available as small units that can be picked up easily in one hand and placed where needed, or as large, heavy units equipped with wheels to move them about. The smaller models work slowly and tip over easier.

Hydraulic jacks use a pump to push hydraulic fluid against a ram that operates the lifting pad. They have seals that are prone to leaking. This is one good reason why you shouldn't work under a vehicle supported by a hydraulic jack. If the seals leak, the jack will lose pressure and the vehicle will slowly (or quickly) fall to the ground.

Jackstands are the safest way to support a vehicle. They are made of heavy metal, and are adjustable for different working levels. Once you have raised the vehicle to a convenient height, the jackstands are adjusted underneath it and the vehicle is lowered onto the stands. Professional jackstands are the easiest to use, but cost the most. Occasionally, if you're very fortunate, they can be picked up used from a service station that is going out of business.

Drive-on ramps are the alternative to jacking and supporting the vehicle. A good set of pressed steel ramps can cost as much as $40–$70, but they are often worth the expense. Be sure to check the angle of the incline on the ramps. With extensive use of front spoilers and air dams on today's vehicles, often there may be clearance problems.

GUIDE TO TOOLS FOR DO-IT-YOURSELF REPAIRS

Column headers (Type of repair):

- Engine tuning
- Filter, oil changing & lube
- Cooling system
- Tire & wheels
- Body care
- Body repair
- Brakes
- Battery
- Starting/charging
- Stereo & radio
- Washers & wipers
- Air conditioning
- Towing & R/V
- Lighting
- Shock absorbers & suspension
- Safety services
- Exhaust systems
- Maintenance

Tools needed

Basic level
- pliers
- screwdrivers
- hammers
- wrenches
- hacksaw
- cable/terminal cleaners
- spark plug gage
- tire pressure gage
- battery hydrometer
- antifreeze hydrometer
- trouble light
- oil can
- workbench
- jacks
- drive-on ramps
- safety stands
- bench vise
- socket set
- oil drain pan
- tread depth gage
- lug wrench
- fender covers
- fire extinguisher
- first aid kit
- grease gun
- funnels

Average level
- bench grinder
- soldering gun
- tach/dwell meter
- timing light
- punches and chisels
- files
- inspection mirror
- electric drill
- wire wheels
- thickness gages
- compression tester
- continuity tester
- brake adjusting tool
- torque wrench
- hex-key wrenches
- terminal crimper/stripper
- magnet
- ruler
- putty knife/scraper

Advanced level
- micrometers
- battery charger
- volt/amp/ohmmeter
- tubing tools
- screw extractors
- taps, dies, thread file
- pullers
- power tools
- stud puller
- belt tension gage

Legend: ■ Need to have ▨ Nice to have

88521C01

Shop Supplies

♦ **See Figures 50 and 51**

When you plan your shop supplies, you should follow the same format as you used for your tools—if you intend to perform only basic level work, you need only acquire a minimum number of supplies, and so forth.

At the basic level, you're going to need mostly replacement fluids. Things such as motor oil, antifreeze, automatic transmission fluid and brake fluid should be kept on hand. You'll also need some clean rags or wiping towels and some hand cleaner.

At the average level, things get a little more complex. You'll probably need chassis and wheel bearing grease, spare hoses and belts, plugs, penetrating oil, parts cleaner and a variety of other supplies.

88521P26

Fig. 50 Hand cleaners have gone high-tech! Lotion, cream, and even citrus. Make sure you have some on hand.

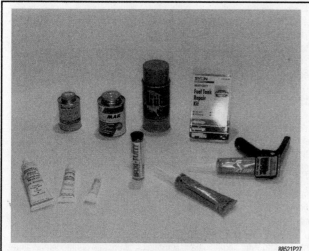

88521P27

Fig. 51 Shop sealants and adhesives come in a variety of applications. Always read the package before use.

The list of supplies needed for the advanced level could be endless, but if you're operating at the advanced level, you probably already have most supplies. Look at the list prepared here, keeping in mind that it's only a partial list, and these are all just suggestions. Remember the advanced level includes all the other levels as well.

SEALANTS

♦ **See Figures 52, 53 and 54**

If you're not already familiar with the terms "aerobic," "anaerobic" and "RTV", you probably should be. These are the kinds of sealant that have replaced many cork and rubber gaskets on vehicle assemblies.

The terms refer to the curing properties of the sealant. Aerobic means that the sealant cures in the presence of air and can be used on flexible flanges and between machined parts. However, it should not be used where it might squeeze out and plug small passages. Parts must be assembled immediately or the sealant will harden.

RTV sealant is another name for a type of aerobic sealant, standing for Room Temperature Vulcanizing. Aerobic sealants are often identified as RTV

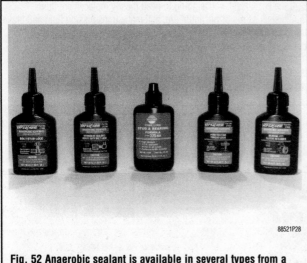

Fig. 52 Anaerobic sealant is available in several types from a variety of manufacturers

Fig. 54 RTV comes in various colors indicating specific applications. Once again read the package.

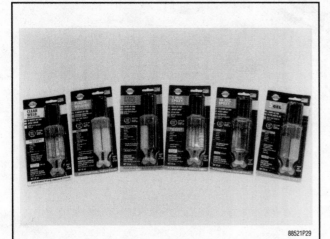

Fig. 53 Epoxy systems are available for metal and plastics and have different drying times

silicone rubber compounds, under names such as GM, GE, Permatex®, Devcon®, Dow Corning, MOPAR®, FelPro®, Loctite®, or Versa Chem®.

Anaerobic sealants are those that cure in the absence of air. In other words, the sealant will not cure (harden) until the parts are assembled and the air is denied. Anaerobic sealants are for use between smooth, machined surfaces, but should not be used between flexible mounting flanges. They should also be applied sparingly in a continuous bead to a clean surface.

Uncured aerobic or RTV sealants can be wiped off with a rag. Cured sealants can be removed with a scraper, wire brush or common shop solvents.

Universal Thread Sealant

There are more thread sealants than can be counted. Add to these the several sealant tapes now on the market and the confusion can be great. Mechanics should be aware of the anaerobic sealant with Teflon® filler that can be used on all joints. (GM Truck has adopted it as universal

sealant.) "Pipe Sealant with Teflon" is applied to threads. It creates an instant seal, but does not cure for 24 hours. This permits making changes if needed. Once hardened it prevents vibration-induced loosening.

How to Use Sealants

Anaerobics: Clean surfaces with solvent and apply bead to one surface. Material will not begin to cure until parts are assembled. Sealing is effective in half an hour. Full cure is complete in 2½–10 hours depending upon temperature. Cold slows cure.

Aerobic or Silicone sealants: Clean and dry surfaces. Apply bead and let cure for two hours. To make a gasket that will cling to only one surface, apply bead to one surface and allow it to cure. Then apply grease to other surface, and assemble. Or, to make a gasket that will bond to both surfaces, apply and assemble. This will provide maximum blowout resistance. Material will cure to depth of ¼ inch in 24 hours.

When to Use Sealants

The basic guide in choosing a sealant is the size of the gap. Anaerobic materials are used only on smooth, rigid, machine-surfaced flanges which have a total gap less than .030 inch (.301mm). Silicones are used in parts that may flex (such as metal-stamping covers) and which have gaps that are more than .030 inch (.301mm) but not more than 0.25 inch (6.35mm). Both materials are impervious to the normal automotive fluids such as gas, oil, coolants and hydraulics. Anaerobics have a temperature range of — 60–300°F (15–149°C), and silicones will handle—100– 450°F (38–232°C).

Anaerobics: Common applications for the anaerobic materials include fuel pumps, timing covers, oil pumps, water pumps, thermostat housings, oil filter adapters, manual transmission housings, differential covers and other rigid parts. Bear in mind that anaerobic materials add rigidity to the assembly because they help lock the surfaces.

Aerobic or Silicone sealants: Many silicone applications involve stamped metal housings such as oil pans, valve covers, and other parts such as intake manifolds, transmission covers, axle covers and rear main bearing seals.

Solvent release: Non-hardening sealants are used to repair cut gaskets on both rigid and flexible assemblies that operate at high temperatures up to 600°F (315°C). On semi-permanent assemblies, the materials set quickly to bolster the conventional gasket. By remaining pliable, they permit easy removal later.

Hardening sealants dry fast and hard and are used on permanent assemblies to aid the conventional gasket, particularly when the flanges are damaged.

Most sealants also aid in assembly by holding the gasket in place during assembly. When such positioning problems are extremely difficult, a gasket adhesive can be used to hold the gasket in perfect alignment during assembly.

Arranging Your Shop

▶ **See Figure 55**

Obviously, the arrangement of your shop depends a great deal on just what kind of shop you have in the first place. If you have very limited floor space, careful use of wall space will be the key to allowing yourself working room. If you're like most of us, you probably have a million things in the

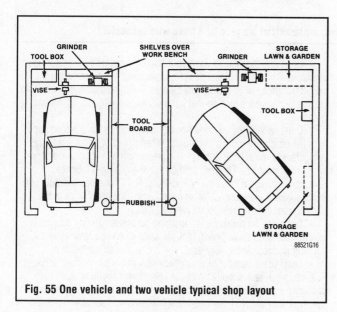

Fig. 55 One vehicle and two vehicle typical shop layout

garage already, which isn't going to help matters. Put up some shelves or get some pegboard to hang tools on. Make sure you have plenty of lighting in the garage. If you don't have enough lights, install some more. There's nothing worse than trying to work by the light of a flashlight or a trouble light. Keep the floor clean and make sure you have adequate ventilation. Keep flammable liquids outside, and anchor all the benches and any heavy equipment you may have.

Servicing Your Vehicle Safely

▶ **See Figures 56 and 57**

It is virtually impossible to anticipate all of the hazards involved with automotive maintenance and service, but care and common sense will prevent most accidents.

The rules of safety for mechanics range from "don't smoke around gasoline," to "use the proper tool for the job." The trick to avoiding injuries is to develop safe work habits and take every possible precaution.

DO'S

- Do keep a fire extinguisher and first aid kit handy.
- Do wear safety glasses or goggles when cutting, drilling, grinding or prying, even if you have 20–20 vision. If you wear glasses for the sake of vision, wear safety goggles over your regular glasses.
- Do shield your eyes whenever you work around the battery. Batteries contain sulfuric acid. In case of contact with the eyes or skin, flush the area with water or a mixture of water and baking soda, then seek immediate medical attention.
- Do use safety stands (jackstands) for any undervehicle service. Jacks are for raising vehicles; jackstands are for making sure the vehicle stays raised until you want it to come down. Whenever the vehicle is raised, block the wheels remaining on the ground and set the parking brake.
- Do use adequate ventilation when working with any chemicals or hazardous materials. Like carbon monoxide, the asbestos dust resulting from some brake lining wear can be hazardous in sufficient quantities.
- Do disconnect the negative battery cable when working on the electrical system. The secondary ignition system contains EXTREMELY HIGH VOLTAGE. In some cases it can even exceed 50,000 volts.
- Do follow manufacturer's directions whenever working with potentially hazardous materials. Most chemicals and fluids are poisonous if taken internally.
- Do properly maintain your tools. Loose hammerheads, mushroomed punches and chisels, frayed or poorly grounded electrical cords, excessively worn screwdrivers, spread wrenches (open end), cracked sockets, slipping ratchets, or faulty droplight sockets can cause accidents.
- Likewise, keep your tools clean; a greasy wrench can slip off a bolt head, ruining the bolt and often harming your knuckles in the process.
- Do use the proper size and type of tool for the job at hand. Do select a wrench or socket that fits the nut or bolt. The wrench or socket should sit straight, not cocked.
- Do, when possible, pull on a wrench handle rather than push on it, and adjust your stance to prevent a fall.
- Do be sure that adjustable wrenches are tightly closed on the nut or bolt and pulled so that the force is on the side of the fixed jaw.
- Do strike squarely with a hammer; avoid glancing blows.
- Do set the parking brake and block the drive wheels if the work requires a running engine.

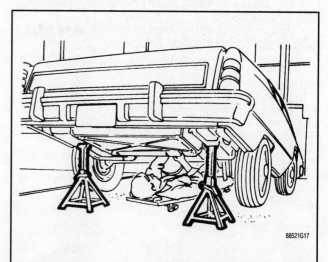

Fig. 56 Always support your vehicle on jackstand while working underneath

**TWO-WIRE CONDUCTOR...
THIRD WIRE GROUNDING
THE CASE**

**THREE-WIRE CONDUCTOR...
GROUNDING THRU
A CIRCUIT**

**THREE-WIRE CONDUCTOR...
ONE WIRE TO A GROUND**

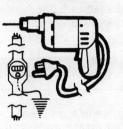

**THREE-WIRE CONDUCTOR...
GROUNDING THRU
AN ADAPTER PLUG**

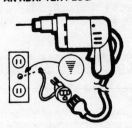

88521G18

Fig. 57 If you're using portable electric tools, make sure they're grounded, preferably at the plug by a three wire connector

DON'TS

• Don't run the engine in a garage or anywhere else without proper ventilation—EVER! Carbon monoxide is poisonous; it takes a long time to leave the human body and you can build up a deadly supply of it in your system by simply breathing in a little every day. You may not realize you are slowly poisoning yourself. Always use power vents, windows, fans and/or open the garage door.

• Don't work around moving parts while wearing loose clothing. Short sleeves are much safer than long, loose sleeves. Hard-toed shoes with neoprene soles protect your toes and give a better grip on slippery surfaces. Jewelry such as watches, fancy belt buckles, beads or body adornment of any kind is not safe working around a vehicle. Long hair should be tied back under a hat or cap.

• Don't use pockets for toolboxes. A fall or bump can drive a screwdriver deep into your body. Even a rag hanging from your back pocket can wrap around a spinning shaft or fan.

• Don't smoke when working around gasoline, cleaning solvent or other flammable material.

• Don't smoke when working around the battery. When the battery is being charged, it gives off explosive hydrogen gas.

• Don't use gasoline to wash your hands; there are excellent soaps available. Gasoline contains dangerous additives which can enter the body through a cut or through your pores. Gasoline also removes all the natural oils from the skin so that bone dry hands will suck up oil and grease.

• Don't service the air conditioning system unless you are equipped with the necessary tools and training. When liquid or compressed gas refrigerant is released to atmospheric pressure it will absorb heat from whatever it contacts. This will chill or freeze anything it touches. Although refrigerant is normally non-toxic, R-12 becomes a deadly poisonous gas in the presence of an open flame. One good whiff of the vapors from burning refrigerant can be fatal.

• Don't use screwdrivers for anything other than driving screws! A screwdriver used as an prying tool can snap when you least expect it, causing injuries. At the very least, you'll ruin a good screwdriver.

• Don't use a bumper or emergency jack (that little ratchet, scissors, or pantograph jack supplied with the vehicle) for anything other than changing a flat! These jacks are only intended for emergency use out on the road; they are NOT designed as a maintenance tool. If you are serious about maintaining your vehicle yourself, invest in a hydraulic floor jack of at least a 1½ ton capacity, and at least two sturdy jackstands.

TYPES OF SEALANTS

Type Product	Description	Characteristics
Lubricants	High temperature anti-seize lubricant	High temp anti-seize lube that does not harden with heat. Prevents corrosion. Good to temperatures of 1800°F.
	Dry spray lubricant with Teflon	Dry spray contains Teflon. Prevents sticking and squeaking on most moving parts, even non-metallic ones. Better than oil, sillcone or graphite.
	Multi-purpose penetrating lubricant	Fast-acting penetrating oil. Also displaces moisture and prevents corrosion when applied prior to assembly.
	Degreasing agent	Cuts grease and washes it away . . . leaves no film or residue. Good on glass, metal or rubber. Excellent on brake assemblies.
Sealers	Thread sealing tape made of Teflon	A tape thread sealant and lubricant made of Teflon in a handy roll. Replaces pipe dopes and hardening sealants.
	High performance thread sealant	Lubricates threads, then seals by hardening without shrinkage or cracking. Vibration resistant.
	Fast, hard-setting gasket sealer	Fast-setting gasket supplement in paste form. Dries to a hard film. Fills voids.
	Pliable, non-hardening gasket sealer	Dries to a pliable seal. Fills voids, protects threaded parts, too.
	Liquid gasket sealer	Brush-on type for non-rubber gaskets before assembly to ease reassembly and insure a leak-resistant seal.
	Spray adhesive sealant	A fast-drying adhesive sealant in an aerosol can.
	Form-in-place gasket compound	Self-forming gasket compound to fill gaps up to .030″ and up to 350°F applications. Can be used as a substitute for a gasket in an emergency when pre-cut soft gaskets are not available.
	Black silicone rubber adhesive and sealant	Room temperature vulcanizing silicone especially useful in sealing joints and threads, or use in attaching weather stripping. Good low temperature flexibility.
Bonders	Clear silicone rubber adhesive and sealant	Room Temperature Vulcanizing silicone dries to a transparent film to function where appearance is vital.
	Instant adhesive	Instant adhesive for high strength bonding of rubber, metal, hard woods and plastic.
	Quick-drying contact adhesive	Quick-drying contact adhesive for bonding all types of gaskets, including rubber, to parts before assembly. Resists impact, water proofs, mends and reinforces.
	General purpose epoxy adhesive	A multi-purpose epoxy that forms a tough bond in minutes.
Lockers	Self-curing locking compound	Self-curing compound replaces lock washers in nut and bolt applications.
	High strength locking compound	High strength version of above, used on sleeves, studs, and other parts that don't need frequent disassembly.
Patchers	Steel reinforced patching compound	Steel reinforced epoxy compound for repair of engine blocks, axle housings, pump castings, body work, etc.
	Aluminum reinforced patching compound	Aluminum reinforced epoxy for use in repairing aluminum castings, aluminum heads or blocks, transmission cases, etc.

88521C03

SHOP SUPPLIES PLANNER

Basic Level	Average level		Advanced level
motor oil	chassis grease	assorted electrical connectors	vacuum hose
antifreeze/coolant	wheel bearing grease	assorted fuses	oil seals for wheel bearings
fuel line antifreeze	penetrating oil	spare battery terminals	gear oil
automatic transmission fluid	parts cleaning solvent	sandpaper	fuel line
power steering fluid	carburetor cleaner	assorted bulbs	thermostat
hand cleaner	oil absorbent compound	solder	assorted gaskets
car wash chemicals	cotter pins	spray paint	muffler clamps and brackets
windshield washer solvent	nut and bolt assortment	spray undercoating	thread repair kit
windshield wiper blades	flat and lock washer assortment	body repair kits	brake system parts
brake fluid	spare belts	battery terminal spray	thermostat
wiping towels (cloth/paper)	spare hoses	gasket/sealer	
electrical tape	hose clamps	fuel filter	
masking tape	radiator cap		
air filter	spare wire		
oil filter	tune-up parts		
	spark plugs		

The Average level is in addition to Basic level; Advanced includes Basic and Average.

88521C02

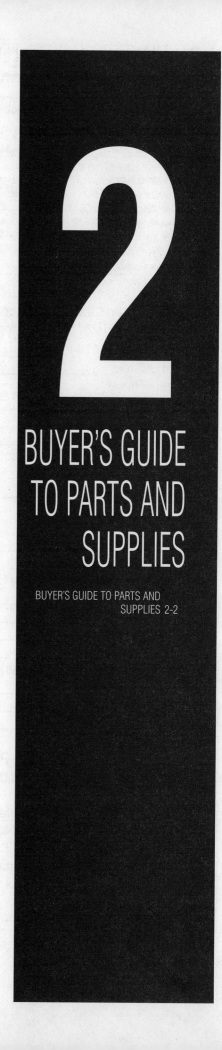

2

BUYER'S GUIDE TO PARTS AND SUPPLIES

BUYER'S GUIDE TO PARTS AND SUPPLIES

♦ **See Figure 1**

Do-it-yourself has become an economic necessity for many of us. It's an opportunity to save some money and have some measure of fun working on the old buggy at the same time. You'll find, if you haven't already, that it's easy to change the oil and filters or handle minor repairs, but you have to be sure you're getting the correct parts, at the best price.

Today, manufacturers and retailers know you're interested in do-it-yourself repairs to save money. That's why you'll find parts packaged or displayed with application charts to help you select the right parts for your vehicle.

Auto supply stores, discount and department stores, automotive jobbers, and other sources sell complete lines of quality parts for auto repair enthusiasts like you. You may want to comparison shop these outlets to see where you can get the most for your money. It's wise to compare price tags and quality all year, instead of expecting to find bargains on infrequent shopping tours. Sales on replacement parts are common. Weekly specials, holiday, and seasonal promotions all offer a chance to save on your automotive needs.

It doesn't really matter whether you buy name brand or store-brand parts. You can save a little money on the store-brand items as opposed to Origi-

---

QUICK REFERENCE SPECIFICATIONS

For quick and easy reference, you can use this form to Jot down frequently used information concerning parts available for your vehicle.

Tune-Up Data

Firing Order_____

Spark Plugs:

  Type (Manufacturer/No.)_____

  Gap (in./mm)_____

Ignition Timing _____

  Vacuum (Connected/Disconnected)_____

Valve Clearance (in./mm)

  Intake_____   Exhaust_____

Capacities

Engine Oil (qts)_____

  With Filter Change_____

  Type of Lubricant Cooling System (qts)_____

Manual Transmission (pts)_____

  Type of Lubricant_____

Transfer Case (pts.)_____

  Type of Lubricant_____

Automatic Transmission (pts)_____

  Type of Lubricant_____

Differential (pts)_____

  Type of Lubricant_____

Commonly Forgotten Part Numbers

Use these spaces to record the part numbers of frequently replaced parts.

PCV VALVE	OIL FILTER
Manufacturer_____	Manufacturer_____
Part No._____	Part No._____
AIR FILTER	FUEL FILTER
Manufacturer_____	Manufacturer_____
Part No._____	Part No._____

88522G01

Fig. 1 Make copies of this chart and keep with your vehicle

nal Equipment Manufacture (OEM) parts, but you may end up replacing them a little sooner if you buy too far down on the price scale.

The main thing is to be sure to get the correct part for your vehicle. An incorrect part can adversely affect your engine performance, fuel economy, and emissions, and will cost you more money and aggravation in the end. To avoid buying the parts piecemeal, many manufacturers have taken to offering do-it-yourself tune-up packages, containing, plugs, rotor, and sometimes distributor cap. Spark plug wires can be purchased already cut to length and ready to install, or as a kit, in which case you cut the necessary lengths yourself.

To get the proper parts for your vehicle, you will probably need to know some or all of the following information:
- Make: Jeep, Saturn, etc.
- Model: Cherokee, SL2 Sedan, etc.
- Year: 1996 (example)
- Engine size: The engine size may be designated in cubic inches (242, 116, etc.) or in cubic centimeters (cc) on imports (1600, 2000, etc.). Usually, it will be given in liters (4.0, 1.9, etc.). If you are not sure, there is usually a designation on the engine or under the hood that tells you the engine size. There may be a letter with the number that you should copy down, too. When in doubt write down all the information you can find it will save you repeated trips to the parts store.
- Number of cylinders: 4, 5, 6, 8, etc., for example
- Carburetor (or fuel injection): If the engine is carbureted, you'll need to know if the carburetor is a 1, 2, 3, or 4 barrel (abbreviated bbl) model. You may also find the word venturi (abbreviated V) used interchangeably with the word barrel when describing carburetors. On fuel injected models you may need to know which injection system is used. This is important because there are instances where a given model in the same year may have two engines with the same displacement, and the only difference may be the injection system. These are usually described on the engine in some sort of acronym SFI, SPFI, MFI, PGMFI, etc. In addition, your fuel-injected engine may be turbo-charged. These conditions will usually have ramifications that will effect other engine and fuel related parts.
- Air conditioner: Yes or No
- Quantity of oil: How many quarts
- Engine code: Since 1981, this code has been important to all domestic and some import vehicles. The engine code is part of the 17 digit Vehicle Identification Number (VIN), which is visible through the front windshield on the driver's side. On GM, Ford and Chrysler vehicles, the engine code is the 8th digit. On many import vehicles the engine must be identified by a tag on the engine or a number stamped on the block, bell housing or other location.

Sources for Parts

There are many sources for the parts you will need. Where you shop for parts will be determined by what kind of parts you need, how much you want to pay, and the types of stores in your neighborhood.

NEW CAR DEALERS

New vehicle dealers usually have parts for your vehicle, but the prices are usually higher than other sources. The dealer carries what are known in the auto trade as Original Equipment Manufacturer (OEM) parts. OEM parts are those supplied by the vehicle manufacturer and are the same parts installed on the vehicle when it was built. Because of the higher overhead expenses, these parts are generally a little more expensive than the same item available through other outlets.

The higher cost of OEM parts does not necessarily indicate a better value, or higher quality. Automotive jobbers and auto discount stores regu-

larly stock high-quality replacement parts in addition to OEM parts. Although manufacturers will recommend that you use OEM parts for replacement or service work, they will also specify that you can use an equivalent replacement part. Many replacement parts are made by or sold by reputable companies and are built to the same specifications as OEM parts. In many cases, replacement parts may even be identical to OEM parts, since many parts manufacturers sell parts to vehicle makers as OEM parts and also sell the same part to other companies, who market the part under a different brand name. The parts you have to be careful of are "gypsy" parts, which are discussed later in this section. Fortunately there are very few of them.

There are some parts for your vehicle—cylinder heads, crankshafts, body parts, and other slow movers—that you will be unlikely to obtain anywhere but at your dealer. These parts are not sold in sufficient quantities to make it attractive for any other outlet to stock them. Many of these parts may be special ordered.

SERVICE STATIONS

Your local service station can supply you with many of the common parts you require; though they stock these parts mainly for their own use in the repair end of the business. The problem, from the consumer's standpoint, is the cost—it will be high. The reason is that the service station operator buys the same part from a jobber that you can buy over the counter. Although he buys at a discount, he must make a profit on the resale of the item, whether through direct sale of the item or as part of repair charges. Really, when your service station sells parts to you over the counter, they are competing with the local parts stores and discount merchandisers, and most service stations do not buy or sell parts in sufficient volume to offer a competitive price. They are in business to sell "service," not to sell parts.

PARTS JOBBER

The local parts jobber, who is usually listed in the yellow pages or whose name can be obtained from the local gas station, supplies most of the parts that are purchased by service stations and repair shops. He also does a sizeable business in over-the-counter parts sales for the do-it-yourselfer, and this may constitute as much as 30% to 50% of his business.

The jobber usually has at least two prices—one for the local mechanic or service station and an over-the-counter retail price. The reason for this is that local mechanic, like the service station, does not pay the retail price for a given part. They pay less than retail (a mechanic's discount may range from 15–40% depending on the item) and mark up the price of the part to their customer, making a profit on the resale. Many jobbers will offer you a 10%–15% discount off the retail prices on over-the-counter sales, and most jobbers run periodic sales on both private brand and brand name do-it-yourself items.

The prices charged by jobbers are usually lower than the new vehicle dealers and service stations but slightly higher than discount or mass merchandisers. The reason is that the jobber is used to dealing with professional mechanics and usually sells name brand or OEM parts. His volume is such that he sells more than a service station, but less than a discount merchandiser does, and thus his prices fall somewhere between the two.

The people who work the counters in the jobber stores and discount stores know about vehicles—often more than the salesperson in the auto section of a department store. Unless they are extremely busy or very rushed, they can usually offer valuable advice on quality parts or tools needed to do the job right.

AUTOMOTIVE CHAIN STORES

Almost every community has one or more convenient automotive chain stores. These stores often offer the best retail prices and the convenience of one-stop shopping for all your automotive needs. Since they cater to the automotive do-it-yourselfer, these stores are almost always-open weekday nights, Saturdays, and Sundays, when the automotive jobbers are usually closed.

Chain stores are the automotive "supermarkets." Hardly a week goes by that they are not running advertised specials or a seasonal promotion of some type. The ads normally appear in the local newspapers and offer substantial savings on both name and store brand items. In contrast to the traditional jobber stores, where most merchandise is located behind the counter, you can walk through the auto chain stores and browse among most products, picking and choosing from a large stock of brand names.

Prices in the auto chain stores will normally be competitive with the discount stores and mass merchandisers, and they will usually be slightly lower than the jobber will. Counter personnel working in the chain and jobber stores are usually familiar with their products and common automotive problems and can offer good advice.

DISCOUNT STORES

The lowest prices for parts are most often found in discount stores or the auto department of mass merchandisers, such as K-Mart, Sears, and Wal-Mart. Parts sold here are name and private brand parts bought in huge quantities, so they can offer a competitive price. Private brand parts are made by major manufacturers and sold to large chains under a store label.

You have to have a good idea of what you're looking for when you buy from these outlets. Many are self-serve, in direct contrast to the older, traditional jobbers where they still look up the part number and get the part for you.

AUTO JUNKYARD

Wrecking yards, junkyards, salvage yards, previously owned parts yards—call them what you will—are good sources of parts, particularly for older vehicles or limited budgets, although most parts available from salvage yards are beyond the scope of this book. Auto wrecking yards range from the incredibly sophisticated computer—run inventories to stumble-bum one-man operations where nobody knows exactly what they have except the inevitable snarling dog.

In most cases, don't expect the wrecking yards to supply the smaller parts. They prefer to deal in complete assemblies. Among the better deals in wrecking yards are engines, transmissions, rear axles, body parts, and wheels. The cost of these parts from a yard is generally about one-half the cost of new parts. Most junkyards are not interested in selling carburetors, voltage regulators, and other small parts, but if they do, their cost will be negligibly less than the cost of rebuilt parts, and rebuilt parts are a far better deal.

Some wrecking yards may have two prices—one if they remove the parts and one if you do it. Most yards will prefer to remove parts themselves, but be careful. Time is money when removing parts, so a lot of yards, particularly the less organized, will remove an engine or rear axle with a cutting torch instead of unbolting it. This makes it necessary for you to buy small parts, such as motor mounts, brake lines, spring hangers, and other hardware, that were destroyed by the cutting torch.

Kinds of Parts

NEW OR REBUILT PARTS

Many times, you will be required to return your old starter, alternator, fuel pump, or carburetor when you buy a new one. These old parts are returned to a professional parts rebuilding service and are reconditioned to be sold over the counter as remanufactured or rebuilt parts.

Most parts stores will carry both new and rebuilt parts. There is nothing wrong with buying remanufactured parts. Many are just as good as the new ones but can be bought at considerable savings. Compare the price and guarantee on a remanufactured part with that of a new part. In general, the higher the quality of a remanufactured part, the closer the price will be to a new part and the better the warranty.

Inordinately low prices for remanufactured parts usually mean shorter parts life and earlier failures. In this case, it will be worthwhile to spend a little extra money for higher quality.

COUNTERFEIT PARTS

Caveat Emptor—let the buyer beware—was a reasonable attitude when the buyer could easily judge the quality of the merchandise he was buying.

However, as automobiles have become increasingly sophisticated, with electronic engine control systems and other hi-tech hardware, there are fewer manifestly clear ways by which to judge the quality of replacement parts.

Reputable manufacturers of replacement parts have built their reputations of repeat business. Their products meet or exceed the Original Equipment (OE) specifications. If they don't perform, you're not going to come back and buy many more of the same.

Counterfeiting, as applied to auto parts, is a broad term that covers any form of deception designed to trick the buyer into believing that he or she is purchasing a part produced by the original equipment manufacturer or a reputable aftermarket manufacturer.

Counterfeit products should not be confused with "generic or no-brand" products such as those found in the food industry. It's fully understood that these types of products are not branded products. The key to counterfeit parts lies in the fact that no attempt is made to identify the source of manufacture and that the counterfeit part and packaging closely resembles the real thing.

Packaging of reputable parts manufacturers is often unique and highly recognizable, but those who buy replacement parts by appearance or packaging alone should beware. Counterfeit parts are made to look like the real thing both in packaging and in appearance.

Counterfeit packaging usually involves the unauthorized use of a registered trademark on the packaging or the simulation of a part using original equipment characteristics and is designed to pass off generally sub-standard parts as the genuine article. Counterfeit parts have the right number of wires and connectors. They look official, durable and reliable.

However, looks are deceiving. Not only can counterfeit parts cost you money in the long run, due to premature failure or an unknown manufacturer who will not guarantee the part's performance, the shortcuts often taken in the manufacture of counterfeit parts could jeopardize your safety or the vehicle's performance. Some counterfeit brake shoes have been found deficient in braking power. Some counterfeit gas tank caps have no safety valves, designed to prevent spillage and fire in case of an accident.

How can you recognize counterfeit parts? Often, it's extremely difficult.

• Buy brand-name products. A name brand manufacturer's reputation for quality can only have been earned by selling quality merchandise.

• Be suspicious of packaging that very closely, but not exactly, replicates the packaging of a known, name brand manufacturer.

• Recognize that in a competitive marketplace, there will be variations in price among reputable manufacturers. Nevertheless, be suspicious of extremely low prices.

• If someone other than you is installing the part, ask to see the package in which it came. Even mechanics are not immune to assuming, mistakenly, that they are buying name brand replacement parts.

• If possible, compare the original equipment part with the replacement part before purchasing the replacement part. There are often subtle differences between counterfeit and original equipment and reputable replacement parts.

Using Automotive Catalogs

▶ **See Figure 2**

To a person looking for a part for his or her vehicle, the catalog is the most important tool to know how to use. Automotive parts catalogs are what you make them—a confusing foreign language or an easy-to-understand reference to get the correct part number, and price the first time.

Almost all manufacturers of hard parts make a catalog listing the part number, application, and sometimes the price of the item. The catalog may take the form of a large book with thousands of entries if the manufacturer makes many parts for a lot of applications, or it may be as simple as a single card if the manufacturer has relatively few variations. If you are purchasing oil filters, air filters, PCV valves, belts, hoses, and similar common parts, you will usually find the catalog near the merchandise in the parts store, though from time to time they will disappear. Wherever they are located and whatever form they take, learning to use them will assure that you get the correct part the first time, saving a lot of time and energy to return parts that don't fit.

With the age of computer databases, more and more parts look-up is done via a terminal on the parts counter. It is important to supply the operator with the correct information regarding your vehicle as discussed earlier. He will enter the vehicle only one time and have access to many different manufactures parts, as opposed to looking up the vehicle, then the part in individual printed catalogs. You may also find mini-computers in product locations on the sales floor for filters, batteries, wiper blades, etc.

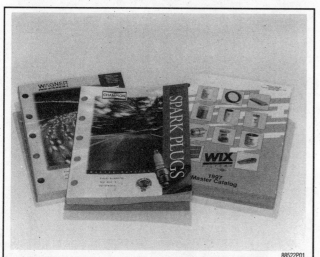

88522P01

Fig. 2 Parts catalogs, giving part number and application, are provided by manufacturers for most replacement parts

GENERAL LAYOUT

Catalogs normally contain a descriptive and dated (sometimes-coded) cover, a table of contents, index, illustrations, and then the meat of the catalog, the applications. The applications are normally arranged two ways: (1) alphabetically by vehicle name, and (2) numerically by part number. Jobbers may store their catalogs using the Weatherly filing system, a three-digit number on the front of the catalog, but this is of little interest to the do-it-yourselfer. What does interest you is the alphabetical listing of vehicles by make and model.

Many manufacturers print their parts catalogs every year, but some only print every two years and supply a supplement during the off year. It is essential to check the date of the catalog to be sure it has the latest information. Working with an outdated catalog is sometimes worse than working with no catalog at all.

LOCATING APPLICATIONS

Let's say you want to look up the spark plug for your 1996 Jeep Cherokee with a 4.0L engine. The first thing you do is find a spark plug catalog and check the date to make sure it is current. Then you look in the index for "Jeep." In this particular catalog, there is no listing by make and model in the index. The spark plug applications are broken down by Automobiles, Vans / Trucks & Buses, and several other listings. If you have an SUV or sport utility vehicle it may be listed either in the Car or Automobile section or in the Truck section depending upon the manufacturer. In this case, turn to the page starting Vans, Trucks & Buses.

Under Vans, Trucks & Buses, you'll find they are broken down into individual makes starting with Acura and working back to Volkswagen. Scan the pages until you find the heading Jeep. Under Jeep, you'll find the applications are further broken by model and year. And then 4-cylinder and 6-cylinder engines. Your Jeep is a 1996 Cherokee and has a 6-cylinder, so look under the appropriate heading. Read across the column from the L6 4.0L entry and find the number of the spark plug.

ABBREVIATIONS & FOOTNOTES

▶ **See Figure 3**

If you have trouble deciphering the abbreviations used in the parts catalog, they are usually identified in the front of the catalog.

The biggest distraction in all automotive catalogs is the footnotes. Asterisks, daggers, numerals, and letters that appear after a part number or listing indicate that you are up against a footnote. If such a notation is present, you must look further for more information. Most likely, you will go to the bottom of the page for an explanation of why the notation was used. In addition, the explanation could be almost anything. Special kits, superceded parts, special applications, and a myriad of other pieces of information all are deserving of footnotes. To get the right part for your vehicle you cannot afford to skip over the footnotes.

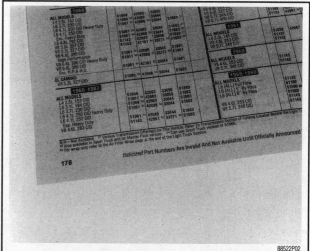

88522P02

Fig. 3 Catalog footnotes are important. They may contain replacement part numbers and other pertinent information.

CROSS-REFERENCE

▶ **See Figure 4**

Many catalogs include a cross-reference so you can double check information. A cross-reference could be from original equipment to independent supplier part numbers, or to application by part number.

➡**Caution should be used when cross-referencing parts. While Original Equipment Manufacturer (OEM) to an aftermarket part number is often a very accurate reference, aftermarket-to-aftermarket references should be double-checked by that particular manufactures application guide.**

COMMON CATALOG MISTAKES

Catalogs are designed for using, not confusing, but it is not unusual for catalog users to make mistakes in tracking down part numbers. Simple goofs are the most common and costly. For instance, often the user will find the correct listing, but then he or she reads across the wrong line. On the other hand, sometimes everything is done correctly, but a mistake is made in copying or trying to remember the part number. Alternatively, you can be mixed up in using a cross-reference, or working with an outdated catalog, or overlooking a footnote. Such mistakes happen every day to even the most experienced. All you can do is try your best to avoid them.

88522P03

Fig. 4 It is a good idea to check the actual number on the part, against the application catalog.

3

FASTENERS

FASTENERS

▶ See Figure 1

➡In most applications, fasteners on vehicles may be reused providing they have not been damaged during a repair. However, in certain special applications where stretch bolts or torque prevailing nuts are used these fasteners must be replaced.

Threaded fasteners are the basic couplers holding your vehicle together. There are many different kinds, but they all fall into three basic types:

Bolts—Bolts go through holes in parts that are attached together and require a nut that is turned onto the other end. A lock-washer of some sort is usually used under the nut.

Studs—Studs are similar to bolts, except that they are threaded at both ends (they have no heads). One end is screwed into a threaded hole and a nut is turned onto the other end. Lock-washers are usually used under the nuts.

Screws—Screws are turned into drilled or threaded holes in metal or other materials.

There are a great variety of screws and bolts, but most are hex headed or slot headed for tightening. Because the fastener is the weakest link in an assembly, it is useful to know the relative strength of the fastener, determined by the size and type of material. It is also important to understand the sizes of bolts, to avoid the expense and work of re-threading stripped holes.

Screws

▶ See Figures 2 and 3

Screws are supplied with slotted, Phillips, Torx® or Allen heads for screwdrivers or with hex heads for wrenches. Most of the screws used on cars and trucks are sheet metal, hexagon or pan type. Occasionally, you'll find a self-tapping sheet metal screw, with slots in the end to form a cutting edge. These types cut their own threads when turned into a hole.

The size of a screw is designated as 8–32, 10–32 or ¼–32. The first number indicates the size of the thread at the root or minor diameter (the diameter of the screw measured from the bottom of the threads on each side) and the second number indicates the number of threads per inch.

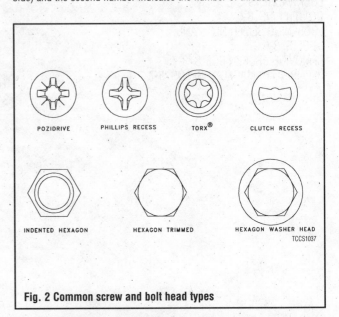

POZIDRIVE   PHILLIPS RECESS   TORX®   CLUTCH RECESS

INDENTED HEXAGON   HEXAGON TRIMMED   HEXAGON WASHER HEAD

TCCS1037

Fig. 2 Common screw and bolt head types

Fig. 1 Keep an assortment of fasteners and hardware neatly sorted in tackle boxes

88523P01

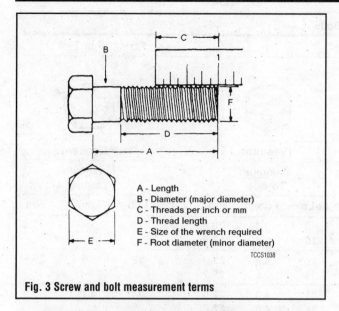

Fig. 3 Screw and bolt measurement terms

A - Length
B - Diameter (major diameter)
C - Threads per inch or mm
D - Thread length
E - Size of the wrench required
F - Root diameter (minor diameter)

Torx® Fasteners

▶ **See Figure 4**

Torx® fasteners have a star shaped head of either an internal or an external design.

These fasteners come in three different types. The most common being internal, these fasteners require a star shaped driver and are frequently found on headlight retainers and adjusters. The second type is external, these fasteners require a star shaped socket and may be found in odd locations such as the wheel cylinder retaining bolts. The third type is tamper resistant, which are used in places that manufacturer's are very serious about avoiding a Do-It-Yourselfer (DIYer) from touching. These look similar to the internal type however, they have a pin in the center of the fastener preventing the use of the standard Torx® driver. They may be found on components that are meant to be serviced only by authorized repair centers.

SAE Bolts

▶ **See Figures 5, 6 and 7**

Many bolts that were once used on domestic cars and trucks maybe measured in inches, and standards for these bolts were established by the Society of Automotive Engineers (SAE). Special markings on the head of the bolt indicate its tensile strength (resistance to breaking). The SAE grade number, corresponding to the special markings, is an indication of the relative strength of the bolt. Grade 0 bolts (no markings) are usually made of a mild steel and are much weaker than a grade 8, usually made from a mild carbon steel alloy, though a grade 0 or 2 bolt is sufficient for most fasteners.

SAE fasteners are also identified by size. As an example, a ⅜–24 bolt means that the major (greatest) thread diameter is ⅜ inch and that there are 24 threads per inch. The head diameter is always ³⁄₁₆ inch larger than the bolt diameter. A ½ 16 bolt would be ½ inch in diameter and have 16 threads per inch. More threads per inch are called "fine" threads and less

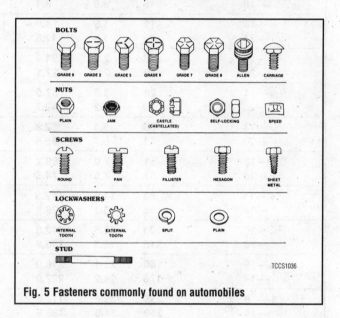

Fig. 5 Fasteners commonly found on automobiles

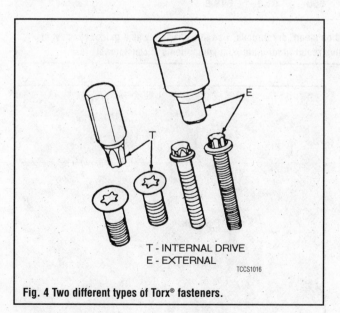

T - INTERNAL DRIVE
E - EXTERNAL

Fig. 4 Two different types of Torx® fasteners.

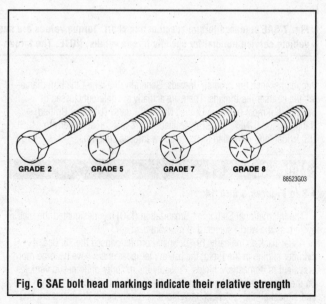

GRADE 2   GRADE 5   GRADE 7   GRADE 8

Fig. 6 SAE bolt head markings indicate their relative strength

SAE Bolts									
SAE Grade Number	**1 or 2**			**5**			**6 or 7**		
Bolt Markings Manufacturers' marks may vary—number of lines always two less than the grade number.									
Usage	**Frequent**			**Frequent**			**Infrequent**		
Bolt Size (inches)—(Thread)	**Maximum Torque**			**Maximum Torque**			**Maximum Torque**		
	Ft-Lb	**kgm**	**Nm**	**Ft-Lb**	**kgm**	**Nm**	**Ft-Lb**	**kgm**	**Nm**
1/4—20	5	0.7	6.8	8	1.1	10.8	10	1.4	13.5
—28	6	0.8	8.1	10	1.4	13.6			
5/16—18	11	1.5	14.9	17	2.3	23.0	19	2.6	25.8
—24	13	1.8	17.6	19	2.6	25.7			
3/8—16	18	2.5	24.4	31	4.3	42.0	34	4.7	46.0
—24	20	2.75	27.1	35	4.8	47.5			
7/16—14	28	3.8	37.0	49	6.8	66.4	55	7.6	74.5
—20	30	4.2	40.7	55	7.6	74.5			
1/2—13	39	5.4	52.8	75	10.4	101.7	85	11.75	115.2
—20	41	5.7	55.6	85	11.7	115.2			
9/16—12	51	7.0	69.2	110	15.2	149.1	120	16.6	162.7
—18	55	7.6	74.5	120	16.6	162.7			
5/8—11	83	11.5	112.5	150	20.7	203.3	167	23.0	226.5
—18	95	13.1	128.8	170	23.5	230.5			
3/4—10	105	14.5	142.3	270	37.3	366.0	280	38.7	379.6
—16	115	15.9	155.9	295	40.8	400.0			
7/8— 9	160	22.1	216.9	395	54.6	535.5	440	60.9	596.5
—14	175	24.2	237.2	435	60.1	589.7			
1— 8	236	32.5	318.6	590	81.6	799.9	660	91.3	894.8
—14	250	34.6	338.9	660	91.3	849.8			

88523G10

Fig. 7 SAE standard torque specification chart. Torque values are based on clean, dry threads. Use this chart only as a guide, check your vehicle service manual for specific torque values. NOTE: The torque value required for aluminum components is considerably less.

threads per inch are "coarse" threads. Generally, the larger the bolt diameter, the coarser the threads. There are actually six different classes of threads, but most bolts are Unified National Coarse (UNC) or Unified National Fine (UNF). The term "Unified" refers to a thread pattern to which US, British and Canadian machine screw threads conform.

Metric Bolts

▶ **See Figures 8 thru 14**

The International Standards Organization (ISO) has designated the metric system as the world standard of measurement.

As far back as the early 1970's when Ford introduced the 2300cc, 4-cylinder engine in the Pinto, the use of metric fasteners have become more prevalent in domestic vehicles. Probably the majority of domestic vehicles on the road today have more metric fasteners than the inch-size (SAE) type and almost all the fasteners on vehicles currently being produced are metric.

The mixture of metric and SAE fasteners on the same vehicle means that you have to be very careful when removing bolts to note their locations and to keep metric nuts and bolts together. At first glance, metric fasteners may

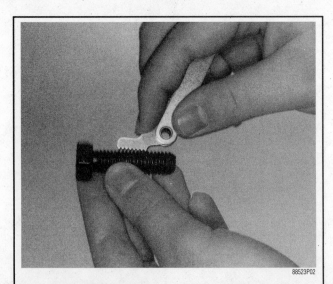

88523P02

Fig. 8 A thread gauge will instantly identify the thread size

Metric Grade	Nominal Diameter (mm)	Corresponds to SAE Grade
4.6	M5 thru M36	1
4.8	M1.6 thru M16	—
5.8	M5 thru M24	2
8.8	M16 thru M36	5
9.8	M1.6 thru M16	—
10.9	M5 thru M36	8
12.9	M1.6 thru M36	—

88523G05

Fig. 9 Metric grade to SAE grade comparison

M1.6 × 0.35	M20 × 2.5
M2 × 0.4	M24 × 3
M2.5 × 0.45	M30 × 3.5
M3 × 0.5	M36 × 4
M3.5 × 0.6	M42 × 4.5
M4 × 0.7	M48 × 5
M5 × 0.8	M56 × 5.5
M6.3 × 1.0	M64 × 6
M8 × 1.25	M72 × 6
M10 × 1.5	M80 × 6
M12 × 1.75	M90 × 6
M14 × 2	M100 × 6
M16 × 2	

88523G08

Fig. 12 The 25 standard metric diameter and pitch combinations

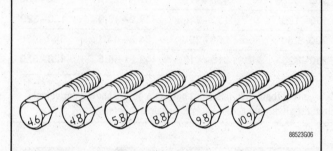

88523G06

Fig. 10 Metric bolts are marked with numbers that indicate the relative strength of the bolt. These numbers have nothing to do with the size of the bolt.

BSW	BSF	UNC	UNF	ISO Metric Size
		10	10	M5
3/16	3/16			
		12	12	M6
1/4	1/4	1/4	1/4	M6
5/16	5/16	5/16	5/16	M8
3/8	3/8	3/8	3/8	M10
7/16	7/16	7/16	7/16	
1/2	1/2	1/2	1/2	M12

88523G09

Fig. 13 Thread forms replaced by ISO Metric

STRENGTH GRADE 6   STRENGTH GRADE 8

STRENGTH GRADE 12   STRENGTH GRADE 14

88523G07

Fig. 11 Typical ISO bolt and nut markings

appear to be the same size as their SAE counterparts, but they're not. While the size may be very close, the pitch of the threads (distance between threads) is different. It is possible to start a metric bolt into a hole with SAE threads and run it down several turns before it binds. Any further tightening will strip the threads. The opposite could occur also; a nut could be run all the way down and be too loose to provide sufficient strength.

Fortunately, metric bolts are marked differently than SAE bolts. An ISO metric bolt larger than 6 mm in diameter has either "ISO M" or "M" embossed on top of the head. In addition, most metric bolts are identified by a number stamped on the bolt head, such as 4.6, 5.8 or 10.9. The number has nothing to do with the size, but does indicate the relative strength of the bolt. The higher the number, the stronger the bolt. Some metric nuts are also marked with a single-digit number to indicate the strength, and some may have the M and strength grade embossed on the flats of the hex.

Metric nuts with an ISO thread are marked on one face of the hex flats with the strength grade (4, 5, 6, 8, 12, and 14). Some nuts with a 4, 5 or 6 strength grade may or may not be marked.

A clock face system is used as an alternate means of strength grade designation. The external chamfers or faces of the nut are marked with a dash at the appropriate hour mark corresponding to the relative strength grade. One dot indicates the 12 o'clock position and, if the grade is above 12, 2 dots identify 12 o'clock.

Metric Bolts						
Relative Strength Marking	4.6, 4.8			8.8		
Bolt Markings		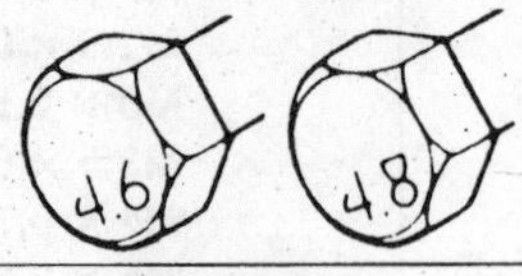			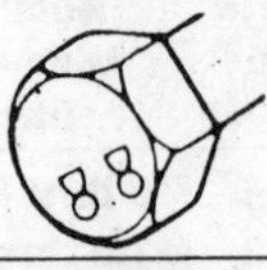	
Usage	Frequent			Infrequent		
Bolt Size	Maximum Torque			Maximum Torque		
Thread Size x Pitch (mm)	Ft-Lb	Kgm	Nm	Ft-Lb	Kgm	Nm
6 x 1.0	2–3	.2–.4	3–4	3–6	.4–.8	5–8
8 x 1.25	6–8	.8–1	8–12	9–14	1.2–1.9	13–19
10 x 1.25	12–17	1.5–2.3	16–23	20–29	2.7–4.0	27–39
12 x 1.25	21–32	2.9–4.4	29–43	35–53	4.8–7.3	47–72
14 x 1.5	35–52	4.8–7.1	48–70	57–85	7.8–11.7	77–110
16 x 1.5	51–77	7.0–10.6	67–100	90–120	12.4–16.5	130–160
18 x 1.5	74–110	10.2–15.1	100–150	130–170	17.9–23.4	180–230
20 x 1.5	110–140	15.1–19.3	150–190	190–240	26.2–46.9	160–320
22 x 1.5	150–190	22.0–26.2	200–260	250–320	34.5–44.1	340–430
24 x 1.5	190–240	26.2–46.9	260–320	310–410	42.7–56.5	420–550

88523G12

Fig. 14 Metric torque specification chart. Torque values are based on clean, dry threads Use this chart only as a guide, check your vehicle service manual for specific torque values. NOTE: The torque value required for aluminum components is considerably less.

The size of a metric fastener is also identified differently than an SAE fastener. A metric fastener could be designated M12 x 2, for example. This means that the major diameter of the threads is 12 mm and that the thread pitch is 2 mm (there are 2 mm between threads). Most importantly, metric threads are not classed by number of threads per inch, but by the distance between the threads, and the distance between threads does not exactly correspond to number of threads per inch (2 mm between threads is about 12.7 threads per inch).

The 25 standard metric diameter and pitch combinations are shown here. The first number in each size is the nominal or root (minor) diameter (mm) and the second number is the thread pitch (mm).

➡**Remember that the nominal bolt diameter is the measurement of the bolt diameter as taken from the bottom of the threads NOT the top (which would be major diameter).**

Nuts

There is a variety of nuts used on vehicles. Slotted and castle (castellated) nuts are designed for use with a cotter pin. These are mainly used for various suspension and wheel bearing fasteners, where it is extremely important that the nuts do not work loose.

Other nuts have a self-locking feature. A soft metal or plastic collar inside the nut is slightly smaller than the bolt threads. When the nut is turned down, the bolt cuts a thread in the collar and the collar material jams in the bolt threads to keep the nut from loosening.

Still other varieties of nuts include jam nuts and speed nuts. A jam nut is merely a second nut which is tightened against the first nut in order to hold the first nut in place. Jam nuts are widely used where an adjustment is involved. A speed nut is a rectangular piece of sheet metal that is pushed down over a screw or stud.

Lockwashers

A lockwasher is a split or toothed washer. It is usually installed between a nut or screw head, and a flat washer or the actual part and is used to help keep a nut or screw from loosening in service. The split washer is crushed flat and locks the nut in place by spring tension, while the toothed lockwasher, usually used for smaller bolts, provides many edges to improve the locking effect.

Cotter Pins

Cotter pins are used with slotted or castle nuts to lock the nut in position (preventing it from loosening or coming off in service). When used, the stud or bolt has a hole in it. When the nut is tightened, you align the slots with the hole so that a pin can be inserted. After the cotter pin is inserted through the nut and bolt, the legs of the cotter pin are bent over to lock the pin in place.

Loosening Seized Nuts and Bolts

▶ **See Figure 15**

Occasionally, nuts and bolts that are rusted resist the ministrations of mere mortals and refuse to budge. Most of the time, penetrating oil or a sharp rap with a hammer will loosen stubborn nuts.

Another method, used in extreme cases, is to saw away two sides of the nut with a hacksaw. The idea is to weaken the nut as much as possible by sawing away two sides as close to the bolt as possible without actually damaging the bolt threads. A wrench will usually remove the remaining portion of the nut. Another option to this method is a special tool called a nutcracker. This tool often resembles a "C"-clamp with a chisel tip (other versions of this tool may be completely round with a tip at the opposite end of the threaded portion). Tightening this tool against the nut splits the nut and it then can be easily removed with a wrench.

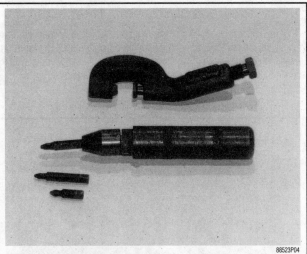

Fig. 15 "C"-clamp type nut cracker (top) and impact driver (bottom) can be used to remove stubborn nuts and bolts

Removing Broken Bolts

♦ See Figure 16

Unfortunately for the do-it-yourselfer learning the feel for how tight is too tight is an acquired skill. Breaking bolts is an unfortunate learning experience for most new mechanics. Most often, the original threads are still in satisfactory condition, however there is no longer any means to turn the bolt. When this occurs you can try to drill the bolt out and rethread the hole using a tap. However, this would probably cause you to go to the next size bolt. The more common method to remove a broken bolt is a tool called a bolt extractor, often referred to as an Easy-Out®. Bolt extractors are available in various shapes and sizes, and are often sold in kits. You will need to know the original bolt size to select the correct tool. Once selected you will drill a small hole in the center of the bolt. Then you will insert and lightly tap the tool into the hole until it is snug. Finally, you can turn the tool and hopefully the remains of the bolt removing them from the hole.

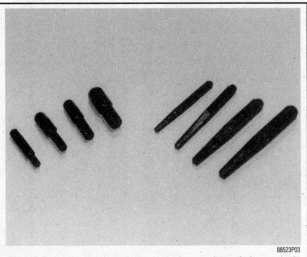

Fig. 16 Bolt or screw extractors come in a variety of shapes and sizes

Repairing Damaged Threads

♦ See Figures 17, 18, 19, 20 and 21

Several methods of repairing damaged threads are available. Heli-Coil®(shown here), Keenserts® and Microdot® are among the most widely used. All involve the same principle—drilling out stripped threads, tapping the hole and installing a pre-wound insert—making welding, plugging and oversize fasteners unnecessary.

Two types of thread repair inserts are usually supplied—a standard type for most inch-coarse, inch-fine, metric-coarse and metric-fine thread sizes and a spark plug type to fit most spark plug port sizes. Consult the individual manufacturer's catalog to determine exact applications. Typical thread repair kits will contain a selection of pre-wound threaded inserts, a tap (corresponding to the outside diameter threads of the insert) and an installation tool. Spark plug inserts usually differ because they require a tap equipped with pilot threads and a combined reamer/tap section. Most manufacturers also supply blister-packed thread repair inserts separately

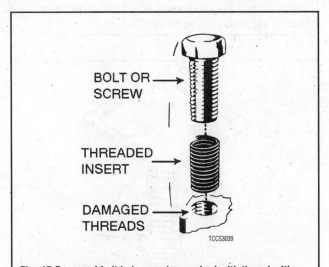

BOLT OR SCREW

THREADED INSERT

DAMAGED THREADS

TCCS3039

Fig. 17 Damaged bolt holes can be repaired with thread with thread repair inserts

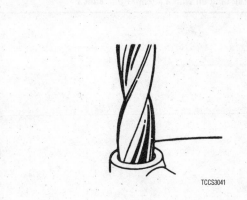

TCCS3041

Fig. 18 Drill out the damaged threads with the specified bit. Drill completely through the hole or to the bottom of the blind hole.

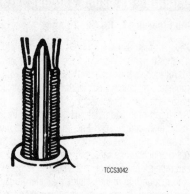

Fig. 19 With the tap supplied, rethread the hole to receive the threaded insert. Keep the tap well oiled and back the tap out frequently to avoid clogging the threads.

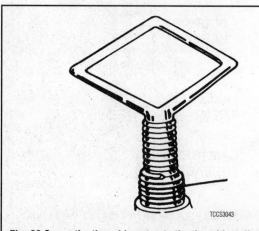

Fig. 20 Screw the thread insert onto the thread installation tool until the tang engages the slot. Screw the insert into the tapped hole until it is ¼–½ turn below the top surface. After installation break the tang off with a hammer and punch.

plus a master kit containing a variety of taps and inserts plus installation tools.

Before effecting a repair to a threaded hole, remove any snapped, broken or damaged bolts or studs. Penetrating oil can be used to free frozen threads; the offending item can be removed with locking pliers or with a screw or stud extractor. After the hole is clear, the thread can be repaired.

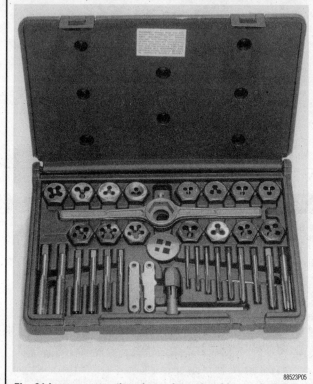

Fig. 21 In some cases threads can be restored by running a tap in the hole, or a die on the bolt

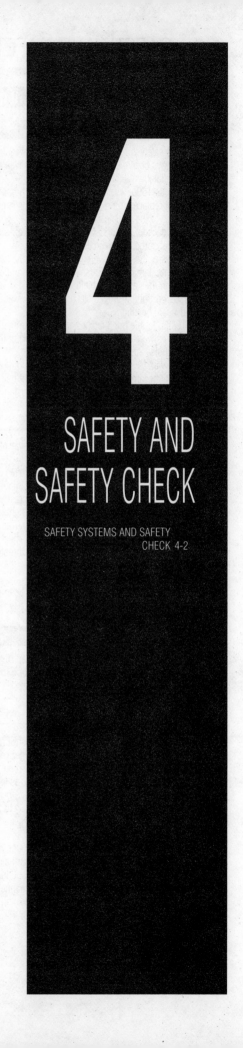

4

SAFETY AND
SAFETY CHECK

SAFETY SYSTEMS AND SAFETY
CHECK 4-2

SAFETY SYSTEMS AND SAFETY CHECK

Automotive Safety

Automotive safety is not a recent invention of Washington legislators. Safety has always been a concern of automakers, even before Federal standards were initiated.

As far back as 1900, when vehicles were still "horseless carriages," the steering wheel replaced the rudder-like steering stick, adding safety as well as convenience to the vehicle.

In the next decade, the industry introduced the all-steel body, rearview mirror, shock absorbers and the electric horn.

Automobiles of the 1920s were revolutionized by steel wheels, twin-beam headlights, laminated windshield glass, hydraulic brakes on all four wheels, balloon tires and windshield wipers.

The 1930s brought improved steering gears, power brakes, defrosters and sealed-beam headlights.

In the 1940s double hood latches, padded instrument panels, and self-adjusting brakes were first used, in addition to one of the most important safety innovations—the turn signal.

In the post-war 1950s, the population of automobiles increased dramatically and safety became even more important. Seat belts, head restraints, energy-absorbing steering wheels and impact-resistant door latches were added to most new vehicles.

The '60s and '70s saw the advent of dual braking systems, collapsible steering columns, wear indicators for various parts of the vehicle, side impact door beams, warning lights and buzzers, seat-belt interlock systems and energy-absorbing bumper systems.

The '80s and '90s brought the addition of improved safety belts, improved side impact protection, head restraints, infant and child seats, and air bag systems. Also, there was a new focus on crash avoidance with the addition of anti-lock brakes and daytime running lights.

There are currently over 60 National Highway Traffic and Safety Administration (NHTSA) standards that directly affect vehicle safety, with more (including revised air bags, improved head restraints, and advanced crash avoidance systems) sure to make it onto the books in the coming years.

Most of the cost of regulatory compliance has been passed on to the consumer in the form of retail price increases.

Crashworthiness

The most important safety feature is actually part of your vehicle's design, which is crashworthiness. This is something to consider when purchasing a new or used vehicle.

VEHICLE SIZE & STRUCTURE

An obvious design characteristic influencing crashworthiness is size. The laws of physics dictate that, all else being equal, larger vehicles are safer than smaller vehicles. In relation to their numbers on the road, small cars have more than twice as many occupant deaths each year as large cars. Some people claim small cars are easier to maneuver in an emergency, so they're less likely to be in crashes. But small cars aren't less likely to be in crashes. Insurance claims for vehicle damage, good indicators of overall crash involvement, are more frequent for small cars than large ones.

How the vehicle structure performs in a crash is another important aspect of crashworthiness. Late model car designs include a strong occupant compartment, or "safety cage," along with front and rear crush zones designed to absorb crash energy in a controlled manner. Good structural designs confine crash damage to the crush zones in all but the worst impacts.

On-Board Warning Systems

▶ See Figures 1 and 2

Turn on the ignition switch in almost any vehicle and watch the instrument panel. The modern automobile has an abundance of warning lights that provide valuable information. The list could include:
- Brake system warning
- Windshield washer fluid level
- Coolant level
- Brake fluid level
- Door ajar
- Headlamp door position
- EGR or Check Engine
- High beam indicator

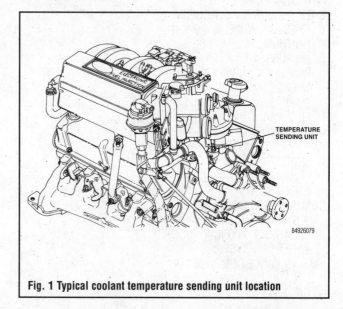

Fig. 1 Typical coolant temperature sending unit location

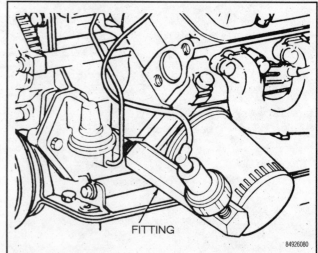

Fig. 2 Oil pressure sending units may be located in a variety of places on the engine

- Seatbelt light
- Cold engine warning
- Turn signals
- Charging system
- Transmission temperature
- ABS or Anti-lock Brake System
- SRS or Supplemental Restraint System
- Brake lining wear indicator light.

The high price of fuel created a demand for yet another light—the fuel economy warning system. When the light comes on, it tells the driver he or she is pushing too hard on the gas pedal. High manifold vacuum equals good gas mileage and vice versa. The system simply reads manifold vacuum from a sensor, and when it drops to a predetermined level, a circuit is completed and the light is lit. This has become in many models what is known as the up-shift light. An arrow on the dash indicates the time to shift into the next gear to obtain optimum fuel economy.

If a warning light comes on, you must find out why. It means there is a problem either in the system being monitored or in the warning lamp circuit. Finding the actual fault is important and not very difficult. However, a wiring diagram may be needed to prevent confusion.

Looking at the typical warning light circuit, you'll see that the bulb is most often supplied with current through the ignition switch. Further examination reveals the most common way of completing the circuit and getting the bulb to light is by means of a sensor, which completes the ground connection. In this case, sensor is a fancy word for a switch that turns on or off according to specific conditions.

Consider a typical oil pressure warning light system. Current from the ignition switch flows through the warning lamp and from there to ground through the oil pressure switch. This particular switch is normally closed and the circuit is complete until the switch opens in response to oil pressure in the engine.

Just the opposite is true with the coolant temperature sensor. It is normally open and only completes the circuit when an internal element expands (in response to heat) to close the contacts. If the vehicle has a cold engine warning lamp, the sensor includes two sets of contacts. One set is normally closed and opens as the internal element expands. This action breaks the ground circuit to the warning lamp. The other set of contacts functions if the temperature rises far enough to close them, turning on the high temperature warning.

If either of the temperature lights is lit while the engine seems normal, just unplugging the wires from the sensor will provide valuable diagnostic information. If the lights remain lit, there's a short to ground in the wiring from the lamp to the sensor. The service needed isn't to the cooling system, but to the warning system.

If the lights go out with the wires unplugged and the engine seems normal, it's entirely possible that the sensor has failed and needs to be replaced. Nevertheless, don't just unplug the wires and forget about them. This could be disastrous for the vehicle owner should a cooling problem develop without warning.

Energy-Absorbing Bumpers

▶ See Figures 3, 4 and 5

Energy-absorbing bumpers in some form, capable of absorbing impact up to 5 mph, have been required by law on passenger vehicles since the early 70's.

On cars of the 70's and 80's it took the form of a piston, charged with an inert gas and a cylinder filled with hydraulic fluid. The cylinder tube is crimped around the piston tube. The crimping is backed by a grease ring to prevent the entrance of moisture and/or dirt. The piston tube is attached to the bumper and the cylinder tube is attached to the frame. Extension is limited by a stop ring.

Some oil wetting is normal due to seepage of the grease ring behind the crimp. Hydraulic fluid leakage in the form of noticeable dripping indicates a failed unit.

Some scuffing of the piston is normal in average use. Obvious damage to the unit, such as dents or torn mounts, indicates a failed unit. Repair is not possible. Defective units must be replaced.

The hydraulic or gas charged bumpers worked as follows: On impact, the bumper makes contact with the barrier. As the bumper is pushed back, hydraulic fluid is pushed past the tapered metering pin, absorbing the impact. As the bumper is stopped, hydraulic fluid in the front chamber has forced the floating piston foreword, compressing the gas to return the bumper. On recovery, compressed gas forces the fluid to return to its original chamber and the bumper is returned to its original position.

Vehicles of the 90's began took on more rounded shapes for increased aerodynamics and fuel efficiency. Many manufacturer's took this opportunity to reduce weight and cost by styling new crushable front bumpers made of

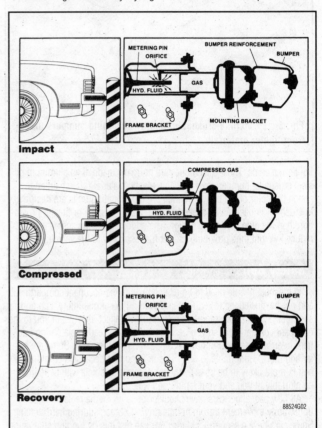

Impact

Compressed

Recovery   88524G02

Fig. 3 Vehicles of the 70's and early 80's used gas charged energy absorbing bumpers

88524G2A

Fig. 4 By the 90's manufacturer's used stylish bumper covers . . .

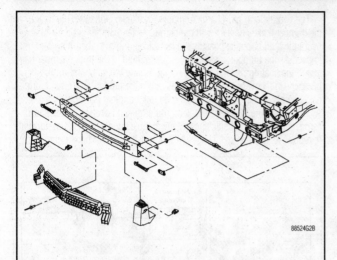

Fig. 5 . . . to hide crushable, energy absorbing bumpers made from lighter materials

lighter materials. These assemblies are normally made of an aluminum or steel crushable bumper covered with a plastic material (often painted to match the color of the body). In addition, the mounting units are designed to crush on impact. As an assembly, this offers the same or greater protection than the older hydraulic design. The added advantage comes with the reduced weight thus providing greater fuel economy to the vehicle.

Safety Belts

In crashes, people need to be retained within the occupant compartment and not be ejected, as to reduce the likelihood of serious injury. Lap and shoulder belts play an important role in this. In effect, they retain you to the occupant compartment so you decelerate with it instead of slamming into hard interior surfaces. But not all belt designs are the same. Some are easier and more comfortable to use . This is important because a comfortable belt is more likely to be used every trip. Choose a vehicle with belts that comfortably fit you and your family, and wear them.

All new passenger cars have shoulder belts on inertia reels that allow upper body movement during normal driving but lock during hard braking. Some cars have a second lock, too. You can test this by tugging sharply on a belt. If it locks, it's dual locking.

Some vehicles have tensioners that activate in more serious frontal crashes to reduce belt slack which, in turn, reduces the risk of head and chest impacts with hard interior surfaces.

Air Bags

▶ **See Figures 6, 7, 8, and 9**

Even the best belt designs can't prevent all head and chest impacts in serious frontal crashes. Air bags help by creating an energy-absorbing cushion between the upper body and steering wheel, instrument panel, or windshield. To get the maximum benefits, you should use a belt and sit away from the bag. This way, you'll be in position with sufficient space for the air bag to inflate rapidly and create a protective buffer.

Driver deaths in frontal crashes are about 20 percent lower with air bags than in similar cars without them. At the time of publication, it has been estimated that more than 2,500 lives have been saved. But in some circumstances, air bags can cause injuries, mostly minor, but occasionally serious or, in rare cases, fatal. The most serious injuries occur when people are

very close to air bags when they first begin to inflate. Some of the deaths have been infants in rear-facing restraints and unrestrained or improperly restrained children. This risk can be eliminated by making sure all youngsters travel in the back seat.

Although different manufacturers' systems vary slightly, the air bag system is composed of a few basic parts. Two sensors located in the area of the front bumper, or in the firewall area, sense the impact. The sensors activate inflator(s) that blow-up a passenger air bag in the right-hand side of the dashboard, and a driver air bag located in the steering wheel hub.

The system has an indicator lamp activated by the ignition key to let you know the system is working. If the car is involved in a frontal crash equivalent to running into a stationary barrier at least 10–12 mph, the sudden deceleration (impact) causes the sensor to activate a gas cartridge that instantly inflates the air bag preventing the occupants from contacting the inside of the vehicle. The air cushions absorb the impact.

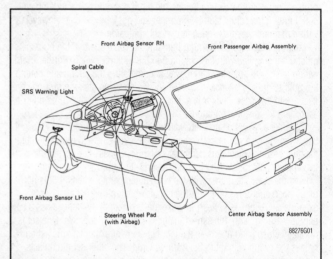

Fig. 6 Typical components of a supplemental restraint system (SRS) air bag

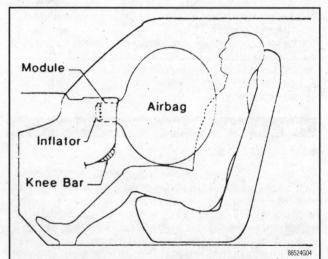

Fig. 7 High mounted passenger air bags are designed to provide head and upper torso restraint in frontal impacts

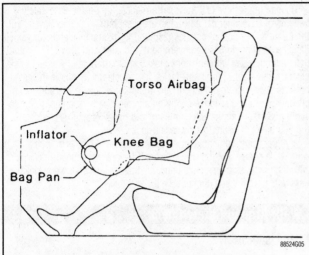

Fig. 8 Low mounted passenger air bags are designed to give lower torso protection in frontal impact situations

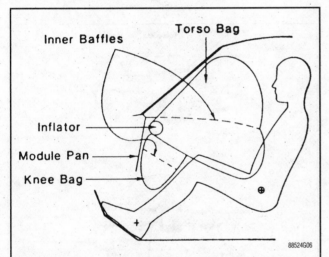

Fig. 9 Driver is protected from frontal impacts using a steering wheel mounted air bag.

The air bags themselves are porous and the air is actually beginning to escape as they are being inflated. The entire process (sensing, inflation and partial deflation) is completed in about ⅟₂₅th of a second, or about the time it takes to blink your eye.

SEATING POSITION

Sitting very close to the steering wheel increases your risk of hitting it in a crash, even if you're using a lap and shoulder belt, and it doesn't allow sufficient space for the air bag. So it's important to position yourself away from the wheel. Choose a vehicle that allows you to comfortably reach the pedals without being close to the wheel. Shorter people who cannot reach pedals without getting too close might consider vehicles equipped with a telescoping adjustment to move the steering wheel away from your chest. And remember that sitting very close to an air bag increases injury risk from the bag itself. This is another reason to position yourself away from the steering wheel.

Side Impact Protection

In side impacts, some of the more serious injuries occur when the force of a crash drives a door into an occupant. All 1997 and later model passenger cars must meet federal side impact crash test requirements intended to address this problem. Vans, pickups, and utility vehicles were not required to meet this standard until the 1999 model year, though many did prior to the deadline. Manufacturers typically have used extra padding to meet this standard, but some also are installing side air bags to protect drivers and right front passengers. Side air bags were fist introduced in some 1997 models including the Audi A8, BMW 5- and 7-series, Cadillac Catera and DeVille, Lexus LS 400, Mercedes E,S,SL classes, and all Volvos.

Head Restraints

To prevent people's heads from being snapped back, causing neck injuries in rear-end crashes, head restraints are required in the front seats of all new passenger vehicles. Rear-seat head restraints aren't required but are found in more and more cars.

All head restraints aren't the same. Some are adjustable, and some are fixed. Head restraints also vary a lot in height and how far they're set back from occupants' head. To prevent neck injuries, it's necessary for head restraints to be directly behind and close to the backs of occupants' heads. Make sure the ones in a car you're considering can be positioned this way. In general, fixed head restraints are preferred because they don't have to be adjusted for different occupants. If the ones in a car you're considering are adjustable, check that they can be positioned behind and close to the back of your head. Make sure they lock when adjusted, because some don't.

Don't be surprised if a head restraint cannot be positioned for adequate protection. Among more than 200 1997 model passenger cars in which the NHTSA measured the head restraints, more than half had poor geometry. Only five vehicles had good head restraint geometry. They were the Honda Civic del Sol, Mercedes E class with restraints that adjust automatically, the Toyota Supra, and two Volvo models — the 850 and 960.

Infant And Child Seats

An infant who can't sit up should be placed in a rear-facing restraint secured by an adult safety belt in a vehicle's back seat. Such restraints provide very good protection but can pose a safety risk if placed in the front seat with a passenger air bag. An inflating bag could hit the restraint with enough force to cause serious injury or death. In vehicles with no rear seat, automakers may install manual cut-off switches for passenger air bags. Drivers of these vehicles should check the passenger bag status before every trip.

✳✳ CAUTION

Don't position an infant in front if there's a passenger air bag!

When infants first outgrow their safety seats and can sit up by themselves, they should travel in special child restraints — again, held in place by adult safety belts in the back seat. When used properly, such restraints provide good crash protection, and they're offered as optional built-ins in the back seats of a number of passenger vehicles. Older children can use either adult safety belts or booster seats to make the adult belts fit better. What's crucial to remember is that infants and children should ride, properly buckled into special restraints or safety belts, in the back seat. This was true before air bags, and it's doubly true now because riding in back puts children out of the paths of inflating air bags.

➡**If children must ride up front, set the seat all the way back. Don't let a child fiddle with radio dials, for example, because this can put the youngster's head too close to the air bag.**

Daytime Running Lights

More of a crash avoidance system than a conventional safety system, many new vehicles are equipped with daytime running lights. Activated by the ignition switch, these typically are high-beam headlights at reduced intensity or low-beam headlights at full or reduced power. The lights, which increase contrast between vehicles and their background to make cars more visible to oncoming drivers, are an inexpensive way to reduce multiple-vehicle daytime crashes. In Canada and other countries where they're required, daytime running lights have reduced daylight, car-to-car crashes. Such lights aren't currently required on new cars in the United States, but they're permitted.

Anti-lock Brakes

One of the greatest contributions to automotive safety was the advent of anti-lock braking systems. Anti-lock braking systems (ABS) allows maintaining directional control of the vehicle during braking. While benefits from ABS can be derived on dry pavement driving, the most substantial benefits are witnessed under adverse traction conditions.

Braking systems operate on the principle that motion energy is removed from the vehicle in the form of heat and dissipated. The brake calipers squeeze the brake pads against the rotors and slow the rotors. This does not stop the vehicle; the friction of the road surface against the tires is what actually slows the vehicle. The brakes merely provide the retarding force for the tires. If the tires can not maintain a level of traction with the road surface, the best braking system can not slow the vehicle.

If during braking, 1 or more tires hit a section of low traction, the braking force applied by the calipers will overwhelm the available traction at the tire contact patch. As a result the tire will slide instead of roll. If we look at the contact patch of the tire as the car rolls down the road, we would see that the tire has a relative speed of zero compared to the ground. Under braking the relative may increase so there is a slight percentage of slip between the tire and the road surface. A small percentage of slip is acceptable and friction force will rise, slowing the car. If the percentage rises too high and the tire is no longer rolling, the friction force drops tremendously and the tire can not provide lateral or longitudinal traction.

Driving in the wet or snow, loose gravel or sand, or any other kind of low traction surface can cause the tires to lock and loose directional stability. ABS monitors the rotation of the tires and compares the speed of each. If the speed of 1 or more tires drop drastically below that of the others during braking, the ABS controller will cut hydraulic pressure to that wheel until it is rotating at the same speed as the others. This will provide the best chance of maintaining directional control of the vehicle.

ABS can not perform miracles. If the laws of physics are exceeded, the car can leave the roadway. ABS can only help to maintain control. Go too fast into a turn and mash the brakes, ABS or not, the tires can only do so much and control may be lost. Driving too fast in the rain or snow is a recipe for trouble. ABS is a tool to make driving safer, not a cure-all for bad driving habits.

ABS can be useful in dry ground driving in the same way it is in low traction situations.

Despite impressive test track performance, the on-the-road safety benefits of passenger car anti-locks are disappointing. They haven't cut the frequency or cost of crashes resulting in insurance claims for vehicle damage. Recent studies by government, industry, and the NHTSA found that cars equipped with anti-lock brakes are in more fatal single-vehicle crashes than cars without anti-locks. It's not clear why this is the case, but it is suspected that many drivers don't know how to use anti-locks effectively. Trained to brake gently on slippery roads or pump brakes to avoid a skid, drivers have to "unlearn" old behavior and use hard, continuous brake pressure to activate anti-locks.

If you anticipate driving a lot on slick roads, such brakes may be a worthwhile choice. But remember that anti-locks aren't "super" brakes allowing you to stop on a dime under all circumstances. And don't take risks you'd avoid if you did not have the anti-locks.

Walk-Around Safety Check

➧ **See Figure 10**

Take a few minutes to walk around your car or truck every now and then, especially during a long trip. Checking out all of the things that affect your driving safety won't take more than five minutes and could uncover a small problem before it gets dangerous or expensive.

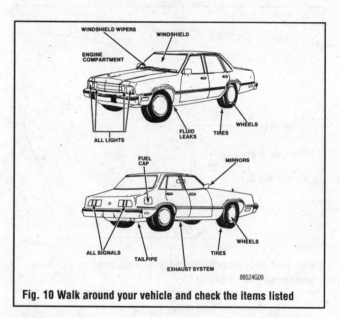

Fig. 10 Walk around your vehicle and check the items listed

TIRES AND WHEELS

➧ **See Figures 11 and 12**

Check for uneven wear patterns, excessive wear, nails, cuts or other damage. Uneven wear may indicate alignment problems in the front end or uneven inflation pressure. Check the inflation pressure with a gauge.

LIGHTING SYSTEM

Check the headlights, turn signals and taillights for proper operation. Look at the operation of all exterior lights while someone else operates them.

Fig. 11 Carefully check the sidewalls for any signs of damage

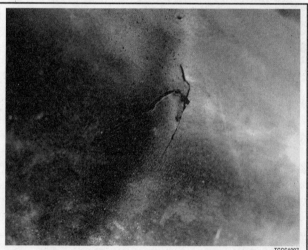

Fig. 12 Sidewall damage like this can lead to dangerous conclusions

Clean the headlights with a rag. You'll be amazed at the difference it makes at night.

MIRRORS

Be sure that the mirrors are clean and adjusted properly for the best view of what's behind you.

WINDSHIELD & WIPERS

Clean the windshield for maximum visibility. While you're about it, take a quick look at the wiper blades. They should be in good condition for when they're needed.

TAILPIPE

Checking the color of the tailpipe is a good habit to get into. It can provide a quick check on how your engine is operating.

On a long trip, or when the car has been run at highway speeds for a while, the inside of the tailpipe should be a light gray or white. This indicates that the engine is running properly.

FLUID LEAKS

Look for fuel, oil, or water leaks. The location of the spots under the vehicle can give a clue to the source of the leak, just as the color of the spots gives valuable clues.

* Red is probably automatic transmission fluid.
* Black or brown is most likely engine oil or axle lube.
* Clear water will usually come from the air conditioning condenser on a hot day.
* Greenish or Orange colored water is usually antifreeze.

It's normal for the air conditioner to drip a small amount of water under the front of the vehicle when it's used on a hot day.

FUEL CAP

If you just stopped for fuel, be sure that the fuel cap was put back.

UNDERHOOD CHECK

* Engine oil—Check the engine oil level.
* Coolant—Check the radiator coolant level in the reservoir.
* Battery— Visually check battery cables and connections.
* Automatic transmission—Check the fluid level.
* Master cylinder—Check the fluid level.
* Power Steering—Check the fluid level.
* Windshield washer—Check the fluid level.
* Belts & hoses—Visually check all belts and hoses for wear.

➡**In addition to the items listed above there are cases with some manufacturer's where odd components such as manual transmission/transaxles and front differentials many be equipped with a dipstick found underhood for fluid level check. If you are unsure of a dipstick on your vehicle, check with the owners manual.**

MAINTENANCE COMPONENT LOCATIONS—TYPICAL FRONT WHEEL DRIVE VEHICLE

1. Vehicle Identificaiton Number (VIN) plate
2. Brake booster
3. Brake fluid reservoir
4. Underhood fuse and relay box
5. Battery
6. Transmission fluid level dipstick
7. Air cleaner
8. Ignition coil pack
9. Spark plugs (under cover)
10. Engine oil filler cap
11. Radiator cap
12. Windshield washer fluid reservoir
13. Power steering fluid reservoir
14. Coolant reservoir
15. Positive Crankcase Ventilation (PCV) valve
16. Engine oil level dipstick

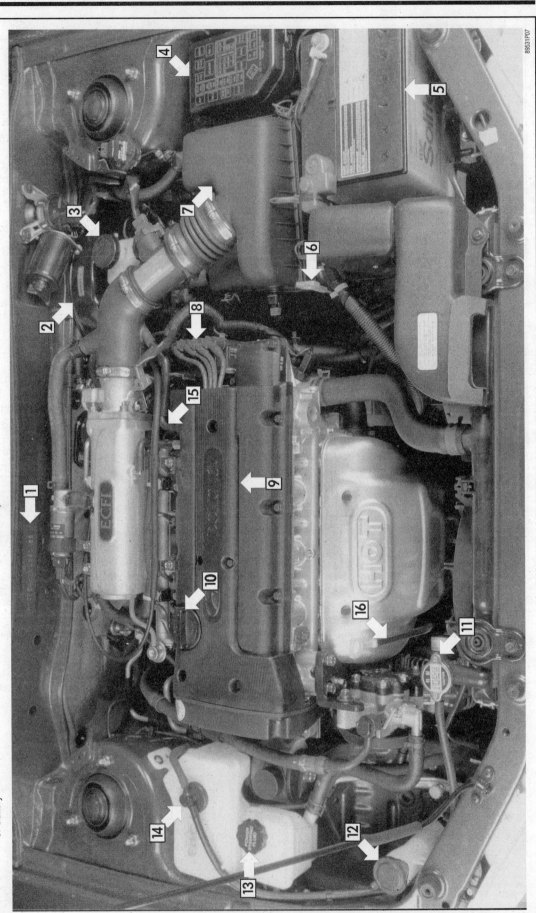

89531P07

MAINTENANCE COMPONENT LOCATIONS—TYPICAL REAR WHEEL DRIVE VEHICLE

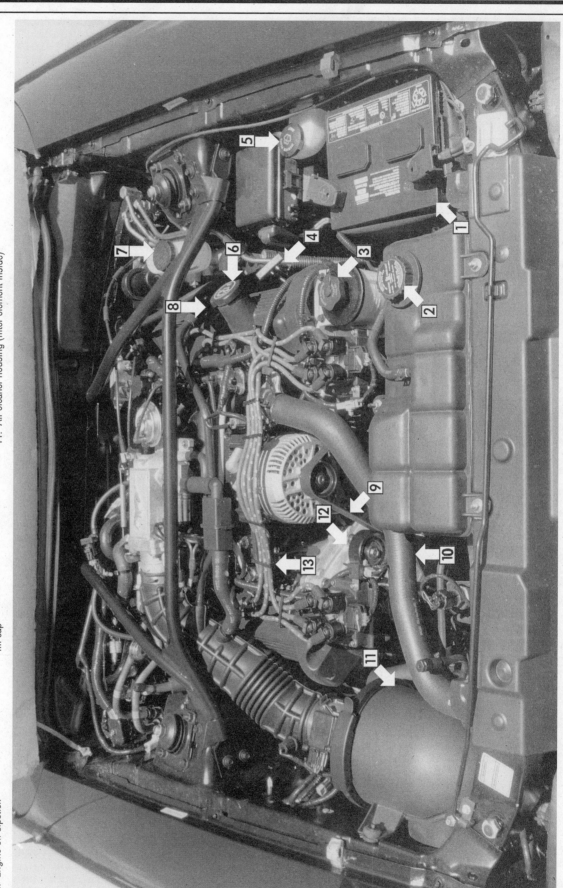

1. Battery
2. Cooling system reservoir and fill cap
3. Power steering fluid reservoir and fill cap
4. Engine oil dipstick
5. Windshield washer reservoir and fill cap
6. Engine oil fill cap
7. Brake master cylinder fluid reservoir and fill cap
8. PCV valve
9. Accessory drive belt
10. Upper radiator hose
11. Air cleaner housing (filter element inside)
12. Accessory drive belt automatic tensioner
13. Spark plug wires

88231P72

Safety on the Road

▶ See Figure 13

While you're on the road, pay attention to your vehicle, it may be trying to tell you something. Look, listen, smell and feel for possible problems. Warning signals come in many forms—noises, different handling and vibrations.

SIGHTS

▶ See Figure 14

Part of any walk-around inspection of your vehicle should include checking underneath for spots and drips. Get into the habit of doing this regularly, especially after the vehicle has been driven for a while.

Red spots under the transmission area indicate leaking transmission fluid. Try to find out where the leak is coming from. It could be the problem is as simple as an overfilled transmission. The fluid could be foaming out the dipstick tube and running down the case.

Rust spots of water under the front of the vehicle may indicate a leaking radiator; leaking radiator hoses or simply overflows from the radiator or air conditioning condenser.

Dark oil spots under a differential probably indicate that the differential cover bolts are loose and should be tightened. Oil spots under the engine can mean anything from leaking valve cover gaskets (the oil runs down the engine) to a host of more serious problems. Try to find the source of the leak and fix it.

HIGHWAY EMERGENCY CHECKLIST

Item	Where to Carry it		
	Car	Glove Comp.	Trunk
Fire extinguisher	●		
This manual	●		
Coins for meters and phone		●	
Tire Gauge		●	
Flashlight		●	
First aid kit		●	
Road maps		●	
Spare fuses		●	
Flares			●
Lug wrench/Jack			●
Jumper cables			●
Hand tools			●
Paper towels/rags			●
Work gloves			●
Hand cleaner			●
Plastic jug of water			●
Duct tape			●
Silicone spray lube			●

88524G08

Fig. 13 Important items to carry in every vehicle

COMMON SENSE GUIDE TO SAFETY

Sight	Besides routine inspection, be alert to the very appearance. Look for sagging on either end or side, puddles underneath or anything that doesn't look right.
Sound	If you've got a strange noise, try to associate it with a particular function, such as braking or accelerating. Then you'll know where to look for it.
Smell	Smells are deceptive. Does it smell like burned rubber, oil, or insulation? Gas or exhaust fumes point out leaks in their systems.
Feel	If car handles strangely, is it a constant feel, or does it only pull while braking? Associate behavior of car with particular action.

88524G10

Fig. 14 Let your senses be your guide to safe operation of your vehicle

FEEL

All good drivers learn to recognize when the vehicle is behaving differently than normal. Vibrations often preface great many mechanical problems that can be located and corrected before they become serious. Be suspicious of any vibrations that are out-of-the-ordinary—be alert and train yourself to recognize the warning signs.

SMELL

▶ See Figures 15 and 16

Strange odors are often a clue to something gone (or about to go) wrong.
- An overheated radiator gives off a steamy vapor and a mild odor something like burning paint. It should warn you to check the temperature gauge or to stop and check the coolant level.

MECHANICAL VIBRATION DIAGNOSIS

Vibration Category	Correction Codes For Vibrations Within Specific mph Ranges								
	10	20	30	40	50	60	70	80	90
Vehicle Speed Sensitive				UJ and TEB	WB	TRR	TB / PSY	TLR	
Torque Sensitive		UJA		UJ and TEB				UJA	
Engine Speed Sensitive		EA / DEM							

Diagnosis Chart Correction Codes

ADB—Accessory Drive Belts. Excessive wear or looseness may cause droning noise or flutter.

AN—Rear Axle Noise. May be caused by gears or bearings.

DEM—Damaged Engine Mounts. May allow engine or accessories to contact body.

EA—Engine Accessories. Loose or broken accessories: power steering pump, air conditioning compressor, alternator, water pump, etc.

PSY—Propeller Shaft and Yokes. Undercoating, runout, and balance not a cause for vibration below 45 mph. Possible cause of audible vibration only between 55 and 75 mph.

TB—Tire Balance. Not a cause of vibration below 30 mph. Dynamic unbalance not a cause below 40 mph. Check balance of wheels and tires.

TEB—Transmission Extension Housing Bushing. Looseness usually accompanied by oil seal leakage.

TLR—Tire and Wheel Lateral Runout. Not usually a cause of vibration below 60 mph.

TRR—Tire and Wheel Radial Runout. Not a cause of vibration below 20 mph. The speed required to cause vibration increases as runout decreases.

TW—Tire Wear. Uneven wear patterns (cupped) may generate a singing whine at higher speeds and degenerate to a growl at lower speeds and may be accompanied by vibration similar to that caused by wheel bearings.

UJ—Universal Joints. Universal joints can cause vibrations at any speed.

UJA—Universal Joint Angles. Incorrect angles may cause mechanical vibration below 15 mph and mechanical or audible vibration between 30 and 55 mph.

WB—Wheel Bearings. If rough or damaged, will cause a growling or grinding noise at low speeds, or a whining noise at high speeds. Loose wheel bearings can cause mechanical vibrations at 50 to 60 mph.

AUDIBLE VIBRATION DIAGNOSIS

Vibration Category	Correction Codes For Vibrations Within Specific mph Ranges								
	10	20	30	40	50	60	70	80	90
Vehicle Speed Sensitive				UJA / UJ and TEB	WB	TW	PSY		
Torque Sensitive					AN / UJ and TEB				
Engine Speed Sensitive		DEM	ADB		EA				

88524G11

Fig. 15 Vibration diagnosis charts

• Overheated brake linings give off a strong definite odor of something burning. Usually overheated linings are accompanied by squeaking sounds from the wheels, indicating that the linings are glazed from heat. The best thing to do is stop and let the brakes cool for about half an hour, but have the brakes checked as soon as possible.

• Burning oil or grease is a strong, pungent odor, usually more noticeable when the vehicle is not moving. Occasionally, there will be wisps of smoke coming from under the hood. The problem could be as simple as oil leaking from valve cover gaskets onto hot exhaust manifolds, or it could be just accumulated grease from a long overdue engine cleaning.

• A frequent smell associated with catalytic converters is the rotten egg smell, which is unmistakable for anything else. One of the byproducts of the reaction in the catalytic converter is sulfur dioxide (SO_2), which is responsible for the odor. It does not necessarily indicate a malfunction, but is extremely unpleasant.

NOISES

Noises are the most common indicator of something gone wrong in your car, and also the most difficult to interpret. Noises come in hundreds of variations (knocks, rattles, squeaks, grinds, etc.), each with its own particular sound and nearly impossible to describe accurately. The other problem is recognizing when the sound is perfectly normal and when it spells trouble.

Virtually any part can make almost any noise if the conditions are right. A stethoscope, piece of hose or a metal rod can be used carefully to pinpoint sounds coming from various parts.

Noise	Description	Could be Caused By
Buzz	A humming sound (bzzzz)	A buzz or whistle can be caused by a defective radiator cap. If loosening the cap stops the noise, replace the cap. Other causes include foreign debris on the radiator, loose radiator or fan, or a loose shroud.
Clang	Metallic ringing similar to the sound of a bell	This is normally due to a failing U-joint and you will hear it as you back off, or step on the gas. U-joints are serviced by replacement.
Click (tick)	A quick, sharp sound similar to a loud clock	A tick while starting is typical of older electrical fuel pumps and is not a malfunction. Other causes are stone in the tire tread (frequency varies with speed), damaged wheel bearing, shredded fan belt, windshield wiper motor/transmission, differential or transmission gears, heater motor, lack of radio suppression, or improperly adjusted valves.
Grinding Grating Growling	A harsh rubbing sound, like parts rubbing or scraping A deeper grinding sound	Check the fluid level in the power steering pump. U-joints will also occasionally make a grinding noise, as will a starter drive that is not engaging or disengaging completely. Other causes include a bad throwout bearing, dragging brakes, something non-metallic in contact with the brakes or brake drum, worn transmission gears, bad water pump or loose water pump pulley or fan belt contacting the shroud.
Hiss	A high pitched sound like steam escaping (sssssssss...)	The usual cause of this type of sound is steam escaping from the radiator or a broken hose, although it can be produced by a vacuum leak, a leaking tire, or a loose spark plug. All of these are fairly easy to cure. Other causes are wind leaks around the body or windows, or a plugged PCV valve. Watch the oil fill hole; if smoke is coming out accompanied by a hiss, chances are you have worn piston rings.
Howl	A prolonged wailing sound	A howling sound is usually from the transmission gears (check the fluid level before assuming the worst), but could also be due to wind leaks around the body or windows.
Hum	A low droning noise (hummmmmm...)	A hum from the rear probably indicates a defective rear axle, especially if it is louder coasting, but before having it torn down, check other causes. Snow tires produce a constant hum, as do certain road surfaces. Check the rear axle oil level, wheel bearings and U-joints.
Knock	A pounding or striking of metal parts	A constant knocking noise is usually due to worn crankshaft or connecting rod bearings. A knock under load can be caused by worn connecting rod bearings, fuel octane too low, or loose wrist pins in the piston. Remove a spark plug wire from each cylinder in turn. If the knock stops, you've located the cylinder.
Rattle	Rapid succession of sharp sounds	Rattles are normal to the aging process. If it doesn't seem to affect the handling or running of the car, don't worry.
Squeal	A prolonged, shrill squeaking	A squeal normally comes from an improperly tightened fan belt, but could be due to a bad water pump, brakes not fully releasing, improper toe-in, worn brake linings, low tires or worn alternator bearings.
Thud, Thump	A dull knocking sound	These sounds are caused by low, flat-spotted or out-of-round tires, worn U-joints (they give a slight thud as you let off the gas), loose battery or contents of the trunk, bad throwout bearing (check by applying and releasing the clutch), excessive play in the crankshaft or broken engine mounts.

88524G12

Fig. 16 Noise diagnosis chart

5

FUELS AND LUBRICANTS

FUELS AND LUBRICANTS

Fluid Disposal

Used fluids such as engine oil, transmission fluid, ethylene-glycol antifreeze and brake fluid are hazardous wastes and must be disposed of properly. Before draining any fluids, consult with your local authorities; in many areas waste oil, etc. is being accepted as a part of recycling programs. A number of service stations and auto parts stores are also accepting waste fluids for recycling.

Be sure of the recycling center's policies before draining any fluids, as many will not accept different fluids that have been mixed together.

Gasoline

Gasoline is a hydrocarbon (composed of hydrogen and carbon), produced by refining crude oil or petroleum. When gasoline burns, these compounds separate into hydrogen and carbon atoms and unite with oxygen atoms. The results obtained from burning gasoline are dependent on its most important characteristics: octane rating, volatility, lead content, and density.

OCTANE RATING

▶ **See Figure 1**

Simply put, the octane rating of a gasoline is its ability to resist knock, a sharp metallic noise resulting from detonation or uncontrolled combustion in the cylinder. Knock can occur for a variety of reasons, one of which is the incorrect octane rating for the engine in your vehicle. To understand why knock occurs, you must understand why knock doesn't occur. So let's look at the normal combustion process.

Under normal operating conditions, the firing of the spark plug initiates the burning of the fuel air mixture in the combustion chamber. Once the plug fires, a wall of flame starts outward from the plug in all directions at once. This flame front moves evenly and rapidly throughout the entire combustion chamber until the entire fuel/air mixture is burned. This even, rapid progress of the burning fuel/air mixture is highly dependent on the octane rating of the gasoline.

If the octane rating is too low, the last part of the compressed fuel/air mixture may ignite before the flame front reaches it, in effect creating two areas of combustion within the cylinder. However, while the original combustion is proceeding at a carefully controlled rate, this new combustion is simply a sudden sharp explosion. This abrupt increase in pressure is what creates the knocking sound in the combustion chamber.

As far as the piston is concerned, the damage inflicted by the increase in pressure (caused by the sudden explosion) is exactly like striking the piston top with a heavy hammer. Knock is very damaging to the engine, since it causes extraordinary wear to bearings, piston crowns, and other vital engine parts. Engines can actually be destroyed through excessive engine knock.

Engine knock can be controlled by using a gas with the proper octane rating. Octane measurements made under laboratory conditions have led to "Research" and "Motor" octane ratings. In general, the research octane number tends to be about 6–10 points higher than the motor octane rating (for what is essentially the same gasoline). Since the early seventies, most octane ratings on gas pumps have been the average of the research and motor octane numbers. For instance, if the gasoline formerly had a research octane rating of 100, and a motor octane rating of 90, the octane rating found on the pump now would be 95.

Your owner's manual will probably indicate the type of gasoline and octane recommended for use in your vehicle. However, octane requirements can vary according to the vehicle and the conditions under which it is operating. If you encounter sustained engine knock, wait until your tank is nearly empty, and then try a gasoline with a higher octane rating. Don't needlessly overbuy—it's a waste of money to buy gasoline of a higher octane than your engine requires in order to satisfy its anti-knock need.

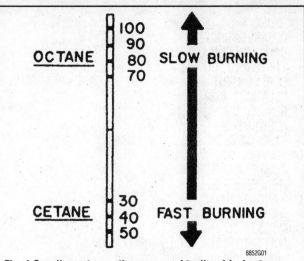

Fig. 1 Gasoline octane rating compared to diesel fuel cetane rating

As a new vehicle is driven, combustion deposits build up and the octane requirement increases until an equilibrium level, normally between four and six octane numbers higher than the new-vehicle requirement, is reached. Other factors which can increase the octane an engine requires are higher air or engine temperatures, lower altitudes, lower humidity, a more advanced ignition spark timing, a leaner fuel/air mixture, sudden acceleration, and frequent stop-and-go driving which increases the build-up of combustion chamber deposits.

CATALYTIC CONVERTERS & UNLEADED FUEL

Since 1975, most vehicles have been equipped with catalytic converters, making the use of unleaded fuel mandatory. All vehicles equipped with catalytic converters have a restricted filler neck opening that will only permit the use of the smaller nozzle used on unleaded gas pumps. The use of leaded gas will not harm the engine, but will destroy the effectiveness of the converter and void your warranty.

LEAD CONTENT

Older, higher-compression engines usually required a gasoline with a higher octane rating. The most efficient way of increasing the octane rating of a gasoline was to add a compound called tetraethyl lead. Should circumstances force you to use a low-lead or no-lead gasoline with lower octane than the vehicle manufacturer specifies in an older lead fuel vehicle, you should temporarily retard the ignition timing very slightly in order to lessen the possibility of knocking. Some vehicles, though designed to operate on leaded gasoline, may be able to use low-lead and no-lead fuels. Again, experimentation is helpful in determining the gasoline octane that your vehicle and your driving require.

VOLATILITY

The volatility of any liquid is its ability to vaporize, and gasoline must vaporize in order to burn. A highly volatile gasoline will help a cold engine start easily and run smoothly while it is warming up. However, the use of a highly volatile gasoline in warm weather tends to cause vapor lock on carbureted engines. Vapor lock is a condition in which the gasoline actually vaporizes before it arrives at the carburetor jet where vaporization is supposed to take place. This premature vaporization may occur in the fuel line, fuel pump, or in a section of the carburetor. When use of highly volatile fuel leads to vapor lock, the engine becomes starved for fuel and will either lose power or stall. Although refiners vary the percentage of volatile fuel in their gasoline according to season and locality, vapor lock is more likely to occur in the early spring, when some stations may not have received supplies of less volatile gasoline.

DENSITY

Density is another property of gasoline, which can affect your fuel economy. It indicates how much chemical energy the gasoline contains. Density is generally measured in BTU's per gallon (the BTU, or British Thermal Unit, is a standard unit of energy), and usually varies less than 2% among most gasoline but can vary as much as 4–8%. This indicates that gas mileage could vary by as much as 4–8%, depending on the density of the gasoline you happen to choose.

ADDITIVES

➡ **The Environmental Protection Agency (EPA), through the Clean Air Act, has required that detergent additives, also referred to as Deposit Control Additives (DCAs) be added to all gasoline from January 1, 1995.**

Practically as important as octane rating and volatility are the additives that refiners put into their gasoline. Carburetor/Fuel injection detergent additives help clean the tiny passages in the carburetor or fuel injectors, ensuring consistent fuel/air mixtures necessary for smooth running and good gas mileage. Other additives are used to help control combustion chamber deposits, gum formation, rust, and wear. One additive you may have noticed in your vehicle is manganese. Since the advent of the catalytic converter and the resultant widespread use of unleaded gas, manganese has been used in many fuels as an anti-knock additive in unleaded gasoline. Manganese works, but it leaves reddish deposits on spark plugs. So, if you pull your spark plugs and notice that they are covered with what looks like rust, don't panic. It's only manganese and it's as harmless as the lead deposits it replaces.

GASOLINE BLENDS

The disruption of oil supplies from the Middle East in the 70's spurred an effort to try to curb the U.S. dependence on foreign petroleum sources. Interest in alternative fuels was also created by the reduction or elimination of lead anti-knock additives in gasoline. The lead was removed because of its incompatibility with the catalytic converter, now standard on almost every car and light truck.

Ethanol

Ethanol has attracted the most attention as a blend. It can be fermented from a variety of bases, including grain and sugar cane, much the same way wine is produced from grapes. The U.S. Environmental Protection Agency (EPA) allows a 10% ethanol mixture with gasoline and it is being sold as "super unleaded" or "premium unleaded" gasoline, gasohol, or with no specific identification.

Methanol

Methanol comes from natural gas, but the technology can produce it from coal, wood and a variety of other materials. Like ethanol, methanol raises the octane of gasoline and reduces engine "knock" or "ping", without affecting the efficiency of the catalytic converter. A 5% blend of methanol may raise the octane rating at the pump by 1–1.5 numbers.

Methanol also reduces carbon monoxide exhaust emissions, but the trade-off can be high:

• Methanol has an adverse effect on fuel economy, especially in late model vehicles. A 5% blend of methanol with gasoline has an energy content 2.5% less than gasoline.

• Evaporative emissions rise substantially when methanol is blended with gasoline. In addition, methanol may increase the oxides of nitrogen emissions and affect the capacity of the charcoal in the evaporative emissions canister.

• Methanol causes both hot and cold weather driveability problems. Methanol can change the stoichiometric (chemically correct) air/fuel ratio in the fuel delivery system. The higher volatility of the fuel increases the chance of vapor lock in carbureted vehicles and the increased heat of vaporization of methanol increases cold start and stalling problems in winter.

• Methanol, when water is present even in trace (minute) amounts will separate gasoline into 2 layers—gasoline rich on top and alcohol and water on the bottom. The net effect is unsatisfactory vehicle operation. Since the engine draws fuel from the bottom of the tank, it will not run properly, even at idle. Some refiners add heavier alcohol, known as "cosolvents", to counter the separation, but they are not 100% effective.

• Methanol has an effect on the parts of the fuel system and is measured more in time than in mileage. Rubber, plastic and metal fuel system components in most motor vehicles were designed for use with gasoline and are subject to attack by methanol blended fuels. Water tends to cling to methanol, and any water in the fuel tank will be carried through the entire fuel system. Metal components (excluding brass) are subject to water corrosion. Plastic and rubber compounds tend to swell, lose strength and stretch when subjected to high concentrations of methanol.

Several fuel suppliers are successfully marketing blends of methanol and cosolvents with gasoline, but the long-term effects on engines and fuel systems are not known and vehicle manufacturers will not give unqualified sanction to the use of methanol blended fuels.

Check your owner's manual to be sure.

Reformulated Gasoline

The Environmental Protection Agency (EPA), through the Clean Air Act, has mandated the use of reformulated gasoline in certain areas of the country from January 1, 1995.

Reformulated (RFP), is gasoline that the composition has been changed to reduce vehicle emissions. Reformulated gasoline has lower levels of volatile compounds and benzene. RFP also contains an oxygenate such as ether or ethanol.

Any oxygenated fuel will reduce fuel economy, this is true simply because it has less combustible material per gallon. But, because of the reduction of volatile compounds, vehicles which are in poor mechanical condition may also experience an increased hesitation after start-up.

Reformulated gasoline differs from oxygenated fuel in that it is intended for year round use with reduced emissions, whereas oxygenated fuels are designed to reduce carbon monoxide levels during the winter season.

Diesel Fuel

Because of their unique compression-ignition principle, diesel engines run on fuel oil instead of gasoline. The fuel is injected into the cylinder at the end of the compression stroke and the heat of compression ignites the mixture. Diesel fuel used in automotive applications comes in two grades, No. 1 diesel fuel and No. 2 diesel fuel. No. 1 diesel is the more volatile of the two and is designed for engines that will operate under varying load and speed conditions. No. 2 diesel is designed for a relatively uniform speed and high loads.

CETANE NUMBER

The cetane number of a diesel fuel refers to the ease with which a diesel fuel ignites. Don't confuse cetane ratings with octane ratings. Octane ratings refer to the slowing or controlling of the burning of gasoline. Cetane ratings refer only to the ease or speed of the ignition of diesel fuel. High cetane numbers mean that the fuel will ignite with relative ease or that it ignites well at low temperatures.

VISCOSITY

Viscosity is the ability of a liquid to flow. Water, for instance, has a low viscosity since it flows so easily. The viscosity of diesel fuel is important since it must be low enough that it flows easily through the injection system, while at the same time being high enough to lubricate the moving parts in the injection system. No. 2 diesel fuel has a higher viscosity than No. 1, which means it lubricates better, but does not flow as well. Because of this and its lower cetane rating, No. 2 diesel is not as satisfactory as No. 1 in extremely cold weather.

One more word on diesel fuels. No matter what you've heard elsewhere, don't thin diesel fuel with gasoline in cold weather. The lighter gasoline, which is more explosive, will cause rough running at the very least, and may cause extensive engine damage if enough is used.

Oils and Additives

Three ways you can improve your vehicle's mileage and insure that it delivers good economy for a longer time are:
1. Understand the functions of oil in your engine.
2. Choose the proper oil for various operating conditions.
3. Change the oil and filter changed at the recommended intervals.

THE FUNCTIONS OF ENGINE OIL

What does oil do in your vehicle's engine? If you answered "lubricate"; you're only partially right. While oil is primarily a lubricant, it also performs a number of other functions that are vital to the life and performance of your engine.

In addition to being a lubricant, oil also dissipates heat and makes parts run cooler; it helps reduce engine noise; it combats rust and corrosion of metal surfaces; it acts as a seal for pistons, rings, and cylinder walls; it combines with the oil filter to remove foreign substances from the engine.

When combustion occurs, temperatures can reach 2000–3000°F. (1093–1648°C), while pistons can easily reach a temperature of 1000°F (537°C). The high heat load travels down the connecting rods to the bearings. Both tin and lead are commonly used in bearings and become very soft around 350°F (177°C).

Oil in the crankcase can reach 250°F (121°C) after warm-up and is supplied to the bearings at these temperatures.

As the oil circulates, it picks up heat, and may be 50°F (10°C) hotter than the crankcase oil. Flow and circulation of the oil keeps the bearings at a safe heat level and is essential to limiting bearing temperatures. A continuous circulation of large quantities of oil is essential to long engine life.

TYPES OF ENGINE OIL

▶ See Figures 2 and 3

Engine oil service classifications have been provided by the American Petroleum Institute and include "S" (normal gasoline engine use) and "C" (commercial and fleet) applications. The following chart compares the latest API oil classifications with those previously used.

The American Petroleum Institute (API) SH quality level is a performance upgrade for gasoline engine oils from the API SG category. The American Society for Testing and Materials (ASTM) establishes engine tests for motor oils. Passing limits for these tests are the same for API SH oils as they were for API SG lubricants. However, the Chemical Manufacturers Association (CMA) has applied a Multiple Test Acceptance Criteria (MTAC), which is a statistically based methodology, to ASTM engine tests used to evaluate candidate oil.

The MTAC is:
• For oil run once, test data for each parameter must be a pass.
• For oil run twice, the average value of each parameter must be a pass.
• For oil run three or more times, one test may be discarded, and the average value of retained test data for each parameter must be a pass.

Previously for API SG and earlier categories, a pass in each engine test was sufficient regardless of the number of failures on the candidate oil before a test pass was obtained. Therefore, oils could be approved by failing a number of tests and bouncing one through for a pass.

In order to be certain that API SH oils can pass the ASTM engine tests to which MTAC have been applied, higher additive levels and a balancing of the chemical additive formula are required. More highly refined base oils

Fig. 2 The API donut symbol

88525G02

Fig. 3 Look for the API certification symbol when choosing a brand of engine oil

TCCS1235

are also helpful in meeting API SH specifications. The MTAC applied to ASTM engine tests results in performance improvements outlined below.

TEST CRITERIA (HOW OILS ARE RATED)

• Engine Rust
• High Temperature Oil Oxidation (oil deterioration)
• Piston Varnish
• Engine Varnish
• Engine Sludge
• Cam & Lifter Wear
• Bearing Wear
• Fuel Economy Improvement
Performance Improvement Over API SG
• Less rust
• Improved oxidation protection
• Less varnish
• Less sludge
• Less wear
• Better, fuel economy

Passing the ASTM Sequence tests with performance improvements over API SG allows oil to be labeled API SH and display the API donut symbol.

Thus far, we've discussed API SH. Now we'll talk about the tie-in with ILSAC. The American Automobile Manufacturers Association (AAMA) and the Japanese Automobile Manufacturers Association (JAMA), through an organization called the International Lubricant Standardization and Approval Committee (ILSAC), jointly developed and approved a specification for gasoline-fueled passenger car engine oils identified as GF-1. API and ILSAC have agreed on a single set of specifications that meet both API SH and ILSAC GF-1 with the exception of fuel economy and SAE grades approved. That is, in order to meet GF-1 an oil must meet API SH and the Energy Conserving II (EC-II) requirements. EC-II oil provides a 2.7% fuel economy improvement over reference oil in an ASTM fuel economy test that uses a laboratory engine. API SH has no energy conserving requirements. ILSAC GF-1 specifications apply to 0W-X, 5W-X and 10W-X oils where X can be 20, 30, 40 or 50. In contrast, API SH applies to all viscosity grades (multigrades and monogrades).

Shown in the illustration are the ILSAC Certification Mark and the API Donut Symbol. The ILSAC Certification Mark must be displayed on the front of an oil container. An oil with the ILSAC Mark meets all physical, chemical and performance requirements (ASTM engine tests) of API SH and is Energy Conserving II. Its viscosity grade is 0W-X, 5W-X or 10W-X.

The API Donut Symbol can be displayed anywhere on the container for oils meeting the API SH chemical, physical and performance requirements. All viscosity grades are included and the oil does not have to be EC-II approved.

API designation SH and ILSAC designation GF-1 were introduced by the petroleum industry on August 1, 1993.

The API designation SJ has been adopted to engine oils available after 1996 and has replaced the former SH designation at the time of publication. The API SH designation may still be used in conjunction with an API C-service category.

Previously there were two energy conserving oil categories: **ENERGY CONSERVING AND ENERGY CONSERVING II**. These may appear on the label as: EC or EC II. Effective as of October 1996 there is only one EC designation that is EC. The EC and EC II that were used in conjunction with API Service Category SH became obsolete after August 1997.

EC used in conjunction with API SH: These oils have produced a fuel economy improvement of 1.5 percent or greater over a standard reference oil in an ASTM test procedure. Oils meeting this requirement display the ENERGY CONSERVING will have a label in the lower portion of the donut shaped API Service Symbol.

EC II used in conjunction with API SH: These oils have produced a fuel economy improvement of 2.7 percent or greater over a standard reference oil in an ASTM test procedure. Oils meeting this requirement display the ENERGY CONSERVING II will have a label in the lower portion of the donut shaped API Service Symbol.

EC used in conjunction with API SJ: These oils have produced a fuel economy improvement of 1.4 percent or more (0W-20 and 5W-20 viscosity grades), 1.1 percent or more (other 0W- and 5W-multiviscosity grades), or 0.5 percent or more (low-multi viscosity grades and all other viscosity grades). Oils that meet this requirement and are properly licensed may display "Energy Conserving" in the lower portion of the API Service Symbol in conjunction with API Service Category SJ in the upper portion.

OIL VISCOSITY

▶ **See Figure 4**

In addition to meeting the SH or SJ classification of the American Petroleum Institute, your oil should be of a viscosity suitable for the outside temperature in which you'll be driving.

Oil must be thin enough to get between the close tolerances of the moving parts it must lubricate. Once there, it must be thick enough to separate them with a slippery oil film. If the oil is too thin it won't separate the parts, if it's too thick it can't squeeze between them in the first place either way, excess friction and wear takes place. To complicate matters, cold-morning starts require thin oil to reduce engine resistance, while high-speed driving requires thick oil, which can lubricate vital engine parts at temperatures up to 250°F (121°C).

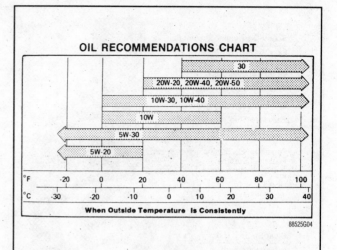

Fig. 4 Typical oil grade recommendation chart—check your owners manual for specific manufacturers recommendations

According to the Society of Automotive Engineers' viscosity classification system, an oil with a high viscosity number (e.g., 40) will be thicker than one with a lower number (e.g., 10W). The "W" in 10W indicates that the oil is desirable for use in winter driving. Using special additives, multiple-viscosity oils are available to combine easy starting at cold temperatures with engine protection at turnpike speeds. For example, 10W-40 oil will have the viscosity of 10W oil when the engine is cold and that of 40 oil when the engine is warm. The use of such oil will decrease engine resistance and improve your gas mileage during short trips in which the oil doesn't have a chance to warm up.

Some of the more popular multiple-viscosity oils are 5W-30, 10W-30, 10W-40, 15W-40, 20W-40, 20W-50, and 5W-50.

Consult your owner's manual or a reputable oil dealer for the recommended viscosity range for your vehicle and the outside temperature in which it operates.

ADDITIVES

▶ **See Figures 5 and 6**

High-quality engine oil will include a number of chemical compounds known as additives. These are blended in at the refinery and fall into the following categories.

Pour point depressants help cold starting by making the oil flow more easily at low temperatures. Otherwise, the oil would tend to be a waxy substance just when you need it the most.

Oxidation and bearing corrosion inhibitors help to prevent the formation of gummy deposits which can take place when engine oil oxidizes under high temperatures. In addition, these inhibitors place a protective coating on sensitive bearing metals, which would otherwise be attacked by the chemicals, formed by oil oxidation.

Rust and corrosion inhibitors protect against water and acids formed by the combustion process. Water is physically separated from the metal parts vulnerable to rust, and corrosive acids are neutralized by alkaline chemicals. The neutralization of combustion acids is an important key to long engine life.

Detergents and dispersants use teamwork. Detergents clean up the products of normal combustion and oxidation while dispersants keep them suspended until they can be removed by means of the filter or an oil change. Foam inhibitors prevent the tiny air bubbles that can be caused by fast moving engine parts whipping air into the oil. Foam can also occur when the oil level falls too low and the oil pump begins sucking up air instead of oil (like when the kids finish a milkshake). Without foam inhibitors, these tiny air bubbles would cause hydraulic valve lifters to collapse and reduce engine performance and economy significantly.

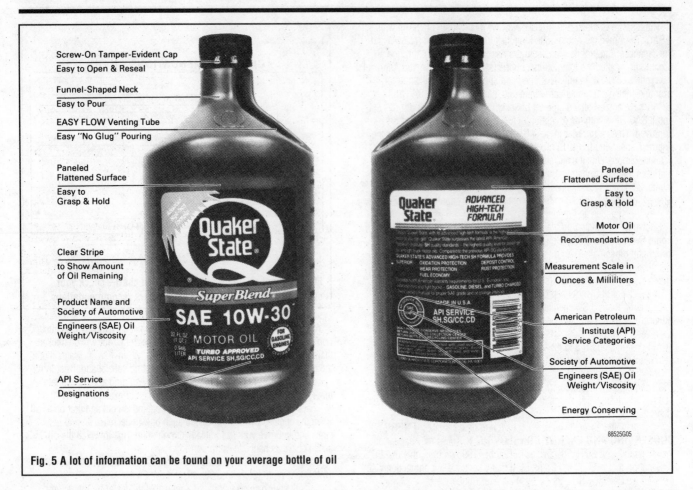

Screw-On Tamper-Evident Cap
Easy to Open & Reseal

Funnel-Shaped Neck
Easy to Pour

EASY FLOW Venting Tube
Easy "No Glug" Pouring

Paneled
Flattened Surface
Easy to
Grasp & Hold

Clear Stripe
to Show Amount
of Oil Remaining

Product Name and
Society of Automotive
Engineers (SAE) Oil
Weight/Viscosity

API Service
Designations

Paneled
Flattened Surface

Easy to
Grasp & Hold

Motor Oil
Recommendations

Measurement Scale in
Ounces & Milliliters

American Petroleum
Institute (API)
Service Categories

Society of Automotive
Engineers (SAE) Oil
Weight/Viscosity

Energy Conserving

Fig. 5 A lot of information can be found on your average bottle of oil

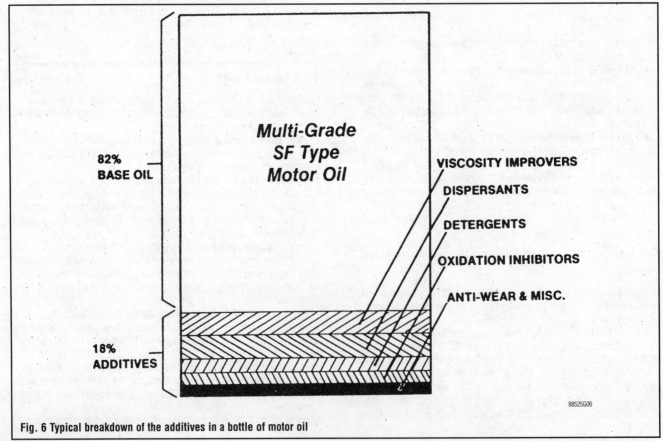

82%
BASE OIL

Multi-Grade
SF Type
Motor Oil

VISCOSITY IMPROVERS

DISPERSANTS

DETERGENTS

OXIDATION INHIBITORS

ANTI-WEAR & MISC.

18%
ADDITIVES

Fig. 6 Typical breakdown of the additives in a bottle of motor oil

Viscosity index improvers reduce the rate at which an oil thins out when the temperature climbs. These additives are what make multiple-viscosity oils possible. Without them, single-weight oil, which permitted easy starting on a cold morning, might thin out and cause you to lose your engine on a hot afternoon. If you use multiple-viscosity oil, it's this additive that helps your gas mileage during those short trips in cold weather.

Friction modifiers and extreme pressure additives are valuable in so-called boundary lubrication, where there is metal-to-metal contact due to the absence or breaking down of the oil film between moving parts. Friction modifiers, or anti-wear agents, deposit protective surface films that reduce the friction and heat of metal-to-metal contact. Extreme pressure additives work by reacting chemically with metal surfaces involved in high-pressure contact.

SYNTHETIC OILS

▶ **See Figure 7**

There are excellent synthetics and fuel-efficient oils available that, under the right circumstances, can help provide better fuel mileage and better engine protection. However, these advantages come at a price, which can be significantly more expensive than the cost per quart of conventional motor oils.

Before pouring any synthetic oils into your vehicle's engine, you should consider the condition of the engine and the type of driving you do. Also, check the manufacturer's warranty conditions regarding the use of synthetics.

Generally, it is best to avoid the use of synthetic oil in both brand new and older, high mileage engines. New engines require a proper break-in, and the synthetics are so slippery that they can prevent this. Most manufacturers recommend that you wait at least 5000 miles (8000 km) before switching to a synthetic oil. Conversely, older engines are looser and tend to loose more oil. Synthetics will slip past worn parts more readily than regular oil. If your vehicle already leaks oil (due to bad seals or gaskets), it will probably leak more with a slippery synthetic inside.

Consider your type of driving. If most of your accumulated mileage is on the highway at higher, steadier speeds, a synthetic oil will reduce friction and probably help deliver fuel mileage. Under such ideal highway conditions, the oil change interval can be extended, as long as the oil filter will operate effectively for the extended life of the oil. If the filter can't do its job for this extended period, dirt and sludge will build up in your engine's crankcase, sump, oil pump and lines, no matter what type of oil is used. If using synthetic oil in this manner, you should continue to change the oil filter at the recommended intervals.

Vehicles used under harder, stop-and-go, short hop circumstances should always be serviced more frequently, and for these vehicles, synthetic oil may not be a wise investment. Because of the necessary shorter change interval needed for this type of driving, you cannot take advantage of the long recommended change interval of most synthetic oils.

Most synthetic oils have been tested under the types of extreme conditions that you hope you will never duplicate within your engine. Under conditions of extreme heat, these oils can offer an additional level of protection which you cannot find in most conventional oils. Because of this, synthetic oils are popular for applications such as towing, racing or desert operation. They are also popular with those who are looking for that extra level of protection against engine wear or damage. Consider all of these factors if you are thinking about using synthetic oils.

Handling Used Motor Oil

✳✳ CAUTION

It has been demonstrated that continuous contact with used motor oil can cause skin cancer in laboratory animals. It has also been documented that some substances found to cause cancer in laboratory animals can also cause cancer in humans. Therefore, it is important and prudent to minimize skin contact with used motor oil.

Skin contact with used motor oil can be minimized by following these safety precautions:
- DO follow work practices that minimize the amount of skin exposed and the length of time used oil stays on the skin.
- DO thoroughly wash off used oil as soon as possible with soap and water.
- DO wear long-sleeved shirts and use gloves made of material that oil cannot penetrate.
- DO remove and launder oil soaked clothing promptly. Discard oil soaked shoes.
- DON'T use kerosene, gasoline or other thinners to wash oil off the skin. They remove the skin's natural oils and can cause dryness or have serious toxic effects.
- DON'T over-use waterless hand cleaners. They also remove the skin's protective barriers.
- DON'T put oil rags in your pocket. This can cause prolonged skin contact.

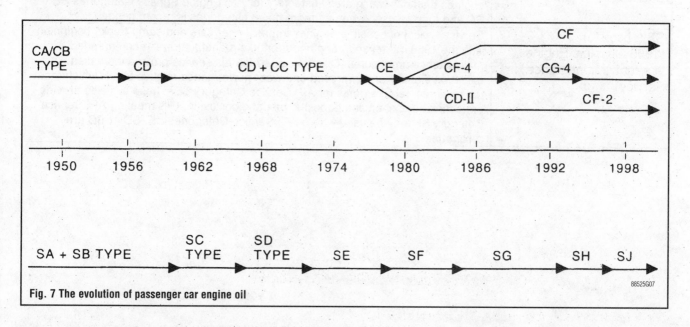

Fig. 7 The evolution of passenger car engine oil

MOTOR OIL GUIDE

The American Petroleum Institute (API) has classified and identified oil according to its use. The API service recommendations are listed on the oil can and all car manufacturers use API letters to indicate recommended oils. Almost all oils meet or exceed the highest service rating (SJ), but viscosity should be selected to match the highest anticipated temperature before the next oil change. S = Gasoline C = Diesel

API Symbol	Use & Definition
SA (obsolete) (Formerly for utility gasoline and diesel engine service)	Service typical of older engines operated under such mild conditions that the protection afforded by compounded oils is not required. This category has no performance requirements and oils in this category should not be used in any engine unless specifically recommended by the equipment manufacturer.
SB (obsolete) (Minimum Duty Gasoline Engine Service)	Service typical of older gasoline engines operated under such mild conditions that only minimum protection afforded by compounding is desired. Oils designed for this service have been used since the 1930's and provide only anti-scuff capability and resistance to oil oxidation and bearing corrosion. They should not be used In any engine unless specifically recommended by the equipment manufacturer.
SC (obsolete) (1964 Gasoline Engine Warranty Service)	Service typical of gasoline engines in 1964 through 1967 models of passenger cars and trucks operating under engine manufacturers' warranties in effect during those model years. Oils designed for this service provide control of high and low-temperature deposits, wear, rust, and corrosion in gasoline engines.
SD (obsolete) (1968 Gasoline Engine Warranty Maintenance Service)	Service typical of gasoline engines in 1968 through 1970 models of passenger cars and some trucks operating under engine manufacturers' warranties in effect during those model years. Also may apply to certain 1971 and/or later models as specified (or recommended) in the owners' manuals. Oils designed for this service provide more protection against high- and low-temperature engine deposits, wear, rust and corrosion in gasoline engines than oils which are satisfactory for API Engine Service Category SC and may be used when API Engine Service Category SC is recommended.
SE (obsolete) (1972 Gasoline Engine Warranty Maintenance Service)	Service typical of gasoline engines in passenger cars and some trucks beginning with 1972 and certain 1971 models operating under engine manufacturers' warranties. Oils designed for this service provide more protection against oil oxidation, high-temperature engine deposits, rust and corrosion in gasoline engines than oils which are satisfactory for API Engine Service Categories SD or SC and may be used when either of these categories is recommended.
SF (obsolete) (1980 Gasoline Engine Warranty Maintenance Service)	Service typical of gasoline engines in passenger cars and some trucks beginning with the 1980 model operating under engine manufacturers' recommended maintenance procedures. Oils developed for this service provide increased oxidation stability and improved anti-wear performance relative to oils which meet the minimum requirements for API Service Category SE. These oils also provide protection against engine deposits, rust and corrosion. Oils meeting API Service Category SF may be used where API Service Categories SE, SD or SC are recommended.

88525C01

API Symbol	Use & Definition
SG (obsolete) (1989 Gasoline Engine Warranty Maintenance Service)	Service typical of gasoline engines in passenger cars, vans and light trucks beginning with the 1989 model year operating under manufacturer's recommended maintenance procedures. Category SG quality oils include the performance properties of API Service Category CC. (Certain manufacturers of gasoline engines require oils also meeting API Service Category CD). Oils developed for this service provide improved control of engine deposits, oil oxidation and engine wear relative to oils developed for previous categories. These oils also provide protection against rust and corrosion. Oils meeting API Service Category SG may be used where API Service Categories SF, SE, SF/CC or SE/CC are recommended.
SH (1993 Gasoline Engine Warranty Maintenance Service)	Service typical of gasoline engines in present and earlier passenger cars, vans and light trucks operating under vehicle manufacturer recommended maintenance procedures. Engine oils developed for this category provide performance exceeding the minimum performance requirements for API SG, which it is intended to replace, in the areas of deposit control, oil oxidation, wear, rust and corrosion. Engine oils meeting the API SH designation have been tested according to the Chemical Manufacturers Association (CMA) Product Approval Code of Practice, may utilize the API Base Oil Interchange and Viscosity Grade Engine Testing Guidelines and may be used where API Service Category SG and earlier categories have been recommended.
SJ (1997 Gasoline Engine Warranty Maintenance Service)	API Service Category SJ was adopted for use in describing engine oils available in 1996. These oils are for use in service typical of gasoline engines in current and earlier passenger car, sport utility vehicle, van, and light truck operations under vehicle manufacturers' recommended maintenance procedures. Engine oils that meet the API Service Category SJ designation may be used where API Service Category SH and earlier categories have been recommended. Engine oils that meet the API Service Category SJ designation have been tested in accordance with the CMA Code, may use the API Base Oil Interchangeability Guidelines and the API Guidelines for SAE Viscosity-Grade Engine Testing. Engine oils that meet these requirements may display API Service Category SJ in the upper portion of the API Service Symbol.
CA (obsolete) (Light Duty Diesel Engine Service)	Service typical of diesel engines operated in mild to moderate duty with high-quality fuels and occasionally has included gasoline engines in mild service. Oils designed for this service provide protection from bearing corrosion and from ring belt deposits in some naturally aspirated diesel engines when using fuels of such quality that they impose no unusual requirements for wear and deposit protection. They were widely used in the late 1940's and 1950's but should not be used in any engine unless specifically recommended by the equipment manufacturer.
CB (obsolete) (Moderate Duty Diesel Engine Service)	Service typical of diesel engines operated in mild to moderate duty, but with lower quality fuels which necessitate more protection from wear and deposits. Occasionally has included gasoline engines in mild service. Oils designed for this service were introduced in 1949. Such oils provide necessary protection from bearing corrosion and from high temperature deposits in normally aspirated diesel engines with higher sulfur fuels.
CC (obsolete) (Moderate Duty Diesel and Gasoline Engine Service)	Service typical of lightly supercharged diesel engines operated in moderate to severe duty and has included certain heavy duty gasoline engines. Oils designed for this service were introduced in 1961 and used in many trucks and In industrial and construction equipment and farm tractors. These oils provide protection from high temperature deposits in lightly supercharged diesels and also from rust, corrosion, and low temperature deposits in gasoline engines.

API Symbol	Use & Definition
CD (obsolete) (Severe Duty Diesel Engine Service)	Service typical of supercharged diesel engines in high speed, high output duty requiring highly effective control of wear and deposits. Oils designed for this service were introduced in 1955, and provide protection from bearing corrosion and from high temperature deposits in supercharged diesel engines when using fuels of a wide quality range.
CD-II (obsolete) (Two-Stroke Diesel Engine Service)	Service typical of two-stroke cycle diesel engines requiring highly effective control over wear and deposits. Oils designed for this service also meet all performance requirements of API Service Category CD.
CE (obsolete) (Turbocharged or Supercharged Heavy Duty Diesel Engine Service)	Service typical of turbocharged or supercharged heavy duty diesel engines manufactured since 1983 and operated under both low-speed, high-load and high-speed, high-load conditions. Oils designed for this service may also be used when previous API engine service categories for diesel engines are recommended.
CF (Indirect Injected Diesel Engine Service)	This Category denotes service typical of indirect injected diesel engines, and other diesel engines which use a broad range of fuel types including those using fuel with higher sulfur content, for example, over 0.5% wt. Effective control of piston deposits, wear and copper-containing bearing corrosion is essential for these engines which may be naturally aspirated, turbocharged or supercharged. Oils designated for this service have been in existence since 1994. Oils designated for this service may also be used when API service category CD is recommended.
CF-2 (Two Stroke Cycle Diesel Engine Service)	This Category denotes service typical of two-stroke cycle engines requiring highly effective control over cylinder and ring-face scuffing and deposits. Oils designated for this service have been in existence since 1994 and may also be used when API Service Category CD-his recommended. These oils do not necessarily meet the requirements of CF or CF-4 unless passing test requirements for these categories.
CF-4 (1990 Diesel Engine Service)	This category was adopted in 1990 and describes oils for use in high-speed, four-stroke-cycle, diesel engines. API CF-4 oils exceed the requirements of the CE category providing improved control of oil consumption and piston deposits. These oils should be used in place of CD oils. They are particularly suited for on-highway, heavy duty truck applications. When combined with the appropriate "5" category, for example SG, they can also be used in gasoline and diesel powered personal vehicles such as automobiles, light trucks and vans when recommended by the vehicle or engine manufacturer.
CG-4 (Severe Duty Diesel Engine Service)	This Category describes oils for use in high-speed four-stroke cycle diesel engines used on both heavy-duty on-highway (less than 0.05% wf. sulfur fuel) and off highway (less than 0.5% wt. sulfur fuel) applications. CG-4 oils provide effective control over high temperature piston deposits, wear, corrosion, foaming, oxidation stability and soot accumulation. These oils are especially effective in engines designed to meet 1994 exhaust emission standards and may also be used in engines requiring API Service Categories CD, CE and CF-4. Oils designated for this service have been in existence since January 1995.

88271C02

Environmental Issues

Used motor oil is a valuable resource, but it can be a pollution problem if not disposed of properly. The following guidelines should be used when disposing of used motor oil:

- DO put used motor oil in a clean plastic container with a tight lid.
- DO take used motor oil to a collection point or put out for curbside recycling, as available.
- DON'T dump used motor oil in the trash, on roads, down drains or sewers, or on the ground.
- DON'T mix used motor oil with anything else (paint, gasoline, solvent, antifreeze, etc.).

Fluids and Greases

TYPES OF GREASE

▶ **See Figure 8**

National Lubricating Grease Institute Certification Mark

It has long been recognized that the diversity of specifications for Automotive Greases, established by the Original Equipment Manufacturer (OEM), have made it difficult, if not impossible, for the marketer of lubricating greases to make available all the many specified products. With the issuance of specification ASTM D 4950 Standard Classification and Specification for Automotive Service Grease, it has become possible to offer the products needed to provide proper service of automotive equipment. This ASTM specification includes two Performance Groups: chassis lubricants (letter designation L) and wheel bearing lubricants (letter designation G). Performance categories within these Groups result in two letter designations for chassis greases (LA and LB), and three for wheel bearing greases (GA, GB, and GC). The automotive industry is in general agreement that the highest performance category in each group (LB and GC) is suitable for service lubrication.

The NLGI has developed an identifying symbol, i.e., the NLGI Certification Mark. The OEM's Owner's Manuals, which illustrate this Mark, advise users to use only those greases that incorporate the Mark into their product label.

Since only the highest performance categories are acceptable to OEM, only categories LB and GC will be authorized for use with the Mark. The three versions of the Mark are shown in the illustration.

CHASSIS GREASES

Most late-model vehicles no longer require chassis lubrication, but for those that do, the correct grease is generally an EP (extreme pressure) chassis lube. There's not really much problem, since it's about the only thing you can get in a cartridge refill that will fit in your hand-operated grease gun, if you lube your own vehicle. Also, check for the new NLGI performance ratting mentioned.

WHEEL BEARING LUBRICANT

There are two types of wheel bearing lubricant, low temperature and high temperature. The high temperature wheel bearing lubricant is the only one suitable for modern vehicles. Also, check for the new NLGI performance ratting mentioned earlier.

MASTER CYLINDER FLUID

➡ **Always check your vehicle's owners manual (if available) or even the cap on the master cylinder reservoir before adding brake fluid. DOT 3 and 4 are very similar fluids, though one may be specifically recommended by your particular manufacturer. DOT 5 (silicone fluid) is rarely used, but it is not compatible with systems designed for DOT 3 or 4 and, if used in the wrong system, would cause damage to the seals and other rubber components.**

Brake fluid is used for both the brake master cylinder and the clutch master cylinder (if your vehicle is equipped with a hydraulic clutch). Use only brake fluid rated DOT 3 or 4 or conforming to SAE Standard J1709. The rating can be found on the container. Brake fluid is typically hydroscopic, meaning it tends to absorb water from the atmosphere, both in the vehicle and on the shelf. This is a good reason to change fluid at recommended intervals, and always use fresh brake fluid. Don't buy more than you are going to use, and purchase small containers rather than large so that you can keep them sealed for future use.

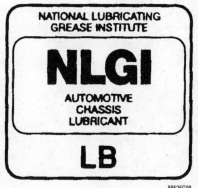

Fig. 8 The NLGI identification symbols

❊❊ WARNING

Brake fluid makes a wonderful paint remover. Be careful not to spill any on painted surfaces.

AUTOMATIC TRANSMISSION FLUID

Automatic transmission fluids can be broken down into two types, Dexron® III and Ford type F. These fluids are specific to the transmission using them. Don't assume that all Ford vehicles use type F, they don't!

• Dexron® III, sometime referred to as multi-purpose ATF. This replaces the old Type A, Suffix A, was recommended by GM, Chrysler and AMC between 1956–1967. It also supercedes Dexron® and Dexron® II fluids. Ford vehicles 1977 and later with the C6 transmission or the Jatco transmission in the Granada and Monarch also use this fluid. Ford refers to this fluid as Mercon®, or transmissions where type H or CJ where recommended.

• Type F fluid is recommended by Ford Motor Co. for most late model Fords and certain imports, and contains certain frictional compounds required for proper operation in these transmissions.

There is not much of a problem here, since the bottles are clearly marked to indicate the type of fluid. If you are in doubt, check your owner's manual.

GEAR LUBRICANTS

The American Petroleum Institute has developed specific lubricant service designations for automotive manual transmissions and axles, each designation referring to the performance required from a gear lubricant for a specific type of automotive service. These designations also recognize the possibility that lubricants may be developed for more than one service classification and consequently may be so designated. The system of designations replaces all previous API gear lubricant designations.

API GL-1—Designates the type of service characteristics of automotive spiral-bevel and worm gear axles as well as some manually operated transmissions operating under such mild conditions of low unit pressures and sliding velocities that straight mineral oil can be used satisfactorily. Oxidation and rust inhibitors, defoamers and pour depressants may be utilized to improve the characteristics of lubricants for this service. Frictional modifiers and extreme pressure agents shall not be utilized.

API GL-2—Designates the type of service characteristics of automotive type worm gear axles operating under such conditions of load, temperature and sliding velocities that lubricants satisfactory for API GL-1 service will not suffice. (obsolete)

API GL-3—Designates the type of service characteristics of manual transmissions and spiral-bevel axles operating under moderately severe conditions of speed and load. These service conditions require a lubricant having load carrying capacities greater than those which will satisfy API GL-1 service, but below the requirements of lubricants satisfying API GL-4 service. (obsolete)

API GL-4—Designates the type of service characteristics of gears, particularly hypoid in passenger cars and other automotive equipment operated under high-speed: shock-load, low-torque, and low-speed: high-torque conditions.

API GL-5—Designates the type of service characteristics of gears, particularly hypoid in passenger cars and other automotive equipment operated under high-speed: shock-load, low-torque, and low-speed: high-torque conditions.

MANUAL TRANSMISSION LUBRICANT

Many manual transmissions use gear oil viscosity of about SAE 80W or 90 grade. This is a gear oil viscosity and has nothing to do with motor oil viscosity. For instance, SAE 80W gear oil can have the same viscosity characteristics as SAE 40 or 50 motor oil.

However, not all manual transmissions use gear oil. For years, Chrysler Corporation specified the use of automatic transmission fluid in their manual transmission vehicles. Some transaxles, both foreign and domestic, use either ATF or engine oil to lubricate the transmission. For this reason, it is always best to consult your owner's manual or your dealer if you are unsure about what sort of lubricant to use in your manual transmission.

DRIVE AXLE LUBRICANTS

Most conventional drive axles use gear oil viscosity of about 80W or 90 grade. Consult your owner's manual for more detail. Limited-slip or Positraction® rear axles usually .require a special lubricant or in some cases, it is available as an additive, which is available from the dealer or parts store. If you do have a limited-slip differential, make sure you use only the correct lubricant, as the use of the incorrect lubricant can destroy the differential.

POWER STEERING FLUID

Power steering pumps are ordinarily lubricated with power steering fluid. Use the correct type for the vehicle. Check the owner's manual if you are unsure.

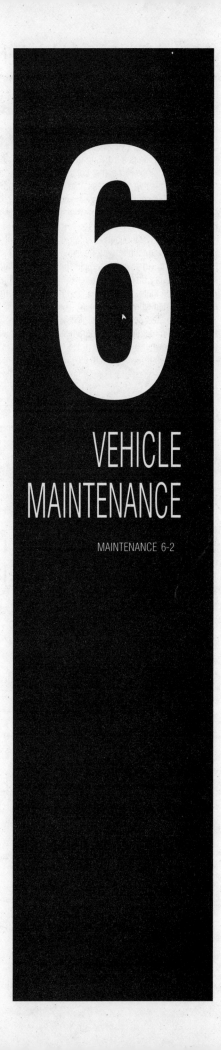

6

VEHICLE MAINTENANCE

MAINTENANCE 6-2

MAINTENANCE

Benefits of Proper Maintenance

The automobile is a truly amazing machine. It is expected to function under a wide range of weather conditions and other adverse conditions, yet it often is subjected to careless hard driving and indifferent maintenance. Recommended service intervals are often ignored by the same vehicle owners that wouldn't let a week go by without vacuuming all the rugs in the house.

Today the automobile is an integral part of our life. We have come to rely on the proper functioning of the family vehicle and seldom, if ever, make a time allowance in case the vehicle should fail to start. We expect it to start and move every time, and fortunately, most of the time it does. However, the rare instance that it doesn't, causes the owner to forget the thousands of times it started without a problem. The irony is that, chances are, the vehicle failed to start because of neglect.

A periodic maintenance program such as the one in this book can keep the vehicle owner more aware of the condition of his or her vehicle and will save money in three important areas—fuel economy, emissions and performance.

Maintenance Intervals

▶ See Figures 1, 2, 3, 4 and 5

BUT THE OWNER'S MANUAL IS DIFFERENT?

We have provided a maintenance interval chart which is based on general industry standards. The time and mileage given are the most conservative figures (low end recommendations), and therefore should be sufficient to meet or beat most manufacturer's warranty requirements. If you have an owner's manual for your vehicle, we would still recommend that you consult it and see what the manufacturer specifically recommends (there may be some odd or atypical components on your vehicle that require special attention).

Because this chart is designed to cover all vehicles, we may have included items which are not applicable to your exact model (for instance, many vehicles use hydraulic valve lifters, making periodic adjustment of the valve clearance unnecessary). So when looking at items on the chart, remember to check if they are applicable to your vehicle (using an owner's manual or a Chilton manual written specifically for your model).

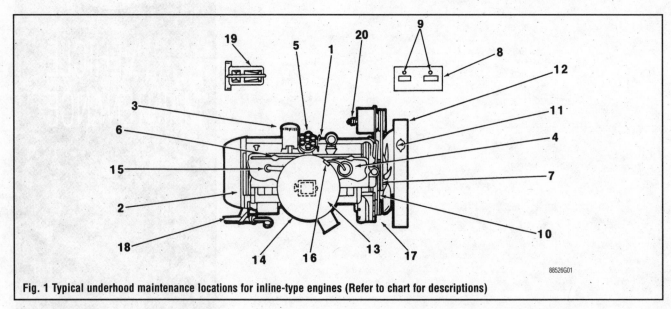

Fig. 1 Typical underhood maintenance locations for inline-type engines (Refer to chart for descriptions)

88526G01

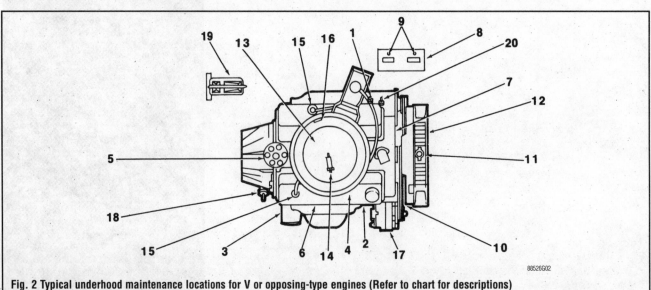

Fig. 2 Typical underhood maintenance locations for V or opposing-type engines (Refer to chart for descriptions)

88526G02

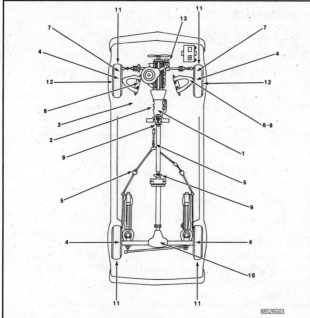

Fig. 3 Typical body and undervehicle maintenance locations (Refer to chart for descriptions)

Fig. 5 Special tools make lubrication easier, from left to right: Oil Suction Gun; Oil Can; Funnel; Grease Gun; and Wheel Bearing Packers

Also, keep in mind that we may have included items which we believe are very important, even if your particular manufacturer does not. Brake fluid is one item of which not all manufacturers require periodic replacement in order to keep in warranty. But, that doesn't change the fact that brake fluid is hydroscopic meaning that it absorbs moisture from the atmosphere. Over time moisture in the brake system will lead to corrosion and damage to internal parts. Also, a sufficient level of moisture in the fluid can dramatically lower its boiling point. Should temperatures during hard braking (mountain driving, trailer towing, racing, etc) allow the brake fluid to boil, you could experience and sudden and complete loss of braking ability. So if you plan on keeping a vehicle for any length of time, and/or you use it under harsh conditions (such as towing or racing), you would be wise to follow our fluid replacement guidelines.

BUT THE REPLACEMENT PART IS DIFFERENT?

Another thing to remember is that maintenance intervals may vary with the type of replacement parts which are used. Spark plugs and synthetic

Fig. 4 Typical lubricants, from left to right: Engine Oil; Gear Oil; ATF; Wheel Bearing Grease; Brake Fluid; Chassis Grease; White Grease; and Silicone Spray

oils are two good examples of this. Although we have suggested changing your oil and filter every 3,000 miles, use of a synthetic oil may allow you to lengthen or even double this mileage, IF your usage fits the proper patterns (highway miles, above freezing, with little stop-and-go and no excessive speeds . . .). The recommendation we give for spark plugs is based on conventional plugs with an electronic ignition system, which probably covers most vehicles on the road. If you have an antique that uses a points ignition, well then you will probably have to replace the plugs more often. But, if you use special plugs, like the increasingly popular long-life Platinum plugs, you may easily be able to double the recommended replacement interval. The key here is to pay attention to the directions supplied with your replacement parts (and if you have never replaced an item before, check with the manufacturer for suggestions about original equipment).

IS MY DRIVING "NORMAL" OR "SEVERE"?

Sometimes we are puzzled at how manufacturer's chose the term "Normal" for the style of driving which most refer to in their maintenance charts as the opposite of "Severe." Check your owner's manual and you will likely see that you are NOT normal. Sorry to be the one to tell you, but it's probably true.

You see, to be "Normal" according to most manufacturer's driving and maintenance recommendations you would have to: Drive the car for more than 10 miles or so (to make sure it properly warms up) almost every time you start it (never under freezing conditions, but not in excessive heat, dry or dusty conditions either). Most miles would have to be on the highway, NOT stop-and-go (few red lights or stop signs), with no excessive idling (in traffic or curbside), but NOT at excessive speeds. Well, some of you reading this will find that this applies . . . but most won't.

If ALL of these conditions apply, then most manufacturers call your driving style "Severe" and lump it in with trailer towing, racing, cab or delivery driving or even police or fire vehicle usage. The truth is that most usage probably falls somewhere in between. Actual severe usage, such as those that we have just listed, should require a LOT of attention to all of the various systems of a car (including early replacement of all fluids). But, the average person, who does not race or tow, will be fine with the 3,000 mile/3 month engine oil change and most of the other recommendations we have given. If you compare those recommendations with your manufacturer, you will probably find that they have listed those intervals for "SEVERE" usage and not "NORMAL." Maybe it is just a play on words. Just remember that it is your money (that you are driving around every day) and possibly even your life (kept safe by tires and brakes . . .) so remember the general rule, maintenance is cheaper than repair. Don't be afraid of not being "Normal." Go ahead and admit that your driving is "Severe" and maintain your vehicle to match.

UNDERHOOD MAINTENANCE INTERVALS

This chart gives minimum maintenance intervals by miles or time, whichever comes first, based on average of 12,000 miles per year. The recommendations given are general industry standards, and may be more strict than your manufacturer's schedules. Obviously, the type of driving you do will also affect your maintenance program. Refer to Fig. 1 and Fig. 2 for service locations. Note: This chart is an attempt to cover all vehicles, please refer to your owners manual for factory recommended service intervals.

Service Location	Item	Check Every
	Engine	
1	Check oil, add if necessary	Fuel Stop
2	Drain oil	3000 miles/3 months
3	Replace oil filter	3000 miles/3 months
4*	Check valve clearance, adjust if necessary	12,000 miles/12 months
	Ignition System	
6*	Replace spark plugs	18-30,000 miles/18-24 months
6*	Check spark plug wires	12,000 miles/12 months
6*	Replace spark plug wires	At least every 36,000 miles/3 years
5*	Replace distributor cap/rotor	12,000 miles/12 months
7*	Check/adjust ignition timing	12,000 miles/12 months
	Battery	
9	Check/clean terminals and cables	3000 miles/3 months
	Starter and Alternator	
9	Check electrical connections	3000 miles/3 months
10†	Check/adjust drive belt	3000 miles/3 months
10†	Replace drive belt	At least every 24,000 miles/2 years
	Cooling System	
11	Check coolant level	1000 mlies/1 month
12	Check condition of radiator hoses	1000 miles/1 month
11	Check condition of radiator cap	1000 miles/1 month
10†	Check/adjust drive belt	3000 miles/3 months
10†	Replace drive belt	At least every 24,000 miles/2 years
12	Clean radiator of debris	3000 miles/3 months
12	Drain/replace coolant	12,000 miles/12 months (Each Fall)
	Fuel & Emissions System	
16*	Clean crankcase breather	12,000 miles/12 months
13	Replace air filter	12,000 miles/12 months
14	Replace fuel filter	12,000 miles/12 months
15*	Check PCV valve	12,000 miles/12 months
10*†	Check/adjust air pump belt tension	3,000 miles/3 months
10*†	Replace drive belt	At least every 24,000 miles/2 years
	Air Conditioning	
12	Clean condenser grille	3000 miles/3 months
17	Check for leaks at connections	3000 miles/3 months
10*†	Check/adjust compressor belt	3,000 miles/3 months
10*†	Replace compressor drive belt	At least every 24,000 miles/2 years
	Automatic transmission	
18*	Check fluid level/condition	6000 miles/6 months
	Brakes	
19	Check brake master cylinder fluid level	1000 miles/1 month
19	Replace brake fluid	At least every 2 years
	Hydraulic Clutch	
19*	Check clutch master cylinder fluid level	1000 miles/1 month
19*	Replace hydraulic clutch fluid	At least every 2 years
	Power Steering	
20*	Check pump fluid level	3000 miles/3 months
10*†	Replace drive belt	At least every 24,000 miles/2 years
10*†	Check drive belt tension	3000 miles/1 month

(*) Denotes items that may not be applicable to all vehicles.

(†) Most modern accessory drive systems utilize one serpentine belt rather than numerous individual belts.
   New drive belts will stretch with use. Recheck the tension of a newly installed belt after 200 miles.

88526C01

BODY AND UNDERVEHICLE MAINTENANCE INTERVALS

This chart gives minimum maintenance intervals by miles or time, whichever comes first, based on average of 12,000 miles per year. The recommendations given are general industry standards, and may be more strict than your manufacturer's schedules. Obviously, the type of driving you do will also affect your maintenance program. Refer to Fig. 1 and Fig. 2 for service locations. Note: This chart is an attempt to cover all vehicles, please refer to your owners manual for factory recommended service intervals.

Service Location	Item	Check Every
	Automatic Transmission/Transaxle	
1	Change fluid	24,000 miles /2 years
1	Replace filter or clean screen	24,000 miles /2 years
	Manual Transmission/Transaxle	
2	Check lubricant level	3000 miles/3 months
2	Change lubricant	24,000 miles/2 years
	Transfer Case	
2*	Check lubricant level	3000 miles/3 months
2*	Change lubricant	24,000 miles/2 years
	Clutch	
3	Check clutch pedal free-play	6000 miles/6 months
2*	Lubricate shift and/or pedal linkage	6000 miles/6 months
	Brakes	
4	Check condition of brake pads or shoes	6000 miles/6 months
4	Check wheel cylinders, return springs, calipers, hoses, drums and/or rotors	6000 miles/6 months
5	Adjust parking brake	As necessary
	Suspension	
6	Check shock absorbers/struts	12,000 miles/12 months
7	Check tires for abnormal wear	1000 miles/1 month
8*	Lubricate front end	3000 miles/3 months
	Driveshaft	
9*	Lubricate U-joints	6000 miles/6 months
	CV-Joints/Boots	
6, 10*	Check for damage, wear and/or tears	3000 miles/3 months
	Drive Axles	
10	Check level of drive axle fluid	6000 miles/6 months
10	Replace drive axle fluid	24,000 mlies/2 years
	Tires	
7	Check tires for abnormal wear	1000 miles/1 month
11	Clean tread of debris	As necessary
12	Check tire pressure	Each fuel stop/2 weeks
11	Rotate tires	6000 miles/6 months
11	Check tread depth	6000 miles/6 months
	Wheels	
12	Clean wheels	As necessary
12	Check wheel weights	Each fuel stop/2 weeks (when you check tire pressure)
11	Rotate wheel/tire	6000 miles/6 months
	Windshield wipers	
	Check and clean wiper blades	3000 miles/3 months
	Replace wiper blades	12,000 miles/12 months
	Lubricate linkage and pivots	6000 miles/6 months
	Check hoses and clean nozzles	3000 miles/3 months
	Windshield	
	Clean glass	Each fuel stop
	Air Conditioner	
13	Operate air conditioner for a few minutes	Once a week

(*) Denotes items that may not be applicable to all vehicles.

88526C02

RECOMMENDED LUBRICANTS

Every manufacturer has specific recommendations for fluids and lubricants used in their vehicles Note: This chart is an attempt to cover all vehicles, please refer to your owners manual for factory recommended lubricants

Part	Lubricant
Engine	Engine oil API service rated SJ (gasoline engines) or CD (diesel engines) Viscosity determined by anticipated temperatures before next oil change or as recommended by the manufacturer
Automatic transmission	Automatic Transmission Fluid (ATF): Dexron III® / Mercon or Type F
Manual transmission/transaxle	SAE 80W-90 gear lubricant (API-GL4), ATF or engine oil Refer to the vehicles owner manual for specific fluid requirements
Transfer Case	SAE 80W-90 gear lubricant (API-GL4), ATF or engine oil Refer to the vehicles owner manual for specific fluid requirements
Power steering pump	Power steering fluid or ATF Refer to vehicles owner manual for specific fluid recommendations
Conventional drive axle	SAE 80W-90 through 90W-140 gear lubricant (API-GL4 minimum) Refer to the vehicles owner manual for specific fluid requirements
Limited slip drive axle	SAE 80W-90 through 90W-140 gear lubricant (API-GL5) Refer to the vehicles owner manual for specific fluid requirements NOTE: Special limited slip additive may be required
Wheel bearings	High melting point, long fiber wheel bearing grease
Brake master cylinder	Heavy duty brake fluid meeting DOT-3 specification or as noted on the cap
Clutch master cylinder	Heavy duty brake fluid meeting DOT-3 specification or as noted on the cap
Manual steering gear, suspension, ball joints, U-joints, clutch and gear shift linkage, steering linkage and other chassis lubrication points	Lithium base, multi-purpose chassis lubricant
Doors, hood, trunk and tailgate locks, seat tracks, parking brake	White grease
Accelerator linkage, door hinges, trunk and hood hinges	SAE 30 engine oil
Lock cylinders	Silicone spray lubricant or thin oil applied to key and inserted in lock
Weather stripping	Silicone spray lubricant

88526C03

7

TUNE-UP

TUNE-UP

➡The word "tune-up" actually applies only to older vehicles, on which you can perform the traditional work associated with the term—spark plug replacement, ignition contact point replacement, dwell adjustment, ignition timing adjustment and carburetor idle and mixture adjustment. For today's vehicles engine performance maintenance is a more accurate term. All modern cars and light trucks are equipped electronic ignition (no points) and at least one on-board computer that automatically adjusts items like the ignition timing, fuel mixture and idle speed. In fact, on modern computer-controlled vehicles, it's impossible to adjust these yourself.

An automotive tune-up is an orderly process of inspection, diagnosis, testing, and adjustment that is periodically necessary to maintain peak engine performance or restore the engine to original operating efficiency.

The tune-up is also a good opportunity to perform a general preventive maintenance check on everything in the engine compartment. Look for failed or about to fail components such as loose or damaged wiring, leaking fuel lines, cracked coolant hoses, and frayed belts.

This section will lead you through the various elements of a tune-up in their proper order. The following sections give specific details on how to perform the various procedures. Operations should be performed in the order listed.

Necessary Tools

◆ See Figures 1 and 2

In order to perform a proper tune-up, several specific tools are needed; a tach (only if base idle speed is adjustable), a timing light (if timing is adjustable), a spark plug socket, feeler gauges (the round wire type for gapping plugs), and a compression tester.

On late-model vehicles with electronic ignition, you won't need a dwell-meter since dwell is not adjustable on these vehicles. In addition, keep in mind that some tachometers will not operate on vehicles equipped with electronic ignition, and neither will some timing lights. So before you buy anything, check to be sure it will work on your particular vehicle.

Fig. 1 A variety of tools and gauges are required for spark plug gapping and installation

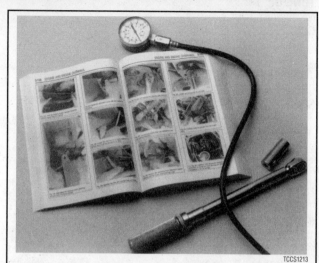

Fig. 2 Accurate information is an important tool, so keep your Chilton Total Car Care for specific instructions

Compression

◆ See Figure 3

Along with vacuum gauge readings and spark plug condition, cylinder compression test results are extremely valuable indicators of internal engine condition. The best professional mechanics automatically check an engine's compression as the first step in a comprehensive tune-up. Obviously, it is useless to try to tune an engine with extremely low or erratic compression readings, since a simple tune-up will not cure the problem. However, before we go any further, it might be wise to review exactly what is compression.

In the description of engine operation in the "Engine" chapter, it is mentioned that, after the intake valve closes, the air/fuel mixture is trapped in the cylinder as the piston rises. The volume of the combustion chamber

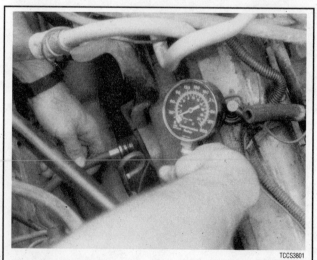

Fig. 3 Checking compression with a screw-in type compression gauge

after the piston reaches top dead center (TDC) is about ⅛ to ⅟₁₁ of the volume of the whole cylinder. Compressing the mixture in this manner raises the pressure and temperature in the combustion chambers during the power stroke, thus improving combustion and increasing the amount of power delivered to the piston on the down stroke. Any leakage in the combustion chamber will reduce the pressure created during the compression stroke.

The pressure created in the combustion chamber may be measured with a gauge that remains at the highest reading it measures during the action of a one-way valve. This gauge is inserted into the spark plug hole. A compression test will uncover many mechanical problems that can cause rough running or poor performance.

CHECKING COMPRESSION

Prepare the engine for a compression test as follows:
1. Run the engine until it reaches operating temperature. The engine is at operating temperature a few minutes after the upper radiator hose gets hot. If the test is performed on a cold engine, the readings will be considerably lower than normal, even if the engine is in perfect mechanical condition.
2. Mark or label the position of the spark plug wires and remove the plug wires from the plugs.
3. Clean all dirt and foreign material from around the spark plugs, and then remove all the plugs. On carbureted vehicles, block the throttle plates wide open.
4. If you are using a hand-held gauge, have an assistant crank the engine over while you hold it in the spark plug hole. The engine should be cranked for at least one full revolution. Probably the best idea is to crank the engine until you record the highest reading possible on that cylinder.
5. Record the compression reading from that cylinder (noting which cylinder it was), and repeat the test for all the other cylinders.

Not all engines will exhibit the same compression readings. In fact, two identical engines may not have the same compression. Generally, the rule of thumb is that the lowest cylinder should be within 25% of the highest (difference between the two readings). The lower limit of normal compression on a V8 engine with normal wear is 100 psi (690 kPa); on a 4- or 6-cylinder engine, it is 90 psi (620 kPa).

LOW COMPRESSION

Compression readings that are generally low indicate worn rings, valves, or pistons, and usually indicate a high-mileage engine. If all cylinders read low, squirt a tablespoon of oil into the cylinder, crank the engine a few times, and recheck compression. If the readings come up to normal, the problem is worn rings, pistons, or cylinders. If compression does not increase, the problem is in the valves.

Low compression in two adjacent cylinders (with normal compression in the other cylinders) indicates a blown head gasket between the low-reading cylinders. Other problems are possible (broken ring, hole burned in a piston), but a blown head gasket is most likely.

CYLINDER LEAK-DOWN TEST

This test requires the use of a cylinder leak-down tester. The cylinder leak-down tester provides a more accurate means for determining the engine condition. By pressurizing each cylinder (one at a time) with a regulated amount of air pressure from a compressor and comparing it to the amount of air pressure in the cylinder, a determination can be made of how much air is escaping around the rings, valves and head gasket. A small amount of leakage is normal.

The cylinder leak-down test will detect the following:
• Improper seating of the exhaust or intake valves.
• Leaks into the water jacket between two adjacent cylinders.

• Any causes for loss of combustion or compression pressure.

The engine is brought to normal operating temperature and turned off. The spark plugs, oil filler cap, and air cleaner are removed. The tester should be calibrated to the manufacturers instructions.

The leak-down test is performed on each cylinder according to the tester manufacturer's instructions. To pinpoint the area of leakage, listen for pressurized air escaping through the throttle body/carburetor, tailpipe and the oil filler cap opening. Also check for bubbles in the radiator coolant:
• Air heard through the throttle body/carburetor means an intake valve is leaking.
• Air escaping through the tailpipe means that an exhaust valve is leaking
• Air coming through the oil filler indicates that air is escaping past the rings
• Bubbles in the radiator means that air is leaking into the cooling system, likely past the head gasket.

Each of the cylinders should leak nearly the same amount of air, with no more than 25 percent leakage. For Example: At 80 psi (552 kPa) input pressure from the air compressor, a minimum of 60 psi (414kPa) should be maintained in the cylinder.

Checking Engine Vacuum

Strictly speaking, vacuum gauge readings are not a necessary part of the everyday tune-up, which is why a vacuum gauge is considered optional equipment. Properly used, however, a vacuum gauge is an extremely useful diagnostic tool.

Spark Plugs

Spark plug life and efficiency depend upon the condition of the engine and the combustion chamber temperatures to which the plug is exposed. These temperatures are affected by many factors, such as compression ratio of the engine, air/fuel mixtures, exhaust emission equipment, and the type of driving you do.

Factory installed plugs are, in a way, compromise plugs, since the factory has no way of knowing what sort of driving you do, but most people never have reason to change their plugs from the factory recommended heat range.

SPARK PLUG HEAT RANGE

▶ See Figure 4

Spark plug heat range is the ability of the plug to dissipate heat. The longer the insulator (or the farther it extends into the engine), the hotter the plug will operate; the shorter the insulator (the closer the electrode is to the block's cooling passages) the cooler it will operate. A plug that absorbs little heat and remains too cool will quickly accumulate deposits of oil and carbon since it is not hot enough to burn them off. This leads to plug fouling and consequently to misfiring. A plug that absorbs too much heat will have no deposits but, due to the excessive heat, the electrodes will burn away quickly and might possibly lead to preignition or other ignition problems. Preignition takes place when plug tips get so hot that they glow sufficiently to ignite the air/fuel mixture before the actual spark occurs. This early ignition will usually cause a pinging during low speeds and heavy loads.

The general rule of thumb for choosing the correct heat range when picking a spark plug is: if most of your driving is long distance, high speed travel, use a colder plug; if most of your driving is stop and go, use a hotter plug. Original equipment plugs are generally a good compromise between the 2 styles and most people never have the need to change their plugs from the factory recommended heat range.

USING A VACUUM GAUGE

White needle = steady needle   Dark needle = drifting needle

The vacuum gauge is one of the most useful and easy-to-use diagnostic tools. It is inexpensive, easy to hook up, and provides valuable information about the condition of your engine.

Indication: Normal engine in good condition

Gauge reading: Steady, from 17–22 in./Hg.

Indication: Sticking valve or ignition miss

Gauge reading: Needle fluctuates from 15–20 in./Hg. at idle

Indication: Late ignition or valve timing, low compression, stuck throttle valve, leaking carburetor or manifold gasket.

Gauge reading: Low (15–20 in./Hg.) but steady

Indication: Improper carburetor adjustment, or minor intake leak at carburetor or manifold

NOTE: Bad fuel injector O-rings may also cause this reading.

Gauge reading: Drifting needle

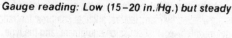

Indication: Weak valve springs, worn valve stem guides, or leaky cylinder head gasket (vibrating excessively at all speeds).

NOTE: A plugged catalytic converter may also cause this reading.

Gauge reading: Needle fluctuates as engine speed increases

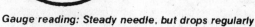

Indication: Burnt valve or improper valve clearance. The needle will drop when the defective valve operates.

Gauge reading: Steady needle, but drops regularly

Indication: Choked muffler or obstruction in system. Speed up the engine. Choked muffler will exhibit a slow drop of vacuum to zero.

Gauge reading: Gradual drop in reading at idle

Indication: Worn valve guides

Gauge reading: Needle vibrates excessively at idle, but steadies as engine speed increases

TCCS3C01

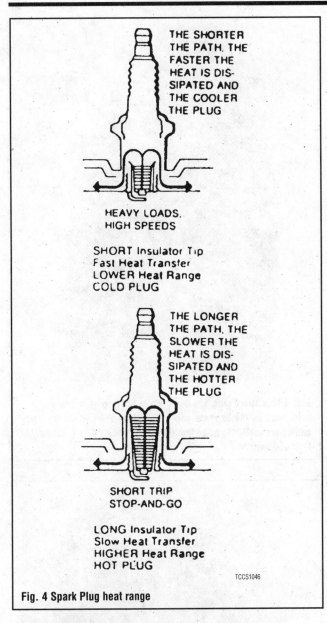

THE SHORTER
THE PATH, THE
FASTER THE
HEAT IS DIS-
SIPATED AND
THE COOLER
THE PLUG

HEAVY LOADS,
HIGH SPEEDS

SHORT Insulator Tip
Fast Heat Transfer
LOWER Heat Range
COLD PLUG

THE LONGER
THE PATH, THE
SLOWER THE
HEAT IS DIS-
SIPATED AND
THE HOTTER
THE PLUG

SHORT TRIP
STOP-AND-GO

LONG Insulator Tip
Slow Heat Transfer
HIGHER Heat Range
HOT PLUG

TCCS1046

Fig. 4 Spark Plug heat range

TCCS2135

Fig. 5 A normally worn spark plug should have light tan or gray deposits on the firing tip (electrode)

READING SPARK PLUGS

◆ **See Figures 5 thru 12**

Your spark plugs are the single most valuable indicator of your engine's internal condition. Study your spark plugs carefully every time you remove them. Compare them to illustrations shown to identify the most common plug conditions.

REPLACING SPARK PLUGS

➡**New technologies in spark plug and ignition system design have pushed the recommended replacement interval to 60,000 miles (96,540 km) or even 100,000 miles (160,900 km). However, this depends on vehicle usage and driving conditions. This holds true unless internal engine wear or damage and/or improperly operating emissions controls cause plug fouling. If you suspect this, you may wish to remove and inspect the plugs before the recommended mileage. Most platinum plugs should not be cleaned or regapped. If you find their condition unsuitable, they should be replaced.**

A set of standard spark plugs usually requires replacement after about 20,000–30,000 miles (32,180–48,270 km) on vehicles with electronic ignition. These figures are dependent on your particular style of driving, how-

TCCS2136

Fig. 6 A carbon-fouled plug, identified by soft, sooty black deposits, may indicate an improperly tuned vehicle. Check the air cleaner, ignition components and the engine control system.

TCCS2137

Fig. 7 A physically damaged spark plug may be evidence of severe detonation in that cylinder. Watch that cylinder carefully between services, as a continued detonation will not only damage the plug, but could also damage the engine

TCCS2139

Fig. 9 This spark plug has been left in the engine too long, as evidenced by the extreme gap—Plugs with such an extreme gap can cause misfiring and stumbling accompanied by a noticeable lack of power

TCCS2138

Fig. 8 An oil-fouled spark plug indicates an engine with worn piston rings and/or bad valve seals allowing excessive oil to enter the combustion chamber

TCCS2140

Fig. 10 A bridged or almost bridged spark plug, identified by the build-up between the electrodes caused by excessive carbon or oil build-up on the plug

ever. The electrode on a new spark plug has a sharp edge, but with use, this edge becomes rounded by wear, causing the plug gap to increase. In normal operation, plug gap increases about 0.001 inch (0.25mm) for every 1,000–2,500 miles (1,609–4,022 km). As the gap increases, the plug's voltage requirement also increases. It requires a greater voltage to jump the wider gap and about two to three times as much voltage to fire a plug at high speeds than at idle. The improved air/fuel ratio control of modern fuel injection combined with the higher voltage output of modern ignition systems will often allow an engine to run significantly longer on a set of standard spark plugs, but keep in mind that efficiency will drop as the gap widens (along with fuel economy and power).

Tools needed for spark plug replacement include a ratchet handle, short extension, spark plug socket (there are two types; either 13/16 inch or 5/8 inch, depending upon the type of plug), a combination spark plug gauge and gapping tool, and a can of penetrating oil or an anti-seize type grease for engines with aluminum heads.

When removing spark plugs, work on one at a time. Don't start by removing the plug wires all at once, because unless you number them, they may become mixed up. Take a minute before you begin and number the wires with tape. The best location for numbering is near where the wires come out of the cap.

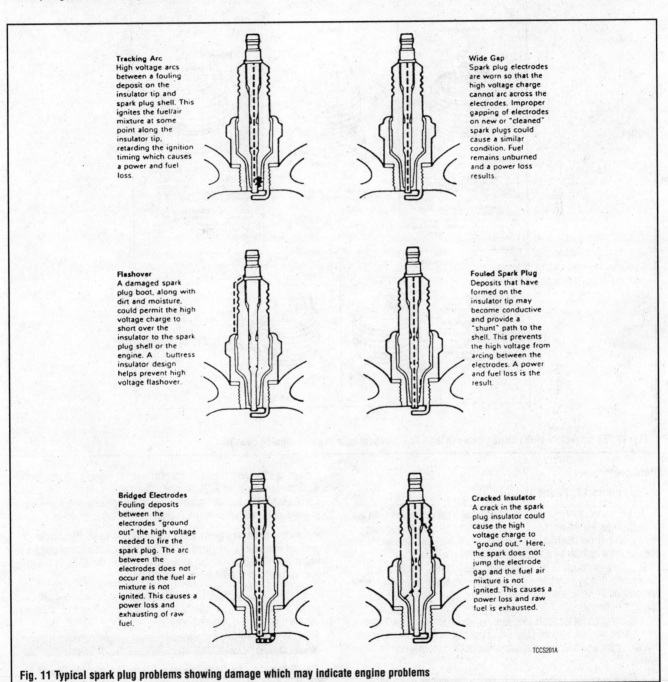

Tracking Arc
High voltage arcs between a fouling deposit on the insulator tip and spark plug shell. This ignites the fuel/air mixture at some point along the insulator tip, retarding the ignition timing which causes a power and fuel loss.

Wide Gap
Spark plug electrodes are worn so that the high voltage charge cannot arc across the electrodes. Improper gapping of electrodes on new or "cleaned" spark plugs could cause a similar condition. Fuel remains unburned and a power loss results.

Flashover
A damaged spark plug boot, along with dirt and moisture, could permit the high voltage charge to short over the insulator to the spark plug shell or the engine. A buttress insulator design helps prevent high voltage flashover.

Fouled Spark Plug
Deposits that have formed on the insulator tip may become conductive and provide a "shunt" path to the shell. This prevents the high voltage from arcing between the electrodes. A power and fuel loss is the result.

Bridged Electrodes
Fouling deposits between the electrodes "ground out" the high voltage needed to fire the spark plug. The arc between the electrodes does not occur and the fuel air mixture is not ignited. This causes a power loss and exhausting of raw fuel.

Cracked Insulator
A crack in the spark plug insulator could cause the high voltage charge to "ground out." Here, the spark does not jump the electrode gap and the fuel air mixture is not ignited. This causes a power loss and raw fuel is exhausted.

TCCS201A

Fig. 11 Typical spark plug problems showing damage which may indicate engine problems

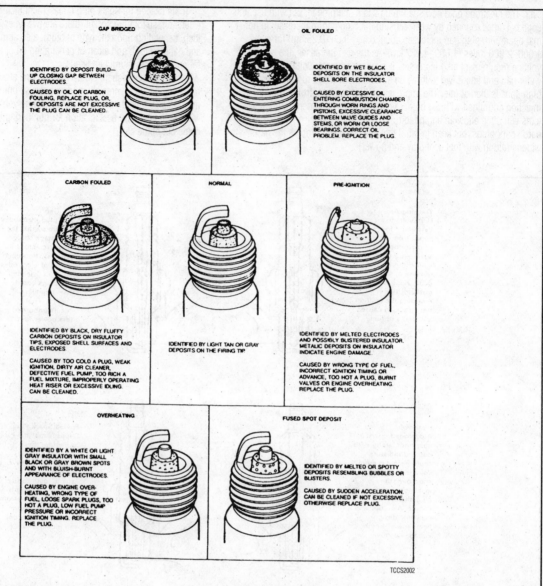

GAP BRIDGED
IDENTIFIED BY DEPOSIT BUILD—UP CLOSING GAP BETWEEN ELECTRODES.
CAUSED BY OIL OR CARBON FOULING. REPLACE PLUG, OR, IF DEPOSITS ARE NOT EXCESSIVE THE PLUG CAN BE CLEANED.

OIL FOULED
IDENTIFIED BY WET BLACK DEPOSITS ON THE INSULATOR SHELL BORE ELECTRODES.
CAUSED BY EXCESSIVE OIL ENTERING COMBUSTION CHAMBER THROUGH WORN RINGS AND PISTONS, EXCESSIVE CLEARANCE BETWEEN VALVE GUIDES AND STEMS, OR WORN OR LOOSE BEARINGS. CORRECT OIL PROBLEM. REPLACE THE PLUG.

CARBON FOULED
IDENTIFIED BY BLACK, DRY FLUFFY CARBON DEPOSITS ON INSULATOR TIPS, EXPOSED SHELL SURFACES AND ELECTRODES.
CAUSED BY TOO COLD A PLUG, WEAK IGNITION, DIRTY AIR CLEANER, DEFECTIVE FUEL PUMP, TOO RICH A FUEL MIXTURE, IMPROPERLY OPERATING HEAT RISER OR EXCESSIVE IDLING. CAN BE CLEANED.

NORMAL
IDENTIFIED BY LIGHT TAN OR GRAY DEPOSITS ON THE FIRING TIP

PRE-IGNITION
IDENTIFIED BY MELTED ELECTRODES AND POSSIBLY BLISTERED INSULATOR. METALIC DEPOSITS ON INSULATOR INDICATE ENGINE DAMAGE.
CAUSED BY WRONG TYPE OF FUEL, INCORRECT IGNITION TIMING OR ADVANCE, TOO HOT A PLUG, BURNT VALVES OR ENGINE OVERHEATING. REPLACE THE PLUG.

OVERHEATING
IDENTIFIED BY A WHITE OR LIGHT GRAY INSULATOR WITH SMALL BLACK OR GRAY BROWN SPOTS AND WITH BLUISH-BURNT APPEARANCE OF ELECTRODES.
CAUSED BY ENGINE OVERHEATING, WRONG TYPE OF FUEL, LOOSE SPARK PLUGS, TOO HOT A PLUG, LOW FUEL PUMP PRESSURE OR INCORRECT IGNITION TIMING. REPLACE THE PLUG.

FUSED SPOT DEPOSIT
IDENTIFIED BY MELTED OR SPOTTY DEPOSITS RESEMBLING BUBBLES OR BLISTERS.
CAUSED BY SUDDEN ACCELERATION. CAN BE CLEANED IF NOT EXCESSIVE, OTHERWISE REPLACE PLUG.

TCCS2002

Fig. 12 The inspection of the spark plugs can tell you a lot about your engines running condition

Removal

▶ **See Figures 13, 14 and 15**

1. Disconnect the negative battery cable, and if the vehicle has been run recently, allow the engine to thoroughly cool. Attempting to remove plugs from a hot cylinder head could cause the plugs to seize and damage the threads in the cylinder head. Especially on aluminum heads!

2. Check for access to the plugs on your vehicle. You may be able to gain access directly from the engine compartment, or you may have to raise and support the vehicle on jackstands to get them from underneath or through a wheel well.

3. Carefully twist the spark plug wire boot to loosen it, then pull upward and remove the boot from the plug. Be sure to pull on the boot and not on the wire, otherwise the connector located inside the boot may become separated.

➡**A spark plug wire removal tool is recommended as it will make removal easier and help prevent damage to the boot and wire assembly.**

4. Using compressed air (and SAFETY GLASSES), blow any water or debris from the spark plug well to assure that no harmful contaminants are allowed to enter the combustion chamber when the spark plug is removed. If compressed air is not available, use a rag or a brush to clean the area. Compressed air is available from both an air compressor or from compressed air in cans which may be obtained at photography stores.

➡**Remove the spark plugs when the engine is cold, if possible, to prevent damage to the threads. If plug removal is difficult, apply a few drops of penetrating oil to the area around the base of the plug, and allow it a few minutes to work.**

5. Using a spark plug socket that is equipped with a rubber insert to properly hold the plug, turn the spark plug counterclockwise to loosen and remove the spark plug from the bore.

❊❊ WARNING

AVOID the use of a flexible extension on the socket. Use of a flexible extension may allow a shear force to be applied to the plug. A shear force could break the plug off in the cylinder head, leading to costly and frustrating repairs. In addition, be sure to support the ratchet with your other hand—this will also help prevent the socket from damaging the plug.

Fig. 13 To remove the boot, twist it gently on the spark plug. Sometimes a boot puller tool comes in handy.

Fig. 14 Brush away any dirt from around the plug, so that none will fall into the hole after the plug is removed.

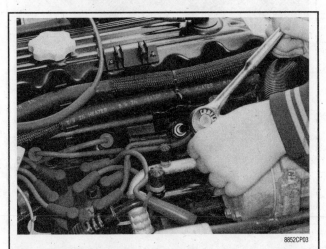

Fig. 15 Remove the spark plug using the proper size socket and necessary extensions. Be sure the socket is seated correctly on the plug and turn it counterclockwise to remove it.

Gapping

♦ See Figures 16 and 17

Check spark plug gap before installation. The ground electrode (the L-shaped one connected to the body of the plug) must be parallel to the center electrode and the specified size wire must pass between the electrodes with a slight drag.

➡ **NEVER adjust the gap platinum type spark plug. These plugs have a thin layer of platinum on the electrodes which may be easily damaged with a gapping tool or feeler gauge. Platinum spark plugs are pregapped at the factory for your specific application and require no adjustment.**

Always check the gap on new conventional type plugs as they are not always set correctly at the factory. Do not use a flat feeler gauge when measuring the gap on a used plug, because the reading may be inaccurate. A round-wire type gapping tool is the best way to check the gap. The correct gauge should pass through the electrode gap with a slight drag. If you're in doubt, try 1 size smaller and 1 larger. The smaller gauge should go through easily, while the larger one shouldn't go through at all. Wire gapping tools usually have a bending tool attached. Use that to adjust the side electrode until the proper distance is obtained. Never attempt to bend the center elec-

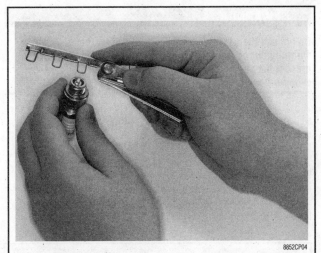

Fig. 16 Checking the spark plug gap with a wire type feeler gauge

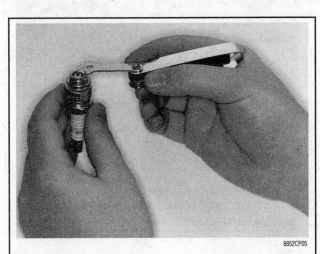

Fig. 17 To adjusting the spark plug gap, use the proper tool as shown. The use of other tools or pliers will risk breaking the electrode.

trode. Also, be careful not to bend the side electrode too far or too often as it may weaken and break off within the engine, requiring removal of the cylinder head to retrieve it.

Installation

▶ See Figure 18

1. Inspect the spark plug boot for tears or damage. If a damaged boot is found, the spark plug wire must be replaced. As mentioned earlier, this is an excellent time to check each of the spark plug wires for proper resistance and/or for damage.

2. Using a wire feeler gauge, check and adjust the spark plug gap. When using a gauge, the proper size should pass between the electrodes with a slight drag. The next larger size should not be able to pass while the next smaller size should pass freely.

3. Apply a thin coating of anti-seize on the thread of the plug. This is extremely important on aluminum head engines.

4. Carefully thread the plug into the bore by hand. If resistance is felt before the plug is almost completely threaded, back the plug out and begin threading again. In small, hard to reach areas, an old spark plug wire and boot could be used as a threading tool. The boot will hold the plug while you twist the end of the wire and the wire is supple enough to twist before it would allow the plug to crossthread.

✳✳ WARNING

Do not use the spark plug socket to thread the plugs. Always carefully thread the plug by hand or using an old plug wire to prevent the possibility of crossthreading and damaging the cylinder head bore.

5. Carefully tighten the spark plug. If the plug you are installing is equipped with a crush washer, seat the plug, then tighten about ¼ turn to crush the washer. Whenever possible, spark plugs should be tightened to the factory specification.

6. Apply a small amount of silicone dielectric compound to the end of the spark plug lead or inside the spark plug boot to prevent sticking, then install the boot to the spark plug and push until it clicks into place. The click may be felt or heard, then gently pull back on the boot to assure proper contact.

Fig. 18 Coat the threads of the plug with "anti-seize" grease and start the plug in by hand to avoid cross-threading. Tighten the plug to the factory specification.

Spark Plug Wires

CHECKING & REPLACING

▶ See Figures 19 and 20

At every tune-up/inspection, visually check the spark plug cables for burns cuts, or breaks in the insulation. Check the boots and the nipples on the distributor cap and/or coil. Replace any damaged wiring. If no physical damage is obvious, the wires can be checked with an ohmmeter for excessive resistance.

Every 30,000 miles (48270 km) or so, the resistance of the wires should be checked with an ohmmeter. Wires with excessive resistance will cause misfiring and may make the engine difficult to start. In addition worn wires will allow arcing and misfiring in damp weather. Generally, the useful life of the cables is 30,000–45,000 miles (48,270–72,405 km), though some late-model vehicles use newer long-life wires that could last up to 100,000 miles (160,900 km) in some circumstances.

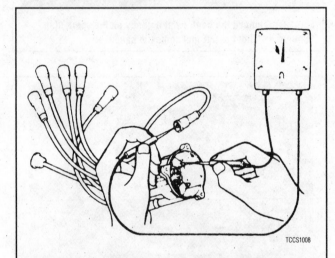

Fig. 19 Checking plug wire resistance through the distributor cap with an ohmmeter

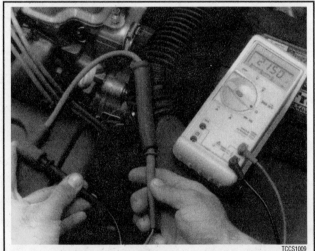

Fig. 20 On distributorless ignition systems, the ignition wires must be checked alone, since there is no cap

To check resistance on vehicles with a distributor ignition, remove the distributor cap and leave the wires connected to the cap. Connect one lead of the ohmmeter to the corresponding electrode inside the cap and the other lead to the spark plug terminal (remove it from the spark plug for the test). Replace any wire that shows over 50,000 ohms. (Generally speaking, resistance should not run over 35,000 ohms and 50,000 ohms should be considered the outer limit of acceptability.)

Test the coil wire by connecting the ohmmeter between the center contact in the cap and either of the primary terminals at the coil. If the total resistance of the coil and wire is more than 25,000 ohms, remove the wire from the coil and check the resistance of the wire alone. If the resistance is higher than 15,000 ohms, replace the wire.

For vehicles with distributorless ignition use the specifications below as a guide to check you wire resistance. Connect one lead of the ohmmeter to the coil end of the cable and the other lead to the spark plug terminal (remove it from the spark plug for the test). Replace any wire that shows over 50,000 ohms.

Wire resistance is a function of length, and the longer the wire, the greater the resistance. Thus, if the wires on your vehicle are longer than the factory originals, resistance will be higher and quite possibly outside of these limits.

- 0–15 in. (0–38 cm) — 3000–10,000 ohms
- 15–25 in. (38–64 cm) — 4000–15,000 ohms
- 25–35 in. (64–89 cm) — 6000–20,000 ohms
- Over 35 in. (89 cm) — 5000–10,000 ohms per 12 in. (30 cm)

When installing a new set of spark plug wires, replace the wires one at a time so there will be no confusion. Start by replacing the longest wire first. Install the boot firmly over the spark plug. Route the wire the same as the original. Insert the nipple firmly into the tower on the distributor cap. Repeat the process for each wire.

➡If the spark plug wires have become unserviceable due to time and wear, it is probably a good idea to replace the distributor cap and rotor as well.

Distributor Service

DISTRIBUTOR CAP & ROTOR

▶ **See Figures 21 and 22**

➡**One often overlooked part of cap inspection are the terminals on the underside. Small burn spots or deposits of corrosion here can lead to engine misfiring.**

At every tune-up, visually check the distributor cap and rotor for damage, burns or corrosion. Check the spark plug towers and their terminals

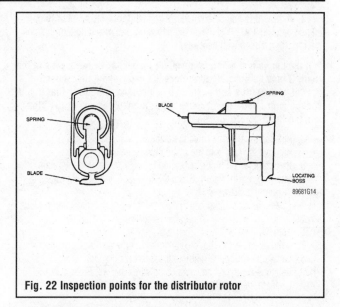

Fig. 22 Inspection points for the distributor rotor

under the cap to be sure they are free of corrosion that would inhibit proper spark distribution. Replace any damaged or worn components.

Inspect the rotor for cracks, excessive burning of the contacts, and mechanical damage, and replace as necessary. Slightly burned contacts should be sanded smooth.

While primary wiring is less perishable than the secondary circuit, it should be checked for cracked insulation or loose connections. Tighten connections or replace wires as necessary.

➡**If the spark plug wires have become unserviceable due to time and wear, it is probably a good idea to replace the cap and rotor as well.**

Removal & Installation

▶ **See Figures 23, 24, 25 and 26**

1. Disconnect the negative battery cable for safety.

➡**Some late-model vehicles, use spark plug wires and distributor caps that are already numbered for ease of service, double-check this before disconnecting any wires. Besides, even if the OEM cap and wires were numbered doesn't mean that the replacements will be to. Be sure make a quick sketch to follow during installation.**

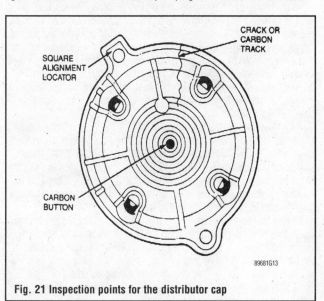

Fig. 21 Inspection points for the distributor cap

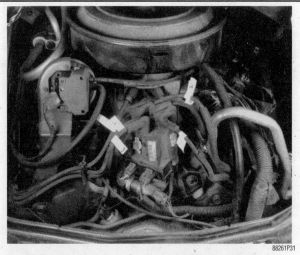

Fig. 23 Tag all spark plug wires and matching cap terminals before removal

2. If the cap is being completely removed (for replacement or for engine service) TAG all of the spark plug wires and matching terminals on the cap, then disconnect the wires.

➡**If the cap is just being removed for inspection or for access to the rotor, it may be possible to remove the cap without disconnecting any/all of the wires and position it aside. Just remember that if you change your mind and disconnect 2 or more wires you MUST stop and tag them before proceeding.**

3. Release the distributor cap retainers.
4. Remove the cap from the distributor assembly.
5. If you are replacing or inspecting the rotor, check for any retaining screws and remove, if present. Grasp the rotor and gently pull upward to remove it from the shaft.
6. Check the distributor cap and rotor for wear or damage and replace, if necessary.

To install:

7. If removed, install the rotor to the top of the distributor shaft.
8. Install the cap to the distributor assembly
9. As tagged, connect any spark plug wires that were removed.
10. Connect the negative battery cable.

Fig. 24 Release the distributor hold-down screws or clamps

Fig. 25 Remove the cap for inspection, replacement or access to the rotor

Fig. 26 Remove any retaining screws from the rotor, then carefully pull the rotor from the distributor shaft

Ignition Timing

➡**On many late-model vehicles the ignition timing is completely controlled by the on-board computer and is not adjustable. The following is a generic procedure for a point of reference. Check the under hood emissions sticker or refer to Chilton's Total Car Care for specific information on your vehicle.**

GENERAL INFORMATION

Ignition timing is the measurement, in degrees of crankshaft rotation, of the point at which the spark plugs fire in each of the cylinders. It is measured in degrees before or after Top Dead Center (TDC) of the compression stroke.

Because it takes a fraction of a second for the spark plug to ignite the mixture in the cylinder, the spark plug must fire a little before the piston reaches TDC. Otherwise, the mixture will not be completely ignited as the piston passes TDC and the full power of the explosion will not be used by the engine.

The timing measurement is given in degrees of crankshaft rotation before the piston reaches TDC (BTDC). If the setting for the ignition timing is 5° BTDC, the spark plug must fire 5° before each piston reaches TDC. This only holds true, however, when the engine is at idle speed.

As the engine speed increases, the pistons go faster. The spark plugs have to ignite the fuel even sooner if it is to be completely ignited when the piston reaches TDC. To do this, distributors have various means of advancing the spark timing as the engine speed increases. On older vehicles, this was accomplished by centrifugal weights within the distributor along with a vacuum diaphragm mounted on the side of the distributor. Later vehicles are equipped with an electronic spark timing system in which no vacuum or mechanical advance is used, instead all timing changes electronically based on signals from various sensors.

If the ignition is set too far advanced (BTDC), the ignition and expansion of the fuel in the cylinder will occur too soon and tend to force the piston down while it is still traveling up. This causes engine ping. If the ignition spark is set too far retarded, after TDC (ATDC), the piston will have already passed TDC and started on its way down when the fuel is ignited. This will cause the piston to be forced down for only a portion of its travel. This will result in poor engine performance and lack of power.

Timing marks usually consist of a notch on the rim of the crankshaft pulley and a scale of degrees attached to the front of the engine (often on the engine front cover). The notch corresponds to the position of the piston in the No. 1 cylinder. A stroboscopic (dynamic) timing light is used, which is hooked into the circuit of the No. 1 cylinder spark plug. Every time the spark plug fires, the timing light flashes. By aiming the timing light at the timing marks while the engine is running, the exact position of the piston within the cylinder can be easily read since the stroboscopic flash makes the mark on the pulley appear to be standing still. Proper timing is indicated when the notch is aligned with the correct number on the scale.

→Never pierce a spark plug wire in order to attach a timing light or perform tests. The pierced insulation will eventually lead to an electrical arc and related ignition troubles.

Since your vehicle most likely has an electronic ignition, you should use a timing light with an inductive pickup. This pickup simply clamps onto the No. 1 spark plug wire, eliminating the adapter. It is not susceptible to cross-firing or false triggering, which may occur with a conventional light, due to the greater voltages produced by electronic ignition.

SERVICE PRECAUTIONS

✳✳ WARNING

Some older electronic diagnostic equipment and service tachometers may not be compatible with electronic ignition systems, consult your manufacturer before using such equipment.

- The distributor needs no periodic lubrication, for the engine lubrication system lubricates the lower bushing and an oil reservoir lubricates the upper bushing.
- Since there are no points in the electronic ignition systems, NO manual dwell adjustment is necessary or possible.
- The material used in the construction of the spark plug wires is very soft and pliable. These wires can withstand high heat and carry a higher voltage. It is very important that the wires be routed correctly, for they are highly susceptible to scuffing and/or cutting.

✳✳ WARNING

When removing a spark plug wire, be sure to twist the boot and then pull on it to remove it. Do NOT pull on the wire to remove it.

ADJUSTMENT

▶ See Figures 27 and 28

Ignition timing on most late model engines is controlled by the electronic engine control system and does NOT need to be periodically checked and adjusted. If the distributor has been removed for engine service or if all

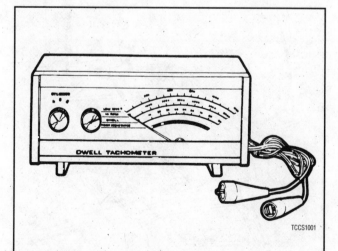

Fig. 27 A Dwell-Tach may be used to set the idle speed while making the timing adjustment

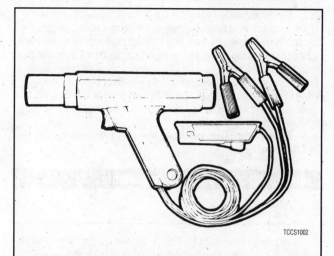

Fig. 28 Typical inductive DC powered timing light. The inductive clamp goes around the number 1 plug wire.

other causes of a driveability problem have been resolved and the timing is suspect, the initial (base) timing may be checked and adjusted.

✳✳ WARNING

Timing adjustment procedures are specific to the type of ignition system used on your vehicle. For specific adjustment procedures refer to a Chilton's Total Car Care manual and check the underhood emission label. Below is a generic timing procedure to be used as a reference only.

Ignition timing is adjusted by loosening the distributor locking device and turning the distributor in the engine. The steps below outline the steps in checking and adjusting the ignition timing.

The following procedure requires the use of a distributor wrench and a timing light. When using a timing light, be sure to consult the manufacturer's recommendations for installation and usage.

1. Refer to the ignition timing specifications, listed on the Vehicle Emissions Control Information (VECI) label, located in the engine compartment and follow the instructions. If the label is missing you MUST obtain the correct replacement in order to assure the proper timing procedures are being followed for YOUR engine.
2. Start and run the engine until it reaches normal operating temperature.

✳✳ CAUTION

NEVER run the engine in a sealed garage. Open all doors and windows, and if possible, use vents or fans to provide further ventilation. Carbon Monoxide that is prevalent in exhaust gas can quickly build-up in your blood, preventing oxygen from reaching your brain. This can cause serious injury or even DEATH.

3. Disable the electronic ignition advance system (usually known as Ignition Control or IC). This is usually done by disconnecting the "Set Timing" connector. The location and procedure for this will vary from vehicle to vehicle.
4. Connect a timing light to the engine:
   a. If using a non-inductive type, connect an adapter between the No. 1 spark plug and the spark plug wire; DO NOT puncture the spark plug wire, for this will allow arching which will cause engine misfiring.
   b. If using an inductive type, clamp it around the No. 1 spark plug wire.
   c. If using a magnetic type, place the probe in the connector located near the damper pulley; this type must be used with special electronic timing equipment.

5. Start the engine and allow it to idle at normal operating temperature. Aim the timing light at the timing mark on the damper pulley (be careful because the strobe affect of the timing light will make moving engine parts appear to be standing still); a line on the damper pulley will align with the timing mark. If necessary (to adjust the timing), loosen the distributor hold-down clamp and slowly turn the distributor slightly to align the marks. When the alignment is correct, tighten the hold-down bolt, and then re-check the timing with the light to be sure it did not change while you were tightening the distributor bolt.

6. Turn the engine **OFF**, remove the timing light and reset the "Set Timing" connector.

Idle Speed and Mixture Adjustments

CARBURETED ENGINES

The different combinations of emission systems application on the various available engines have resulted in a great variety of tune-up specifications. Most vehicles should have a decal conspicuously placed in the engine compartment giving tune-up specifications.

Many late model engines utilize electronically controlled feedback carburetors and there are no periodic mixture adjustments, necessary or possible. Slow (curb) idle speeds can often be set using the speed screw at the throttle valve on the carburetor. When setting the curb idle speed, be sure the engine is at normal operating temperature and that all of the conditions on the vehicle emission control information label have been met.

FUEL INJECTED ENGINES

Engines covered by this manual may be equipped with a variety of fuel injection systems including: Throttle Body Injection (TBI), Multi-Port Fuel Injection (MPFI), and others. Although each of these systems contain some of their own unique engine control components, what they all share is full computer control of the idle air supply and of all fuel delivery. The fuel injection computer module regulates idle speeds and supplies the correct amount of fuel during all engine operating conditions. No periodic adjustments are necessary or possible. If the engine is suspected of maintaining an incorrect idle speed, refer to a Chilton's Total Car Care manual for information regarding the self-diagnostic features of the engine computer and emission control systems and for information regarding the fuel delivery systems.

Valve Adjustment

⬥ **See Figures 29, 30, 31 and 32**

As the valve tip and the valve actuating components wear, excessive clearance develops between these components leading to reduced engine performance and valve noise, commonly called "valve tap." Several methods have been developed to compensate for this excessive clearance. In most vehicles, this clearance is automatically adjusted by a component called the hydraulic valve lifter, sometimes called the hydraulic lash adjuster.

This type of lifter is actually a very small cylinder and piston. When the engine is running, the lifter is constantly exposed to engine oil that has been pressurized by the engine oil pump. As the valve components wear, more oil is pumped into the lifter thereby reducing the clearance in the valvetrain components. If this type of system becomes noisy, suspect low oil pressure and/or excessive wear on valvetrain components. The exact cause should be determined and the appropriate parts replaced.

Many V6 and V8 OHV engines use a stamped steel rocker arm that pivots on a stud near the center of the cylinder head. The rocker arm is held in position by a pivot ball and nut. These engines utilize hydraulic lifters and after the initial installation, if done properly, requires no further adjustment.

Fig. 29 Adjust the valve lash by unlocking the nut, turning the adjustment screw and testing with a feeler gauge

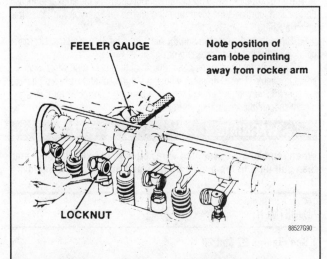

FEELER GAUGE

Note position of cam lobe pointing away from rocker arm

LOCKNUT

Fig. 30 Overhead camshaft engine with adjustable rocker arm/cam follower

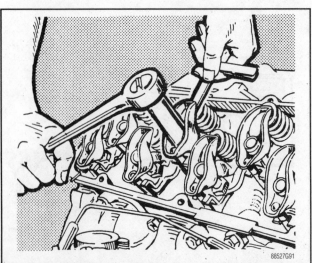

Fig. 31 Typical overhead valve V engine with adjustable rocker arms

89701P68

Fig. 32 Different size shims are used to adjust the clearance on engines where the camshaft works directly on the valve

Some vehicle manufacturers still utilize a manually adjusted valvetrain system. This system incorporates a screw and a jam nut, also called a lock-nut, usually located on the rocker arm or cam follower near the tip of the valve. Clearance is adjusted by inserting the correct size feeler gauge between the rocker arm and valve tip, then after loosening the locknut, adjust the screw until a slight drag is felt on the feeler gauge as it is moved between the two components.

Some engines utilize shims to take up excessive clearance in the valve-train. This system may be used on engines where the camshaft is located directly over the valve. The shim is positioned in a small bucket on the valve between the cam lobe and the valve. Shims are available in many different thicknesses. The thickness of the new shim must be calculated to determine the exact shim to use. The thickness of the new shim should equal the measured clearance minus the specification given by the manufacturer plus the thickness of the initial shim. This new shim should then be placed on the valve instead of the old shim.

Exact valve adjustment procedures for all cars is impossible to detail here, but the most common types of adjustments have been discussed and should serve as a general guide. For specific, detailed instructions, please refer to a Chilton's Total Car Care Manual.

The following are tips that can make valve adjustment a little easier and more accurate:

• Before removing a valve cover, be sure to have a valve cover gasket on hand, if a replacement is required on your model.

• When making static adjustments (engine **OFF**), be sure that the base of the cam lobe is facing the valve or lifter when adjusting that particular valve. In other words, the valve must be in the fully closed position in order to assure an accurate measurement.

• Check if the valves should be adjusted with the engine "HOT" or "COLD."

• On very old cars or high performance machines with solid lifters, if you set the valves with the engine running, run the engine as slow as possible.

• The feeler gauge should pass through with a slow steady drag. On old vehicles with the engine running, if you force the gauge or the engine misses when the gauge is inserted, the clearance is too tight.

• It is better to have the clearance a little loose than a little tight. Valves adjusted too tight will cause valve burning.

Tune-Up Check List

ELECTRONIC IGNITION

On an electronic ignition system, the basic tune-up procedures are as follows.

• Remove spark plugs.

• Test compression in each cylinder.

• Clean and/or replace spark plugs and gap spark plugs to manufacturer's specifications and install in engine.

• If applicable, check the distributor cap and rotor for cracks and wear. Replace if necessary.

• Use tachometer to set idle speed to specifications (If adjustable).

• Use timing light to set initial timing. (Most electronic ignition systems do not require adjustments.)

The list above represents only the "bare bones" facts about tune-ups. Other functions that could be performed are using an emissions analyzer to check for compliance with emissions standards and for fuel economy, and measuring vacuum and checking for leaks with a vacuum gauge.

USING A VACUUM GAUGE

White needle = steady needle *Dark needle = drifting needle*

The vacuum gauge is one of the most useful and easy-to-use diagnostic tools. It is inexpensive, easy to hook up, and provides valuable information about the condition of your engine.

Indication: Normal engine in good condition

Gauge reading: Steady, from 17–22 in./Hg.

Indication: Sticking valve or ignition miss

Gauge reading: Needle fluctuates from 15–20 in./Hg. at idle

Indication: Late ignition or valve timing, low compression, stuck throttle valve, leaking carburetor or manifold gasket.

Gauge reading: Low (15–20 in./Hg.) but steady

Indication: Improper carburetor adjustment, or minor intake leak at carburetor or manifold

NOTE: Bad fuel injector O-rings may also cause this reading.

Gauge reading: Drifting needle

Indication: Weak valve springs, worn valve stem guides, or leaky cylinder head gasket (vibrating excessively at all speeds).

NOTE: A plugged catalytic converter may also cause this reading.

Gauge reading: Needle fluctuates as engine speed increases

Indication: Burnt valve or improper valve clearance. The needle will drop when the defective valve operates.

Gauge reading: Steady needle, but drops regularly

Indication: Choked muffler or obstruction in system. Speed up the engine. Choked muffler will exhibit a slow drop of vacuum to zero.

Gauge reading: Gradual drop in reading at idle

Indication: Worn valve guides

Gauge reading: Needle vibrates excessively at idle, but steadies as engine speed increases

TCCS3C01

8

THE ENGINE

THE ENGINE

How it Works

▶ **See Figures 1, 2, 3, 4 and 5**

The basic piston engine is a metal block containing a series of chambers. The upper engine block is usually an iron or aluminum alloy casting, consisting of outer walls that form hollow jackets around the cylinder walls. The lower block, which provides a number of rigid mounting points for the bearings that hold the crankshaft in place, is known as the crankcase. The hollow jackets of the upper block add rigidity to the engine and contain the liquid coolant that carries heat away from the cylinders and other engine parts.

An air-cooled engine block consists of a crankcase that provides a rigid mounting for the crankshaft and has studs to hold the cylinders in place. The cylinders are individual, single-wall castings, finned for cooling, and they are usually bolted to the crankcase, rather than cast integrally with the block.

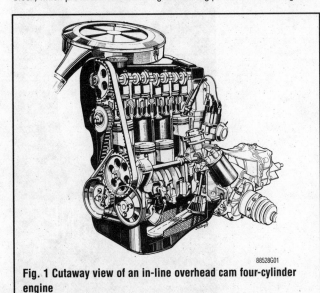

Fig. 1 Cutaway view of an in-line overhead cam four-cylinder engine

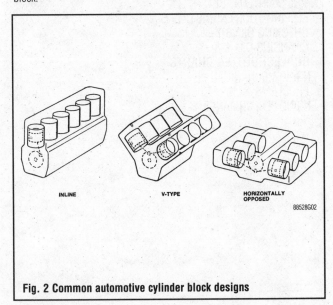

INLINE   V-TYPE   HORIZONTALLY OPPOSED

88528G02

Fig. 2 Common automotive cylinder block designs

THE FOUR STROKE CYCLE

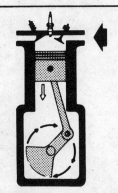 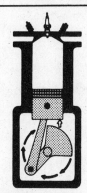 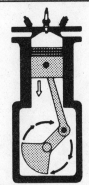 

1. Intake

The intake stroke begins with the piston near the top of its travel. As the piston begins its descent, the exhaust valve closes fully, the intake valve opens and the volume of the combustion chamber begins to increase, creating a vacuum. As the piston descends, an air/fuel mixture is drawn from the carburetor into the cylinder through the intake manifold. The intake stroke ends with the intake valve closed just after the piston has begun its upstroke.

2. Compression

As the piston ascends, the fuel/air mixture is forced into the small chamber machined into the cylinder head. This compresses the mixture until it occupies ⅛th to 1/11th of the volume that it did at the time the piston began its ascent. This compression raises the temperature of the mixture and increases its pressure, increasing the force generated by the expansion of gases during the power stroke.

3. Ignition

The fuel/air mixture is ignited by the spark plug just before the piston reaches the top if its stroke so that a very large portion of the fuel will have burned by the time the piston begins descending again. The heat produced by combustion increases the pressure in the cylinder, forcing the piston down with great force.

4. Exhaust

As the piston approaches the bottom of its stroke, the exhaust valve begins opening and the pressure in the cylinder begins to force the gases out around the valve. The ascent of the piston then forces nearly all the rest of the unburned gases from the cylinder. The cycle begins again as the exhaust valve closes, the intake valve opens and the piston begins descending and bringing a fresh charge of fuel and air into the combustion chamber.

88528G03

Fig. 3 The four-stroke cycle of a basic two-valve, carbureted gasoline, spark ignition engine (multi-valve and fuel injected engines operate the same way)

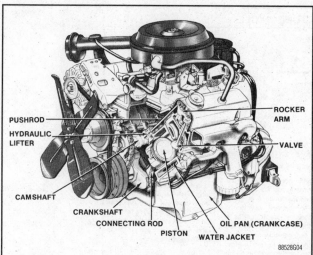

Fig. 4 Cutaway view of a V6 gasoline powered overhead valve engine

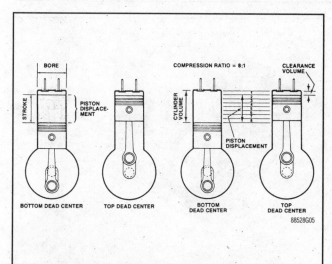

Fig. 5 Basic engine cylinder dimensions. The ratio between the total cylinder and clearance volume is the compression ratio.

In a water-cooled engine, only the cylinder head is bolted to the block (usually on top). The water pump is mounted directly to the block.

The crankshaft is a long iron or steel shaft (and sometimes aluminum in more high-tech or high performance applications) mounted rigidly at a number of points in the bottom of the crankcase. The crankshaft is free to turn and contains several counterweighted crankpins (one centered under each cylinder) that are offset several inches from the center of the crankshaft and turn in a circle as the crankshaft turns. Pistons are connected to the crankpins by steel connecting rods. The rods connect the pistons at their upper ends with the crankpins at their lower ends. Circular rings seal the small space between the pistons and wall of the cylinders.

When the crankshaft spins, the pistons move up and down in the cylinders, varying the volume of each cylinder, depending on the position of the piston. At least two openings in each cylinder head (above the cylinders) allow the intake of the air/fuel mixture and the exhaust of burned gasses. After intake, the pistons compress the fuel mixture at the top of the cylinder, the fuel is ignited, and, as the pistons are forced downward by the expansion of burning fuel, the connecting rods convert the up and down motion of the pistons into rotary (turning) motion of the crankshaft. A round flywheel at the rear of the crankshaft provides a large, stable mass to smooth out the rotation.

The cylinder heads form tight covers for the tops of the cylinders and contain chambers into which the fuel mixture is forced as it is compressed by the pistons reaching the upper limit of their travel. Each combustion chamber contains at least one intake valve, one exhaust valve, and one spark plug per cylinder (depending on the design). The tips of the spark plugs protrude into the combustion chambers.

The valve in each opening of the cylinder head is opened and closed by the action of the camshaft. The camshaft is driven by the crankshaft through a gear, chain, or belt at 1/2 crankshaft speed (the camshaft gear is twice the size of the crankshaft gear). The valves are operated either through rocker arms and pushrods (overhead valve and some overhead cam engines) or directly by the camshaft using cam followers which usually contain shims for adjustment (overhead cam engine).

Lubricating oil is stored in a pan at the bottom of the engine and is force-fed to all parts of the engine by a gear-type pump, driven from the crankshaft. The oil lubricates the entire engine and seals the piston rings, giving good compression.

THE DIESEL ENGINE

▶ **See Figures 6 and 7**

Diesel engines, like gasoline powered engines, have a crankshaft, pistons, camshaft, etc. In addition, four-stroke diesels require four piston strokes for the complete combustion cycle, exactly like a gasoline engine. The difference lies in how the fuel mixture is ignited. A diesel engine does not rely on a conventional spark ignition to ignite the fuel mixture. Instead, heat produced by compressed air in the combustion chamber ignites the fuel and produces a power stroke. This is known as a compression-ignition engine.

No fuel enters the cylinder on the intake stroke, only air. Since only air is present on the intake stroke, only air is compressed on the compression stroke. At the end of the compression stroke, fuel is sprayed into the combustion chamber and the mixture ignites.

The fuel/air mixture ignites because of the very high temperatures generated by the high compression ratios used in diesel engines. Typically, the compression ratios used in automotive diesels run anywhere from 16:1–23:1. A typical spark-ignition engine has a ratio of about 8:1–10:1. This is why a spark-ignition engine, which continues to run after you have shut off the engine, is said to be "dieseling." It is running on combustion chamber heat alone.

Designing an engine to ignite on its own combustion chamber heat poses certain problems. For instance, although a diesel engine has no need for a coil, spark plugs, or a distributor, it does need what are known as "glow plugs." These look like spark plugs, but are only used to warm the combustion chambers when the engine is cold. Without these plugs, cold starting would be impossible. Also, since fuel timing (rather than spark timing) is critical to a diesel's operation, all diesel engines are fuel-injected rather than carbureted, since the precise fuel metering necessary is not possible with a carburetor.

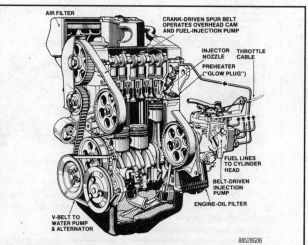

Fig. 6 Cutaway view of an in-line overhead cam four-cylinder diesel engine. Note the similarity to the gasoline engine shown earlier.

THE DIESEL FOUR STROKE CYCLE

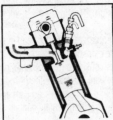

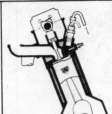
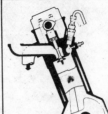

1. Air Intake

Rotation of the crankshaft drives a toothed belt which turns the camshaft, opening the intake valve. As the piston moves down, a vacuum is created, sucking fresh air into the cylinder, past the open intake valve.

2. Air Compression

As the piston moves up, both valves are closed and the air is compressed about 23 times smaller than its original volume. The compressed air reaches a temperature of about 1650°F., far above the temperature needed to ignite diesel fuel.

3. Fuel Injection and Compression

As the piston reaches the top of the stroke, the air temperature is at its maximum. A fine mist of fuel is sprayed into the pre-chamber where it ignites and the flame front spreads rapidly into the combustion chamber. The piston is forced downward by the pressure (about 500 psi) of expanding gasses.

4. Exhaust

As the energy of combustion is spent and the piston begins to move upward again, the exhaust valve opens and burned gasses are forced out past the open valve. As the piston starts down, the exhaust valve closes, intake valve opens, and the air intake stroke begins again.

88528G07

Fig. 7 The four-stroke operating principal applied to a diesel engine

THE WANKEL ENGINE

▶ **See Figures 8 and 9**

Like a conventional piston engine, the Wankel engine is an internal combustion engine and operates on a four-stroke cycle. Also, it runs on gasoline and the spark is generated by a conventional distributor-coil ignition system. However, the similarities end there.

In a Wankel engine, the cylinders are replaced by chambers, and the pistons are replaced by rotors. The chambers are not circular, but have a curved circumference that is identified as an epitrochoid. An epitrochoid is the curve described by a given point on a circle as the circle rolls around the periphery of another circle which is twice the radius of the generating circle.

The rotor is three-cornered, with curved sides. All three corners are in permanent contact with the epitrochoidal surface as the rotor moves around the chamber. This motion is both orbital and rotational, as the rotor is mounted off center. The crankshaft of a piston engine is replaced by a rotor shaft, and crank throws are replaced by eccentrics. Each rotor is carried on an eccentric. Any number of rotors is possible, but most engines have one or two rotors. The valves of the piston engine are replaced by ports in the Wankel engine housing. They are covered and uncovered by the path of the rotor.

88528G08

Fig. 8 Cutaway view of a two rotor Wankel rotary engine

THE ROTARY ENGINE POWER CYCLE

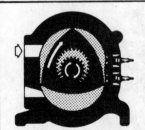
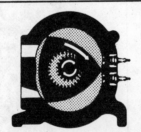

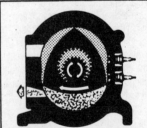

1. Intake.

Fuel/air mixture is drawn into combustion chamber by revolving rotor through intake port (upper left). No valves or valve-operating mechanism needed.

2. Compression.

As rotor continues revolving, it reduces space in chamber containing fuel and air. This compresses mixture.

3. Ignition.

Fuel/air mixture now fully compressed. Leading spark plug fires. A split-second later, following plug fires to assure complete combustion.

4. Exhaust.

Exploding mixture drives rotor, providing power. Rotor then expels gases through exhaust port.

88528G09

Fig. 9 The path of the rotor in the Wankel engine. Note the constantly varying shape of the combustion chamber and the two spark plugs per cylinder.

One of the important differences between the Wankel rotary engine and the piston engine is in the operational cycle. In the piston engine, all the events take place at the top end of the cylinder (intake, compression, expansion, and exhaust). The events are spaced out in time only. The Wankel engine is the opposite. The events occur at the same time but at different places around the rotor-housing surface.

The intake phase takes place next to the intake port and overlaps with the area used for compression. Expansion takes place opposite the ports, and the exhaust phase takes place in the area preceding the exhaust port, overlapping with the latter part of the expansion phase. All three rotor faces are engaged in one of the four phases at all times.

Turbocharging & Supercharging

♦ **See Figures 10, 11 and 12**

Turbocharging, sometimes called supercharging, has been under investigation practically since the invention of the automobile. Gottlieb Daimler, generally credited with development of the first auto, sought to boost the volumetric efficiency of his first vertical gasoline engine in 1885, but was unable to make it work. It wasn't until 1921 that Mercedes-Benz introduced the first production supercharged vehicles.

Between 1921 and the end of World War II, various companies exploited the use of superchargers and turbochargers for racing, marine, and large truck engines. In 1962, General Motors introduced the Oldsmobile F-85 Jetfire, powered by a turbocharged V8 engine and quickly followed that with a turbocharged version of the Chevrolet Corvair. With gasoline prices going rapidly out of sight, the number of manufacturers offering turbocharging has rapidly increased as manufacturers try to maintain performance, reduce engine size and emissions, and increase fuel economy, all at the same time. Models available run the gamut from the Porsche Turbo and the Volkswagen Turbodiesel to the Supercharged Pontiac.

The word turbocharger is an abbreviation of the word turbo supercharging. Although there is a difference between turbocharging and supercharging, the principle is the same—to drive a small compressor which will increase the quantity of fuel/air mixture going into the combustion chamber as it is needed, increasing the volumetric efficiency of the engine and increasing the power output.

Supercharging accomplishes this by operating the compressor mechanically, through a gear-driven shaft. The supercharger is normally activated on demand, when the accelerator pedal is pushed to the floor. A turbocharger is actually a small turbine, which uses exhaust gasses to spin a turbine wheel mounted on a common shaft with a compressor. As the turbine turns at high speed, it causes the compressor to pack a greater charge of air into the engine's cylinders.

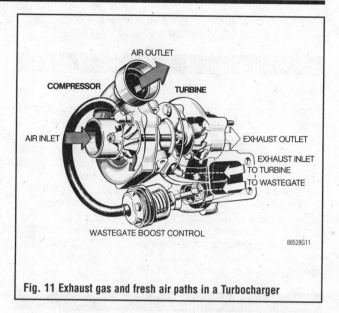

Fig. 11 Exhaust gas and fresh air paths in a Turbocharger

In both systems, air enters through an air intake, passes through an air cleaner, and travels through a duct (usually funnel shaped) to the compressor inlet portion of the turbocharger. From there air is forced through a diffuser into the intake manifold, to the individual cylinders.

The turbocharger itself and the principles involved are extremely simple, but sophisticated engineering problems are created by application. The most critical problem is controlling the manifold or boost pressure. This is the amount of additional boost or pressure created by the turbocharger. The boost must be controlled or the engine will begin to detonate and eventually burn holes in the pistons and self-destruct.

The solution lies in the wastegate or safety valve, which is keyed to intake manifold pressure, exhaust pressure, or a combination of both. At a predetermined pressure, the wastegate valve will open, allowing some of the exhaust gas to pass directly into the exhaust system bypassing the turbocharger. This keeps the intake manifold pressure at a preset maximum.

The second problem with turbocharging is the generally inconsistent quality of gasoline available. If the octane of the fuel is unpredictable, then so is the point at which the engine begins to detonate, making it difficult to set the maximum manifold pressure. The answer to this problem is a knock sensor, a device that detects the harmful pressure waves of detonation in the cylinders and instantly retards the ignition timing to prevent detonation.

The turbocharger itself spins at a maximum speed of about 110,000 rpm at highway speeds and is capable of supplying boost pressure of up to 60–70 psi

Fig. 10 A few of the additional components required for a turbocharged engine. Clockwise from the left: exhaust manifold, exhaust plenum, wastegate assembly, throttle body adapter, and intake manifold.

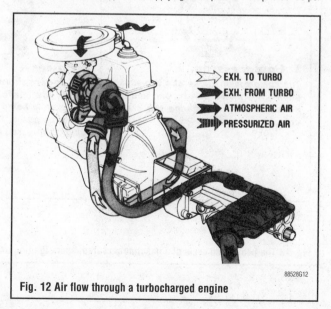

Fig. 12 Air flow through a turbocharged engine

(413–483kPa) on professional racing engines. However, for the average auto or light truck, 3–9 psi is about the maximum boost pressure expected.

Two Stroke Engines

▶ See Figure 13

Although currently out of production, several vehicles imported into the United States used two-stroke engines. These operated with only a compression stroke and a power stroke. Intake of fuel and air mixture and expulsion of exhaust gases takes place between the power and compression strokes while the piston is near the bottom of its travel. Ports in the cylinder walls replace the cylinder head valves of the four-stroke engine. The crankcase is kept dry of oil, and the entire engine is lubricated by mixing the oil with the fuel so that a fine mist of oil covers all moving parts.

The ports are designed so the fuel and air are trapped in the engine's crankcase during most of the down stroke of the piston. This makes the crankcase into a compression chamber that force-feeds the combustion chambers after the ports are uncovered. The pistons serve as the valves, covering the ports whenever they should be closed.

Engine Identification

▶ See Figure 14

It is important for servicing and ordering parts, to know which engine you have. The place to start identifying an engine is with the Vehicle Identification Number (VIN) of the vehicle. The VIN is visible through the windshield on the driver's side of the dash and contains data encoded into a lengthy combination of letters and numbers. A specific letter or number is used to designate the installed engine. Beginning in 1981, all

Fig. 14 The VIN is visible through the driver's side windshield.

domestic manufacturers adopted a uniform, 17-digit VIN. The tenth digit of the VIN indicates the model year and the eighth digit indicates the engine code.

Some import manufacturers also follow this rule. Others only use the tenth digit for the model year. In most cases, the engine designation is also located on a tag or a stamped number located on the engine block or bell housing. Check with your dealer or Chilton's Total Car Care manual for more information.

THE TWO STROKE CYCLE

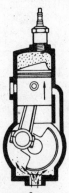

1. Compression
The compression stroke of a two-stroke engine; the intake port is open and the air/fuel mixture is entering the crankcase.

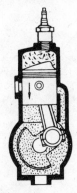

2. Power
The power stroke of a two-stroke engine; the intake port is closed, and the piston is being forced down by the expanding gases. The air/fuel mixture is being compressed in the crankcase.

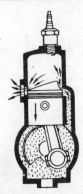

3. Exhaust
The exhaust stroke of a two-stroke engine; the piston travels past the exhaust port, thus opening it, then past the intake port, opening that. As the exhaust gases flow out, the air/fuel mixture flows in due to being under pressure in the crankcase. The next stroke of the piston is the compression stroke and the series of events starts over again.

Fig. 13 The two-stroke cycle of a gasoline-powered, spark ignition engine

Engine Maintenance

▶ See Figure 15

KEEPING YOUR ENGINE CLEAN

▶ See Figure 16

There are a variety of cleaners and degreasers available to help you keep your engine and engine compartment clean. No one wants to work on an engine that is nearly invisible underneath the grease. The most effective way to clean an engine is to steam clean it. However, this takes equipment that the average backyard mechanic does not ordinarily have, though steam cleaning is available at some car washes. It is possible, of course, to have your engine professionally steam cleaned, although this is generally not necessary unless the engine is extraordinarily dirty. Ordinary commercial degreasers, available at auto parts stores, will generally do the job.

CHECKING OIL

▶ See Figures 17, 18, 19 and 20

Maintaining the correct oil level in your vehicle is probably the single most important item of periodic engine maintenance you can perform. There are many reasons an engine uses oil, but keep in mind that it is not unusual for even a showroom-fresh vehicle to use oil at the rate of about 1000 miles (1609 km) to the quart. Therefore, it can be assumed that almost every engine will use a certain amount of oil.

Frequent oil checks are a necessity. Make it a habit to check the oil at least once a week, or at every gas stop. When checking the oil, the engine should be warm, but not running, and the vehicle should be parked on a level surface. Be sure to give the oil a few minutes to drain back into the pan from the upper regions of the engine. Otherwise, you will get a false reading.

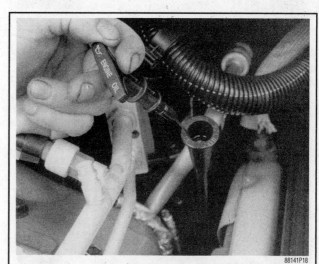

ENGINE MAINTENANCE INTERVALS
To keep your engine operating efficiently, maintain it at the following intervals.

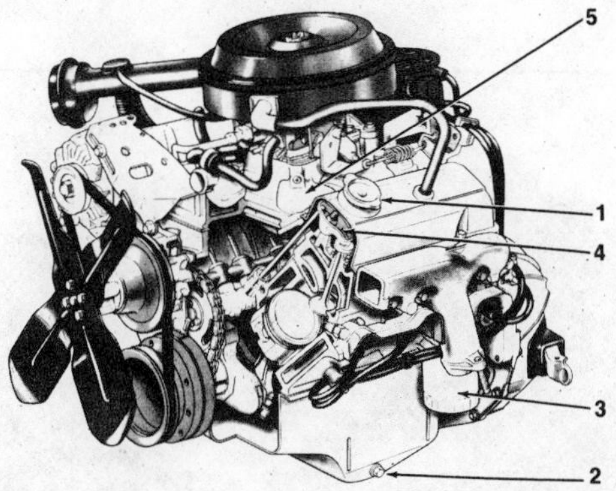

88528G14

Fig. 15 Common engine maintenance intervals—1.Check oil; 2.Change oil; 3.Change filter; 4.Check valves if adjustable; 5.Clean and degrease engine

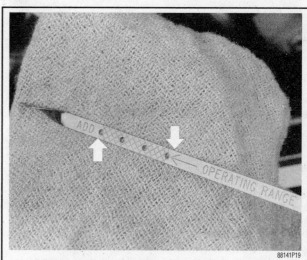

88141P18

Fig. 17 Locate and remove the dipstick, wipe it clean and insert it into the dipstick tube, making sure it is fully inserted

88528P03

Fig. 16 Always cover the distributor and or ignition coils, along with all engine electronics when washing the engine.

88141P19

Fig. 18 While holding the dipstick, read the oil in relation to the marks on the stick (it should be between them)

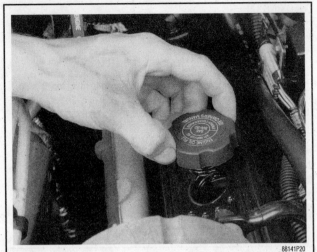

Fig. 19 Locate and remove the oil filler cap. Most late-model filler caps are marked

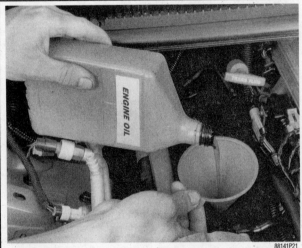

Fig. 20 Add clean oil to the engine until the correct level is indicated on the dipstick. Do not overfill the crankcase with oil!

Follow these simple steps to check your oil level:

1. Make sure the vehicle is parked on level ground.

2. When checking the oil level, it is best for the engine to be at normal operating temperature, although checking the oil immediately after stopping will lead to a false reading. Wait a few minutes after turning off the engine to allow the oil to drain back into the crankcase.

3. Open the hood and locate the dipstick that normally will be in a guide tube mounted to the engine block. Pull the dipstick from its tube, wipe it clean (using a clean, lint free rag) and then reinsert it.

4. Pull the dipstick out again and holding it VERTICALLY (so that the oil cannot flow up the dipstick, giving a false high indication), read the oil level. The oil should be between the FULL and ADD marks on the dipstick. If the oil level is below the ADD mark, add oil of the proper viscosity through the capped opening (usually in the valve or camshaft cover, and sometimes in a filler tube).

➡Some dipsticks do not say FULL and ADD, they may say F and A, or they might just have 2 dots or lines. In any case, the upper of the two marks is used to indicate the full oil level, while the lower of the 2 marks (usually is the one quart low mark) means it is time to add oil.

5. Insert the dipstick and check the oil level again after adding any oil. Be sure not to overfill the crankcase and waste the oil. Excess oil will generally be consumed at an increased rate.

✷✷ WARNING

DO NOT overfill the crankcase. It may result in oil-fouled spark plugs, oil leaks caused by oil seal failure or engine damage due to oil foaming.

CHANGING OIL

▶ **See Figures 21 thru 33**

An oil change is not difficult. Actually, it is one of the simplest (and most valuable) operations you can perform on your vehicle. Although it may seem somewhat complicated at first glance, if you follow these simple instructions, you'll discover that it's not as tough as you may have first thought. All you need is oil, a filter, a drain pan of some type, a funnel, a wrench to fit the drain plug, and the appropriate oil filter wrench.

➡**Although many vehicle manufacturers recommend changing the filter at the first oil change and then every other oil change, we recommend changing the filter with each service. It is a small price to pay for extra protection.**

Fig. 21 Oil change containers make oil changes clean and easy. Remember to drain the filter into the pan and always recycle your used motor oil

Fig. 22 There is a wide verity of filter wrenches available from several specialty tool manufacturers. You may have to experiment to find the correct combination for your vehicle

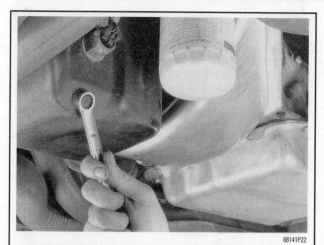

Fig. 23 Locate the drain plug on the oil pan. Use a wrench or a socket to loosen the plug. Use care, the engine and oil should be HOT!

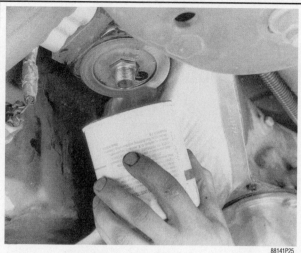

Fig. 26 . . . then remove the oil filter from its mounting. Check that the gasket came off with the filter

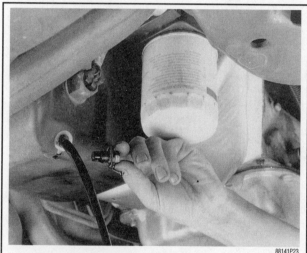

Fig. 24 Quickly withdraw the drain plug and move your hands away, allowing the oil to drain completely

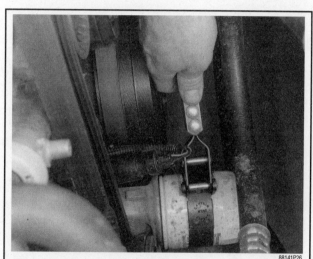

Fig. 27 Oil filters may be located on various positions. In this example, the oil filter is mounted to the front of the engine

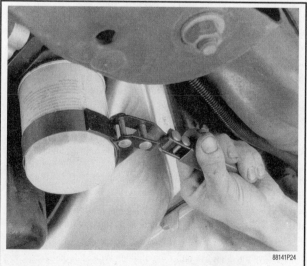

Fig. 25 Use an appropriate filter wrench to loosen the filter . . .

Fig. 28 Coat the new oil filter gasket with clean engine oil

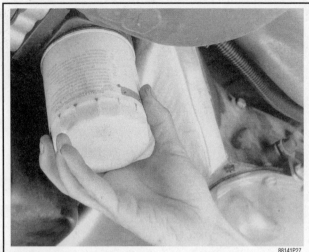

Fig. 29 Always install the oil filter by hand. Never use an oil filter wrench for installation

Fig. 30 Locate and remove the oil filler cap

Fig. 31 Use a funnel to add the proper amount of engine oil

✳✳ CAUTION

The EPA warns that prolonged contact with used engine oil may cause a number of skin disorders, including cancer! You should make every effort to minimize your exposure to used engine oil. Protective gloves should be worn when changing the oil. Wash your hands and any other exposed skin areas as soon as possible after exposure to used engine oil. Soap and water, or waterless hand cleaner should be used.

Under normal operating conditions, many manufacturers recommend the oil to be changed every 7500 miles (12,000 km) or 6 months, whichever occurs first. When driving conditions frequently include dusty or polluted areas, trailer towing, idling for long periods of time, low speed operation, when operating at temperatures below freezing or driving short distances (under 4 miles or 6.4km), change the oil and filter more frequently. Under these circumstances, oil has a greater chance of building up sludge and contaminants which could damage your engine. If your vehicle use fits into one or more of these categories (as it does for most vehicles), it is suggested that the oil and filter be changed every 3000 miles (5000 km) or 3 months, whichever comes first.

The oil should be disposed of properly after it is drained from the vehicle. Store the oil in a suitable container and take the container to an official oil recycling station. Most gas stations or oil and lube facilities will take the used oil at little or no expense to you.

Oil should always be changed after the engine has been running long enough to bring it up to normal operating temperature. Hot oil will flow more easily and will carry more contaminants than will cold oil. The oil drain plug is located on the bottom of the oil pan (bottom of the engine, underneath the car). The oil filter is usually a spin-on canister located on the bottom or side of most engines. In some instances the filter may be in a replacement cartridge located in a housing on the engine or in the engine oil pan.

To change the oil and filter:

1. Run the engine until it reaches normal operating temperature.

2. On most cars, you will have to raise the front of the vehicle and support it safely using a suitable pair of jackstands. Alternately, you can use a pair of ramps just be sure to check for adequate clearance between the ramp and any bodywork on the front of the vehicle. Always block the rear wheels. On many trucks and Sport Utility Vehicles (SUV's), you may have access without raising. The oil will often drain more effectively if the vehicle is level.

3. Locate the drain plug on the bottom of the oil pan. Slide a drain pan of a suitable capacity under the oil pan. Wipe the drain plug and surrounding area clean using an old rag.

4. Loosen the drain plug using a ratchet, short extension and socket or a box-wrench. Turn the plug out by hand, using a rag to shield your fingers from the hot oil. By keeping an inward pressure on the plug as you unscrew it, oil won't escape past the threads and you can remove it without being burned by hot oil.

➡**Although a rare occurrence, there are a few vehicles with more than one oil pan drain plug. This is necessary on vehicles where the oil pan is shaped to accommodate suspension components. Be sure to check your oil pan for a second plug, especially if the pan straddles a crossmember.**

5. Quickly withdraw the plug and move your hands out of the way. Allow the oil to drain completely into the pan, then install and carefully tighten the drain plug. Be careful not to overtighten the drain plug, otherwise you'll be buying a new pan or a replacement plug for stripped threads.

➡**If the drain plug is equipped with a removable washer or gasket, check its condition and replace, if necessary, to provide a leak-proof seal.**

6. Move the drain pan under the oil filter. With spin-on filters, use a strap-type or cap-type filter wrench to loosen and remove the oil filter from the engine block.. Keep in mind that it's holding about one quart of

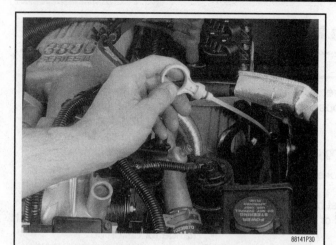

Fig. 32 Start the engine and run for a few minutes. Stop the engine, wait a for the oil to drain down, then remove the engine oil dipstick . . .

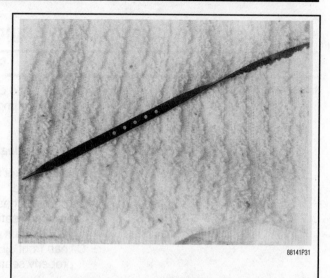

Fig. 33 . . . and check the oil level on the dipstick

hot, dirty oil. On cartridge filters, open the filter housing using an appropriate wrench for access to the filter element

✳✳ WARNING

On cartridge type oil filters, pay close attention to any gaskets or O-rings that seal the cover to the housing. They must be in good shape and proper position during assembly or leaks will occur.

7. Empty the old filter into the drain pan and properly dispose of the filter.

➡ Some vehicles have used cartridge type filters which are actually installed into the bottom of the oil pan.

8. Check that the gasket came off with the filter or cartridge housing. Using a clean rag, wipe off the filter adapter on the engine block. Be sure that the rag doesn't leave any lint which could clog an oil passage.

9. Coat the rubber gasket on the filter with fresh oil, then spin it onto the engine by hand. When the gasket touches the adapter surface, give it another ½–¾ turn (but no more, or you'll squash the gasket and it may leak).

10. Refill the engine with the correct amount of fresh oil. Please refer to your owners manual for the correct capacity. Fill the engine slowly, checking the level often.

11. Check the oil level on the dipstick. Before the engine is run (and the filter is filled with oil), it is normal for the level to be a slightly above the full mark. Start the engine and allow it to idle for a few minutes. Check for leaks at the filter and the drain plug.

Troubleshooting Engine Mechanical Problems

Problem	Cause	Solution
External oil leaks	• Cylinder head cover RTV sealant broken or improperly seated	• Replace sealant; inspect cylinder head cover sealant flange and cylinder head sealant surface for distortion and cracks
	• Oil filler cap leaking or missing	• Replace cap
	• Oil filter gasket broken or improperly seated	• Replace oil filter
	• Oil pan side gasket broken, improperly seated or opening in RTV sealant	• Replace gasket or repair opening in sealant; inspect oil pan gasket flange for distortion
	• Oil pan front oil seal broken or improperly seated	• Replace seal; inspect timing case cover and oil pan seal flange for distortion
	• Oil pan rear oil seal broken or improperly seated	• Replace seal; inspect oil pan rear oil seal flange; inspect rear main bearing cap for cracks, plugged oil return channels, or distortion in seal groove
	• Timing case cover oil seal broken or improperly seated	• Replace seal
	• Excess oil pressure because of restricted PCV valve	• Replace PCV valve
	• Oil pan drain plug loose or has stripped threads	• Repair as necessary and tighten
	• Rear oil gallery plug loose	• Use appropriate sealant on gallery plug and tighten
	• Rear camshaft plug loose or improperly seated	• Seat camshaft plug or replace and seal, as necessary
Excessive oil consumption	• Oil level too high	• Drain oil to specified level
	• Oil with wrong viscosity being used	• Replace with specified oil
	• PCV valve stuck closed	• Replace PCV valve
	• Valve stem oil deflectors (or seals) are damaged, missing, or incorrect type	• Replace valve stem oil deflectors
	• Valve stems or valve guides worn	• Measure stem-to-guide clearance and repair as necessary
	• Poorly fitted or missing valve cover baffles	• Replace valve cover
	• Piston rings broken or missing	• Replace broken or missing rings
	• Scuffed piston	• Replace piston
	• Incorrect piston ring gap	• Measure ring gap, repair as necessary
	• Piston rings sticking or excessively loose in grooves	• Measure ring side clearance, repair as necessary
	• Compression rings installed upside down	• Repair as necessary
	• Cylinder walls worn, scored, or glazed	• Repair as necessary

88528C01

Troubleshooting Engine Mechanical Problems

Problem	Cause	Solution
Excessive oil consumption (cont.)	• Piston ring gaps not properly staggered	• Repair as necessary
	• Excessive main or connecting rod bearing clearance	• Measure bearing clearance, repair as necessary
No oil pressure	• Low oil level	• Add oil to correct level
	• Oil pressure gauge, warning lamp or sending unit inaccurate	• Replace oil pressure gauge or warning lamp
	• Oil pump malfunction	• Replace oil pump
	• Oil pressure relief valve sticking	• Remove and inspect oil pressure relief valve assembly
	• Oil passages on pressure side of pump obstructed	• Inspect oil passages for obstruction
	• Oil pickup screen or tube obstructed	• Inspect oil pickup for obstruction
	• Loose oil inlet tube	• Tighten or seal inlet tube
Low oil pressure	• Low oil level	• Add oil to correct level
	• Inaccurate gauge, warning lamp or sending unit	• Replace oil pressure gauge or warning lamp
	• Oil excessively thin because of dilution, poor quality, or improper grade	• Drain and refill crankcase with recommended oil
	• Excessive oil temperature	• Correct cause of overheating engine
	• Oil pressure relief spring weak or sticking	• Remove and inspect oil pressure relief valve assembly
	• Oil inlet tube and screen assembly has restriction or air leak	• Remove and inspect oil inlet tube and screen assembly. (Fill inlet tube with lacquer thinner to locate leaks.)
	• Excessive oil pump clearance	• Measure clearances
	• Excessive main, rod, or camshaft bearing clearance	• Measure bearing clearances, repair as necessary
High oil pressure	• Improper oil viscosity	• Drain and refill crankcase with correct viscosity oil
	• Oil pressure gauge or sending unit inaccurate	• Replace oil pressure gauge
	• Oil pressure relief valve sticking closed	• Remove and inspect oil pressure relief valve assembly
Main bearing noise	• Insufficient oil supply	• Inspect for low oil level and low oil pressure
	• Main bearing clearance excessive	• Measure main bearing clearance, repair as necessary
	• Bearing insert missing	• Replace missing insert
	• Crankshaft end-play excessive	• Measure end-play, repair as necessary
	• Improperly tightened main bearing cap bolts	• Tighten bolts with specified torque
	• Loose flywheel or drive plate	• Tighten flywheel or drive plate attaching bolts
	• Loose or damaged vibration damper	• Repair as necessary

Troubleshooting Engine Mechanical Problems

Problem	Cause	Solution
Connecting rod bearing noise	• Insufficient oil supply	• Inspect for low oil level and low oil pressure
	• Carbon build-up on piston	• Remove carbon from piston crown
	• Bearing clearance excessive or bearing missing	• Measure clearance, repair as necessary
	• Crankshaft connecting rod journal out-of-round	• Measure journal dimensions, repair or replace as necessary
	• Misaligned connecting rod or cap	• Repair as necessary
	• Connecting rod bolts tightened improperly	• Tighten bolts with specified torque
Piston noise	• Piston-to-cylinder wall clearance excessive (scuffed piston)	• Measure clearance and examine piston
	• Cylinder walls excessively tapered or out-of-round	• Measure cylinder wall dimensions, rebore cylinder
	• Piston ring broken	• Replace all rings on piston
	• Loose or seized piston pin	• Measure piston-to-pin clearance, repair as necessary
	• Connecting rods misaligned	• Measure rod alignment, straighten or replace
	• Piston ring side clearance excessively loose or tight	• Measure ring side clearance, repair as necessary
	• Carbon build-up on piston is excessive	• Remove carbon from piston
Valve actuating component noise	• Insufficient oil supply	• Check for: (a) Low oil level (b) Low oil pressure (c) Wrong hydraulic tappets (d) Restricted oil gallery (e) Excessive tappet to bore clearance
	• Rocker arms or pivots worn	• Replace worn rocker arms or pivots
	• Foreign objects or chips in hydraulic tappets	• Clean tappets
	• Excessive tappet leak-down	• Replace valve tappet
	• Tappet face worn	• Replace tappet; inspect corresponding cam lobe for wear
	• Broken or cocked valve springs	• Properly seat cocked springs; replace broken springs
	• Stem-to-guide clearance excessive	• Measure stem-to-guide clearance, repair as required
	• Valve bent	• Replace valve
	• Loose rocker arms	• Check and repair as necessary
	• Valve seat runout excessive	• Regrind valve seat/valves
	• Missing valve lock	• Install valve lock
	• Excessive engine oil	• Correct oil level

88528C03

Troubleshooting Engine Performance

Problem	Cause	Solution
Hard starting (engine cranks normally)	• Faulty engine control system component • Faulty fuel pump • Faulty fuel system component • Faulty ignition coil • Improper spark plug gap • Incorrect ignition timing • Incorrect valve timing	• Repair or replace as necessary • Replace fuel pump • Repair or replace as necessary • Test and replace as necessary • Adjust gap • Adjust timing • Check valve timing; repair as necessary
Rough idle or stalling	• Incorrect curb or fast idle speed • Incorrect ignition timing • Faulty EGR valve operation • Faulty PCV valve air flow • Faulty TAC vacuum motor or valve • Air leak into manifold vacuum • Faulty distributor rotor or cap • Improperly seated valves • Incorrect ignition wiring • Faulty ignition coil • Restricted air vent or idle passages • Restricted air cleaner	• Adjust curb or fast idle speed (If possible) • Adjust timing to specification • Test EGR system and replace as necessary • Test PCV valve and replace as necessary • Repair as necessary • Inspect manifold vacuum connections and repair as necessary • Replace rotor or cap (Distributor systems only) • Test cylinder compression, repair as necessary • Inspect wiring and correct as necessary • Test coil and replace as necessary • Clean passages • Clean or replace air cleaner filter element
Faulty low-speed operation	• Restricted idle air vents and passages • Restricted air cleaner • Faulty spark plugs • Dirty, corroded, or loose ignition secondary circuit wire connections • Faulty ignition coil high voltage wire • Faulty distributor cap	• Clean air vents and passages • Clean or replace air cleaner filter element • Clean or replace spark plugs • Clean or tighten secondary circuit wire connections • Replace ignition coil high voltage wire (Distributor systems only) • Replace cap (Distributor systems only)
Faulty acceleration	• Incorrect ignition timing • Faulty fuel system component • Faulty spark plug(s) • Improperly seated valves • Faulty ignition coil	• Adjust timing • Repair or replace as necessary • Clean or replace spark plug(s) • Test cylinder compression, repair as necessary • Test coil and replace as necessary

88528C04

Troubleshooting Engine Performance

Problem	Cause	Solution
Faulty high speed operation	• Incorrect ignition timing	• Adjust timing (if possible)
	• Faulty advance mechanism	• Check advance mechanism and repair as necessary (Distributor systems only)
	• Low fuel pump volume	• Replace fuel pump
	• Wrong spark plug air gap or wrong plug	• Adjust air gap or install correct plug
	• Partially restricted exhaust manifold, exhaust pipe, catalytic converter, muffler, or tailpipe	• Eliminate restriction
	• Restricted vacuum passages	• Clean passages
	• Restricted air cleaner	• Cleaner or replace filter element as necessary
	• Faulty distributor rotor or cap	• Replace rotor or cap (Distributor systems only)
	• Faulty ignition coil	• Test coil and replace as necessary
	• Improperly seated valve(s)	• Test cylinder compression, repair as necessary
	• Faulty valve spring(s)	• Inspect and test valve spring tension, replace as necessary
	• Incorrect valve timing	• Check valve timing and repair as necessary
	• Intake manifold restricted	• Remove restriction or replace manifold
	• Worn distributor shaft	• Replace shaft (Distributor systems only)
Misfire at all speeds	• Faulty spark plug(s)	• Clean or relace spark plug(s)
	• Faulty spark plug wire(s)	• Replace as necessary
	• Faulty distributor cap or rotor	• Replace cap or rotor (Distributor systems only)
	• Faulty ignition coil	• Test coil and replace as necessary
	• Primary ignition circuit shorted or open intermittently	• Troubleshoot primary circuit and repair as necessary
	• Improperly seated valve(s)	• Test cylinder compression, repair as necessary
	• Faulty hydraulic tappet(s)	• Clean or replace tappet(s)
	• Faulty valve spring(s)	• Inspect and test valve spring tension, repair as necessary
	• Worn camshaft lobes	• Replace camshaft
	• Air leak into manifold	• Check manifold vacuum and repair as necessary
	• Fuel pump volume or pressure low	• Replace fuel pump
	• Blown cylinder head gasket	• Replace gasket
	• Intake or exhaust manifold passage(s) restricted	• Pass chain through passage(s) and repair as necessary
Power not up to normal	• Incorrect ignition timing	• Adjust timing
	• Faulty distributor rotor	• Replace rotor (Distributor systems only)

88528C05

Troubleshooting Engine Performance

Problem	Cause	Solution
Power not up to normal (cont.)	• Incorrect spark plug gap	• Adjust gap
	• Faulty fuel pump	• Replace fuel pump
	• Faulty fuel pump	• Replace fuel pump
	• Incorrect valve timing	• Check valve timing and repair as necessary
	• Faulty ignition coil	• Test coil and replace as necessary
	• Faulty ignition wires	• Test wires and replace as necessary
	• Improperly seated valves	• Test cylinder compression and repair as necessary
	• Blown cylinder head gasket	• Replace gasket
	• Leaking piston rings	• Test compression and repair as necessary
Intake backfire	• Improper ignition timing	• Adjust timing
	• Defective EGR component	• Repair as necessary
	• Defective TAC vacuum motor or valve	• Repair as necessary
Exhaust backfire	• Air leak into manifold vacuum	• Check manifold vacuum and repair as necessary
	• Faulty air injection diverter valve	• Test diverter valve and replace as necessary
	• Exhaust leak	• Locate and eliminate leak
Ping or spark knock	• Incorrect ignition timing	• Adjust timing
	• Distributor advance malfunction	• Inspect advance mechanism and repair as necessary (Distributor systems only)
	• Excessive combustion chamber deposits	• Remove with combustion chamber cleaner
	• Air leak into manifold vacuum	• Check manifold vacuum and repair as necessary
	• Excessively high compression	• Test compression and repair as necessary
	• Fuel octane rating excessively low	• Try alternate fuel source
	• Sharp edges in combustion chamber	• Grind smooth
	• EGR valve not functioning properly	• Test EGR system and replace as necessary
Surging (at cruising to top speeds)	• Low fuel pump pressure or volume	• Replace fuel pump
	• Improper PCV valve air flow	• Test PCV valve and replace as necessary
	• Air leak into manifold vacuum	• Check manifold vacuum and repair as necessary
	• Incorrect spark advance	• Test and replace as necessary
	• Restricted fuel filter	• Replace fuel filter
	• Restricted air cleaner	• Clean or replace air cleaner filter element
	• EGR valve not functioning properly	• Test EGR system and replace as necessary

88528C06

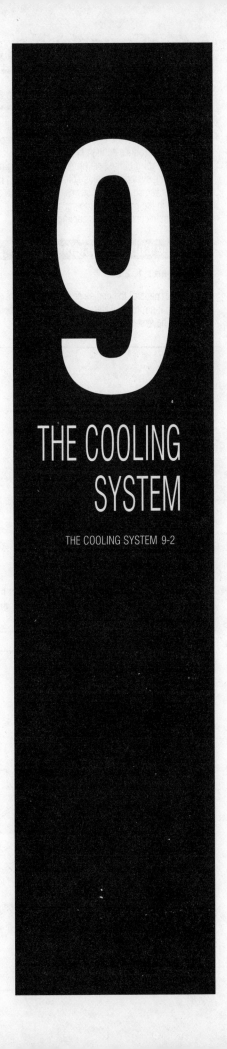

9

THE COOLING
SYSTEM

THE COOLING SYSTEM

Your engine needs a cooling system to protect it from self-destruction. Burning gases inside the cylinders can reach a temperature of 4500°F (2500°C) and produce enough heat to melt a 200 lb. engine block.

About one-third of the heat produced in the engine must be carried away by the cooling system. Some is utilized for heating the passenger compartment. Moreover, strange as it seems, your vehicle's air conditioner produces heat in the process of cooling and dehumidifying the air. This heat must also be dispersed by the cooling system.

How the Cooling System Works

▶ **See Figures 1, 2 and 3**

The main parts of the engine cooling system are the radiator, pressure cap, hoses, thermostat, water pump, fan, and fan belt (except on electric fan engines). The system is filled with coolant, which should be a 50–50 mixture of antifreeze and water. No matter where you live or how hot or cold the weather becomes, the mixture should be maintained the year around.

The water pump and engine cooling fan are mounted on the same shaft and driven by a belt connected to the engine. The pump draws coolant from the bottom of the radiator and forces it through passages surrounding the hot area—the cylinders, combustion chambers, valves and spark plugs. From there the coolant flows through a hose into the top of the radiator, then downward through tubes attached to cooling fins and surrounded by air passages. Heat is transferred from the coolant to air forced through the radiator passages by the fan and the forward motion of the vehicle.

Some GM vehicles may be equipped with a reverse-flow cooling system which operates differently than a conventional type cooling system. The specialized components of this system include a gear-driven water pump with cast internal cross-over passages, an inlet-side thermostat and a pressurized high fill coolant reservoir. In this system, coolant is routed from the water pump, directly to the cylinder heads. When the heads are adequately cooled, any

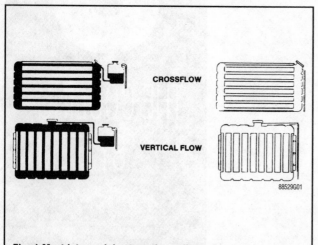

Fig. 1 Most late model automotive radiators have coolant recovery systems as shown on left, early model non-recovery systems shown on right.

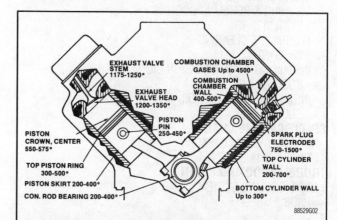

Fig. 2 The internal combustion engine converts about one-third of the heat it develops into power. Another third is lost in the exhaust system and the remaining third must be carried away by the cooling system. The operating temperatures (given in the Fahrenheit scale) are typical of a modern engine.

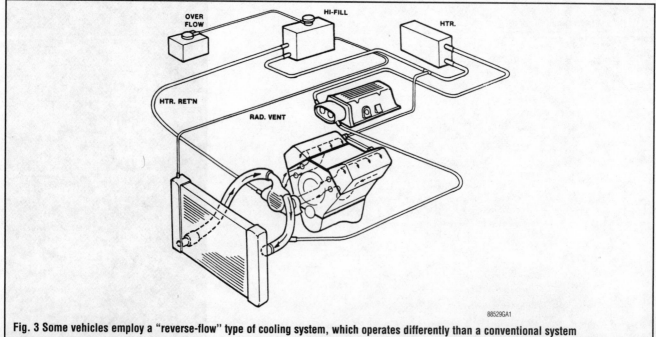

Fig. 3 Some vehicles employ a "reverse-flow" type of cooling system, which operates differently than a conventional system

accumulated vapors are vented off, and the coolant then circulates through the engine block. After the coolant leaves the engine block, it returns to the water pump, moving through an internal passage into the radiator. There is a thermostat on the inlet side of the pump which meters the coolant temperature as it flows from the radiator and tries to enter the water pump casting. The water pump, which is driven by the camshaft, which is the center of the system, has cast internal passages which route coolant through the engine without sending it through the intake manifold, eliminating possible leaks. The gear-driven pump ensures coolant flow even if the drive belt breaks. The reverse-flow cooling system is advantageous because it reduces the overall cooling system pressure and basically eliminates pitting or disintegration of the water pump and seal. In addition, routing the coolant to the cylinder heads first promotes higher bore temperatures and less ring bore friction, increasing output and horsepower. Due to the increased temperature of the cylinder walls, which created higher oil temperatures, engines with reverse-flow cooling systems may be equipped with an engine oil cooler or use synthetic oil.

WHAT IS COOLANT

❊❊ CAUTION

When draining the coolant, keep in mind that cats and dogs are attracted by ethylene glycol antifreeze, and are quite likely to drink any that is left in an uncovered container or in puddles on the ground. This will prove fatal in sufficient quantity. Always drain the coolant into a leak-proof container. To avoid injuries from scalding fluid and steam, DO NOT remove the radiator cap while the engine and radiator are still HOT. The best way to dispose of coolant is through an approved recycling center.

Ethylene Glycol

Coolant in most late model vehicles is at least 50–50 mixture of ethylene glycol and water. This mixture in older vehicles was required not only in the winter to prevent freezing, but also to prevent corrosion in aluminum cooling systems, and to provide lubricants to the water pump. Modern vehicles with air-conditioning must also use it in the summer as well.

Late-model vehicle manufacturers also require their engines to run at a higher temperature because it results in better engine efficiency and improves the effectiveness of emission control devices. This temperature is controlled by the thermostat, most of which are in the 192°F (89°C)—195°F (91°C) range.

Good quality antifreezes also contain water pump lubricants, rust inhibitors, and other corrosion inhibitors along with acid neutralizers. Ethylene-Glycol antifreeze mixtures should not remain in the cooling system beyond one year.

Propylene Glycol

Appearing in the early 90's a new, less-toxic antifreeze/coolant emerged. This is a propylene glycol base. As compared to ethylene glycol, propylene glycol is less toxic and safer for humans, pets, and wildlife in the environment. Its coolant and engine protection properties are similar to the ethylene glycol coolant listed above. Most of the coolant providers now offer a choice between Ethylene Glycol or Propylene Glycol based products.

Silicate-free Coolant

The cooling systems on some 1996 and later vehicles were originally filled with silicate-free coolant. The fluid is easily identified because of its orange color (instead of the green we have come to expect from most types of ethylene glycol antifreeze). If your cooling system is filled with DEX-COOL® or other silicate-free coolant, then no periodic service is required, other than fluid level checks, for 100,000 miles (160,000 km) or 5 years, whichever comes first. However, if you add a silicate coolant to the system (even in small amounts) premature engine, heater core or radiator corrosion may result. In addition, the coolant will have to be changed sooner (12,000 miles (19,300 km) or every year, just like other vehicles not using DEX-COOL® or other Silicate-free coolant).

CONTROLLING THE TEMPERATURE

It's important to get the coolant up to normal operating temperature as quickly as possible to ensure smooth engine operation, free flow of oil, and ample heat for the occupants. When the engine is cold, the thermostat blocks the passage from the cylinder head to the radiator and sends coolant on a shortcut to the water pump. The cooling fluid is not exposed to the blast of air from the radiator, so it warms up rapidly. As temperature increases, the thermostat gradually opens and allows coolant to flow through the radiator.

Cooling systems on older vehicles were limited to a maximum temperature of 212°F (100°C)—the boiling point of water. To get rid of the extra heat generated by more powerful engines, automatic transmissions, and air conditioning, modern vehicles have pressurized systems using a 50–50 mixture of antifreeze and water which enables them to operate at temperatures up to 263°F (129.4°C) without boiling. At this temperature, plain water alone would boil away.

TRANSMISSION OIL COOLER

Automatic transmission oil is cooled by a small, separate radiator, usually located in the lower tank or alongside the main radiator. While the only purpose of the engine coolant is to keep the block and upper engine components cool, the transmission oil has three functions. It hydraulically operates the transmission, lubricates the transmission internal components and also keeps the transmission within proper operating temperature range.

Most vehicles can benefit from the installation of a transmission oil cooler, especially if the vehicle is used to pull a trailer or for some other kind of heavy service.

ENGINE OIL COOLER

Some vehicles, particularly high performance or diesel engines, are equipped with an engine oil cooler. The oil cooler can be located in one of the radiator tanks (similar to the transmission oil cooler), or mounted separately, near the front of the engine, on aftermarket applications. Also, there is usually an adapter mounted between the engine block and the oil filter. If the cooler is mounted in a radiator tank, heat is dissipated from the oil to the coolant. A separate oil cooler usually looks like a small radiator and heat is dispersed from the tubes and fins in the cooler to the air passing through the cooler. The purpose of the cooler is to reduce the temperature of the oil, preventing oxidation and increasing the oil's lubricating and protecting properties.

ELECTRIC COOLING FANS

▶ See Figure 4

Many late model vehicles are equipped with an electric cooling fan or an auxiliary electric cooling fan. These fans are usually operated by a thermostatically controlled switch located in the cylinder head, radiator tank, or intake manifold. When the thermostatic switch reaches a specified temperature, the contacts close providing current to the motor. As the temperature lowers to the specified range, the contacts open thus shutting off the cooling fan.

The thermostatic switches may be used to complete the ground side of the fan motor, they may trigger a relay to provide power to the fan motor, or they may send a signal to a computer to energize the fan motor.

On some air conditioner equipped vehicles, the fan motor is energized at all times the air conditioner is operating. This increases the airflow through the air conditioning condenser and the radiator.

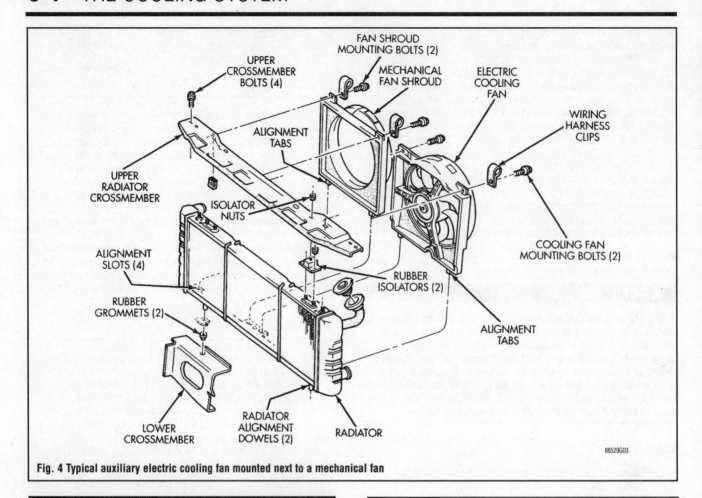

Fig. 4 Typical auxiliary electric cooling fan mounted next to a mechanical fan

What to Do When the Engine Overheats

♦ See Figures 5, 6, 7, 8 and 9

☀☀ CAUTION

Never remove the radiator cap under any conditions while the engine is hot! Failure to follow these instructions could result in damage to the cooling system, engine and/or personal injury. To avoid having scalding hot coolant or steam blow out of the radiator, use extreme care whenever you are removing the radiator cap. Wait until the engine has cooled, then wrap a thick cloth around the radiator cap and turn it slowly to the first stop. Step back while the pressure is released from the cooling system. When you are sure the pressure has been released, press down on the radiator cap (still have the cloth in position) turn and remove the radiator cap.

Air conditioning, automatic transmission, and power-operated accessories put an extra burden on the engine cooling system. The temperature light or gauge is designed to activate as the engine begins to overheat. This gives the driver a chance to correct the cause of overheating with minimum delay. If you are stuck in heavy traffic and the temperature gauge shows the engine is overheating or the temperature light comes on, shut off the air conditioner.

If your vehicle has a belt driven fan, whenever you come to a stop, shift into neutral and speed up the engine a little to increase circulation of the coolant and air flow from the fan. Most front wheel drive vehicles now have electric cooling fans. Increasing the engine speed won't help on these vehicles.

If the temperature light turns on or the temperature gauge indicates overheating when the air conditioner is running, follow these steps:

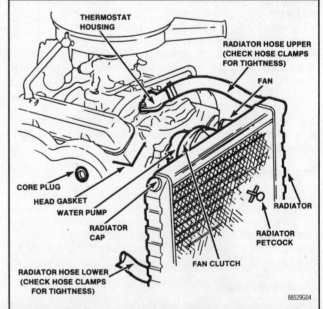

Fig. 5 Loss of coolant is not usually a mystery if you know what to look for. Coolant leaks usually show up as a puddle of coolant on the garage floor or driveway. External coolant leaks are likely to occur at: loose hose clamps, leaking hoses, leaking radiator, leak at the thermostat, leak at the radiator petcock, loose water pump bolts, a failed water pump seal, faulty radiator cap, loose freeze plugs, or a leaking heater core (this will sometimes leak coolant inside the passenger compartment).

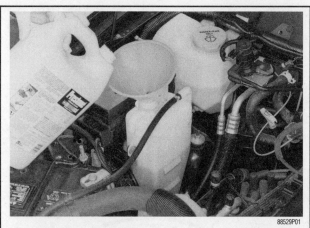

Fig. 6 Vehicles with coolant overflow systems use a plastic bottle to catch the expanding coolant. These are sealed systems and the radiator cap should not be removed. Check the coolant level and add coolant through the reservoir

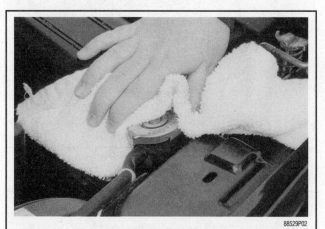

Fig. 7 On vehicles without coolant overflow systems special care should be taken when removing the radiator cap. Allow the system to cool and use a rag to prevent burns and slowly release the system pressure.

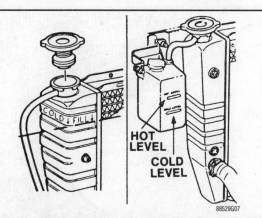

Fig. 8 Coolant level should be 1–2 inches (25–50mm) —below the filler neck on systems without coolant recovery (left). This allows for coolant expansion within the tank. On coolant recovery systems (right), maintain the level at the mark indicated on the reservoir.

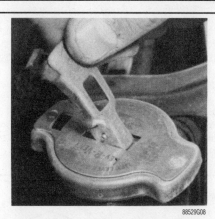

Fig. 9 Lever-type radiator caps were used on systems without coolant overflow. These make releasing the pressure safer and easier. When the system is under pressure, simply lifting the lever will release the system pressure allowing the safe removal of the cap.

1. Turn off the air conditioning, then turn the heater on and the blower motor on high. Turning the heater and blower motor on will help get rid of some of the extra heat from the engine.

2. If the light doesn't go out in about a minute, pull over in a safe place and set the parking brake. Then place the transmission selector lever in park.

3. Don't turn off the engine, instead, speed up the engine (on vehicles with belt driven fans only) so it sounds as if it's idling twice as fast as normal. Lift the engine hood and check for fluid leaks at the radiator hoses, radiator, or radiator overflow outlet. Check to see that drive belts are intact, fan is turning (either the mechanical or electric fan), and radiator cap is sealed. The overheating should subside.

4. When the overheating has passed, proceed on the road a little slower, and don't resume normal driving for 10 minutes.

5. If the radiator starts boiling over, pull off the road as soon as possible. Shut off the engine. When the boiling stops, raise the hood, but don't touch the radiator cap. Allow the system to cool.

6. On vehicles without coolant overflow systems, place a cloth over the cap and slowly turn it to the first notch to relieve the pressure. Remove the cap, start the engine, and slowly add water, or a water/coolant mixture if possible. Replace the cap.

7. On vehicles with coolant overflow systems, simply add a water/coolant mixture to the reservoir.

8. Never open the radiator cap when the engine is hot; the release of pressure will precipitate boiling and further overheating and may scald anyone nearby in the process. If the engine is losing coolant, or a fan belt is broken or loose, or if the overheating persists, stop the engine until the cause of the overheating is corrected.

9. At the first opportunity, check the system to find out why it overheated. Refill with the correct mix of the antifreeze and water.

Cooling System Maintenance

♦ **See Figure 10**

At least once a year on Glycol based coolants, the engine cooling system should be inspected, flushed, and refilled with fresh coolant. If the coolant is left in the system too long, it loses its ability to prevent rust and corrosion. If the coolant has too much water, it won't protect against freezing.

Silicate free coolants such as DEX-COOL® can go for 100,000 miles (160,000 km) or 5 years, whichever comes first. However, if you add a silicate coolant to the system (even in small amounts) premature engine, heater core or radiator corrosion may result. In addition, the coolant will have to be changed sooner (12,000 miles (19,300 km) or every year, just like other vehicles not using DEX-COOL® or other Silicate-free coolant).

The pressure cap should be checked for signs of age or deterioration. The fan belt and other drive belts should be inspected and adjusted to the proper tension. If a belt is cracked, frayed along the edges, or shows signs of peeling, it should be replaced before it fails and causes problems that are more serious.

Leaves, dead insects, and other debris should be removed from the surfaces of the radiator and the air conditioning condenser so air can get through. Hose clamps should be tightened, and soft or cracked hoses replaced. Damp spots or accumulations of rust or dye near hoses, water pump, or other areas indicate possible leakage, which must be corrected before filling the system with fresh coolant.

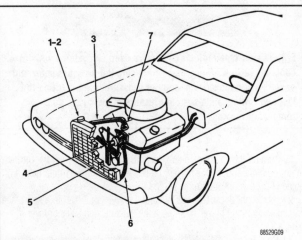

Fig. 10 Check these components of the cooling system: Coolant level (1); Radiator cap (2); Radiator hoses (3); Drive belts (4); Clean radiator (5); Change coolant (6); Thermostat (7)

CHECKING COOLANT LEVEL

> **❈❈ CAUTION**
>
> **Never remove the radiator cap under any conditions while the engine is hot! Failure to follow these instructions could result in damage to the cooling system, engine and/or personal injury. To avoid having scalding hot coolant or steam blow out of the radiator, use extreme care whenever you are removing the radiator cap. Wait until the engine has cooled, then wrap a thick cloth around the radiator cap and turn it slowly to the first stop. Step back while the pressure is released from the cooling system. When you are sure the pressure has been released, press down on the radiator cap (still have the cloth in position) turn and remove the radiator cap.**

Once a month or every 1000 miles (1600 km), whichever comes first, check the level of the coolant in the radiator. If you do a lot of hard driving or trailer pulling, check more often.

On vehicles without a coolant overflow system the coolant level should be checked on a cold engine. If there is a chance the engine is hot, cover the radiator cap with a heavy cloth. Turn the radiator cap to the first stop and let the pressure release. The pressure is gone when the hissing stops. Push down on the cap and turn it all the way around to remove it.

Most late-model vehicles come equipped with a coolant recovery system. They allow coolant that would normally overflow to be caught in an expansion tank; it will automatically be drawn back into the radiator when the coolant cools down. Radiator caps for these systems are not interchangeable. Replace only with the proper cap for the system.

On vehicles without coolant recovery systems keep the coolant level 1–2 inches (25–50mm) below the filler neck on a cold engine. On vehicles equipped with a coolant recovery system, simply check the level in the

plastic tank, located near the radiator. On these types, top off the coolant in the plastic tank, not the radiator. Only when doing a complete refill should you add to the radiator, then the overflow tank.

If the coolant level is constantly low, check for leaks.

CHECKING THE RADIATOR CAP

▶ **See Figure 11**

While you are checking the coolant level, check the radiator cap for a worn or cracked gasket. If the cap doesn't seal properly, fluid will be lost and the engine will overheat. A worn cap should be replaced with a new one.

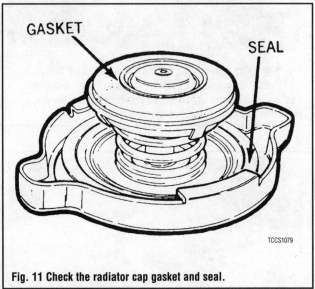

Fig. 11 Check the radiator cap gasket and seal.

CLEANING RADIATOR OF DEBRIS

▶ **See Figure 12**

Periodically clean any debris—leaves, paper, insects, etc.—from the radiator fins. Pick the large pieces off by hand. The smaller pieces can be washed away with water pressure from a hose.

Carefully straighten any bent radiator fins. Be careful, the fins are very soft.

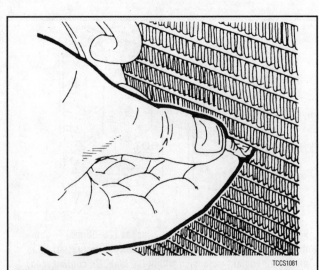

Fig. 12 Keep the radiator and air conditioning condenser clear of debris, bug and leaves

DRIVE BELTS

Modern Drive Belts Don't Show Their Age

On today's vehicles, it's very difficult to tell the difference between an automotive drive belt with 50,000 miles (80,450 km) of wear, and another belt with 10,000 miles (16,090 km) of wear. A basic change in engine belt construction—one that produced a longer-lasting belt—also makes it difficult to spot indications of belt wear.

Virtually all automotive drive belts produced in the U.S. and Europe are made without a cover. These "bandless" belts don't show wear like their predecessors. Although bandless belts are designed to outlast banded belts on similar drives, they provide no early warning of failure.

There are two main causes of drive belt failure. The most common is fatigue of the load-bearing, tensile cords leading to belt failure from the inside out. Tensile cord failure is due to a gradual weakening of the tensile cords that results from a combination of side stress, bending stress, and centrifugal force imposed on the belt as it travels around the pulleys.

Because this type of failure takes place inside the belt, there is no easy way to determine when the belt is about to break. Statistics show the chance of drive belt failure on an average vehicle goes up sharply after four years.

For this reason, many drive belt manufacturers recommend that all engine drive belts be replaced on a four-year basis.

In this way, the replacement can be done at the vehicle owner's convenience, rather than on an emergency basis.

The other major cause of drive belt failure is improper tension. This causes the belt to slip as it travels around the pulleys, generating heat build-up. Excessive heat eventually causes the rubber compounds in the belt to break down, and crack, leading to belt failure.

Indicators of belt tension problems include:
- Belt squeal, especially on the fan or power steering drives.
- Battery discharge sometimes caused by a slipping alternator belt.
- Excessive sidewall wear that allows the belt to ride lower than normal in the pulley grooves.
- Absences of overcord (the belt's top protective covering).
- Excessive cracking, or rib chunking (pieces of the ribs breaking off). Keep in mind that serpentine belts do tend to form small cracks across the backing. If the only wear you find is in the form of one or more cracks across the backing and NOT parallel to the ribs, the belt is still good and does not need to be replaced.

In addition, small engine compartments on today's vehicles make belts more susceptible to heat and contamination from petroleum products. High temperatures can cause belts to dry, harden and crack. If a belt becomes oil soaked, it cannot grip the pulley. Petroleum products also break down the rubber compounds in the belt.

The best way to check belt tension is with a tension gauge. Because of smaller engine compartments and shorter belt spans between pulleys, the old finger deflection method of checking tension are not as accurate.

Belt Inspection

▶ See Figures 13, 14, 15, 16 and 17

❊❊ WARNING

DO NOT use belt dressings in an attempt to extend belt life. Belt dressing will soften the belt, causing deterioration. Oil or grease contamination on the belt or pulleys will have the same effect. Keep the drive belt system clear of oil, grease, coolant or other contaminants.

Accessory drive belts are of two types, V-belts (conventional, cogged and multi-ribbed) and serpentine (multi-ribbed) belts. A V-belt rides in V-shaped pulleys to rotate various accessories, such as the power steering pump, air conditioner compressor, alternator/generator, water pump, and air pump. Only the inside of a V-belt is used, unlike a serpentine belt which utilizes both sides. V-belts typically operate one or two accessories per belt,

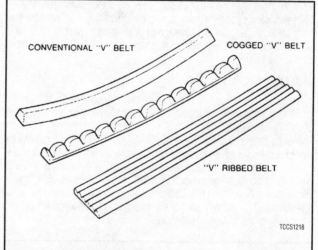

Fig. 13 There are typically three types of accessory drive belts found on vehicles today

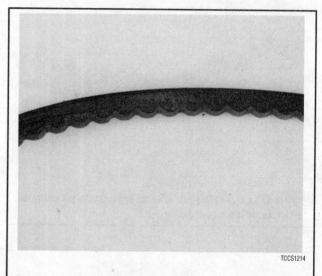

Fig. 14 An example of a healthy drive belt

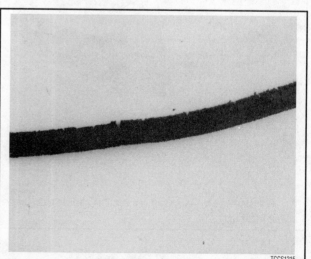

Fig. 15 Deep cracks in this belt will cause flex, building up heat that will eventually lead to belt failure

whereas a single serpentine belt can power all of the accessories. V-belts and a few serpentine belts require periodic adjustment because the belts are under tension and stretch over time. Most serpentine belts utilize an automatic belt tensioner that constantly provides the proper tension to the belt.

V-BELTS

Many vehicles utilize one or more V-belts to drive engine accessories (such as the alternator, water pump, power steering pump or A/C compressor off the crankshaft.

V-belts should be checked every 3,000 miles (4,800 km) or 3 months for evidence of wear such as cracking, fraying and incorrect tension. Determine the belt tension at a point halfway between the pulleys by pressing on the belt with moderate thumb pressure. The belt should deflect about ¼ inch (6mm) over a 7–10 inch (178–254mm) span, or ½ inch (13mm) over a 13–16 inch (330–406mm) span. If the deflection is found too much or too little, perform the tension adjustments.

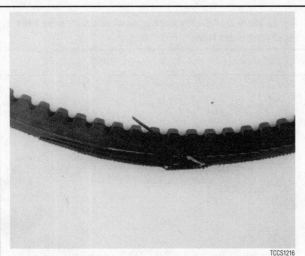

Fig. 16 The cover of this belt is worn, exposing the critical reinforcing cords to excessive wear

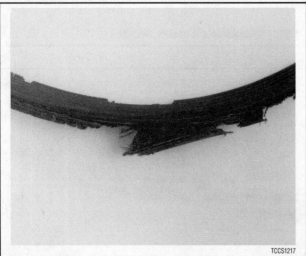

Fig. 17 Installing too wide a belt can result in serious belt wear and/or breakage

SERPENTINE BELTS

▶ See Figures 18 and 19

Many late model vehicles utilize one ribbed, serpentine belt to drive engine accessories, such as the alternator, water pump, power steering pump or A/C compressor off the crankshaft.

The serpentine belt and pulleys should be inspected every 3,000 miles (4,800 km) or 3 months for evidence of wear such as excessive cracking (on serpentine belts, some cracking is normal), fraying, incorrect alignment and incorrect tension. Proper maintenance of the belt and pulleys can extend normal belt life.

1. Visually check the belt for signs of damage. Routine inspection may reveal cracks in the belt ribs. These cracks will not impair belt performance and are NOT a basis for belt replacement. HOWEVER, if your inspection reveals that sections of the belt are missing, the belt must be replaced to avoid a possible failure.

Fig. 18 Serpentine drive belts require little attention other than periodic inspection or replacement

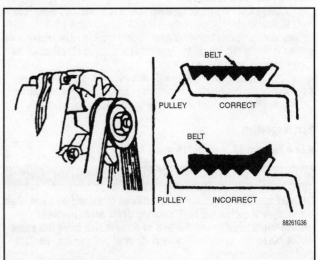

Fig. 19 When checking the serpentine belt, be sure it is properly seated in each of the pulleys

2. Visually check the belt for proper routing (when compared with the engine compartment label). Make sure the belt is fully seated on all pulleys.

3. Check the automatic drive belt tensioner. The belt is considered serviceable if no wear or damage was found in the previous visual inspections and if the arrow on the tensioner assembly is pointing within the acceptable used belt length range on the tensioner spindle.

PULLEY INSPECTION

▶ See Figure 20

Pulley inspection is most easily accomplished with the drive belt removed so you can freely turn the pulleys and to provide an unobstructed view of each pulley.

1. Visually inspect each of the pulleys for chips, nicks, cracks, tool marks, bent sidewalls, severe corrosion or other damage. Replace any pulley showing these signs as they will eventually lead to belt failure.

2. Place a straightedge or position a length of string across any 2 pulleys making sure it touches all points. When using string, be sure it is straight and not bent at one spot in order to contact all points on the pulley.

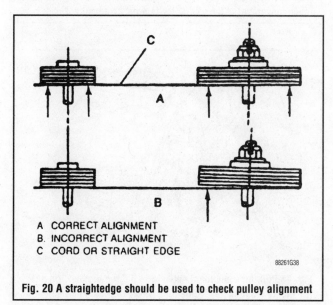

A CORRECT ALIGNMENT
B INCORRECT ALIGNMENT
C CORD OR STRAIGHT EDGE

88261G38

Fig. 20 A straightedge should be used to check pulley alignment

➡An assistant is helpful to hold the straightedge or string during the next steps.

3. Turn each pulley ½ revolution and recheck with the straightedge or string.

4. Full contact must be made at all points checked. If contact is not made at all of the points, the pulley may be warped or the shaft may be bent. Replace any damaged parts to assure proper belt life.

Adjusting Tension

✳✳ CAUTION

On vehicles with an electric cooling fan, disable the power to the fan by disengaging the fan motor wiring connector or removing the negative battery cable before replacing or adjusting the drive belts. Otherwise, the fan may engage even though the ignition is OFF.

V-BELTS

If a belt tension gauge is not available, you can adjust tension using the deflection measurements, but this is not as exact. Keep in mind that too tight or too loose an adjustment can damage the components that the belt drives. Too tight will increase preload on the bearings, leading to early failure, while too loose could cause slippage or jerky movements. Of the two possibilities, you would prefer the belt to be a little loose, rather than a little tight. The belt should deflect about ¼ inch (6mm) over a 7–10 inch (178–254mm) span, or ½ inch (13mm) over a 13–16 inch (330–406mm) span.

If a belt tension gauge is available:

1. If the belt is cold, operate the engine (at idle speed) for 15 minutes; the belt will seat itself in the pulleys allowing the belt fibers to relax or stretch. If the belt is hot, allow it to cool, until it is warm to the touch.

➡A used belt is one that has been rotated at least one complete revolution on the pulleys. This begins the belt seating process and it must never be tensioned to the new belt specifications.

2. Disconnect the negative battery cable for safety.

3. Loosen the component-to-mounting bracket bolts.

4. Place a Belt Tension Gauge, place the tension gauge at the center of the belt between the longest span.

5. Applying belt tension pressure, adjust the drive belt tension.

6. While holding the correct tension on the component, tighten the component-to-mounting bracket bolt.

7. When the belt tension is correct, remove the tension gauge and connect the negative battery cable.

SERPENTINE BELTS

Most late model vehicles are equipped with a single serpentine belt and spring loaded tensioner. The proper belt adjustment is automatically maintained by the tensioner, therefore, no periodic adjustment is needed until the pointer is past the scale on the tensioner. For more information, please refer to the information on serpentine belt and pulley inspection found earlier in this section.

Drive Belt Routing

A label is normally provided in the engine compartment which details the proper belt routing for the original engine installed in that vehicle. Check the routing label (or vehicle emission control information label) for an illustration which resembles your motor first. If no label is present or if the label does not match your engine (perhaps an engine swap was performed on older vehicles before you were the owner).

Drive Belt Replacement

✳✳ CAUTION

On vehicles with an electric cooling fan, disable the power to the fan by disengaging the fan motor wiring connector or removing the negative battery cable before replacing or adjusting the drive belts. Otherwise, the fan may engage even though the ignition is OFF.

V-BELTS

▶ See Figures 21, 22, 23, 24 and 25

1. Disconnect the negative battery cable for safety.

2. Depending upon the vehicle application, either loosen the component-to-mounting bracket bolts and pivot the component inward or turn the threaded adjuster rod to create some slack in the belt.

3. Slip the drive belt from the pulleys and remove it from the engine.

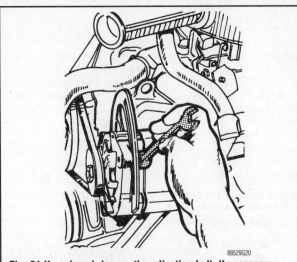

Fig. 21 If equipped, loosen the adjusting bolt. If necessary, loosen the bolt that the component pivots on.

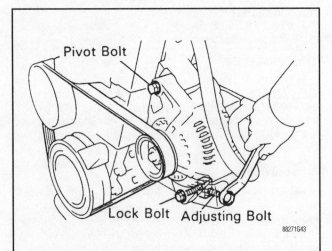

Fig. 22 Some vehicles use a threaded adjusting bolt to increase or decrease tension on the belt

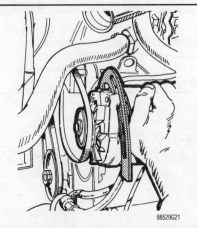

Fig. 23 Push the component in until there is enough slack in the belt to remove it. Remove the belt from the component pulley and the crankshaft pulley. If the component belt is behind another belt, the interfering belt will also have to be removed.

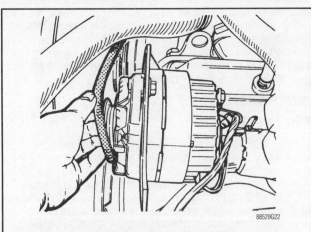

Fig. 24 Install the new belt over the crankshaft and component pulleys. Be sure you have the correct belt. It should fit even with the top of the pulley groove and should not require too much movement of the alternator to properly tension it.

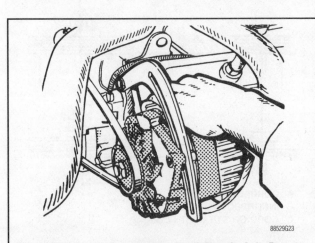

Fig. 25 Pull the component outward to tighten the belt. Do not pry on the component. Tighten the alternator adjusting bolt and pivot bolts (if loosened). Check the belt tension, and recheck it in about 200 miles; new belts will stretch with use.

➡️If the engine uses more than one belt, it may be necessary to remove other belts that are in front of the one being removed.

4. To install, reverse the removal procedures. Adjust the component drive belt tension.

SERPENTINE BELTS

♦ See Figures 26, 27 and 28

For serpentine belts, replacement is a relatively simple matter of rotating the tensioner off the belt (to relieve tension) and holding the tensioner in this position as the belt is slipped from its pulley. Depending on the model, engine and year of production, there are various methods of rotating the tensioner, but most require a breaker bar, large ratchet or wrench.

1. Before you begin, visually confirm the belt routing to the engine compartment label (if present). If you cannot make a match (perhaps it is not the original motor), scribble your own diagram before proceeding.

2. Disconnect the negative battery cable for safety.

3. Install the appropriate sized breaker bar, wrench, or socket to the tensioner arm or pulley, as applicable.

Fig. 26 Many vehicles have an underhood belt routing diagram, in this case, it is located on a belt guard

Fig. 27 Use a breaker bar or ratchet and socket, as necessary, to rotate the belt tensioner . . .

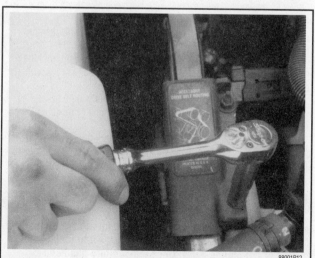

Fig. 28 . . . then remove the serpentine belt from the accessory pulleys

4. Rotate the tensioner and slip the belt from the tensioner pulley.

5. Once the belt is free from the tensioner, CAREFULLY rotate the tensioner back into position. DO NOT allow the tensioner to suddenly snap into place or damage could occur to the assembly.

6. Slip the belt from the remaining pulleys (this can get difficult if there is little room to work between components). Work slowly and be patient.

7. Once the belt is free, remove it from the engine compartment.

To install:

8. Route the belt over all the pulleys except one, and the tensioner. Refer to engine compartment label, or your own notes before beginning.

9. Rotate the tensioner pulley and hold it while you finish slipping the belt into position. Slowly allow the tensioner into contact with the belt. DO NOT allow the tensioner to suddenly snap into place or damage could occur to the assembly.

10. Run your hand around the pulleys to make sure the belt ribs are properly seated in the pulley grooves.

❋❋ WARNING

Improper belt seating will cause the belt to fail in a short period.

11. Connect the negative battery cable.

RADIATOR HOSES

Inspection

◆ See Figures 29, 30, 31 and 32

Upper and lower radiator hoses along with the heater hoses should be checked for deterioration, leaks and loose hose clamps at every 1,000 miles (1,600 km) or one-month. This may sound excessive, however if you're under the hood it is a good habit to look at your cooling system. A quick visual inspection could discover a weakened hose that might have left you stranded if it had remained unrepaired.

Whenever you are checking the hoses, make sure the engine and cooling system are cold. Visually inspect for cracking, rotting or collapsed hoses, and replace as necessary. Run your hand along the length of the hose. If a weak or swollen spot is noted when squeezing the hose wall, the hose should be replaced.

Removal & Installation

1. Remove the radiator pressure cap or coolant overflow pressure cap, as applicable.

Fig. 29 The cracks developing along this hose are a result of age-related hardening

Fig. 30 A hose clamp that is too tight can cause older hoses to separate and tear on either side of the clamp

Fig. 31 A soft spongy hose (identifiable by the swollen section) will eventually burst and should be replaced

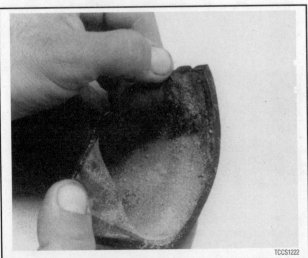

Fig. 32 Hoses are likely to deteriorate from the inside if the cooling system is not periodically flushed

✳✳ CAUTION

Never remove the pressure cap while the engine is running, or personal injury from scalding hot coolant or steam may result. If possible, wait until the engine has cooled to remove the pressure cap. If this is not possible, wrap a thick cloth around the pressure cap and turn it slowly to the stop. Step back while the pressure is released from the cooling system. When you are sure all the pressure has been released, use the cloth to turn and remove the cap.

2. Position a clean container under the radiator and/or engine drain-cock or plug, then open the drain and allow the cooling system to drain to an appropriate level. For some upper hoses, only a little coolant must be drained. To remove hoses positioned lower on the engine, such as a lower radiator hose, the entire cooling system must be emptied.

✳✳ CAUTION

When draining coolant, keep in mind that cats and dogs are attracted by ethylene glycol antifreeze, and are quite likely to drink any that is left in an uncovered container or in puddles on the ground. This will prove fatal in sufficient quantity. Always drain coolant into a leak-proof container.

3. Loosen the hose clamps at each end of the hose requiring replacement. Clamps are usually either of the spring tension type (which require pliers to squeeze the tabs and loosen) or of the screw tension type (which require screw or hex drivers to loosen). Pull the clamps back on the hose away from the connection.

4. Twist, pull and slide the hose off the fitting, taking care not to damage the neck of the component from which the hose is being removed.

➡**If the hose is stuck at the connection, do not try to insert a screwdriver or other sharp tool under the hose end in an effort to free it, as the connection and/or hose may become damaged. Heater connections especially may be easily damaged by such a procedure. If the hose is to be replaced, use a single-edged razor blade to make a slice along the portion of the hose that is stuck on the connection, perpendicular to the end of the hose. Do not cut deep to prevent damaging the connection. The hose can then be peeled from the connection and discarded.**

5. Clean both hose mounting connections. Inspect the condition of the hose clamps and replace them, if necessary.

To install:

6. Dip the ends of the new hose into clean engine coolant to ease installation.

7. Slide the clamps over the replacement hose, then slide the hose ends over the connections into position.

8. Position and secure the clamps at least ¼ inch (6mm) from the ends of the hose. Make sure they are located beyond the raised bead of the connector.

9. Close the radiator or engine drains and properly refill the cooling system with the clean drained engine coolant or a suitable mixture of antifreeze and water.

10. If available, install a pressure tester and check for leaks. If a pressure tester is not available, run the engine until normal operating temperature is reached (allowing the system to naturally pressurize), then check for leaks.

✳✳ CAUTION

If you are checking for leaks with the system at normal operating temperature, BE EXTREMELY CAREFUL not to touch any moving or hot engine parts. Once temperature has been reached, shut the engine OFF, and check for leaks around the hose fittings and connections that were removed earlier.

DRAINING & REFILLING COOLING SYSTEM

▶ See Figures 33, 34, and 35

✳✳ CAUTION

When draining the coolant, keep in mind that cats and dogs are attracted by ethylene glycol antifreeze, and are quite likely to drink any that is left in an uncovered container or in puddles on the ground. This will prove fatal in sufficient quantity. Always drain the coolant into a leak-proof container. Coolant should be reused unless it is contaminated or several years old. To avoid injuries from scalding fluid and steam, DO NOT remove the radiator cap while the engine and radiator are still HOT.

➡The cooling systems on some 1996 and later vehicles were originally filled with silicate-free coolant. The fluid is easily identified because of its orange color (instead of the green we have come to expect from most types of ethylene glycol antifreeze). If your cooling system is filled with DEX-COOL® or other silicate-free coolant, then no periodic service is required, other than fluid level checks, for 100,000 miles (161,000 km) or 5 years, whichever comes first. However, if you add a silicate coolant to the system (even in small amounts) premature engine, heater core or radiator corrosion may result. In addition, the coolant will have to be changed sooner (12,000 miles (19,300 km) or every year, just like other vehicles not using DEX-COOL® or other Silicate-free coolant).

➡This is a generic procedure intended to be used on most vehicles. Certain models may not be equipped with conventional radiator fill caps and are usually checked only through the recovery tank. In addition, some vehicles require system bleeding procedures. For these vehicles please refer to a Chilton's Total Car Care manual.

1. When the engine is cool, remove the radiator cap using the following procedures.
   a. Slowly rotate the cap counterclockwise to the detent.
   b. If any residual pressure is present, WAIT until the hissing noise stops.
   c. After the hissing noise has ceased, press down on the cap and continue rotating it counterclockwise to remove it.
2. Place a fluid catch pan under the radiator, open the radiator drain valve and, if access is possible, remove the engine drain plugs, then drain the coolant.
3. Close the drain valve and, if removed, install the engine drain plugs.
4. Empty the coolant reservoir and flush it.
5. Using the correct mixture (AND TYPE, refer your owners manual) of antifreeze, fill the radiator to about ½ inch (13mm) from the bottom of the filler neck.
6. Start the engine and allow it to idle as the engine warms-up. As the thermostat is opened, air which was trapped in the engine should be expelled, causing the fluid level in the radiator to drop. Add fresh coolant/water mixture until the level reaches the bottom of the filler neck.
7. Add some of the coolant/water mixture to the coolant tank, but don't go above the ADD or COLD mark at this time.
8. Install the radiator cap (make sure the arrows align with the overflow tube).
9. Run the engine until it reaches the operating temperatures, then check the recovery tank and add fluid (if necessary).

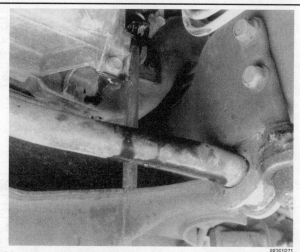
Fig. 33 To prevent a mess when draining the radiator, place a plastic tube over the radiator petcock

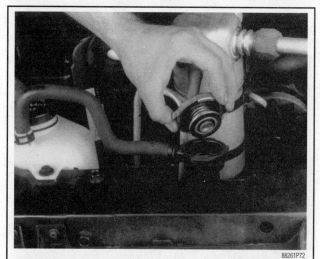
Fig. 34 When refilling the system, pour coolant directly into the radiator first.

Fig. 35 If additional coolant is needed, it should be added to the tank

COOLING SYSTEM CAPACITY CHART

Cooling System	QUARTS OF ANTIFREEZE REQUIRED								
Capacity (QTS.)	3	4	5	6	7	8	9	10	11
6	−34°								
7	− 17								
8	−7	−34°							
9	0	−21							
10	4	−12	−34°						
11	8	−6	−23						
12	10	0	−15	−34°					
13		3	−9	−25					
14		6	−5	−17	−34°				
15		8	0	−12	−26				
16		10	2	−7	−19	−34°			
17			5	−4	−14	−27			
18			7	0	−10	−21	−34°		
19			9	2	−7	−16	−28		
20			10	4	−3	−12	−22	−34°	

For Best Year Round Operation under all driving conditions, install a 50/50 mix of ANTIFREEZE and water. Protects against freeze-ups down to −34°F. Protects against boilover up to 266°F.*

***Using a 15-lb. pressure cap in good condition**

88529G31

FLUSHING & CLEANING THE SYSTEM

The cooling system should be drained, thoroughly flushed and refilled at least every 30,000 miles or 24 months. These operations should be done with the engine cold, especially if a backpressure flushing kit is being used. Completely draining, flushing and refilling the cooling system at least every two years will remove accumulated rust, scale and other deposits. Coolant in late model vehicles is a 50/50 mixture of ethylene glycol and water for year round use. Use a good quality antifreeze with water pump lubricants, rust inhibitors and other corrosion inhibitors along with acid neutralizers.

There are many products available for cooling system flushing, including power flushing equipment or adapters to attach your garden hose. If a backpressure flushing kit is used, it is recommended that the thermostat be temporarily removed in order to allow free flow to the system with cold water. Always follow the kit or cleaner manufacturer's instructions and make sure the product is compatible with your vehicle.

Most flushing compounds attack metals and SHOULD NOT remain in the cooling system for more than a few minutes. Be sure to use a neutralizer in the cooling system IMMEDIATELY after a descaling solvent has been used. Keep in mind that for extremely hard, stubborn coatings, such as lime scale, a stronger solution may be necessary. HOWEVER, the corrosive action of the stronger solution will affect the thin metals of the radiator, thereby reducing its operating life. A COMPLETE flushing and rinsing is mandatory if this is attempted.

1. Make sure the engine is cool and the vehicle is parked on a level surface, then remove the radiator neck cap, if equipped, and the recovery tank cap in order to relieve system pressure.

2. Position a large drain pan under the vehicle, then drain the existing antifreeze and coolant by opening the radiator petcock and/or engine drains.

3. Close the radiator/engine drains, as applicable and fill the system with water.

4. Add a can of quality radiator flush.

5. Idle the engine until the upper radiator hose gets hot and the thermostat has opened. This will allow the solution to fully circulate through the system.

6. Drain the system again.

7. Repeat this process until the drained water is clear and free of scale.

8. Close all drains and connect all the hoses.

9. If equipped with a coolant recovery system, flush the reservoir with water and leave empty.

10. Determine the capacity of your coolant system. Through the radiator filler neck or reservoir, add a 50/50 mix of quality antifreeze (ethylene glycol) and water to provide the desired protection.

11. Leave the radiator pressure cap or reservoir cap off, then start and run the engine until the thermostat heats up and opens, this will allow air to bleed from the system and provide room for additional coolant to be added to the system.

12. Add additional coolant to the radiator or reservoir, as necessary to bring the coolant mixture up to the proper level.

13. Stop the engine and check the coolant level.

14. Check the level of protection with an antifreeze tester, then install the radiator pressure or reservoir cap, as applicable.

15. Start and run the engine to normal operating temperature, then check the system for leaks.

TROUBLESHOOTING BASIC COOLING SYSTEM PROBLEMS

The most common troubles you'll have with your car's cooling system will show up as overheating. It will first show up when the high temperature warning light (on the dash) comes on or when the temperature gauge shows abnormally high operating temperatures (above 230°F.). Occasionally, a weakened hose will rupture and cause immediate overheating.

YOUR CAR'S ENGINE OVERHEATS BECAUSE...	YOUR CAR'S HEATER DOES NOT PRODUCE HEAT BECAUSE...	YOUR CAR'S ENGINE WARMS UP SLOWLY BECAUSE...
COOLANT LEVEL IS LOW—Check and correct level	THE THERMOSTAT IS STUCK—Replace the thermostat	THE THERMOSTAT IS STUCK OPEN—Replace the thermostat
LOOSE OR BROKEN FAN BELT—Tighten or replace fan belt	THE HEATER CORE IS CLOGGED—Have the heater core checked	
FAULTY RADIATOR CAP—Replace cap	HEATER CONTROL IS FAULTY—Check the control mechanism	
INACCURATE GAUGE OR WARNING LIGHT—Have gauge and sending unit checked		
CLOGGED COOLING SYSTEM—Drain coolant and flush system		
DEBRIS ON RADIATOR—Clean the radiator		
THERMOSTAT STUCK CLOSED—Replace thermostat		
WATER PUMP IS FAULTY—Have water pump checked and/or replaced		
ANTIFREEZE HAS BEEN USED TOO LONG—Drain coolant and fill with fresh mix.		
WATER HAS HIGH MINERAL CONTENT—		
Radiator HOSE HAS WEAKENED AND COLLAPSED—Replace hose		
IGNITION TIMING IS RETARDED—Check and set ignition timing		
ENGINE OIL LEVEL IS LOW—Check and refill engine oil		
CYLINDER HEAD GASKET LEAKS—This is usually accompanied by bubbles in the radiator (engine running) and poor compression in the cylinders adjacent to the leak.		

88529C01

INSTALLING A TRANSMISSION OIL COOLER

If your vehicle is used primarily on hilly or mountainous roads, or as a towing vehicle, you can probably benefit from the installation of an additional automatic transmission oil cooler. The increased load of a trailer or hilly terrain, causes an increase in the temperature of the automatic transmission fluid. Heat is the worst enemy of an automatic transmission. As the temperature of the fluid increases, the life of the fluid decreases.

It is essential, therefore, that you install an automatic transmission cooler. The cooler, which consists of a multi-tube, finned heat exchanger, is usually installed in front of the radiator or air conditioning compressor, and hooked in-line with the transmission cooler tank inlet line. Follow the cooler manufacturer's installation instructions.

Select a cooler of at least adequate capacity, based upon the gross weights of the vehicle and, if necessary, trailer.

Cooler manufacturers recommend that you use an aftermarket cooler in addition to, and not instead of, the present cooling tank in your radiator. If you do want to use it in place of the radiator cooling tank, get a cooler at least two sizes larger than normally necessary.

➡️**A transmission cooler can, sometimes, cause slow or harsh shifting in the transmission during cold weather, until the fluid has a chance to come up to normal operating temperature. Some coolers can be purchased with or retrofitted with a temperature bypass valve which will allow fluid flow through the cooler only when the fluid has reached above a certain operating temperature.**

INSTALLING AN ENGINE OIL COOLER

Some vehicles may be equipped with an original equipment oil cooler and adapter. On these vehicles, the oil cooler is usually built into the side of the radiator, with the adapter mounted between the engine block and oil filter. However, if your vehicle did not come equipped with one, you may want to install an aftermarket engine oil cooler and adapter. Although the adapter for most aftermarket and OEM kits are installed in basically the same manner, aftermarket coolers are usually not integral with the radiator, as OEM coolers are. Aftermarket coolers are usually separate radiator units, which get mounted near the vehicle's radiator. When installed an engine oil cooler assembly, make sure to follow the manufacturer's instructions.

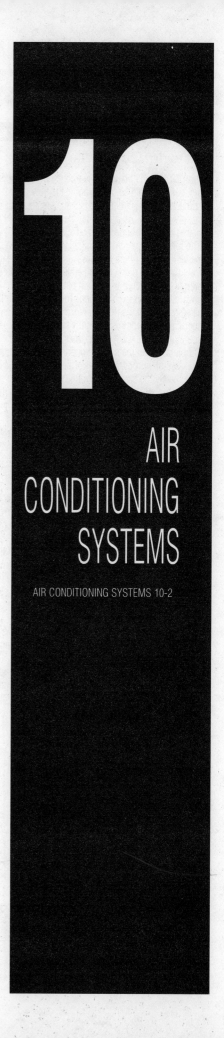

10

AIR
CONDITIONING
SYSTEMS

AIR CONDITIONING SYSTEMS 10-2

AIR CONDITIONING SYSTEMS

Theory of Air Conditioning

▶ **See Figure 1**

In order to understand how air conditioning works, it is necessary to understand several basic laws about the flow of heat. While it may seem puzzling to talk about heat in the same breath as air conditioning, heat is your only concern. An air conditioner does not cool the air, but rather, removes the heat from a confined space.

The law of entropy states that all things must eventually come to the same temperature; there will always be a flow of heat between adjacent objects that are at different temperatures. When two objects at different temperatures are placed next to each other, heat will flow from the warmer of the two objects to the cooler one. The rate at which heat is transferred depends on how large the difference is between their temperatures. If the temperature difference is great, the transfer of heat will be great, and if the temperature difference lessens, the transfer of heat will be reduced until both objects reach the same temperature. At that point, heat transfer stops.

Because of entropy, the interior of an automobile tends to remain at approximately the same temperature as the outside air. To cool an automobile interior, you have to reverse the natural flow of heat, no matter how thoroughly insulated the compartment might be. The heat which the body metal and glass absorb from the outside must constantly be removed.

The refrigeration cycle of the air conditioning system removes the heat from a vehicle's interior by making use of another law of heat flow, the theory of latent heat. This theory says that during a change of state, a material can absorb or reject heat without changing its temperature. A material is changing its state when it is freezing, thawing, boiling or condensing. Changes of state differ from ordinary heating and cooling in that they occur without the temperature of the substance changing, although they cause a visible change in the form of the substance. While many materials can exist in solid, liquid, or gaseous form, the best example is plain water.

Water is a common material that can exist in all three states. Below 32°F (0°C), it exists as ice. Above 212°F (100°C), at sea level air pressure, it exists as steam, which is a gas. Between these two temperatures, it exists in its liquid form.

Since a change in state occurs at a constant temperature, it follows that a material can exist as both a liquid and a gas at the same temperature without any exchange of heat between the two states. As an example, when water boils, it absorbs heat without changing the temperature of the resulting gas (steam).

The change from a solid to a liquid and vice versa is always practically the same for a given substance—32°F (0°C) for water—but the tempera-

ture at which a liquid will boil or condense depends upon the pressure. For example, water will boil at 212°F (100°C), but only at sea level. The boiling point drops slightly at higher altitudes, where the atmospheric pressure is lower. We also know that raising the pressure 15 lbs. above normal air pressure in an automobile cooling system will keep the water from boiling until the temperature reaches about 260°F (127°C)

One additional aspect of the behavior of a liquid at its boiling point must be clarified to understand how a refrigeration cycle works. Since liquid and gas can exist at the same temperature, either the evaporation of liquid or the condensation of gas can occur at the same temperature and pressure conditions. It's just a matter of whether the material is being heated or cooled.

As an example, when a pan of water is placed on a hot stove, the heat travels from the hot burner to the relatively cool pan and water. When the water reaches it's boiling point, its temperature will stop rising, and all the additional heat forced into it by the hot burner will be used to turn the liquid material into a gas (steam). The gas thus contains slightly more heat than the liquid material.

If the top of the pan were now to be held a couple of inches above the boiling water, two things would happen. First, droplets of liquid would form on the lower surface of the lid. Second, the top would get hot very quickly. The top becomes hot because the heat originally used to turn the water into steam is being recovered. As the vapor encounters the cooler surface of the metal, heat is removed from it and transferred to the metal. This heat is the same heat that was originally required to change the water into a vapor, and so it again becomes a liquid.

Since water will boil only at 212°F (100°C) and above, it follows that the steam must have been 212°F (100°C) when it reached the top and must have remained that hot until it became a liquid. The cooling effect of the top (which started out at room temperature) caused the steam to condense, but both the boiling and the condensation took place at the same temperature.

To sum up, refrigeration is the removal of heat from a confined space and is based on three assumptions:

1. Heat will only flow from a warm substance to a colder substance.

2. A refrigerant can exist as both a liquid and a gas at the same temperature if it is at its "boiling point." A refrigerant at its boiling point will boil and absorb heat from its surroundings if the surroundings are warmer than the refrigerant. A refrigerant at its boiling point will condense and become liquid, losing heat to its surroundings, if they are cooler than the refrigerant.

3. The boiling point of the refrigerant depends upon the pressure of the refrigerant, rising as the pressure rises and falling as the pressure falls.

The operation of the refrigeration cycle illustrates how these three laws are put to use.

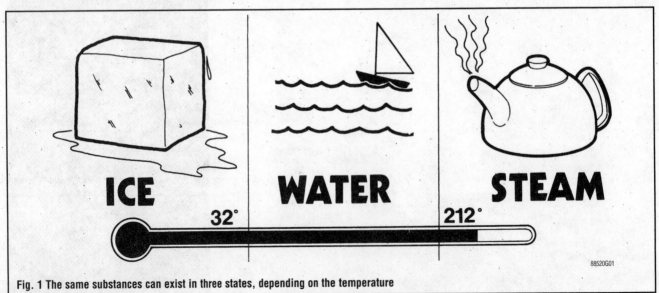

Fig. 1 The same substances can exist in three states, depending on the temperature

88520G01

How the Air Conditioner Works

REFRIGERATION CYCLE

▶ See Figure 2

Any automotive air conditioning system employs four basic parts—a mechanical compressor, driven by the vehicle's engine; an expansion valve, which is a restriction the compressor pumps against; and two heat exchangers, the evaporator and the condenser. In addition, there is the refrigerant that flows through this system.

The belt-driven compressor uses engine power to compress and circulate the refrigerant gas throughout the system. The refrigerant passes through the condenser on its way from the compressor outlet to the expansion valve. The condenser is located outside the passenger compartment, usually in front of the vehicle's radiator. The refrigerant passes from the expansion valve to the evaporator, and after passing through the evaporator tubing, it is returned to the compressor through its inlet. The evaporator is located inside the vehicle's passenger compartment.

When the compressor starts running, it pulls refrigerant from the evaporator coil and forces it into the condenser coil, thus lowering the evaporator pressure and increasing the condenser pressure. When proper operating pressures have been established, the expansion valve will open and allow refrigerant to return to the evaporator as fast as the compressor is removing it. Under these conditions, the pressure at each point in the system will reach a constant level, but the condenser pressure will be much higher than the evaporator pressure.

The pressure in the evaporator is low enough for the boiling point of the refrigerant to be well below the temperature of the vehicle's interior. Therefore, the liquid will boil, remove heat from the interior, and pass from the evaporator as a gas. The heating effect produced as the refrigerant passes through the compressor keeps the gas from liquefying and causes it to be discharged from the compressor at very high temperatures. This hot gas passes into the condenser. The pressure on this side of the system is high enough so that the boiling point of the refrigerant is well beyond the outside temperature. The gas will cool until it reaches its boiling point, and then condense to a liquid as heat is absorbed by the outside air. The liquid refrigerant is then forced back through the expansion valve by the condenser pressure.

(minus 6°C). If liquid R-12 is spilled into the open air, it would be seen for a brief period as a rapidly boiling, clear liquid.

R-12 was nearly an ideal refrigerant. It operated at low pressure and condenses easily at the temperature ranges found in automotive air conditioning systems. It is also non-corrosive, non-toxic (except when exposed to an open flame), and nonflammable. However, due to its low boiling point and the fact that it is stored under pressure, certain safety measures must be observed when working around the air conditioning system. Unfortunately it was discovered the carbo-floro-carbons (CFC's) which were chemicals in the same group as dichlorodifluoromenthane, which you know as R-12 or Freon were depleting the ozone layer of the atmosphere.

On December 31, 1995, CFC-12 production essentially ended in the U.S. However to avoid release into the atmosphere it is still legal to use the existing stockpiles of CFC-12.

The replacement for CFC-12 has been a non-CFC refrigerant R-134a. This has been used since the 1994 model year. Some of the older R-12 systems are being changed over to R-134a but this can be a costly and complicated process on some vehicles.

There is a third category for refrigerants that substitute CFC-12, these also contain ozone depleting HCFC's such as R-22, R142b, and R-124.

There are strict governmental regulations enforced by the clean air act of 1990 section 609. These include specific regulations for the use and handling of each of the three types of refrigerants.

Governmental Regulations

THE CLEAN AIR ACT 1990—SECTION 609

Our Threatened Ozone Layer

▶ See Figure 3

The ozone layer acts as a blanket in the stratosphere that protects us from harmful Ultra Violet (UV) radiation. Scientists worldwide believe that man-made chemicals such as CFC-12 (also known by the trade name Freon) are rapidly destroying this layer of gas 10–30 miles (16–48 km) above the earth's surface. Strong UV radiation breaks the CFC-12

Refrigerant

A liquid with a low boiling point must be used to make practical use of the heat transfer that occurs when a liquid boils. Refrigerant-12 (R-12) is the refrigerant that was universally used in automotive air conditioning systems. At normal temperatures, it is a colorless, odorless gas that is slightly heavier than air. Its boiling point at atmospheric pressure is −21.7°F

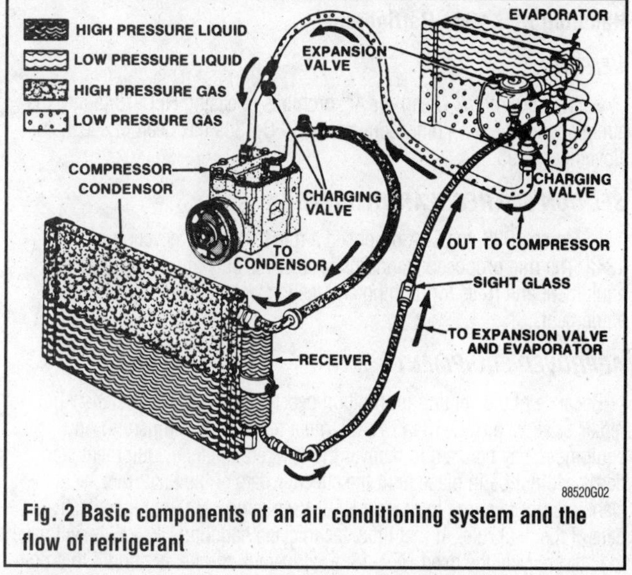

Fig. 2 Basic components of an air conditioning system and the flow of refrigerant

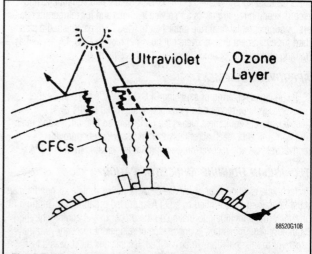

Fig. 3 Refrigerant causes harm by depleting the ozone layer to protect us from ultra violet rays of the sun

molecules apart, releasing chlorine. A single chlorine atom can destroy over one hundred thousand ozone molecules. Ozone loss in the atmosphere is likely to lead to an increase in cataracts and skin cancer, which is now one of the fastest growing forms of cancer, and could weaken the human immune system. In the U.S., one person dies of skin cancer every hour. Agriculture, as well as plant and animal life, may also be dramatically affected.

Remember that ozone is "good up high, bad nearby": even though it protects us when it is in the stratosphere, ozone at ground level can be harmful to breathe and is a prime ingredient in smog. Many man-made sources such as tailpipe emissions from vehicles contribute to ground-level ozone.

Global Action to Protect the Ozone Layer

The United States has joined over 160 countries as a party to the international treaty known as the Montreal Protocol. All developed countries agreed to phase out production of most ozone-depleting substances, including CFC's, by the end of 1995. The 1990 Clean Air Act Amendments (the Act) incorporated this production ban date and directed the EPA to develop regulations to maximize recycling, ban nonessential uses, develop labeling requirements and examine safe alternatives for ozone-depleting substances.

Impact of Motor Vehicle Air Conditioners

One of the largest uses of CFC-12 in the U.S. is as a refrigerant in Motor Vehicle Air Conditioners (MVACs). Section 609 of the Act gives the EPA the authority to establish requirements to prevent the release of refrigerants during the servicing of MVACs and to require recycling of refrigerants. Widespread refrigerant recycling reduces the demand for virgin CFC-12 and thus extends the time that it will be available. The following sections describe the requirements of the law and its potential impact on the service industry.

Handling CFC-12

VENTING

Another section of the Clean Air Act, section 608, prohibits releasing CFC-12 into the atmosphere. The prohibition on venting CFC-12 has been in effect since 1992.

SECTION 609 REGULATORY HISTORY

The original regulation promulgated under section 609 was published in July 1992. That regulation established standards for equipment that recovers and recycles CFC-12 refrigerant from motor vehicle air conditioners, rules for training and testing technicians to handle this equipment, and record-keeping requirements for service facilities and for refrigerant retailers. A supplemental final rule published in May 1995 established a standard for equipment that recovers but does not recycle CFC-12, as well as training and testing technicians to handle this equipment.

APPROVED EQUIPMENT

Technicians repairing or servicing CFC-12 MVACs must use either recover/recycle or recover-only equipment approved by the EPA. Recover/recycle equipment cleans the refrigerant so that oil, air and moisture contaminants reach acceptably low levels. A list of approved recover/recycle and recover-only equipment is available from the EPA.

TECHNICIAN TRAINING AND CERTIFICATION

Technicians who repair or service CFC-12 motor vehicle air conditioners must be trained and certified by an EPA-approved organization. Training programs must include information on the proper use of equipment, the regulatory requirements, the importance of refrigerant recovery, and the effects of ozone depletion. To be certified, technicians must pass a test demonstrating their knowledge in these areas. A list of approved testing programs is available from the EPA.

RECORDKEEPING REQUIREMENTS

Service shops must certify to the EPA that they own approved CFC-12 equipment. If refrigerant is recovered and sent to a reclamation facility, the name and address of that facility must be kept on file.

SALES RESTRICTIONS

▶ See Figure 4

Section 609 has long prohibited the sale of small cans of ozone-depleting refrigerants to anyone other than a certified technician. The sale of any size container of CFC-12 to anyone other than certified technicians was prohibited under section 608 of the Act beginning on November 14, 1994. This provision is intended to discourage "do-it-yourselfers" who recharge their own air conditioners. Such individuals often release refrigerant because they typically do not have access to recovery/recycling equipment. The EPA encourages "do-it-yourselfers" to bring their vehicles to certified technicians who can properly fix air conditioners using approved equipment. This avoids damage to A/C equipment by improper charging and helps to protect the environment.

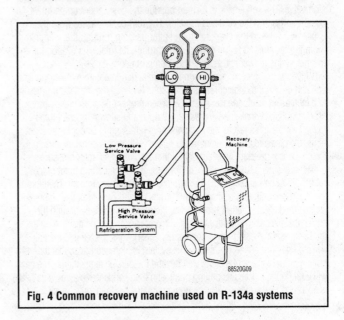

Fig. 4 Common recovery machine used on R-134a systems

Handling HFC-134a Refrigerant

VENTING

Section 608 of the Clean Air Act prohibits releasing HFC-134a into the atmosphere. The prohibition on venting HFC-134a has been in effect since November 1995.

SECTION 609 REGULATORY HISTORY

In March 1996, the EPA proposed a rule to require recycling of HFC-134a. The rule proposed standards for recover-only and recover/recycle equipment and rules for training and testing technicians to handle this equipment.

APPROVED EQUIPMENT

Because of the venting prohibition described above, technicians who repair or service HFC-134a MVACs must recover the refrigerant. Any equipment may be used to recover the refrigerant, since equipment standards will not be in place until the effective date of the final rule. Technicians are not required to recycle HFC-134a refrigerant until the effective date of the final rule. At that time, technicians handling HFC-134a will have to either recycle the used HFC-134a refrigerant on-site, or send it to an off-site reclamation facility to be purified to ARI Standard 700, before it can be used to recharge A/C equipment.

After the effective date of the rule, the EPA will make available a list of approved recover/recycle and recover-only HFC-134a equipment.

CONVERTING CFC-12 EQUIPMENT FOR USE WITH HFC-134A

EPA regulations prohibit technicians from changing fittings on the same unit back and forth so that the unit is used for CFC-12 in the morning, HFC-134a in the afternoon, then back to CFC-12 again, etc.

EPA regulations specify that when equipment is converted for use with a new refrigerant, the converted unit must be able to meet the applicable equipment standard set forth in the regulations. CFC-12 equipment may be permanently converted for use with HFC-134a under certain conditions. The EPA intends to issue regulations placing certain restrictions on these retrofits in the future. Those restrictions may require that the manufacturer's service representative rather than the automotive service technician perform the retrofit, that a unit may only be retrofitted if retrofit procedures have been certified by an independent testing laboratory such as Underwriters Laboratories, and that an appropriate label is affixed to the unit. In addition, the retrofitted unit must meet the technical specifications of SAE standard J2210 and must have the capacity to purify used refrigerant to SAE standard J2099 for safe and direct return to the air conditioner following repairs.

In the absence of any EPA regulations, a service facility may perform such a retrofit, or may have the equipment manufacturer's service representative perform the retrofit, as long as the fittings are changed in accordance with the EPA's Significant New Alternative Policy (SNAP) program regulations. The Agency cautions technicians, however, that although recovering a given refrigerant using permanently converted equipment is legal, it may not be technically desirable. The equipment is designed to be compatible with specific refrigerants, and incompatible materials may cause short circuits, damage to seals, and compressor failure. Technicians should check with the recovery equipment manufacturer for recommendations about the recovery of refrigerants other than the refrigerant the equipment was originally intended to recover. Conversion of recovery equipment for use with other refrigerants may also invalidate any warranties offered by the equipment manufacturer.

TECHNICIAN TRAINING AND CERTIFICATION

Before the final rule is published and goes into effect, technicians repairing or servicing HFC-134a MVACs do not need to be trained and certified to handle HFC-134a. After the effective date of the rule, however, technicians who repair or service HFC-134a MVACs must be trained and certified by an EPA-approved organization. If a technician is already trained and certified to handle CFC-12, he will not need to be recertified to handle HFC-134a.

RECORDKEEPING REQUIREMENTS

Service shops must certify to the EPA that they own approved HFC-134a equipment.

➡**This certification is a one-time requirement, so that if a shop purchased a piece of CFC-12 recycling equipment in the past, and sent the certification to the EPA, the shop does not need to send a second certification to the EPA when it purchases a second piece of equipment, no matter what refrigerant that equipment is designed to handle. If refrigerant is recovered and sent to a reclamation facility, the shop must retain the name and address of that reclaimer.**

SALES RESTRICTIONS

At the time of publishing, there is no restriction on the sale of HFC-134a, so anyone may purchase it. The EPA will issue a proposed rule under section 608 of the Act that will include a proposal to restrict the sale of HFC-134a so that only technicians certified under sections 608 and 609 may purchase it. After the proposed rule is published, the EPA will review comments from the public on the proposal and will then publish a final rule sometime in late 1998.

Handling Other Refrigerants that Substitute for CFC-12

VENTING SUBSTITUTE REFRIGERANTS

Other than HFC-134a, all EPA-accepted refrigerants that substitute for CFC-12 in motor vehicles, and that are currently on the market, are blends that contain ozone-depleting HCFC's such as R-22, R-142b and R-124.

Section 608 of the Clean Air Act prohibits venting any of these new blend substitutes into the atmosphere. The prohibition on venting these ozone-depleting blends has been in effect since 1992.

SECTION 609 REGULATORY HISTORY

When the March 1996 proposed rule that requires recycling of HFC-134a was published in final form in the summer of 1997, it also established a standard for equipment that is designed to recover, but not recycle, any single, specific blend substitute refrigerant.

RECOVER ONLY EQUIPMENT

Technicians recovering these blend refrigerants must use EPA-approved equipment. As noted above, the final rule contains a standard for equipment designed to recover, but not recycle, a single, specific blend refrigerant. It may be possible to convert a piece of CFC-12 recover-only equipment so that it meets this standard—see the discussion on equipment conversions that follows this topic.

The EPA is currently working with independent testing laboratories and with equipment manufacturers to devise equipment that can recover, but not recycle, not only multiple blend refrigerants, but also contaminated CFC-12 and HFC-134a. Within the next year, the EPA will propose a standard for this type of equipment. The EPA expects that this equipment should be available by the 1998 A/C season.

CONVERTING CFC-12 RECOVER-ONLY EQUIPMENT FOR USE WITH BLEND SUBSTITUTES

The EPA regulations prohibit technicians from changing fittings on the same unit back and forth so that the unit is used for CFC-12 in the morning, a blend substitute in the afternoon, another blend substitute the next morning, HFC-134a the next afternoon, etc.

The EPA regulations specify that when equipment is converted for use with a refrigerant other than the refrigerant for which the equipment was originally intended, the converted unit must be able to meet the applicable equipment standard set forth in the regulations. CFC-12 recover-only equipment may be permanently converted for use with single, specific blend refrigerants under certain conditions. The EPA intends to issue regulations placing certain restrictions on these retrofits in the future. Those restrictions may require that the manufacturer's service representative rather than the automotive service technician perform the retrofit, that a unit may only be retrofitted if retrofit procedures have been certified by an independent testing laboratory such as Underwriters Laboratories, and that an appropriate label is affixed to the unit. In addition, the retrofitted unit has to meet the technical specifications of the EPA standard.

RECYCLING EQUIPMENT

The EPA regulations currently prohibit technicians from recycling blend substitute refrigerants, and the Agency is not aware of any equipment currently on the market designed to recycle any of these blends. After recovering the blend refrigerant from the MVAC system, it must, therefore, be sent off-site for reclamation.

The EPA is working with independent testing laboratories and with equipment manufacturers to determine whether recycling equipment can be developed to service these blends, without jeopardizing the health or safety of the technician and the integrity of the MVAC system. If it is possible to develop such equipment, the EPA will work with equipment and refrigerant manufacturers and with independent testing laboratories to develop an appropriate standard for the equipment.

CONVERTING CFC-12 RECOVER/RECYCLE EQUIPMENT FOR USE WITH BLEND SUBSTITUTES

At the time of publication, the EPA also currently prohibits the conversion of existing CFC-12 or HFC-134a recycling equipment for either temporary or permanent use with a blend refrigerant. In the future, the EPA may issue regulations allowing these conversions but placing certain restrictions on who performs the conversions, what models may be converted, etc.

TECHNICIAN TRAINING AND CERTIFICATION

Technicians who repair or service MVACs with these refrigerants must be trained and certified by an EPA-approved organization. If a technician is already trained and certified to handle CFC-12 or HFC-134a, he will not need to be recertified to handle the blend refrigerants.

RECORDKEEPING REQUIREMENTS

Service facilities that work on vehicles that use blend substitutes must certify to the EPA that they own approved equipment designed to service these refrigerants. Note that this certification is a one-time requirement, so that if a shop purchased a piece of CFC-12 or HFC-134a recycling equipment in the past, and sent the certification to the EPA, the shop does not need to send a second certification to the EPA when it purchases a second piece of equipment, no matter what refrigerant that equipment is designed to handle. If refrigerant is recovered and sent to a reclamation facility, the shop must retain the name and address of that reclaimer.

SALES RESTRICTIONS

Because these blends contain HCFC's, Section 608 regulations prohibit the sale of any size container of any of these blend refrigerants to anyone other than certified technicians. This prohibition began in November, 1994.

Retrofitting Vehicles to Alternative Refrigerants

Although section 609 of the Act does not govern retrofitting, section 612 of the Act, which describes the EPS's Significant New Alternatives Policy (SNAP) program, does require that when retrofitting a CFC-12 vehicle for use with another refrigerant, the technician must first extract the CFC-12, must cover the CFC-12 label with a label that indicates the new refrigerant in the system and other information, and must affix new fittings unique to that refrigerant.

In addition, if a technician is retrofitting a vehicle to a refrigerant that contains R-22, the technician must ensure that only barrier hoses are used in the A/C system. Finally, if the system includes a pressure relief device, the technician must install a high-pressure compressor shutoff switch to prevent the compressor from increasing pressure until the refrigerant is vented.

Revisions to the Section 609 Rules and Regulations

Although these rules were current at the time of publication, revisions and additional information can be obtained through the Environmental Protection Agency. Contact the EPA through their hotline (800) 296–1996, or on the World Wide Web at http://epa.gov/ozone

Air Conditioning Safety Precautions

▶ See Figure 5

There are two particular hazards associated with air conditioning systems and they both relate to the refrigerant gas.

First, R-12 and R-134a are an extremely cold substance. When exposed to the atmosphere, it will instantly freeze any surface it comes in contact with, including your eyes. The other hazard relates to fire. Although normally non-toxic, R-12 refrigerant gas becomes highly poisonous in the presence of an open flame. In fact, one good whiff of the vapors formed by burning refrigerant can be fatal. So keep all forms of fire (including cigarettes) well clear of the air conditioning system.

Any repair work to an air conditioning system should be left to a professional. **Do not, under any circumstances,** attempt to loosen or tighten any fittings or perform any work other than that outlined here.

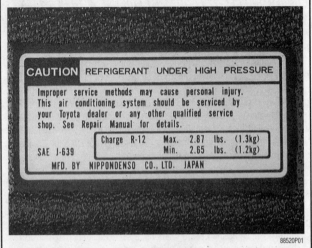

Fig. 5 Check the label on your vehicle to see what type of refrigerant is used

System Service & Repair

➥It is recommended that the A/C system be serviced by an EPA Section 609 certified automotive technician utilizing a refrigerant recovery/recycling machine.

The do-it-yourselfer should not service his/her own vehicle's A/C system for many reasons, including legal concerns, personal injury, environmental damage and cost. The following are some of the reasons why you may decide not to service your own vehicle's A/C system.

According to the U.S. Clean Air Act, it is a federal crime to service or repair (involving the refrigerant) a Motor Vehicle Air Conditioning (MVAC) system for money without being EPA certified. It is also illegal to vent R-12 and R-134a refrigerants into the atmosphere. Selling or distributing A/C system refrigerant (in a container that contains less than 20 pounds of refrigerant) to any person whom is not EPA 609 certified is also not allowed by law.

State and/or local laws may be stricter than the federal regulations, so be sure to check with your state and/or local authorities for further information. For further federal information on the legality of servicing your A/C system, call the EPA Stratospheric Ozone Hotline.

➥Federal law dictates that a fine of up to $25,000 may be levied on people convicted of venting refrigerant into the atmosphere. Additionally, the EPA may pay up to $10,000 for information or services leading to a criminal conviction of the violation of these laws.

When servicing an A/C system you run the risk of handling or coming in contact with refrigerant, which may result in skin or eye irritation or frostbite. Although low in toxicity (due to chemical stability), inhalation of concentrated refrigerant fumes is dangerous and can result in death; cases of fatal cardiac arrhythmia have been reported in people accidentally subjected to high levels of refrigerant. Some early symptoms include loss of concentration and drowsiness.

➥Generally, the limit for exposure is lower for R-134a than it is for R-12. Exceptional care must be practiced when handling R-134a.

In addition, R-12 refrigerant can decompose at high temperatures (near gas heaters or open flame), that may result in hydrofluoric acid, hydrochloric acid and phosgene (a fatal nerve gas).

R-12 refrigerant can damage the environment because it is a Chlorofluorocarbon (CFC), which has been proven to add to ozone layer depletion, leading to increasing levels of UV radiation. UV radiation has been linked with an increase in skin cancer, suppression of the human immune system, an increase in cataracts, damage to crops, damage to aquatic organisms, an increase in ground-level ozone, and increased global warming.

R-134a refrigerant is a greenhouse gas which, if allowed to vent into the atmosphere, will contribute to global warming (the Greenhouse Effect).

It is usually more economically feasible to have a certified MVAC automotive technician perform A/C system service on your vehicle. Some possible reasons for this are as follows:

• While it is illegal to service an A/C system without the proper equipment, the home mechanic would have to purchase an expensive refrigerant recovery/recycling machine to service his/her own vehicle.

• Since only a certified person may purchase refrigerant—according to the Clean Air Act, there are specific restrictions on selling or distributing A/C system refrigerant—it is legally impossible (unless certified) for the home mechanic to service his/her own vehicle. Venting refrigerant in an illegal fashion exposes one to the risk of paying a $25,000 fine to the EPA.

R-12 REFRIGERANT CONVERSION

▶ **See Figure 6**

If your vehicle still uses R-12 refrigerant, one way to save A/C system costs down the road is to investigate the possibility of having your system converted to R-134a. The older R-12 systems can be easily converted to R-134a refrigerant by a certified automotive technician by installing a few new components and changing the system oil.

The cost of R-12 is steadily rising and will continue to increase, because it is no longer imported or manufactured in the United States. Therefore, it is often possible to have an R-12 system converted to R-134a and recharged for less than it would cost to just charge the system with R-12.

If you are interested in having your system converted, contact local automotive service stations for more details and information.

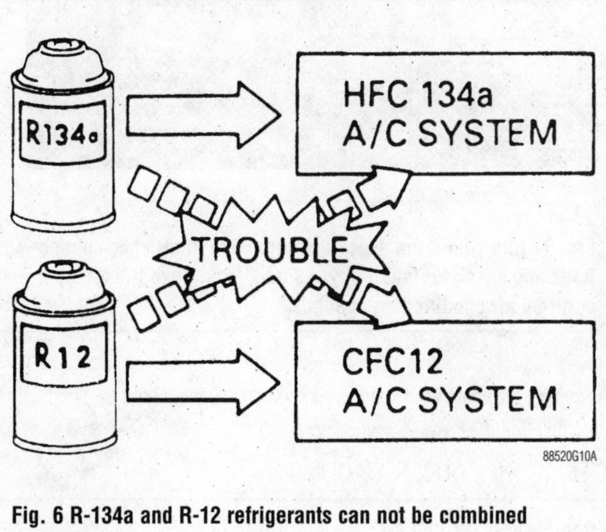

Air Conditioning Maintenance

▶ **See Figures 7, 8, 9 and 10**

Although the A/C system should not be serviced by the do-it-yourselfer, preventive maintenance can be practiced and A/C system inspections can be performed to help maintain the efficiency of the vehicle's A/C system. For preventive maintenance, perform the following:

• The easiest and most important preventive maintenance for your A/C system is to be sure that it is used on a regular basis. Running the system for five minutes once a week (no matter what the season) will help ensure that the seals and all internal components remain lubricated.

➡**Some newer vehicles automatically operate the A/C system compressor whenever the windshield defroster is activated. When running, the compressor lubricates the A/C system components; therefore, the A/C system would not need to be operated each month.**

Fig. 7 A coolant tester can be used to determine the freezing and boiling levels of the coolant in your vehicle

Fig. 8 View of a common compressor and service fittings

Fig. 6 R-134a and R-12 refrigerants can not be combined together

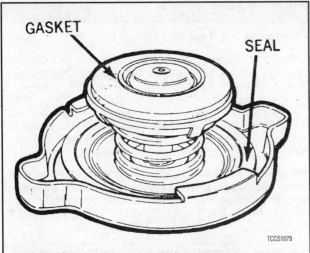

Fig. 9 To ensure efficient cooling system operation, inspect the radiator cap gasket and seal

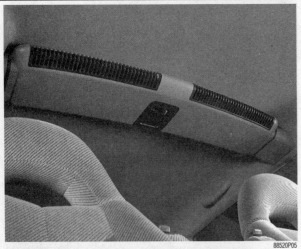

Fig. 10 On vehicles so equipped, don't forget to check the rear A/C vents for dirt or debris

• In order to prevent heater core freeze-up during A/C operation, it is necessary to maintain proper antifreeze protection. Use a hand-held coolant tester (hydrometer) to periodically check the condition of the antifreeze in your engine's cooling system.

➡**Antifreeze should not be used longer than the manufacturer specifies.**

• For efficient operation of an air conditioned vehicle's cooling system, the radiator cap should have a holding pressure that meets manufacturer's specifications. A cap that fails to hold these pressures should be replaced.

• Any obstruction of or damage to the condenser configuration will restrict airflow that is essential to its efficient operation. It is, therefore, a good rule to keep this unit clean and in proper physical shape.

➡**Bug screens that are mounted in front of the condenser (unless they are original equipment) are regarded as obstructions.**

• The condensation drain tube expels any water that accumulates on the bottom of the evaporator housing into the engine compartment. If this tube is obstructed, the air conditioning performance can be restricted and condensation buildup can spill over onto the vehicle's floor.

System Inspection

Although the A/C system should not be serviced by the do-it-yourselfer, preventive maintenance can be practiced and A/C system inspections can be performed to help maintain the efficiency of the vehicle's A/C system. For A/C system inspection, perform the following:

The easiest and often most important check for the air conditioning system consists of a visual inspection of the system components. Visually inspect the air conditioning system for refrigerant leaks, damaged compressor clutch, abnormal compressor drive belt tension and/or condition, plugged evaporator drain tube, blocked condenser fins, disconnected or broken wires, blown fuses, corroded connections and poor insulation.

CHECKING FOR OIL LEAKS

◆ **See Figure 11**

Refrigerant leaks show up as oily areas on the various components because the compressor oil is transported around the entire system along with the refrigerant. Look for oily spots on all the hoses and lines, and especially on the hose and tubing connections. If there are oily deposits,

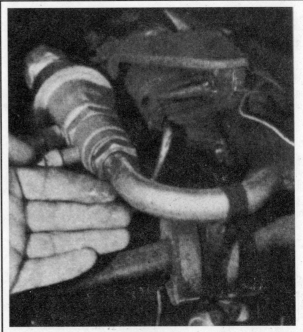

Fig. 11 Run your hand along the underside of all hose connections and check for leaks. If you find a leak, have it fixed by a certified air conditioning specialist.

the system may have a leak, and you should have it checked by a certified air conditioning specialist.

KEEPING THE CONDENSER CLEAR

◆ **See Figures 12 and 13**

Periodically inspect the front of the condenser for bent fins or foreign material (dirt, bugs, leaves, etc.). If any cooling fins are bent, straighten them carefully. You can remove any debris with a stiff bristle brush.

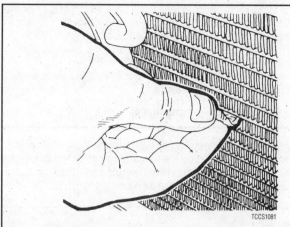

Fig. 12 The position of the condenser in front of the radiator makes it particularly susceptible to collecting debris. Periodically, remove the accumulated bugs, leaves and other trash from the condenser.

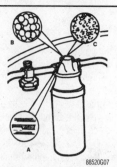

Fig. 14 Oils streaks (A), constant bubbles (B) or foam (C) indicate there is not enough refrigerant in the system. Occasional bubbles during the initial operation are normal. A clear sight glass indicates a proper charge of refrigerant or no refrigerant at all, which can be determined by the presence of cold air at the outlets in the vehicle. If the glass is clouded with a milky white substance, have the receiver/dryer checked by a certified air conditioning specialist.

Fig. 13 On models with rear A/C, make sure to clean and inspect the rear condenser also

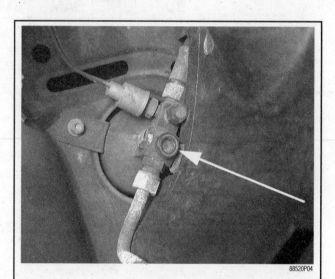

Fig. 15 Look through the sight glass for refrigerant flow

CHECKING THE COMPRESSOR BELT

➡For belt inspection, adjustment and replacement please refer to the chapter on the Cooling System.

CHECKING THE REFRIGERANT LEVEL

There are two ways to check refrigerant level. On vehicles equipped with sight glasses, checking the refrigerant level is a simple matter. Many late model vehicles, however, do not have a sight glass, and you have to check the temperature of the lines to determine the refrigerant level.

With Sight Glass

▶ See Figures 14 and 15

The sight glass is normally located in the head of the receiver/drier. The receiver/drier is not hard to locate. It's a large metal cylinder that looks something like a fire extinguisher. Sometimes the sight glass is located in

one of the metal lines leading from the top of the receiver/drier. Once you've found it, wipe it clean and proceed as follows:

1. With the engine and the air conditioning system running, look for the flow of refrigerant through the sight glass. If the air conditioner is working properly, you'll be able to see a continuous flow of clear refrigerant through the sight glass, with perhaps an occasional bubble at very high temperatures.

2. Cycle the air conditioner on and off to make sure what you are seeing is clear refrigerant. Since the refrigerant is clear, it is possible to mistake a completely discharged system for one that is fully charged. Turn the system off and watch the sight glass. If there is refrigerant in the system, you'll see bubbles during the off cycle. If you observe no bubbles when the system is running, and the airflow from the unit in the vehicle is delivering cold air, everything is OK.

3. If you observe bubbles in the sight glass while the system is operating, the system is low on refrigerant. Have it checked by a professional.

4. Oil streaks in the sight glass are an indication of trouble. Most of the time, if you see oil in the sight glass, it will appear as a series of streaks, although occasionally it may be a solid stream of oil. In either case, it means that part of the charge has been lost.

Without Sight Glass

▶ **See Figure 16**

On vehicles that are not equipped with sight glasses, it is necessary to feel the temperature difference in the inlet and outlet lines at the receiver/drier to gauge the refrigerant level. Use the following procedure:

1. Locate the receiver/drier. It will generally be up front near the condenser. It is shaped like a small fire extinguisher and will always have two lines connected to it. One line goes to the expansion valve and the other goes to the condenser.

2. With the engine and the air conditioner running, hold a line in each hand and gauge their relative temperatures. If they are the same approximate temperatures, the system is correctly charged.

3. If the line from the expansion valve to the receiver/drier is a lot colder than the line from the receiver/drier to the condenser, then the system is overcharged. It should be noted that this is an extremely rare condition.

4. If the line that leads from the receiver/drier to the condenser is a lot colder than the other line, the system is undercharged.

5. If the system is undercharged or overcharged, have it checked by a professional air conditioning mechanic.

OPERATE THE AIR CONDITIONER PERIODICALLY

Many problems can be avoided by simply running the air conditioner at least once a week, regardless of the season. Simply let the system run for at least five minutes a week (even in the winter), and you'll keep the internal parts lubricated as well as preventing the hoses from hardening.

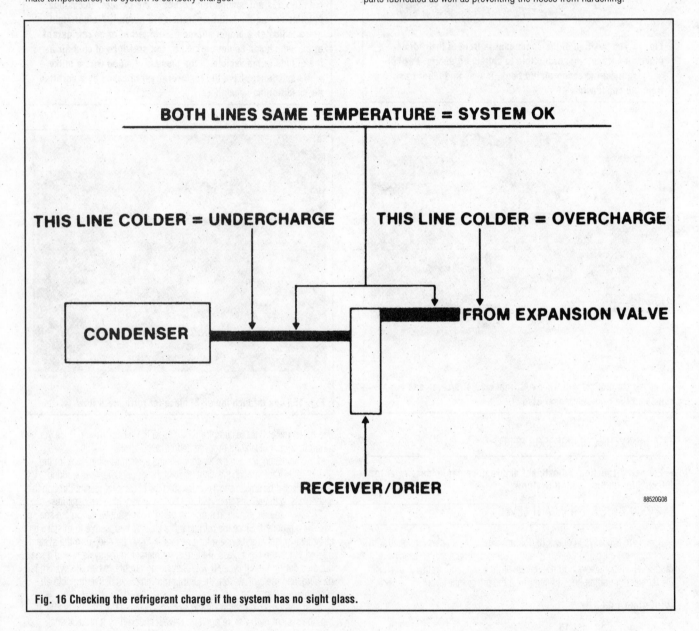

Fig. 16 Checking the refrigerant charge if the system has no sight glass.

AIR-CONDITIONING SYSTEM MAINTENANCE INTERVALS

Your car's air conditioning system will work efficiently if it is maintained at these intervals

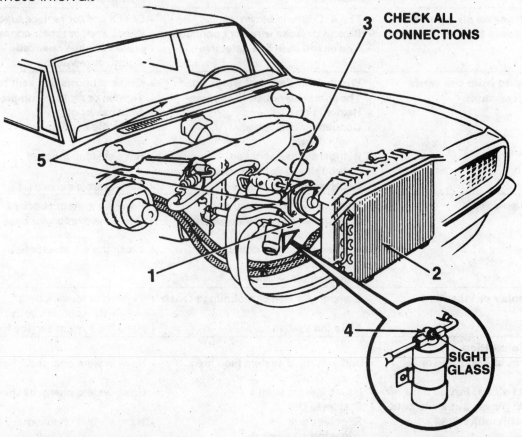

CHECK ALL CONNECTIONS

SIGHT GLASS

1. **Check/adjust drive belt***	**Every 1000 miles or 1 month**
2. **Check/clean condenser**	**Every 3000 miles or 3 months**
3. **Check for refrigerant leaks**	**Every 3000 miles or 3 months**
4. **Check refrigerant level**	**Every 3000 miles or 3 months**
5. **Operate compressor**	**Once a week for a few minutes (regardless of season)**

88520C01

TROUBLESHOOTING BASIC AIR CONDITIONING PROBLEMS

Most problems with the air conditioning system are best left to experts with the knowledge and proper equipment. There are, however, a number of problems that you can check out yourself.

Problem	Is Caused By	What to Do
There's little or no air coming from the vents (and you're sure it's on)	• The A/C fuse is blown • Broken or loose wires or connections • The on/off switch is defective	• Check and/or replace fuse • Check and/or repair connections • Have switches checked and/or replaced
The air coming from the vents is not cool enough	• Windows and air vent wings open • The compressor belt is slipping • Heater is on • Condenser is clogged with debris • Refrigerant has escaped through a leak in the system • Receiver/drier is plugged	• Close windows and vent wings • Tighten or replace compressor belt • Shut heater off • Clean the condenser • Have system checked • Have system serviced
The air has an odor	• Vacuum system is disrupted • Odor producing substances on the evaporator case • Condensation has collected in the bottom of the evaporator housing	• Have the system checked/repaired • Clean the evaporator case • Clean the evaporator housing drains
System is noisy or vibrating	• Compressor belt or mountings loose • Air in the system	• Tighten or replace belt; tighten mounting bolts • Have the system serviced

Sight glass condition
   Constant bubbles, foam or oil streaks
   Clear sight glass, but no cold air
   Clear sight glass, but air is cold
   Clouded with milky fluid
	• Undercharged system (see text)
	• No refrigerant at all
	• System is OK
	• Receiver/drier is leaking desiccant
		• Have system charged/checked
		• Have system charged/checked
		• Have system checked

Large difference in temperature of lines	• System undercharged	• Have system charged/checked

88520C02

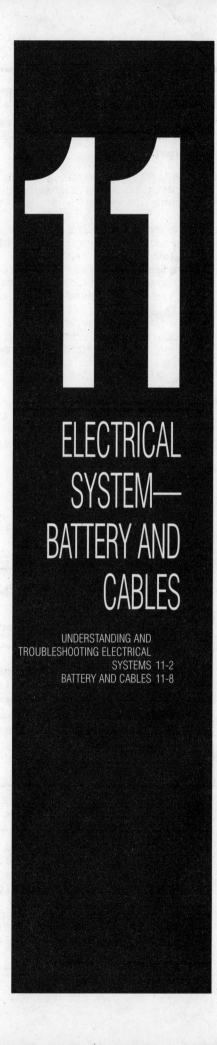

11

ELECTRICAL SYSTEM— BATTERY AND CABLES

UNDERSTANDING AND TROUBLESHOOTING ELECTRICAL SYSTEMS

Basic Electrical Theory

▶ See Figure 1

For any 12 volt, negative ground, electrical system to operate, the electricity must travel in a complete circuit. This simply means that current (power) from the positive terminal (+) of the battery must eventually return to the negative terminal (-) of the battery. Along the way, this current will travel through wires, fuses, switches and components. If, for any reason, the flow of current through the circuit is interrupted, the component fed by that circuit will cease to function properly.

Perhaps the easiest way to visualize a circuit is to think of connecting a light bulb (with two wires attached to it) to the battery—one wire attached to the negative (-) terminal of the battery and the other wire to the positive (+) terminal. With the two wires touching the battery terminals, the circuit would be complete and the light bulb would illuminate. Electricity would follow a path from the battery to the bulb and back to the battery. It's easy to see that with longer wires on our light bulb, it could be mounted anywhere. Further, one wire could be fitted with a switch so that the light could be turned on and off.

The normal automotive circuit differs from this simple example in two ways. First, instead of having a return wire from the bulb to the battery, the current travels through the frame of the vehicle. Since the negative (-) battery cable is attached to the frame (made of electrically conductive metal), the frame of the vehicle can serve as a ground wire to complete the circuit. Secondly, most automotive circuits contain multiple components which receive power from a single circuit. This lessens the amount of wire needed to power components on the vehicle.

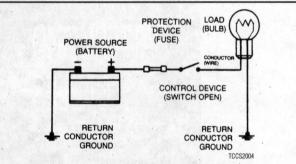

Fig. 1 This example illustrates a simple circuit. When the switch is closed, power from the positive (+) battery terminal flows through the fuse and the switch, and then to the light bulb. The light illuminates and the circuit is completed through the ground wire back to the negative (-) battery terminal. In reality, the two ground points shown in the illustration are attached to the metal frame of the vehicle, which completes the circuit back to the battery

HOW DOES ELECTRICITY WORK: THE WATER ANALOGY

Electricity is the flow of electrons—the subatomic particles that constitute the outer shell of an atom. Electrons spin in an orbit around the center core of an atom. The center core is comprised of protons (positive charge) and neutrons (neutral charge). Electrons have a negative charge and balance out the positive charge of the protons. When an outside force causes the number of electrons to unbalance the charge of the protons, the elctrons will split off the atom and look for another atom to balance out. If this imbalance is kept up, electrons will continue to move and an electrical flow will exist.

Many people have been taught electrical theory using an analogy with water. In a comparison with water flowing through a pipe, the electrons would be the water and the wire is the pipe.

The flow of electricity can be measured much like the flow of water through a pipe. The unit of measurement used is amperes, frequently abbreviated as amps (a). You can compare amperage to the volume of water flowing through a pipe. When connected to a circuit, an ammeter will measure the actual amount of current flowing through the circuit. When relatively few electrons flow through a circuit, the amperage is low. When many electrons flow, the amperage is high.

Water pressure is measured in units such as pounds per square inch (psi); The electrical pressure is measured in units called volts (v). When a voltmeter is connected to a circuit, it is measuring the electrical pressure.

The actual flow of electricity depends not only on voltage and amperage, but also on the resistance of the circuit. The higher the resistance, the higher the force necessary to push the current through the circuit. The standard unit for measuring resistance is an ohm Ω. Resistance in a circuit varies depending on the amount and type of components used in the circuit. The main factors which determine resistance are:

• Material—some materials have more resistance than others. Those with high resistance are said to be insulators. Rubber materials (or rubber-like plastics) are some of the most common insulators used in vehicles as they have a very high resistance to electricity. Very low resistance materials are said to be conductors. Copper wire is among the best conductors. Silver is actually a superior conductor to copper and is used in some relay contacts, but its high cost prohibits its use as common wiring. Most automotive wiring is made of copper.

• Size—the larger the wire size being used, the less resistance the wire will have. This is why components which use large amounts of electricity usually have large wires supplying current to them.

• Length—for a given thickness of wire, the longer the wire, the greater the resistance. The shorter the wire, the less the resistance. When determining the proper wire for a circuit, both size and length must be considered to design a circuit that can handle the current needs of the component.

• Temperature—with many materials, the higher the temperature, the greater the resistance (positive temperature coefficient). Some materials exhibt the opposite trait of lower resistance with higher temperatures (negative temperature coefficient). These principles are used in many of the sensors on the engine.

OHM'S LAW

There is a direct relationship between current, voltage and resistance. The relationship between current, voltage and resistance can be summed up by a statement known as Ohm's law.

Voltage (E) is equal to amperage (I) times resistance (R): $E = I \times R$
Other forms of the formula are $R = E/I$ and $I = E/R$

In each of these formulas, E is the voltage in volts, I is the current in amps and R is the resistance in ohms. The basic point to remember is that as the resistance of a circuit goes up, the amount of current that flows in the circuit will go down, if voltage remains the same.

The amount of work that the electricity can perform is expressed as power. The unit of power is the watt (w). The relationship between power, voltage and current is expressed as:

Power (W) is equal to amperage (I) times voltage (E): $W = I \times E$

This is only true for direct current (DC) circuits; The alternating current formula is a tad different, but since the electrical circuits in most vehicles are DC type, we need not get into AC circuit theory.

Electrical Components

POWER SOURCE

Power is supplied to the vehicle by two devices: The battery and the alternator. The battery supplies electrical power during starting or during periods when the current demand of the vehicle's electrical system exceeds the output capacity of the alternator. The alternator supplies electrical current when the engine is running. Just not does the alternator supply the current needs of the vehicle, but it recharges the battery.

The Battery

In most modern vehicles, the battery is a lead/acid electrochemical device consisting of six 2 volt subsections (cells) connected in series, so that the unit is capable of producing approximately 12 volts of electrical pressure. Each subsection consists of a series of positive and negative plates held a short distance apart in a solution of sulfuric acid and water.

The two types of plates are of dissimilar metals. This sets up a chemical reaction, and it is this reaction which produces current flow from the battery when its positive and negative terminals are connected to an electrical load. The power removed from the battery is replaced by the alternator, restoring the battery to its original chemical state.

The Alternator

On some vehicles there isn't an alternator, but a generator. The difference is that an alternator supplies alternating current which is then changed to direct current for use on the vehicle, while a generator produces direct current. Alternators tend to be more efficient and that is why they are used.

Alternators and generators are devices that consist of coils of wires wound together making big electromagnets. One group of coils spins within another set and the interaction of the magnetic fields causes a current to flow. This current is then drawn off the coils and fed into the vehicles electrical system.

GROUND

Two types of grounds are used in automotive electric circuits. Direct ground components are grounded to the frame through their mounting points. All other components use some sort of ground wire which is attached to the frame or chassis of the vehicle. The electrical current runs through the chassis of the vehicle and returns to the battery through the ground (-) cable; if you look, you'll see that the battery ground cable connects between the battery and the frame or chassis of the vehicle.

➡ **It should be noted that a good percentage of electrical problems can be traced to bad grounds.**

PROTECTIVE DEVICES

▶ **See Figure 2**

It is possible for large surges of current to pass through the electrical system of your vehicle. If this surge of current were to reach the load in the circuit, the surge could burn it out or severely damage it. It can also overload the wiring, causing the harness to get hot and melt the insulation. To prevent this, fuses, circuit breakers and/or fusible links are connected into the supply wires of the electrical system. These items are nothing more than a built-in weak spot in the system. When an abnormal amount of current flows through the system, these protective devices work as follows to protect the circuit:

• Fuse—when an excessive electrical current passes through a fuse, the fuse "blows" (the conductor melts) and opens the circuit, preventing the passage of current.

• Circuit Breaker—a circuit breaker is basically a self-repairing fuse. It will open the circuit in the same fashion as a fuse, but when the surge subsides, the circuit breaker can be reset and does not need replacement.

• Fusible Link—a fusible link (fuse link or main link) is a short length of special, high temperature insulated wire that acts as a fuse. When an excessive electrical current passes through a fusible link, the thin gauge wire inside the link melts, creating an intentional open to protect the circuit. To repair the circuit, the link must be replaced. Some newer type fusible links are housed in plug-in modules, which are simply replaced like a fuse, while older type fusible links must be cut and spliced if they melt. Since this link is very early in the electrical path, it's the first place to look if nothing on the vehicle works, yet the battery seems to be charged and is properly connected.

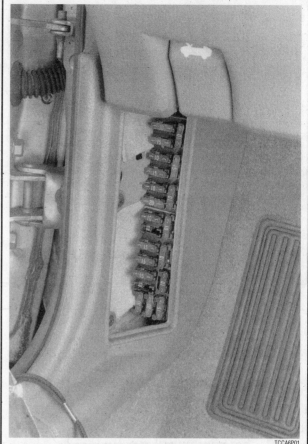

TCCA6P01

Fig. 2 Most vehicles use one or more fuse panels. This one is located on the driver's side kick panel

---

❋❋ CAUTION

Always replace fuses, circuit breakers and fusible links with identically rated components. Under no circumstances should a component of higher or lower amperage rating be substituted.

SWITCHES & RELAYS

▶ **See Figures 3 and 4**

Switches are used in electrical circuits to control the passage of current. The most common use is to open and close circuits between the battery and the various electric devices in the system. Switches are rated according to the amount of amperage they can handle. If a sufficient amperage rated switch is not used in a circuit, the switch could overload and cause damage.

Some electrical components which require a large amount of current to operate use a special switch called a relay. Since these circuits carry a large amount of current, the thickness of the wire in the circuit is also greater. If this large wire were connected from the load to the control switch, the switch would have to carry the high amperage load and the fairing or dash would be twice as large to accommodate the increased size of the wiring harness. To prevent these problems, a relay is used.

Relays are composed of a coil and a set of contacts. When the coil has a current passed though it, a magnetic field is formed and this field causes the contacts to move together, completing the circuit. Most relays are normally open, preventing current from passing through the circuit, but they can take any electrical form depending on the job they are intended to do. Relays can be considered "remote control switches." They allow a smaller

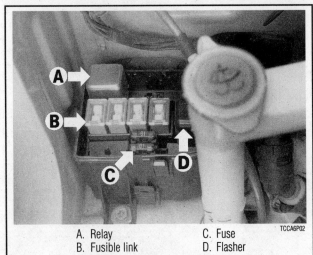

A. Relay   C. Fuse
B. Fusible link   D. Flasher

TCCA6P02

Fig. 3 The underhood fuse and relay panel usually contains fuses, relays, flashers and fusible links

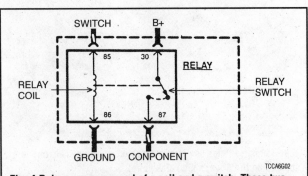

TCCA6G02

Fig. 4 Relays are composed of a coil and a switch. These two components are linked together so that when one operates, the other operates at the same time. The large wires in the circuit are connected from the battery to one side of the relay switch (B+) and from the opposite side of the relay switch to the load (component). Smaller wires are connected from the relay coil to the control switch for the circuit and from the opposite side of the relay coil to ground

current to operate devices that require higher amperages. When a small current operates the coil, a larger current is allowed to pass by the contacts. Some common circuits which may use relays are the horn, headlights, starter, electric fuel pump and other high draw ciruits.

LOAD

Every electrical circuit must include a "load" (something to use the electricity coming from the source). Without this load, the battery would attempt to deliver its entire power supply from one pole to another. This is called a "short circuit."All this electricity would take a short cut to ground and cause a great amount of damage to other components in the circuit by developing a tremendous amount of heat. This condition could develop sufficient heat to melt the insulation on all the surrounding wires and reduce a multiple wire cable to a lump of plastic and copper.

WIRING & HARNESSES

The average vehicle contains meters and meters of wiring, with hundreds of individual connections. To protect the many wires from damage and to keep them from becoming a confusing tangle, they are organized into bun-

dles, enclosed in plastic or taped together and called wiring harnesses. Different harnesses serve different parts of the vehicle. Individual wires are color coded to help trace them through a harness where sections are hidden from view.

Automotive wiring or circuit conductors can be either single strand wire, multi-strand wire or printed circuitry. Single strand wire has a solid metal core and is usually used inside such components as alternators, motors, relays and other devices. Multi-strand wire has a core made of many small strands of wire twisted together into a single conductor. Most of the wiring in an automotive electrical system is made up of multi-strand wire, either as a single conductor or grouped together in a harness. All wiring is color coded on the insulator, either as a solid color or as a colored wire with an identification stripe. A printed circuit is a thin film of copper or other conductor that is printed on an insulator backing. Occasionally, a printed circuit is sandwiched between two sheets of plastic for more protection and flexibility. A complete printed circuit, consisting of conductors, insulating material and connectors for lamps or other components is called a printed circuit board. Printed circuitry is used in place of individual wires or harnesses in places where space is limited, such as behind instrument panels.

Since automotive electrical systems are very sensitive to changes in resistance, the selection of properly sized wires is critical when systems are repaired. A loose or corroded connection or a replacement wire that is too small for the circuit will add extra resistance and an additional voltage drop to the circuit.

The wire gauge number is an expression of the cross-section area of the conductor. Vehicles from countries that use the metric system will typically describe the wire size as its cross-sectional area in square millimeters. In this method, the larger the wire, the greater the number. Another common system for expressing wire size is the American Wire Gauge (AWG) system. As gauge number increases, area decreases and the wire becomes smaller. An 18 gauge wire is smaller than a 4 gauge wire. A wire with a higher gauge number will carry less current than a wire with a lower gauge number. Gauge wire size refers to the size of the strands of the conductor, not the size of the complete wire with insulator. It is possible, therefore, to have two wires of the same gauge with different diameters because one may have thicker insulation than the other.

It is essential to understand how a circuit works before trying to figure out why it doesn't. An electrical schematic shows the electrical current paths when a circuit is operating properly. Schematics break the entire electrical system down into individual circuits. In a schematic, usually no attempt is made to represent wiring and components as they physically appear on the vehicle; switches and other components are shown as simply as possible. Face views of harness connectors show the cavity or terminal locations in all multi-pin connectors to help locate test points.

CONNECTORS

▶ **See Figures 5 and 6**

Three types of connectors are commonly used in automotive applications—weatherproof, molded and hard shell.

• Weatherproof—these connectors are most commonly used where the connector is exposed to the elements. Terminals are protected against moisture and dirt by sealing rings which provide a weathertight seal. All repairs require the use of a special terminal and the tool required to service it. Unlike standard blade type terminals, these weatherproof terminals cannot be straightened once they are bent. Make certain that the connectors are properly seated and all of the sealing rings are in place when connecting leads.

• Molded—these connectors require complete replacement of the connector if found to be defective. This means splicing a new connector assembly into the harness. All splices should be soldered to insure proper contact. Use care when probing the connections or replacing terminals in them, as it is possible to create a short circuit between opposite terminals. If this happens to the wrong terminal pair, it is possible to damage certain components. Always use jumper wires between connectors for circuit checking and NEVER probe through weatherproof seals.

• Hard Shell—unlike molded connectors, the terminal contacts in hard-shell connectors can be replaced. Replacement usually involves the use of

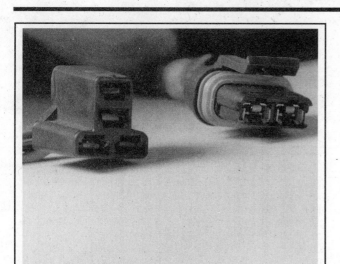

Fig. 5 Hard shell (left) and weatherproof (right) connectors have replaceable terminals

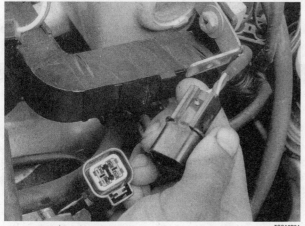

Fig. 6 Weatherproof connectors are most commonly used in the engine compartment or where the connector is exposed to the elements

a special terminal removal tool that depresses the locking tangs (barbs) on the connector terminal and allows the connector to be removed from the rear of the shell. The connector shell should be replaced if it shows any evidence of burning, melting, cracks, or breaks. Replace individual terminals that are burnt, corroded, distorted or loose.

Test Equipment

Pinpointing the exact cause of trouble in an electrical circuit is most times accomplished by the use of special test equipment. The following describes different types of commonly used test equipment and briefly explains how to use them in diagnosis. In addition to the information covered below, the tool manufacturer's instructions booklet (provided with the tester) should be read and clearly understood before attempting any test procedures.

JUMPER WIRES

✳✳ CAUTION

Never use jumper wires made from a thinner gauge wire than the circuit being tested. If the jumper wire is of too small a

gauge, it may overheat and possibly melt. Never use jumpers to bypass high resistance loads in a circuit. Bypassing resistances, in effect, creates a short circuit. This may, in turn, cause damage and fire. Jumper wires should only be used to bypass lengths of wire or to simulate switches.

Jumper wires are simple, yet extremely valuable, pieces of test equipment. They are basically test wires which are used to bypass sections of a circuit. Although jumper wires can be purchased, they are usually fabricated from lengths of standard automotive wire and whatever type of connector (alligator clip, spade connector or pin connector) that is required for the particular application being tested. In cramped, hard-to-reach areas, it is advisable to have insulated boots over the jumper wire terminals in order to prevent accidental grounding. It is also advisable to include a standard automotive fuse in any jumper wire. This is commonly referred to as a "fused jumper". By inserting an in-line fuse holder between a set of test leads, a fused jumper wire can be used for bypassing open circuits. Use a 5 amp fuse to provide protection against voltage spikes.

Jumper wires are used primarily to locate open electrical circuits, on either the ground (-) side of the circuit or on the power (+) side. If an electrical component fails to operate, connect the jumper wire between the component and a good ground. If the component operates only with the jumper installed, the ground circuit is open. If the ground circuit is good, but the component does not operate, the circuit between the power feed and component may be open. By moving the jumper wire successively back from the component toward the power source, you can isolate the area of the circuit where the open is located. When the component stops functioning, or the power is cut off, the open is in the segment of wire between the jumper and the point previously tested.

You can sometimes connect the jumper wire directly from the battery to the "hot" terminal of the component, but first make sure the component uses 12 volts in operation. Some electrical components, such as fuel injectors or sensors, are designed to operate on about 4 to 5 volts, and running 12 volts directly to these components will cause damage.

TEST LIGHTS

♦ See Figure 7

The test light is used to check circuits and components while electrical current is flowing through them. It is used for voltage and ground tests. To use a 12 volt test light, connect the ground clip to a good ground and probe wherever necessary with the pick. The test light will illuminate when voltage is detected. This does not necessarily mean that 12 volts (or any particular amount of voltage) is present; it only means that some voltage is present. It is

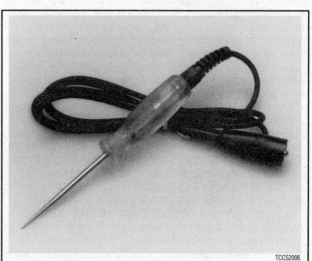

Fig. 7 A 12 volt test light is used to detect the presence of voltage in a circuit

advisable before using the test light to touch its ground clip and probe across the battery posts or terminals to make sure the light is operating properly.

✱✱ WARNING

Do not use a test light to probe electronic ignition, spark plug or coil wires. Never use a pick-type test light to probe wiring on computer controlled systems unless specifically instructed to do so. Any wire insulation that is pierced by the test light probe should be taped and sealed with silicone after testing.

Like the jumper wire, the 12 volt test light is used to isolate opens in circuits. But, whereas the jumper wire is used to bypass the open to operate the load, the 12 volt test light is used to locate the presence of voltage in a circuit. If the test light illuminates, there is power up to that point in the circuit; if the test light does not illuminate, there is an open circuit (no power). Move the test light in successive steps back toward the power source until the light in the handle illuminates. The open is between the probe and a point which was previously probed.

The self-powered test light is similar in design to the 12 volt test light, but contains a 1.5 volt penlight battery in the handle. It is most often used in place of a multimeter to check for open or short circuits when power is isolated from the circuit (continuity test).

The battery in a self-powered test light does not provide much current. A weak battery may not provide enough power to illuminate the test light even when a complete circuit is made (especially if there is high resistance in the circuit). Always make sure that the test battery is strong. To check the battery, briefly touch the ground clip to the probe; if the light glows brightly, the battery is strong enough for testing.

➡**A self-powered test light should not be used on any computer controlled system or component. The small amount of electricity transmitted by the test light is enough to damage many electronic automotive components.**

MULTIMETERS

Multimeters are an extremely useful tool for troubleshooting electrical problems. They can be purchased in either analog or digital form and have a price range to suit any budget. A multimeter is a voltmeter, ammeter and ohmmeter (along with other features) combined into one instrument. It is often used when testing solid state circuits because of its high input impedance (usually 10 megaohms or more). A brief description of the multimeter main test functions follows:

• Voltmeter—the voltmeter is used to measure voltage at any point in a circuit, or to measure the voltage drop across any part of a circuit. Voltmeters usually have various scales and a selector switch to allow the reading of different voltage ranges. The voltmeter has a positive and a negative lead. To avoid damage to the meter, always connect the negative lead to the negative (-) side of the circuit (to ground or nearest the ground side of the circuit) and connect the positive lead to the positive (+) side of the circuit (to the power source or the nearest power source). Note that the negative voltmeter lead will always be black and that the positive voltmeter will always be some color other than black (usually red).

• Ohmmeter—the ohmmeter is designed to read resistance (measured in ohms) in a circuit or component. Most ohmmeters will have a selector switch which permits the measurement of different ranges of resistance (usually the selector switch allows the multiplication of the meter reading by 10, 100, 1,000 and 10,000). Some ohmmeters are "auto-ranging" which means the meter itself will determine which scale to use. Since the meters are powered by an internal battery, the ohmmeter can be used like a self-powered test light. When the ohmmeter is connected, current from the ohmmeter flows through the circuit or component being tested. Since the ohmmeter's internal resistance and voltage are known values, the amount of current flow through the meter depends on the resistance of the circuit or component being tested. The ohmmeter can also be used to perform a continuity test for suspected open circuits. In using the meter for making continuity checks, do not be concerned with the actual resistance readings. Zero resistance, or any ohm reading, indicates continuity in the circuit. Infinite resistance indicates

an opening in the circuit. A high resistance reading where there should be none indicates a problem in the circuit. Checks for short circuits are made in the same manner as checks for open circuits, except that the circuit must be isolated from both power and normal ground. Infinite resistance indicates no continuity, while zero resistance indicates a dead short.

✱✱ WARNING

Never use an ohmmeter to check the resistance of a component or wire while there is voltage applied to the circuit.

• Ammeter—an ammeter measures the amount of current flowing through a circuit in units called amperes or amps. At normal operating voltage, most circuits have a characteristic amount of amperes, called "current draw" which can be measured using an ammeter. By referring to a specified current draw rating, then measuring the amperes and comparing the two values, one can determine what is happening within the circuit to aid in diagnosis. An open circuit, for example, will not allow any current to flow, so the ammeter reading will be zero. A damaged component or circuit will have an increased current draw, so the reading will be high. The ammeter is always connected in series with the circuit being tested. All of the current that normally flows through the circuit must also flow through the ammeter; if there is any other path for the current to follow, the ammeter reading will not be accurate. The ammeter itself has very little resistance to current flow and, therefore, will not affect the circuit, but it will measure current draw only when the circuit is closed and electricity is flowing. Excessive current draw can blow fuses and drain the battery, while a reduced current draw can cause motors to run slowly, lights to dim and other components to not operate properly.

Troubleshooting Electrical Systems

When diagnosing a specific problem, organized troubleshooting is a must. The complexity of a modern automotive vehicle demands that you approach any problem in a logical, organized manner. There are certain troubleshooting techniques, however, which are standard:

• Establish when the problem occurs. Does the problem appear only under certain conditions? Were there any noises, odors or other unusual symptoms? Isolate the problem area. To do this, make some simple tests and observations, then eliminate the systems that are working properly. Check for obvious problems, such as broken wires and loose or dirty connections. Always check the obvious before assuming something complicated is the cause.

• Test for problems systematically to determine the cause once the problem area is isolated. Are all the components functioning properly? Is there power going to electrical switches and motors. Performing careful, systematic checks will often turn up most causes on the first inspection, without wasting time checking components that have little or no relationship to the problem.

• Test all repairs after the work is done to make sure that the problem is fixed. Some causes can be traced to more than one component, so a careful verification of repair work is important in order to pick up additional malfunctions that may cause a problem to reappear or a different problem to arise. A blown fuse, for example, is a simple problem that may require more than another fuse to repair. If you don't look for a problem that caused a fuse to blow, a shorted wire (for example) may go undetected.

Experience has shown that most problems tend to be the result of a fairly simple and obvious cause, such as loose or corroded connectors, bad grounds or damaged wire insulation which causes a short. This makes careful visual inspection of components during testing essential to quick and accurate troubleshooting.

Testing

OPEN CIRCUITS

◆ **See Figure 8**

This test already assumes the existance of an open in the circuit and it is used to help locate the open portion.
  1. Isolate the circuit from power and ground.

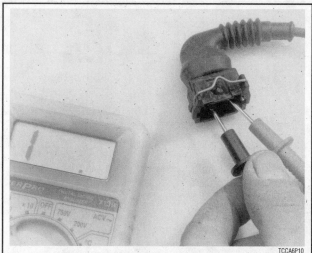

Fig. 8 The infinite reading on this multimeter (1 .) indicates that the circuit is open

2. Connect the self-powered test light or ohmmeter ground clip to the ground side of the circuit and probe sections of the circuit sequentially.

3. If the light is out or there is infinite resistance, the open is between the probe and the circuit ground.

4. If the light is on or the meter shows continuity, the open is bewtween the probe and the end of the circuit toward the power source.

SHORT CIRCUITS

➡Never use a self-powered test light to perform checks for opens or shorts when power is applied to the circuit under test. The test light can be damaged by outside power.

1. Isolate the circuit from power and ground.

2. Connect the self-powered test light or ohmmeter ground clip to a good ground and probe any easy-to-reach point in the circuit.

3. If the light comes on or there is continuity, there is a short somewhere in the circuit.

4. To isolate the short, probe a test point at either end of the isolated circuit (the light should be on or the meter should indicate continuity).

5. Leave the test light probe engaged and sequentially open connectors or switches, remove parts, etc. until the light goes out or continuity is broken.

6. When the light goes out, the short is between the last two circuit components which were opened.

VOLTAGE

This test determines voltage available from the battery and should be the first step in any electrical troubleshooting procedure after visual inspection. Many electrical problems, especially on computer controlled systems, can be caused by a low state of charge in the battery. Excessive corrosion at the battery cable terminals can cause poor contact that will prevent proper charging and full battery current flow.

1. Set the voltmeter selector switch to the 20V position.

2. Connect the multimeter negative lead to the battery's negative (-) post or terminal and the positive lead to the battery's positive (+) post or terminal.

3. Turn the ignition switch **ON** to provide a load.

4. A well charged battery should register over 12 volts. If the meter reads below 11.5 volts, the battery power may be insufficient to operate the electrical system properly.

VOLTAGE DROP

▶ **See Figure 9**

When current flows through a load, the voltage beyond the load drops. This voltage drop is due to the resistance created by the load and also by small resistances created by corrosion at the connectors and damaged insulation on the wires. The maximum allowable voltage drop under load is critical, especially if there is more than one load in the circuit, since all voltage drops are cumulative.

1. Set the voltmeter selector switch to the 20 volt position.

2. Connect the multimeter negative lead to a good ground.

3. Operate the circuit and check the voltage prior to the first component (load).

4. There should be little or no voltage drop in the circuit prior to the first component. If a voltage drop exists, the wire or connectors in the circuit are suspect.

5. While operating the first component in the circuit, probe the ground side of the component with the positive meter lead and observe the voltage readings. A small voltage drop should be noticed. This voltage drop is caused by the resistance of the component.

6. Repeat the test for each component (load) down the circuit.

7. If a large voltage drop is noticed, the preceding component, wire or connector is suspect.

Fig. 9 This voltage drop test revealed high resistance (low voltage) in the circuit

RESISTANCE

▶ **See Figures 10 and 11**

✱✱ WARNING

Never use an ohmmeter with power applied to the circuit. The ohmmeter is designed to operate on its own power supply. The normal 12 volt electrical system voltage could damage the meter!

1. Isolate the circuit from the vehicle's power source.

2. Ensure that the ignition key is **OFF** when disconnecting any components or the battery.

3. Where necessary, also isolate at least one side of the circuit to be checked, in order to avoid reading parallel resistances. Parallel circuit

TCCA6P08

Fig. 10 Checking the resistance of a coolant temperature sensor with an ohmmeter. Reading is 1.04 kilohms

resistances will always give a lower reading than the actual resistance of either of the branches.

4. Connect the meter leads to both sides of the circuit (wire or component) and read the actual measured ohms on the meter scale. Make sure the selector switch is set to the proper ohm scale for the circuit being tested, to avoid misreading the ohmmeter test value.

Wire and Connector Repair

Almost anyone can replace damaged wires, as long as the proper tools and parts are available. Wire and terminals are available to fit almost any need. Even the specialized weatherproof, molded and hard shell connectors are now available from aftermarket suppliers.

Be sure the ends of all the wires are fitted with the proper terminal hardware and connectors. Wrapping a wire around a stud is never a permanent solution and will only cause trouble later. Replace wires one at a time to avoid confusion. Always route wires exactly the same as the factory.

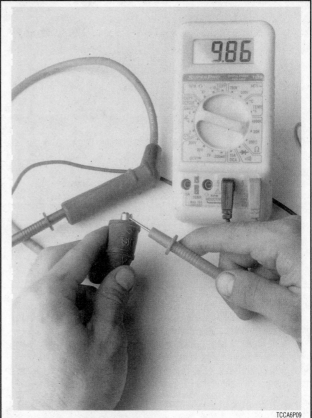

TCCA6P09

Fig. 11 Spark plug wires can be checked for excessive resistance using an ohmmeter

➡**If connector repair is necessary, only attempt it if you have the proper tools. Weatherproof and hard shell connectors require special tools to release the pins inside the connector. Attempting to repair these connectors with conventional hand tools will damage them.**

BATTERY AND CABLES

Battery Components

All batteries used in modern automotive applications are of the lead-acid storage type. Essentially, a lead-acid storage battery is an electro-chemical device for storing energy in chemical form so that this energy can be released as electricity when connected to an outside circuit. A battery can perform this operation repeatedly.

PLATE GRIDS

♦ See Figure 12

The plate grids are the vital elements of the battery, for they support the active material, and although they are not an active part in the production of electricity, they must be a good conductor to support the flow of electricity. There are two types of plates—positive plates and negative plates. The positive plates consist of a grid over which active lead peroxide is placed. This dark brown crystalline material has a high degree of porosity in order to allow the electrolyte to penetrate the plate freely. Negative plates are grids pasted with a type of lead referred to as sponge lead, which is simply finely ground lead. Grinding the lead allows the electrolyte to penetrate the grid.

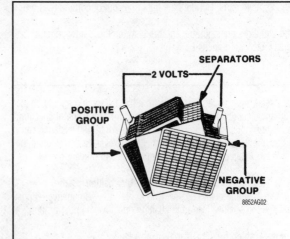

8852AG02

Fig. 12 Compound battery element or cell showing positive plates, negative plates, and separators

There may be any number of plates used in a battery; it all depends on how much energy you want to store. The more plates (or the larger the plates), the more energy the battery can store and release. The negative plates will always outnumber the positive plates by one for reasons of improved performance.

SEPARATORS

No positive plate may touch a negative plate, or all the plates in the cell will lose their stored energy. This is called a short (or short circuit). To prevent the plates from touching, thin sheets of non-conductive porous material called separators are used. These are placed between every positive and negative plate.

BATTERY ELEMENTS

▶ **See Figures 13, 14 and 15**

An element is the desired number of positive and negative plates placed together with a separator between each plate. The simplest unit you could construct would be a single positive plate and a single negative plate, kept apart by a porous separator. This would be a single element. If this element

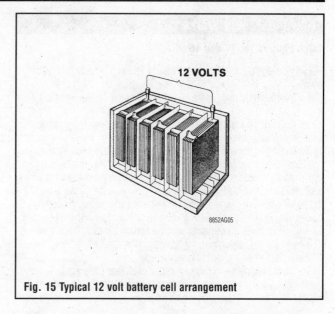

Fig. 15 Typical 12 volt battery cell arrangement

is put in a solution of sulfuric acid and water (electrolyte), a simple two-volt cell is formed. Electricity will flow if these plates are connected to an electrical load. When six of these cells are connected in series, a group or battery of cells is formed. This battery of cells will produce six times as much electrical pressure as a simple two-volt cell, or 12 volts.

ELECTROLYTE

Electrolyte is a mixture of sulfuric acid and water. Ordinarily, the electrolyte used in a fully charged battery contains about 25% sulfuric acid and 75% water. The strength or percentage of the sulfuric acid in the solution is measured by its specific gravity, that is, the density of the electrolyte versus the density of pure water. The specific gravity or electrolyte strength of a fully charged battery is in the range of 1.260–1.275. This means that its electrolyte is at least 1.260 times heavier than pure water. This is only true at 80°F (27°C) however. Above or below that temperature, the reading must be corrected to allow for the temperature. See the section on checking electrolyte level.

CONTAINERS & TERMINALS

Battery containers are simply tanks which hold all the various elements; plates, separators and electrolyte. Usually, the case is constructed of molded hard rubber or polypropylene (plastic). The containers are designed to withstand extremes of heat and cold, as well as shock. In addition, all containers have a series of bridges (usually four) on the bottom. The elements rest on these bridges, allowing a space for the active material to settle during the life of the battery.

The battery terminals are the external electrical connections. They are connected inside the battery to the positive plates (+ terminal) and the negative plates (- terminal). For years, the terminals were located on the top of the battery, and in many cases, still are. However, side terminal batteries have been developed to minimize or eliminate the problem of dirt, acid spray, or moisture corroding the terminals or cables.

COVERS & VENT CAPS

Most "maintenance-free" or "lifetime" batteries were designed to eliminate the need for periodic checking and addition of electrolyte. For this reason, most of these batteries are sealed (meaning they do not have removable covers or vent caps). Vent plugs or covers are used on older, conventional style batteries and on some newer "maintenance-free" units for a number of reasons. In addition to keeping impurities out of the battery, the vent plugs provide a convenient way to check and/or add electrolyte.

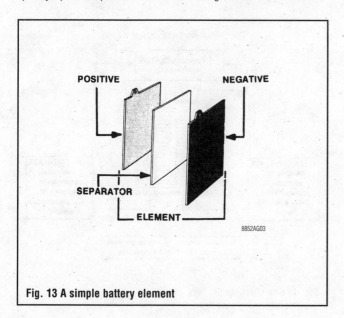

Fig. 13 A simple battery element

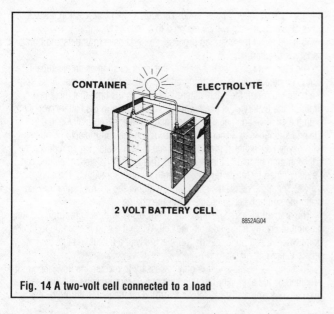

Fig. 14 A two-volt cell connected to a load

How the Battery Works

▶ See Figures 16, 17 and 18

Every storage battery used in an automobile has three essential functions:

1. To provide current for the starter and ignition system when cranking.

2. To provide current (in addition to alternator current) to operate the radio, lights, etc.

3. To act as a voltage stabilizer or reservoir in the electrical system.

While the first two functions are obvious, the third may require some explanation. To understand it, first consider the battery and alternator (or generator) as opposing forces. Current will flow from the greater force to the lesser force. For example, after running the starter motor, the battery will be discharged since some of the acid has been absorbed into the plates. If the vehicle is driven immediately, which is usually the case, current will flow back into the battery from the alternator. The voltage regulator will cut off the current when the battery is recharged.

The most important attribute of a lead-acid storage battery is its chemical reversibility. This means that unlike a dry cell battery, a storage battery is capable of being recharged by passing an electric current through it in

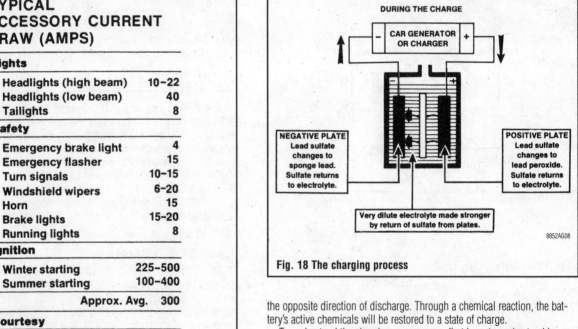

Fig. 17 The discharge process

Fig. 18 The charging process

TYPICAL ACCESSORY CURRENT DRAW (AMPS)

Lights	
Headlights (high beam)	10–22
Headlights (low beam)	40
Tailights	8
Safety	
Emergency brake light	4
Emergency flasher	15
Turn signals	10–15
Windshield wipers	6–20
Horn	15
Brake lights	15–20
Running lights	8
Ignition	
Winter starting	225–500
Summer starting	100–400
Approx. Avg.	300
Courtesy	
Cigarette lighter	15–20
Interior lights	10–15
Instrument panel lights	4
Entertainment	
Radio	10
Stereo Tape	10
Electric antenna	20
Comfort	
Air conditioner	10
Heater	20–30
Defroster	15–30
Electric seat	20
Electric windows	20–30

8852AG06

Fig. 16 Typical battery current draw

the opposite direction of discharge. Through a chemical reaction, the battery's active chemicals will be restored to a state of charge.

To understand the charging process, you first have to understand how a battery is discharged.

The discharge process in a battery is begun as soon as an electrical circuit is completed, such as turning on the vehicle lights. Current flows from the battery through the positive terminal. During the time that there is a drain on the battery (it is discharging), sulfuric acid in the battery works on both the positive and negative plates' active material, normally lead peroxide and sponge lead respectively. Hydrogen in the sulfuric acid combines with oxygen available at the positive plate to form water, which reduces the concentration of acid in the electrolyte. This is why the state of charge can be determined by measuring the strength (specific gravity) of the electrolyte. The more dense the solution, the higher the charge. The more like water the solution becomes, the lower the charge.

The amount of acid consumed by the plates is in direct proportion to the amount of energy removed from the cell. When the acid is used up to the point where it can no longer deliver electricity at a useful voltage, the battery is effectively discharged.

To recharge the battery, it is only necessary to reverse the flow of current provided by the alternator through the positive terminal and out the negative battery terminal. The sulfate that formed on the plates during discharge is changed back to sponge lead, and the sulfur returns to the electrolyte, forming sulfuric acid again. At the positive plate, the lead sulfate changes to lead peroxide and returns even more sulfuric acid to the electrolyte.

Battery Rating System

Under the battery rating system, there are two standards used to determine battery power. When purchasing a battery for a cold climate, Cold Cranking Amps (CCA) is the most important factor. In a warm climate, look for a higher Reserve Capacity (RC) rating.

The CCA rating is used for measuring battery-starting performance, and provides an approximate relationship between battery size and engine size. The most important factor is sizing the battery's CCA rating to meet or exceed, depending on the climate, the vehicle's OEM cranking requirement. As batteries age, they are less capable of producing cold cranking amps.

➡**When replacing a battery, you should always choose a battery with AT LEAST as high a CCA rating. It is usually a good idea to purchase a battery with a higher rating to assure proper vehicle starting.**

The reserve capacity rating is used for measuring electrical capacity. It shows how long (in minutes) the battery will operate the vehicle's electrical system in case of a charging system failure. The reserve capacity is the number of minutes a fully charged battery at 80°F (27°C) can be discharged at 25 amps until the voltage falls below 10.5 volts. For example, if your battery has a reserve capacity rating of 135, this means you have approximately 2 hours and 15 minutes to get to a service station before the battery "dies." If more reserve capacity is required, two or more 12-volt batteries can be connected in parallel.

Battery Maintenance

Difficulty in starting accounts for almost half of the service calls that the American Automobile Association (AAA) makes each year.

A survey by Champion Spark Plug Company indicated that roughly one third of all vehicles experienced one "can't start" condition in a given year.

When a vehicle won't start, most people blame the battery when, in fact, it may be that the battery has run down in a futile attempt to start a vehicle with other problems.

Battery output is affected by ambient temperatures; the battery becomes less efficient at low temperatures, while the power required to start the engine becomes greater. All this means that it pays to keep your battery in good shape, so that power is there when it's needed.

GENERAL MAINTENANCE

A battery that is not sealed must be checked periodically for electrolyte level. You cannot add water to a sealed maintenance-free battery (though not all maintenance-free batteries are sealed); however, a sealed battery must also be checked for proper electrolyte level, as indicated by the color of the built-in hydrometer "eye."

Always keep the battery cables and terminals free of corrosion. Check these components about every three months, or 3000 miles (4800 km). Refer to the removal, installation and cleaning procedures outlined in this section.

Keep the top of the battery clean, as a film of dirt can help completely discharge a battery that is not used for long periods. A solution of baking soda and water may be used for cleaning, but be careful to flush this off with clear water. DO NOT let any of the solution into the filler holes on non-sealed batteries. Baking soda neutralizes battery acid and will de-activate a battery cell.

Batteries in vehicles which are not operated on a regular basis can fall victim to parasitic loads (small current drains which are constantly drawing current from the battery). Normal parasitic loads may drain a battery on a vehicle that is in storage and not used for 6–8 weeks. Vehicles that have additional accessories such as a cellular telephone, an alarm system or other devices that increase parasitic load may discharge a battery sooner. If the vehicle is to be stored for 6–8 weeks in a secure area and the alarm

system, if present, is not necessary, the negative battery cable should be disconnected at the onset of storage to protect the battery charge.

Remember that constantly discharging and recharging will shorten battery life. Take care not to allow a battery to be needlessly discharged.

BATTERY FLUID

▶ **See Figure 19**

Check the battery electrolyte level at least once a month, or more often in hot weather or during periods of extended vehicle operation. On non-sealed batteries, the level can be checked either through the case on translucent batteries or by removing the cell caps on opaque-case types. The electrolyte level in each cell should be kept filled to the split ring inside each cell, or the line marked on the outside of the case.

If the level is low, add only distilled water through the opening until the level is correct. Each cell is separate from the others, so each must be checked and filled individually. Distilled water should be used, because the chemicals and minerals found in most drinking water are harmful to the battery and could significantly shorten its life.

If water is added in freezing weather, the vehicle should be driven several miles to allow the water to mix with the electrolyte. Otherwise, the battery could freeze.

Although some maintenance-free batteries have removable cell caps for access to the electrolyte, the electrolyte condition and level on all sealed maintenance-free batteries must be checked using the built-in hydrometer "eye." The exact type of eye varies between battery manufacturers, but most apply a sticker to the battery itself explaining the possible readings. When in doubt, refer to the battery manufacturer's instructions to interpret battery condition using the built-in hydrometer.

➡**Although the readings from built-in hydrometers found in sealed batteries may vary, a green eye usually indicates a properly charged battery with sufficient fluid level. A dark eye is normally an indicator of a battery with sufficient fluid, but one that may be low in charge. In addition, a light or yellow eye is usually an indication that electrolyte supply has dropped below the necessary level for battery (and hydrometer) operation. In this last case, sealed batteries with an insufficient electrolyte level must usually be discarded.**

TCCA1P08

Fig. 19 Add only distilled water to prolong battery life

Checking the Specific Gravity

▶ **See Figures 20, 21 and 22**

A hydrometer is required to check the specific gravity on all batteries that are not maintenance-free. On batteries that are maintenance-free, the spe-

Fig. 20 On non-maintenance free batteries with translucent cases, the electrolyte level can be viewed through the case; on other types (such as the one shown), the cell caps must be removed

Fig. 21 Check the specific gravity of the battery's electrolyte with a hydrometer

SPECIFIC GRAVITY (@ 80° F.) AND CHARGE

Specific Gravity Reading (use the minimum figure for testing)

Minimum	Battery Charge
1.260	100% Charged
1.230	75% Charged
1.200	50% Charged
1.170	25% Charged
1.140	Very Little Power Left
1.110	Completely Discharged

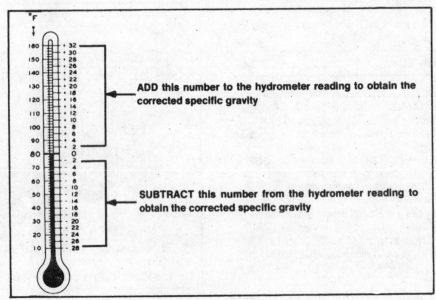

ADD this number to the hydrometer reading to obtain the corrected specific gravity

SUBTRACT this number from the hydrometer reading to obtain the corrected specific gravity

Fig. 22 The effects of temperature on specific gravity reading. Add or subtract, depending on temperature

cific gravity is checked by observing the built-in hydrometer "eye" on the top of the battery case. Check with your battery's manufacturer for proper interpretation of its built-in hydrometer readings.

✳✳ CAUTION

Battery electrolyte contains sulfuric acid. If you should splash any on your skin or in your eyes, flush the affected area with plenty of clear water. If it lands in your eyes, get medical help immediately.

The fluid (sulfuric acid solution) contained in the battery cells will tell you many things about the condition of the battery. Because the cell plates must be kept submerged below the fluid level in order to operate, maintaining the fluid level is extremely important. In addition, because the specific gravity of the acid is an indication of electrical charge, testing the fluid can be an aid in determining if the battery must be replaced. A battery in a vehicle with a properly operating charging system should require little maintenance, but careful, periodic inspection should reveal problems before they leave you stranded.

As stated earlier, the specific gravity of a battery's electrolyte level can be used as an indication of battery charge. At least once a year, check the specific gravity of the battery. It should be between 1.20 and 1.26 on the gravity scale. Most auto supply stores carry a variety of inexpensive battery testing hydrometers. These can be used on any non-sealed battery to test the specific gravity in each cell.

The battery testing hydrometer has a squeeze bulb at one end and a nozzle at the other. Battery electrolyte is sucked into the hydrometer until the float or pointer is lifted from its seat. The specific gravity is then read by noting the position of the float/pointer. If gravity is low in one or more cells, the battery should be slowly charged and checked again to see if the gravity has come up. Generally, if after charging, the specific gravity of any two cells varies more than 50 points (0.50), the battery should be replaced, as it can no longer produce sufficient voltage to guarantee proper operation.

CHECKING THE CHARGE ON MAINTENANCE-FREE BATTERIES

♦ See Figures 23 and 24

Although some maintenance-free batteries have removable cell caps for access to the electrolyte, the electrolyte condition and level on all sealed maintenance-free batteries must be checked using the built-in hydrometer "eye." The exact type of eye varies between battery manufacturers, but most apply a sticker to the battery itself explaining the possible readings. When

in doubt, refer to the battery manufacturer's instructions to interpret battery condition using the built-in hydrometer.

➡**Although the readings from built-in hydrometers found in sealed batteries may vary, a green eye usually indicates a properly charged battery with sufficient fluid level. A dark eye is normally an indicator of a battery with sufficient fluid, but one that may be low in charge. In addition, a light or yellow eye is usually an indication that electrolyte supply has dropped below the necessary level for battery (and hydrometer) operation. In this last case, sealed batteries with an insufficient electrolyte level must usually be discarded.**

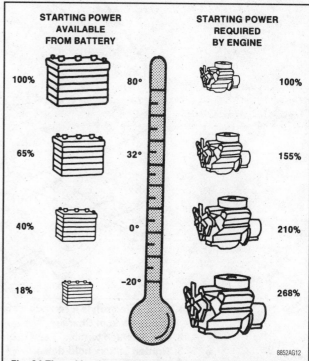

Fig. 24 The colder the weather, the healthier the battery has to be to provide sufficient starting power

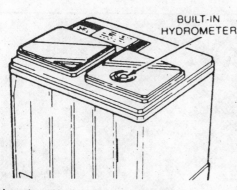

Location of indicator on sealed battery

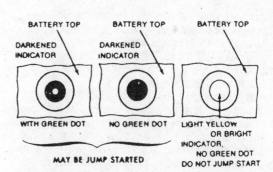

Check the appearance of the charge indicator on top of the battery before attempting a jump start; if it's not green or dark, do not jump start the car

Fig. 23 A typical sealed (maintenance-free) battery with a built-in hydrometer—note that the hydrometer eye may vary between manufacturers; always refer to the battery's label

BATTERY MAINTENANCE INTERVALS
Your car's battery will perform efficiently if it is maintained at these intervals.

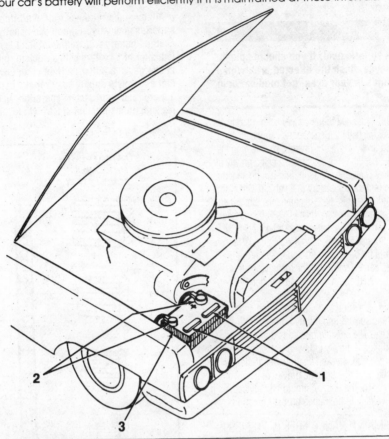

1. **Check electrolyte level/add water**	**Every month or 1000 miles**
Check State of Charge	
2. **Check/clean terminals and cables**	**Every 3 months or 3000 miles**
3. **Tighten battery hold-downs**	**As needed**

8852AC01

BATTERY TERMINALS

▶ **See Figures 25 thru 35**

Every 3 months or 3000 miles (4800 km), the battery terminals and cable clamps should be cleaned. Loosen the clamps and remove the cables, negative cable first. On batteries with top mounted posts, the use of a puller specially made for this purpose is recommended. These are inexpensive and available in most auto parts stores. Side terminal battery cables are secured with a small bolt.

Clean the cable clamps and the battery terminal with a wire brush, until all corrosion, grease, etc., is removed and the metal is shiny. It is especially important to clean the inside of the clamp thoroughly (a wire brush is useful here), since a small deposit of foreign material or oxidation there will prevent a sound electrical connection and inhibit either starting or charging. Special tools are available for cleaning these parts, one type for conventional top post batteries and another type for side terminal batteries. It is also a good idea to apply some dielectric grease to the terminal, as this will aid in the prevention of corrosion.

After the clamps and terminals are clean, reinstall the cables, negative cable last; DO NOT hammer the clamps onto battery posts. Tighten the clamps securely, but do not distort them. Give the clamps and terminals a thin external coating of grease after installation, to retard corrosion.

Check the cables at the same time that the terminals are cleaned. If the insulation is cracked or broken, or if its end is frayed, that cable should be replaced with a new one of the same length and gauge.

8852AP01

Fig. 25 On top post style batteries, clean the top of the case with a solution of baking soda and water, or with a spray-on battery cleaner

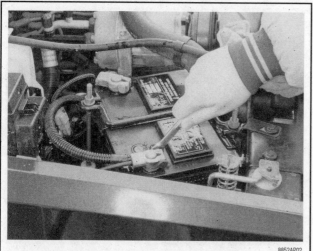

Fig. 26 On top post style batteries, loosen the terminal (cable clamp) retaining nut, then remove the terminal from the post

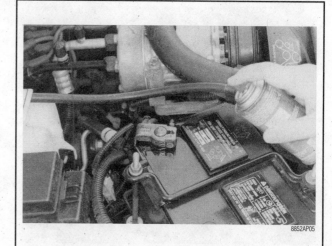

Fig. 29 Reinstall the cables and apply a liberal amount of petroleum jelly or battery terminal protectant spray to the terminals

Fig. 27 Clean the top post style terminal with a special tool. Use the pointed end of the brush to clean inside the terminal until it shines

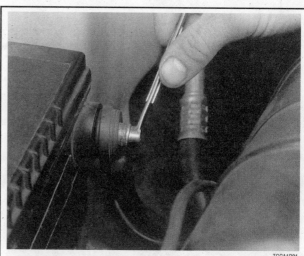

Fig. 30 On side terminal style batteries, loosen the terminal retaining bolt . . .

Fig. 28 With the other end of the tool, use a rotating motion to clean the post until it shines

Fig. 31 . . . then remove the terminal from the battery

Fig. 32 Use a wire brush to gently clean the cable terminal and retaining bolt . . .

Fig. 33 . . . along with the battery's terminal

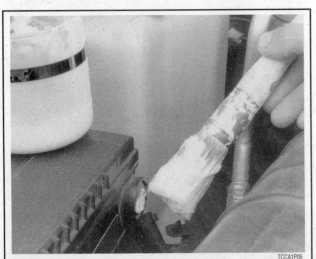

Fig. 34 Clean the battery's side terminals with a solution of baking soda and water, or with a spray-on battery cleaner

Fig. 35 A light coating of dielectric grease will help guard against corrosion

Replacing Battery Cables

Battery cables don't go bad very often, but like anything else, they can wear out. If the cables on your car are cracked, frayed or broken, they should be replaced.

When working on any electrical component on the vehicle, it is always a good idea to disconnect the negative (-) battery cable. This will prevent potential damage to many sensitive electrical components such as the Engine Control Module (ECM), radio, alternator, etc.

Replace the cables with one of the same length, or you will increase resistance and possibly cause hard starting. Smear the battery posts with a light film of petroleum jelly, or a battery terminal protectant spray once you've installed the new cables. If you replace the cables one at a time, you won't mix them up.

➡️Any time you disengage the battery cables, it is recommended that you disconnect the negative (-) battery cable first. This will prevent you from accidentally grounding the positive (+) terminal to the body of the vehicle when disconnecting it, thereby preventing damage to the electrical system.

Before you disconnect the cable(s), first turn the ignition to the **OFF** position. This will prevent a draw on the battery which could cause arcing (electricity trying to ground itself to the body of a vehicle, just like a spark plug jumping the gap) and, of course, damaging some components such as the alternator diodes. This will also prevent damage to the electronic control module.

When the battery cable(s) are reconnected (negative cable last), be sure to check that your lights, windshield wipers and other electrically operated safety components are all working correctly. If your vehicle contains an Electronically Tuned Radio (ETR), don't forget to also reset your radio stations. Ditto for the clock.

Jump Starting

◆ See Figure 36

Whenever a vehicle is jump started, precautions must be followed in order to prevent the possibility of personal injury. Remember that batteries contain a small amount of explosive hydrogen gas which is a by-product of battery charging. Sparks should always be avoided when working around batteries, especially when attaching jumper cables. To minimize the possibility of accidental sparks, follow the procedure carefully.

❋❋ CAUTION

NEVER hook the batteries up in a series circuit or the entire electrical system will go up in smoke, including the starter!

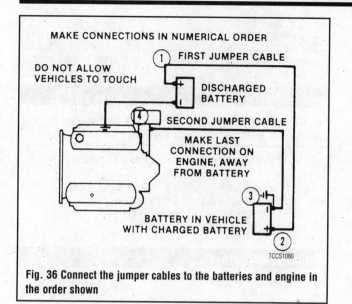

MAKE CONNECTIONS IN NUMERICAL ORDER

DO NOT ALLOW VEHICLES TO TOUCH

① **FIRST JUMPER CABLE**

DISCHARGED BATTERY

④ **SECOND JUMPER CABLE**

MAKE LAST CONNECTION ON ENGINE, AWAY FROM BATTERY

③

BATTERY IN VEHICLE WITH CHARGED BATTERY

②

TCCS1080

Fig. 36 Connect the jumper cables to the batteries and engine in the order shown

Vehicles equipped with a diesel engine may utilize two 12 volt batteries. If so, the batteries are connected in a parallel circuit (positive terminal to positive terminal, negative terminal to negative terminal). Hooking the batteries up in parallel circuit increases battery cranking power without increasing total battery voltage output. Output remains at 12 volts. On the other hand, hooking two 12 volt batteries up in a series circuit (positive terminal to negative terminal, positive terminal to negative terminal) increases total battery output to 24 volts (12 volts plus 12 volts).

JUMP STARTING PRECAUTIONS

- Be sure that both batteries are of the same voltage. Vehicles covered by this manual and most vehicles on the road today utilize a 12 volt charging system.
- Be sure that both batteries are of the same polarity (have the same terminal, in most cases NEGATIVE grounded).
- Be sure that the vehicles are not touching or a short could occur.
- On serviceable batteries, be sure the vent cap holes are not obstructed.
- Do not smoke or allow sparks anywhere near the batteries.
- In cold weather, make sure the battery electrolyte is not frozen. This can occur more readily in a battery that has been in a state of discharge.
- Do not allow electrolyte to contact your skin or clothing.

JUMPER CABLES

There are four things to consider when buying jumper cables:

Conductor (Cable)

Cables are usually made from copper, which minimizes power loss due to heating of the conductor, since copper has less resistance to electrical current (more resistance produces more heat). Aluminum is sometimes used, but the gauge size should be at least two numbers smaller to deliver the same power. The package should say "all copper conductor"; if not, push the insulation back to be sure it is copper.

The gauge (size) of the conductor is also important. The smaller the gauge numbers the larger the wire. A larger conductor will carry more current longer, without overheating.

Clamps

Check the feel of the clamps. They should resist twisting from side to side, have a strong spring and good gripping power. A higher amperage rating means the clamps will withstand more current.

Insulation

The conductor is insulated with vinyl or rubber to protect the user. Quality cables will retain their flexibility in sub-zero temperatures without cracking or breaking.

Length

Buy the shortest cables possible to safely do the job. Longer cables mean increased resistance and power loss, but they should be at least 8–10 feet to reach between two vehicles.

JUMP STARTING PROCEDURE

Single Battery Gasoline Engine Models

1. Make sure that the voltages of the 2 batteries are the same. Most batteries and charging systems are of the 12 volt variety.
2. Pull the jumping vehicle (with the good battery) into a position so the jumper cables can reach the dead battery and that vehicle's engine. Make sure that the vehicles do NOT touch.
3. Place the transmissions of both vehicles in **Neutral** (MT) or **P** (AT), as applicable, then firmly set their parking brakes.

➡**If necessary for safety reasons, the hazard lights on both vehicles may be operated throughout the entire procedure without significantly increasing the difficulty of jumping the dead battery.**

4. Turn all lights and accessories OFF on both vehicles. Make sure the ignition switches on both vehicles are turned to the **OFF** position.
5. Cover the battery cell caps with a rag, but do not cover the terminals.
6. Make sure the terminals on both batteries are clean and free of corrosion or proper electrical connection will be impeded. If necessary, clean the battery terminals before proceeding.
7. Identify the positive (+) and negative (-) terminals on both batteries.
8. Connect the first jumper cable to the positive (+) terminal of the dead battery, then connect the other end of that cable to the positive (+) terminal of the booster (good) battery.
9. Connect one end of the other jumper cable to the negative (-) terminal on the booster battery and the final cable clamp to an engine bolt head, alternator bracket or other solid, metallic point on the engine with the dead battery. Try to pick a ground on the engine that is positioned away from the battery in order to minimize the possibility of the 2 clamps touching should one loosen during the procedure. DO NOT connect this clamp to the negative (-) terminal of the bad battery.

✴✴ CAUTION

Be very careful to keep the jumper cables away from moving parts (cooling fan, belts, etc.) on both engines.

10. Check to make sure that the cables are routed away from any moving parts, then start the donor vehicle's engine. Run the engine at moderate speed for several minutes to allow the dead battery a chance to receive some initial charge.
11. With the donor vehicle's engine still running slightly above idle, try to start the vehicle with the dead battery. Crank the engine for no more than 10 seconds at a time and let the starter cool for at least 20 seconds between tries. If the vehicle does not start in 3 tries, it is likely that something else is also wrong or that the battery needs additional time to charge.
12. Once the vehicle is started, allow it to run at idle for a few seconds to make sure that it is operating properly.
13. Turn ON the headlights, heater blower and, if equipped, the rear defroster of both vehicles in order to reduce the severity of voltage spikes and subsequent risk of damage to the vehicles' electrical systems when the cables are disconnected. This step is especially important to any vehicle equipped with computer control modules.
14. Carefully disconnect the cables in the reverse order of connection. Start with the negative cable that is attached to the engine ground, then the

negative cable on the donor battery. Disconnect the positive cable from the donor battery and finally, disconnect the positive cable from the formerly dead battery. Be careful when disconnecting the cables from the positive terminals not to allow the alligator clips to touch any metal on either vehicle or a short and sparks will occur.

Dual Battery Diesel Models

▶ **See Figure 37**

Some diesel model vehicles utilize two 12 volt batteries, one on either side of the engine compartment. The batteries are connected in a parallel circuit (positive terminal to positive terminal and negative terminal to negative terminal). Hooking the batteries up in a parallel circuit increases battery cranking power without increasing total battery voltage output. The output will remain at 12 volts. On the other hand, hooking two 12 volt batteries in a series circuit (positive terminal to negative terminal and negative terminal to positive terminal) increases the total battery output to 24 volts (12 volts plus 12 volts).

✱✱ WARNING

Never hook the batteries up in a series circuit or the entire electrical system will be damaged, including the starter motor.

In the event that a dual battery vehicle needs to be jump started, use the following procedure:

1. Turn the heater blower motor **ON** to help protect the electrical system from voltage surges when the jumper cables are connected and disconnected.
2. Turn all lights and other switches **OFF**.

➡**The battery cables connected to one of the diesel vehicle's batteries may be thicker than those connected to its other battery. (The passenger side battery often has thicker cables.) This set-up allows relatively high jump starting current to pass without damage. If so, be sure to connect the positive jumper cable to the appropriate battery in the disabled vehicle. If there is no difference in cable thickness, connect the jumper cable to either battery's positive terminal. Similarly, if the donor vehicle also utilizes two batteries, the jumper cable connections should be made to the battery with the thicker cables; if there is no difference in thickness, the connections can be made to either donor battery.**

3. Connect the end of a jumper cable to one of the disabled diesel's positive (+) battery terminals, then connect the clamp at the other end of the same cable to the positive terminal (+) on the jumper battery.

4. Connect one end of the other jumper cable to the negative battery terminal (-) on the jumper battery, then connect the other cable clamp to an engine bolt head, alternator bracket or other solid, metallic point on the disabled vehicle's engine. DO NOT connect this clamp to the negative terminal (-) of the disabled vehicle's battery.

✱✱ CAUTION

Be careful to keep the jumper cables away from moving parts (cooling fan, belts, etc.) on both engines.

5. Start the engine on the vehicle with the good battery and run it at a moderate speed.
6. Start the engine of the vehicle with the discharged battery.
7. When the engine starts on the vehicle with the discharged battery, remove the cable from the engine block before disconnecting the cable from the positive terminal.

Battery Chargers

▶ **See Figures 38 and 39**

Before using any battery charger, consult the manufacturer's instructions for its use.

Battery chargers are electrical devices that change house Alternating Current (AC) to a lower voltage of Direct Current (DC) that can be used to charge an auto battery. There are two types of battery chargers—manual and automatic.

➡**On diesel-engine vehicles, do not operate the glow plug system while using an external battery charger to charge the battery.**

A manual battery charger must be physically disconnected when the battery has become fully charged. If not, the battery can be overcharged, and possibly fail. Excess charging current at the end of the charging cycle will heat the electrolyte, resulting in loss of water and active material, substantially reducing battery life. As a rule, on manual chargers, when the ammeter on the charger registers half the rated amperage of the charger, the battery is fully charged. This can vary, and it is recommended to use a hydrometer to accurately measure state of charge.

Automatic battery chargers have an important advantage—they can be left connected (for instance, overnight) without the possibility of overcharging the battery. Automatic chargers are equipped with a sensing device to allow the battery charge to taper off to near zero as the battery becomes fully charged. When charging a low or completely discharged battery, the meter will read close to full rated output. If only partially discharged, the initial reading may be less than full rated output, as the charger responds to the condition of the battery. As the battery continues to charge, the sensing device monitors the state of charge and reduces the charging rate. As the rate of charge tapers to zero amps, the charger will continue to supply a few milliamps of current—just enough to maintain a charged condition.

Battery and Charging Safety Precautions

Always follow these safety precautions when charging or handling a battery.

1. Wear eye protection when working around batteries. Batteries contain corrosive acid and produce explosive gas a byproduct of their operation. Acid on the skin should be neutralized with a solution of baking soda and water made into a paste. In case acid contacts the eyes, flush with clear water and seek medical attention immediately.
2. Avoid flame or sparks that could ignite the hydrogen gas produced by the battery and cause an explosion. Connection and disconnection of cables to battery terminals is one of the most common causes of sparks.
3. Always turn a battery charger off, before connecting or disconnecting the leads. When connecting the leads, connect the positive lead first, then the negative lead, to avoid sparks.
4. When lifting a battery, use a battery carrier or lift at opposite corners of the base.

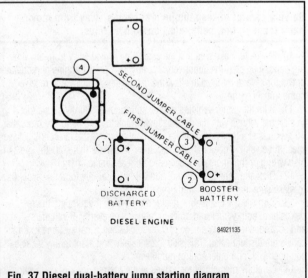

Fig. 37 Diesel dual-battery jump starting diagram

APPROXIMATE CHARGING TIME

Specific Gravity	Charger Rated Output		
Before Charging*	4 amps	6 amps	10 amps
1.250	———Charge at 2 amps or less———		
1.225	2-4 hrs	2-3 hrs	½-1 hr
1.200	5-7 hrs	3-5 hrs	1-2 hrs
1.175	8-10 hrs	5-7 hrs	2-4 hrs
1.150	10-14 hrs	6-8 hrs	3-5 hrs

*Temperature corrected—check with hydrometer

   NOTE: Due to condition temperature, etc. a given battery may require more or less time. This chart is only a guide. Check the state of charge periodically with a hydrometer.

8852AC05

Fig. 38 Battery charging time chart

Fig. 39 Typical battery charger hook-up with battery in the vehicle (negative ground vehicle). Connect the positive (+) cable to the battery and the negative (-) cable to a good engine ground

TCCA1P10

Fig. 40 After disconnecting the battery cables, unfasten the retaining bolt . . .

   5. Be sure there is good ventilation in a room where the battery is being charged.

   6. Do not attempt to charge or load-test a maintenance-free battery when the charge indicator dot is yellow or clear, or otherwise indicating insufficient electrolyte..

   7. Disconnect the negative battery cable if the battery is to remain in the vehicle during the charging process.

   8. Be sure the ignition switch is **OFF** before connecting or turning the charger ON. Sudden power surges can destroy electronic components.

   9. Use proper adapters to connect charger leads to side terminal batteries.

   10. When turning the charger **ON**, slowly increase the charge rate. If gassing or spewing occurs, turn the charger **OFF**.

Battery Replacement

▶ See Figures 40 thru 45

   When a battery finally dies (and it will not hold a charge), it is often very difficult to get the car and the battery to a shop to have a new battery installed. Usually, you wind up taking the old battery out of the vehicle and exchanging it for a new battery. Most stores will give a credit for the old battery.

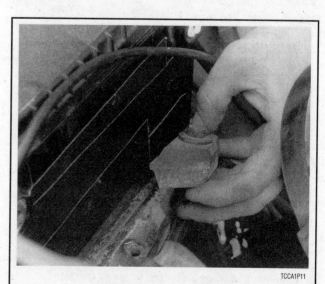

TCCA1P11

Fig. 41 . . . and remove the battery's hold-down clamp

→Always disconnect the ground cable (usually negative) first, and connect it last. This will eliminate a potentially "shocking experience."

1. Disconnect the battery terminals, as described earlier under Battery Maintenance. Be sure to use the correct method of terminal removal, depending on whether the battery has top posts or side terminals.

2. Unfasten the battery's hold-down clamp or hardware. Inspect the hold-down for damage, and replace if necessary.

→Some batteries are equipped with a strap type handle, which makes them easier to hold and maneuver.

3. Remove the battery from the vehicle and place it out of the way.

4. Clean the battery tray or compartment with a solution of baking soda and water. After removing any rust and/or flaking paint, you may want to spray on a coating of primer or paint to lessen any further decay.

5. Install the replacement battery and hold-down clamp or hardware. Be sure that the terminals face the correct direction and that the battery is securely positioned.

6. Clean the battery cable clamps (top post type) or terminals and retaining bolts (side terminal type) with the proper type of tool or wire brush. If installing a used battery, be sure that its top posts or side terminals are also clean.

7. Attach the positive cable (the one running to the starter or relay) to the battery's positive (+) post or terminal, then attach the negative cable to the battery's negative (-) post or terminal. Gently tighten the cable clamp nuts (top post type) or terminal retaining bolts (side terminal type).

8. Treat each battery terminal and cable clamp/retaining bolt with a light coating of petroleum jelly or a protective spray to retard corrosion.

Fig. 44 . . . and apply a solution of baking soda and water . . .

Fig. 42 Lift the battery from the vehicle. Be sure to use the strap handle, if so equipped

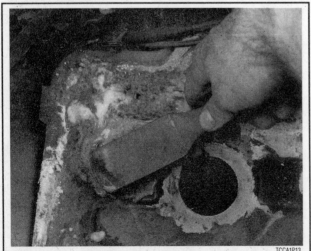

Fig. 43 Before installing the battery, scrape off any loose deposits from the battery tray . . .

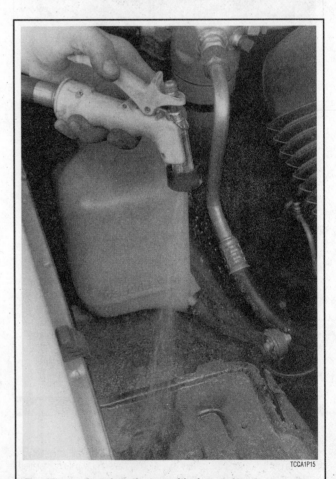

Fig. 45 . . . then rinse the tray with clean water

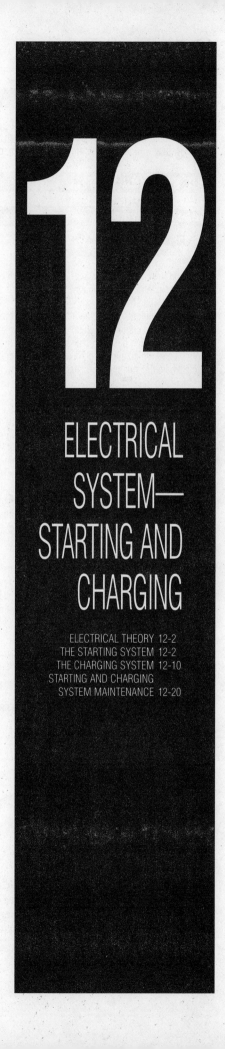

12

ELECTRICAL SYSTEM— STARTING AND CHARGING

ELECTRICAL THEORY

The first step in understanding a vehicle's starting and charging systems is to learn about basic electricity. For more information on electrical circuits, how they work and how to troubleshoot them, please refer to the information on "Understanding and Troubleshooting Electrical Systems" elsewhere in this manual.

THE STARTING SYSTEM

General Information

▶ **See Figures 1, 2, 3 and 4**

The starting system includes the battery, starter motor, solenoid, ignition switch, and in some cases, a starter relay. An inhibitor (neutral safety) switch is included in the starting system circuit to prevent the vehicle from being started while in gear.

When the ignition key is turned to the **START** position, current flows and energizes the starter's solenoid coil. The energized coil becomes an electromagnet which pulls the plunger into the coil, the plunger closes a set of contacts which allow high current to reach the starter motor. On models where the solenoid is mounted on the starter, the plunger also serves to push the starter pinion to mesh with the teeth on the flywheel/flexplate.

To prevent damage to the starter motor when the engine starts, the pinion gear incorporates an over-running (one-way) clutch which is splined to the starter armature shaft. The rotation of the running engine may speed the rotation of the pinion but not the starter motor itself.

The starting of the engine signals the driver to release the ignition key from the start position, stopping the flow of current to the solenoid or relay. The plunger is pulled out of contact with the battery-to-starter cables by a coil spring, and the flow of electricity is interrupted to the starter. This weakens the magnetic fields and the starter ceases its rotation. As the solenoid plunger is released, its movement also pulls the starter drive gear from its engagement with the engine flywheel.

Some starting systems employ a starter relay in addition to the solenoid. This relay may be located under the instrument panel, in the kick panel or in the fuse/relay center under the hood. This relay is used to reduce the amount of current the starting (ignition) switch must carry.

There may be one other component included in the starting system; on vehicles with automatic transmissions, a neutral safety switch (often referred to by many various names by the different manufacturers, such as: transmission range sensor, neutral safety switch, park/neutral switch, etc.) on the side of the transmission is wired to the relay or solenoid. Its function is to prevent activation of the starter (by creating an open circuit) when the transmission is in any gear other than **P** (park) or **N** (neutral). The vehicle can only be started in **P** or **N**. Most manual transmission vehicles have a clutch switch to prevent starting the vehicle unless the clutch is depressed.

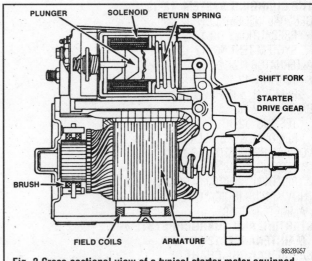

Fig. 2 Cross-sectional view of a typical starter motor equipped with a starter mounted solenoid

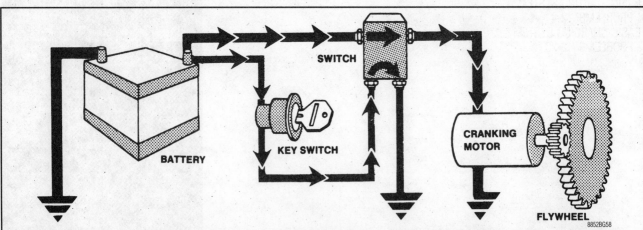

Fig. 1 A typical starting system converts electrical energy into mechanical energy to turn the engine. The components are: Battery, to provide electricity to operate the starter; Ignition switch, to control the energizing of the starter relay or solenoid; Starter relay or solenoid, to make and break the circuit between the battery and starter; Starter, to convert electrical energy into mechanical energy to rotate the engine; Starter drive gear, to transmit the starter rotation to the engine flywheel

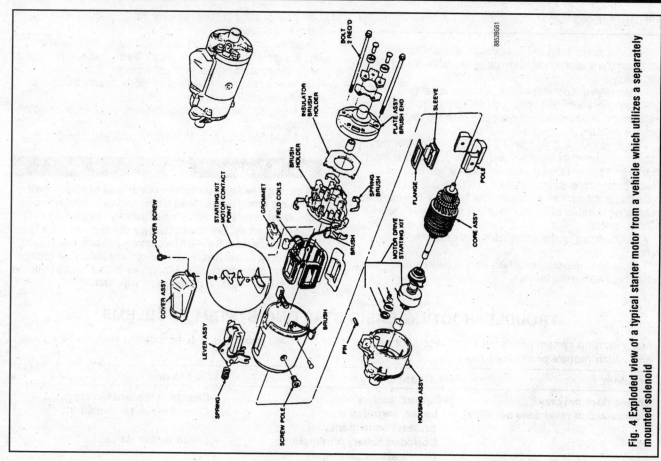

Fig. 4 Exploded view of a typical starter motor from a vehicle which utilizes a separately mounted solenoid

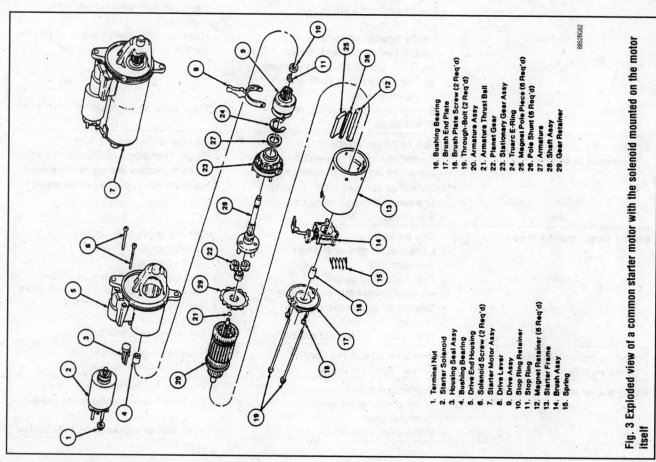

1. Terminal Nut
2. Starter Solenoid
3. Housing Seal Assy
4. Bushing Bearing
5. Drive End Housing
6. Solenoid Screw (2 Req'd)
7. Starter Motor Assy
8. Drive Lever
9. Drive Assy
10. Stop Ring Retainer
11. Stop Ring
12. Magnet Retainer (6 Req'd)
13. Starter Frame
14. Brush Assy
15. Spring
16. Bushing Bearing
17. Brush End Plate
18. Brush Plate Screw (2 Req'd)
19. Through-Bolt (2 Req'd)
20. Armature Assy
21. Armature Thrust Ball
22. Planet Gear
23. Stationary Gear Assy
24. Truarc E-Ring
25. Magnet Pole Piece (6 Req'd)
26. Pole Shunt (6 Req'd)
27. Armature
28. Shaft Assy
29. Gear Retainer

Fig. 3 Exploded view of a common starter motor with the solenoid mounted on the motor itself

PRECAUTIONS

To prevent damage to the on-board computer, alternator and regulator, the following precautionary measures must be taken when working with the electrical system.
- Wear safety glasses when working on or near the battery.
- Don't wear a watch with a metal band when servicing the battery. Serious burns can result if the band completes the circuit between the positive battery terminal and ground.
- Be absolutely sure of the polarity of a booster battery before making connections. Connect the cables positive to positive, and negative to negative. Connect positive cables first and then make the last connection to ground on the body of the booster vehicle so that arcing cannot ignite hydrogen gas that may have accumulated near the battery. Even momentary connection of a booster battery with the polarity reversed will damage the alternator diodes.
- Disconnect both vehicle battery cables before attempting to charge a battery.
- Be cautious when using metal tools around a battery to avoid creating a short circuit between the terminals.
- When installing a battery, make sure that the positive and negative cables are not reversed.
- When jump-starting the car, be sure that like terminals are connected. This also applies to using a battery charger. Reversed polarity will burn out the alternator and regulator in a matter of seconds.
- Never operate the alternator with the battery disconnected or on an otherwise uncontrolled open circuit.
- Always disconnect the battery ground cable before disconnecting the alternator lead.
- Always disconnect the battery (negative cable first) when charging it.

System Testing

➡A good quality digital multimeter with at least 10 megohm/volt impedance should be used when testing modern automotive circuits. These meters can accurately detect very small amounts of voltage, current and resistance. This type of meter also has a high internal resistance that will not load the circuit being tested. Loading the circuit causes inaccurate readings, and may cause damage to sensitive computer circuits. Although we are not testing computer circuits in this section, accuracy is very important.

TROUBLESHOOTING BASIC STARTING SYSTEM PROBLEMS

Many starting system problems are the result of neglect. This chart will show you which problems you can fix yourself and which require professional service.

Problem	Is Caused by	What to do
Engine does not crank (Solenoid or relay does not click)	• "Dead" battery • Loose, corroded or broken connections • Corroded battery terminals (lights will usually light) • Faulty ignition switch • Faulty neutral safety switch or clutch switch (To test: push on brake pedal, hold key in start position and move shift lever or clutch pedal) • Defective starter switch, relay or solenoid.	• Charge or replace battery • Clean or repair connections • Clean terminals • Have ignition switch checked/replaced • Have neutral safety switch or clutch switch checked or replaced • Have defective component replaced
Engine will not crank (Solenoid or relay clicks)	• Low or "dead" battery • Corroded battery terminals or cables • Defective starter solenoid or relay • Defective starter motor (if current is passed through relay or solenoid)	• Charge or replace battery • Clean or replace terminals or cables • Have defective component replaced • Have starter replaced or overhauled
Starter motor cranks slowly	• Low battery • Loose, corroded or broken connections • Cable size too small • Internal starter motor problems • Engine oil too heavy • Ignition timing too far advanced	• Charge or replace battery • Clean, repair or replace connections • Replace with proper size cable • Have starter replaced or overhauled • Use proper oil viscosity for temperature • Set timing to specifications
Starter spins, but will not crank engine	• Broken starter drive gear • Broken flywheel teeth	• Have drive gear replaced • Have flywheel checked
Noisy starter motor	• Starter mounting loose • Worn starter drive gear or flywheel teeth • Worn starter bushings	• Tighten mounting bolts • Have starter or flywheel checked • Have starter replaced or overhauled

8852BC01

WITH STARTER MOUNTED SOLENOID

◆ **See Figures 5 and 6**

1. Check the battery and clean the connections as follows:

a. If the battery cells have removable caps, check the water level. Add distilled water if low. Load test the battery and charge if necessary. See Battery Testing in this section for the procedure.

b. Remove the cables and clean them with a wire brush. Reconnect the cables.

2. Check the starter motor ground circuit with a voltage drop test as follows:

a. Set the meter to read DC voltage on the lowest possible scale.

b. Connect the negative lead of your multimeter to the negative terminal of the battery.

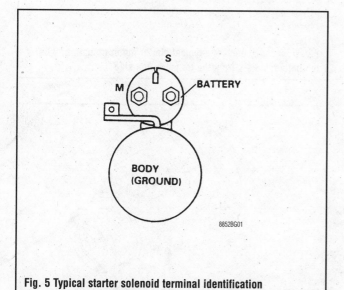

Fig. 5 Typical starter solenoid terminal identification

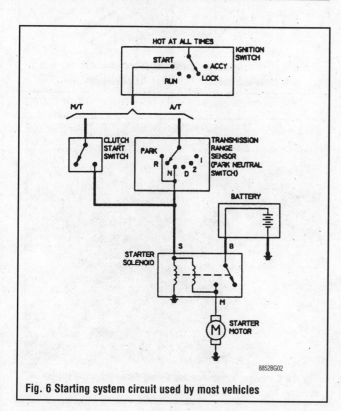

Fig. 6 Starting system circuit used by most vehicles

c. Connect the positive lead to the body of the starter. Make sure the starter mounting bolts are tight. The meter should read 0.2 volts or less. If the voltage reading is greater, remove and clean the negative battery connection on the engine block. The voltage reading should now be within specification: if not, replace the negative battery cable.

3. Check the motor feed circuit with a voltage drop test as follows:

a. Disconnect the coil wire or the fuel injector harness to prevent the engine from starting.

b. Connect the positive lead of your meter to the positive terminal of the battery.

c. Connect the negative meter lead to the motor feed terminal. The motor feed terminal comes out of the body of the starter motor and connects to the solenoid.

d. Turn the ignition key to the **START** position. The meter should read 0.2 volts or less. If the voltage reading is greater, remove and clean the positive battery connection on the starter solenoid. The voltage reading should now be within specification, if not replace the positive battery cable.

e. Connect the coil wire or fuel injector harness.

4. Check for battery voltage at the **S** terminal on the starter solenoid as follows:

a. Disconnect the coil wire or the fuel injector harness to prevent the engine from possible starting.

b. Set the meter to read battery voltage. Move it to the next higher range if set on the 2 volt scale.

c. Connect the positive lead to the **S** terminal on the starter solenoid and the negative lead to a good ground.

d. Turn the ignition key to the **START** position and crank the engine. The meter should read battery voltage. If battery voltage is not present, check the inhibitor (neutral safety) switch, fuse(s) and wiring between the ignition switch and starter solenoid. If battery voltage is present at the **S** terminal on the solenoid and the starter does not operate, replace the starter and solenoid assembly.

e. Connect the coil wire or fuel injector harness.

WITH EXTERNAL SOLENOID

➡**Not all solenoids are mounted on the starter motor. Some models use a solenoid (relay) mounted on the inner fender or firewall. Both types of solenoids serve to make the connection between the battery and starter motor. Trace the wires for positive identification. The small wire comes from the ignition switch, one large cable from the battery and the other large cable to the starter. The terminals are S, B and M respectively.**

1. Check the battery and clean the connections as follows:

a. If the battery cells have removable caps, check the water level. Add distilled water if low. Load test the battery and charge if necessary. See Battery Testing in this section for the procedure.

✳✳ CAUTION

Alway remove the negative battery cable first, and install it last.

b. Remove the cables and clean them with a wire brush. Disconnect and clean the cables on the solenoid in the same manner. Reconnect the cables on the solenoid, then the battery.

2. Check the starter motor ground circuit with a voltage drop test as follows:

a. Set the meter to read DC voltage on the lowest possible scale.

b. Connect the negative lead of your multimeter to the negative terminal of the battery.

c. Connect the positive lead to the body of the starter. Make sure the starter mounting bolts are tight. The meter should read 0.2 volts or less. If the voltage reading is greater, remove and clean the negative battery connection on the engine block. The voltage reading should now be within specification; if not, replace the negative battery cable.

3. Check the motor feed circuit with a voltage drop test as follows:

a. Disconnect the coil wire or the fuel injector harness to prevent the engine from starting.

b. Connect the positive lead of your meter to the positive terminal of the battery.

c. Connect the negative meter lead to the motor feed terminal at the starter. This is the heavy cable on the starter. Turn the ignition key to the **START** position and crank the engine. The meter should read 0.2 volts or less. If the voltage reading is greater, remove and clean the positive battery connections on the starter and solenoid. The voltage reading should now be within specification; if not, replace the positive battery cable.

d. Connect the coil wire or fuel injector harness.

4. Check for battery voltage at the **S** terminal on the starter solenoid as follows:

a. Disconnect the coil wire or the fuel injector harness to prevent the engine from starting.

b. Set the meter to read battery voltage. Move it to next higher range, if previously set on the 2 volt scale.

c. Connect the positive lead to the **S** terminal on the starter solenoid and the negative lead to a good ground.

d. Turn the ignition key to the **START** position. The meter should read battery voltage. If battery voltage is not present, check the inhibitor (neutral safety) switch, fuse(s) and wiring between the ignition switch and starter solenoid. If battery voltage is present at the **S** and **B** terminals but not at the motor feed terminal, replace the solenoid. If battery voltage is present at all three terminals and the starter does not operate, replace the starter motor.

e. Connect the coil wire or fuel injector harness.

Starter Motor

REMOVAL & INSTALLATION

▶ **See Figures 7 thru 13**

1. Disconnect the negative battery cable.

2. Remove all components necessary to gain access to the starter motor (such as exhaust pipes, air intake ducts, hoses, brackets and heat shields)

3. If equipped, remove any wiring covers from the starter motor, then disconnect the wiring from the starter. In some cases, the wiring may be more accessible after removing the mounting bolts and moving the starter.

4. Remove the starter mounting bolts, if not already done.

5. Remove the starter assembly from the vehicle. In some cases, the starter will have to be turned to a different angle to clear obstructions. Don't

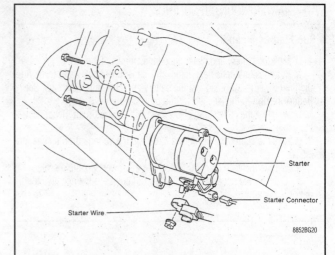

Fig. 8 Exploded view of a typical starter motor mounting, with the bolts installed from the transmission side

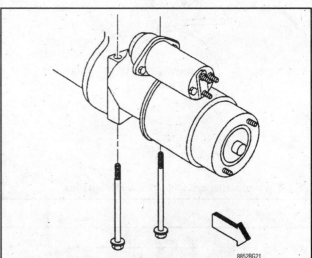

Fig. 9 Exploded view of a typical starter motor mounting, with the bolts installed from the bottom of the starter motor

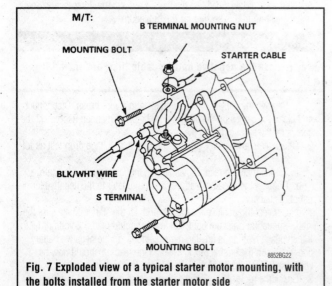

Fig. 7 Exploded view of a typical starter motor mounting, with the bolts installed from the starter motor side

Fig. 10 If equipped, remove the wiring cover from the starter motor . . .

Fig. 11 . . . then loosen the starter motor wiring terminal fasteners

Fig. 12 Label and disengage the wiring harnesses from the starter motor, carefully positioning them out of the way

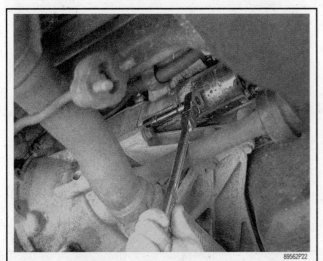

Fig. 13 Loosen the starter motor mounting bolts, then remove the motor from the vehicle

loose any shims that may fall out from between the starter and the mounting boss, they will need to be returned to their original position when installing the starter. The shims are used to adjust the clearance between the starter pinion and flywheel/flexplate teeth.

To install:

6. If necessary, measure and adjust the pinion-to-ring gear clearance.

7. Position the shim (if any) and the starter motor on the mounting boss. Tighten the mounting bolts securely.

8. Connect the wiring, if not already done.

9. Install any components that were removed to gain access to the starter.

10. Connect the negative battery cable.

ADJUSTMENTS

Starter Pinion Depth

♦ See Figures 14 and 15

➥This procedure is used to diagnose starter noise caused by incorrect clearance between the starter pinion and flywheel while the starter is engaged.

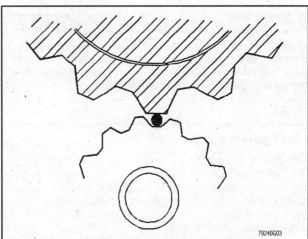

Fig. 14 Use a wire gauge (black dot) to measure the clearance between the tip of the flywheel tooth (top gear) to the bottom of the pinion teeth (bottom gear)

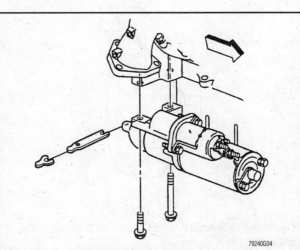

Fig. 15 To adjust the pinion clearance, shims are placed between the starter motor mounting surface on the engine and the starter motor

1. Raise and safely support the front of the vehicle securely.
2. Remove the flywheel cover.
3. Inspect the flywheel for chipped or missing teeth, abnormal wear, cracks and warpage. Replace the damaged component, if any, and continue with the procedure.
4. Make sure the vehicle is in Park or Neutral. Apply the parking brake.
5. Have an assistant slowly and smoothly rotate the crankshaft in the normal direction of rotation.
6. Slowly move a piece of chalk toward the edge of the flywheel until it just touches, which will highlight the high spot of the ring gear.
7. Disconnect the negative battery cable.
8. Turn the high spot of the flywheel to the area of the starter drive pinion.
9. Using a wire gauge, measure the clearance between the tip of the ring gear tooth and the bottom of the pinion gear teeth. Clearance should generally be 0.02–0.06 in. (0.5–1.5mm).
10. Add or remove shims to adjust the clearance, if needed.
11. Install the flywheel cover.
12. Lower the vehicle to the floor.
13. Connect the negative battery cable.

Generally, add shims if the starter whines after the engine starts, and remove shims if the starter whines only during cranking.

Starter Relay

→The starter relay is usually located in the fuse/relay panel. Depending on the manufacturer, it may be in the engine compartment, under the dash or behind a kick panel. Refer to the owner's manual for the location of the fuse/relay box.

TESTING

♦ See Figures 16 and 17

1. Turn the ignition **OFF**.
2. Remove the relay.
3. Locate the two terminals on the relay which are connected to the coil windings. Check the relay coil for continuity. Connect the negative meter lead to terminal **85** and positive meter lead to terminal **86**. There should be continuity. If not, replace the relay.
4. Check the operation of the internal relay contacts, as follows:

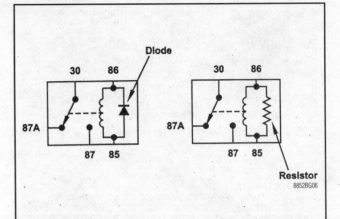

Fig. 17 Terminal identification of the most common types of relays. Diodes and resistors in the relay prevent voltage spikes, induced when the current is removed from the coil, from damaging electronic components

a. Connect the meter leads to terminals **30** and **87**. Meter polarity does not matter for this step.
b. Apply positive battery voltage to terminal **86** and ground to terminal **85**. The relay should click as the contacts are drawn toward the coil and the meter should indicate continuity. Replace the relay if your results are different.

Solenoid

TESTING

♦ See Figures 18 and 19

1. Disconnect the negative battery cable.
2. Remove the wire connections from the starter solenoid.
3. Using a self-powered test light or ohmmeter, check for continuity between the following:
• Solenoid **B** terminal and solenoid case or ground terminal—no continuity

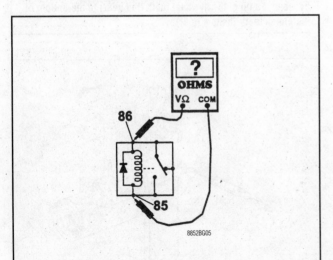

Fig. 16 Use an ohmmeter to check for circuit continuity of the coil in the relay

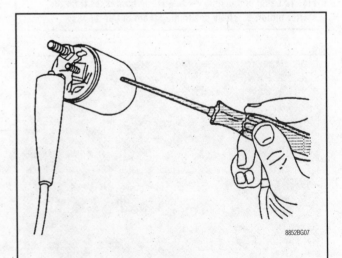

Fig. 18 Test the starter solenoid internal windings with a self-powered test light—starter mounted solenoid shown

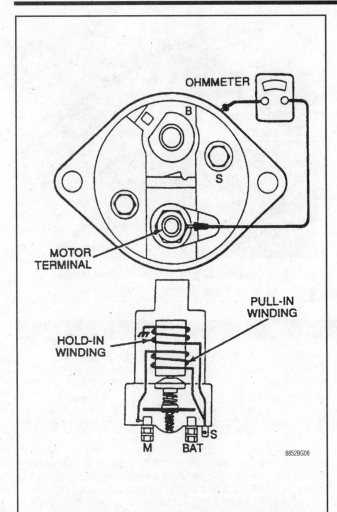

Fig. 19 Use an ohmmeter as shown to test a starter solenoid's internal windings—externally mounted solenoid shown

Fig. 20 To remove an externally mounted starter solenoid, remove any covers from the wiring terminals, if equipped

Fig. 21 Detach any push-on connectors by pulling them straight off of the terminal . . .

- **S** terminal and solenoid case or ground terminal—continuity
- **S** terminal and **M** terminal—continuity
- **M** terminal and solenoid case or ground terminal—continuity

4. If the actual results of the test are different than indicated, replace the starter solenoid.

REMOVAL & INSTALLATION

▶ **See Figures 20, 21, 22, 23 and 24**

➡**This procedure is for externally mounted starter solenoids only. For solenoids mounted on the starter, we recommend replacing the complete assembly.**

1. Disconnect the negative battery cable.
2. Remove the wiring from the starter solenoid. Label the wires and the corresponding terminals if necessary for installation.
3. Remove the fasteners securing the solenoid to the fender or firewall.
4. Remove the solenoid.

To install:

5. Clean the solenoid mounting and the solenoid to ensure good electrical contact.
6. Install the solenoid.
7. Connect the wiring to the proper terminals.
8. Connect the negative battery cable.

Fig. 22 . . . or remove secured wires by loosening the cable retaining nut(s) and separating the cable(s) from the solenoid . . .

Fig. 23 . . . then loosen the solenoid retaining fasteners . . .

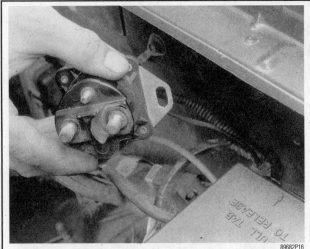

Fig. 24 . . . and remove the solenoid—note that this solenoid is mounted on the inside of one of the front fenders

THE CHARGING SYSTEM

General Information

▶ **See Figures 25 thru 30**

A typical charging system contains an alternator (generator), drive belt, battery, voltage regulator and the associated wiring. The charging system, like the starting system is a series circuit with the battery wired in parallel. After the engine is started and running, the alternator takes over as the source of power and the battery then becomes part of the load on the charging system.

Some vehicle manufacturers use the term generator instead of alternator. Many years ago there used to be a difference, now they are one and the same. The alternator, which is driven by the belt, consists of a rotating coil of laminated wire called the rotor. Surrounding the rotor are more coils of laminated wire that remain stationary (which is how we get the term stator) just inside the alternator case. When current is passed through the rotor via the slip rings and brushes, the rotor becomes a rotating magnet with, of course, a magnetic field. When a magnetic field passes through a conductor (the stator), alternating current (A/C) is generated. This A/C current is rectified, turned into direct current (D/C), by the diodes located within the alternator.

The voltage regulator controls the alternator's field voltage by grounding one end of the field windings very rapidly. The frequency varies according to current demand. The more the field is grounded, the more voltage and current the alternator produces. Voltage is maintained at about 13.5–15 volts. During high engine speeds and low current demands, the regulator will adjust the voltage of the alternator field to lower the alternator output voltage. Conversely, when the vehicle is idling and the current demands

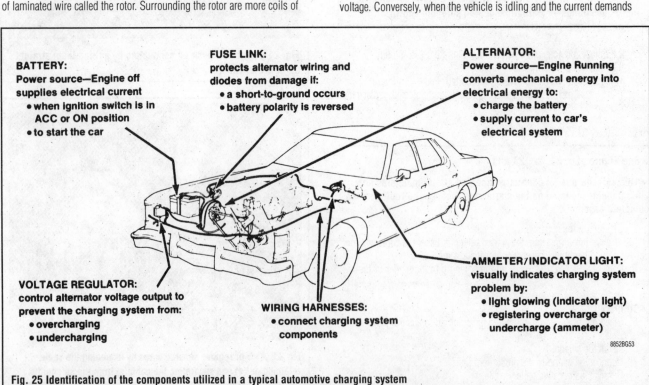

BATTERY:
Power source—Engine off supplies electrical current
● when ignition switch is in ACC or ON position
● to start the car

FUSE LINK:
protects alternator wiring and diodes from damage if:
● a short-to-ground occurs
● battery polarity is reversed

ALTERNATOR:
Power source—Engine Running converts mechanical energy into electrical energy to:
● charge the battery
● supply current to car's electrical system

VOLTAGE REGULATOR:
control alternator voltage output to prevent the charging system from:
● overcharging
● undercharging

WIRING HARNESSES:
● connect charging system components

AMMETER/INDICATOR LIGHT:
visually indicates charging system problem by:
● light glowing (indicator light)
● registering overcharge or undercharge (ammeter)

Fig. 25 Identification of the components utilized in a typical automotive charging system

may be high, the regulator will increase the field voltage, increasing the output of the alternator. Some vehicles actually turn the alternator off during periods of no load and/or wide open throttle. This was designed to reduce fuel consumption and increase power. Depending on the manufacturer, voltage regulators can be found in different locations, including inside or on the alternator, on the fender or firewall and even inside the PCM.

Drive belts are often overlooked when diagnosing a charging system failure. Check the belt tension on the alternator pulley and replace/adjust the belt. A loose belt will result in an undercharged battery and a no-start condition. This is especially true in wet weather conditions when the moisture causes the belt to become more slippery.

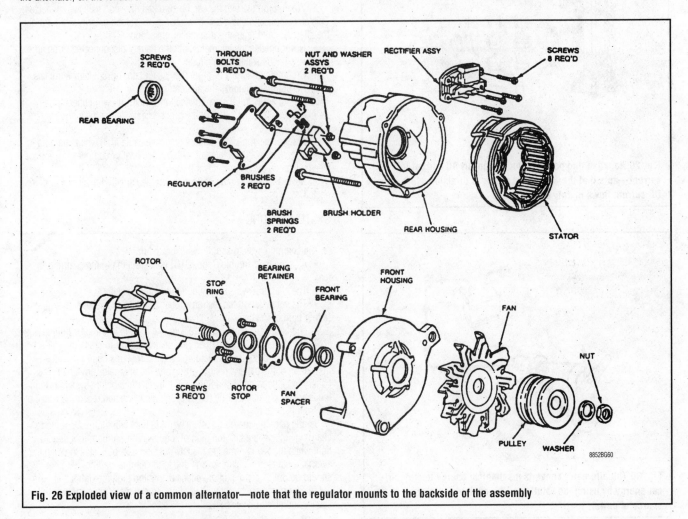

Fig. 26 Exploded view of a common alternator—note that the regulator mounts to the backside of the assembly

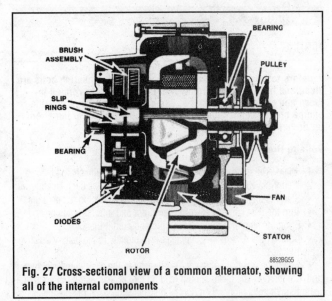

Fig. 27 Cross-sectional view of a common alternator, showing all of the internal components

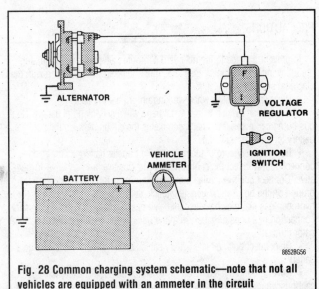

Fig. 28 Common charging system schematic—note that not all vehicles are equipped with an ammeter in the circuit

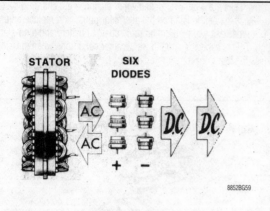

Fig. 29 Negative and positive diodes convert AC current into DC current—note that the AC current reverses direction while the DC current flows in only one direction

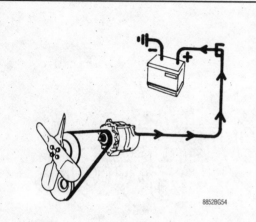

Fig. 30 The alternator converts mechanical energy into electrical energy by using the rotation of the engine's crankshaft as a source of power

PRECAUTIONS

To prevent damage to the on-board computer, alternator and regulator, the following precautionary measures must be taken when working with the electrical system:

• Wear safety glasses when working on or near the battery.

• Don't wear a watch with a metal band when servicing the battery. Serious burns can result if the band completes the circuit between the positive battery terminal and ground.

• Be absolutely sure of the polarity of a booster battery before making connections. Connect the cables positive-to-positive, and negative-to-negative. Connect positive cables first, and then make the last connection to ground on the body of the booster vehicle so that arcing cannot ignite hydrogen gas that may have accumulated near the battery. Even momentary connection of a booster battery with the polarity reversed will damage alternator diodes.

• Disconnect both vehicle battery cables before attempting to charge a battery.

• Never ground the alternator or generator output or battery terminal. Be cautious when using metal tools around a battery to avoid creating a short circuit between the terminals.

• Never ground the field circuit between the alternator and regulator.

• Never run an alternator or generator without load unless the field circuit is disconnected.

• Never attempt to polarize an alternator.

• When installing a battery, make sure that the positive and negative cables are not reversed.

• When jump-starting the car, be sure that like terminals are connected. This also applies to using a battery charger. Reversed polarity will burn out the alternator and regulator in a matter of seconds.

• Never operate the alternator with the battery disconnected or on an otherwise uncontrolled open circuit.

• Do not short across or ground any alternator or regulator terminals.

• Do not try to polarize the alternator.

• Do not apply full battery voltage to the field (brown) connector.

• Always disconnect the battery ground cable before disconnecting the alternator lead.

• Always disconnect the battery (negative cable first) when charging it.

• Never subject the alternator to excessive heat or dampness. If you are steam cleaning the engine, cover the alternator.

• Never use arc-welding equipment on the car with the alternator connected.

SYSTEM TESTING

The charging system should be inspected if:

• A Diagnostic Trouble Code (DTC) is set relating to the charging system

• The charging system warning light is illuminated

• The voltmeter on the instrument panel indicates improper charging (either high or low) voltage

• The battery is overcharged (electrolyte level is low and/or boiling out)

• The battery is undercharged (insufficient power to crank the starter)

The starting point for all charging system problems begins with the inspection of the battery, related wiring and the alternator drive belt. The battery must be in good condition and fully charged before system testing. If a Diagnostic Trouble Code (DTC) is set, diagnose and repair the cause of the trouble code first.

If equipped, the charging system warning light will illuminate if the charging voltage is either too high or too low. The warning light should light when the key is turned to the **ON** position as a bulb check. When the alternator starts producing voltage due to the engine starting, the light should go out. A good sign of voltage that is too high are lights that burn out and/or burn very brightly. Over-charging can also cause damage to the battery and electronic circuits.

Alternator

TESTING

➡Before testing, make sure all connections and mounting bolts are clean and tight. Many charging system problems are related to loose and corroded terminals or bad grounds. Don't overlook the engine ground connection to the body, or the tension of the alternator drive belt.

Voltage Drop Test

1. Make sure the battery is in good condition and fully charged.
2. Perform a voltage drop test of the positive side of the circuit as follows:

• Start the engine and allow it to reach normal operating temperature.

• Turn the headlamps, heater blower motor and interior lights on.

• Bring the engine to about 2,500 rpm and hold it there.

• Connect the negative (-) voltmeter lead directly to the battery positive (+) terminal.

• Touch the positive voltmeter lead directly to the alternator B+ output stud, not the nut. The meter should read no higher than about 0.5 volts. If it does, then there is higher than normal resistance between the positive side of the battery and the B+ output at the alternator.

• Move the positive (+) meter lead to the nut and compare the voltage reading with the previous measurement. If the voltage reading drops substantially, then there is resistance between the stud and the nut.

➡**The theory is to keep moving closer to the battery terminal one connection at a time in order to find the area of high resistance (bad connection).**

3. Perform a voltage drop test of the negative side of the circuit as follows:

a. Start the engine and allow it to reach normal operating temperature.

b. Turn the headlamps, heater blower motor and interior lights ON.

c. Bring the engine to about 2,500 rpm and hold it there.

d. Connect the negative (-) voltmeter lead directly to the negative battery terminal.

e. Touch the positive (+) voltmeter lead directly to the alternator case or ground connection. The meter should read no higher than about 0.3 volts. If it does, then there is higher than normal resistance between the battery ground terminal and the alternator ground.

f. Move the positive (+) meter lead to the alternator mounting bracket, if the voltage reading drops substantially then you know that there is a bad electrical connection between the alternator and the mounting bracket.

➡**The theory is to keep moving closer to the battery terminal one connection at a time in order to find the area of high resistance (bad connection).**

Current Output Test

◗ **See Figure 31**

1. Perform a current output test as follows:

➡**The current output test requires the use of a volt/amp tester with battery load control and an inductive amperage pick-up. Follow the manufacturer's instructions on the use of the equipment.**

a. Start the engine and allow it to reach normal operating temperature.

b. Apply the parking brake and turn OFF all electrical accessories.

c. Connect the tester to the battery terminals and cable according to the instructions.

d. Bring the engine to about 2,500 rpm and hold it there.

e. Apply a load to the charging system with the rheostat on the tester. Do not let the voltage drop below 12 volts.

f. The alternator should deliver to within 10% of the rated output. If the amperage is not within 10% and all other components test good, replace the alternator.

Alternator Isolation Test

◗ **See Figures 32, 33 and 34**

On some models it is possible to isolate the alternator from the regulator by grounding the **F** (field) terminal. Grounding the **F** terminal removes the regulator from the circuit and forces full alternator output. On alternators equipped with internal regulators, we recommend replacing the complete assembly if either the alternator or regulator is defective.

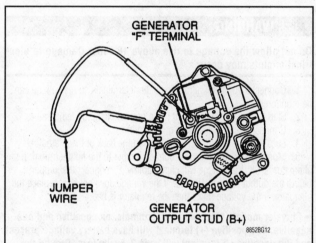

Fig. 32 Use a jumper wire to ground the F terminal in order to force the alternator into full output mode—typical Motorcraft alternator field terminal locations

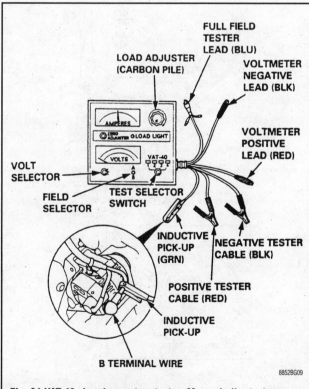

Fig. 31 VAT-40 charging system tester. Many similar testers are available that perform equally as well

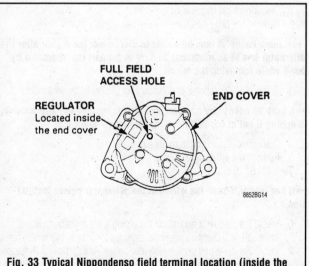

Fig. 33 Typical Nippondenso field terminal location (inside the access hole) on the back of the alternator

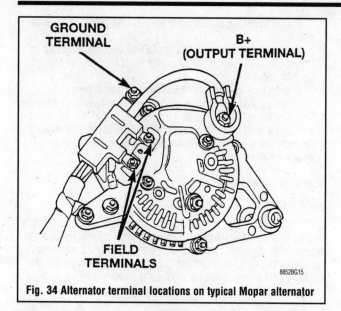

Fig. 34 Alternator terminal locations on typical Mopar alternator

✳✳ WARNING

Do not allow the voltage to rise above 18 volts. Damage to electrical circuits may occur.

1. Connect a voltmeter across the battery terminals so the voltage can be monitored.
2. Start the engine and allow it reach normal operating temperature.
3. Connect a jumper lead to a good ground.
4. Locate the field terminal (negative) on the back of the alternator.
5. Momentarily connect the grounded jumper to the field terminal. If the alternator is OK, the voltage will climb rapidly. Disconnect the jumper before the output reaches 18 volts. If the voltage does not rise, replace the alternator. If the voltage rises, then the regulator is bad.

➡**Chrysler models have two field terminals, one positive and one negative. The positive (+) terminal will have battery voltage present and the negative (-) terminal will have 3–5volts less. Ground the negative (-) terminal when testing this type of alternator.**

REMOVAL & INSTALLATION

▶ **See Figures 35 thru 44**

1. Disconnect the negative battery cable.
2. Remove the drive belt from the alternator pulley.

➡**In some cases, it may be easier to disconnect the wiring after the alternator has been removed. Be sure to support the alternator by hand while removing the wiring.**

3. Remove any components necessary for access to the alternator.

➡**It may be necessary on some vehicles to remove the alternator by dropping it out of the bottom of the engine compartment.**

4. Disconnect the wiring from the alternator.
5. Remove the alternator.
To install:

➡**If necessary, attach the wiring to the alternator before installation.**

6. Install the alternator and attach the wiring if not already done.
7. Install all necessary components removed for access to the alternator.
8. Install the drive belt on the alternator pulley. Adjust the belt if necessary.
9. Connect the negative battery cable.

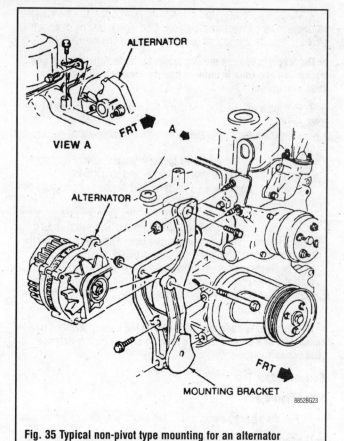

Fig. 35 Typical non-pivot type mounting for an alternator

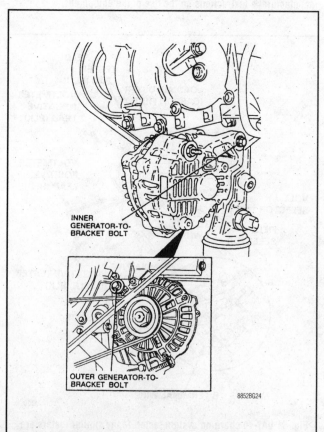

Fig. 36 Common pivot type mounting for an alternator

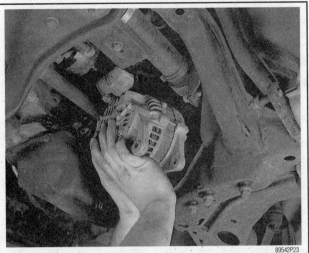

Fig. 37 For models on which it is necessary to drop the alternator out the bottom of the engine compartment . . .

Fig. 38 . . . remove the alternator by moving any components in the way, such as crossmembers . . .

Fig. 39 . . . or exhaust pipes

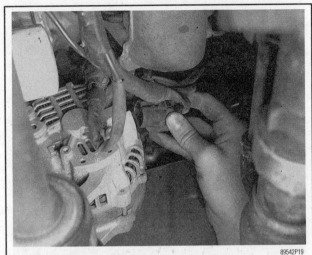

Fig. 40 Once access is gained, detach all wiring from the alternator . . .

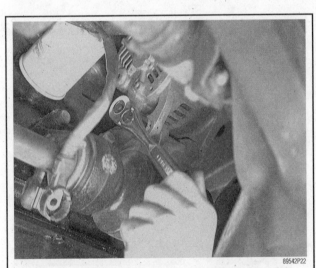

Fig. 41 . . . then loosen the alternator mounting bolts and lower the alternator from the vehicle

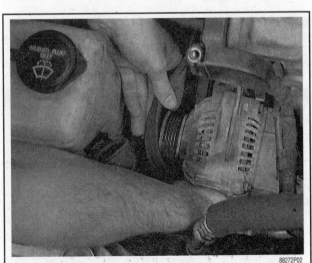

Fig. 42 For models on which the alternator can be removed from the top of the engine compartment, remove the drive belt . . .

Fig. 43 . . . then disconnect all wiring from the alternator

Fig. 44 Loosen the mounting bolts and lift the alternator out of the engine compartment

Battery

TESTING

✳✳ CAUTION

If the battery shows signs of freezing, cracking, leaking, loose posts or low electrolyte level, do not attempt to test, charge or jump start. Internal arcing may occur and cause the battery to explode. Always replace a battery that is physically damaged. If only the water level is low and the battery can be filled, add distilled water to the proper level. When charging, disconnect the battery cables, attach the connections to the battery first,

then turn the charger ON. Never disconnect the battery cable(s) while the engine is running. Always wear safety glasses when servicing the battery.

Specific Gravity Test

◗ See Figure 45

The fluid (sulfuric acid solution) contained in the battery cells will tell you many things about the condition of the battery. Because the cell plates must be kept submerged below the fluid level in order to operate, maintaining the fluid level is extremely important. And, because the specific gravity of the acid is an indication of electrical charge, testing the fluid can be an aid in determining if the battery must be replaced. A battery in a vehicle with a properly operating charging system should require little maintenance, but careful, periodic inspection should reveal problems before they leave you stranded.

At least once a year, check the specific gravity of the battery. It should be between 1.20 and 1.26 on the gravity scale. Most auto supply stores carry a variety of inexpensive battery testing hydrometers. These can be used on any non-sealed battery to test the specific gravity in each cell.

Draw some of the electrolyte from the battery into the until the float in the hydrometer is lifted from its seat. Read the specific gravity indicated by the position of the float. If the specific gravity is low in one or more cells, the battery should be slowly charged and checked again to see if the gravity has come up. Generally, if after charging, the specific gravity between any two cells varies more than 50 points (0.50), the battery should be replaced, as it can no longer produce sufficient voltage to guarantee proper operation.

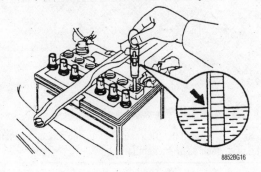

Except Maintenance-Free Battery

Fig. 45 To inspect the specific gravity of a battery cell, draw some battery fluid into the hydrometer and read the value indicated by the float inside the tester

No Load Voltage Test

◗ See Figures 46 and 47

1. Perform a no load voltage test to determine the state of charge by doing the following:

a. If the battery has just been charged, remove the surface charge by turning on the headlamps for 15 seconds, then let the voltage stabilize for about 5 minutes before making any measurements.

b. Disconnect the negative battery cable.

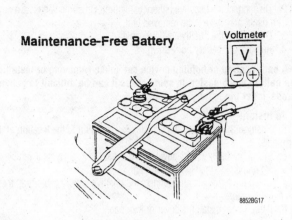

Maintenance-Free Battery

Voltmeter

8852BG17

Fig. 46 On maintenance free batteries, measure the battery voltage to determine the state of charge

Open Circuit Voltage	
Open Circuit Volts	Charge Percentage
11.7 volts or less	0%
12.0 volts	25%
12.2 volts	50%
12.4 volts	75%
12.6 volts or more	100%

8852BG10

Fig. 47 Compare the actual voltage measured with these values to determine the percent of charge based on no load test results

   c. Measure the battery voltage with a good voltmeter.
   d. Compare the readings to the chart to determine the state of charge.

High Capacity Discharge Test

▶ See Figure 48

1. Perform a high capacity discharge test to determine the cranking capacity as follows:
   a. Fully charge the battery.
   b. Connect a VAT-40 or equivalent load tester to the battery.
   c. Apply a load equal to ½ of the Cold Cranking Amp (CCA) rating of the battery for 15 seconds. The CCA is usually found on the battery label, if not, apply a load equal to 200 amps.
   d. If the voltmeter reading falls below 9.6 volts at 70°F (21°C) or more, the battery should be replaced. The minimum battery voltage will be lower depending on the ambient temperature. Refer to the chart for testing in temperatures lower than 70°F (21°C).

Load Test Temperature		
Minimum Voltage	Temperature	
	°F	°C
9.6 volts	70° and above	21° and above
9.5 volts	60°	16°
9.4 volts	50°	10°
9.3 volts	40°	4°
9.1 volts	30°	-1°
8.9 volts	20°	-7°
8.7 volts	10°	-12°
8.5 volts	0°	-18°

8852BG11

Fig. 48 High capacity discharge test minimum allowable voltage/temperature values

Parisitic Draw Test

▶ See Figure 49

➡A good quality Digital Multimeter (DMM) with at least 10 megohm/volt impedance should be used when testing modern automotive circuits. These meters can accurately detect very small amounts of voltage, current and resistance. This type of meter also has a high internal resistance that will not load the circuit being tested. Loading the circuit gives inaccurate readings and may cause damage to sensitive computer circuits.

This test measures the amount of current that the vehicle draws while it is parked and not in use. A small amount of current should be flowing for such things as the on-board computer memory, automatic climate control, clock, and radio station presets. If there is a short in the vehicle electrical system or something has been left on, the excess current draw will eventually drain the battery and cause a no-start condition.

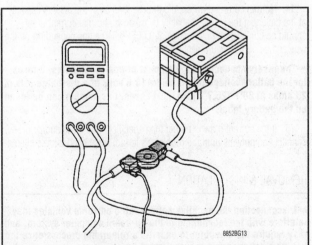

8852BG13

Fig. 49 Before starting the parasitic draw test, install a battery disconnect switch between the negative battery cable and the battery terminal, as shown

1. Be sure all accessories are turned **OFF**. Disconnect the negative battery cable.

2. Install a battery quick-disconnect switch (such as GM Parasitic Draw Test Switch J 38758) between the negative cable and the negative battery terminal. A battery disconnect switch will work in most cases.

3. Road test the vehicle while activating all accessories including the radio and air conditioning. Then, turn all accessories **OFF**.

4. Turn the vehicle **OFF** and open the hood.

5. If equipped, disable the underhood light.

6. Allow approximately 20 minutes for the vehicle computer system(s) to power down.

7. Connect one end of a jumper with a 10 amp fuse to the side of the quick-disconnect switch closest to the negative battery terminal. Be sure the jumper is on the metal part of the switch.

8. Connect the remaining end of the jumper to the other side of the switch closest to the negative battery cable.

✳✳ WARNING

Do not connect the multimeter to the circuit if more than 10 amps are flowing. Damage to the meter may occur.

9. Open the switch so all current flows through the jumper with the 10 amp fuse. If the fuse blows, there is more than 10 amps flowing in the circuit. This indicates that a component was left on (glove box light or other accessory) or there is a short in the electrical system. Find and correct the cause of the large current flow, then continue with this test.

10. If the fuse does not blow, close the disconnect switch and remove the jumper.

11. Set the multimeter to read 10 amps.

12. Connect the multimeter leads in place of the jumper used previously. When the switch is opened, current will flow through the meter.

13. The current draw should now be below 2 amps. If not, then something in the vehicle has been left on. Find the cause and correct it. When the current is less than 2 amps, set the meter to the 2 amp range. This will allow you to measure small amounts of current.

✳✳ WARNING

Do not open the door of the vehicle. The interior lights coming on will blow the fuse of the meter while on the 2 amp range.

14. Normal current draw should be less than ¼ of the reserve capacity of the battery. If the reserve capacity is unknown, normal current draw should be somewhere in the range of 0.005–0.040 amps depending on the type and amount of equipment on the vehicle.

➡**The reserve capacity is the amount of time, in minutes, it takes for the battery voltage to fall below 10.5 volts at a discharge rate of 25 amps at 80°F (26.7°C). In most cases, this number can be found on the battery label.**

15. If the current draw is higher than specified, pull fuses and/or disconnect components until the problem is found. Don't overlook the alternator connection.

REMOVAL & INSTALLATION

➡**Disconnecting the negative battery cable on some vehicles may interfere with the functioning of the on-board computer system, and may require the computer to undergo a relearning process once the negative battery cable is reconnected.**

1. Turn the ignition key to the **OFF** position.

2. Disconnect the negative battery cable first. On some vehicles, a cover or trim panel may have to be removed first.

3. Disconnect the positive battery cable.

4. Remove the battery hold-down.

➡**A battery strap or holding device can make removing or installing the battery much easier. In some cases it can be difficult to get your hands under the battery.**

To install:

5. Position the battery in the vehicle. Pay attention to the location of the terminals.

6. Install the battery hold-down. A loose battery may cause a vehicle fire or severe damage to the electrical system.

7. Clean the terminals and connect the positive battery cable first, then the negative cable.

8. If equipped, install the cover or trim panel.

Voltage Regulator

TESTING

➡**Most regulators are integral (built in) to the alternator or Powertrain Control Module (PCM). If the regulator is found to be defective on these models, the alternator or PCM should be replaced.**

For voltage regulator testing, refer to Alternator Isolation Test.

REMOVAL & INSTALLATION

▶ **See Figures 50 and 51**

➡**The following procedure is only for voltage regulators mounted on the back (outside) of the alternator or elsewhere in the engine compartment.**

1. Disconnect the negative battery cable.

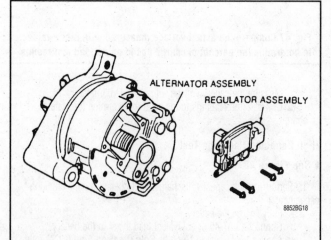

ALTERNATOR ASSEMBLY

REGULATOR ASSEMBLY

8852BG18

Fig. 50 Typically Motorcraft regulators are mounted on the outside case of the alternator

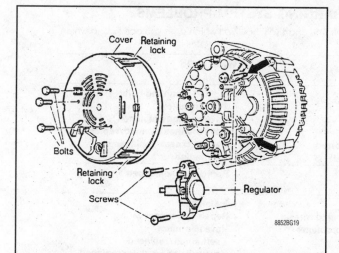

Fig. 51 The regulator on a common Bosch alternator is mounted under a cover on the rear of the alternator

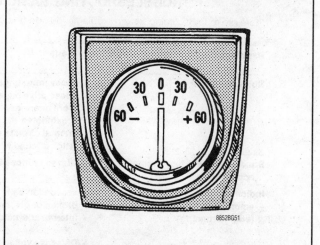

Fig. 52 Your vehicle may be equipped with an ammeter gauge, an indicator of charging system condition

2. If equipped, remove the exterior alternator cover to expose the regulator. Do not disassemble the alternator case that houses the rotor and stator.

3. If equipped, disengage the electrical connector from the regulator.

4. Remove the regulator mounting screws and remove the regulator.

To install:

5. Position the regulator in its original position and install the mounting screws.

6. Connect any wiring that was removed from the regulator.

7. If equipped, install the cover.

8. Connect the negative battery cable.

The Warning Indicator Light or Ammeter

▶ See Figures 52 and 53

➡ Frequently a loose or slipping belt is the cause of a glowing or flickering alternator warning light.

Most modern vehicles have an indicator light located on the dash to alert the driver of a malfunction in the charging system. It is also used to pass a small amount of battery current to the alternator rotor to excite and produce the magnetic field until the alternator begins to charge and can assume this function itself.

Because the bulb circuit is connected to the battery and alternator sides, any movement of current between the two units will cause the bulb to light. As the alternator begins to charge and the produced voltage reaches the battery voltage, the current between the two units ceases to move and the bulb will go out. If either the battery or the alternator should fail as the vehicle is being driven, the difference of voltage between the two units will allow current to flow and the bulb to light, warning the driver of a malfunction.

Fig. 53 Voltmeters may also be used to indicate battery and charging system status

An ammeter also indicates the condition of the charging system. A low battery will be indicated by a high charging current toward (+) side of the gauge. A wiring short or faulty accessory will show as a high rate of discharge toward (-) side of the gauge. It's normal for the gauge to move a slight amount in either direction.

TROUBLESHOOTING BASIC CHARGING SYSTEM PROBLEMS

There are many charging system problems you can fix yourself. This chart will show you which ones you can fix and which ones require professional service.

Problem	Is Caused by	What to Do
Noisy Alternator	• Loose mountings • Loose drive pulley • Worn bearings • Brush noise • Internal circuits shorted (High pitched whine)	• Tighten mounting bolts • Tighten pulley • Have bearings replaced • Have brushes cleaned/replaced • Have alternator replaced or overhauled
Squeal when starting engine or accelerating	• Glazed or loose belt	• Replace or adjust belt
Indicator light remains on or ammeter indicates discharge (engine running)	• Broken fan belt • Broken or disconnected wires • Internal alternator problems • Defective voltage regulator	• Install belt • Repair or connect wiring • Have alternator overhauled/replaced • Have voltage regulator replaced
Car light bulbs continually burn out—battery needs water continually	• Alternator/regulator overcharging	• Have voltage regulator/alternator overhauled or replaced
Car lights flare on acceleration	• Battery low • Internal alternator/regulator problems	• Charge or replace battery • Have alternator/regulator overhauled or replaced
Low voltage output (alternator light flickers continually or ammeter needle wanders)	• Loose or worn belt • Dirty or corroded connections • Internal alternator/regulator problems	• Replace or adjust belt • Clean or replace connections • Have alternator or regulator overhauled or replaced

8852BC03

STARTING AND CHARGING SYSTEM MAINTENANCE

The only periodic maintenance that can be performed on the starting and charging systems is to inspect the electrical cables and wires for fraying and breakage (refer to the section on "Battery and Cables" in this manual), and to inspect the alternator drive belt for proper tension, wear or damage and replace or adjust the belt as necessary (please refer to the "Cooling System" section for information on drive belts). Follow the maintenance intervals in this section, but make a general visual check each time the hood is opened.

STARTING AND CHARGING SYSTEM MAINTENANCE INTERVALS

To keep the starting and charging system operating efficiently, it should be maintained at the following intervals.

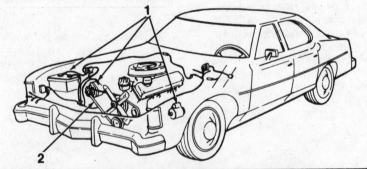

1. Check electrical cables/connections at:
    Battery
    Relay or solenoid
    Starter
    Alternator
	Every 3 months/3000 miles

2. Check condition/adjust drive belt Replace drive belt	Every 3 months/3000 miles* As necessary*

*New drive belts will stretch with use. Recheck the tension of new belts after 200 miles of use.

8852BC02

13

ELECTRICAL SYSTEM— IGNITION

IGNITION SYSTEM 13-2

IGNITION SYSTEM

There are many different types of ignition systems. Most of these systems can be placed into one of three distinct groups: the conventional breaker point type ignition systems (in use since the early 1900's); the electronic ignition systems (popular since the mid 70's); and the distributorless ignition system (introduced in the mid 80's).

The automotive ignition system has two basic functions: it must control the spark and timing of the spark plug firing to match varying engine requirements, and it must increase battery voltage to a point where it will overcome the resistance offered by the spark plug gap and fire the plug.

The first step in understanding a vehicle's ignition system is to learn about basic electricity. For more information on electrical circuits, how they work and how to troubleshoot them, please refer to the information on "Understanding and Troubleshooting Electrical Systems" elsewhere in this manual.

How the Ignition System Works

POINT-TYPE IGNITION SYSTEM

▶ **See Figures 1, 2 and 3**

An automotive ignition system is divided into two electrical circuits (The primary and secondary circuits). The primary circuit carries low voltage. This circuit operates only on battery current and is controlled by the breaker points and the ignition switch. The secondary circuit consists of the secondary windings in the coil, the high tension lead between the distributor and the coil (commonly called the coil wire) on external coil distributors, the distributor cap, the distributor rotor, the spark plug leads, and the spark plugs.

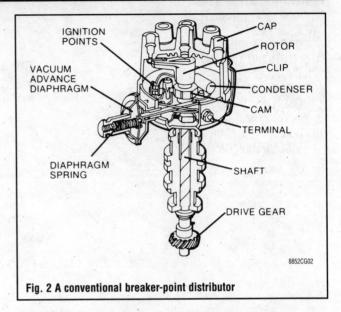

Fig. 2 A conventional breaker-point distributor

The distributor is the controlling element of the system. It switches the primary current on and off and distributes the current to the proper spark plug each time a spark is needed. The distributor is a stationary housing surrounding a rotating shaft. The shaft is driven at one-half engine speed by the engine's camshaft through the distributor drive gears. A cam near the top of the distributor shaft has one lobe for each cylinder of the engine. The cam operates the contact points, which are mounted on a plate within the distributor housing.

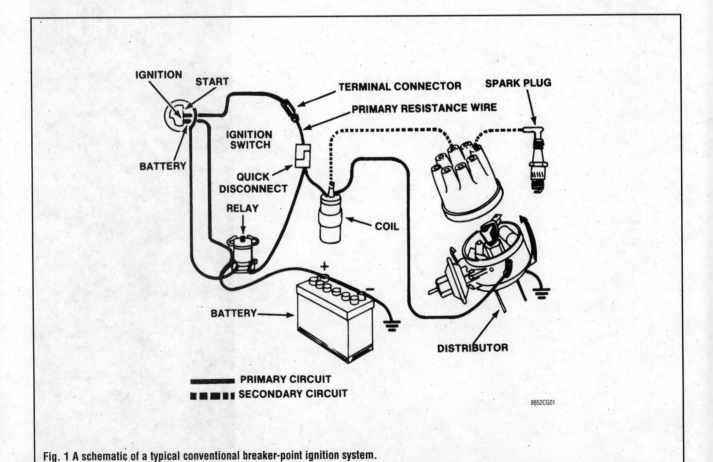

Fig. 1 A schematic of a typical conventional breaker-point ignition system.

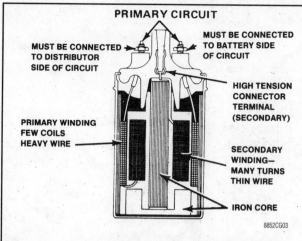

PRIMARY CIRCUIT

MUST BE CONNECTED TO DISTRIBUTOR SIDE OF CIRCUIT

MUST BE CONNECTED TO BATTERY SIDE OF CIRCUIT

HIGH TENSION CONNECTOR TERMINAL (SECONDARY)

PRIMARY WINDING FEW COILS HEAVY WIRE

SECONDARY WINDING— MANY TURNS THIN WIRE

IRON CORE

8852CG03

Fig. 3 Cutaway view of a conventional coil. The primary windings connect to the small terminals on the top of the coil, while the secondary winding connects to the central tower

A rotor is attached to the top of the distributor shaft. When the distributor cap is in place, a spring-loaded piece of metal in the center of the cap makes contact with a metal strip on top of the rotor. The outer end of the rotor passes very close to the contacts connected to the spark plug leads around the outside of the distributor cap.

The coil is the heart of the ignition system. Essentially, it is nothing more than a transformer which takes the relatively low voltage (12 volts) available from the battery and increases it to a point where it will fire the spark plug as much as 40,000 volts. The term "coil" is perhaps a misnomer since there are actually two coils of wire wound about an iron core. These coils are insulated from each other and the whole assembly is enclosed in an oil-filled case. The primary coil, which consists of relatively few turns of heavy wire, is connected to the two primary terminals located on top of the coil. The secondary coil consists of many turns of fine wire. It is connected to the high-tension connection on top of the coil (the tower into which the coil wire from the distributor is plugged).

Under normal operating conditions, power from the battery is fed through a resistor or resistance wire to the primary circuit of the coil and is then grounded through the ignition points in the distributor (the points are closed). Energizing the coil primary circuit with battery voltage produces current flow through the primary windings, which induces a very large, intense magnetic field. This magnetic field remains as long as current flows and the points remain closed.

As the distributor cam rotates, the points are pushed apart, breaking the primary circuit and stopping the flow of current. Interrupting the flow of primary current causes the magnetic field to collapse. Just as current flowing through a wire produces a magnetic field, moving a magnetic field across a wire will produce a current. As the magnetic field collapses, its lines of force cross the secondary windings, inducing a current in them. Since there are many more turns of wire in the secondary windings, the voltage from the primary windings is magnified considerably up to 40,000 volts.

The voltage from the coil secondary windings flows through the coil high-tension lead to the center of the distributor cap, where it is distributed by the rotor to one of the outer terminals in the cap. From there, it flows through the spark plug lead to the spark plug. This process occurs in a split second and is repeated every time the points open and close, which is up to 1500 times a minute in a 4-cylinder engine at idle.

To prevent the high voltage from burning the points, a condenser is installed in the circuit. It absorbs some of the force of the surge of electrical current that occurs during the collapse of the magnetic field. The condenser consists of several layers of aluminum foil separated by insulation. These layers of foil are capable of storing electricity, making the condenser an electrical surge tank.

Voltages just after the points open may reach 250 volts because of the amount of energy stored in the primary windings and the subsequent magnetic field. A condenser which is defective or improperly grounded will not absorb the shock from the fast-moving stream of electricity when the points open and the current can force its way across the point gap, causing pitting and burning.

ELECTRONIC IGNITION SYSTEMS

◆ See Figure 4

The need for higher mileage, reduced emissions and greater reliability has led to the development of the electronic ignition systems. These systems generate a much stronger spark which is needed to ignite leaner fuel mixtures. Breaker point systems needed a resister to reduce the operating voltage of the primary circuit in order to prolong the life of the points. The primary circuit of the electronic ignition systems operate on full battery voltage which helps to develop a stronger spark. Spark plug gaps have widened due to the ability of the increased voltage to jump the larger gap. Cleaner combustion and less deposits have led to longer spark plug life.

On some systems, the ignition coil has been moved inside the distributor cap. This system is said to have an internal coil as opposed to the conventional external one.

Electronic Ignition systems are not as complicated as they may first appear. In fact, they differ only slightly from conventional point ignition systems. Like conventional ignition systems, electronic systems have two circuits: a primary circuit and a secondary circuit. The entire secondary circuit is the same as in a conventional ignition system. In addition, the section of the primary circuit from the battery to the battery terminal at the coil is the same as in a conventional ignition system.

Electronic ignition systems differ from conventional ignition systems in the distributor component area. Instead of a distributor cam, breaker plate, points, and condenser, an electronic ignition system has an armature (called by various names such as a trigger wheel, reluctor, etc.), a pickup coil (stator, sensor, etc.), and an electronic control module.

Essentially, all electronic ignition systems operate in the following manner: With the ignition switch turned on, primary (battery) current flows from the battery through the ignition switch to the coil primary windings. Primary current is turned on and off by the action of the armature as it revolves past the pickup coil or sensor. As each tooth of the armature nears the pickup coil, it creates a voltage that signals the electronic module to turn off the coil primary current. A timing circuit in the module will turn the current on again after the coil field has collapsed. When the current is off, however, the magnetic field built up in the coil is allowed to collapse, which

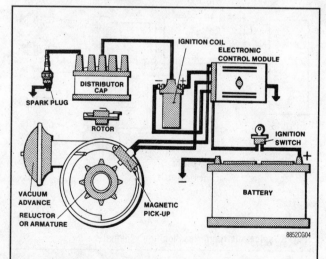

IGNITION COIL

ELECTRONIC CONTROL MODULE

DISTRIBUTOR CAP

SPARK PLUG

ROTOR

IGNITION SWITCH

VACUUM ADVANCE

RELUCTOR OR ARMATURE

MAGNETIC PICK-UP

BATTERY

8852CG04

Fig. 4 Typical electronic ignition system. Note its basic similarity to a conventional system

causes a high voltage in the secondary windings of the coil. It is now operating on the secondary ignition circuit, which is the same as in a conventional ignition system.

Troubleshooting electronic ignition systems ordinarily requires the use of a voltmeter and/or an ohmmeter. Sometimes the use of an ammeter is also required. Because of differences in design and construction, troubleshooting is specific to each system. A complete troubleshooting guide for you particular application can be found in the Chilton's Total Car Care manual.

DISTRIBUTORLESS IGNITION SYSTEMS

▶ **See Figures 5 and 6**

The third type of ignition system is the distributorless ignition. The spark plugs are fired directly from the coils. The spark timing is controlled by an Ignition Control Unit (ICU) and the Engine Control Unit (ECU). The distributorless ignition system may have one coil per cylinder, or one coil for each pair of cylinders.

Some popular systems use one ignition coil per two cylinders. This type of system is often known as the waste spark distribution method. In this system, each cylinder is paired with the cylinder opposite it in the firing order (usually 1–4, 2–3 on 4-cylinder engines or 1–4, 2–5, 3–6 on V6 engines). The ends of each coil secondary leads are attached to spark plugs for the paired opposites. These two plugs are on companion cylinders, cylinders that are at Top Dead Center (TDC) at the same time. But, they are paired oppsites, because they are always at opposing ends of the 4 stroke engine cycle. When one is at TDC of the compression stroke, the other is at TDC of the exhaust stroke. The one that is on compression is said to be the event cylinder and one on the exhaust stroke, the waste cylinder. When the coil discharges, both plugs fire at the same time to complete the series circuit.

Since the polarity of the primary and the secondary windings are fixed, one plug always fires in a forward direction and the other in reverse. This is different than a conventional system firing all plugs the same direction each time. Because of the demand for additional energy; the coil design, saturation time and primary current flow are also different. This redesign of the system allows higher energy to be available from the distributorless coils, greater than 40 kilovolts at all rpm ranges.

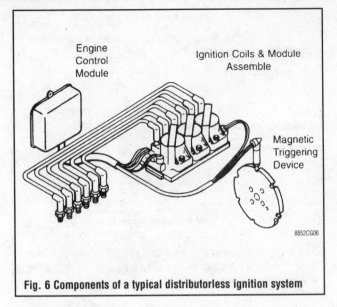

Fig. 6 Components of a typical distributorless ignition system

The Direct Ignition System (DIS) uses either a magnetic crankshaft sensor, camshaft position sensor, or both, to determine crankshaft position and engine speed. This signal is sent to the ignition control module or engine control module which then energizes the appropriate coil.

The advantages of no distributor in theory is:
- No timing adjustments
- No distributor cap and rotor
- No moving parts to wear out
- No distributor to accumulate moisture and cause starting problems
- No distributor to drive thus providing less engine drag

The major components of a distributorless ignition are:
- ECU or Engine Control Unit
- ICU or Ignition Control Unit
- Magnetic Triggering Device such as the Crankshaft Position Sensor and the Camshaft Position Sensor
- Coil Packs

IGNITION TIMING

▶ **See Figures 7 and 8**

Ignition timing is the measurement, in degrees of crankshaft rotation, of the point at which the spark plugs fire in each of the cylinders. It is measured in degrees before or after Top Dead Center (TDC) of the compression stroke.

Because it takes a fraction of a second for the spark plug to ignite the mixture in the cylinder, the spark plug must fire a little before the piston reaches TDC. Otherwise, the mixture will not be completely ignited as the piston passes TDC and the full power of the explosion will not be used by the engine.

Ignition timing on many of today's vehicles is controlled by the engine control computer and is not adjustable. However the timing can be read using a scan tool connected to the data link connector.

The timing measurement is given in degrees of crankshaft rotation before the piston reaches TDC (BTDC). If the setting for the ignition timing is 5° BTDC, the spark plug must fire 5° before each piston reaches TDC. This only holds true, however, when the engine is at idle speed.

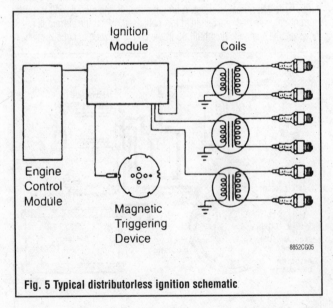

Fig. 5 Typical distributorless ignition schematic

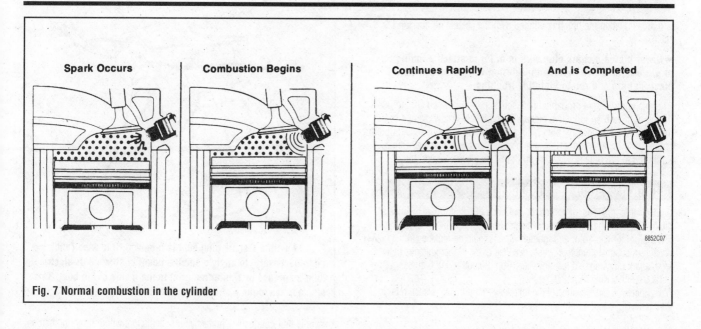

Spark Occurs   **Combustion Begins**   **Continues Rapidly**   **And is Completed**

8852C07

Fig. 7 Normal combustion in the cylinder

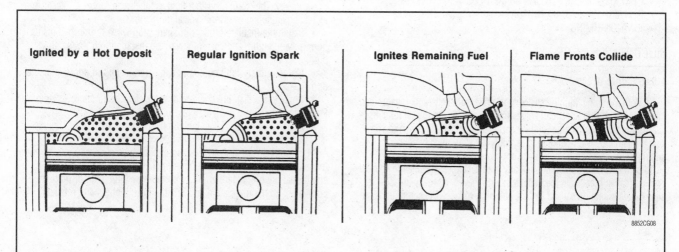

Ignited by a Hot Deposit   **Regular Ignition Spark**   **Ignites Remaining Fuel**   **Flame Fronts Collide**

8852CG08

Fig. 8 Preignition—this is just what the name implies, ignition of the fuel charge prior to the time of the spark. Any hot spot within the combustion chamber such as glowing carbon deposits, rough metallic edges, or overheated spark plugs can cause preignition.

As the engine speed increases, the pistons go faster. The spark plugs have to ignite the fuel even sooner if it is to be completely ignited when the piston reaches TDC. To do this, distributors have various means of advancing the spark timing as the engine speed increases. On older vehicles, this was accomplished by centrifugal weights within the distributor along with a vacuum diaphragm mounted on the side of the distributor. Later vehicles are equipped with an electronic spark timing system in which no vacuum or mechanical advance is used, instead all timing changes electronically based on signals from various sensors.

If the ignition is set too far advanced (BTDC), the ignition and expansion of the fuel in the cylinder will occur too soon and tend to force the piston down while it is still traveling up. This causes engine ping. If the ignition spark is set too far retarded, after TDC (ATDC), the piston will have already passed TDC and started on its way down when the fuel is ignited. This will cause the piston to be forced down for only a portion of its travel. This will result in poor engine performance and lack of power.

Timing marks usually consist of a notch on the rim of the crankshaft pulley and a scale of degrees attached to the front of the engine (often on the engine front cover). On some engines, the timing marks are found on the clutch or torque converter housing. A small hole in the housing and a notch on the flywheel or torque converter are used to check and adjust the timing. The notch corresponds to the position of the piston in the No. 1 cylinder. A stroboscopic (dynamic) timing light is used, which is hooked into the circuit of the No. 1 cylinder spark plug. Every time the spark plug fires, the timing light flashes. By aiming the timing light at the timing marks while the engine is running, the exact position of the piston within the cylinder can be easily read since the stroboscopic flash makes the mark on the pulley appear to be standing still. Proper timing is indicated when the notch is aligned with the correct number on the scale.

➡**Never pierce a spark plug wire in order to attach a timing light or perform tests. The pierced insulation will eventually lead to an electrical arc and related ignition troubles.**

Since your vehicle probably has electronic ignition, you should use a timing light with an inductive pickup. This pickup simply clamps onto the No. 1 spark plug wire, eliminating the adapter. It is not susceptible to cross-firing or false triggering, which may occur with a conventional light, due to the greater voltages produced by electronic ignition.

Ignition System Maintenance

Electronic ignitions, of course, do not need distributor maintenance as often as conventional point type systems, however nothing lasts forever. The distributor cap, rotor and ignition wires should be replaced at the manufacturers suggested interval. Also, because of the higher voltages delivered, spark plugs should last anywhere from 30,000–60,000 miles (48000–96500 Km).

For periodic maintenance of the following components, please refer to the "Tune-Up" section in this manual.
- SPARK PLUGS
- CHECKING AND REPLACING SPARK PLUG WIRES
- DISTRIBUTOR CAP AND ROTOR
- IGNITION TIMING

SILICONE LUBRICANTS

▶ **See Figure 9**

Modern electronic ignition systems generate extremely high voltages and heat. The spark plug boots can soften and actually fuse to the ceramic insulator of the spark plugs after long exposures to high temperature and voltage. If this happens, the boot (and possibly the wire) must be replaced, adding to the cost and complexity of a tune-up.

To help alleviate this condition, many manufacturers use silicone compounds (called greases in the trade, although they're not really greases) to slow the deterioration caused by heat and high voltage. The compounds are

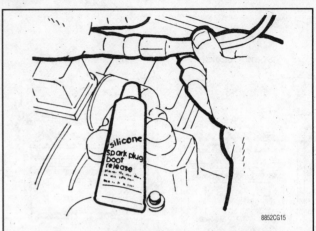

Fig. 9 Anytime a spark plug boot is removed, it is wise (and often necessary) to apply a small amount of silicone di-electric tune-up grease or similar material to the inside of the boot. This also applies to the distributor end of the spark plug wire.

generally non-conductive, protective lubricants that will not dry out, harden, or melt away. They form a weather-tight seal between rubber or plastic and metal and are found in several typical locations:
- Inside the insulating boots of spark plug wires to improve insulation, prevent aging, and ease removal and installation from the spark plug.
- Inside primary ignition circuit cable connectors to improve insulation.
- Apply to the distributor and rotor cap electrodes to improve Radio Frequency Interference (RH) suppression.
- Under the GM Hall Effect Ignition (HEI) control module to improve heat transfer.

Most domestic manufacturers supply the silicone compounds through their own parts departments in one-application packages or supply a small quantity of the compounds with the new rotor, cap, or module. Equivalent compounds are also available from jobbers and retailers.

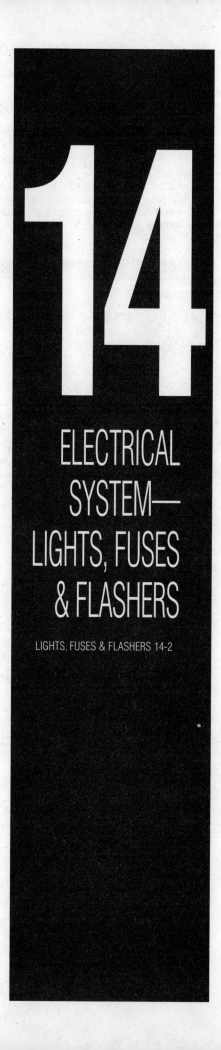

14

ELECTRICAL SYSTEM— LIGHTS, FUSES & FLASHERS

LIGHTS, FUSES & FLASHERS 14-2

LIGHTS, FUSES & FLASHERS

Modern vehicles use dozens of bulbs to light everything from the road to the ashtray. Servicing the system is easy; over half of all lighting problems are caused by burned out bulbs, corroded sockets or burned out fuses.

The first step in understanding a vehicle's lights, fuses and flashers is to learn about basic electricity. For more information on electrical circuits, how they work and how to troubleshoot them, please refer to the information on "Understanding and Troubleshooting Electrical Systems" elsewhere in this manual

Light Bulbs

▶ **See Figures 1, 2, 3 and 4**

Small bulbs, used for most automotive applications, come in several basic types—single contact bayonet base, double contact bayonet base with opposed or staggered indexing lugs, cartridge types for a small, flat installation, and wedge—base light bulbs.Small bulbs show a broken filament when burned-out and are easily replaced. Turn them about ¼ turn and pull them from the socket. The single contact bayonet base is usually used for instrument panel lights in a small snap-in socket. The major difficulty in replacing these is finding them.

The double contact bayonet base is commonly used for turn signals, parking and taillights. The staggered indexing lugs allow one-way installation so the filament connection is correct. These bulbs are reached by removing the lens or light assembly; inside the trunk is also a common place to hide the light housings.

Don't forget to install the gasket under the lens or housing, if one is used. The gasket seals out moisture, a major cause of bulb troubles. While the bulb is out of the socket, check the socket for corrosion and if necessary, clean it.

Poor grounding is a major cause of non-functioning bulbs, especially when the bulb filaments are OK. Scraping the terminal sockets and polishing the bulb contacts is frequently all that's required. Also, check the ground between the bulb housing and the fender, and between the fender and the body. The electricity has to get back to the ground (negative) side of the battery. If it can't because of poor grounding, the bulb won't work. Many times, running a ground wire from the bulb housing directly to the frame of the vehicle is easier than trying to make a ground through rusted sheet metal.

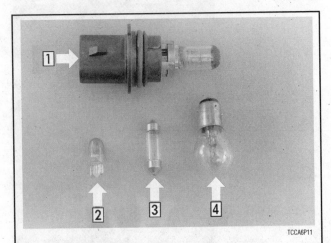

TCCA6P11

1. Halogen headlight bulb
2. Side marker light bulb
3. Dome light bulb
4. Turn signal/brake light bulb

Examples of various types of automotive light bulbs

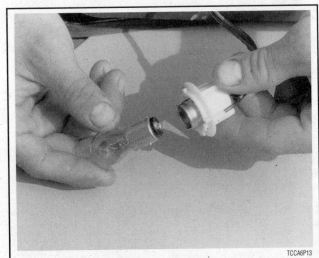

TCCA6P13

Fig. 3 Depress and twist this type of bulb counterclockwise, then pull the bulb straight from its socket

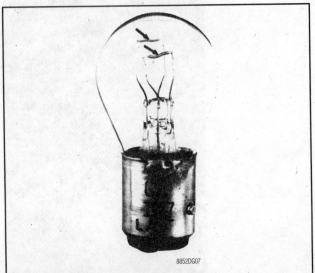

8852DG07

Fig. 2 Burned bulbs show a broken filament (arrows)

TCCA6P15

Fig. 4 Disengage the spring clip which retains one tapered end of this dome light bulb, then withdraw the bulb

Headlights

▶ **See Figures 5 and 6**

In the good old days, headlights where the one part for the vehicle that were easy to figure out. They were round sealed beams and you either had two or four mounted on the front of your vehicle. Nothing stays simple very long. New styling brought on rectangular headlights. This alone doubled the number of possibilities. Even more design changes and lowered hood lines brought out the small rectangular and even the mini-quad (the smallest size sealed beam). This brought the possible number of sealed beam configurations to seven.

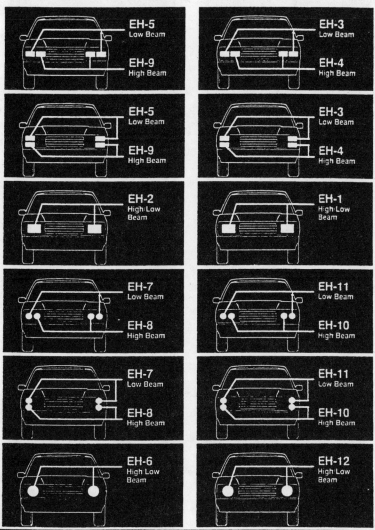

HEADLAMP BULBS

Bulb/Headlamp Number	Customer I.D.#	Bulb/Headlamp Number	Customer I.D.#	Bulb/Headlamp Number	Customer I.D.#
89	EB-6	13050	EB-10	H4651	EH-4
158	EB-8	4000	EH-7	H4656	EH-3
194	EB-7	4001/5001	EH-8	H5001	EH-10
1034	EB-4	4651	EH-9	H5006	EH-11
1073	EB-5	4652	EH-5	H6024	EH-12
1156	EB-3	6014	EH-6	H6054	EH-1
1157	EB-2	6052	EH-2	H6545	EH-13
12100	EB-9			H9004	EB-1

8852DG08

Fig. 5 Common headlight configurations

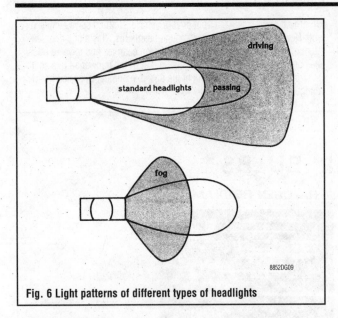

Fig. 6 Light patterns of different types of headlights

Fig. 7 To replace most sealed beam headlights, start by loosening the retaining ring fastener(s) . . .

For years, European vehicles used halogen capsule headlight assemblies. It wasn't until the late 80's that the Department of Transportation (DOT) approved the use for these in U.S. vehicles. This added three new possibilities to the existing sealed beams. However, what this meant to the automaker's was that they could design composite aerodynamic headlight assemblies that could conform to every body design and they can share these common replaceable halogen capsule bulbs.

Practically all late model cars and light trucks use halogen lights. The halogen lights increase the candlepower of the headlight from 75,000 to almost 150,000 and boosts the distance a driver can see at night by almost 20% over the old tungsten lights. Automaker's started installing them on top-of-the-line models in 1980 and they went to wide spread use on 1981 and later models.

Like the old tungsten lights, the halogen lights use a tungsten filament, but it is contained in a halogen gas environment, which allows the filament to be heated to a much higher temperature to produce a much brighter and whiter light. They also require less power, so that a smaller and lighter alternator can be used.

HEADLIGHT REPLACEMENT

▶ See Figures 7, 8, 9 and 10

On most vehicles, light bulb replacement is a simple matter. On sealed beam units, the retaining ring is removed (by loosening the clamp and/or removing the retaining bolts), then the beam is pulled forward so the electrical connector can be unplugged.

On most halogen vehicles the bulb is replaced from behind the lamp assembly. Usually it is just a matter of opening the hood, unscrewing the lock ring on the bulb socket and/or the bulb socket itself and withdrawing the assembly from the back of the lamp. Once the socket is exposed you can remove the old halogen bulb and install the replacement.

✳✳ WARNING

NEVER touch the glass of a halogen bulb! If you touch the glass, you fingers will leave behind natural skin oils which will create a hot spot on the bulb, burning it out LONG BEFORE the natural end of its life. Most halogen bulbs contain a metallic coated tip which can be safely handled and, of course, you can always handle it by the plastic base.

Fig. 8 . . . then remove the retaining ring to free the headlight

Fig. 9 Pull the lamp forward and unplug the wiring harness, then install the replacement bulb

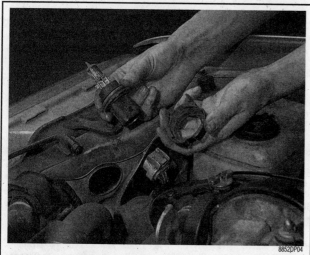

Fig. 10 Most new vehicles require only halogen bulb replacement

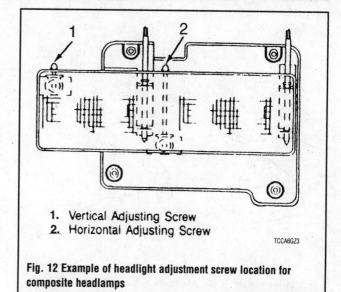

1. Vertical Adjusting Screw
2. Horizontal Adjusting Screw

TCCA6GZ3

Fig. 12 Example of headlight adjustment screw location for composite headlamps

AIMING THE HEADLIGHTS

▶ See Figures 11, 12, 13 and 14

The headlights must be properly aimed to provide the best, safest road illumination. The lights should be checked for proper aim and adjusted as necessary. Certain state and local authorities have requirements for headlight aiming; these should be checked before adjustment is made.

✸✸ CAUTION

About once a year, when the headlights are replaced or any time front end work is performed on your vehicle, the headlights should be accurately aimed by a reputable repair shop using the proper equipment. Headlights not properly aimed can make it virtually impossible to see and may blind other drivers on the road, possibly causing an accident. Note that the following procedure is a temporary fix, until you can take your vehicle to a repair shop for a proper adjustment.

Headlight adjustment may be temporarily made using a wall, as described below, or on the rear of another vehicle. When adjusted, the lights should not glare in oncoming car or truck windshields, nor should they illuminate the passenger compartment of vehicles driving in front of you. These adjustments are rough and should always be fine-tuned by a repair shop which is equipped with headlight aiming tools. Improper adjustments may be both dangerous and illegal.

For most of the vehicles, horizontal and vertical aiming of each sealed beam unit is provided by two adjusting screws which move the retaining ring and adjusting plate against the tension of a coil spring. There is no adjustment for focus; this is done during headlight manufacturing.

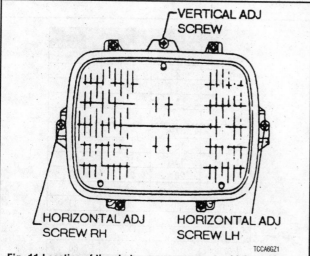

Fig. 11 Location of the aiming screws on most vehicles with sealed beam headlights

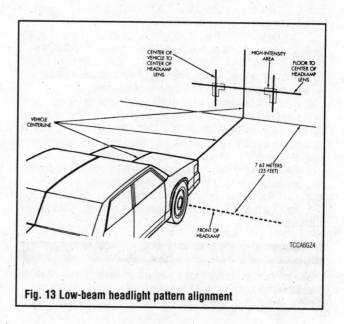

Fig. 13 Low-beam headlight pattern alignment

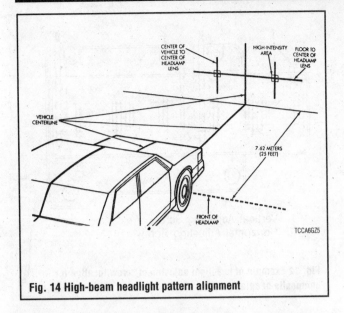

Fig. 14 High-beam headlight pattern alignment

➡ On vehicles with composite headlights, the assembly is bolted into position, no adjustment should be necessary or possible. Some applications, however, may be bolted to an adjuster plate or may be retained by adjusting screws. If so, follow this procedure when adjusting the lights, BUT always have the adjustment checked by a reputable shop.

Before removing the headlight bulb or disturbing the headlamp in any way, note the current settings in order to ease headlight adjustment upon reassembly. If the high or low beam setting of the old lamp still works, this can be done using the wall of a garage or a building:

1. Park the vehicle on a level surface, with the fuel tank about ½ full and with the vehicle empty of all extra cargo (unless normally carried). The vehicle should be facing a wall which is no less than 6 feet (1.8m) high and 12 feet (3.7m) wide. The front of the vehicle should be about 25 feet from the wall.

2. If aiming is to be performed outdoors, it is advisable to wait until dusk in order to properly see the headlight beams on the wall. If done in a garage, darken the area around the wall as much as possible by closing shades or hanging cloth over the windows.

3. Turn the headlights **ON** and mark the wall at the center of each light's low beam, then switch on the brights and mark the center of each light's high beam. A short length of masking tape which is visible from the front of the vehicle may be used. Although marking all four positions is advisable, marking one position from each light should be sufficient.

4. If neither beam on one side is working, and if another like-sized vehicle is available, park the second one in the exact spot where the vehicle was and mark the beams using the same-side light. Then switch the vehicles so the one to be aimed is back in the original spot. It must be parked no closer to or farther away from the wall than the second vehicle.

5. Perform any necessary repairs, but make sure the vehicle is not moved, or is returned to the exact spot from which the lights were marked. Turn the headlights **ON** and adjust the beams to match the marks on the wall.

6. Have the headlight adjustment checked as soon as possible by a reputable repair shop.

Fuses, Fusible Links and Circuit Breakers

All wires must be insulated and protected from overload. If the insulation breaks (creating a path for electricity that was not intended) or if the circuit is overloaded, the fuse, circuit breaker or fusible link that protects the circuit will "blow."

FUSES

▶ See Figures 15, 16, 17, 18 and 19

Fuses never blow because of high voltage. High amperage in the circuit, greater than the capacity of the fuse, causes the metal strip to heat up, melt and open the circuit, preventing the flow of electricity. A fuse could carry 200 volts as well as 2 volts, but will only tolerate its rated amperage and about 10% to handle minor current surges before it blows.

Auto fuses come in several designs, but all usually consist of a zinc strip or a piece of wire. Heavier load fuses have a notch in the middle of the zinc strip. The wider section at each end is to give better temperature-carrying capability. The heat from a temporary overload is transferred to the wider metal and slows fuse burnout. In case of a heavy overload, the metal strip will melt in a fraction of a second and protect the circuit.

The old glass fuse, used in older model vehicles is primarily used in accessory applications today. On all late model vehicles, you'll likely find a fuse that is different from the old glass tube fuse. It's a miniaturized, blade-type design that is referred to as ATC, ATM, or MAX fuse. The "blade-type" was developed in conjunction with the smaller fuse block. Fuses of different ratings are interchangeable but amperage ratings are molded in color-coded numbers that match the fuse ratings on the fuse block. The following chart identifies the amperage and color code.

Normally the fuse box is somewhere under the dash or in the engine compartment. Burned out fuses are readily identified by the burned zinc element in the middle of the glass, plastic, or ceramic insulator. Small, inexpensive plastic tools are available to easily replace a burned fuse. Never replace a fuse with one of a higher load capacity (the amperage is usually stated on the fuse).

Most people's reaction when a fuse blows is simply to replace it and see if the problem reoccurs. Well, if the new fuse blows too, then there is something wrong with that circuit meaning you should figure out the problem and fix it rather than just continuing to replace fuses. Check the wiring to the components that are run off the blown fuse, look for bad connections, cuts, breaks or shorts which would allow the circuit to complete without the proper load or which would add such a large additional load that the fuse would blow. Sometimes just wiggling the harness will be enough to stop the problem (remove a short or make a better connection), BUT, unless you find the broken wire or fasten the loose connector, the fuse will likely blow again later.

	ATC	ATM	MAX
Black	1		
Gray	2	2	
Violet	3	3	
Pink	4	4	
Tan	5	5	
Brown	7½	7½	
Red	10	10	50
Lt. Blue	15	15	60
Yellow	20	20	20
Clear	25	25	
Green	30	30	30
Amber	40		70
Orange			40
Natural			80

Fig. 15 Blade-type fuses—color code denotes amperage

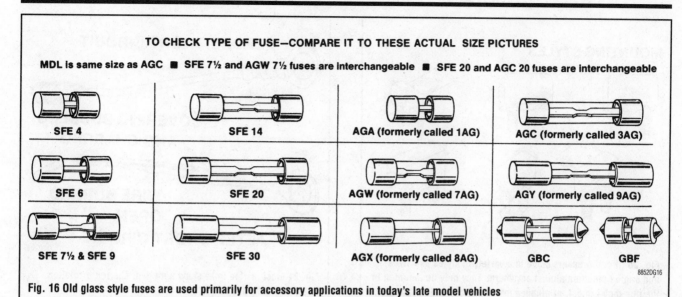

TO CHECK TYPE OF FUSE—COMPARE IT TO THESE ACTUAL SIZE PICTURES

MDL is same size as AGC ■ SFE 7½ and AGW 7½ fuses are interchangeable ■ SFE 20 and AGC 20 fuses are interchangeable

SFE 4	SFE 14	AGA (formerly called 1AG)	AGC (formerly called 3AG)
SFE 6	SFE 20	AGW (formerly called 7AG)	AGY (formerly called 9AG)
SFE 7½ & SFE 9	SFE 30	AGX (formerly called 8AG)	GBC GBF

Fig. 16 Old glass style fuses are used primarily for accessory applications in today's late model vehicles

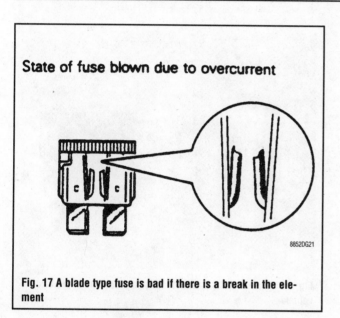

State of fuse blown due to overcurrent

Fig. 17 A blade type fuse is bad if there is a break in the element

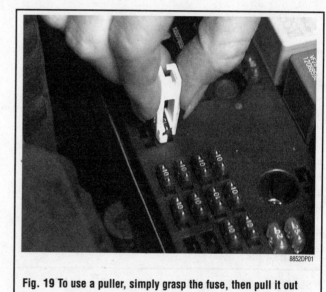

Fig. 19 To use a puller, simply grasp the fuse, then pull it out

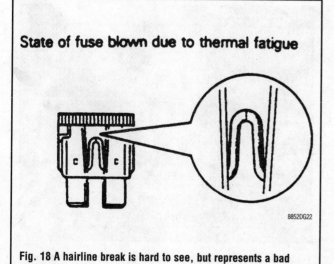

State of fuse blown due to thermal fatigue

Fig. 18 A hairline break is hard to see, but represents a bad fuse too

CIRCUIT BREAKERS

▶ **See Figure 20**

Circuit breakers are sealed assemblies that perform the same job as the fuse, but in case of an overload, will cut current for an instant. Unlike a fuse, things will return to normal. They rarely go bad but must be replaced with an identical unit should one blow. As with fuses, if a circuit breaker continues to fail, the source of the trouble should be found and corrected.

The main advantage of a circuit breaker over a fuse is what happens when the circuit breaker does its job. When a fuse blows, it becomes trash, while the circuit breaker can cool and reset (to be used over and over again). For this reason, circuit breakers tend to be used to protect high load circuits, on which an occasional overload is expected. Accessories such as power windows or seats which use powerful motors (which might occasionally draw too high an amperage if they encounter mechanical resistance) are good candidates for circuit breaker protection.

You never know exactly where to look for a circuit breaker, but many times, they are located near the fuse box or near the component they protect. On some vehicles, the circuit breaker that protects the headlights is an integral part of the headlight switch, which must be replaced in its entirety.

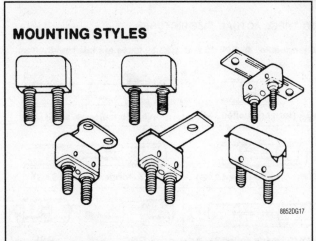

MOUNTING STYLES

8852DG17

Fig. 20 Circuit breakers come in a variety of styles and sizes, and can be mounted almost anywhere. They may be mounted in the line they protect, or plugged into the circuit at the fuse box.

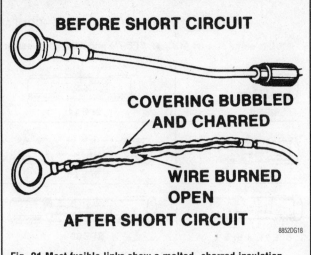

BEFORE SHORT CIRCUIT

COVERING BUBBLED AND CHARRED

WIRE BURNED OPEN

AFTER SHORT CIRCUIT

8852DG18

Fig. 21 Most fusible links show a melted, charred insulation when they burn out

Circuit breakers are designed to offer a variety of performance characteristics including three types of reset.

➡**Always follow the OEM's recommendations when replacing circuit breakers. Replace only with the same type breaker in aftermarket applications.**

• Type I—Automatic reset—Circuit breaker automatically resets after opening, if the fault still exists, the breaker will continue to cycle between ON and OFF positions until the overload is corrected. These devices are sometimes called "cycling breakers."

• Type II—Modified reset—The circuit breaker will remain tripped (in the OFF position) as long as there's power to the circuit due to an internal resistor. Type II breakers can be reset by turning off the circuit, or by turning off the ignition switch. These devices are sometimes called "noncycling breakers."

• Type III—Manual reset—The circuit breaker will remain tripped (in the OFF position) until an indicator button or lever is manually reset.

FUSIBLE LINKS & MAXI FUSES

◆ **See Figures 21, 22 and 23**

Fusible links are a piece of wire about 6" long which is spliced into another wire, usually a gauge or two smaller than the wire it protects. Fusible links can be found almost anywhere. Many times they are identified by a colored flag on the link, or by a loop to make it stand out from other wires, and are usually the same color as the protected circuit. Some fusible links may burn in half with no change in appearance, but most are covered with a special insulation that will bubble and char when the fusible link burns.

Fusible links should always be replaced with an original-equipment type; never use a standard piece of wire.

1. Disconnect the negative battery cable.
2. Disconnect the eyelet of the fuse link from the component.
3. Cut the other end of the fuse link from the wiring harness at the splice.
4. Connect the eyelet end of a new fuse link to the component.
5. Splice the open end of the new fuse link into the wiring harness.
6. Solder the splice with rosin-core solder and wrap the splice with electrical tape. This splice must be soldered. See "Tools and Supplies" for tips on soldering.
7. Connect the negative battery cable.
8. Start the engine to check that the new connections complete the circuit.

On most modern vehicles the fusible link has been replaced by the maxi fuse. The maxi fuse is a much larger version of the common standard size fuse (designed to carry the large loads of fusible links) and which have the advantage of being replaced much more easily than the old style fusible link.

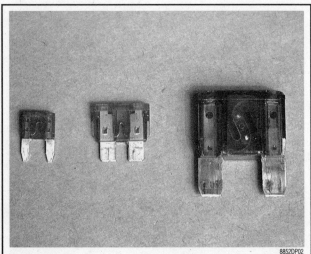

8852DP02

Fig. 22 Mini, standard and maxi fuses are used in most newer vehicles

8852DP03

Fig. 23 A maxi fuse can be pulled out of the block in the same manner as a standard fuse

Flashers

▶ **See Figure 24**

The flasher consists of a blade and resistance ribbon, which holds the blade in a bent position, until the flasher-circuit is activated. Current flows through the ribbon, heating it so that it elongates and relaxes its tension on the blade. The blade snaps away from the ribbon, breaking the circuit. In the absence of current, the ribbon cools rapidly and shrinks in length until the blade is pulled back into contact with the ribbon. This heating and cooling cycle causes the flashing action in the circuit. Essentially, the flasher is a timed relay, the timing of which is dependent upon the current in the circuit and the mechanical design of the flasher itself.

Flashers are found in all sorts of out-of-the-way places. They are usually small metal or plastic (round or square) units that plug into the fuse box, and they operate the turn signal indicators and the hazard warning system. These don't go bad very often, but suspect the flasher if all the bulbs are in good condition. Conversely, check the bulbs first, because the flashers are designed to stop working if one of the bulbs burns out alerting the driver to a potential problem.

If you can't find the flasher right away, turn on the ignition and the turn signals and start hunting for the noise. When you find it, you'll be able to feel the vibration in the relay. Most flashers plug in and can usually be replaced by feel, even if you can't see them.

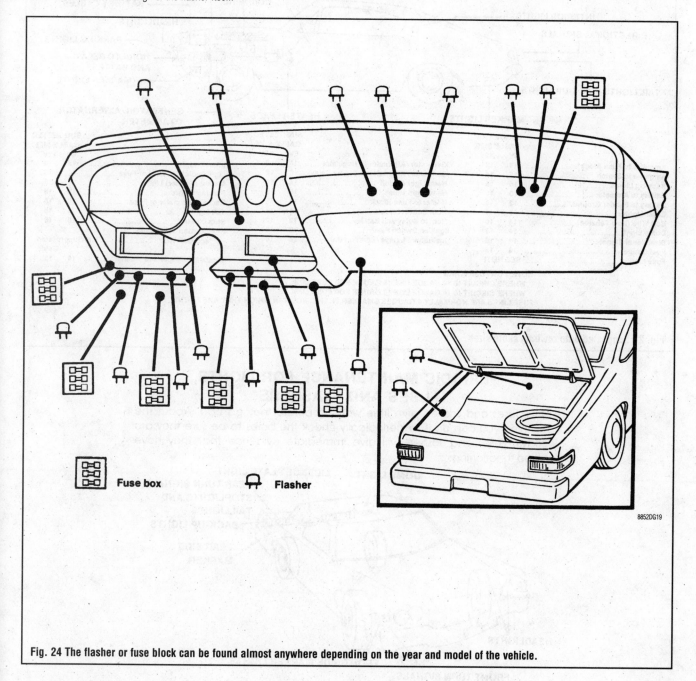

Fuse box   Flasher

8852DG19

Fig. 24 The flasher or fuse block can be found almost anywhere depending on the year and model of the vehicle.

Rewiring

▶ **See Figure 25**

Almost anyone can replace frayed or otherwise damaged wires, as long as the proper tools and parts are available. Automotive wire termi-

nals and connectors are available to fit almost any need. Be sure the ends of all wires are fitted with the proper terminal hardware and connectors. Wrapping a wire around a stud is never a permanent solution and will only cause trouble later. Be sure that wires are replaced one at a time to avoid confusion, and route them neatly and out-of-the-way.

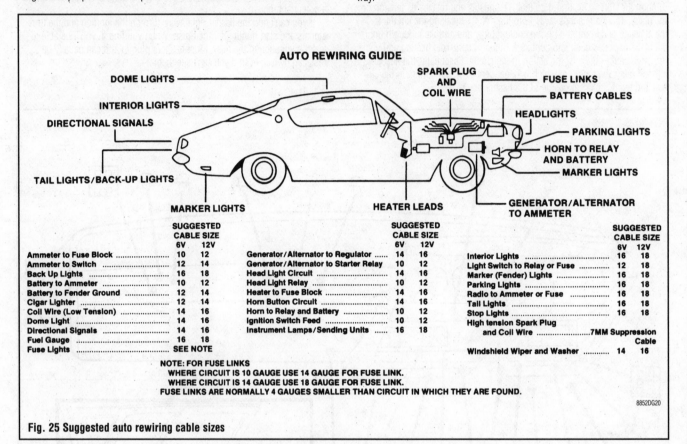

AUTO REWIRING GUIDE

	SUGGESTED CABLE SIZE	
	6V	12V
Ammeter to Fuse Block	10	12
Ammeter to Switch	12	14
Back Up Lights	16	18
Battery to Ammeter	10	12
Battery to Fender Ground	12	14
Cigar Lighter	12	14
Coil Wire (Low Tension)	14	16
Dome Light	14	16
Directional Signals	14	16
Fuel Gauge	16	18
Fuse Lights	SEE NOTE	

	SUGGESTED CABLE SIZE	
	6V	12V
Generator/Alternator to Regulator	14	16
Generator/Alternator to Starter Relay	10	12
Head Light Circuit	14	16
Head Light Relay	10	12
Heater to Fuse Block	14	16
Horn Button Circuit	14	16
Horn to Relay and Battery	10	12
Ignition Switch Feed	10	12
Instrument Lamps/Sending Units	16	18

	SUGGESTED CABLE SIZE	
	6V	12V
Interior Lights	16	18
Light Switch to Relay or Fuse	12	18
Marker (Fender) Lights	16	18
Parking Lights	16	18
Radio to Ammeter or Fuse	16	18
Tail Lights	16	18
Stop Lights	16	18
High tension Spark Plug and Coil Wire	7MM Suppression Cable	
Windshield Wiper and Washer	14	16

NOTE: FOR FUSE LINKS
WHERE CIRCUIT IS 10 GAUGE USE 14 GAUGE FOR FUSE LINK.
WHERE CIRCUIT IS 14 GAUGE USE 18 GAUGE FOR FUSE LINK.
FUSE LINKS ARE NORMALLY 4 GAUGES SMALLER THAN CIRCUIT IN WHICH THEY ARE FOUND.

8852DG20

Fig. 25 Suggested auto rewiring cable sizes

PERIODIC MAINTENANCE FOR LIGHTS, FUSES AND FLASHERS

Lights, fuses and flashers give little warning before they go bad. About the only thing you can do is to periodically check the bulbs to be sure they are working. Fuses and flashers will give immediate evidence that they have ceased functioning.

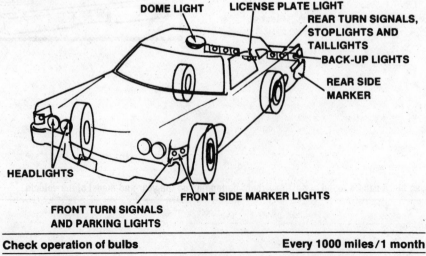

Check operation of bulbs   **Every 1000 miles/1 month**

8852DC01

TROUBLESHOOTING BASIC LIGHTING PROBLEMS

The ability to see and be seen is vital to safety. Fortunately, most lighting problems are relatively uncomplicated and easily corrected.

The Problem	Is Caused By	What to Do
Lights		
One or more lights don't work, but others do	• Defective bulb(s) • Blown fuse(s) • Dirty fuse clips or light sockets • Poor ground circuit	• Replace bulb(s) • Replace fuse(s) • Clean connections • Run ground wire from light socket housing to car frame
Lights burn out quickly	• Incorrect voltage regulator setting or defective regulator • Poor battery/alternator connections	• Have voltage regulator checked/replaced • Check battery/alternator connections
Lights go dim	• Low/discharged battery • Alternator not charging • Corroded sockets or connections • Low voltage output	• Check battery • Check drive belt tension; repair or replace alternator • Clean bulb and socket contacts and connections • Have voltage regulator checked/replaced
Lights flicker	• Loose connection • Poor ground • Circuit breaker operating (short circuit)	• Tighten all connections • Run ground wire from light housing to car frame • Check connections and look for bare wires
Lights "flare"—Some flare is normal on acceleration—if excessive, see "Lights Burn Out Quickly"	• High voltage setting	• Have voltage regulator checked/adjusted
Lights glare—approaching drivers are blinded	• Lights adjusted too high • Rear springs or shocks sagging • Rear tires soft	• Have headlights aimed • Check rear springs/shocks • Check/correct rear tire pressure
Turn Signals		
Turn signals don't work in either direction	• Blown fuse • Defective flasher • Loose connection	• Replace fuse • Replace flasher • Check/tighten all connections
Right (or left) turn signal only won't work	• Bulb burned out • Right (or left) indicator bulb burned out • Short circuit	• Replace bulb • Check/replace indicator bulb • Check/repair wiring
Flasher rate too slow or too fast	• Incorrect wattage bulb • Incorrect flasher	• Replace bulb • Replace flasher (use a variable load flasher if you pull a trailer)
Indicator lights do not flash (burn steadily)	• Burned out bulb • Defective flasher	• Replace bulb • Replace flasher
Indicator lights do not light at all	• Burned out indicator bulb • Defective flasher	• Replace indicator bulb • Replace flasher

8852DC02

TROUBLESHOOTING BASIC TURN SIGNAL AND FLASHER PROBLEMS

Most problems in the turn signals or flasher system, can be reduced to defective flashers or bulbs, which are easily replaced. Occasionally, problems in the turn signals are traced to the switch in the steering column, which will require professional service.

F=Front   R=Rear   ✷=Lights off   O=Lights on

Problem		What to Do
Turn signals light, but do not flash	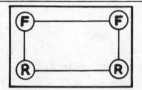	• **Replace the flasher**
No turn signals light on either side	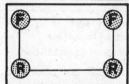	• **Check the fuse. Replace if defective.** • **Check the flasher by substitution.** • **Check for open circuit, short circuit or poor ground.**
Both turn signals on one side don't work	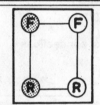	• **Check for bad bulbs.** • **Check for bad ground in both housings.**
One turn signal light on one side doesn't work	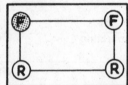	• **Check and/or replace bulb.** • **Check for corrosion in socket. Clean contacts.** • **Check for poor ground at socket.**
Turn signal flashes too fast or too slow	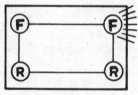	• **Check any bulb on the side flashing too fast. A heavy-duty bulb is probably installed in place of a regular bulb.** • **Check the bulb flashing too slow. A standard bulb was probably installed in place of a heavy-duty bulb.** • **Check for loose connections or corrosion at the bulb socket.**
Indicator lights don't work in either direction		• **Check if the turn signals are working.** • **Check the dash indicator lights.** • **Check the flasher by substitution.**

One indicator light doesn't light		• **On systems with 1 dash indicator:**
		  See if the lights work on the same side. Often the filaments have been reversed in systems combining stoplights with taillights and turn signals.
		  Check the flasher by substitution.
		• **On systems with 2 indicators:**
		  Check the bulbs on the same side.
		  Check the indicator light bulb.
		  Check the flasher by substitution.

8852DC03

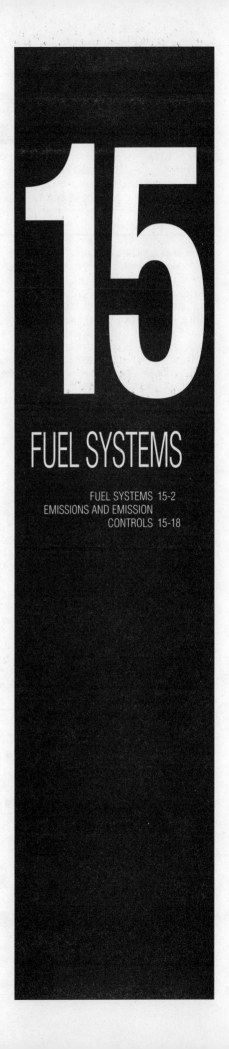

15

FUEL SYSTEMS

FUEL SYSTEMS

The Fuel Delivery System

The fuel delivery system consists of all the components which supply the engine with fuel. This includes the tank itself, all the lines, one or more fuel filters, a fuel pump (mechanical or electric), and the fuel metering components (carburetor or fuel injection system).

FUEL TANK

Fuel tanks are normally located at the rear of the vehicle, although on rear or mid engine vehicles they are usually located at the front. The tank contains a fuel gauge sending unit, a filler tube and on most fuel injected vehicles, a fuel pump. In most tanks, there is also a fine mesh screen "sock" attached to the pickup tube. This is used to filter out large particles which could easily clog the fuel lines, fuel pump and fuel filter.

Since the advent of emission controls, tanks are equipped with a control system to prevent fuel vapor from being discharged into the atmosphere. A vent line in the tank is connected to an activated carbon or charcoal filled canister in the engine compartment. Vapors from the tank are stored in this canister, until they can be purged later for combustion in the engine. On many carbureted engines, the float bowl is also vented to this canister.

FUEL PUMP

Mechanical Pumps

♦ **See Figures 1 and 2**

Mechanical pumps are usually found on carbureted engines or on engines that utilize a mechanical fuel injection system.

Mechanical fuel pumps on carbureted engines are usually mounted on the side of the engine block or cylinder head and operated by an eccentric on the engine's camshaft. The rocker arm of the pump rests against the camshaft eccentric, and as the camshaft rotates, it actuates the rocker arm. Some engines use a pushrod between the rocker arm and camshaft eccentric. Inside the fuel pump, the rocker arm is connected to a flexible diaphragm. A spring, mounted underneath, maintains pressure on the diaphragm. As the rocker arm is actuated, it pulls the diaphragm down and then releases it. Once the diaphragm is released, the spring pushes it back up. This continual diaphragm motion causes a partial vacuum and pressure in the space above the diaphragm. The vacuum draws the fuel from the tank and the pressure pushes it toward the carburetor or injection pump. A check valve is used in the pump to prevent fuel from being pumped back into the tank.

| 1. Fuel pump | 2. Insulator | 3. Fuel hose ports |

Fig. 2 Some mechanical pumps are mounted to the cylinder head, rather than the engine block

Certain mechanical fuel injection systems also utilize a mechanical fuel pump, typically some diesel engines and early gasoline fuel injection systems. Many of them use a fuel pump essentially identical to the carbureted fuel system's. Some, however, use a vane type fuel pump mounted directly to the injection pump/fuel distributor assembly. The injection pump/fuel distributor assembly is driven by the timing belt, chain or gears which in turn drives the fuel pump. The vanes draw the fuel in through the inlet port then squeeze the fuel into a tight passage. The fuel then exits pressurized through the outlet port.

Electric Pumps

♦ **See Figures 3 and 4**

There are two general types of electric fuel pumps: the impeller type and the bellows type. Electric pumps can be found on all types of fuel systems.

The impeller type pump uses a vane or impeller that is driven by an electric motor. These pumps are often mounted in the fuel tank, though they are sometimes found below or beside the tank. The vanes or impeller draw the fuel in through the inlet port then squeeze the fuel into a tight passage. This pressurizes the fuel. The pressurized fuel then exits through the outlet port.

The bellows type pump is rare. This pump is ordinarily mounted in the engine compartment and contains a flexible metal bellows operated by an electromagnet. As the electromagnet is energized, it pulls the metal bellows up—this draws the fuel from the tank into the pump. When the electromagnet is de-energized, the bellows returns to its original position. A check valve closes to prevent the fuel from returning to the tank. The only place for the fuel to go now is through the outlet port.

FUEL FILTERS

In addition to the mesh screen attached to the pickup tube, all fuel systems have at least one other filter located somewhere between the fuel tank and the fuel metering components. On some models, the filter is part of the fuel pump itself, on others, it is located in the fuel line, and still others locate the filter at the carburetor or throttle body inlet.

Inline and Spin On Filters

♦ **See Figures 5, 6, 7 and 8**

Inline and spin on filters are located between the fuel pump and fuel metering components. They are connected to fuel lines either by clamps, banjo bolts, flare fittings or quick-disconnect fittings. Most are "throw-

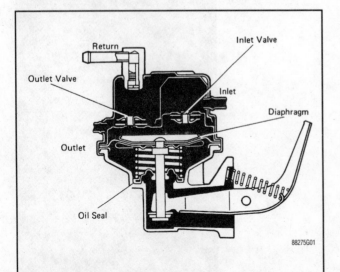

Fig. 1 Cutaway view of a common mechanical fuel pump

Return
Inlet Valve
Outlet Valve
Inlet
Diaphragm
Outlet
Oil Seal

88275G01

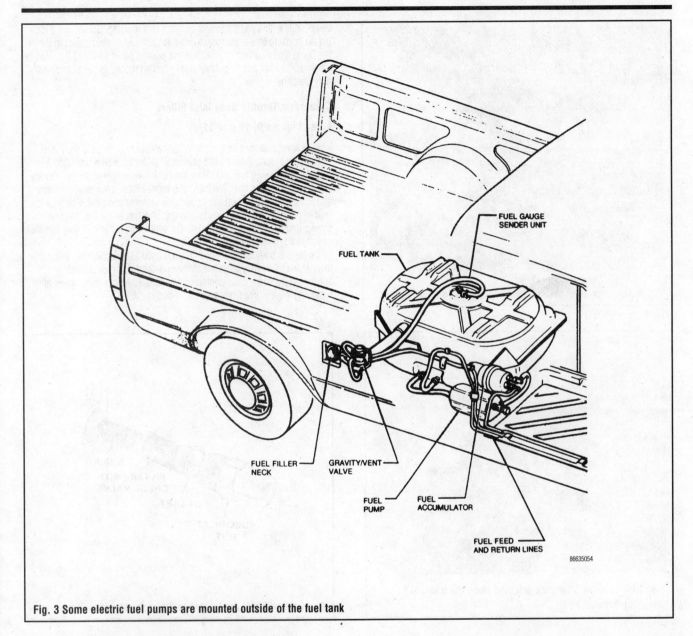

FUEL GAUGE
SENDER UNIT

FUEL TANK

FUEL FILLER
NECK

GRAVITY/VENT
VALVE

FUEL
PUMP

FUEL
ACCUMULATOR

FUEL FEED
AND RETURN LINES

86635054

Fig. 3 Some electric fuel pumps are mounted outside of the fuel tank

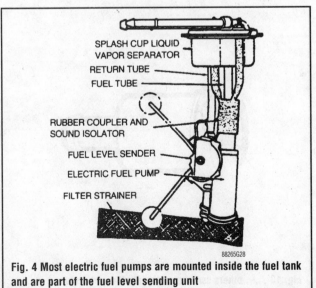

SPLASH CUP LIQUID
VAPOR SEPARATOR

RETURN TUBE

FUEL TUBE

RUBBER COUPLER AND
SOUND ISOLATOR

FUEL LEVEL SENDER

ELECTRIC FUEL PUMP

FILTER STRAINER

88265G28

Fig. 4 Most electric fuel pumps are mounted inside the fuel tank
and are part of the fuel level sending unit

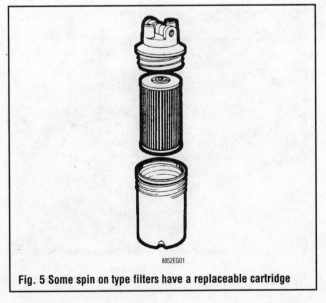

8852EG01

Fig. 5 Some spin on type filters have a replaceable cartridge

Fig. 6 This type of disposable inline filter is secured by clamps

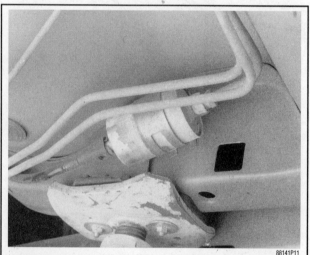

Fig. 7 Many inline filters are mounted along the frame rail under the vehicle . . .

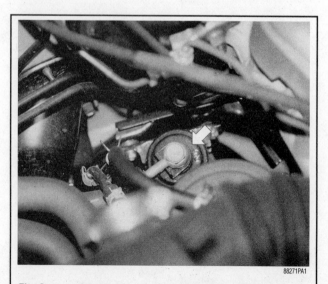

Fig. 8 . . . others can be found in the engine compartment

away" units with a paper element encased in a housing. Some have a clear plastic housing that allows you to view the amount of dirt trapped in the filter. Some filters consist of a replaceable pleated paper cartridge installed in a permanent filter housing. Their use is limited mostly to diesel and heavy-duty gasoline engines.

Carburetor/Throttle Body Inlet Filters

◗ See Figures 9, 10 and 11

Fuel filters can also be located in the carburetor or throttle body inlet.

For carburetors, they consist of a small paper or bronze filter that is installed in the inlet housing. They are extremely simple in design and are about as efficient as an inline type. The bronze filter is the least common and must be installed with the small cone section facing out. One type is held in place by a threaded metal cap that attaches to the fuel line and screws into the carburetor fuel inlet. On another type, the fuel filter threads directly into the carburetor.

On throttle body units, these filters are used as a supplement to the primary inline filter. They usually consist of a conical screen, similar in appearance to an air conditioning orifice tube. They can be accessed after removing the fuel line from the throttle body unit.

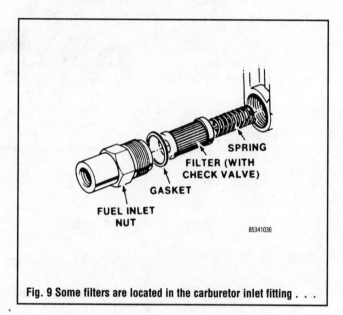

Fig. 9 Some filters are located in the carburetor inlet fitting . . .

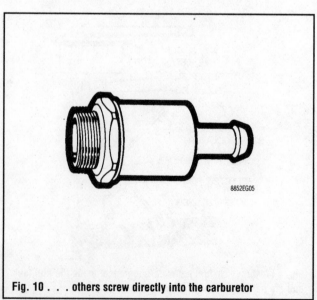

Fig. 10 . . . others screw directly into the carburetor

Fig. 11 Some filter elements are made of sintered bronze

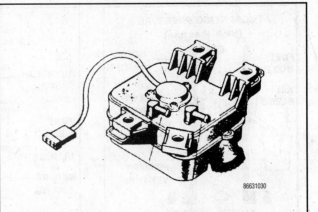

Fig. 13 Remote fuel/water separator units are usually mounted next to the fuel tank

FUEL/WATER SEPARATOR

▶ See Figures 12 and 13

This is usually found on diesel cars and trucks. It can either be part of the fuel filter housing or it can be a separate remote unit all together. Most operate as a two-stage filter. The lower stage removes dirt particles down to about 1 micron in size and allows the water to form large droplets. In the second stage, fuel freely passes through the filter, but water will not. Water collects in the bottom of the filter housing, and a drain plug on the bottom of the housing is usually provided.

The separate units are usually mounted next to the fuel tank. They collect water as it settles out of the fuel tank. Some may light a warning lamp on the dash when it requires draining.

Carbureted Fuel System

GENERAL INFORMATION

The carburetor is the most complex part of the entire fuel system. Carburetors vary greatly in construction, but they all operate the same way. Their job is to supply the correct mixture of fuel and air to the engine in response to varying conditions.

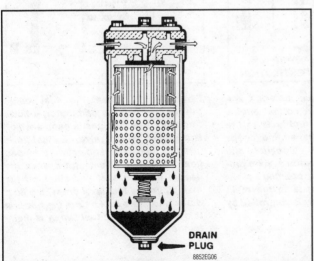

DRAIN PLUG

Fig. 12 Some fuel/water separators are part of the filter housing assembly

Despite their complexity, carburetors function because of a simple physical principle, known as the venturi principle. Air is drawn into the engine by the pumping action of the pistons. As the air enters the top of the carburetor, it passes through a venturi, which is nothing more than a restriction in the throttle bore. The air speeds up as it passes through the venturi, causing a slight drop in pressure. This pressure drop pulls fuel from the float bowl through a nozzle into the throttle bore. It then mixes with the air and forms a fine mist, which is distributed to the cylinders through the intake manifold.

There are six different systems (fuel/air circuits) in a carburetor that make it work. The way these systems are arranged in the carburetor determines the carburetor's size and shape:

1. Float system
2. Idle and low-speed system
3. Main metering system
4. Power system
5. Accelerator pump system
6. Choke system

It is hard to believe that the little single-barrel carburetor used on 4- or 6-cylinder engines have the same basic systems as the enormous 4-barrel carburetors used on many V8 engines. Of course, the 4-barrels have more throttle bores ("barrels") and a lot of other hardware you won't find on the single-barrels. However, all carburetors are similar, and if you understand a simple single-barrel, you can use that knowledge to understand a 4-barrel. If you'll study the explanations of the various systems, you'll discover that carburetors aren't as tricky as you thought they were. In fact, they're simple, considering the job they have to do.

Electronic feedback carburetors operate under the same principal as conventional carburetors, with the added benefit of reducing emissions through the use of electronic controls. The system utilizes electronic signals, generated by an exhaust gas oxygen sensor, throttle position sensor, coolant temperature sensor and a barometric or manifold pressure sensor to precisely control the air/fuel mixture ratio in the carburetor. This, in turn, allows the engine to produce exhaust gases of the proper composition, permitting the use of a 3-way catalyst. The 3-way catalyst is designed to convert 3 pollutants (1) hydrocarbons (HC), (2) carbon monoxide (CO), and (3) oxides of Nitrogen (NOx) into harmless substances.

➡**Note that the presence of an oxygen sensor on carbureted engines does not automatically mean it uses a feedback controlled carburetor. Some manufacturers used an oxygen sensor to control the secondary air injection system, not the carburetor.**

There are three main types of feedback controlled carburetors:

7. Air in the idle air bleed and fuel in the main metering circuits is controlled with an electric solenoid.
8. Air in the idle air bleed and main metering circuits is controlled with an electric solenoid.
9. Air in the idle air bleed and fuel in the main metering circuits is controlled by a vacuum modulator.

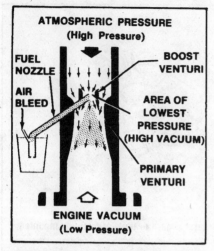

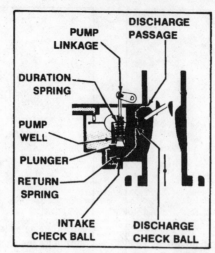

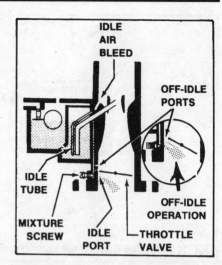

The venturi principle in operation. The pumping action of the pistons creates a vacuum which is amplified by the venturi in the carburetor. This pressure drop will pull fuel from the float bowl through the fuel nozzle. Unfortunately, there is not enough suction present at idle or low speed to make this system work, which is why the carburetor is equipped with an idle and low speed circuit.

Accelerator pump system. When the throttle is opened, the air flowing through the venturi starts flowing faster almost immediately, but there is a lag in the flow of fuel out of the main nozzle. The result is that the engine runs lean and stumbles. It needs an extra shot of fuel just when the throttle is opened. This shot is provided by the accelerator pump, which is nothing more than a little pump operated by the throttle linkage that shoots a squirt of fuel through a separate nozzle into the throat of the carburetor.

Idle and low-speed system. The vacuum in the intake manifold at idle is high because the throttle is almost completely closed. This vacuum is used to draw fuel into the engine through the idle system and keep it running. Vacuum acts on the idle jet (usually a calibrated tube that sticks down into the main well, below the fuel level) and sucks the fuel into the engine. The idle mixture screw is there to limit the amount of fuel that can go into the engine.

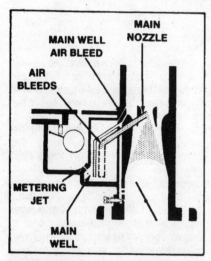

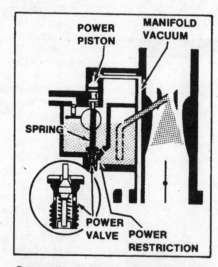

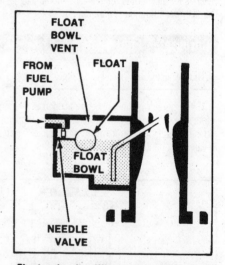

The main metering system may be the simplest system of all, since it is simply the venturi principle in operation. At cruising speeds, the engine sucks enough air to constantly draw fuel through the main fuel nozzle. The main fuel nozzle or jet is calibrated to provide a metering system. The metering system is necessary to prevent an excess amount of fuel flowing into the intake manifold, creating an overly rich mixture.

Power circuit. The main metering system works very well at normal engine loads, but when the throttle is in the wide-open position, the engine needs more fuel to prevent detonation and give it full power. The power system provides additional fuel by opening up another passage that leads to the main nozzle. This passageway is controlled by a power valve.

Float circuit. When the fuel pump pushes fuel into the carburetor, it flows through a seat and past a needle which is a kind of shutoff valve. The fuel flows into the float bowl and raises a hinged float so that the float arm pushes the needle into the seat and shuts off the fuel. When the fuel level drops, the float drops and more fuel enters the bowl. In this way, a constant fuel supply is maintained.

8852EG07

There are 2 operating modes in the feedback controlled carburetor system: open loop and closed loop. When the engine is cold, the system will be operating in the open loop mode. During that time, the air/fuel ratio will be fixed at a richer level. This will allow proper engine warm up and driveability. In open loop operation, the oxygen sensor signal is ignored and the computer does not compensate for an overly rich or lean mixture. On some vehicles, air injection (from the secondary air injection system) will be diverted upstream in the exhaust manifold to help heat the oxygen sensor. During closed loop operation, the air/fuel ratio is varied by the computer. The signal from the oxygen sensor is no longer ignored. Through the use of a mixture control solenoid or vacuum modulator, the air/fuel ratio can be adjusted by metering the air in the air bleeds and/or fuel in the fuel metering circuits. If equipped, air injection is now diverted downstream to the catalytic converter to help promote the catalyst reaction.

It's important to remember that carburetors seldom give trouble during normal operation. Other than changing the fuel and air filters and making sure the idle speed and mixture are OK at every tune-up, there's not much maintenance you can perform on the average carburetor. On feedback controlled carburetors, periodic idle speed and mixture adjustments aren't necessary.

Since they have so few moving parts, there isn't a lot in a carburetor to wear out. The only parts you might occasionally have trouble with are the throttle shaft, accelerator pump, float and maybe the power valve. On feedback controlled carburetors, you may also have trouble with the mixture control solenoid or vacuum modulator. Ordinarily, carburetor problems are caused by dirt or gummy fuel deposits. Most other so-called carburetor problems are caused by other sources such as faulty breaker points, ignition timing, spark plugs, or even a clogged air filter. If you suspect a problem in your carburetor, be sure you check everything else first.

CARBURETOR CIRCUITS

Principal sub-assemblies on most carburetor models include a bowl cover, carburetor body and throttle body. A thick gasket between the throttle body and main body retards heat transfer to the fuel in order to help resist fuel percolation in warm weather. To correctly identify the carburetor model, always check the part number stamped on the main body or attached tag. The carburetor includes four basic fuel metering systems. The idle system provides a mixture for smooth idle and a transfer system for low speed operation. The main metering system provides an economical mixture for normal cruising conditions (and a fuel regulator solenoid/vacuum modulator on feedback systems). The accelerator system provides additional fuel during acceleration. The power enrichment system provides a richer mixture when high power output is desired.

In addition to these 4 basic systems, there is a float system that constantly supplies the fuel to the basic metering systems. A choke system temporarily enriches the mixture to aid in starting and running a cold engine.

Float System

▶ **See Figure 14**

The purpose of the float circuit is to maintain an adequate supply of liquid fuel at the proper, predetermined level in the bowl for use by the idle, acceleration pump, power and main metering circuits. One or 2 separate float circuits may be used, each circuit containing a float assembly, needle and a seat. All circuits are supplied with fuel from the fuel bowl.

All fuel enters the fuel bowl through the fuel inlet fitting in the carburetor body. The fuel inlet needle seats directly in the fuel inlet fitting. The fuel inlet needle is controlled by a float and a lever which is hinged by a float shaft.

The fuel inlet system must constantly maintain the specified level of fuel as the basic fuel metering systems are calibrated to deliver the proper mixture only when the fuel is at this level. When the fuel level in the bowl drops, the float also drops permitting additional fuel to flow past the fuel inlet needle into the bowl.

Idle System

▶ **See Figure 15**

Fuel used during curb idle and low-speed operation flows through the main metering jet into the main well. A connecting idle well intersects the

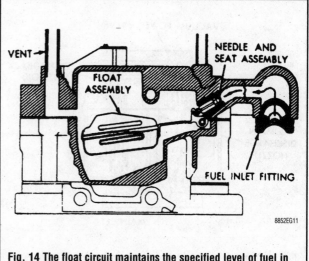

Fig. 14 The float circuit maintains the specified level of fuel in the fuel bowl

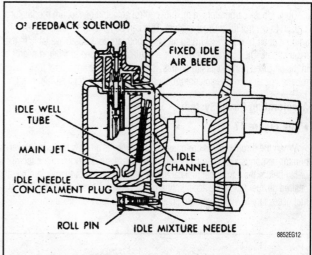

Fig. 15 Common idle system diagram—feedback system shown, others similar

main well. An idle tube is installed in the idle well. Fuel travels up the idle well and mixes with air which enters through the idle air bleed located in the bowl cover. At curb idle the fuel and air mixture flows down the idle channel and is further mixed or broken up by air entering the idle channel through the transfer slot above the throttle plate. The idle system is equipped with a restrictor in the idle channel, located between the transfer slot and the idle port, which limits the maximum attainable idle mixture. During low speed operation the throttle plate moves exposing the transfer slot and fuel begins to flow through the transfer slot as well as the idle port. As the throttle plates are opened further and engine speed increases, the air flow through the carburetor also increases. This increased air flow creates a vacuum in the venturi and the main metering system begins to discharge fuel.

Main Metering System

▶ **See Figure 16**

As the throttle valve(s) continue opening, the air flow through the carburetor increases and creates a low pressure area in the venturi. This low pressure causes fuel to flow from the fuel bowl through the main jets and into the main wells. Air from the main air bleed mixes with the fuel through holes in the sides of main well tube. The mixture is then drawn from the main well tube and discharged through the venturi nozzle. As air flow through the carburetor increases, the amount of air/fuel mixture discharged also increases.

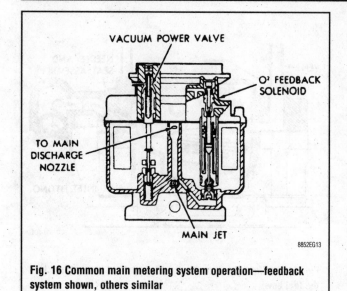

Fig. 16 Common main metering system operation—feedback system shown, others similar

On feedback carburetors, a mixture control solenoid or vacuum modulator is used to control the air/fuel mixture. This can be done by regulating the amount of air bleed or fuel (in some cases both are controlled) available to the main circuit. The solenoid or modulator actuates a stepped or tapered needle in the air bleed or main jets to do this. By controlling the amount of fuel released or air bled, the solenoid/modulator regulates the total air/fuel mixture.

Accelerating Pump System

▶ See Figure 17

When the throttle plates are opened suddenly, the air flow through the carburetor responds almost immediately. However, there is a brief time interval or lag before the additional fuel can move into the system and maintain the desired air/fuel ratio. The accelerating pump provides a measured amount of fuel necessary to insure smooth engine operation upon acceleration.

When the throttle is opened, the pump plunger actuates the pump piston or diaphragm. This closes the intake check valve, forcing fuel out through the discharge passage and out through the pump jets. At higher speeds, pump discharge is no longer necessary to insure smooth acceleration. The external pump linkage is so constructed that less pump stroke is available when the throttle is in the higher speeds positions.

As the throttle is closed, the pump piston or diaphragm returns to its rest position and fuel is drawn into the pump well as the check valve opens.

Power Enrichment System

▶ See Figures 18 and 19

During high speed (or low manifold vacuum) the carburetor must provide a richer mixture than is needed when the engine is running at cruising

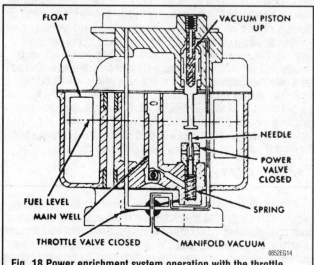

Fig. 18 Power enrichment system operation with the throttle valve closed

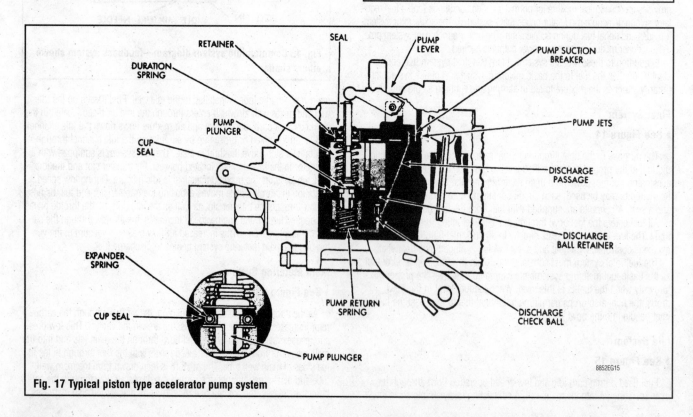

Fig. 17 Typical piston type accelerator pump system

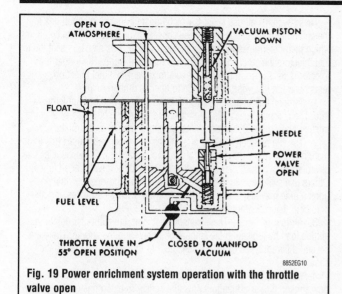

Fig. 19 Power enrichment system operation with the throttle valve open

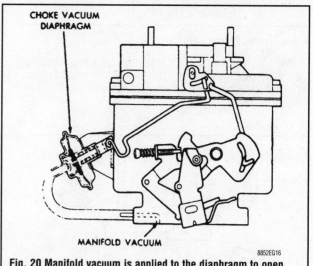

Fig. 20 Manifold vacuum is applied to the diaphragm to open the choke valve

speed. Added fuel for power operation is supplied by a power enrichment system. There are both vacuum and mechanically controlled systems.

On vacuum controlled systems, a passage in the throttle body transmits manifold vacuum to the piston chamber in the bowl cover. Under light throttle and light load conditions, there is sufficient vacuum acting on the vacuum piston to overcome the piston spring tension. When the throttle valves are opened more, vacuum that is acting on the piston is bled to atmosphere and manifold vacuum is closed off, insuring proper mixture for this throttle opening. The vent port is right in line with the throttle shaft, which has a small hole drilled through it. When the throttle valve is opened sufficiently, the hole in the throttle shaft will line up with the port in the base of the carburetor, venting the piston vacuum chamber to atmosphere and allowing the spring loaded piston to open the power valve. As engine power demands are reduced, and the throttle valve begins to close, manifold vacuum increases. The increased vacuum acts on the vacuum piston, overcoming the tension of the piston spring. This closes the power valve and shuts off the added supply of fuel which is no longer required.

On mechanical systems, metering rods are directly actuated by the throttle linkage. As the throttle is opened towards the wide-open position, the metering rods are lifted from their jets. This allows additional fuel to pass.

Choke System

▶ **See Figure 20**

The choke provides the richer air/fuel mixture required for starting and operating a cold engine. There are both automatic and manual chokes.

On automatic chokes, a bi-metal spring inside the choke housing (or in a well in the intake manifold) pushes the choke valve toward the closed position. When the engine starts, manifold vacuum is applied to the choke diaphragm through a hose from the throttle body. This adjustment of the choke valve opening when the engine starts is called vacuum kick. Manifold vacuum alone is not strong enough to provide the proper degree of choke opening during the entire choking period. The force of air rushing past the partially open choke valve provides the additional opening force. As the engine warms up, manifold heat transmitted to the choke housing relaxes the bi-metal spring until it eventually permits the choke to open fully. On some carburetors, an electric heater assists engine heat to open the choke rapidly in summer temperatures.

On carburetors with manual chokes, there is lever or knob in the vehicle which actuates the choke linkage through a cable. Before the car is started, the choke lever is pulled by the driver. The further the lever is pulled, the further the choke plate closes. After the vehicle starts and begins to warm up, the driver begins to push the lever back, opening the choke valve.

Carburetors are also equipped with choke unloaders. This is a mechani-

cal linkage that opens the choke valve when the accelerator pedal is held wide-open. This is mainly used to help start a cold engine that has been flooded. Opening the choke valve leans the mixture by reducing fuel flow and allowing additional air to pass.

Additonal Carburetor Systems

Some carburetors are also equipped with various control solenoids. These are the most common:

1. Mixture control solenoids/vacuum modulators—These are used on feedback carburetors to control the fuel mixture. Through the use of these mixture control solenoids or modulators, the air/fuel ratio can be adjusted by metering the amount of air available to the air bleeds and/or fuel in the fuel metering circuits.

2. Fuel cut-off valves—The valves can be either vacuum or electrically controlled. They help prevent dieseling or run-on after the car is shut off. Fuel is shut off to the idle circuit, main circuit or both.

3. Anti-diesel solenoids—These solenoids allow the throttle valve to close after the car is turned off to prevent dieseling or run-on. When the ignition key is first turned **ON**, the solenoid actuates the throttle linkage to open the throttle valve(s) slightly. When the key is turned **OFF**, the solenoid retracts, allowing the throttle valves to close.

4. Idle-up solenoids—These solenoids open the throttle valve slightly to allow for an increase in idle speed. They are used when the vehicle is under a heavy electrical load or the air conditioning is turned on.

5. Idle speed motors—These are stepper motors used on feedback carburetors. They maintain the proper idle speed, as determined by the computer, by actuating the throttle lever.

Fuel Injection Systems

GENERAL INFORMATION

Fuel injection systems have been used on vehicles for many years. The earliest ones were purely mechanical. As technology advanced, electronic fuel injection systems became more popular. Early mechanical and electronic fuel injection systems did not use feedback controls. As emissions became more of a concern, feedback controls were adapted to both types of fuel injection systems.

Both mechanical and electronic fuel injection systems can be found on gasoline engines. Diesel engines are most commonly found with mechanical type systems, although the newest generations of these engines have been using electronic fuel injection. Following is a description of the most common fuel injection systems.

MULTI-PORT FUEL INJECTION

▶ **See Figures 21 and 22**

This is the most common type of fuel injection system found today. Regardless of the manufacturer, they all function in the same basic way. On these systems an equal amount of fuel is delivered to each cylinder.

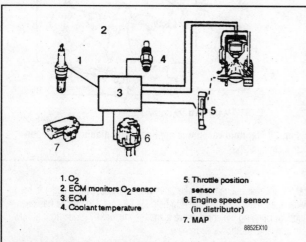

1. O₂

$$1.\ O_2$$
2. ECM monitors O₂ sensor
3. ECM
4. Coolant temperature
5. Throttle position sensor
6. Engine speed sensor (in distributor)
7. MAP

8852EX10

Fig. 21 The computer monitors several signals to determine injector pulse width. Non-feedback systems do not use an oxygen sensor

These systems all use sensors which transmit operating conditions to the computer. Information from these sensors is processed by the computer which then determines the proper air/fuel mixture. This signal is sent the to fuel injectors which open and inject fuel into their ports. The longer the injector is held open, the richer the fuel mixture. Most fuel injection systems need the following information to operate properly:

1. Temperature sensors—This includes both air and coolant temperature. The computer uses this information to determine how rich or lean the mixture should be. The colder the temperature, the richer the mixture.

2. Throttle position sensors or switches—The computer uses this information to determine the position of the throttle valve(s). Some vehicles use sensors which relay the exact position of the throttle valve(s) at all times. Others use switches which only relay closed and wide-open throttle positions (some may also use a mid-throttle switch). These switches and sensors help determine engine load.

3. Airflow sensors—These sensors also help the computer determine engine load by indicating the amount of air entering the engine. There are several different types of airflow sensors, but in the end, they all do the same job.

4. Manifold pressure sensors—If a vehicle is not equipped with an airflow sensor, it uses a manifold pressure sensor to determine engine load (Note that some vehicles with an airflow sensor may also have a manifold pressure sensor. This is used as a fail-safe if the airflow sensor fails). As engine load increases, so does intake manifold air pressure.

5. Engine speed and position sensors—Engine speed/position sensors can be referenced from the crankshaft, camshaft or both. In addition to helping determine engine load, these sensors also tell the computer when the injectors should be fired.

These systems operate at a relatively high pressure (usually at least 30 psi). To control the fuel pressure, a fuel pressure regulator is used. As engine load increases, more fuel pressure is needed. This is due to the

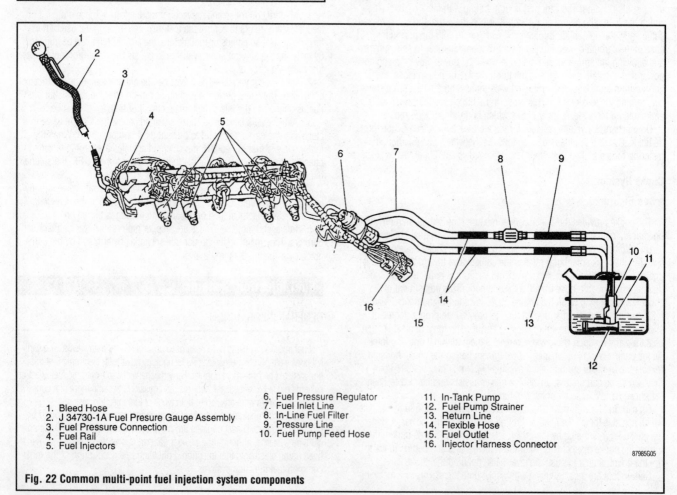

1. Bleed Hose
2. J 34730-1A Fuel Presure Gauge Assembly
3. Fuel Pressure Connection
4. Fuel Rail
5. Fuel Injectors
6. Fuel Pressure Regulator
7. Fuel Inlet Line
8. In-Line Fuel Filter
9. Pressure Line
10. Fuel Pump Feed Hose
11. In-Tank Pump
12. Fuel Pump Strainer
13. Return Line
14. Flexible Hose
15. Fuel Outlet
16. Injector Harness Connector

87985G05

Fig. 22 Common multi-point fuel injection system components

richer mixture (more fuel needed) and to overcome the increased air pressure in the ports. Any unused fuel is diverted back to the fuel tank using a return line.

The fuel injectors can be fired as a batch, a bank or sequentially. On batch fire systems, all of the injectors are fired simultaneously, usually at top dead center of the compression stroke for cylinder number one. Bank fire systems are divided into two separate injector banks. The first bank fires when cylinder number one is at top dead center of the compression stroke. The second bank is usually fired when the number one cylinder is at top dead center of the exhaust stroke. On sequential systems, each injector is fired as its cylinder is at top dead center of its compression stroke. This tends to be the most fuel efficient system.

Feedback fuel injection systems use an oxygen sensor to precisely monitor the air/fuel mixture. Using the signal generated by the oxygen sensor, the computer varies the pulse-width of the fuel injectors. The longer the injector on time (longer pulse width) the richer the fuel mixture.

CENTRAL MULTI-PORT INJECTION

▶ **See Figures 21, 23 and 24**

This system is very similar to the standard multi-port injection system. The main difference lies in the location and construction of the fuel injector(s). Instead of an injector positioned at each intake manifold port, the injector(s) are centrally located in the intake manifold plenum assembly (hence the name central multi-port).

The main component of the system is the fuel meter body. This houses the fuel injector(s), pressure regulator and poppet nozzle/hose assemblies. A hose with a poppet valve extends from the bottom of the fuel injector(s). These hoses are routed to the individual cylinders. The poppet valves handle the atomization of the fuel rather the injector itself as in standard multiport systems.

Early systems used one fuel injector for all the cylinders and are batch fired. Later systems use an injector for each cylinder and are fired sequentially.

THROTTLE BODY INJECTION

▶ **See Figures 21 and 25**

The appearance of throttle body injection systems is similar to the carbureted fuel system. Although not as efficient as multi-port systems, it does offer better driveability and lower emissions than carbureted systems.

The fuel injector(s) is mounted vertically above the throttle plate(s). The throttle body assembly also houses the fuel pressure regulator. These systems typically run at lower pressure compared to multi-port systems. This is mostly due to the fact that pressure in the intake manifold does not have to be overcome. Since the injector(s) is mounted above the throttle plate, fuel is actually drawn into the intake system. Other than this, the actual operation of the throttle body injection system is similar to the multi-port system.

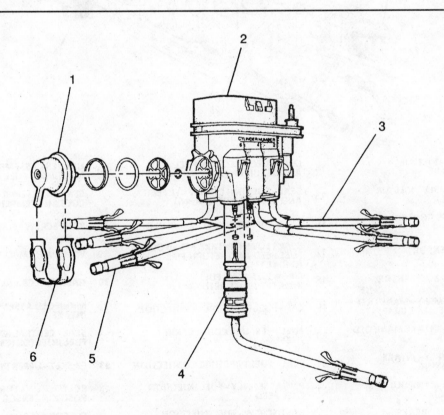

1. Regulator Assembly
2. Fuel Meter Body
3. Flexible Fuel Line
4. Injector Assembly
5. Poppet Nozzle
6. Regulator Retainer

87985G17

Fig. 23 Exploded view of the fuel meter body

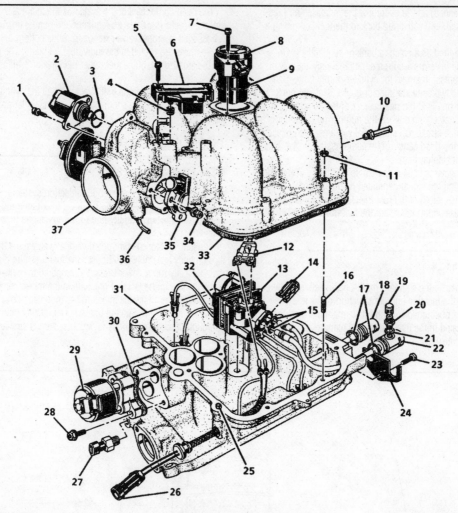

1	BOLT/SCREW - IDLE AIR CONTROL VALVE	**14**	CLIP - FUEL INJECTION FUEL FEED AND RETURN PIPE	**26**	HARNESS ASSEMBLY - CENTRAL MULTIPORT FUEL INJECTOR WIRING
2	VALVE ASSEMBLY - IDLE AIR CONTROL (IAC)	**15**	SEAL - FUEL INJECTION FUEL FEED AND RETURN PIPE (O-RING)	**27**	SENSOR ASSEMBLY - ENGINE COOLANT TEMPERATURE (ECT)
3	SEAL - IDLE AIR CONTROL VALVE (O-RING)	**16**	STUD - UPPER INTAKE MANIFOLD	**28**	BOLT/SCREW - EGR VALVE
4	SEAL - MAP SENSOR	**17**	SEAL - LOWER INTAKE MANIFOLD FUEL FEED AND RETURN PIPE (O-RING)	**29**	VALVE ASSEMBLY - EGR
5	BOLT/SCREW - MAP SENSOR	**18**	PIPE ASSEMBLY - FUEL INJECTION FUEL RETURN	**30**	GASKET - EGR VALVE
6	SENSOR ASSEMBLY - MANIFOLD ABSOLUTE PRESSURE (MAP)	**19**	CAP - FUEL PRESSURE CONNECTION	**31**	MANIFOLD ASSEMBLY - LOWER INTAKE
7	BOLT/SCREW - INTAKE MANIFOLD TUNING VALVE	**20**	FUEL PRESSURE CONNECTION ASSEMBLY	**32**	SEAL - CENTRAL MULTIPORT FUEL INJECTOR (CMFI)
8	VALVE ASSEMBLY - INTAKE MANIFOLD TUNING	**21**	SEAL - FUEL PRESSURE CONNECTION	**33**	GASKET - UPPER INTAKE MANIFOLD
9	SEAL - INTAKE MANIFOLD VALVE (O-RING)	**22**	PIPE ASSEMBLY - FUEL INJECTION FUEL FEED	**34**	BOLT/SCREW - THROTTLE POSITION SENSOR
10	FITTING - POWER BRAKE BOOSTER VACUUM	**23**	BOLT/SCREW - FUEL INJECTION FUEL FEED AND RETURN PIPE RETAINER	**35**	SENSOR ASSEMBLY - THROTTLE POSITION (TP) SENSOR
11	NUT - UPPER INTAKE MANIFOLD	**24**	RETAINER - FUEL INJECTION FUEL FEED AND RETURN PIPE	**36**	TUBE - FUEL VAPOR CANISTER PURGE
12	CONNECTOR ASSEMBLY - CENTRAL MULTIPORT FUEL INJECTOR WIRING HARNESS	**25**	PIN - UPPER INTAKE MANIFOLD LOCATING	**37**	MANIFOLD ASSEMBLY - UPPER INTAKE (WITH THROTTLE BODY)
13	INJECTOR ASSEMBLY - CENTRAL MULTIPORT FUEL INJECTOR (CMFI)				

Fig. 24 The fuel meter body is located inside the plenum assembly

88265G59

Fig. 25 Common throttle body injection system operation

8. Fuel supply
10. Fuel return
13. Pressure regulator (part of fuel meter cover)
14. Idle air control (IAC) valve (shown open)
16. Fuel injector
17. Fuel injector terminals
18. Ported vacuum sources*
19. Manifold vacuum source*
20. Throttle valve

88265G36

BOSCH CONTINUOUS INJECTION SYSTEMS

▶ **See Figure 26**

CIS System

The Continuous Injection System (CIS) is an independent mechanical system. The basic operating principle is to continuously inject fuel into the intake side of the engine by means of an electric pump. The amount of fuel delivered is metered by an air flow measuring device. Some CIS systems are feedback controlled.

The primary fuel circuit consists of an electric pump, which pulls fuel from the tank. Fuel then passes through an accumulator. The accumulator is basically a container in the fuel line. It houses a spring-loaded diaphragm that provides fuel damping and delays pressure build-up when the engine is first started. When the engine is shut down, the expanded chamber in the accumulator keeps the system under enough pressure for good hot restarts with no vapor locking. Fuel flows through a large, paper element filter to the mixture control assembly.

The mixture control assembly is the heart of the CIS system. It houses the airflow sensor and the fuel distributor. The air sensor is a round plate attached to a counterbalanced lever. The plate and lever are free to move up-and-down on a fulcrum. Accelerator pedal linkage connects to a throttle butterfly, which is upstream (closer to the manifold and intake valves) of the air sensor. Stepping on the accelerator pedal opens the throttle valve. Increased air, demanded by the engine, is sucked through the air cleaner and around the air sensor plate.

In the air funnel, where the air sensor plate is located, the quantity of intake air lifts the plate until an equilibrium is reached between air flow and hydraulic counter-pressure acting on the lever through a plunger. This is the control plunger. In this balanced position, the plunger stays at a level in the

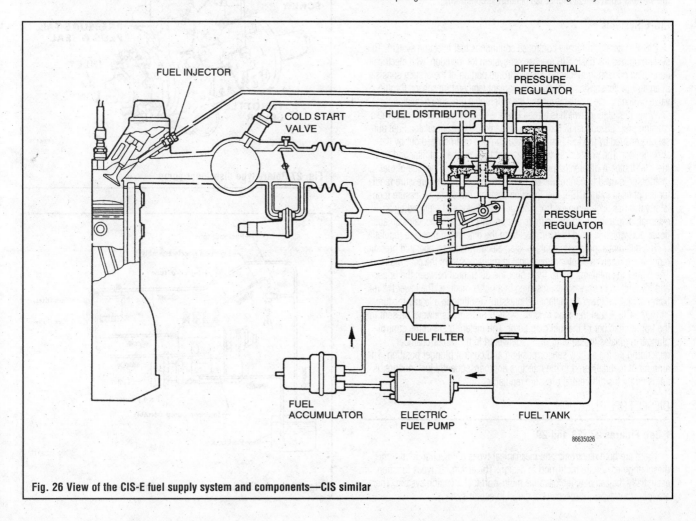

FUEL INJECTOR

COLD START VALVE

FUEL DISTRIBUTOR

DIFFERENTIAL PRESSURE REGULATOR

PRESSURE REGULATOR

FUEL FILTER

FUEL ACCUMULATOR

ELECTRIC FUEL PUMP

FUEL TANK

86635026

Fig. 26 View of the CIS-E fuel supply system and components—CIS similar

fuel distributor to open small metering slits, one for each cylinder in the engine. Fuel under controlled pressure from the pump goes through the slits to the injectors' supply opening. The slit meters the right amount of fuel.

In order to maintain a precise fuel pressure, a pressure regulator, or pressure relief valve, is located in the primary fuel circuit of the fuel distributor. Excess fuel is diverted back to the tank through a return line. To make sure the amount of fuel going through the control plunger slits depends only on their area, an exact pressure differential must always be maintained at the openings. This pressure is controlled by a differential-pressure valve. There's one valve for each cylinder. The valve consists of a spring loaded steel diaphragm and an outlet to the injectors. The diaphragm separates the upper and lower chambers.

The valve keeps an exact pressure differential of 1.42 psi between upper chamber pressure and lower chamber pressure. Both pressures act on the spring loaded steel diaphragm which opens the outlet to the injectors. The size of the outlet opening is always just enough to maintain that 1.42 psi pressure differential at the metering slit. The diaphragm opens more if a larger amount of fuel flows. If less fuel enters the upper chamber, the diaphragm opens less and less fuel goes to the injectors. An exact pressure differential between upper and lower chamber is kept constant. Diaphragm movement is actually only a thousandths of an inch (few hundreths of a millimeter). On feedback controlled CIS systems, a frequency valve regulates the pressure differential at the metering slits and as a result is able to control mixture ratio. The frequency valve uses a signal from a control unit which is generated by an oxygen sensor.

The control pressure regulator can alter the pressure on the control plunger according to engine and outside air temperature. For warm-up running, it lowers the pressure so that the air sensor plate can go higher for the same air flow. This exposes more metering slit area, and more fuel flows for a richer mixture. For cold starts, a separate injector is used to squirt fuel into the intake manifold. This injector is electronically controlled. A thermo-time switch, screwed into the engine, limits the amount of time the valve is open and at higher temperatures, cuts it off.

CIS-E Systems

CIS-E is an electronically controlled continuous fuel injection system. This system utilizes the basic CIS mechanical system for injection, with electrically controlled correction functions. The electronic portion of the system consists of an airflow sensor position indicator, coolant temperature sensor, throttle valve switches, idle air stabilizer and the differential pressure regulator.

When the ignition switch is turned **ON**, the electric fuel pump is activated causing pressurized fuel to move from the tank to the accumulator. Fuel pulsations exerted by the fuel pump are then damped or smoothed out by the accumulator. The pressurized fuel is directed through the fuel filter and to the fuel distributor. A differential pressure regulator located on the side of fuel distributor is used to control the air/fuel mixture. The control pressure regulator is not used in the CIS-E fuel injection system. The system pressure regulator valve has been removed from the fuel distributor and replaced by an external, diaphragm type, pressure regulator. This regulator contains an additional port which is used to return fuel from the differential pressure regulator.

The differential pressure regulator is an electro-magnetic operated pressure regulator. It receives an electronic signal in milliamps from the control unit. The higher the milliamp signal the higher the differential between the upper and lower chamber pressures, resulting in a richer mixture. The lower the milliamp signal the lower the differential pressure resulting in a leaner mixture.

In the CIS-E fuel injection system, system pressure is always present in the upper chamber of the fuel distributor. The metering slit in the control plunger regulates the amount of fuel delivered to the upper chamber depending on the airflow sensor position and control plunger position. The amount of fuel delivered to the injectors and consequently fuel mixture, is adjusted by the differential pressure regulator.

DIESEL FUEL INJECTION

♦ **See Figures 27, 28 and 29**

There are both electronic and mechanical types of injection found on diesel engines; all are multi-port in design. The electronic types function essentially the same as the gasoline multi-port fuel injection system. There are four main types of mechanical diesel injection systems:

1. Inline or rotary distributor pump
2. Individual control pump
3. Common rail
4. Unit injection

The inline or rotary distributor pump is one of the most common types of diesel injection found. This type of pump pressurizes and distributes fuel for each of the cylinders. Fuel from the fuel filter flows from the transfer pump (usually a vane type pump attached to the distributor pump assembly) to the distributor pump itself. The fuel is pressurized inside the distributor pump to approximately 1800 psi (12,411 kPa). This high pressure fuel is then directed to an injector at the appropriate cylinder. The injector atomizes the fuel for proper combustion.

The individual control pump system use a separate high pressure pump and metering unit for each cylinder. The high pressure pumps are fed fuel from a transfer pump. The plungers have helix cut grooves which allow them to meter fuel. By rotating the plunger, the effective stroke is changed and the amount of fuel fed to injectors is metered. The plungers themselves are cam operated. The injector atomizes the fuel for proper combustion.

On common rail systems, a high pressure pump feeds fuel to the injectors through a common rail. The injectors are actuated by a cam, pushrod and rocker arm assembly. The amount of fuel delivered depends on how long the injector is open. A wedge mechanism varies the effective length of

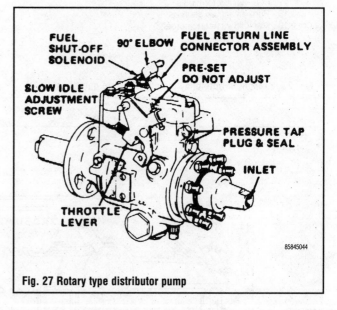

Fig. 27 Rotary type distributor pump

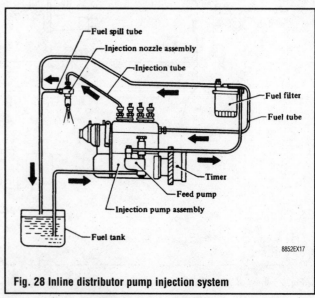

Fig. 28 Inline distributor pump injection system

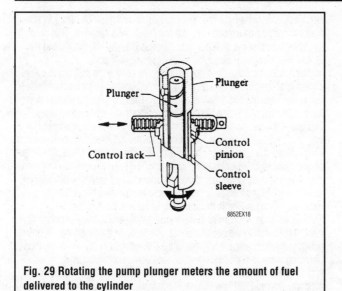

Fig. 29 Rotating the pump plunger meters the amount of fuel delivered to the cylinder

the pushrod, which controls how long the injector is open. The injector also atomizes the fuel for proper combustion.

Unit injections systems also use an individual injector for each cylinder. The injector also contains a high pressure pump and metering assembly, fed by a transfer pump. The injectors are cam operated. Rotating the pump plunger in the injector meters the amount of fuel delivered to the cylinder. In addition, the injector atomizes the fuel for proper combustion.

ROCHESTER MECHANICAL FUEL INJECTION

▶ **See Figure 30**

The first hurdle is understanding the design of this fuel injection system. This is best done by thinking of the unit as three separate systems, interlocked to accomplish a common function. The first system is the air meter and this simultaneously furnishes the fuel meter with an assessment of the load demands of the engine and feeds air to the intake manifold. The intake manifold is designed to ram charge the air as it distributes it to the cylinders. The fuel meter evaluates the air meter signal and furnishes the correct amount of fuel to the nozzles where it is injected into the engine.

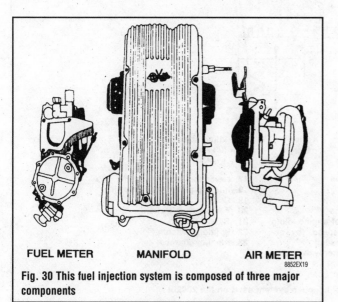

FUEL METER   MANIFOLD   AIR METER

8852EX19

Fig. 30 This fuel injection system is composed of three major components

Air Meter

▶ **See Figure 31**

The air meter consists of three sub-components: the throttle valve, cold enrichment valve and diffuser cone assembly, all of which is contained within the meter housing. Later, air meters were modified to the extent that a choke piston was added and the choke valve stop was relocated in the diffuser cone. This allows an initial choke opening of 10° that increases to 30° after an initial cold start. The throttle valve regulates the flow of air into the manifold and is mechanically actuated by the accelerator pedal. The diffuser cone, suspended in the bore of the air meter inlet, functions as an annular venturi and accelerates the airflow between the cone and the meter housing. The air meter houses the previously mentioned components plus the idle and main venturi signal systems.

The main venturi vacuum signals are generated at the venturi as the incoming air rushes over an annular opening formed between the air meter body and piezometer ring. They are then transmitted through a tube to the main control diaphragm in the fuel meter. The venturi signal measures the flow of air into the engine and automatically controls the air/fuel ratio. The one exception to this is at idle speeds.

Idle air requirements are handled differently by the fuel injection method. Approximately 40% of the idle-speed airflow enters the engine through the nozzle block air connections tapped into the air meter body. Part of the remaining 60% flows past the throttle valve, which is preset against a fixed stop. The remainder enters the idle air by-pass passage that is controlled by the large idle-speed adjusting screw. Idle speed is adjusted by turning this screw in or out.

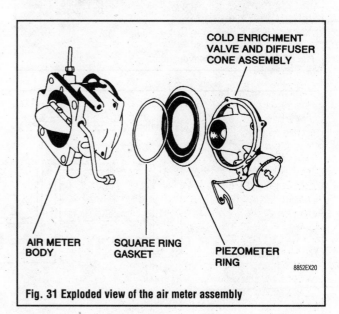

COLD ENRICHMENT VALVE AND DIFFUSER CONE ASSEMBLY

AIR METER BODY   SQUARE RING GASKET   PIEZOMETER RING

8852EX20

Fig. 31 Exploded view of the air meter assembly

Fuel Meter

The fuel meter's float-controlled fuel reservoir is basically the same as that found in conventional carburation. The fuel meter receives fuel from the regular engine fuel pump. The incoming fuel is routed through fuel filter before entering the main reservoir of the fuel meter, where the high-pressure gear pump picks it up. This high-pressure spur-gear type pump is completely submerged in the lower part of the fuel meter main reservoir. A distributor-powered, flexible shaft drives the pump at ½ engine speed. Fuel pressures span a range of near zero to 200 psi, according to engine speed. Fuel not used by the engine reenters the fuel meter through a fuel control system. Some fuel meters contain a vent screen and baffle which helps to stabilize the air/fuel mixture.

Fuel Control System

♦ **See Figure 32**

The fuel control system regulates fuel pressure (flow) from the fuel pump to the nozzles. This flow is controlled by the amount of fuel that is spilled or recirculated from the high-pressure pump, through the nozzle block and back to the fuel meter spill ports. This is accomplished by a three-piece spill plunger or disc that is located between the gear pump and the nozzles.

When high fuel flow is required, it moves downward, closing the spill ports to the fuel meter reservoir and concentrating the flow to the nozzle

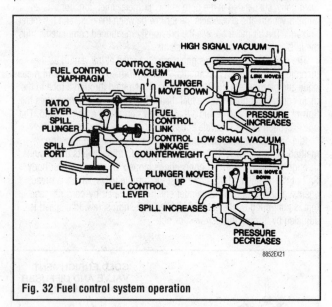

Fig. 32 Fuel control system operation

circuits. Correspondingly, the spill plunger or disc must be raised to allow the spill ports to be exposed when a low fuel flow is required. This causes the main output of the gear pump to by-pass the nozzles circuits and reenter the meter reservoir through the now opened spill ports.

The accelerator pedal does not mechanically control the spill plunger. Fuel control is accomplished by a precisely counterbalanced linkage system sensitive to fuel pressure and diaphragm vacuum. Thus the slightest change in venturi vacuum signal on the main control diaphragm will activate the linkage. One end of the fuel control lever pivots on the roller end of an arm called the ratio lever. When the increased vacuum above the diaphragm forces the control lever upward, the lever pivots on the ration lever's and pushes the spill plunger or disc downward. This closes the spill ports and steps up fuel flow to the nozzles. When decreased vacuum above the diaphragm reverses the pivot action, fuel pressure forces the spill plunger upward and permits the spill ports to by-pass fuel into the reservoir, thus fuel flow to the nozzles is reduced.

The diaphragm vacuum-to-fuel pressure ration, and subsequent air/fuel ratio, is regulated by the position of the ratio lever. As the ration lever changes position, the mechanical advantage of the linkage system also changes, thus providing the correct air/fuel ration for each driving condition. As long as engine manifold vacuum exceeds 8 in. Hg, the ration lever remains at the economy stop and fuel flow follows the dictates of the main control diaphragm vacuum. A sudden decrease in manifold vacuum moves the ratio lever to the power stop. The resulting increase in the mechanical advantage of the linkage system closes the spill ports and increases fuel flow to the nozzles.

KUGELFISCHER MECHANICAL FUEL INJECTION

♦ **See Figure 33**

In the Kugelfischer mechanical fuel injection system, fuel and air are inducted separately through the injection pump and the throttle manifold butterfly. Fuel is injected into the intake manifold behind the open intake valve under high pressure.

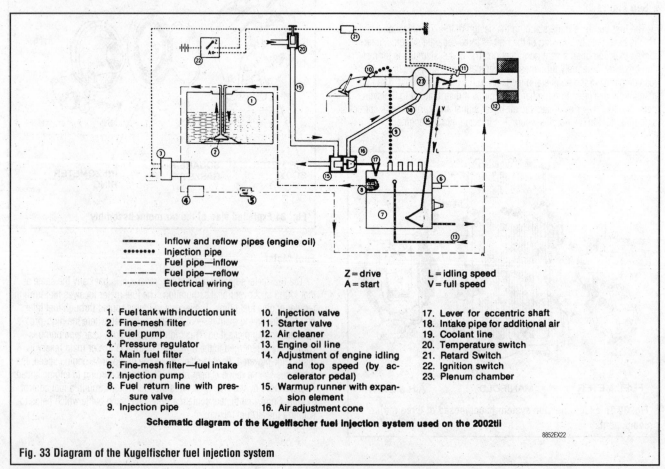

Line legend	
--------	Inflow and reflow pipes (engine oil)
••••••••	Injection pipe
– – – –	Fuel pipe—inflow
–·–·–	Fuel pipe—reflow
··········	Electrical wiring

Z = drive   L = idling speed
A = start   V = full speed

1. Fuel tank with induction unit
2. Fine-mesh filter
3. Fuel pump
4. Pressure regulator
5. Main fuel filter
6. Fine-mesh filter—fuel intake
7. Injection pump
8. Fuel return line with pressure valve
9. Injection pipe
10. Injection valve
11. Starter valve
12. Air cleaner
13. Engine oil line
14. Adjustment of engine idling and top speed (by accelerator pedal)
15. Warmup runner with expansion element
16. Air adjustment cone
17. Lever for eccentric shaft
18. Intake pipe for additional air
19. Coolant line
20. Temperature switch
21. Retard Switch
22. Ignition switch
23. Plenum chamber

Schematic diagram of the Kugelfischer fuel injection system used on the 2002tii

Fig. 33 Diagram of the Kugelfischer fuel injection system

The electric fuel pump pumps fuel from the tank through a fine-mesh filter in the tank and a filter in the fuel line. The fuel flows through the expansion container, the main fuel filter, and into the injector pump. Excess fuel and any air bubbles are routed back to the tank via a return line. This ensures that the fuel is always kept cool and free of bubbles.

The injection pump camshaft is belt-driven from the engine crankshaft. Four pumping pistons, operating in firing order sequence, inject the required amount of fuel. The amount of fuel injected depends on engine load and speed.

Fuel injection volume is regulated by engine load. The accelerator pedal is connected with throttle butterfly and the lever on the injection pump. When the pedal is depressed, the throttle butterfly moves and the stroke length of the pump piston is governed by the regulating cam, depending on throttle opening. Fuel injection volume is also regulated by engine speed. The stroke of the pump piston is governed by the injection pump governor.

When the engine is started, fuel is injected into the intake manifold by a solenoid valve. The duration time of injection depends on the coolant temperature.

When the injection pump pressure reaches approximately 435-551 psi, each injection valve opens. Intake air flows through the air cleaner and the throttle manifold butterfly to the manifold plenum chamber, and from there through the 4 manifold branches to the combustion chambers.

Fuel System Maintenance

The major components of the fuel system are usually quite reliable in themselves. Fuel system maintenance basically consists of a routine visual inspection and fuel filter replacement. If equipped, the fuel/water separator should be periodically drained.

SERVICE PRECAUTIONS

Safety is an important factor when servicing the fuel system. Failure to conduct maintenance and repairs in a safe manner may result in serious personal injury. Maintenance and testing of the vehicle's fuel system components can be accomplished safely and effectively by adhering to the following rules and guidelines.

• To avoid the possibility of fire and personal injury, always disconnect the negative battery cable unless the repair or test procedure requires that battery voltage be applied.

• Always relieve the fuel system pressure prior to disconnecting any fuel system component (injector, fuel rail, pressure regulator, etc.), fitting or fuel line connection. Exercise extreme caution whenever relieving fuel system pressure to avoid exposing skin, face and eyes to fuel spray. Please be advised that fuel under pressure may penetrate the skin or any part of the body that it contacts.

• Always place a shop towel or cloth around the fitting or connection prior to loosening to absorb any excess fuel due to spillage. Ensure that all fuel spillage is quickly removed from engine surfaces. Ensure that all fuel soaked cloths or towels are deposited into a suitable waste container.

• Always keep a dry chemical (Class B) fire extinguisher near the work area.

• Do not allow fuel spray or fuel vapors to come into contact with a spark or open flame.

• Always use a backup wrench and a flare nut (line) wrench when loosening and tightening fuel line connection fittings. This will prevent unnecessary stress and torsion to fuel line piping. Always follow the proper torque specifications.

• Always replace worn fuel fitting O-rings. Do not substitute fuel hose where fuel pipe is installed.

RELIEVING FUEL SYSTEM PRESSURE

Fuel system pressure can be relieved a variety of ways. Some vehicles feature a self-bleed feature—system pressure automatically bleeds down after a period of time. Even if your vehicle has this feature, it is still a good idea to relieve any residual pressure.

If your vehicle is equipped with a fuel pressure test port (usually a Schrader valve), it can be bled from that point. The best way to do this is by attaching a fuel pressure tester gauge hose to the valve. Place the other end of the hose in a container and allow the fuel to bleed off. Often, a vehicle may not have this port, or you may not have a fuel pressure tester. If this is the case, unplug the electrical connector from the fuel pump. Start the engine and allow it to run until it stalls out. Try cranking the engine a couple of more times. The fuel system pressure should now be relieved. When you undo any fittings, wrap a rag around it to prevent any residual pressure from spraying out.

SYSTEM INSPECTION

▶ **See Figure 34**

The fuel system should be routinely inspected for leaks. Check all the fuel lines for cracks, leaks and deformation. Fittings are usually the most common points for leaks to develop. Leaks sometimes also develop at the fuel injectors as the sealing O-rings age. Any type of damage or leaks should be fixed immediately.

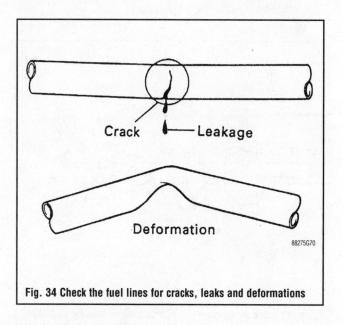

Fig. 34 Check the fuel lines for cracks, leaks and deformations

FUEL FILTER REPLACEMENT

▶ **See Figures 35, 36 and 37**

As described before, there are several different types of fuel filters. Use this procedure as a guide for removing the fuel filter. For specific procedures, refer to a Chilton's Total Car Care manual for your vehicle.

1. Read the service precautions and relieve the fuel system pressure.
2. Locate your fuel filter, then determine what type you have.
3. If necessary remove any shields or clamps securing the filter.
4. For fuel filters located inside mechanical fuel pumps, remove the fastener securing the pump cover. Remove the filter screen and clean or replace with a new one. If a gasket is used, replace it. Reinstall the cover.
5. For filters treaded into the carburetor or throttle body, simply unthread the inlet (or filter itself) and remove the filter. Be sure to note the way the filter and spring (if equipped) came out for installation purposes. Install the new filter (in the proper direction) with a new gasket, if equipped.
6. For spin on type filters, simply unscrew the filter assembly from its mounting boss. An oil filter strap wrench can be used to help loosen the filter. On some models, the filter is a throw-away type. On models with a replaceable cartridge, dispose of the cartridge and clean the housing. Install the new filter assembly—be sure not to overtighten it.

7. As described earlier, inline filters can be attached to the fuel lines several different ways. If your filter is secured with clamps, simply undo them and remove the filter. Inspect the clamps and replace if damaged. Other filters use flare type fittings, banjo bolt connections or a combination of these. Use a wrench or socket to remove the banjo type fitting. On flare type fittings, use a backup wrench on the stationary fitting and a line wrench on the flare nut fitting. The filter can now be removed from the vehicle. Be sure to replace any gaskets with new ones (yes, even the copper washers). Some inline filters are secured to the lines with quick-connect fittings. These usually require special tools to disengage them. Luckily these tools are usually available at local parts stores and are fairly inexpensive. Make sure the fitting connections are clean before disconnecting them. Any sealing O-rings should be replaced upon filter installation. Be sure the sealing surfaces are clean.

8. After the filter is reinstalled, start the engine and check for leaks. If the filter is secured by clamps, be sure to secure it before starting the engine. It may take several tries to start the car. This is normal—the system must reprime itself. Some vehicles with mechanical injection may have a priming plunger on the injection pump. If equipped, use this to reprime the fuel system. Correct any fuel leaks necessary.

9. Install any protective shields, if equipped.

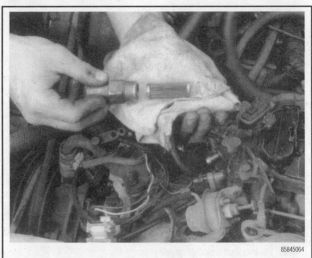

Fig. 36 Be sure to note the way the filter and spring came out for installation purposes—inlet type filter

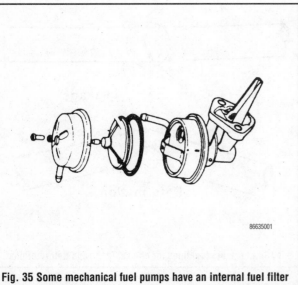

Fig. 35 Some mechanical fuel pumps have an internal fuel filter

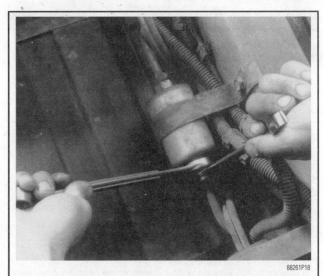

Fig. 37 Use a backup wrench to keep the lines from twisting

EMISSIONS AND EMISSION CONTROLS

Air Pollution

The earth's atmosphere, at or near sea level, consists approximately of 78 percent nitrogen, 21 percent oxygen and 1 percent other gases. If it were possible to remain in this state, 100 percent clean air would result. However, many varied sources allow other gases and particulates to mix with the clean air, causing our atmosphere to become unclean or polluted.

Some of these pollutants are visible while others are invisible, with each having the capability of causing distress to the eyes, ears, throat, skin and respiratory system. Should these pollutants become concentrated in a specific area and under certain conditions, death could result due to the displacement or chemical change of the oxygen content in the air. These pollutants can also cause great damage to the environment and to the many man made objects that are exposed to the elements.

To better understand the causes of air pollution, the pollutants can be categorized into 3 separate types, natural, industrial and automotive.

NATURAL POLLUTANTS

Natural pollution has been present on earth since before man appeared and continues to be a factor when discussing air pollution, although it causes only a small percentage of the overall pollution problem. It is the direct result of decaying organic matter, wind born smoke and particulates from such natural events as plain and forest fires (ignited by heat or lightning), volcanic ash, sand and dust which can spread over a large area of the countryside.

Such a phenomenon of natural pollution has been seen in the form of volcanic eruptions, with the resulting plume of smoke, steam and volcanic ash blotting out the sun's rays as it spreads and rises higher into the atmosphere. As it travels into the atmosphere the upper air currents catch and carry the smoke and ash, while condensing the steam back into water vapor. As the water vapor, smoke and ash travel on their journey, the smoke dissipates into the atmosphere while the ash and moisture settle back to earth in a trail hundreds of miles long. In some cases, lives are lost and millions of dollars of property damage result.

INDUSTRIAL POLLUTANTS

Industrial pollution is caused primarily by industrial processes, the burning of coal, oil and natural gas, which in turn produce smoke and fumes. Because the burning fuels contain large amounts of sulfur, the principal ingredients of smoke and fumes are sulfur dioxide and particulate matter. This type of pollutant occurs most severely during still, damp and cool weather, such as at night. Even in its less severe form, this pollutant is not confined to just cities. Because of air movements, the pollutants move for miles over the surrounding countryside, leaving in its path a barren and unhealthy environment for all living things.

Working with Federal, State and Local mandated regulations and by carefully monitoring emissions, big business has greatly reduced the amount of pollutant introduced from its industrial sources, striving to obtain an acceptable level. Because of the mandated industrial emission clean up, many land areas and streams in and around the cities that were formerly barren of vegetation and life, have now begun to move back in the direction of nature's intended balance.

AUTOMOTIVE POLLUTANTS

The third major source of air pollution is automotive emissions. The emissions from the internal combustion engines were not an appreciable problem years ago because of the small number of registered vehicles and the nation's small highway system. However, during the early 1950's, the trend of the American people was to move from the cities to the surrounding suburbs. This caused an immediate problem in transportation because the majority of suburbs were not afforded mass transit conveniences. This lack of transportation created an attractive market for the automobile manufacturers, which resulted in a dramatic increase in the number of vehicles produced and sold, along with a marked increase in highway construction between cities and the suburbs. Multi-vehicle families emerged with a growing emphasis placed on an individual vehicle per family member. As the increase in vehicle ownership and usage occurred, so did pollutant levels in and around the cities, as suburbanites drove daily to their businesses and employment, returning at the end of the day to their homes in the suburbs.

It was noted that a smoke and fog type haze was being formed and at times, remained in suspension over the cities, taking time to dissipate. At first this "smog," derived from the words "smoke" and "fog," was thought to result from industrial pollution but it was determined that automobile emissions shared the blame. It was discovered that when normal automobile emissions were exposed to sunlight for a period of time, complex chemical reactions would take place.

It is now known that smog is a photo chemical layer which develops when certain oxides of nitrogen (NOx) and unburned hydrocarbons (HC) from automobile emissions are exposed to sunlight. Pollution was more severe when smog would become stagnant over an area in which a warm layer of air settled over the top of the cooler air mass, trapping and holding the cooler mass at ground level. The trapped cooler air would keep the emissions from being dispersed and diluted through normal air flows. This type of air stagnation was given the name "Temperature Inversion."

Temperature Inversion

In normal weather situations, surface air is warmed by heat radiating from the earth's surface and the sun's rays. This causes it to rise upward, into the atmosphere. Upon rising it will cool through a convection type heat exchange with the cooler upper air. As warm air rises, the surface pollutants are carried upward and dissipated into the atmosphere.

When a temperature inversion occurs, we find the higher air is no longer cooler, but is warmer than the surface air, causing the cooler surface air to become trapped. This warm air blanket can extend from above ground level to a few hundred or even a few thousand feet into the air. As the surface air is trapped, so are the pollutants, causing a severe smog condition. Should this stagnant air mass extend to a few thousand feet high, enough air movement with the inversion takes place to allow the smog layer to rise above ground level but the pollutants still cannot dissipate. This inversion can remain for days over an area, with the smog level only rising or lowering from ground level to a few hundred feet high. Meanwhile, the pollutant levels increase, causing eye irritation, respiratory problems, reduced visibility, plant damage and in some cases, even disease.

This inversion phenomenon was first noted in the Los Angeles, California area. The city lies in terrain resembling a basin and with certain weather conditions, a cold air mass is held in the basin while a warmer air mass covers it like a lid.

Because this type of condition was first documented as prevalent in the Los Angeles area, this type of trapped pollution was named Los Angeles Smog, although it occurs in other areas where a large concentration of automobiles are used and the air remains stagnant for any length of time.

Heat Transfer

Consider the internal combustion engine as a machine in which raw materials must be placed so a finished product comes out. As in any machine operation, a certain amount of wasted material is formed. When we relate this to the internal combustion engine, we find that through the input of air and fuel, we obtain power during the combustion process to drive the vehicle. The by-product or waste of this power is, in part, heat and exhaust gases with which we must dispose.

The heat from the combustion process can rise to over 4000°F (2204°C). The dissipation of this heat is controlled by a ram air effect, the use of cooling fans to cause air flow and a liquid coolant solution surrounding the combustion area to transfer the heat of combustion through the cylinder walls and into the coolant. The coolant is then directed to a thin-finned, multi-tubed radiator, from which the excess heat is transferred to the atmosphere by 1 of the 3 heat transfer methods, conduction, convection or radiation.

The cooling of the combustion area is an important part in the control of exhaust emissions. To understand the behavior of the combustion and transfer of its heat, consider the air/fuel charge. It is ignited and the flame front burns progressively across the combustion chamber until the burning charge reaches the cylinder walls. Some of the fuel in contact with the walls is not hot enough to burn, thereby snuffing out or quenching the combustion process. This leaves unburned fuel in the combustion chamber. This unburned fuel is then forced out of the cylinder and into the exhaust system, along with the exhaust gases.

Many attempts have been made to minimize the amount of unburned fuel in the combustion chambers due to quenching, by increasing the coolant temperature and lessening the contact area of the coolant around the combustion area. However, design limitations within the combustion chambers prevent the complete burning of the air/fuel charge, so a certain amount of the unburned fuel is still expelled into the exhaust system, regardless of modifications to the engine.

Automotive Emissions

Before emission controls were mandated on internal combustion engines, other sources of engine pollutants were discovered along with the exhaust emissions. It was determined that engine combustion exhaust produced approximately 60 percent of the total emission pollutants, fuel evaporation from the fuel tank and carburetor vents produced 20 percent, with the final 20 percent being produced through the crankcase as a by-product of the combustion process.

EXHAUST GASES

The exhaust gases emitted into the atmosphere are a combination of burned and unburned fuel. To understand the exhaust emission and its composition, we must review some basic chemistry.

When the air/fuel mixture is introduced into the engine, we are mixing air, composed of nitrogen (78 percent), oxygen (21 percent) and other gases (1 percent) with the fuel, which is 100 percent hydrocarbons (HC), in a semi-controlled ratio. As the combustion process is accomplished, power is produced to move the vehicle while the heat of combustion is transferred to the cooling system. The exhaust gases are then composed of nitrogen, a diatomic gas (N_2), the same as was introduced in the engine, carbon dioxide (CO_2), the same gas that is used in beverage carbonation, and water vapor (H_2O). The nitrogen (N_2), for the most part, passes through the engine unchanged, while the oxygen (O_2) reacts (burns) with the hydrocarbons (HC) and produces the carbon dioxide (CO_2) and the water vapors (H_2O). If this chemical process would be the only process to take place, the exhaust emissions would be harmless. However, during the combustion process, other compounds are formed which are considered dangerous. These pollutants are hydrocarbons (HC), carbon monoxide (CO), oxides of nitrogen (NOx) oxides of sulfur (SOx) and engine particulates.

Hydrocarbons

Hydrocarbons (HC) are essentially fuel which was not burned during the combustion process or which has escaped into the atmosphere through fuel evaporation. The main sources of incomplete combustion are rich air/fuel mixtures, low engine temperatures and improper spark timing. The main sources of hydrocarbon emission through fuel evaporation on most vehicles used to be the vehicle's fuel tank and carburetor float bowl.

To reduce combustion hydrocarbon emission, engine modifications were made to minimize dead space and surface area in the combustion chamber. In addition, the air/fuel mixture was made more lean through the improved control which feedback carburetion and fuel injection offers and by the addition of external controls to aid in further combustion of the hydrocarbons outside the engine. Two such methods were the addition of air injection systems, to inject fresh air into the exhaust manifolds and the installation of catalytic converters, units that are able to burn traces of hydrocarbons without affecting the internal combustion process or fuel economy.

To control hydrocarbon emissions through fuel evaporation, modifications were made to the fuel tank to allow storage of the fuel vapors during periods of engine shut-down. Modifications were also made to the air intake system so that at specific times during engine operation, these vapors may be purged and burned by blending them with the air/fuel mixture.

Carbon Monoxide

Carbon monoxide is formed when not enough oxygen is present during the combustion process to convert carbon (C) to carbon dioxide (CO_2). An increase in the carbon monoxide (CO) emission is normally accompanied by an increase in the hydrocarbon (HC) emission because of the lack of oxygen to completely burn all of the fuel mixture.

Carbon monoxide (CO) also increases the rate at which the photo chemical smog is formed by speeding up the conversion of nitric oxide (NO) to nitrogen dioxide (NO_2). To accomplish this, carbon monoxide (CO) combines with oxygen (O_2) and nitric oxide (NO) to produce carbon dioxide (CO_2) and nitrogen dioxide (NO_2). ($CO + O_2 + NO = CO_2 + NO_2$).

The dangers of carbon monoxide, which is an odorless and colorless toxic gas are many. When carbon monoxide is inhaled into the lungs and passed into the blood stream, oxygen is replaced by the carbon monoxide in the red blood cells, causing a reduction in the amount of oxygen supplied to the many parts of the body. This lack of oxygen causes headaches, lack of coordination, reduced mental alertness and, should the carbon monoxide concentration be high enough, death could result.

Nitrogen

Normally, nitrogen is an inert gas. When heated to approximately 2500°F (1371°C) through the combustion process, this gas becomes active and causes an increase in the nitric oxide (NO) emission.

Oxides of nitrogen (NOx) are composed of approximately 97–98 percent nitric oxide (NO). Nitric oxide is a colorless gas but when it is passed into the atmosphere, it combines with oxygen and forms nitrogen dioxide (NO_2). The nitrogen dioxide then combines with chemically active hydrocarbons (HC) and when in the presence of sunlight, causes the formation of photochemical smog.

OZONE

To further complicate matters, some of the nitrogen dioxide (NO_2) is broken apart by the sunlight to form nitric oxide and oxygen. ($NO_2 +$ sunlight =

NO + O). This single atom of oxygen then combines with diatomic (meaning 2 atoms) oxygen (O_2) to form ozone (O_3). Ozone is one of the smells associated with smog. It has a pungent and offensive odor, irritates the eyes and lung tissues, affects the growth of plant life and causes rapid deterioration of rubber products. Ozone can be formed by sunlight as well as electrical discharge into the air.

The most common discharge area on the automobile engine is the secondary ignition electrical system, especially when inferior quality spark plug cables are used. As the surge of high voltage is routed through the secondary cable, the circuit builds up an electrical field around the wire, which acts upon the oxygen in the surrounding air to form the ozone. The faint glow along the cable with the engine running that may be visible on a dark night, is called the "corona discharge." It is the result of the electrical field passing from a high along the cable, to a low in the surrounding air, which forms the ozone gas. The combination of corona and ozone has been a major cause of cable deterioration. Recently, different and better quality insulating materials have lengthened the life of the electrical cables.

Although ozone at ground level can be harmful, ozone is beneficial to the earth's inhabitants. By having a concentrated ozone layer called the "ozonosphere," between 10 and 20 miles (16–32 km) up in the atmosphere, much of the ultra violet radiation from the sun's rays are absorbed and screened. If this ozone layer were not present, much of the earth's surface would be burned, dried and unfit for human life.

Oxides Of Sulfur

Oxides of sulfur (SOx) were initially ignored in the exhaust system emissions, since the sulfur content of gasoline as a fuel is less than 1/10 of 1 percent. Because of this small amount, it was felt that it contributed very little to the overall pollution problem. However, because of the difficulty in solving the sulfur emissions in industrial pollution's and the introduction of catalytic converter to the automobile exhaust systems, a change was mandated. The automobile exhaust system, when equipped with a catalytic converter, changes the sulfur dioxide (SO_2) into sulfur trioxide (SO_3).

When this combines with water vapors (H_2O), a sulfuric acid mist (H_2SO_4) is formed and is a very difficult pollutant to handle since it is extremely corrosive. This sulfuric acid mist that is formed, is the same mist that rises from the vents of an automobile battery when an active chemical reaction takes place within the battery cells.

When a large concentration of vehicles equipped with catalytic converters are operating in an area, this acid mist may rise and be distributed over a large ground area causing land, plant, crop, paint and building damage.

Particulate Matter

A certain amount of particulate matter is present in the burning of any fuel, with carbon constituting the largest percentage of the particulates. In gasoline, the remaining particulates are the burned remains of the various other compounds used in its manufacture. When a gasoline engine is in good internal condition, the particulate emissions are low but as the engine wears internally, the particulate emissions increase. By visually inspecting the tail pipe emissions, a determination can be made as to where an engine defect may exist. An engine with light gray or blue smoke emitting from the tail pipe normally indicates an increase in the oil consumption through burning due to internal engine wear. Black smoke would indicate a defective fuel delivery system, causing the engine to operate in a rich mode. Regardless of the color of the smoke, the internal part of the engine or the fuel delivery system should be repaired to prevent excess particulate emissions.

Diesel and turbine engines emit a darkened plume of smoke from the exhaust system because of the type of fuel used. Emission control regulations are mandated for this type of emission and more stringent measures are being used to prevent excess emission of the particulate matter. Electronic components are being introduced to control the injection of the fuel at precisely the proper time of piston travel, to achieve the optimum in fuel ignition and fuel usage. Other particulate after-burning components are being tested to achieve a cleaner emission.

Good grades of engine lubricating oils should be used, which meet the manufacturers specification. Cut-rate oils can contribute to the particulate emission problem because of their low flash or ignition temperature point.

Such oils burn prematurely during the combustion process causing emission of particulate matter.

The cooling system is an important factor in the reduction of particulate matter. The optimum combustion will occur, with the cooling system operating at a temperature specified by the manufacturer. The cooling system must be maintained in the same manner as the engine oiling system, as each system is required to perform properly in order for the engine to operate efficiently for a long time.

CRANKCASE EMISSIONS

Crankcase emissions are made up of water, acids, unburned fuel, oil fumes and particulates. These emissions are classified as hydrocarbons (HC) and are formed by the small amount of unburned, compressed air/fuel mixture entering the crankcase from the combustion area (between the cylinder walls and piston rings) during the compression and power strokes. The head of the compression and combustion help to form the remaining crankcase emissions.

Since the first engines, crankcase emissions were allowed into the atmosphere through a road draft tube, mounted on the lower side of the engine block. Fresh air came in through an open oil filler cap or breather. The air passed through the crankcase mixing with blow-by gases. The motion of the vehicle and the air blowing past the open end of the road draft tube caused a low pressure area (vacuum) at the end of the tube. Crankcase emissions were simply drawn out of the road draft tube into the air.

To control the crankcase emission, the road draft tube was deleted. A hose and/or tubing was routed from the crankcase to the intake manifold so the blow-by emission could be burned with the air/fuel mixture. However, it was found that intake manifold vacuum, used to draw the crankcase emissions into the manifold, would vary in strength at the wrong time and not allow the proper emission flow. A regulating valve was needed to control the flow of air through the crankcase.

Testing, showed the removal of the blow-by gases from the crankcase as quickly as possible, was most important to the longevity of the engine. Should large accumulations of blow-by gases remain and condense, dilution of the engine oil would occur to form water, soots, resins, acids and lead salts, resulting in the formation of sludge and varnishes. This condensation of the blow-by gases occurs more frequently on vehicles used in numerous starting and stopping conditions, excessive idling and when the engine is not allowed to attain normal operating temperature through short runs.

EVAPORATIVE EMISSIONS

Gasoline fuel is a major source of pollution, before and after it is burned in the automobile engine. From the time the fuel is refined, stored, pumped and transported, again stored until it is pumped into the fuel tank of the vehicle, the gasoline gives off unburned hydrocarbons (HC) into the atmosphere. Through the redesign of storage areas and venting systems, the pollution factor was diminished, but not eliminated, from the refinery standpoint. However, the automobile still remained the primary source of vaporized, unburned hydrocarbon (HC) emissions.

Fuel pumped from an underground storage tank is cool but when exposed to a warmer ambient temperature, will expand. Before controls were mandated, an owner might fill the fuel tank with fuel from an underground storage tank and park the vehicle for some time in warm area, such as a parking lot. As the fuel would warm, it would expand and should no provisions or area be provided for the expansion, the fuel would spill out of the filler neck and onto the ground, causing hydrocarbon (HC) pollution and creating a severe fire hazard. To correct this condition, the vehicle manufacturers added overflow plumbing and/or gasoline tanks with built in expansion areas or domes.

However, this did not control the fuel vapor emission from the fuel tank. It was determined that most of the fuel evaporation occurred when the vehicle was stationary and the engine not operating. Most vehicles carry 5–25 gallons (19–95 liters) of gasoline. Should a large concentration of vehicles be parked in one area, such as a large parking lot, excessive fuel vapor emissions would take place, increasing as the temperature increases.

To prevent the vapor emission from escaping into the atmosphere, the fuel systems were designed to trap the vapors while the vehicle is stationary, by sealing the system from the atmosphere. A storage system is used to collect and hold the fuel vapors from the carburetor (if equipped) and the fuel tank when the engine is not operating. When the engine is started, the storage system is then purged of the fuel vapors, which are drawn into the engine and burned with the air/fuel mixture.

Emission Control Systems

When viewed as a whole, emission control systems can be extremely confusing. However, it is possible to ease some of the confusion by dividing the overall emissions system into several easily understood smaller systems.

There are five popular systems used to reduce emissions: the crankcase ventilation system, the evaporative emission control system, the Exhaust Gas Recirculation (EGR) system, the air injection system and the catalytic converter system. In addition to these emission systems, some vehicles incorporate an electronically controlled fuel system (feedback system) which further reduces emissions.

➡ Not all vehicles are equipped with these emission systems.

CRANKCASE VENTILATION SYSTEMS

◆ See Figures 38 and 39

Since the early sixties, all cars have been equipped with crankcase ventilation systems.

When the engine is running, a small portion of the gases which are formed in the combustion chamber leak past the piston rings and enter the crankcase. Since these gases are under pressure, they tend to escape from the crankcase and enter the atmosphere. If these gases are allowed to remain in the crankcase for any length of time, they contaminate the engine oil and cause sludge to build up in the crankcase. If the gases are allowed to escape to the atmosphere, they pollute the air with unburned hydrocarbons. The job of the crankcase ventilation system is to recycle these gases back into the engine combustion chamber where they are reburned.

The crankcase (blow-by) gases are recycled as the engine is running by drawing clean filtered air through the air filter and into the crankcase. As the air passes through the crankcase, it picks up the combustion gases and carries them out of the crankcase, through the oil separator, through the PCV valve or orifice, and into the induction system. As they enter the intake manifold, they are drawn into the combustion chamber where they are reburned.

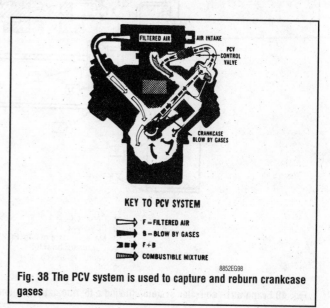

KEY TO PCV SYSTEM

⇨ F = FILTERED AIR
➡ B = BLOW BY GASES
▨▶ F + B
▥▷ COMBUSTIBLE MIXTURE

8852EG98

Fig. 38 The PCV system is used to capture and reburn crankcase gases

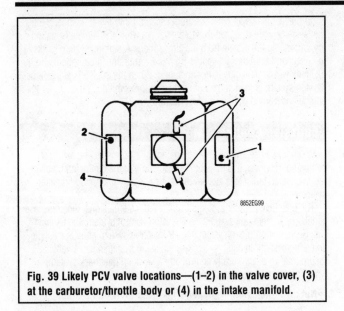

Fig. 39 Likely PCV valve locations—(1–2) in the valve cover, (3) at the carburetor/throttle body or (4) in the intake manifold.

The most critical component in the system is the PCV valve that controls the amount of gases that are recycled. At low engine speeds, the valve is partially closed, limiting the flow of gases. As engine speed increases, the valve opens to admit greater quantities of air to the intake manifold. Some systems do not use a PCV valve. They simply use a restrictor or orifice in the ventilation hose to meter the crankcase gases.

If the PCV valve/orifice becomes blocked or plugged, the gases cannot be vented from the crankcase. Since they are under pressure, they will find their own way out of the crankcase. This alternate route is usually a weak oil seal or gasket in the engine. As the gas escapes by the gasket, it usually creates an oil leak. Besides causing oil leaks, a clogged PCV valve also allows these gases to remain in the crankcase for an extended period, promoting the formation of sludge in the engine.

EVAPORATIVE EMISSION CONTROL SYSTEM

▶ See Figures 40 and 41

The evaporative emission control system is designed to prevent fuel tank and carburetor bowl (if equipped) vapors from being emitted into the atmosphere. Fuel vapors are absorbed and stored by a fuel vapor charcoal canister. The canister stores them until certain engine conditions are met and the vapors can be purged and burned by the engine.

The charcoal canister purge cycle is controlled different ways: either by a thermostatic vacuum switch, a solenoid or by a timed vacuum source. The thermostatic switch is installed in the coolant passage and prevents canister purge when the engine is below a certain temperature. The solenoid is usually controlled by a computer and is used on feedback controlled fuel systems. The computer determines when canister purge is appropriate. Depending on the system, this can be engine operating temperature, engine speed, evaporative system pressure or any combination of these. The timed vacuum source uses a manifold vacuum controlled diaphragm to control canister purge. When the engine is running, full manifold vacuum is applied to the top tube of the purge valve which lifts the valve diaphragm and opens the valve.

A vent located in the fuel tank, allows fuel vapors to flow to the charcoal canister. A tank pressure control valve, used on some high altitude applications, prevents canister purge when the engine is not running. The fuel tank cap does not normally vent to the atmosphere, but is designed to provide both vacuum and pressure relief.

AIR INJECTION SYSTEMS

▶ See Figure 42

Introducing a controlled amount of air into the exhaust stream promotes further oxidation of the gases. This in turn reduces the amount of carbon monoxide and hydrocarbons. The carbon monoxide and hydrocarbons are converted to carbon dioxide and water, the harmless by-products of combustion. Some systems use an air pump, while other use negative exhaust pulses to draw air (pulse air).

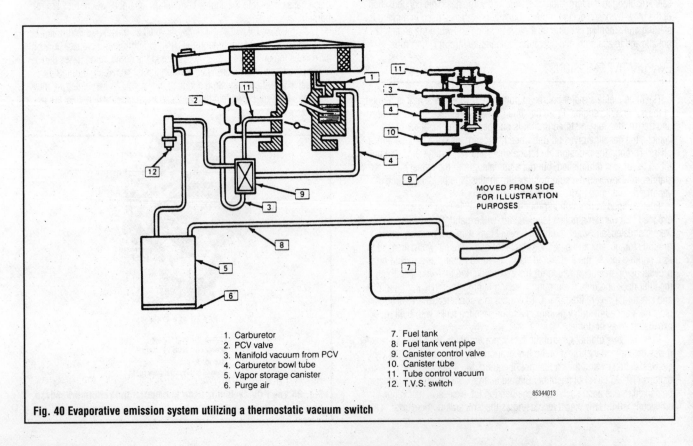

MOVED FROM SIDE
FOR ILLUSTRATION
PURPOSES

1. Carburetor
2. PCV valve
3. Manifold vacuum from PCV
4. Carburetor bowl tube
5. Vapor storage canister
6. Purge air
7. Fuel tank
8. Fuel tank vent pipe
9. Canister control valve
10. Canister tube
11. Tube control vacuum
12. T.V.S. switch

Fig. 40 Evaporative emission system utilizing a thermostatic vacuum switch

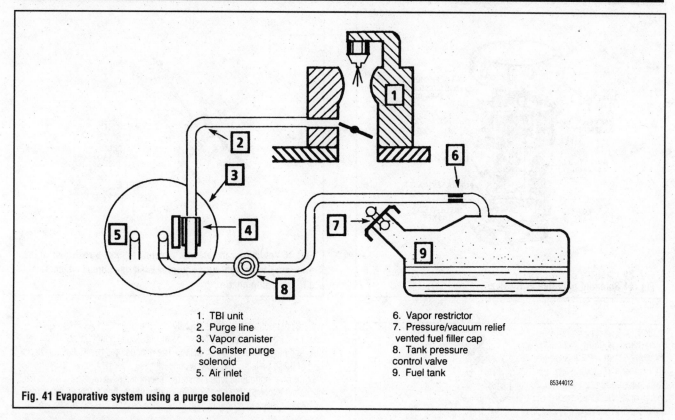

1. TBI unit
2. Purge line
3. Vapor canister
4. Canister purge solenoid
5. Air inlet
6. Vapor restrictor
7. Pressure/vacuum relief vented fuel filler cap
8. Tank pressure control valve
9. Fuel tank

85344012

Fig. 41 Evaporative system using a purge solenoid

The air pump, usually driven by a belt, simply pumps air under a pressure of only a few pounds into each exhaust port. Between the nozzles and the pump is a check valve to keep the hot exhaust gases from flowing back into the pump and hoses thereby destroying them. Most pumps also utilize a gulp valve or a diverter valve. Early systems used a gulp valve, while later systems use diverter valves. They both operate on the same principle. During deceleration, as the throttle is closed, the fuel mixture tends to get too rich. If the air continued to be pumped during deceleration, an explosion in the exhaust system could occur that could blow the muffler apart. During deceleration, the air is either diverted into the atmosphere or into the intake system.

On pulse air systems, clean air (from the air cleaner) is drawn through a silencer, the check valve(s) and then into the exhaust ports. The negative exhaust pulses opens the reed valve in the check valve assembly, allowing air to flow into the exhaust port.

Some feedback controlled vehicles utilize an oxdizing catalytic converter. Under certain operating conditions, the air is diverted into the catalytic converter to help oxdize the exhaust gases.

EXHAUST GAS RECIRCULATION (EGR) SYSTEMS

♦ See Figures 43, 44 and 45

The EGR system's purpose is to control oxides of nitrogen (NOx) which are formed during the combustion process. NOx emissions at low combustion temperatures are not severe, but when the combustion temperatures go over 2500° F, the production of NOx in the combustion chambers shoots way up. The end products of combustion are relatively inert gases derived from the exhaust gases. These are redirected (under certain conditions)

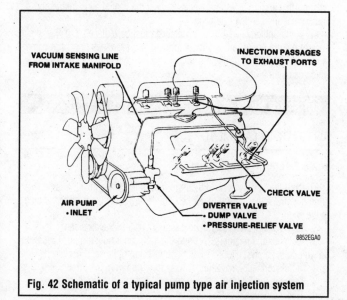

VACUUM SENSING LINE FROM INTAKE MANIFOLD

INJECTION PASSAGES TO EXHAUST PORTS

CHECK VALVE

AIR PUMP
• INLET

DIVERTER VALVE
• DUMP VALVE
• PRESSURE-RELIEF VALVE

8852EGA0

Fig. 42 Schematic of a typical pump type air injection system

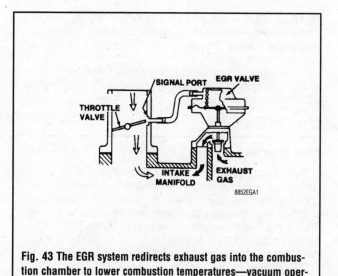

SIGNAL PORT   EGR VALVE

THROTTLE VALVE

INTAKE MANIFOLD   EXHAUST GAS

8852EGA1

Fig. 43 The EGR system redirects exhaust gas into the combustion chamber to lower combustion temperatures—vacuum operated EGR valve

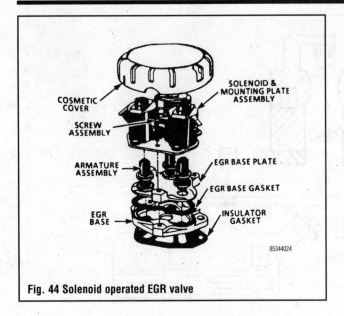

Fig. 44 Solenoid operated EGR valve

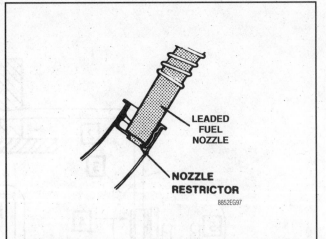

Fig. 46 Vehicles with catalytic converters have a restrictor in the filler neck to prevent filling from leaded gas pumps which have a larger pump nozzle

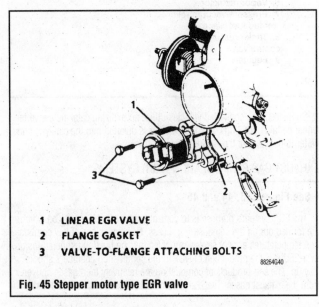

1   LINEAR EGR VALVE

2   FLANGE GASKET

3   VALVE-TO-FLANGE ATTACHING BOLTS

Fig. 45 Stepper motor type EGR valve

through the EGR valve and back into the combustion chamber. These inert gases displace a certain amount of oxygen in the chamber. Since not as much oxygen is present, the explosion is not as hot. This helps lower peak combustion temperatures.

The EGR valve can either be actuated by a vacuum diaphragm, a solenoid or a stepper motor. On feedback controlled vehicles, the EGR system is controlled by the computer.

CATALYTIC CONVERTER

▶ See Figure 46

The catalytic converter is a muffler-like container built into the exhaust system to aid in the reduction of exhaust emissions. The catalyst element is coated with a noble metal such as platinum, palladium, rhodium or a combination of them. When the exhaust gases come into contact with the catalyst, a chemical reaction occurs which reduces the pollutants into harmless substances such as water and carbon dioxide. Oxidizing catalysts require the addition of oxygen to spur the catalyst into reducing the engine's HC and CO emissions into H_2O and CO_2.

While catalytic converters are built in a variety of shapes and sizes, they all fall into two general types, the pellet, or bead type and the monolithic

type. Construction may differ slightly, but the object is the same—to present the largest possible surface area to passing exhaust gases. Older vehicles use bead/pellet type converters. The exhaust gas must pass through a bed of these pellets. This type of converter is rather restrictive. The cross-section of a monolithic type converter resembles a honeycomb. The exhaust gases are exposed to a greater amount of surface area in these converters, as a result they are more efficient. They also tend to be less restrictive.

Catalytic Converter Precautions

1. Use only unleaded fuel.
2. Avoid prolonged idling; the engine should run no longer than 20 min. at curb idle and no longer than 10 min. at fast idle.
3. Don't disconnect any of the spark plug leads while the engine is running. If any engine testing procedure requires disconnecting or bypassing a control component, perform the procedure as quickly as possible. A misfiring engine can overheat the catalyst and damage the oxygen sensor.
4. Make engine compression checks as quickly as possible.
5. Whenever under the vehicle or around the catalytic converter, remember that it has a very high outside or skin temperature. During operation, the catalyst must reach very high temperatures to work efficiently. Be very wary of burns, even after the engine has been shut off for a while. Additionally, because of the heat, never park the vehicle on or over flammable materials, particularly dry grass or leaves. Inspect the heat shields frequently and correct any bends or damage.
6. In the unlikely event that the catalyst must be replaced, DO NOT dispose of the old one where anything containing grease, gas or oil can come in contact with it. The catalytic reaction may occur with these substances, which can start a fire.

Emission System Maintenance

AIR FILTER REPLACEMENT

▶ See Figures 47, 48, 49 and 50

The air filter is never very difficult to find. It is always inside a rather large housing either on top of the carburetor/throttle body or off to the side of the engine.

1. Remove any components necessary to access the air cleaner.
2. Unfasten the retainers securing the air cleaner housing lid. These can be wingnuts, screws, clamps or any combination of these. If necessary, label and disconnect any vacuum hoses or wiring from the lid.
3. Remove the lid from the housing and remove the air filter.
4. Clean the inside of the housing of any dirt or debris.

Fig. 47 Remove the retainers securing the air filter cover. Sometimes there are additional hoses that have to be disconnected before the air cleaner cover can be removed

Fig. 48 Remove the old air filter and inspect it

Fig. 49 Wipe the inside of the air filter housing clean before installing the filter

Fig. 50 Be sure that the filter is positioned properly so the gasket seals

5. Inspect the filter. Check the pleats and gasket surfaces for any tears. Hold the filter up to a light; if you can see a glow through it, it is probably OK to be reused. If the filter is too dirty of damaged, replace it.

6. Reinstall the filter in the housing. Be sure it is positioned properly so the gasket seals. Reinstall the lid on the air cleaner housing.

CRANKCASE VENTILATION SYSTEM

▶ See Figures 51 and 52

The crankcase ventilation system should be inspected for clogged, broken or missing hoses. In addition the PCV valve can be tested. A general test is to remove the PCV valve and shake it. If a rattle is heard, the valve is usually OK. A more accurate test is:

1. Connect a tachometer to the engine.
2. With the engine idling, remove the PCV valve from its mount.
3. Check the tachometer reading. Place a finger over the valve or hose opening. Suction should be felt.
4. Check the tachometer again. The engine speed should have dropped at least 50 rpm. It should return to normal when you remove your finger from the opening.

Fig. 51 The PCV valve is easily replaced

Fig. 52 If equipped, check the ventilation filter

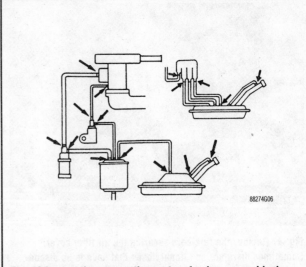

Fig. 53 Inspect the evaporative system for damage and leaks

5. If the engine does not change speed or if the change is less than 50 rpm, the hose is clogged or the valve is defective. Check the hose first. If the hose is not clogged, replace the PCV valve.

6. Test the new valve to make sure that it is operating properly.

The PCV valve itself is fairly easy to replace. It can usually be pulled from the ventilation hose or a grommet in the valve cover. Some are threaded into the valve cover—simply unplug the hose and unthread it from the valve cover with a wrench.

If equipped, check the crankcase ventilation system filter. This is usually located in the air cleaner. Replace if clogged with oil residue.

EVAPORATIVE EMISSION SYSTEM

▶ See Figure 53

The evaporative emission system is relatively maintenance free, but should still be inspected periodically. Inspect all the hoses, fittings and canister for damage. If the canister is cracked or leaking fuel, it must be replaced. Some canisters have a replaceable air filter. They are usually located on the bottom of the canister. Remove the canister from its mount and turn it over—if it appears black and clogged, simply pull it out and replace it.

EXHAUST GAS RECIRCULATION (EGR) SYSTEM

The EGR system is maintenance free. However, it is a good idea to periodically check that none of the components are damaged (damaged vacuum hoses or wiring, leaking exhaust crossover pipes).

AIR INJECTION SYSTEM

▶ See Figure 54

The air injection system should be inspected periodically. Check for damaged hoses, defective check valves and proper belt tension (refer to the cooling system section for belt tension information). Defective check valves are usually indicated by excessive heat bluing (metal is a dark blue color) or rust, causing them to leak.

CATALYTIC CONVERTER

Other than checking for exhaust leaks or damaged heat shielding, the catalytic converter is maintenance free.

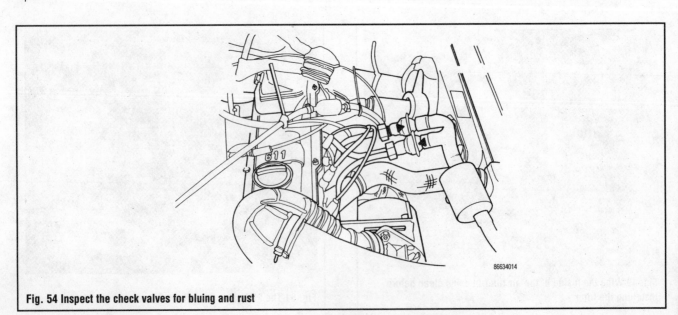

Fig. 54 Inspect the check valves for bluing and rust

FUEL AND EMISSIONS SYSTEM
MAINTENANCE INTERVALS

Your car's fuel and emissions systems will work efficiently if it is maintained at these intervals.

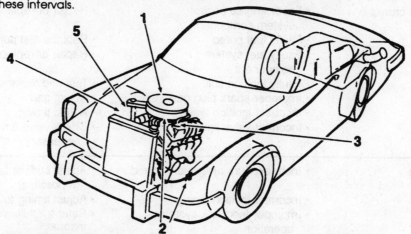

1. **Replace air filter and crankcase breather filter**   Every 12,000 miles/12 months
2. **Replace fuel filter**   Every 12,000 miles/12 months
3. **Check/replace PCV valve**   Check every 12,000 miles/12 months
   Replace every 24,000 miles/2 years

4. **Replace carbon canister filter element**   Every 15,000 miles
5. **Check/adjust air pump belt tension**   Every 3000 miles/3 months*

*New belts will stretch. Check tension after new belt is installed after 200 miles.

8852EC02

Troubleshooting Engine Performance

Problem	Cause	Solution
Hard starting (engine cranks normally)	• Faulty engine control system component	• Repair or replace as necessary
	• Faulty fuel pump	• Replace fuel pump
	• Faulty fuel system component	• Repair or replace as necessary
	• Faulty ignition coil	• Test and replace as necessary
	• Improper spark plug gap	• Adjust gap
	• Incorrect ignition timing	• Adjust timing
	• Incorrect valve timing	• Check valve timing; repair as necessary
Rough idle or stalling	• Incorrect curb or fast idle speed	• Adjust curb or fast idle speed (If possible)
	• Incorrect ignition timing	• Adjust timing to specification
	• Improper feedback system operation	• Refer to Chilton's Total Car Care manual
	• Faulty EGR valve operation	• Test EGR system and replace as necessary
	• Faulty PCV valve air flow	• Test PCV valve and replace as necessary
	• Faulty TAC vacuum motor or valve	• Repair as necessary
	• Air leak into manifold vacuum	• Inspect manifold vacuum connections and repair as necessary
	• Faulty distributor rotor or cap	• Replace rotor or cap (Distributor systems only)
	• Improperly seated valves	• Test cylinder compression, repair as necessary
	• Incorrect ignition wiring	• Inspect wiring and correct as necessary
	• Faulty ignition coil	• Test coil and replace as necessary
	• Restricted air vent or idle passages	• Clean passages
	• Restricted air cleaner	• Clean or replace air cleaner filter element
Faulty low-speed operation	• Restricted idle air vents and passages	• Clean air vents and passages
	• Restricted air cleaner	• Clean or replace air cleaner filter element
	• Faulty spark plugs	• Clean or replace spark plugs
	• Dirty, corroded, or loose ignition secondary circuit wire connections	• Clean or tighten secondary circuit wire connections
	• Improper feedback system operation	• Refer to Chilton's Total Car Care manual
	• Faulty ignition coil high voltage wire	• Replace ignition coil high voltage wire (Distributor systems only)
	• Faulty distributor cap	• Replace cap (Distributor systems only)
Faulty acceleration	• Incorrect ignition timing	• Adjust timing
	• Faulty fuel system component	• Repair or replace as necessary
	• Faulty spark plug(s)	• Clean or replace spark plug(s)
	• Improperly seated valves	• Test cylinder compression, repair as necessary
	• Faulty ignition coil	• Test coil and replace as necessary

Troubleshooting Engine Performance

Problem	Cause	Solution
Faulty acceleration (cont.)	• Improper feedback system operation	• Refer to Chilton's Total Car Care manual
Faulty high speed operation	• Incorrect ignition timing • Faulty advance mechanism	• Adjust timing (if possible) • Check advance mechanism and repair as necessary (Distributor systems only)
	• Low fuel pump volume • Wrong spark plug air gap or wrong plug	• Replace fuel pump • Adjust air gap or install correct plug
	• Partially restricted exhaust manifold, exhaust pipe, catalytic converter, muffler, or tailpipe	• Eliminate restriction
	• Restricted vacuum passages • Restricted air cleaner	• Clean passages • Cleaner or replace filter element as necessary
	• Faulty distributor rotor or cap	• Replace rotor or cap (Distributor systems only)
	• Faulty ignition coil • Improperly seated valve(s)	• Test coil and replace as necessary • Test cylinder compression, repair as necessary
	• Faulty valve spring(s)	• Inspect and test valve spring tension, replace as necessary
	• Incorrect valve timing	• Check valve timing and repair as necessary
	• Intake manifold restricted	• Remove restriction or replace manifold
	• Worn distributor shaft	• Replace shaft (Distributor systems only)
	• Improper feedback system operation	• Refer to Chilton's Total Car Care manual
Misfire at all speeds	• Faulty spark plug(s) • Faulty spark plug wire(s) • Faulty distributor cap or rotor	• Clean or relace spark plug(s) • Replace as necessary • Replace cap or rotor (Distributor systems only)
	• Faulty ignition coil • Primary ignition circuit shorted or open intermittently • Improperly seated valve(s)	• Test coil and replace as necessary • Troubleshoot primary circuit and repair as necessary • Test cylinder compression, repair as necessary
	• Faulty hydraulic tappet(s) • Improper feedback system operation • Faulty valve spring(s)	• Clean or replace tappet(s) • Refer to Chilton's Total Car Care manual • Inspect and test valve spring tension, repair as necessary
	• Worn camshaft lobes • Air leak into manifold	• Replace camshaft • Check manifold vacuum and repair as necessary
	• Fuel pump volume or pressure low • Blown cylinder head gasket • Intake or exhaust manifold passage(s) restricted	• Replace fuel pump • Replace gasket • Pass chain through passage(s) and repair as necessary
Power not up to normal	• Incorrect ignition timing • Faulty distributor rotor	• Adjust timing • Replace rotor (Distributor systems only)

8852EC21

Troubleshooting Engine Performance

Problem	Cause	Solution
Power not up to normal (cont.)	• Incorrect spark plug gap	• Adjust gap
	• Faulty fuel pump	• Replace fuel pump
	• Faulty fuel pump	• Replace fuel pump
	• Incorrect valve timing	• Check valve timing and repair as necessary
	• Faulty ignition coil	• Test coil and replace as necessary
	• Faulty ignition wires	• Test wires and replace as necessary
	• Improperly seated valves	• Test cylinder compression and repair as necessary
	• Blown cylinder head gasket	• Replace gasket
	• Leaking piston rings	• Test compression and repair as necessary
	• Improper feedback system operation	• Refer to Chilton's Total Car Care manual
Intake backfire	• Improper ignition timing	• Adjust timing
	• Defective EGR component	• Repair as necessary
	• Defective TAC vacuum motor or valve	• Repair as necessary
Exhaust backfire	• Air leak into manifold vacuum	• Check manifold vacuum and repair as necessary
	• Faulty air injection diverter valve	• Test diverter valve and replace as necessary
	• Exhaust leak	• Locate and eliminate leak
Ping or spark knock	• Incorrect ignition timing	• Adjust timing
	• Distributor advance malfunction	• Inspect advance mechanism and repair as necessary (Distributor systems only)
	• Excessive combustion chamber deposits	• Remove with combustion chamber cleaner
	• Air leak into manifold vacuum	• Check manifold vacuum and repair as necessary
	• Excessively high compression	• Test compression and repair as necessary
	• Fuel octane rating excessively low	• Try alternate fuel source
	• Sharp edges in combustion chamber	• Grind smooth
	• EGR valve not functioning properly	• Test EGR system and replace as necessary
Surging (at cruising to top speeds)	• Low fuel pump pressure or volume	• Replace fuel pump
	• Improper PCV valve air flow	• Test PCV valve and replace as necessary
	• Air leak into manifold vacuum	• Check manifold vacuum and repair as necessary
	• Incorrect spark advance	• Test and replace as necessary
	• Restricted fuel filter	• Replace fuel filter
	• Restricted air cleaner	• Clean or replace air cleaner filter element
	• EGR valve not functioning properly	• Test EGR system and replace as necessary
	• Improper feedback system operation	• Refer to Chilton's Total Car Care manual

8852EC22

16

WINDSHIELD WIPERS AND WASHERS

WINDSHIELD WIPERS AND WASHERS

Windshield Wipers

▶ See Figure 1

The first windshield wipers were an inside, hand-operated crank connected to an outside arm holding a rubber wiper blade, and operated back and forth by the driver. Later, for the convenience of the passenger, a blade and arm was installed on the passenger's side of the windshield and connected to the arm on the driver's side by linkage and operated in tandem with the driver's wiper.

This was unsatisfactory and was replaced by the vacuum wiper motor that operated the wiper arms using the vacuum from the vehicle engine. This type of motor was used as late as the early '20's, mounted along the roof line and later moved to the cowl panel, directly below the windshield.

The major difficulty plaguing the vacuum motor was its inability to maintain a constant wiper blade speed. As the engine vacuum was lowered (when the vehicle went uphill for instance), the wipers would stop and cause visibility problems. Vacuum holding tanks with one-way check valves and mechanical vacuum pumps were used to maintain a constant vacuum supply, but as the vehicle designs changed, the windshield became larger and the wiper motor's work load increased. The added workload could not be handled by vacuum wipers.

Vacuum wipers gave way to electric wiper motors, first installed on vehicles as an option as early as 1940. The electric motor was dependable and could operate the wipers independent of the fluctuation in engine vacuum, and by 1972; all original equipment vacuum wiper motor installations had ceased.

Electric wiper motors are generally multiple speed units, with delayed or intermittent units used as options. A delayed or intermittent wiper control is used in a mist or light drizzle when the wipers are not continually needed. An adjustable time interval of three to twenty seconds is usually provided for the delayed wiper operation. Depending upon the manufacturer, the vehicle may be equipped with multiple or adjustable intermittent settings that allow the driver to better control the wiper delay interval as necessary for the weather conditions.

➡Some import vehicles use delay wipers which are timed using an electronic control unit. The unit will vary the delay based on vehicle speed, slowing or almost stopping the wipers while you are sitting at a light.

HOW THE ELECTRIC WIPER MOTOR WORKS

The electric wiper motor is a permanent magnet, rotary electric motor. A worm gear machined on the armature shaft drives the output shaft and gear through an idler gear and shaft. The output shaft operates the output arm, which is connected to the wiper linkage. As the electric motor revolves the output arm, the linkage is forced to move in a back and forth motion.

The speed of the electric motor is controlled by resistors, located on or in the control switch, and connected to the wiper motor electrical windings. The control switch directs the current through certain circuits of the wiper motor, as the driver desires.

WIPER LINKAGE

Regardless of the type of drive motor used, the wiper linkage remains the same.

As the drive output arm is revolved or moved back and forth by the operation of the wiper motor, the force of this movement is transmitted by the linkage, to the linkage pivots, to which the wiper arms and blades are attached. As the linkage pivots are forced to rotate, the arms and blades move on the windshield in a predetermined arc.

Two types of linkages are used—depressed and non-depressed. The depressed types are hidden below the hood line when in the park position, while the non-depressed types are visible above the hood line when in their park position.

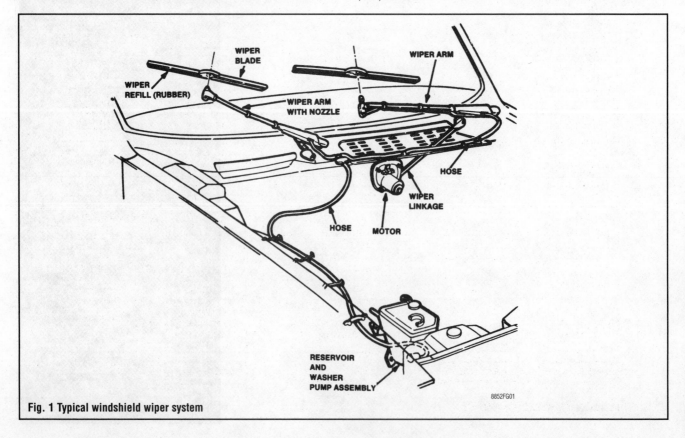

Fig. 1 Typical windshield wiper system

Windshield Washers

Windshield washers are installed in different vehicles in different ways.

All late model vehicles have the washers operated by electric motors, mounted separately or mounted in combination with the wiper motor. All types are controlled by the driver.

The nozzle arrangements are different in the respect that the locations can range from a single base with adjustable offset nozzles, to a single nozzle for the right and left sides, mounted on the cowl panel and individually aimed at the windshield.

Another location of the washer nozzles are on the wiper arms, distributing the fluid spray over the windshield as the arms go through their cleaning arcs.

On certain models, the washer pump can be activated and the wipers will automatically start and stop after a pre determined time, while on others the wipers must be stopped manually.

Plastic or rubber tubing is used to route the washer fluid from the reservoir, through the pump and check-valves, and to the washer nozzles.

TROUBLESHOOTING BASIC WINDSHIELD WIPER PROBLEMS

Most windshield wiper problems are traced to the motor, but there are a few areas to eliminate before assuming the motor is bad.

TROUBLESHOOTING ELECTRIC WIPERS

The Problem	Is Caused By	What to Do
Wipers do not operate— Wiper motor heats up or hums	• Internal motor defect • Bent or damaged linkage • Arms improperly installed on linkage pivots	• Have motor serviced • Repair or replace linkage • Position linkage in park and reinstall wiper arms
Wipers do not operate— No current to motor	• Fuse or circuit breaker blown • Loose, open or broken wiring • Defective switch • Defective or corroded terminals • No ground circuit for motor or switch	• Replace fuse or circuit breaker • Repair wiring and connections • Replace switch • Repair or clean terminals • Repair ground circuits
Wipers do not operate— Motor runs	• Linkage disconnected or broken	• Connect wiper linkage or replace broken linkage

8852FC02

Fig. 2 Troubleshooting windshield wipers

TROUBLESHOOTING BASIC WINDSHIELD WASHER PROBLEMS

Windshield washer problems can usually be traced to minor details such as clogged hoses or jets. Check the little things before assuming the worst.

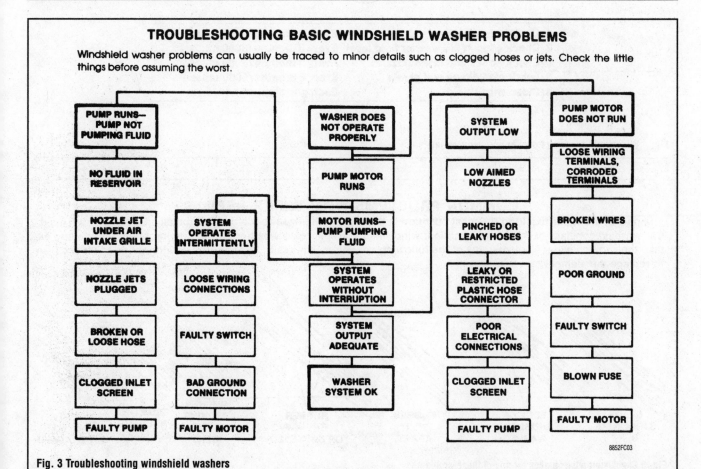

8852FC03

Fig. 3 Troubleshooting windshield washers

Wiper and Washer Maintenance

♦ **See Figure 4**

CHANGING WIPER BLADES

♦ **See Figure 5**

First, don't forget that many vehicles have rear wipers as well as front wipers.

Normally, the wiper blade rubber refills should be changed at least once a year, depending upon the type of weather and the amount of use. If the wipers receive greater than average use or if the vehicle is left outdoors much of the time, both the blades and the refills should be replaced more often.

The blade base should be inspected for kinks along the frame, bent or broken lever or yoke jaws and broken or rusted blade saddles at each refill replacement.

Always replace refills or blades in pairs. If one side has worn out, the other side is likely to follow suit in the near future.

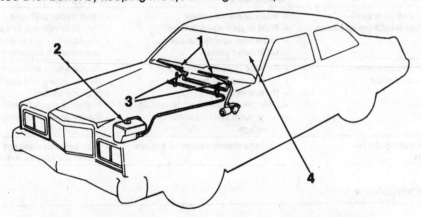

WINDSHIELD WIPER AND WASHER MAINTENANCE INTERVALS

Windshield wiper problems can be kept to a minimum and you'll be able to see a lot better by keeping the system in good shape.

1. Check wiper blades	Every 3 months/3000 miles
2. Check windshield washer fluid level	Every 3 months/3000 miles
Check hoses and clean nozzles	Every 3 months/3000 miles
3. Lubricate linkage and pivots	Every 6 months/6000 miles
4. Clean windshield	Each gas stop

8852FC01

Fig. 4 Windshield wiper and washer maintenance intervals

COMMON PROBLEMS WITH WIPER REFILLS

The part of the wiper requiring the most attention is the wiper refill, or rubber strip that actually wipes the windshield. Car washes, constant back-and-forth motion, windshield solvents, cold weather and the drying effects of the sun all take their toll on wiper elements. Any of the following conditions will result in poor wiper performance and are cause to replace the element.

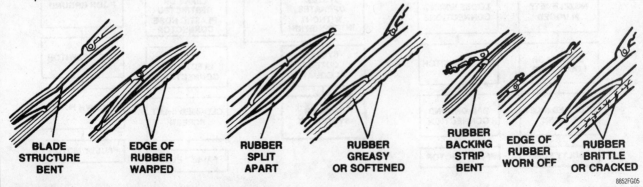

BLADE STRUCTURE BENT   EDGE OF RUBBER WARPED   RUBBER SPLIT APART   RUBBER GREASY OR SOFTENED   RUBBER BACKING STRIP BENT   EDGE OF RUBBER WORN OFF   RUBBER BRITTLE OR CRACKED

8852FG05

Fig. 5 Check your wiper blades for any of these problems

Chattering is the noise and the jerking motion resulting from the wiper blade rubber getting hard and not gliding smoothly over the windshield.

Make sure the wiper blade and rubber is properly installed and in good condition. If the rubber is soft and pliable, chattering should not occur.

Worn linkage and connections can also cause chattering of the wiper blades.

WIPER MOTOR & LINKAGE LUBRICATION

The wiper motor, regardless of the type used, does not require regular maintenance. It is sometimes located in an inaccessible position and can only be exposed by removal of cover panels or other parts when replacement is necessary. If the linkage pivot arms or pivot shafts are exposed, apply a silicone spray lubricant to them at least twice a year.

CLEANING THE WINDSHIELD

The windshield should be kept clean to avoid grinding the dirt into the wiper blades and scratching the glass.

Keep waxes and solvents from the windshield. Waxes leave an invisible film that can create a serious hazard when rain or road grime becomes mixed in the wax coating. The wiper blades cannot cut through this coating during their cleaning action. Clean the waxes from the windshield surface as soon as possible, using commercial cleaners designed for this purpose.

Keep solvents from the windshield to avoid damage to the wiper blade rubber and to the sealing rubber of the windshield. Certain solvents can destroy the rubber by swelling or disintegration. Use only solutions that have been designed for use on the windshield surface.

WINTER WIPER MAINTENANCE

♦ See Figure 6

If you live in the Snow Belt or your area is subjected to freezing rains, remove any packed snow or ice from the windshield before starting and stopping the wiper motor.

If the blades are frozen to the glass or snow is packed over them, starting the wiper motor can result in bent linkage, bent arms, blades, and possible internal motor damage.

Clean the park position area of packed snow and ice, remembering that the arms and blades will stop at a lower position than the lowest point of the normal wiper blade sweep. This can cause the wiper motor to continue to run which can result in blown fuses or circuit breakers, or internal damage to the wiper motor.

As the wiper blades free themselves from the glass, lift them carefully to prevent the rubber from cracking or tearing. Clean the snow and ice from the rubber before using them.

Similarly, with the washer system, make sure the nozzles are always free of snow and ice. Be sure a non-freezing solution (available as pre-mix or concentrate) is added to the washer fluid. Follow the instructions on the solution container when mixing.

NOZZLE ADJUSTMENT

Centered Single Post—Fixed Position Nozzles

This type of nozzle is usually located on the rear center of the hood panel, directly in front of the windshield. It is mounted in a fixed position and can only be adjusted by loosening the whole nozzle body retainer, which is located under the hood. By loosening the body-retaining nut from under the hood, the nozzle body can be turned to provide the best spray discharge to cover the majority of the windshield area. Tighten the retaining nut while holding the nozzle body in the proper position.

Centered Single Post—Adjustable Nozzles

♦ See Figure 7

This type of nozzle, which is similar to the fixed position nozzle, can ordinarily be found in front of the windshield on the rear center of the hood panel. However, on this type you can move the nozzle in the body to adjust the direction of the washer spray. The nozzle is adjusted with a wrench, screwdriver or pliers. If the nozzle has no gripping area, the adjustment is done by inserting a stiff wire into the nozzle aperture and moving the nozzle in the direction desired. When using the wire as an adjuster tool, do not force the nozzles; the wire could be broken within the nozzle aperture.

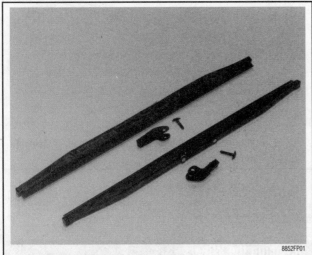

Fig. 6 Winter wipers are rubber covered to prevent freeze-up in ice and snow conditions.

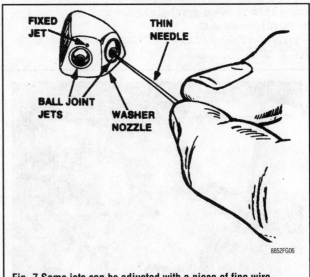

Fig. 7 Some jets can be adjusted with a piece of fine wire

Individual Nozzles

▶ **See Figure 8**

A tab is normally fastened to the nozzle stem to assist in the aiming of the nozzle. If a tab is not present, use a pair of pliers and gently move the nozzle in the proper direction.

By following the mixing instructions on the solution container, fill the reservoir to the specified height with the proper mixture.

Using a long pin or a piece of fine wire, loosen any dirt deposited in the nozzles, hoses or screens. Rinse the exposed areas with clear water.

Operate the pump or motor and flush the washer system out with the new solution until all traces of deposits are gone.

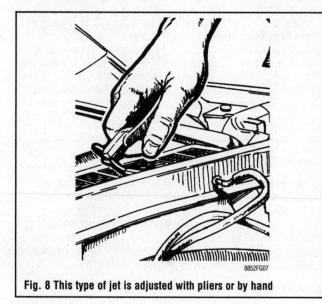

Fig. 8 This type of jet is adjusted with pliers or by hand

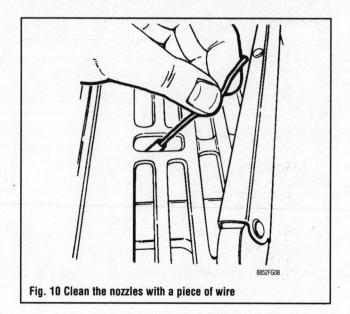

Fig. 10 Clean the nozzles with a piece of wire

Wiper Arm Nozzles

No adjustment is necessary on this type nozzle as the aperture is centered on the wiper arm and moves with the arm action.

WINDSHIELD WASHERS

▶ **See Figures 9, 10 and 11**

If the bottom of the washer fluid reservoir has accumulations of dirt, remove it from the vehicle, clean the inside thoroughly, and reinstall, connecting all hoses and wires.

Examine the plastic or rubber hoses for cracks or breaks, and replace them as needed.

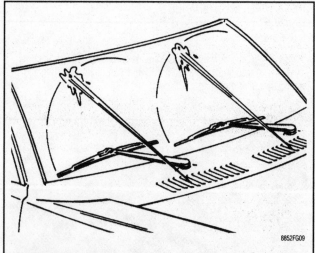

Fig. 11 Washer nozzles should be adjusted to hit the windshield above center

Observe the washer nozzle aim and if necessary, correct it, remembering that the washer nozzles are provided in different forms and have different methods of adjustment.

Servicing the Wipers

It may be necessary to move the wiper arms and blades higher on the windshield before attempting to replace the arms, blades or refills.

Turn the ignition switch on first, and then turn the wiper switch on. When the wipers are in their farthest point of their arc, turn the ignition switch off. Mark the position of the arms so that the replacement will be installed in the same location as the original.

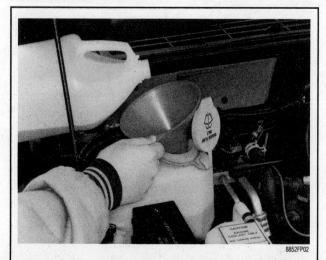

Fig. 9 Check the solution level in the washer reservoir. Also, check the screen in the bottom of the pick-up tube for clogging.

ELEMENT (REFILL) CARE & REPLACEMENT

▶ **See Figures 12 thru 18**

For maximum effectiveness and longest element life, the windshield and wiper blades should be kept clean. Dirt, tree sap, road tar and so on will cause streaking, smearing and blade deterioration if left on the glass. It is advisable to wash the windshield carefully with a commercial glass cleaner at least once a month. Wipe off the rubber blades with the wet rag afterwards. Do not attempt to move wipers across the windshield by hand; damage to the motor and drive mechanism will result.

To inspect and/or replace the wiper blade elements, place the wiper switch in the **LOW** speed position and the ignition switch in the **ACC** position. When the wiper blades are approximately vertical on the windshield, turn the ignition switch to **OFF**.

Examine the wiper blade elements. If they are found to be cracked, broken or torn, they should be replaced immediately. Replacement intervals will vary with usage, although ozone deterioration usually limits element life to about one year. If the wiper pattern is smeared or streaked, or if the blade chatters across the glass, the elements should be replaced. It is easiest and most sensible to replace the elements in pairs.

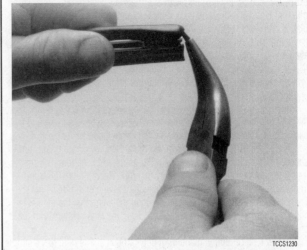
Fig. 14 On Trico® wiper blades, the tab at the end of the blade must be turned up . . .

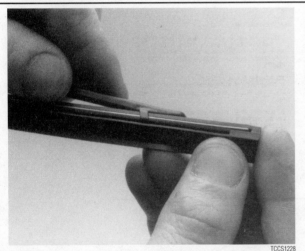
Fig. 12 To remove and install a Lexor® wiper blade refill, slip out the old insert and slide in a new one

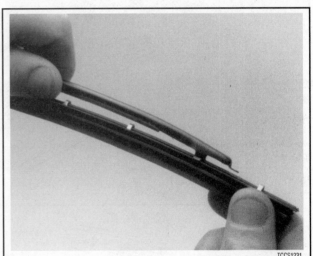
Fig. 15 . . . then the insert can be removed. After installing the replacement insert, bend the tab back

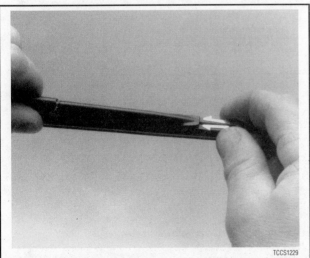
Fig. 13 On Pylon® inserts, the clip at the end has to be removed prior to sliding the insert off

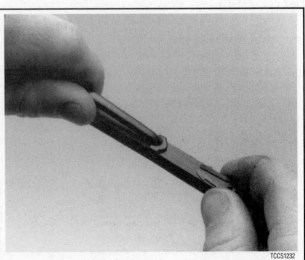
Fig. 16 The Tripledge® wiper blade insert is removed and installed using a securing clip

If your vehicle is equipped with aftermarket blades, there are several different types of refills and your vehicle might have any kind. Aftermarket blades and arms rarely use the exact same type blade or refill as the original equipment. Here are some typical aftermarket blades; not all may be available for your vehicle:

The Anco® type uses a release button that is pushed down to allow the refill to slide out of the yoke jaws. The new refill slides back into the frame and locks in place.

Some Trico® refills are removed by locating where the metal backing strip or the refill is wider. Insert a small screwdriver blade between the frame and metal backing strip. Press down to release the refill from the retaining tab.

Other types of Trico® refills have two metal tabs which are unlocked by squeezing them together. The rubber filler can then be withdrawn from the frame jaws. A new refill is installed by inserting the refill into the front frame jaws and sliding it rearward to engage the remaining frame jaws. There are usually four jaws; be certain when installing that the refill is engaged in all of them. At the end of its travel, the tabs will lock into place on the front jaws of the wiper blade frame.

Another type of refill is made from polycarbonate. The refill has a simple locking device at one end which flexes downward out of the groove into which the jaws of the holder fit, allowing easy release. By sliding the new refill through all the jaws and pushing through the slight resistance when it reaches the end of its travel, the refill will lock into position.

To replace the Tridon® refill, it is necessary to remove the wiper blade. This refill has a plastic backing strip with a notch about 1 in. (25mm) from the end. Hold the blade (frame) on a hard surface so that the frame is tightly bowed. Grip the tip of the backing strip and pull up while twisting counter-clockwise. The backing strip will snap out of the retaining tab. Do this for the remaining tabs until the refill is free of the blade. The length of these refills is molded into the end and they should be replaced with identical types.

Because there are many different brands of wiper refills, not every type is specified here. Keep in mind that most types of refills are similar, and replacement usually just requires unfastening any retainers to free the element, then removing it from the wiper arm. During installation, place the new wiper element on the arm and secure it properly. Regardless of the type of refill used, be sure to follow the part manufacturer's instructions closely. Make sure that all of the frame jaws are engaged as the refill is pushed into place and locked. If the metal blade holder and frame are allowed to touch the glass during wiper operation, the glass could be scratched.

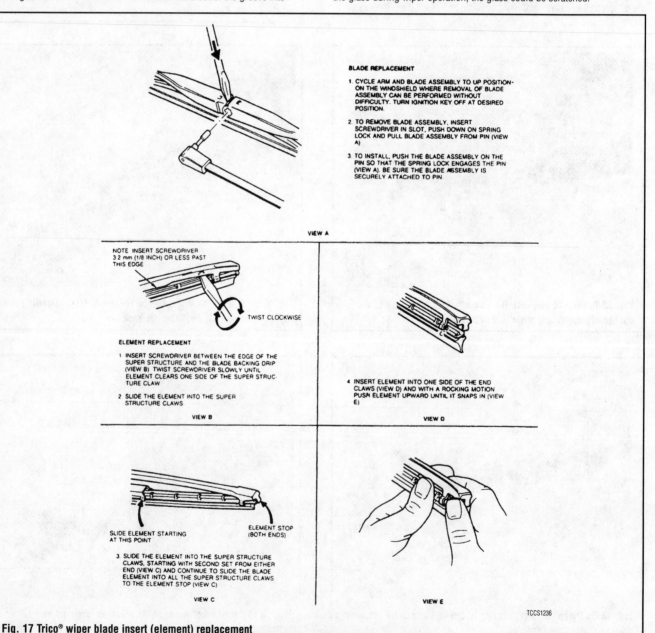

BLADE REPLACEMENT

1. CYCLE ARM AND BLADE ASSEMBLY TO UP POSITION- ON THE WINDSHIELD WHERE REMOVAL OF BLADE ASSEMBLY CAN BE PERFORMED WITHOUT DIFFICULTY. TURN IGNITION KEY OFF AT DESIRED POSITION.

2. TO REMOVE BLADE ASSEMBLY, INSERT SCREWDRIVER IN SLOT, PUSH DOWN ON SPRING LOCK AND PULL BLADE ASSEMBLY FROM PIN (VIEW A)

3. TO INSTALL, PUSH THE BLADE ASSEMBLY ON THE PIN SO THAT THE SPRING LOCK ENGAGES THE PIN (VIEW A). BE SURE THE BLADE ASSEMBLY IS SECURELY ATTACHED TO PIN

VIEW A

NOTE INSERT SCREWDRIVER 3 2 mm (1/8 INCH) OR LESS PAST THIS EDGE

TWIST CLOCKWISE

ELEMENT REPLACEMENT

1 INSERT SCREWDRIVER BETWEEN THE EDGE OF THE SUPER STRUCTURE AND THE BLADE BACKING DRIP (VIEW B) TWIST SCREWDRIVER SLOWLY UNTIL ELEMENT CLEARS ONE SIDE OF THE SUPER STRUCTURE CLAW

2 SLIDE THE ELEMENT INTO THE SUPER STRUCTURE CLAWS

VIEW B

4 INSERT ELEMENT INTO ONE SIDE OF THE END CLAWS (VIEW D) AND WITH A ROCKING MOTION PUSH ELEMENT UPWARD UNTIL IT SNAPS IN (VIEW E)

VIEW D

SLIDE ELEMENT STARTING AT THIS POINT

ELEMENT STOP (BOTH ENDS)

3 SLIDE THE ELEMENT INTO THE SUPER STRUCTURE CLAWS, STARTING WITH SECOND SET FROM EITHER END (VIEW C) AND CONTINUE TO SLIDE THE BLADE ELEMENT INTO ALL THE SUPER STRUCTURE CLAWS TO THE ELEMENT STOP (VIEW C)

VIEW C

VIEW E

TCCS1236

Fig. 17 Trico® wiper blade insert (element) replacement

BLADE REPLACEMENT

1. Cycle arm and blade assembly to a position on the windshield where removal of blade assembly can be performed without difficulty. Turn ignition key off at desired position.
2. To remove blade assembly from wiper arm, pull up on spring lock and pull blade assembly from pin (View A). Be sure spring lock is not pulled excessively or it will become distorted.
3. To install, push the blade assembly onto the pin so that the spring lock engages the pin (View A). Be sure the blade assembly is securely attached to pin.

ELEMENT REPLACEMENT

1. In the plastic backing strip which is part of the rubber blade assembly, there is an 11.11mm (7/16 inch) long notch located approximately one inch from either end. Locate either notch.
2. Place the frame of the wiper blade assembly on a firm surface with either notched end of the backing strip visible.
3. Grasp the frame portion of the wiper blade assembly and push down until the blade assembly is tightly bowed.
4. With the blade assembly in the bowed position, grasp the tip of the backing strip firmly, pulling up and twisting C.C.W. at the same time. The backing strip will then snap out of the retaining tab on the end of the frame.
5. Lift the wiper blade assembly from the surface and slide the backing strip down the frame until the notch lines up with the next retaining tab, twist slightly, and the backing strip will snap out. Continue this operation with the remaining tabs until the blade element is completely detached from the frame.
6. To install blade element, reverse the above procedure, making sure all six (6) tabs are locked to the backing strip before installing blade to wiper arm.

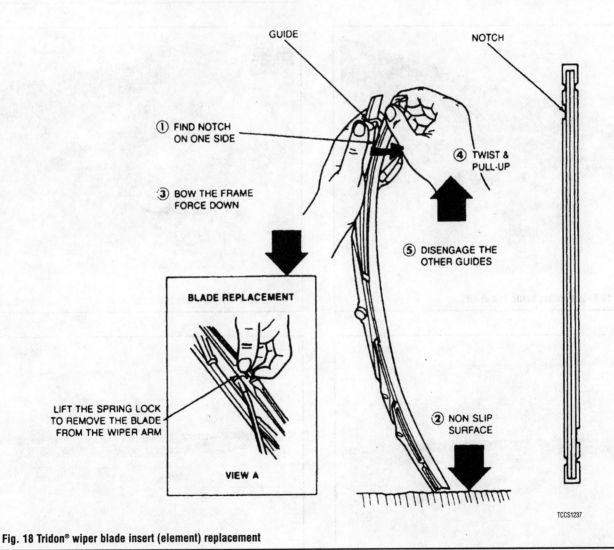

Fig. 18 Tridon® wiper blade insert (element) replacement

WIPER BLADE REPLACEMENT

▶ **See Figures 19 thru 24**

Trico® Bayonet Blade

Press down on the arm to unlatch the top stud. Depress the tab on the saddle and pull the blade from the arm. When installing the blade, the locking studs should snap into place.

Anco® Bayonet Blade

Press inward on the tab and pull the blade from the arm. To install, slide the blade into the arm so that the locking studs snap into place.

Trico® or Anco® Pin Type

Insert a screwdriver into the spring release opening of the blade saddle and depress the spring clip. Pull the blade from the arm. To install, push the blade saddle onto the mounting pin so that the spring clip engages the pin. Be sure that the blade is securely attached to the arm.

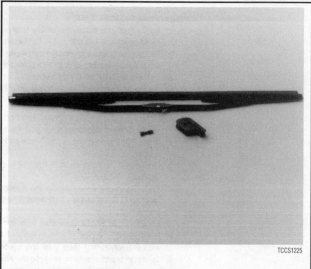

TCCS1225

Fig. 21 Pylon® wiper blade and adapter

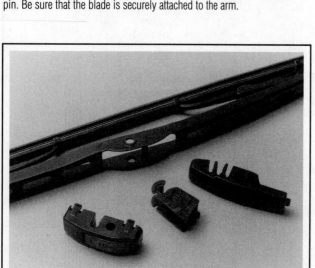

TCCS1223

Fig. 19 Bosch® wiper blade and fit kit

TCCS1226

Fig. 22 Trico® wiper blade and fit kit

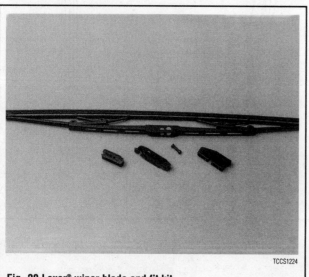

TCCS1224

Fig. 20 Lexor® wiper blade and fit kit

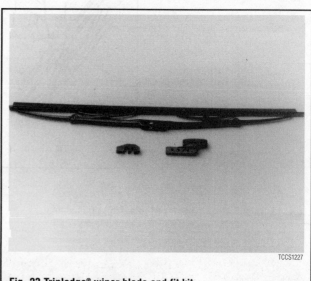

TCCS1227

Fig. 23 Tripledge® wiper blade and fit kit

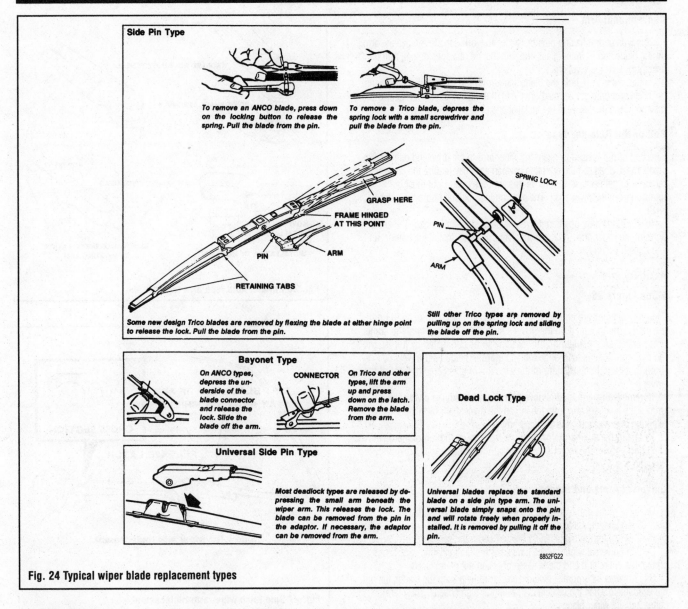

Fig. 24 Typical wiper blade replacement types

Universal Types

Numerous universal blades and adapters have been provided to install other than the original equipment wiper blades.

To install the universal type, push the blade adapter onto the arm until the lugs click into place. Push the blade onto the adapter until the locking lugs click closed. To remove the adapter from the blade, a tab is provided as in the Anco® bayonet type and by pressing on the tab, the adapter can be pulled from the arm.

REPLACING THE WIPER ARM

▶ See Figure 25

The wiper arm attachment to the pivot shaft varies from vehicle to vehicle, and should be known before any attempt is made to remove the arm from the pivot.

Pin and Hole Type

▶ See Figure 26

This type of arm has a pinhole near the arm's pivot pin. To remove the arm, raise the blade end off the glass and insert a 3/32 inch pin or pop rivet into the hole. This locks the arm in the released position, allowing the arm to be lifted off the pivot shaft without the aid of tools.

To install this type of arm, the pin must be left in place. (New service replacement arms have the pins already installed to hold them in the released position). Position the wiper motor in the park position and install the wiper arm over the pivot shaft, in its proper arm-to-glass position. Push the arm downward over the pivot shaft so that the retaining clip will engage the drive head of the pivot shaft. Remove the pin from the wiper arm.

Slide Latch Type

▶ See Figure 27

This wiper arm has a slide latch that locks under the drive head of the pivot shaft. To remove this type, raise the blade end from the glass and at the same time, move the slide latch outward, away from the pivot shaft. This holds the arm in the off-glass position and permits it to be removed from the pivot head without the aid of tools.

To install this type arm, push the wiper arm onto the pivot head while holding the arm in the off-glass position. Push the slide latch into the lock under the pivot shaft. Lower the blade to the windshield. If the blade does not touch the glass, the slide latch is not completely locked.

Conventional Arm

This type of arm has no pins or latches to work with. To remove the arm, lift the blade end from the glass and with the aid of a special tool, pull the assembly from the pivot shaft.

To install the arm, hold the blade and arm in the swing out position and push the arm onto the serrated drive end of the pivot shaft. The special tool may be needed to assist in the installation.

Bolt or Nut Retainer Type

A bolt or nut is used to retain the wiper arm to the drive end of the pivot shaft. These bolts or nuts are often covered and may require the cover to be removed to gain access. To remove this arm, the bolt or nut must be removed from the pivot shaft. The arm can then be lifted from the pivot shaft.

To install the arm, position it over the pivot shaft and engage the serration's of the wiper arm and the pivot shaft drive end. Install the bolt or nut and tighten securely.

Auxiliary Arm

▶ **See Figure 28**

Some vehicles are equipped with a small auxiliary arm in addition to the main arm, mounted on the driver's side. This arm assembly is sometimes called an articulating arm, meaning to be connected by joints, and the main purpose is to change the angle of the blade as it travels through its arc, to clear more of the windshield glass area in front of the driver.

To remove this arm, first remove the main arm from the pivot shaft. Unlock the auxiliary arm from the lug on the pivot shaft, by sliding the retaining clip back onto the auxiliary arm.

To install the auxiliary arm, position the arm on the lug of the pivot shaft and engage the retaining clip. Install the main arm as previously outlined.

Universal Arms and Blades

Universal arms and blades are sold by aftermarket outlets to take the place of original equipment. One such item is an adjustable arm, having an angling swivel for the blade, and a tension controller screw.

Certain universal wiper blades have adapters to fit existing wiper arms, so that the entire arm and blade assembly need not be replaced.

Other blades incorporate a wind deflector to help keep the blades flat on the windshield when the vehicle is traveling at high speeds. These are called anti-lift wiper blades.

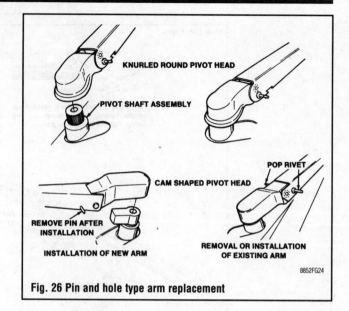

Fig. 26 Pin and hole type arm replacement

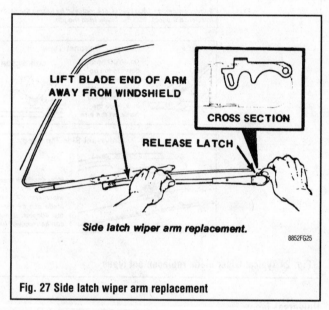

Side latch wiper arm replacement.

Fig. 27 Side latch wiper arm replacement

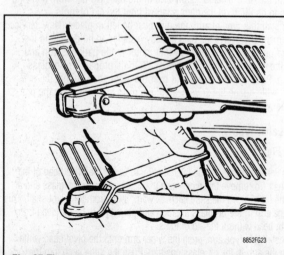

Fig. 25 These two styles of wiper arm removal tools are inexpensive and will remove the arm from the driveshaft without damaging the shaft or arm

Some wiper systems use an auxiliary (articulated) wiper arm. It is secured to an auxiliary pivot by a sliding lock.

Fig. 28 Some wiper systems use an auxiliary (articulated) wiper arm. It is secured to an auxiliary pivot by sliding a lock

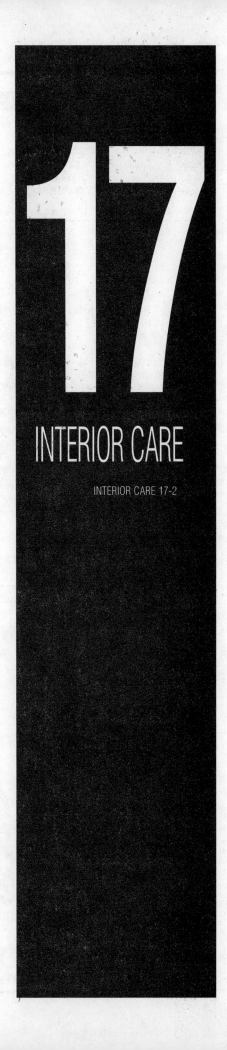

17

INTERIOR CARE

INTERIOR CARE 17-2

INTERIOR CARE

▶ **See Figures 1 and 2**

One way to preserve a "new car" feeling is to keep the interior clean and protected. You have to use some common sense and not let the dirt accumulate. The more dirt that is ground into carpeting and seats, the faster they will wear out. Keep the seats clean and the rugs vacuumed.

Cleaning and Detailing the Interior

▶ **See Figures 3 and 4**

Interior detailing is "super housekeeping" applied to your vehicle. Vehicle carpeting is shampooed much as is your home's carpeting, but

Fig. 1 A virtual plethora of cleaning product are available for today's interiors. Always read the label and test the product on an out of the way area.

Fig. 2 Automotive glass cleaners on the left and glass treatment products on the right

more intensively. Vehicle upholstery—whether vinyl, fabric, or leather—is cleaned of stains using methods and products similar to (or the same as) those used on upholstered furniture, but with greater attention to detail. What cleans your home's windows cleans your vehicle's, but windows and windshield (as well as sunroofs) need more frequent and more careful cleaning. For example, a vehicle with finely finished wood molding can be detailed with the same polish used to protect and brighten fine furniture, but special attention must be given to crevices and contours.

The major difference between a vehicle's interior and your home's is use intensity. Because your vehicle interior is used intensively and subjected to all the abuses that use intensity implies, its detailing must be intensive, differing significantly from routine "housecleaning."

Consider the facts. Depending on your life-style and how much time you spend at home, you may only occasionally use your living room's sofa or any particular upholstered chair. However, driver seat upholstery may be used and unavoidably abused half the hours— and more—of every day. Vehicle carpeting, unlike most home carpeting, is often continuously "tracked"—with dirt, oil, grease, snow and slush. Whereas home carpeting is seldom systematically worn in any one small spot, a driver's right heel, forever nudging the accelerator, first dirties and then sometimes wears through a particular place in vehicle carpeting (unless that particular place is protected by a car mat).

8852GP03

Fig. 3 A professional detailer brushes dirt from a vent directly into the waiting vacuum crevice tool

8852GP04

Fig. 4 Remove outdated service stickers, however when detailing door jams and underhood leave informational stickers in place.

In its lifetime, moreover, your vehicle's interior may become a bedroom (for a quick snooze at a highway rest area), a restaurant, an office, a sick bay, a storeroom, a moving van—you name it.

And all of this use and abuse occurs literally under glass and within the relatively tiny confines of the average vehicle. Use of a home may be spread over 1200– 5000 square feet, or more. A vehicle's interior use takes place in seldom more than 45 square feet. And, in some downsized models, less than half that.

Moreover, unlike your home's carpets and upholstered furniture, or even windows, a vehicle's interior is subjected to extremes of heat, cold, and sunlight. Daily it is exposed to atmospheric pollutants, road grime and contamination from its own and other engines. Even a tightly closed vehicle interior cannot escape all of these natural and unnatural extremes.

Thus, interior detailing, far from being merely routine "housecleaning," aims to restore, wherever possible, a vehicle's interior to its showroom condition and appearance. Anything less may produce a reasonably clean interior, but not one that is detailed.

"Detailed," when it comes to your vehicle's interior, means simply that: minute, painstaking, time-consuming attention to details. See a smidgen of dirt or grime? Get rid of it. An upholstery seam crevice not as clean as the area around it? Clean it. The steering wheel's underneath places begrimed by sweaty hands? Degrime them. An outdated service sticker on a door edge or jamb? Remove it. If it didn't come with the vehicle's interior when you took delivery, or if it did, it shouldn't have, do away with it. That's interior detailing.

DETAILING THE INTERIOR

There is no one "right way" to super-detail your vehicle's interior. But a systematic, orderly way is outlined below:

Carpeting and Fabric Upholstery

- Vacuum
- Shampoo
- Rinse
- Dry
- Protect (optional)

Vinyl Upholstery

- Vacuum
- Clean
- Protect

Leather Upholstery

- Vacuum
- Clean
- Condition/protect

Dashboard, Moldings and Trim (Plastic, Vinyl or Rubber)

- Clean
- Restore
- Protect

Interior Metal, Including Chrome

- Clean
- Polish

Windshield, Windows and Mirrors

- Clean
- Protect (optional)

You can detail the interior piecemeal—say, do the carpeting and upholstery one day, the rest of the interior an other—or get it done with one effort. Doing it in a single shot usually means you'll need to do all of the interior molding, chrome, the dash, windshield, and windows first, before you do the upholstery, because upholstery that seems to have dried requires several hours, or even overnight, to dry thoroughly. Since you don't want to sit on a wet or damp seat while doing the dash, windows, ceiling (headliner), and other interior detailing, it makes sense to do those jobs first.

Vacuuming

▶ See Figures 5, 6 and 7

Any good home vacuum with a plastic (not metal) crevice attachment works well. Portable vacuums, despite their popularity and increased power, generally lack the power to vacuum vehicle carpets as they should be vacuumed. Vacuums at the coin-op places may have power enough, but the clamor of other vehicle owners to use the vacuum you're using, plus the need to keep feeding the meter, often discourages a thorough job.

1. Start with the upholstery. Using the attachment usually used for drapes or window blinds, vacuum seat backs and seats. Push seats forward to get behind and beneath them. On rear seats, don't neglect seat fronts, the back edge of seats facing the rear window, and around armrests.

2. Switch to the plastic crevice tool (plastic rather than metal which, if bent or sharp, risks tearing the fabric, vinyl or leather, or cutting stitching). The crevice tool is for getting deep into upholstery seams and pleats. With one hand working ahead of the tool, spread the upholstery's seams; with the

Fig. 7 In many areas, a vacuum alone can't dislodge all the dirt. Here a soft bristled paintbrush and a vacuum crevice tool work in unison to clean the dashboard nooks and crannies.

Fig. 5 Industrial vacuums have the power necessary for cleaning the vehicle's mats, carpets and upholstery.

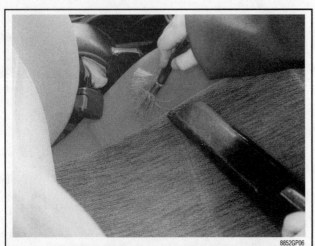

Fig. 6 Whether upholstery is leather, vinyl or fabric, the first step in vacuuming is a soft-bristled brush and the crevice tool of the vacuum, working together to rid the seams of dirt.

other hand, work the crevice tool into the seams. Seams collect a lot of dirt, so you may have to go over them several times.

3. Now vacuum the carpets. Use the drape and blind attachment to vacuum rear carpeting. Unless you have a van, wagon, or motor home, rear carpeting isn't extensive.

4. Move to the front carpeting (under and ahead of seats). Move the seats forward and then backward, to their full forward or rear positions to get under them. This is probably the dirtiest carpeting area in any vehicle. The next dirtiest is the carpeting in front of the driver's seat.

5. With the palm of your hand or a brush, beat the carpeting just ahead of your vacuum tool. Carpet beating dislodges deep-down dirt and brings it to the surface for vacuuming.

6. With the crevice tool, get into crevices of the seat's floor tracks; all around the perimeter of the carpeting, front and back; and especially in the driver's foot area (around the pedals and dimmer switch, if it's located on the floor).

7. Use the crevice tool to vacuum the instrument panel, floor console, and around the windows and windshield molding, especially where the windshield meets the dash. If the crevice tool won't squeeze into this often small but particularly dirty area, use a "detail stick": a 1/8 or 1/4 inch-diameter length of wood doweling wrapped in a clean piece of cloth or cheesecloth.

8. Finally, use the drape and blind attachment to gently vacuum the headliner. The headliner is fragile, so exert minimum pressure on it to avoid damage.

Detailing Fabric Upholstery

You have several methods and product choices as described below. The first two methods are outlined on the following pages.

1. Shampoo fabric upholstery (including cloth, velour, sheepskin, or combination vinyl/fabric upholstery) with a good sudsy household wash product. Some of the choices are:

• A sudsy solution made with liquid hand soap; any good neutral soap and water; a soap made for hand-washing delicate fabrics; fabric and rug shampoos shelved in supermarkets; car-maker upholstery shampoos available from the dealer from whom you bought your vehicle.

• Use a spray-on/wipe-off fabric cleaner

• Hire others to clean it. Arrange to bring your vehicle into the shop of any reputable home carpet/upholstery cleaner. For a usually small fee, someone there will use the shop's heavy-duty equipment to clean your vehicle's upholstery and carpet and to extract the rinse water so as to speed the drying process.

Vehicle cloth is the most difficult type of upholstery material to keep clean or to clean after it becomes dirty or stained. That's one reason pro-detailers usually charge more to clean the interior of a fabric-upholstered vehicle.

SHAMPOOING FABRIC UPHOLSTERY

▶ See Figures 8, 9 and 10

If there's any secret to shampooing a vehicle's upholstery (or, for that matter, vehicle carpeting) it's rinsing. Rinse water must be sucked from upholstery and carpets with a home shop wet-dry vacuum, a carpet wet-dry machine rented from a local supermarket, an extractor, or a vacuum available at coin-op car wash places.

Whatever the fabric cleaner—name-brand or no-name generic—test it first. Try it on a small area of the fabric that normally isn't in view, If what's happening doesn't look right (you detect fading, or a tint of fabric color shows on your cloth), stop right there. Let things dry. Then test another fabric cleaner on another spot.

1. Remove any spots or stains see "How to remove stains," in this chapter.

2. With a soft-bristled brush, gently, but firmly scrub the seats and seatbacks with a circular motion . Get into seams and crevices with the same brush or a toothbrush.

3. Wipe away suds with a damp cloth or sponge .

4. Rinse with clean water. Use as little water as necessary to rinse thoroughly.

Fig. 8 Apply upholstery shampoo with a soft bristled brush

Fig. 9 When scrubbing upholstery, work the suds into the seams and crevices with a toothbrush

Fig. 10 Use an absorbent terry cloth towel to remove the foam.

5. Extract rinse water with a wet-dry vacuum. Or use paper towels and a hair dryer to speed dry the fabric. To avoid scorching, be careful not to hold the dryer too close to the fabric.

6. Allow to dry overnight.

USING SPRAY-ON/WIPE-OFF FABRIC CLEANER

▶ See Figures 11 and 12

✳✳ CAUTION

Always read a product label and heed the maker's advice. Some spray-on vehicle carpet protectors warn: "Keep small children and pets off carpet until thoroughly dry."

➡ The steps listed below are for a specific product that is typical of the spray-on/wipe-off cleaners. Follow manufacturer's instructions for the product you select.

1. Test for colorfastness by cleaning a small, inconspicuous fabric area. Allow to dry. Do not use if color or texture is adversely affected.

2. Shake can vigorously. Hold the spray nozzle 4–6 inches from the fabric. Spray a thin, even layer of foam over a small area . Use a cloth or sponge to remove overspray from adjacent, non-upholstered areas.

Fig. 11 After testing the fabric for colorfastness and for the effect of the cleaner on the texture, hold the can 4–6 inches from the fabric and spray on a thin even coat of cleaner

8852GP12

Fig. 12 Use a damp, clean sponge, work the foam into the fabric with overlapping circular strokes. When the fabric if thoroughly dry, vacuum again.

8852GP13

Fig. 13 Regular treatment with protectants will prevent cracks in the vinyl

3. With a clean, damp sponge, work foam into the upholstery with overlapping, circular strokes. Rinse sponge clean and squeeze dry frequently.

4. Repeat procedure on a small area at a time until entire upholstery is cleaned and protected. Depending on the product, special stain protection may remain after cleaning. It acts to prevent further soiling and stains and helps to maintain the original repellency of upholstery treated with a stain repellent.

5. When upholstery is thoroughly dry, vacuum

Detailing Vinyl Upholstery

Vinyl is the easiest vehicle upholstery to clean, but it is not necessarily the easiest to keep clean. Vinyl collects grime faster than other upholsteries do (you can actually feel the grime). And vinyl, despite claims to the contrary, fades noticeably, especially when subjected to intense sun exposure—as the rear seatback, for one example.

There's really no reason to buy a vinyl product that just cleans, when soap and water—or any of many all-purpose household detergents and cleaners—will do just as well. But, unless you're very careful to rinse the vinyl well and then wipe it dry, soap and some other household cleaners can dull or streak vinyl. Special vinyl cleaners—and they abound—do more than merely clean: most also impart a sheen to vinyl.

1. Optional wash. Using a clean, damp cloth, thoroughly wash vinyl with a mild household detergent or cleaning formula. Some choices: ammonia and water (4–6 tablespoons of ammonia to 1 quart of water); dish-washing detergent and water.

2. Work the solution into seams, seatbacks, along seat, and backrest edges. Use a toothbrush to reach hard-to-reach places.

3. Rinse with clean water. Buff dry with a clean cloth. Allow to dry completely, at least one hour, depending on the weather.

4. Apply a good vinyl cleaner or a combination cleaner protectant. Let it work for a few minutes, then rub dry with a clean cloth. The object is to bring up vinyl's natural sheen.

5. Finally, if you applied a vinyl cleaner, conclude with a straight protectant. Protectants restore vinyl's original color and sheen. Apply with a clean cloth. Let the formula work a few minutes, then buff dry.

RESTORING SUN-FADED VINYL

◆ See Figure 13

A good protectant can sometimes restore nearly original color and sheen to even extremely sun-faded vinyl.

1. Apply the protectant with a cloth and a toothbrush and let it work and penetrate overnight. Next morning, rub and buff off any excess.

2. If restoration is not complete, repeat the process. Three applications and three overnight soak-ins may be necessary— but the results can be amazing.

3. For worst-case sun-faded vinyl upholstery, you may have to repeat the treatment every 3–4 months in summer, less frequently during less sunny seasons.

Detailing Leather Upholstery

Leather is much different from other upholstery materials. If your upholstery is genuine hide, it is perishable. Neglected, it will harden, crack, fade, and, in time, deteriorate into a rash of sand like granules that fall off at the mere brush of an arm. Detailing ensures that your costly leather upholstery will retain its resiliency . . . and its life.

There are several products available for cleaning and preserving leather. Saddle soap, once the conventional cleaner for leather, is seldom used today by pro-detailers. And, yes, some Owner's Manuals still advise doing nothing but wiping leather with a damp cloth, then thoroughly drying.

Before applying any product to leather, test it. Many foreign leathers are topically dyed, meaning they aren't dyed completely through the hide. Non-compatible products will "pull dye"—that is, dye comes off on your cleaning cloth.

On the other hand, many late model American vehicle leathers are coated with a protective plastic. The plastic, usually a PolyVinylChloride (PVC), prevents penetration of any of the various leather cleaners and conditioners. Treat vinyl-coated leather exactly as you'd treat vinyl upholstery. As for leather cleaners/conditioners so essential for "raw," uncoated leather? Forget them. They can't get through the protective plastic barrier.

To test whether your leather upholstery is "raw" or plastic-coated, apply a few drops of clean water to the leather. If the water is easily and quickly absorbed, the leather is uncoated; if the droplets aren't absorbed, the leather probably has a protective coating.

The steps listed below are for a specific brand of leather cleaner and conditioner. Follow manufacturer's instructions on the product you select.

1. With a soft cloth, apply the cleaner in overlapping strokes.

2. Use a soft-bristled toothbrush to work it into seams and crevices. A cleaner's foaming action (use enough cleaner for sufficient foaming) loosens embedded dirt, "floats" dirt from crevices, and cleans the leather.

3. Rinse with clean water and a soft cloth or sponge.

4. While the leather is still damp, apply the conditioner evenly over the entire surface and into crevices and seams. Wipe off excess conditioner with a soft, clean cloth. The conditioner lubricates and restores the leather's suppleness and its rich, natural luster.

5. Allow to dry thoroughly before use.

Detailing Vehicle Carpeting

What cleans the carpets in your home will clean the carpets in your vehicle. The same spot removers that "de-spot" your home's carpeting will de-spot your vehicle's. Carpet-wash solutions sold for supermarket rental carpet cleaning machines generally do an equally good job on your vehicle's carpeting. Cold-water home fabric wash products are also popular with pro-detailers for cleaning both wool and synthetic vehicle carpeting.

Most common household carpet cleaners tend to be "wet formulas." Even when a wet-dry vacuum or extractor is used to pull out most of the water, carpets are still pretty wet and may need several days to thoroughly air dry. Spray-on vehicle carpet formulas do a credible cleaning job without undo wetness.

REMOVING ROAD-SALT STAINS

After vacuuming, but before cleaning and washing carpets, remove any spots or stains (see "How to Remove Stains," in this chapter, for spot-removal techniques). Unlike vehicle upholstery, however, carpet is often tracked with road-salted snow and slush, which not only whiten or gray the carpeting but also stain upon melting. A simple procedure and homemade antidote often rids vehicle carpeting of road-salt stains.

1. Brush away snow and slush. Vacuum remaining residue.
2. If stain remains, remove with a carefully applied saltwater solution: 1 cup of table salt to 1 quart of water.
3. Use a soft-bristled brush or cloth to work the salt solution into the stain place. Feather outward from stain's center to avoid leaving a ring in the carpeting.
4. With stain removed, shampoo the stain area and adjacent carpeting.

CARPET CLEANING WITH A "WET FORMULA"

▶ See Figure 14

1. Clean the dirtier front-seat carpeting first. If your "wet formula" wash solution becomes dirty, mix a new solution before cleaning the backseat carpeting.
2. Apply generous amounts of a "wet formula" with a soft-bristled brush. Use vigorous, circular, overlapping strokes.
3. Work the brush and suds deep into the piling.
4. With a dry, absorbent cloth or paper towels, wipe off any excess.
5. Rinse well and deeply with clean cool or cold water.
6. Soak up the rinse water with paper towels. Or, far better, remove with an extractor or a wet-dry home shop vacuum. Or drive to a coin-op place and use its wet-dry vacuum.
7. Let dry overnight. When nearly or completely dry, fluff carpet's nap with a dry, soft-bristled brush.

8852GP14

Fig. 14 Spray bottle administers "wet formula" to the door trim. Next the trim is scrubbed, rinsed and allowed to dry.

CARPET CLEANING WITH A SPRAY-ON FORMULA

1. Apply spray-on cleaner as outlined step-by-step in the "wet formula" procedure, for spray-on upholstery cleaning.
2. Although some spray-on carpet cleaners may also help to protect newly cleaned vehicle carpets from quickly resoiling, a product designed specifically as a protector gives double protection.

APPLYING CARPET PROTECTANT

The steps listed below are for a specific brand of protector. Follow the manufacturer's instructions on the protector you select.

1. First, test colorfastness. Spray a small amount on a hid den area of carpeting. Wipe with a clean white cloth. If any color shows on the cloth, do not use the product. If no color rub-off shows, proceed.
2. Shake the spray can vigorously. Hold can 4–6 inches from the carpet and make circular, overlapping passes. Spray an even, light coating over the entire carpet area.
3. Protector will foam. The foam will disappear within a few minutes. Wipe any overspray from adjacent, non-carpet areas.
4. Let dry. Protector usually completely dries within about 2 hours.
5. If, after the carpet is dry, any whitish residue remains (evidence that in places you applied too much protector), vacuum that area clean.

Cleaning and Sheening Dashboard, Instrument Panel, and Most In-Vehicle Vinyl, Plastic and Rubber

▶ See Figure 15

The detailing cure-all for restoring the original good looks and sheen of vinyl, rubber and plastics is a protectant. Protectant is wiped on, allowed to work for anywhere from a few minutes to overnight (in the case of badly sun-faded vinyl upholstery), and then wiped and buffed off.

Many driveway detailers, however, neglect one vital first step: cleaning. A protectant cannot work its considerable restorative wonders unless the surface to which it is applied is clean.

PROTECTANT PRE-CLEANING

Whether restoring the dashboard, door moldings, shift console, rubber weather stripping, headrests, sun visors or other in-vehicle appendage,

8852GP15

Fig. 15 Between thorough in-vehicle detailing sessions, wipe the dash every few weeks with a cloth wetted with protectant. Scratches in plastic dial or gauge lenses can be removed with a plastic cleaner, plastic can then be polished with a plastic polish.

clean the surface before applying protectant. You can use an all-purpose cleaner (such as a dishwashing detergent solution, a weak ammonia-water wash, or any of numerous brand name general-purpose cleaners) and soft cloths to thoroughly wash and dry the surface on which you intend to use a protectant. Or you can apply a pre-protectant rub-on/wipe-off cleaner.

APPLYING PROTECTANT

> ✳✳ **CAUTION**
>
> **Since protectants tend to make surfaces slick, do not use on foot pedal rubber (as the brake or accelerator pedals) or on the steering wheel.**

The same protectants that restore vinyl upholstery can restore other in-vehicle plastic, rubber and composite materials.

Protectants do more than simply restore original color. They keep rubber moldings flexible and functioning, protect vinyl from scuffing, and reduce sun-fade.

Protectants need periodic reapplication. To apply, spray or wipe protectant on surface; let it work, then wipe off and buff to a sheen. Most protectants perform better when left on a surface for awhile (for anywhere from a few minutes to several hours), rather than being wiped off immediately.

Detailing Interior Windows, Windshield and Mirrors

▶ **See Figure 16**

For windows, windshield and mirrors, use any good glass cleaner or a weak solution of ammonia and water. Treat interior convertible windows as you did their exteriors, with a scratch-removing plastic cleaner/polish.

8852GP16

Fig. 16 A good quality glass cleaner will remove smoke and haze from the windows

REACHING THE HARD-TO-REACH PLACES

To access the hard-to-reach places in the vehicle interior, use a vacuum's crevice tool, a "detail stick," or a thin, long-handled paint brush. Often dust and dirt can be dislodged with a few zaps of air pressure from an aerosol can of one of the pressurized air products used to rid precision instruments, including camera innards, of dust.

Cleaning and Polishing Interior Chrome

Any good chrome cleaner/polish used to clean and polish exterior chrome can be used to clean and polish interior chrome, as well. However,

the interior application and polishing must be done far more carefully to avoid getting chrome cleaner on upholstery or other interior materials to which chrome trim and strips may be attached. Quick application of masking tape eliminates the risk.

1. Mask what you intend to polish, if masking is applicable.
2. Apply chrome polish with a soft cloth.
3. Work polish into chromed crevices and channels.
4. Wipe off and buff with a clean soft cloth.

Care And Detailing Of Aftermarket-Tinted Windows

If you had your vehicle's windows tinted after you bought the vehicle ("aftermarket-tinted") to reduce glare, reduce ultraviolet fading of upholstery, lessen the work load of air conditioning, or provide privacy, disregard everything this chapter says about the routine way to detail plain glass windows. Yours aren't plain glass. Because their interior sides are coated with a sunscreening film, their detailing may require something more than routine doing.

How much more depends on the kind of film the tinter used. Older-type films are particularly vulnerable to scratching unless you use great care and, most important, a super-soft non-abrasive cleaning cloth, Technology has greatly improved the durability and toughness of the newer tint films. The new films can be safely cleaned much as you would clean your vehicle's untinted glass. If in doubt as to whether your windows are tinted with older- or newer-type film, clean them as though they were the older, more scratch-prone type. If you detail windows tinted with the older-type film as though they were ordinary plain glass, you can destroy the special film with a single cleaning.

Windows tinted after delivery from the factory have a thin layer of tinted plastic film on their in-vehicle surfaces. The film, old or new, is vulnerable to grime (the film's chief enemy), scratches, the mechanical action of a window's mechanism (which can cut, scratch, and groove the tint film), and everyday use.

Detailing window tint films of the older type requires a gentle approach. The number-one rule: Never use a cleaning solution that contains ammonia. To clean, use a mild dishwashing detergent solution: 1 ounce of biodegradable, no-color dishwashing detergent mixed with 20 ounces of distilled water. Use a spray bottle to apply the mix. Spraying, which eliminates application or wiping with cloths, reduces abrasive contact with the film. No-color dishwashing detergent won't cloud or discolor the tint; some colored detergents may.

After spraying solution on the tint film, dry the film with an extremely soft and pliable squeegee, or with a soft sponge. If you have neither, use a super-soft cotton cloth. Avoid using paper towels; no matter how soft they may feel to you, their fibers can scratch the tint films.

The new tint films can be cleaned much as plain glass windows: with any of the usual window cleaning solutions, with soap and water, or with a solution of dishwashing detergent. Once clean, newer films can be dried with very soft paper towels.

Some vehicle owners protect the tint, whatever its type, with a sheet of clear plastic, carefully cut to fit the window exactly. Protective window plastic is available from window-tinting shops.

Application of the plastic is exacting, but easy. (clean the tint film, as described above, and dry. Mix a solution of dishwashing detergent (3—4 squirts of detergent to a quart of water). Wet the window tint with the soapy solution. Lay the plastic over the tint film. With a squeegee, press the plastic to the tint. Working from the center to the extremities of the plastic, squeegee out any soapy water or air bubbles. In two or three days this protective tint sandwich will be dry, and the tint film will be permanently protected.

Besides normal wear and tear, particular things, such as soft drinks spilled on tinted windows not protected by plastic, can deteriorate some types of tint film. So can cigarette smoke, hairspray, and a buildup of road grime. Also, too-tight window rollers and other parts of the window mechanism can squeeze unprotected tint, damaging the film.

One way to reduce damage caused by a window mechanism is to spray-coat the tint with a silicone vinyl protectant. A number of them, available at some auto supply stores and most window-tint shops, are specially formulated for "lubricating" window tint film. Lubrication makes the tint film slightly slippery, helping to reduce window mechanism damage. Lubrication also makes the film more resistant to scratching.

One additional warning: If your vehicle's windows are aftermarket-tinted with the older-type film, especially if the tint is not covered with a plastic protector, don't let the car wash people touch them. Do the tint windows gently (and with the right products) yourself. Car wash window treatment tends to be rough (the cloths they use) and tough (the pressure they use, which is seldom gentle). A single swipe with a rough cloth can leave unprotected older-type tint films permanently disfigured.

In contrast to aftermarket-tinted windows, factory-delivered tinted windows have the tint manufactured in the glass. Factory-tint windows are detailed just like ordinary plain-glass windows.

How To Remove Stains

Fabric upholstery falls victim to all kinds of staining agents.

The first rule is get to work on a stain agent immediately, before it has a chance to set or permanently stain. The second is, if it stains, know what to use to remove the stain best, fastest and safest.

Upholstery fabrics vary greatly. So do stains. But, generally, there is a right way and a right cleaner to handle each type of stain. While getting rid of stains is part of detailing any vehicle's interior, you should always work on stain-causing materials as soon as possible, before they permanently stain the fabric-because it may be weeks or months before you are able to do a thorough interior detailing.

Upholstery fabrics, including the popular velours, stain more easily and are harder to rid of stains than either vinyl or leather. Some pro-detailers charge more to clean auto interiors upholstered in fabric because more work is involved.

Still, you may be surprised how easily the majority of staining agents and their stains disappear from fabric upholstery when you use nothing more than warm water and even how they disappear even more easily when you use a mild "neutral" soap or a dishwashing detergent and water solution.

"Neutral" soap is soap whose pH factor (a measure of acidity or alkalinity on a scale of 0 to 14) is neither acidic nor alkaline. On the pH scale, 7 is neutral. Factor numbers higher than 7 denote increasing alkalinity: numbers lower than 7 denote increasing acidity.

Neutral detailing soaps, as other neutral detailing products, do not harm or remove paint, wax, or other detailing products. Non-neutral detailing products can. When attacking most fabric stains, try soap and water first. Only when that fails should you progress to fabric cleaners, shampoos, and other stain-removing fabric formulas. Use the mildest, least harsh cleaners first (for one example, a very mild ammonia and water solution: 4 parts water to 1 part ammonia). If that fails, dry excess moisture from the area—using paper towels or a hair dryer—and try a slightly stronger fabric cleaner.

Some stains may defy your best efforts. They never entirely fade away, no matter what techniques and cleaners you use, because the staining ingredients have penetrated and indelibly attached to the fibers of the fabric.

In some cases, what appears at first to be a simple spotting job—perhaps just a little suds or cleaner— becomes more complex. For one thing, the stain may "bleed" into the surrounding fabric. Or a ring may form that is more noticeable than the potential stain itself—and can only be gotten rid of by cleaning the entire area, perhaps a whole seatback or seat cushion.

Still, there are methods which work most often in potential stain situations common to vehicle upholstery. Almost all have a single starting point: remove the foreign material, whether it's fruit drink, chewing gum, or something you can't identify.

The removal methods, usually obvious, depend on the foreign material. Paper towels sop up and remove liquids-as blood, juice, and soft drinks. Adhesive materials—road tar and chewing gum, for example— must be scraped off using a dull knife blade. Or, better and beyond error, a stiff piece of cardboard, perhaps a folded match cover with the matches removed (on the chance they might add to the stain).

Assuming you've removed most of the foreign material—at least as much as is visible, the no-longer-visible having soaked or seeped into the fabric—try these specific stain removing methods:

Greasy or Oily Stains

Lipstick. Lipstick is among the more difficult substances to remove because it contains a variety of dyes and oil-like substances with an affinity for fabrics. Application of a quick-dry cleaning solvent—as dry-cleaning fluid (lighter fluid may also work)—may do the trick. So may various powdered fabric cleaners, available from new car dealerships and recommended for cleaning fabrics used in specific makes and models.

Should the powder-to-suds cleaners fail to eradicate stains as stubborn as lipstick, most car-makers—as well as the makers of fabric-detailing products—have available a variety of solvent-type liquid cleaners.

If the lipstick stain is small, test a tiny quarter-inch place, using a cotton swab gingerly dipped (not soaked) in a solvent cleaner. If the fluid won't work on a quarter inch of the lipstick stain, it won't work on any of it. And, frankly, you're probably stuck with the stain.

If, on the other hand, your quarter-inch solvent test significantly or completely removes the stain, use a little of the solvent cleaner on a clean cloth (a piece of cheesecloth works best). Begin at the outside of the stain and gently, without excessive pressure, work inward to the center.

Working from the outside in minimizes accumulation of fluid at the stain's outer edges and thus reduces the chance of the stain "bleeding." Even if you succeed in removing the lipstick, you may create a ring which only a thorough washing of the entire area (seat cushion or seatback) will wholly remove.

Crayons (wax). Wax-type crayon stains are removed much like lipstick.

Oil, grease, butter, margarine, vegetable oil, cosmetic creams. After you have scraped off or otherwise removed the residue, blot lightly with a clean paper towel, taking up the remaining visible residue. Then use a solvent-type fabric cleaner as in "Lipstick," above, carefully working from the outside in. After each solvent application, blot with a clean paper towel. Continue the removal treatment until the visible stain is gone and no more stain is picked up by the blotter.

Road tar and asphalt. These two are difficult to remove and even harder to prevent from permanently staining fabric. One problem: the solvent-type fabric cleaner, which is used on these substances as for "lipstick," dissolves tar and asphalt, risking "bleeding" into adjacent areas. One way to prevent or minimize bleeding is to blot frequently as you work, blotting up with clean paper towels any tar or asphalt dissolved by the cleaner.

Chewing gum. Generally, removing the gum itself solves the problem, unless it's colorful bubble gum, which can stain unless promptly treated. First, use ice cubes to harden the gum. Then as the gum hardens, scrape it from the fabric with a dull knife. A little solvent-type fabric cleaner makes the process easier and, used ahead of your knife and after it, usually removes all gum remnants.

Shoe polish (wax and paste types; see "Water-soluble inks and polishes," below). The procedure described above under "Lipstick" usually works for wax and paste shoe polishes.

Coffee (with cream). The procedure for removing coffee with cream is similar to that described above under "Lipstick"—with some differences. Coffee stains generally cover more fabric area because more substance is usually spilled-say, half a cup of coffee rather than merely a dab of lipstick or a wad of chewing gum. After the solvent/cleaner procedure and a thorough blotting of the last lingering evidence of the cream-laden coffee spill, a ring is often visible. In that case, the entire seat or seatback must be scrubbed with a mild soap solution, blotted, rinsed with clean lukewarm water, and then blotted some more. Finally, the area should be spot-dried with a hair dryer (some plug into the vehicle's cigarette lighter; use an extension cord if yours does not).

When using a hair dryer, hold the nozzle far enough from the fabric to prevent scorching. To test the dryer's heat, lay your hand flat on the fabric and turn on the dryer. Increase the nozzle's distance until you feel heat, but not extreme heat, on your hand. Slower drying is better than permanently disfigured fabric.

Non-Greasy Stains

Scrape or blot away the non-greasy residue. Sponge the area with cool water, then blot semi-dry with clean paper towels. If the stain disappears without leaving a ring, carefully dry the still-moist area with a hair dryer (as noted above, some plug into the vehicle's cigarette lighter; if yours does not, use an extension cord).

If remnants of the stain (or its odor) remain, one of the two procedures outlined below can probably help, depending on the non greasy substance (as discussed on the following pages):

Use a foam-type fabric cleaner such as those available at some dealerships. Mixed with water, as directed on the label, the powder cleanser produces a suds-like foam. Using a clean sponge, spread the suds over the stain area. Don't rub vigorously or saturate the fabric.

When the stain disappears, remove surplus suds with the sponge, then rinse with a clean sponge and water. Wipe up and blot any remaining moisture with a slightly damp paper towel. Immediately dry with a moderate heat source: heat lamp, hair dryer, or air hose. Finally, merge the treated place and surrounding fabric by rubbing gently over the entire fabric area with a clean, slightly dampened soft cloth.

Some spray-on upholstery cleaner/protectors formulated for de-staining cloth or velour auto fabric deposit a fabric protector after the stain has been removed.

Use mild neutral soap or dishwashing detergent and water, followed, if necessary, by judicious use of cleaning fluid or a solvent-type cleaner/spot lifter. Blot the stain with paper towels and dry with a hair dryer or other gentle heat or air source.

Although you have removed the stain, an odor may linger (particularly if the stain was from urine or vomit). If so, after blotting up most of the moisture, and before final forced-heat or air drying, apply a deodorizing mix of baking soda and warm (not hot) water (for example, 1 teaspoon of baking soda mixed in 1 cup of lukewarm water). Apply the mix with a sponge and allow it to remain on the affected area for about a minute. Wipe up the residue with a clean sponge moistened slightly with water. Repeat if necessary. Then rinse the area using a sponge and warm water, blot up excess moisture, and apply heat to dry.

Ammonia and water acts as both an odor-destroyer and acid neutralizer, especially on urine stains. The mix: 5 parts water and 1 part household (colorless) ammonia. Avoid lemon-scented ammonia because of its color.

Coffee (black). Use a foam-type cleaner, as described above, with lukewarm water. Unless coffee is the heavy-residue "Turkish" type, follow directions above. Either procedure should remove black coffee stains.

Catsup. Gently rub stain with cold water. Use neutral soap or dishwashing detergent, if necessary. Be sure your cloth is clean. Keep switching to a clean place on the cloth rather than wiping over the stain place with a catsup-stained section. When the stain is removed, blot and air or heat dry.

Mustard. Mustard produces one of the harder stains to get rid of because its usually intense color acts like a dye. First, scrape off the residue; then sponge the stain with warm water. Use neutral soap or dishwashing detergent for the most stubborn mustard stains. Blot dry.

Fruit juice, soft drinks, wine, fruit, egg. Treatment for all of these non greasy stains is similar. Remove by following directions for using a foam-type fabric cleaner, above. Do not use soap and water, which may set the stain. If the foam cleaner does not remove all the stain, you may also need to use a solvent-type cleaner. Red wine stains, like those from colored soft drinks and egg yolk, are obviously more troublesome and time-consuming to remove than, say, white wine or colorless soft drink stains. Intensely colored stains in this group may need to be treated with a solvent-type cleaner in order to get them to do a total disappearance act.

Urine. Sponge with a lukewarm suds mix (water and suds), then rinse in cold water. Follow this with an ammonia/water mix, applied with a sponge or clean cloth. Let the ammonia and water (see mix formula directions for using mild neutral soap, above) "work" on the stain place for at least one minute. Finally, rinse with a clean, water-wetted cloth or sponge. Blot and heat dry.

Vomit. Vomit sometimes produces a nasty, hard-to-remove stain. After removing residue, sponge with cold water. Follow with a mild soap and warm water wash. Then apply the deodorizing baking soda/water mix (see mix formula directions, above). Conclude with a cold-water sponge rinse. If any stain remains, use a solvent-type cleaner or cleaning fluid. Finally, use a sponge to rinse with cold water, then blot and air/heat dry.

Blood. Do not use soap or hot water on blood. They will set the stain, perhaps permanently. Use nothing but cold water. Soak and rub the area with a clean cloth or sponge soaked in cold water. Keep turning the cloth to a clean place and use clean cold water each time. When the stain is removed, blot and dry.

Combination Stains

Ice cream. As you might suppose, chocolate ice cream stains are harder to remove than vanilla and other less colorful ice creams. Apply hot water on a clean cloth. If stain persists, wash with a warm neutral soap suds solution, followed by a cold, clean water rinse. Dry or let dry. Any remaining stain can usually be gotten rid of with a few dabs of solvent-type cleaner.

Candy (non-chocolate). Rub gently with a clean cloth soaked in hot water. Let dry. Any remaining stain can be erased with gentle dabs of cleaning fluid, using a clean cloth.

Candy (chocolate). Use the same stain-obliterating technique described for non-chocolate candy. In the final cleaning fluid step, continue applying the fluid and blotting with paper towels or an absorbent dry cloth until all stain remnants are blotted up.

Stains from unknown source. Clean with cool water, blot, and dry. Solvent-type cleaner, applied after stain area dries, will usually remove any remaining stain.

Ballpoint pen ink. Stains produced by a ballpoint pen are among the most difficult to remove from auto upholstery (or any other kind of fabric). Sponge-wet with cool water, then with cool water and detergent; follow with a cool water rinse. Persistent ballpoint marks can sometimes be removed with rubbing alcohol applied with a damp, clean cloth.

If that fails, try a solvent-type cleaning fluid. The risk with ballpoint marks is that the ink, liquefied by the various treatment liquids, will spread to the adjacent fabric. One way to minimize potential spreading is by blotting thoroughly (using super-absorbent paper towels) after each application of water, alcohol, or cleaning fluid.

Sometimes all techniques fail, and the fabric is indelibly ink-stained. Much depends on the type of ink.

Water-soluble inks and polishes. Some inks and a few polishes are water-soluble, and they disappear with only a careful cool water treatment, followed by blotting and air or forced drying.

By contrast, ball pens or markers that use indelible ink may, whatever your treatment, stain indelibly.

Today's auto fabrics are often sprayed at the factory with a water- and oil-repellent protectant. Once a fabric stain area is thoroughly dry (seldom in less than a day's time, longer in humid weather and regardless of apparent surface drying by heat or air), renew its factory protection with a quick spray application of a good fabric protector.

Repairing Seats And Dash

Vinyl dashboards and seats are subject to cracking and tearing with hard use. Wear and tear in these areas is very noticeable, but not too difficult to repair. Cloth-covered seats are harder to repair, unless you're handy with a tailor's needle and thread. If you're not and the seams are coming apart, invest in a set of seat covers in lieu of a trip to the upholstery shop.

Any retail auto store sells pre-fitted seat covers at a fraction of the cost of new upholstery. Seat covers are sold as "fits-all" (universal application), or more expensively by make and model of vehicle. Be sure to check if the covers fit bench, bucket or split-back seats. The covers are tied or wired under the seats.

Burn marks in vinyl seats; armrests and dashboards can be repaired with the help of a good vinyl repair kit. Rips in the vinyl and seams that have come apart are slightly more difficult but are well worth the time and effort in the end.

About the best way to repair a rip is to heat both sides of the tear with a hair drier. Lift up the material and place a 2" wide strip of fabric tape under one side of the vinyl. Stretch the other side over the tape and line it up carefully. When you have it lined up, press down. Hold it in place while someone applies vinyl repair liquid over the area to be repaired. Let it dry completely before using it. The repair should look like new and last quite a while.Other methods of repairing vinyl involve vinyl repair compounds that require heat. The kits contain a repair compound, applicator and several different graining papers. If the hole is deep, it will have to be filled with foam or anything to provide a backing. Spread the vinyl patch compound over the blemish. Select a graining paper to closely match the grain of your material and place it over the patch, grain side down. Heat it with an iron set at **COTTON** for about 60 seconds. **DO NOT LET THE IRON CONTACT THE VINYL**. The result should be a long lasting and nearly invisible repair.

Repairing Door Panels

♦ **See Figures 17 thru 22**

It's easy to fix door panels. Treat them the same way you would a vinyl seat. The panels are usually fastened to the door with clips behind the panel. If these won't hold any more, screw or glue the panel in place.

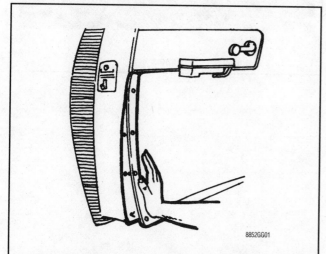

Fig. 17 A few sharp raps with your fist will usually snap a door panel back into place

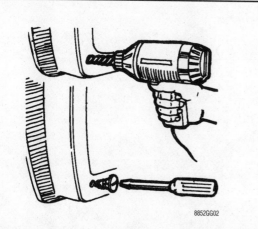

Fig. 18 If the clips are sprung, drill some small holes where the panel is pulled away and install some screws with counter-sunk washers

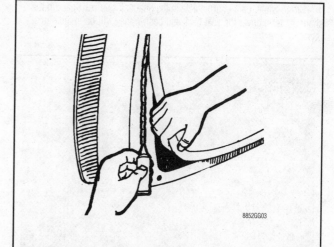

Fig. 19 If drilling holes and screws is not practical, use one of the super-strength glues available

Fig. 20 Use screws and countersunk washers to attach door panels

Keeping The Interior Clean

Once you've gone to the trouble of cleaning the interior, it'll be worth your while to keep it clean. It makes it much easier to clean up the next time around.

Common sense plus these tips will help keep the interior clean.

Vacuum the carpets regularly. The hardest thing to get out of carpets is ground-in dirt.

• If you don't have floor mats, invest in a set. They are much cheaper to replace than carpets and take a lot of the wear carpets would normally get. Don't be too heavy handed with waxes, polishes and dressings. Too much build-up of wax and polish only traps more dirt.

• Don't use dressings or wax on dirty vinyl. Spend a little time to clean it properly before applying a vinyl dressing.

• A combination cleaner/protectant or saddle soap used on vinyl will keep it soft and pliable but will make the seats slippery. A good buffing with a soft cloth will reduce the slippery feeling.

• If your fabric upholstery is new and clean, Scotch-Guard® will keep stains from setting in the fabric and make them easier to clean. However, if the fabric is already dirty or old, you're only wasting your time.

- If possible, park your vehicle in the shade. If you can't park in the shade, at least cover the seat back and dash if they will be in the sun's rays.

- Clean spots and stains as quickly as possible before they have a chance to set in the material. You stand a better chance of completely removing the stain if you remove it while it's wet.

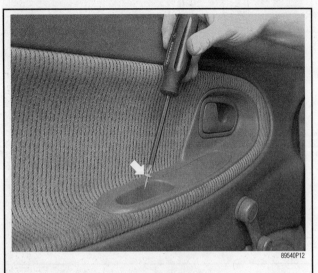

Fig. 21 Door panels are usually retained by screws . . .

Fig. 22 . . . and by snap fasteners

18

DASH GAUGES

DASH GAUGES

◆ See Figures 1 and 2

Most engine problems develop slowly and telegraph their warning signs clearly, if you are equipped to read them. About 25 years ago, the auto industry began a trend to eliminate dash gauges. The oil pressure, ammeter and coolant temperature gauges were replaced with small warning lights—quickly and aptly named "idiot" lights. The difference is that the idiot light tells you when something has already happened; the gauge will tell you when it's starting to happen, and will indicate a trend.

Fortunately, automakers offer gauges as optional equipment, sometimes in addition to the standard warning lights. Equipping your car or truck with gauges in addition to the warning lights can indicate a pattern that will point out irregularities in plenty of time to correct them and save the expense of more serious problems.

As an example, watching the coolant temperature gauge climb slightly above normal over time can indicate slipping belts, low coolant level, worn hoses or incorrect ignition timing. Any of these problems are easily corrected before they cause the warning light to come on, when the engine has already overheated.

As the age of electronics increase the sophistication of the automobile, increased use is being made of the electronic control module and even a separate body control module. These modules are small on-board computers that monitor hundreds of inputs from various sensors on the vehicle. Based on the information they receive, these modules makes decisions to alter ignition timing or alter the fuel metering system.

Manufacturers have also found that the module is capable of handling even more functions than there is a practical use. As a result, more equipment is being offered to feed the driver a constant stream of information—everything from tire pressure to fuel economy to elapsed time or mileage.

Types of Gauges

There are two types of gauges—mechanical and electrical.

MECHANICAL GAUGES

Mechanical gauges measure speed or pressure at the source and send the information to the gauge mechanically. The speedometer and Bourdon tube oil pressure gauges are examples of this type.

Bourdon tube oil pressure gauges are connected directly to a small tube in the main engine oil passage, by a plastic or copper line. The gauge consists of a flattened tube bent in the form of a curve that tends to straighten under engine oil pressure. The curved tube is linked to a needle that registers on a calibrated scale. They are easily distinguished by the copper or nylon line running from the engine to the gauge.

ELECTRICAL GAUGES

Electrical gauges monitor functions at the source and send the information to the gauge electrically.

Thermal (bi-metallic) electric gauges are activated by the difference in the expansion rate of a bi-metal bar. A sending unit controls the flow of current to a heating element coiled around a bimetal bar in the gauge. These gauges can be recognized by a pointer that moves slowly to its position when the ignition is turned ON.

Magnetic electric gauges move the indicator needle by changing the balance between the magnetic pull of two coils built into the gauge. When the ignition is OFF, the needle may rest anywhere. Balance is controlled by the

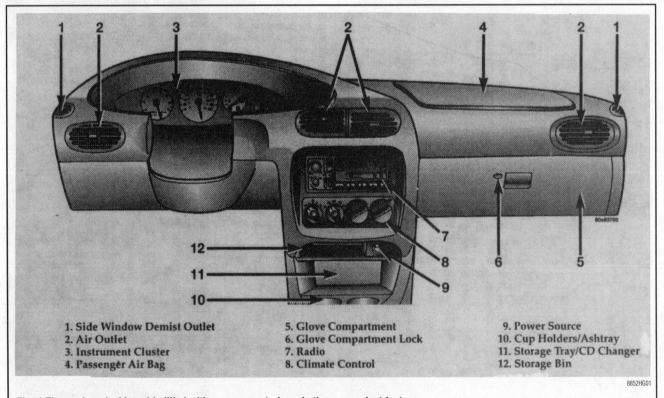

1. Side Window Demist Outlet
2. Air Outlet
3. Instrument Cluster
4. Passenger Air Bag
5. Glove Compartment
6. Glove Compartment Lock
7. Radio
8. Climate Control
9. Power Source
10. Cup Holders/Ashtray
11. Storage Tray/CD Changer
12. Storage Bin

8852HG01

Fig. 1 The modern dashboard is filled with gauges, controls and other convenient features

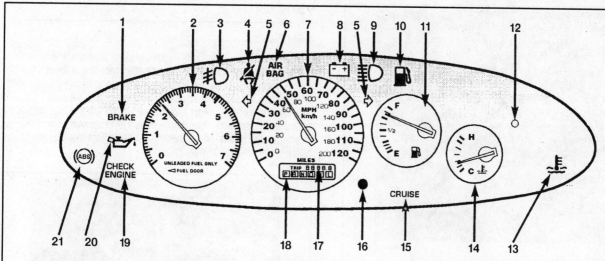

1. Brake System Warning Light
2. Tachometer
3. Fog Light Indicator
4. Seat Belt Reminder Light
5. Turn Signal Indicators

6. Airbag Light
7. Speedometer
8. Charging System Light
9. High Beam Indicator

10. Low Fuel Light
11. Fuel Gauge
12. Security Alarm Light
13. Engine Temperature Warning Light

14. Temperature Gauge
15. Cruise Light
16. Trip Odometer Button
17. Odometer/Trip Odometer

18. Transmission Range Indicator
19. Check Engine Light
20. Oil Pressure Light
21. Anti-Lock Warning Light

Fig. 2 Electronic sensors have replaced mechanical gauges in many applications. A computer with a single logic chip in conjunction with sensors can easily monitor every system of the vehicle, providing warning lights and instant read out of information from tire pressure to fuel economy to elapsed time to your destination

action of a sending unit that will vary current flow, depending on temperature, pressure or movement of a float arm. A magnetic gauge can be recognized by a needle that jumps to its position when the ignition is turned ON. A 90° scale is also the maximum that can be used, since the needle must swing between the poles of a magnet.

Many electric gauges use an instrument voltage regulator to control the supply of voltage to the gauge. This prevents fluctuations in the gauge due to varying voltage.

How to Read Gauges

The problem with gauges is in knowing how to read them; it doesn't do much good to have gauges, if you can't interpret the reading.

Most gauges are marked with green (OK) or red (danger) areas or with calibrated faces. No gauge should be considered totally accurate; an indication of change is far more important than a totally accurate reading.

You should be able to quickly familiarize yourself with the normal readings on the gauges, and to easily spot a sudden or developing change in the readings.

COOLANT TEMPERATURE

♦ See Figure 3

These gauges monitor the temperature of the engine coolant. As the engine warms up, the temperature will probably rise to somewhere around the 180°–200°F (83–94°C) range. If you're stuck in traffic, the temperature will rise slightly. It will also rise slightly immediately after shutting the engine off, because the coolant is not being cooled, but will return to normal when the engine is started.

Variations in temperature as shown on the gauge are not normal, unless you are suddenly caught in heavy traffic or some other conditions cause the temperature to change. Too cool temperatures indicate a faulty thermostat. Too hot readings indicate low coolant level, worn hoses, defective radiator cap, incorrect ignition timing or slipping belts. If the normal operating temperature rises over the course of time, and the above factors are OK, suspect a worn water pump or a clogged system.

Fig. 3 The coolant temperature gauge reads coolant temperature in degrees Fahrenheit or (Centigrade), or may merely be marked "Cold" and "Hot"

OIL PRESSURE

♦ See Figure 4

The oil pressure gauge will tell you if your engine is getting proper lubrication. At fast idle when the engine (and oil) are cold, the pressure will probably be at maximum on the gauge, around 60 psi (413 kPa). Depending on the vehicle, rpm and condition of the engine, oil pressure should be constant, somewhere around 30–40 psi (207–275 kPa) at cruising speed, and less at idle. Under load, you can expect the oil pressure to rise slightly and to fall off with deceleration. Low oil pressure can warn of low oil level, wrong viscosity oil, overheating, clogged oil filter or worn engine (many miles).

Fig. 4 Oil pressure is monitored in pounds per square inch (PSI), (kPa in the metric system), or marked "Low" and "High"

AMMETER

▶ **See Figure 5**

The ammeter will indicate the condition of the charging system.

It will show charge (+) when the battery is being charged and discharge (-) when the battery is being used. Just after cranking the engine, the ammeter will show a charging condition if lights and accessories are OFF. As the energy spent in cranking is restored to the battery, the pointer will gradually move back toward the center, but should stay slightly on the charge (+) side. If the battery is low, it will show a charge condition for an indeterminate period.

At speeds above 30 mph (48 kph), with lights and accessories on, the ammeter should read on the charge side, depending on the condition of the battery. At road speeds, the ammeter should never show discharge. If it does, check the belts or charging system.

A battery that appears to charge rapidly, then discharge rapidly, is failing and replacement time is near. Slower than normal charging rates indicate a slipping belt or a problem in the alternator.

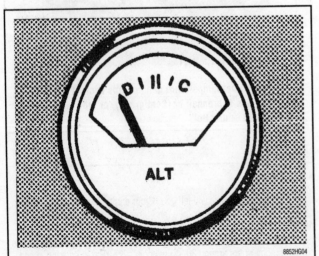

Fig. 5 The ammeter monitors the rate of charge or discharge of the battery

VOLTMETER

▶ **See Figure 6**

Voltmeters are used on some vehicles in place of an ammeter because they give a more complete indication of battery condition. Although the vehicle uses a 12-volt system, the system operates at slightly over 13 volts. If the voltmeter reads under approximately 13 volts after the engine has been running a while, look for slipping belts or too low a voltage regulator setting on vehicles with adjustable regulators. Continuously high (above approximately 15 volts) or low (below 13 volts) voltage may also indicate a defective alternator or defective battery.

Fig. 6 The voltmeter shows the battery condition at any given moment, more accurately than an ammeter

VACUUM GAUGE

▶ **See Figures 7 and 8**

Vacuum gauges are always mechanical types that measure manifold pressure (engine vacuum), which relates directly to fuel consumption.

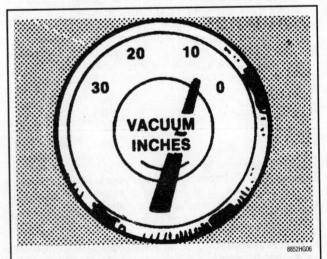

Fig. 7 Vacuum gauges monitor engine vacuum in inches of mercury (in./Hg) or Kilopascals (kPa)

Fig. 8 A normal vacuum gauge can be used to determine the most fuel efficient driving conditions

Engine vacuum varies inversely with engine speed, so you should also drive at the highest indicated vacuum. Try to maintain the highest vacuum under all conditions.

The vacuum gauge readings are also a good indication of the condition of your engine. Actually, the readings are not as important as a steady needle. At idle, the vacuum gauge should show a steady reading of anywhere from 8–16 in. Hg (27–54 kPa) on an engine in good tune and operating condition. A needle that twitches at idle indicates fouled plugs, stuck or worn valves. A low reading at idle that stays low usually means a leaking vacuum hose, incorrect ignition timing or worn valves or valve guides. As engine speed increases, erratic readings may mean a blown head gasket or worn valves.

After the fuel crises of the 70's, the public's interest in fuel economy has given birth to a variation of the vacuum gauge, called a "motor minder." This gauge is a vacuum gauge with words ("Poor," "Fair," "Good" and "Excellent") and color bands (red/yellow/green) replacing the numbers on the face of the vacuum gauge. Since there is a direct correlation between

in./Hg (vacuum) and fuel economy, gauge manufacturers have already interpreted the numbers for the driver.

The latest variant to the vacuum gauge, or the "motor minder" mentioned above is the upshift light. The operating principle is basically the same, there is a sensor monitoring the intake manifold vacuum which then triggers the light telling the driver when to shift to obtain better fuel economy.

TACHOMETER

▶ See Figures 9 and 10

Tachometers are among the most popular of gauges, possibly because of their identification with racing.

They are useful while driving to keep the engine at its most efficient rpm.

Fig. 9 The tachometer measures engine rpm (1000's of engine revolutions per minute).

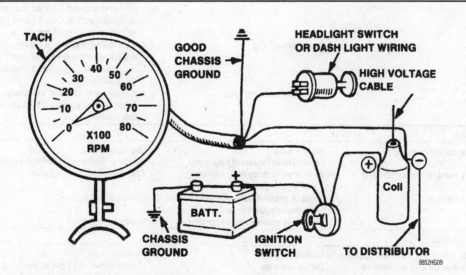

Fig. 10 Most tachometers have only four connections to make. One goes to ground, one to power (ignition switch), one for lights and one to the distributor side of the coil or the trigger side of the ignition module

Installing Add-On Gauges

◆ **See Figure 11**

Before buying gauges, make a survey of likely mounting spots. Gauges should be placed within easy viewing and should not interfere with driving. Give some thought to the location based on priority. The ones you're going to watch the most should be most convenient.

Be sure the gauge faces are clear and readable. They should leave no doubt as to the readings. An accessory mounting bracket is the easiest way to mount gauges, but they can be installed on the dashboard if you want to cut holes in the dash.

Installation is usually a matter of following the manufacturer's instructions for hook-up. Mechanical gauges should be placed where the plumbing for the gauge provides a minimum of routing problems. Be sure all wires are well secured, protected against chafing and have enough slack to absorb engine vibrations. Plastic tap connectors are useful for splicing into wires. These eliminate the need for cutting and taping wires and give a clean, quick connection.

TROUBLESHOOTING BASIC DASH GAUGE PROBLEMS

Most problems with dash gauges can be traced to faulty wiring or a defective sending unit. Occasionally, the gauge itself will be at fault.

The Problem	Is Caused By	What to Do
Coolant Temperature Gauge		
Gauge reads erratically or not at all	• Loose or dirty connections • Defective sending unit • Defective gauge	• Clean/tighten connections • Bi-metal gauge: remove the wire from the sending unit. Ground the wire for an instant. If the gauge registers, replace the sending unit. • Magnetic gauge: Disconnect the wire at the sending unit. With ignition ON gauge should register COLD. Ground the wire; gauge should register HOT.
Ammeter Gauge—Turn Headlights ON (do not start engine). Note reaction		
Ammeter shows charge Ammeter shows discharge Ammeter does not move	• Connections reversed on gauge • Ammeter is OK • Loose connections or faulty wiring • Defective gauge	• Reinstall connections • Nothing • Check/correct wiring • Replace gauge
Oil Pressure Gauge		
Gauge does not register or is inaccurate	• On mechanical gauge, Bourdon tube may be bent or kinked. • Low oil pressure • Defective gauge • Defective wiring • Defective sending unit	• Check tube for kinks or bends preventing oil from reaching the gauge. • Remove sending unit. Idle the engine briefly. If no oil flows from sending unit hole, problem is in engine. • Remove the wire from the sending unit and ground it for an instant with the ignition ON. A good gauge will go to the top of the scale. • Check the wiring to the gauge. If it's OK and the gauge doesn't register when grounded, replace the gauge. • If the wiring is OK and the gauge functions when grounded, replace the sending unit.
All Gauges		
All gauges do not operate All gauges read low or erratically All gauges pegged	• Blown fuse • Defective instrument regulator • Defective or dirty instrument voltage regulator • Loss of ground between instrument voltage regulator and car. • Defective instrument regulator	• Replace fuse • Replace instrument voltage regulator • Clean contacts or replace • Check ground • Replace regulator
Warning Lights		
Light(s) do not come on when ignition is ON, but engine is not started	• Defective bulb • Defective wire • Defective sending unit	• Replace bulb • Check wire from light to sending unit • Disconnect the wire from the sending unit and ground it. Replace the sending unit if the light comes on with the ignition ON.
Light comes on with engine running	• Problem in individual system Defective sending unit	• Check system • Check sending unit (see above)

8852HC01

Fig. 11 Troubleshooting Gauge problems

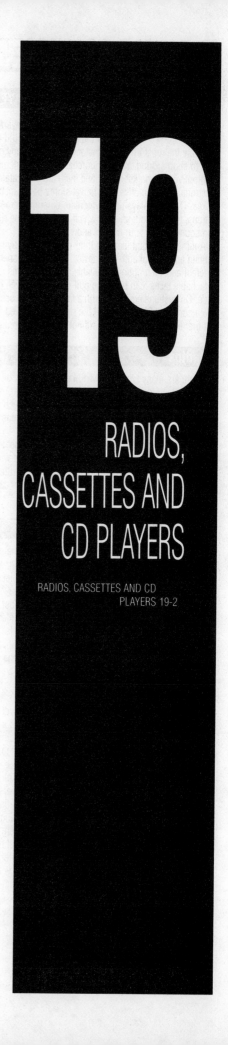

19

RADIOS, CASSETTES AND CD PLAYERS

RADIOS, CASSETTES AND CD PLAYERS

When buying a radio, cassette player or CD player/changer for your vehicle, there are a number of things that you should consider. Price is probably the most important factor when buying any product, so its a good idea to shop around. You can purchase stereo systems from electronic or automotive aftermarket stores and there are also catalog companies. Many electronic or automotive aftermarket stores have functional displays in their stores. These displays usually contain different stereo and speaker combinations, try them out and see which system has the right price, appearance and sound to suit your budget and vehicle.

Another important factor to think about when buying a system is, does it contain any type of anti-theft device? Ask the salesperson to show you the different anti-theft options available. Stereo systems today can come with detachable faces, can be of the pull-out type or even have its own security code. On systems equipped with a factory pre-set security code, the code is like a bankcard PIN number. If the stereo is removed from the vehicle without first entering the code, it will not operate again until the code is entered.

Radios

There are many types of AM-FM radio systems on the market today. Most radios sold or in use today are of the digital push button type. Depending on what type of sound quality, how much you want to spend or what type of features the radio has, should determine what type of radio you purchase.

When you purchase your radio, make sure to get the correct mounting hardware and wiring harness for your vehicle. The wiring harness will allow you to plug the new unit into the existing wiring without cutting.

Most radios (except from the factory), contain a cassette player, CD player or both.

Radio/Cassette Player

If you already have a cassette deck in your home, you'll likely choose one for your vehicle. Radio/cassette prices can vary, with the more expensive units generally offering better tone response, less distortion and greater power output.

The radio/cassette players range from the cheaper basic models, which contain features such as fast forward, rewind and eject with of course the basic radio functions to the more expensive models. The more expensive models include functions such as automatic music search, auto reverse and Dolby noise reduction as well as the basic functions.

If you have limited installation space and want an in dash radio/cassette player combination, this is the way to go.

A variety of products are available from retailer's and catalog companies. Be sure to get a complete custom installation kit with instructions. This should include any special mounting adapters and a wiring harness. The wiring harness will allow you to plug the new unit into the existing wiring or it will allow you to splice the adapter wiring without cutting the original vehicle harness.

If you are replacing an existing unit, try to you pick a unit that fits perfectly in your dashboard. Most radio/cassette players made today are approximately the same size and no cutting of the dashboard or adapters should be required to make it fit. If you are replacing an older, larger system with a new one, most electronic or automotive aftermarket stores sell adapters that will fill the large opening in your dashboard.

When purchasing a radio/cassette player, a system with four-way high-power is one of the keys to great sound. Systems with separate built-in amplifiers for front and rear speakers give you cleaner sound at all volume levels. This is a must if you want to experience the entire range of detail and dynamics your music has to offer. So if you like rolling down the windows or are even thinking about singing along, look for a receiver that offers you at least 8 watts of RMS power x 4 channels.

If you're having a hard time choosing between a new radio/cassette player and an in-dash CD player, then consider a system that gives you the best of both worlds. Many of the radio/cassette players you'll be looking at include controls for an optional CD changer. Mount the changer out of sight in your vehicle, and control it from the driver's seat. You'll be able to enjoy the digital sound quality of multiple CDs, and still listen to all your cassettes, including those mixed tapes you spent years recording.

CARING FOR TAPE CARTRIDGES

Cassettes will give better sound reproduction and last longer if you take care of them.

• Do not expose the tape cartridge to direct sunlight or extremes of temperature.

• If the cartridge is accidentally exposed to high temperatures, allow the tape to run for several minutes at low volume before playing it normally.

• Remove the cartridge from the tape player when not in use.

• Protect the open end of the cartridge from dust and dirt.

• Store tapes with the open end down.

• Never try to pry the cartridge open or pull the tape out.

CLEANING TAPE PLAYERS

▶ See Figure 1

The playback head and capstan accumulate a coating of oxide from the tape. This accumulation can be removed with a cotton swab moistened in denatured alcohol. Hold the cartridge door open and swab the surfaces of the playback head and capstan; dry the parts with a clean cotton swab.

There are also cleaners available in the form of a cassette tape which can be purchased at any music store. Insert the head cleaning tape into player and play the tape as you would any other cassette tape. Follow the manufacturers recommendations on how long you should allow the cleaning tape to run, then remove the tape.

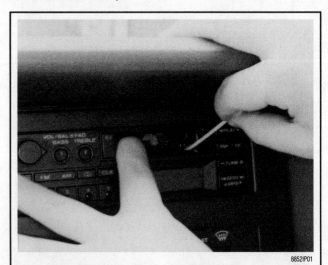

8852IP01

Fig. 1 Clean the tape head and capstan after every few hours of operation with a cotton swab and denatured alcohol

Radio/CD Player

Radio/CD player prices can vary, with the more expensive units generally offering better sound quality, greater power output, and more features.

The digital sound quality allows you to hear exactly what you want to hear in stereo and is highly dependable, offers excellent sound reproduction and a wide range of programming.

1. When buying a radio/CD player, you should find out what products are out on the market, what features are available and what features best suit your needs. A little research into these few things could help you save time and money.

The radio/CD player gives you the option of listening to the radio or enjoying one of your favorite CDs.

The less expensive C/D player will have basic functions such as play, skip or next and will display which track on the disc is currently being played.

The more expensive CD players have the same functions as the basic models as well as features such as intro scan, this feature lets you hear the first few seconds of each track on a tape or a CD. Hit the button again when you hear the song you're looking for and it will play that song. Another features available is random, which permits the playing of the tracks from the CD in a random order. On some models the digital display can show you the name of the CD's artist, track number and the elapsed time of the track playing.

Multi-CD Changers

▶ **See Figures 2 thru 8**

Are you finding it tricky deciding between cassette and compact disc for your vehicle?

Maybe you're in need of hours of continuous music for your road trips, or simply looking for a way to enjoy CDs in your vehicle while keeping your factory radio. All of these are terrific reasons to install a CD changer.

Because these changers install in your trunk, or, in many cases, under your seat or even in your glove box, your changer will be safely out of sight and pose no temptation to would-be thieves.

If you're driving a leased vehicle or cruising in a classic, you may be hesitant to swap out the factory radio for a new in-dash controller. Fortunately, that doesn't mean you have to give up the many advantages of a CD changer. With a hideaway FM modulator, you can get terrific-sounding results playing an add-on changer through your existing FM radio. That means you'll enjoy the sound of digital recordings while keeping your factory receiver and preserving your vehicle's stock appearance.

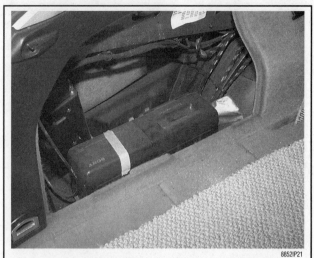
8852IP21

Fig. 3 If applicable, to change or and CDs to the changer you must remove the trim panel

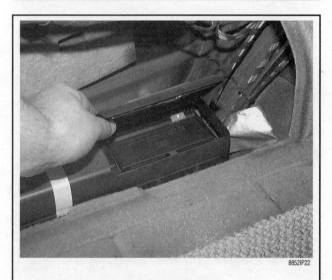
8852IP22

Fig. 4 Lift up the flap covering the CD holder . . .

8852IP20

Fig. 2 Your CD changer may be placed in your trunk behind a trim panel like this

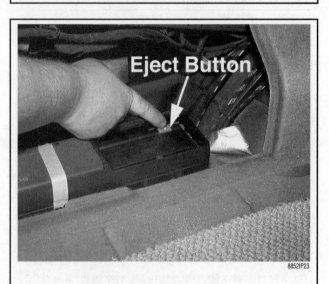
8852IP23

Fig. 5 . . . then press the eject button . . .

Fig. 6 . . . and remove the CD holder from the changer

Fig. 7 To add a CD, simply insert it into a slot in the holder

Fig. 8 To remove a CD, simply push the lever on the side of the holder that corresponds with the slot in which the CD has been placed

Speakers

Speakers are one of the most neglected components of a vehicle stereo system. You can have the best radio or tape player made, but without good speakers, it won't make a bit of difference, because poor-quality speakers create their own distortion and static.

Automotive speakers come in two basic types-flush mount or surface mount. Flush mount (also known as recessed) work best installed in doors, kick panels or rear decks, where they produce best sound and are out of the way. The large, open areas in doors and under the rear deck (behind the speakers) serve as acoustic enclosures, reinforcing the bass tones. Flush-mount speakers come in many different sizes.

Surface-mount (wedge or hang-on) speakers come with their own enclosures made of high-strength ABS plastic. They feature quick and easy installation on almost any flat surface, and can even be installed beneath the dash if they are attached to a flat board. However, the bass tones are not as good because of the reduced baffle space behind the speaker.

Whichever type you choose, a good rule of thumb is, "the heavier the magnet, the better the speaker." A good speaker will have a magnet weighing at least 3–5 ounces (85–141 grams), often as much as 20 ounces (566 grams). In addition, larger speakers (diameter) are more effective, especially for low (bass) tones.

Stereo radios and tape players require the use of at least two speakers to achieve the proper stereo effect, though you can use four or even six. No matter how many speakers you use, remember stereo separation must be side-to-side. The mounting location you pick will usually determine whether flush- or surface-mount speakers are used. Surface-mounted speakers are the easiest to install because they simply bolt in place. Flush-mount speakers produce a better bass response because they use the larger area behind them as a baffle. However, flush mounts are more complex to install.

Before you start cutting holes for them, its smart to make a couple of checks. Will the speaker's location affect the operation of the window crank, convertible top mechanism or removal of the spare tire? If yes, find another location. Also, be sure there's enough room to fit the speaker where you want it. Use a template to help you position the speakers exactly where you want them, and use a hole saw to cut the hole.

Antennas

Like the speakers, the antenna deserves some consideration if optimum performance is expected.

For best reception on AM, the antenna should be extended as high as possible. On FM, the optimum antenna height is approximately 31 inch (787mm); it also happens to work well on AM.

There are several types of antennas. The traditional extendible antenna is seldom seen anymore, giving way to the one-piece stainless steel antenna. These are probably the best compromise, because they are tuned for FM reception and offer the most resistance to casual vandals, who like to break the antennas off parked vehicles.

The windshield antenna supplied with some new vehicles works fine on AM, but leaves something to be desired on FM.

For those to whom price is not important, or who desire the latest in technology, electronic antennas are the thing. These incorporate an amplifier in the base of the antenna to boost the radio signal. Some of the signal in any antenna is lost through the cable before it reaches the receiver. If the signal can be amplified before it enters the cable, a stronger signal will eventually reach the receiver, allowing reception of stations that would normally go unheard.

A retractable antenna is also good idea. This type of antenna allows you to lower or raise your antenna from inside the vehicle. The antenna can be raised or lowered at the push of a button or by turning on and off your radio, depending how the power is supplied to the antenna, through a button or through the radio on/off switch.

Radio Installation

IN-DASH RECEIVERS

In-dash receiver installation is the most attractive and theft-resistant, and is easier now that there are installation kits available for many vehicles.

❋❋ CAUTION

If your model is equipped with a Supplemental Restraint System (SRS), which uses an air bag. Whenever working near any of the SRS components, such as the impact sensors, the air bag module, steering column and instrument panel, disable the SRS. Consult your Chilton Total Car Care manual on how to disable the system.

The best way to attach a custom wiring harness to your new stereo's harness is to use solderless crimp connectors. The wires are usually color-coded and you'll find that it's not very difficult. After determining which wires are to be connected to each other, attach a male end connector to one wire and a female end connector to the other wire and attach the two connectors. This a very effective way of connecting all the wires and is not as permanent or difficult as soldering them, and if for any reason you have to remove the stereo system again it will make it a lot easier. In some cases, the custom harness plugs directly into the bullet connectors on the receiver's harness

Wiring may be a little time consuming, depending on the amount of wires that have to be connected. Most systems have two power leads, one for ignition and main power, while the other is for the clock. The system will also contain positive and negative speaker wires and might have a power wire for an electrically operated antenna. You should connect the clock power wire to a circuit that has power even when the ignition is off. The ignition and main power wire should be connected to a wire that has power only when the ignition key is in the on position. Make sure when you are attaching the speaker wires that you attach the stereo speaker negative wire to the speaker negative wire and the stereo speaker positive wire to the speaker positive wire. If you are unsure of polarity of your speakers (which side is negative and which side is positive), refer to the speaker testing procedure in this section. Follow the manufacturer's wiring diagram for your stereo harness wiring diagram for proper hook-up. Use an aftermarket wiring kit that will mate with your factory wiring harness. This will eliminate the need to cut or splice into the factory wiring harness. If for any reason the wiring kit does not come with your stereo, you can contact the stereo manufacturer and they should be able to supply you with a suitable harness for your vehicle.

➡**There are a few cassette receivers and CD players which are shipped with a plastic or metal locking screw which you need to remove before installation. Your owner's manual will tell you whether this is the case**

Once you've connected the two harnesses, you're ready to take out your old radio and replace it with your new receiver. The other end of the harness simply snaps right into your vehicle's factory radio harness.

There are a few different ways that the stereo could be mounted in your vehicle. If you own an early model American vehicle with knobs instead of buttons, then your stereo is probably what is known as knob mounted.

On some early model foreign models and most late model vehicles the radios will have a flat front and the stereo is mounted in a sleeve in the dashboard. On some models you must use two U-shaped wire tools, sold by most radio suppliers to release the radio from its mount. On other models you must remove parts of the instrument panel to gain access to the stereo sleeve to remove the stereo from the vehicle.

Removing and Installing A Knob Mounted Stereo

▸ **See Figures 9, 10, 11, 12 and 13**

The first step in your installation is removing the existing receiver. Pay close attention to the steps involved in the removal because the process for installing your new receiver will be the same, but in reverse.

➡**Disconnect your negative battery terminal before you get started.**

Remove the knobs and stereo trim panel. Remove the nuts that are on the radio knob posts. Unfasten the radio mounting bracket retainers. There is usually some type of rear bracket support for the radio, so make sure to unfasten any bracket retainers located the rear of the radio. Reach up under the dashboard to grasp the radio, then slide the unit backwards and downwards to remove it from dashboard. Unplug the electrical connections at the rear of the radio and remove the radio.

After you make the appropriate wiring connections and plug in the antenna, slide the new receiver into position on the dashboard. Now test the receiver to make sure it's functioning properly. If everything is OK, install the bracket retainers and the nuts onto the knobs, tighten them until they are snug. Install the stereo trim panel and the knobs.

Fig. 9 Remove the knobs from the front of the radio

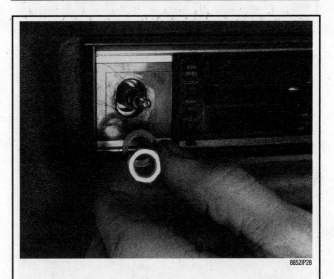

Fig. 10 Remove the nuts and washers located on the knob posts

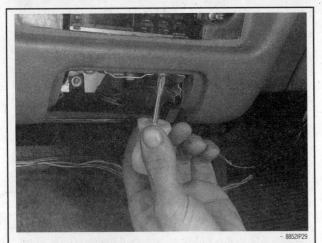

Fig. 11 On some models equipped with a lower or rear mounting bracket, you may have to remove parts of the dash to access the bracket retainers

Fig. 12 If equipped, remove the mounting bracket . . .

Fig. 13 . . . and remove the radio from the dashboard

Removing and Installing A Standard Sleeve Type Stereo

♦ **See Figures 14 thru 20**

The first step in your installation is removing the existing receiver. Pay close attention to the steps involved in the removal because the process for installing your new receiver will be the same, but in reverse.

➡ **Disconnect your negative battery terminal before you get started.**

The sleeve type stereo system uses a standardized rectangular opening in the dash. Instead of separate shafts and a nosepiece, sleeve-style stereos have a continuous flat front.

On some models, you may have to remove a trim panel before accessing the stereo retainers. Most, but not all dashboard trim panels are retained by clips so it is essential that you check for fasteners in the panel before attempting to remove it. Open the glove compartment, remove the ash tray and check under and around the panel for fasteners. If no fasteners are visible, use a prytool to gently and evenly pry all around the outer edges of the trim panel and release its retaining clips. Do not force the trim panel, if the panel will not come off, check again for fasteners or try prying at a different angle on different sections of the panel.

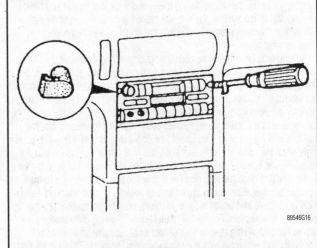

Fig. 14 To remove the radio that is retained by spring clips, you may first have to remove the protective hole covers, if equipped

Fig. 15 Insert the special radio removal tools into the uncovered holes to release the spring clips

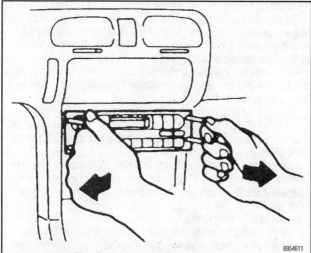

Fig. 16 While maintaining side pressure on the tools, pull the radio straight out of the dash assembly

8954611

Fig. 19 . . . then slide the receiver forward, unplug the antenna cable . . .

89566P55

Fig. 17 When removing a receiver held in place by screws, first remove any trim panels or other components in order to access the radio

89566P57

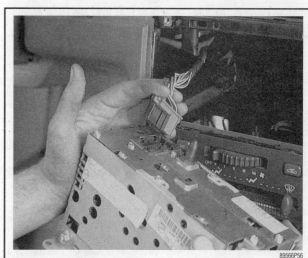

Fig. 20 . . . and the electrical connection, then remove the receiver

89566P56

Fig. 18 Unfasten the receiver retainers . . .

89566P54

While there are many variations among different makes of vehicles, the factory receiver is often secured in a sleeve by spring clips, which you push out of the way using two small tools. Other factory receivers are held in place by screws instead. Most receivers also have some type of rear support. Once you carefully slide the old receiver out, you'll simply disconnect the antenna plug and factory wiring harness

Your case-style stereo may come with a metal mounting sleeve which slides into the dash opening until a small outer lip makes contact with the edges of the opening. (Note: these sleeves usually have a designated top and bottom despite the random appearance of the many holes in them.) Once you put the sleeve in position, bend the tabs on the sleeve out to secure it in place.

After you make the appropriate wiring connections and plug in the antenna, slide the new receiver into the sleeve. Now test the receiver to make sure it's functioning properly. If everything is OK, push the receiver all the way in. On models with spring clips the receiver should click into place. On models attached with screws or bolts, simply tighten the retainers. A trim panel may cover the outer edges of the sleeve and receiver for a clean, custom look.

MULTI-CD CHANGERS

Your vehicle should present a number of good places to mount a disc changer. The most popular locations are in the trunk or under the front passenger seat. Many glove boxes and the areas behind some trim panels are large enough to accommodate a changer.

➡ **Before you get started, disconnect your negative battery terminal, as you would with any other type of installation.**

Make sure the mounting surface you have chosen is rigid enough to support the changer firmly, so it won't become loose during a sudden stop. Avoid mounting your changer on top of your rear deck or anywhere else it will be subject to direct sunlight.

Suspending the changer from the bottom of the rear deck (inside the trunk) is a popular way to go because it keeps it hidden and out of the way and also takes up little or no usable space. However, changing the magazine is a little more cumbersome and running the cable from the front of the vehicle will take more work. If you do decide to go this route, it may save you some time to enlist a second pair of hands. Get a helper to hold the changer in place while you insert the self-tapping screws.

✳✳ CAUTION

When working in the trunk be sure to tape over the latch so you won't become trapped inside accidentally.

One other thing to look out for when you are mounting your changer in this location: Make sure it won't interfere with the torsion bar spring of the trunk lid. Observe how it moves as you close the lid before you settle on the exact mounting spot.

No matter where you put the changer, you'll want to make sure you know what you're screwing the mounting screws into. You certainly don't want to find out the hard way where your fuel tank or brake lines are. Also, check to see that there's enough space for the magazine to be smoothly inserted and removed, and that you can easily access the eject button.

If you want to mount your CD changer at an angle, make sure you set the switch on the side of changer to the correct setting.

If you're mounting your CD changer amplifier in the trunk, run the cables away from any engine control computer harness. This will prevent causing any derivability problems in the harness by minimizing electrical interference.

You will usually have two 12-volt power wires to hook up. One goes to a constant source of power and the other goes to a switched 12-volt source. You'll also have a black ground wire that will be secured beneath a nearby screw that makes contact with the metal body of the vehicle.

If installing a Hideaway Unit (FM modulator), a cable will be run from the FM modulator to the antenna input of your radio, on all other models a cable will be attached from the changer to an input jack on your in-dash radio. If this leaves a lot of slack in your antenna lead, tie it off so it won't fall down and interfere with your pedals.

In most vehicles, you'll be able to find a hole or crevice to slide the cable from the trunk into the passenger compartment. You may have to remove the rear seat to find it.

To hide the cable beneath your carpeting, you will have to remove the door sill. As you pass the cable along the floorboard, make sure it doesn't sit too close to a seat rail, where it could be pinched or damaged when the seat is adjusted.

If you're running the cable up the driver's side, you'll want to make sure it doesn't end up in the way of the pedals or hood latch. Tie it firmly in place with wire ties and coil up any excess cable, so it won't fall on your feet as you drive.

Reconnect your battery cable.

If you have installed an FM modulator type system, play a CD in the changer and search through the FM channels on your radio until you can hear your CD playing, then preset the frequency on which the CD is playing. Once this channel is set remember that your radio is using this channel to pick up the signal from the CD changer.

INSTALLING THE SPEAKERS

▶ **See Figures 21 thru 26**

The most important decision when installing a stereo is the placement of the speakers. Acoustically, the best place for speakers is level with the listeners' ears, and where the baffle (space behind the speakers) is large enough for good bass tones. Unfortunately, most vehicles don't have a space that meets these conditions so you'll have to examine your vehicle carefully. Consider these places as mounting locations for speakers:

• Rear deck—There's plenty of room to act as a baffle, but the speakers are essentially mounted in the trunk, and while the rear deck is at ear level, the speakers face up.

• Under dash—The space under the dash of most vehicles will barely accommodate the radio, let alone a pair of stereo speakers.

• Top of dash—This is a favorite for factory-installed speakers, which can often (though not easily) be replaced if desired.

• Kick panels—Kick panels sometimes cover cavities that make good baffles but frequently only cover the inner fender wall.

• In door—This location is probably the best compromise for a good baffle, good listening position and ease of installation.

• Rear Seat panels—This may be the only place in small vehicles.

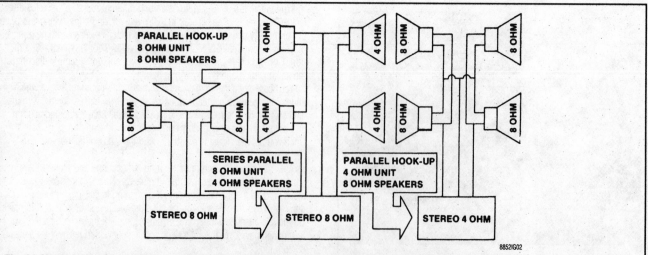

Fig. 21 Check the impedance of your receiver before deciding on speakers. The impedance (ohms) for each speaker should be the same to avoid poor sound or blown speakers. The hook-ups shown here will accommodate multi-speaker installations

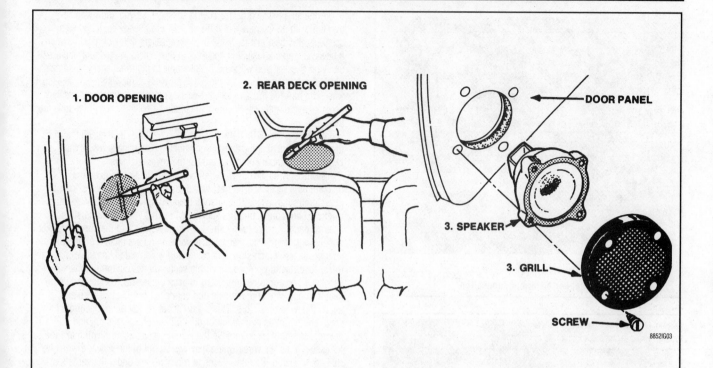

Fig. 22 Whenever you choose to install the speakers, be sure that they will not interfere with window mechanisms, spare tire removal and the like. Also be sure the speaker dimensions will fit in the space available. Mark the hole pattern with a template (1). Cut the fabric with a knife (2) and finish the hole with a saw. Install the speaker grille (3)

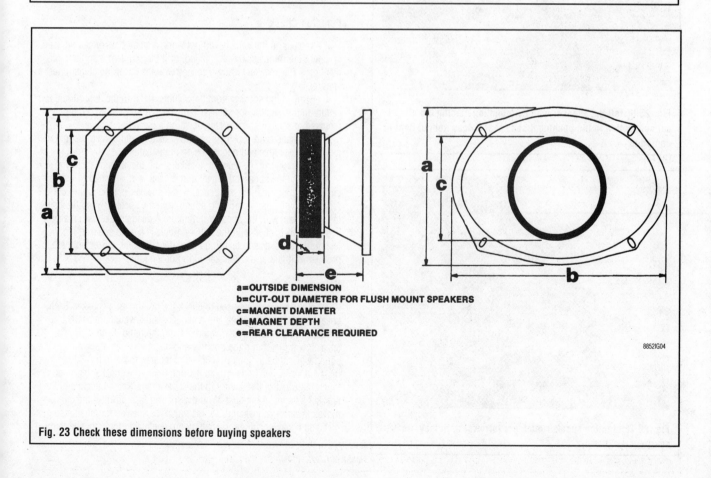

a=OUTSIDE DIMENSION
b=CUT-OUT DIAMETER FOR FLUSH MOUNT SPEAKERS
c=MAGNET DIAMETER
d=MAGNET DEPTH
e=REAR CLEARANCE REQUIRED

Fig. 23 Check these dimensions before buying speakers

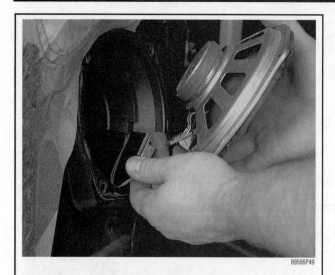

89566P49

Fig. 24 Attach the speaker electrical connection

89566P48

Fig. 25 Install the speaker onto its mounting placing the electrical connection in the opening first so that it does not get bent or damaged

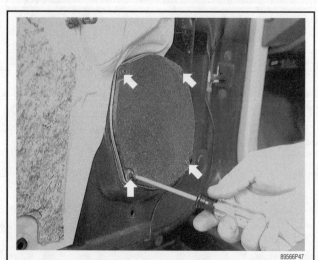

89566P47

Fig. 26 Tighten the speaker retainers (arrows) until they are snug

Decide on a location before buying speakers, so you know whether they'll fit with no interference. If the vehicle was already equipped with speakers, it is best just to install the new speakers in the original locations. If however, you are installing speakers in the vehicle where there was previously no speaker, you will have to cut a hole in the trim panel and sometimes a metal panel. Your speakers will probably come with a template, so when you pick the location for the speaker, mark the template outline very carefully and double check your marks before beginning to cut the hole for the speaker.

Install the speaker mounting hardware in the hole, then attach the wires to the speaker. Install the speaker and tighten its retainers. Install the speaker cover and if equipped, tighten the cover retainers.

It's probably easiest to wire the receiver to the speakers before installing the receiver. The best way to attach the speaker wires to your new stereo's harness is to use solderless crimp connectors. Make sure when you are connecting the speaker wires that you attach the stereo speaker negative wire to the speaker negative wire and the stereo speaker positive wire to the speaker positive wire. If you are unsure of polarity of your speakers (which side is negative and which side is positive), refer to the speaker testing procedure in this section. After determining which speaker wires are to be connected to each other, attach a male end connector to one wire and a female end connector to the other wire and attach the two connectors. This a very effective way of connecting all the wires and is not as permanent or difficult as soldering them, and if for any reason you have to remove the stereo system again it will make it a lot easier. Keep the wires where they will be out of the way and won't be rubbed or chafed. Popular places to run wires are under the carpets or doorsill plates. Where the wires run through a hole, protect them with a rubber grommet.

Be sure to leave enough slack in the wires to open doors, allow for vibration and to connect the wires to the radio.

Once everything is connected, turn the stereo on and check that everything is working properly. Install the stereo.

Function Check

If a speaker in the vehicle will not work, a small battery can be used to determine if the speaker has failed, or if the problem is in the radio itself or in the speaker wiring. Proceed with the following steps to test a speaker.

1. Remove the speaker from the vehicle. Refer to the appropriate procedure in this section for speaker removal and installation. When removed, place the speaker face down on a clean flat surface.

2. Purchase a AA or AAA-size (1.5V) battery and solder a length wire to both the positive and negative side of the battery.

3. Strip ½–1 in. (1–2cm) of insulation off the ends of each wire.

4. To test the speaker, touch 1 end of each wire attached to the battery to each terminal of the speaker. If the speaker is functioning correctly, you will hear a crackling sound from the speaker when the battery makes contact with the speaker terminals. A dead speaker will make no sound when touched with the battery. Replace a dead speaker. If after testing the speaker and learning that it does function correctly, there is a problem with either the speaker wiring or the radio.

Polarity Check

A battery can also be used to check the polarity of a speaker. Each speaker has a positive side and a negative side, which are needed to produce the sound you hear when playing the radio. Even though a speaker will function if the positive and negative wires are reversed, the sound will not be as loud or as clear compared to when they are installed correctly. To determine the polarity of the speaker terminals, touch the wires of the battery to the speaker and watch the cone of the speaker as contact is made. With the speaker face down, if the cone moves towards you when the wires touch the speaker terminals, the positive and negative side of the battery are contacting the opposite terminals on the speaker. Reverse the wires and try again. A properly polarized speaker will move the cone away from you when touched with the battery.

Although this procedure is not as important with speakers that have their respective terminals marked with a plus (+) or a minus (−), many factory speakers do not identify the individual terminals or wires attached to them. This procedure will be most helpful when installing aftermarket speakers into a vehicle using the factory wire harness.

INSTALLING THE ANTENNA

▶ **See Figures 27, 28 and 29**

Antenna installation is usually fairly easy. The biggest problem is fishing the cable through the fender or firewall to connect it with the radio.

The easiest way to install a new antenna is to unhook the antenna from the rear of the radio and tie a piece of wire or fishing line to the old antenna cable. Pull the old antenna and cable from the vehicle pulling the fishing line or wire with it. Untie the fishing line or wire from the old cable and tie it to the new one. Pull on the wire or line and carefully guide the cable through the fender or firewall. Remove the wire or line and connect the cable to the radio.

If the vehicle did not originally have a antenna, install the new antenna following the manufacturers instructions, then route the cable through the firewall or fender and attach it to the radio.

A single-piece antenna is already matched to the FM receiver, but you'll need to adjust the AM portion of the receiver.

Tune the radio to a weak station around 1400 on the AM dial and turn the trimmer adjustment until the station is strongest. The trimmer screw is either on the back or side of the set near the antenna jack, or on the front behind the tuning knob. Wherever it is hidden, it is usually labeled "ANT."

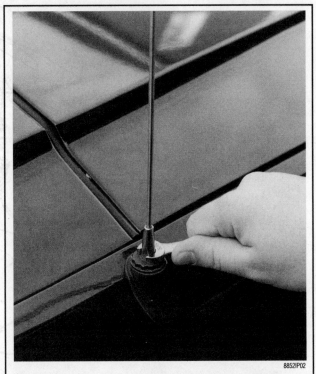

Fig. 27 Remove the cap nut holding the antenna mast. The antenna mast can usually be replaced without disturbing the mount

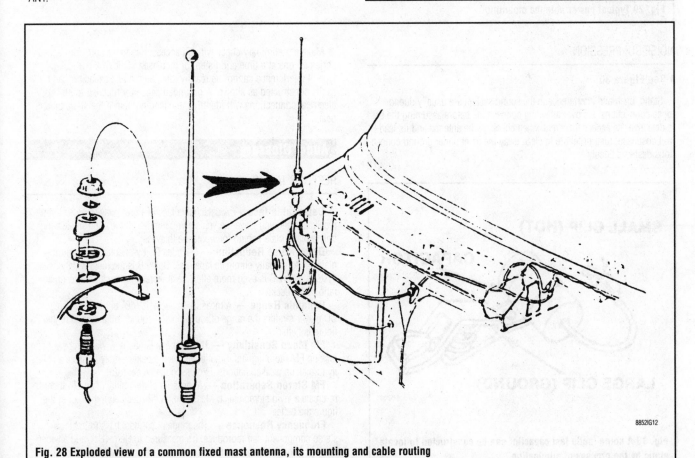

Fig. 28 Exploded view of a common fixed mast antenna, its mounting and cable routing

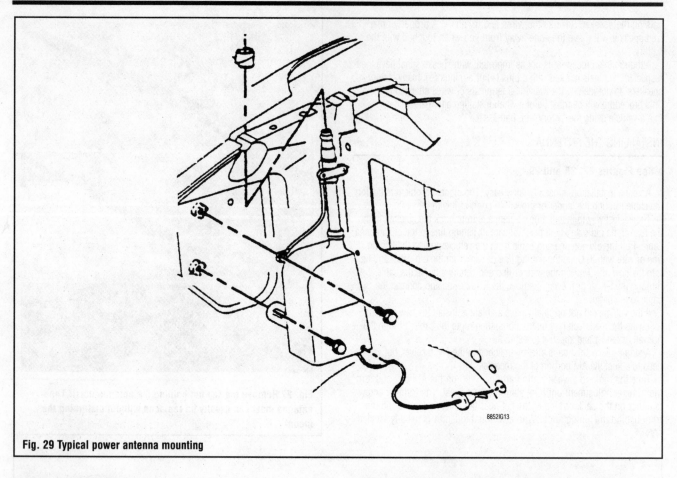

Fig. 29 Typical power antenna mounting

NOISE SUPPRESSION

▶ **See Figure 30**

Static, hash and interference in the sound system are usually due to loose connections. Go over all wiring connections before assuming the set is defective. Be especially careful when checking the antenna and its lead-in. Looseness, rust, or failure to clean away the paint under ground connections destroys fidelity.

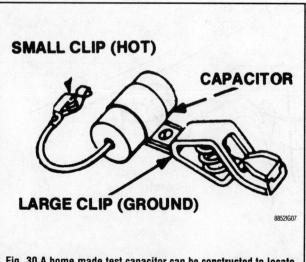

SMALL CLIP (HOT)

CAPACITOR

LARGE CLIP (GROUND)

Fig. 30 A home made test capacitor can be constructed to locate static by the process of elimination

Make a preliminary check with all accessories turned off. Turn accessories on one at a time and listen for increased static. If a particular type of interference cannot be readily identified, a test capacitor can be easily constructed as shown. A grounded capacitor touched to all "hot" electrical connections will identify the offending item if the static disappears.

Audio Glossary

RECEIVER TERMS

Detachable face — A detachable face is a great way to protect your receiver. When you leave the vehicle you remove all the controls, leaving only a blank plate behind for would-be thieves.

Dolby Noise Reduction — Decodes Dolby-encoded tapes during playback to virtually eliminate tape hiss. Dolby B is the most widely used system. Dolby C is even more effective at increasing the signal-to-noise ratio of the deck.

Dynamic Range — A measure in decibels (dB) of how accurately a CD player renders the range of loud and soft sounds on a disc. A higher figure is better.

FM Mono Sensitivity — This figure tells you how well a receiver can pick up FM radio signals. Smaller values are better—they indicate an ability to pick up weaker stations. Expressed in decibel (dBf).

FM Stereo Separation — A measure of the ability of an FM tuner to re-create a vivid stereo effect. Measured, in dB (decibels), the higher the figure the better.

Frequency Response — The range of sounds, bass to treble, a stereo component can reproduce. It's measured in Hertz (Hz), and a wider range is better—the bass will be lower and the treble will be higher. Humans can perceive sounds from 20 to 20,000 Hz. The lowest note on a bass guitar is about 41 Hz. Most male vocalists have a range between 100 and 500 Hz. Cymbals hit about 15,000 Hz.

Illumination — Most in-dash receivers have green or amber illumination which is set by the manufacturer. Models with switchable, 2-way illumination let you select one color or the other in order to match your dash lights. Models with 4-way illumination let you choose the readout or the background in either color.

Install Depth — The length, in inches, of the portion of the stereo that sits behind the dash. It includes an allowance for cables coming out of the unit.

Loudness — This control allows you to boost the lower frequencies in your music to keep it full-sounding, even at lower volumes

Preamp Outputs — Jacks on the rear of the receiver that allow you to use a standard RCA patch cable to add an external amp. Some receivers have two sets, which help if you plan to add a 4-channel amp or a second amp. Some receivers have three sets, one of which is usually intended to be used for a subwoofer amp. In some cases, you can select a low-pass crossover frequency for the second or third set of preamp outputs.

Some receivers offer a "non-fading" set of preamp outputs. Hook your subwoofer amp to the non-fading outputs, and you can fade the regular speakers front to rear without affecting the sound of the subwoofer. Or, if you hook the amp for your main speakers to the non-fading set and your subwoofer amp to the set that fades, you can use the receiver's fader to control the sub's volume.

Preset Scan or Memory Scan — Touch a button and your receiver automatically plays a brief sample of what's on each of your preset radio stations. Touch the button again when you hear something you want to stick with.

RMS Power vs. Peak Power — The amount of continuous power, measured in watts, that an amplifier produces is called RMS power. The higher the RMS figure, the louder and cleaner your music sounds.

Stereo manufacturers often display peak power ratings on the face of their products. Peak power is measured during a brief musical burst, like a dramatic drum accent. The RMS figure is more significant.

IN-DASH CASSETTE PLAYER & CD TERMS

Auto Music Search — Fast-forwards or rewinds to the next song and begins play automatically. Multi-track search skips forward or backward over multiple tracks -hit the fast-forward button three times to skip forward three songs.

Blank Skip — This feature automatically fast-forwards through any silent spots on your tapes.

Full-logic Controls — With a full-logic deck you'll enjoy soft-touch electronic controls, instead of the traditional spring-loaded mechanical buttons. When you insert a cassette, the power load feature takes over and automatically moves it into position. No muscle power is need to eject the tape either—just lightly touch a button, and the tape pops out smoothly. Full-logic decks often offer advanced operational features, including multi-track Music Search, Repeat, and Blank Skip.

Intro Scan — Lets you hear the first few seconds of each track on a tape or a CD. Hit the button again when you hear the song you're looking

for. The scanning feature will stop, and that track will continue playing. This feature is very common among CD players, and is also available on a few cassette receivers.

Power-off Release or Key-off Release — Disengages the pinchroller from the capstan when you turn off the tape deck or turn off your vehicle's engine without first ejecting the tape. Otherwise a crease might form on the pinchroller which would cause the deck to perform poorly. This also prevents damage to tapes left in the player when the power is turned off.

Radio Recall or Automatic Tuner Activation — Automatically plays the radio when a tape is fast-winding. On some receivers, this feature is automatic. On others it's selectable.

Random Play or Shuffle Play — Mixes up the order of songs during playback. Signal-to-Noise Ratio—A measure of how well a cassette or CD player silences background noise. Higher ratings, in decibels (dB), indicate less noise. Tape EQ or Metal Switch—Selects the best equalization response according to the type of tape—normal or high-bias. In some decks it's automatic. Track Repeat—Plays the same track over and over until you turn the feature off.

Travel Presets or Best Tuning Memory — Engage this feature and the receiver automatically loads your presets with the strongest available signals. It makes finding stations easier when you're driving through unfamiliar territory. It also makes loading presets a snap when you first install the receiver or any time your battery runs down or gets disconnected (which wipes out the tuner's preset memory).

CD CHANGER TERMS

FM add-on or FM modulated changers — These are packages that allow you to add a disc changer to any FM vehicle radio, factory systems included. The package consists of a controller and RF (radio frequency) interface and, usually, a changer. By converting the CD audio signal into an FM radio signal, the "station" is simply tuned in on the existing FM radio.

Hideaway Unit — Part of an FM modulator package, this is the RF modulator itself. About the size of a pack of cigarettes, it's typically installed out of sight, behind your receiver.

Intro Scan — This feature lets you press a button to hear the first several seconds of each track on the currently selected disc, or the first several seconds of each disc in the magazine. Depending on its manufacturer, your changer will perform one or both of these tasks.

Repeat — This feature lets you play the currently selected disc track repeatedly or the currently selected disc repeatedly.

Shuffle — This feature lets you play the tracks on the currently selected disc in a random order or play each track on each disc in the changer in a random order.

Custom Programming — Some changer controller combinations let you specify exactly which tracks will play on a CD. Disc title features let you assign each disc a name that will appear on the in-dash display when that disc is loaded. Sony's Custom File Plus systems let you display the titles of all loaded CDs without interrupting playback, and also let you program two separate twelve song sequences.

TROUBLESHOOTING BASIC RADIO PROBLEMS

Radio problems are not normally caused by a defective radio. More often the cause is due to some less obvious fault. Follow the procedures in order before assuming the radio is defective.

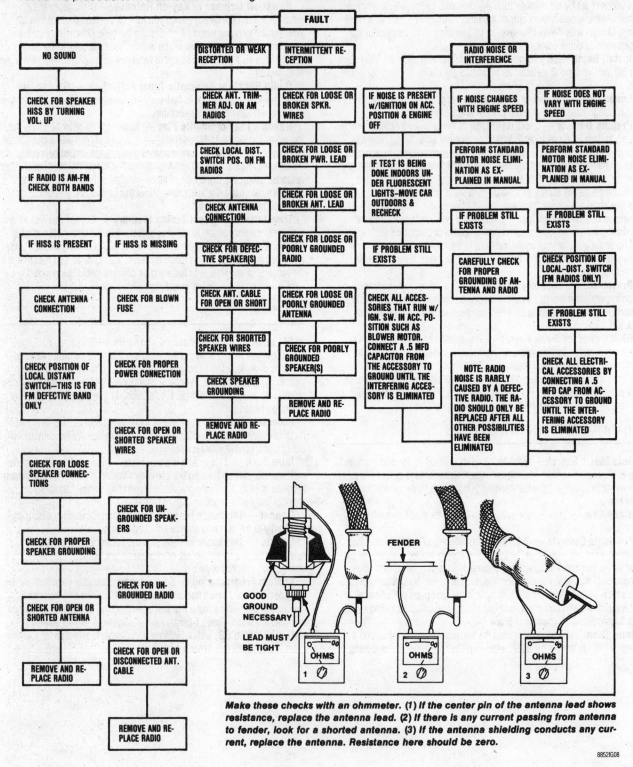

FAULT

NO SOUND
- CHECK FOR SPEAKER HISS BY TURNING VOL. UP
- IF RADIO IS AM-FM CHECK BOTH BANDS
  - IF HISS IS PRESENT
    - CHECK ANTENNA CONNECTION
    - CHECK POSITION OF LOCAL DISTANT SWITCH—THIS IS FOR FM DEFECTIVE BAND ONLY
    - CHECK FOR LOOSE SPEAKER CONNECTIONS
    - CHECK FOR PROPER SPEAKER GROUNDING
    - CHECK FOR OPEN OR SHORTED ANTENNA
    - REMOVE AND RE-PLACE RADIO
  - IF HISS IS MISSING
    - CHECK FOR BLOWN FUSE
    - CHECK FOR PROPER POWER CONNECTION
    - CHECK FOR OPEN OR SHORTED SPEAKER WIRES
    - CHECK FOR UN-GROUNDED SPEAKERS
    - CHECK FOR UN-GROUNDED RADIO
    - CHECK FOR OPEN OR DISCONNECTED ANT. CABLE
    - REMOVE AND RE-PLACE RADIO

DISTORTED OR WEAK RECEPTION
- CHECK ANT. TRIMMER ADJ. ON AM RADIOS
- CHECK LOCAL DIST. SWITCH POS. ON FM RADIOS
- CHECK ANTENNA CONNECTION
- CHECK FOR DEFECTIVE SPEAKER(S)
- CHECK ANT. CABLE FOR OPEN OR SHORT
- CHECK FOR SHORTED SPEAKER WIRES
- CHECK SPEAKER GROUNDING
- REMOVE AND RE-PLACE RADIO

INTERMITTENT RE-CEPTION
- CHECK FOR LOOSE OR BROKEN SPKR. WIRES
- CHECK FOR LOOSE OR BROKEN PWR. LEAD
- CHECK FOR LOOSE OR BROKEN ANT. LEAD
- CHECK FOR LOOSE OR POORLY GROUNDED RADIO
- CHECK FOR LOOSE OR POORLY GROUNDED ANTENNA
- CHECK FOR POORLY GROUNDED SPEAKER(S)
- REMOVE AND RE-PLACE RADIO

- IF NOISE IS PRESENT w/IGNITION ON ACC. POSITION & ENGINE OFF
  - IF TEST IS BEING DONE INDOORS UN-DER FLUORESCENT LIGHTS—MOVE CAR OUTDOORS & RECHECK
  - IF PROBLEM STILL EXISTS
  - CHECK ALL ACCES-SORIES THAT RUN w/ IGN. SW. IN ACC. PO-SITION SUCH AS BLOWER MOTOR. CONNECT A .5 MFD CAPACITOR FROM THE ACCESSORY TO GROUND UNTIL THE INTERFERING ACCES-SORY IS ELIMINATED

RADIO NOISE OR INTERFERENCE
- IF NOISE CHANGES WITH ENGINE SPEED
  - PERFORM STANDARD MOTOR NOISE ELIMI-NATION AS EX-PLAINED IN MANUAL
  - IF PROBLEM STILL EXISTS
  - CAREFULLY CHECK FOR PROPER GROUNDING OF AN-TENNA AND RADIO
  - NOTE: RADIO NOISE IS RARELY CAUSED BY A DEFEC-TIVE RADIO. THE RA-DIO SHOULD ONLY BE REPLACED AFTER ALL OTHER POSSIBILITIES HAVE BEEN ELIMINATED
- IF NOISE DOES NOT VARY WITH ENGINE SPEED
  - PERFORM STANDARD MOTOR NOISE ELIMI-NATION AS EX-PLAINED IN MANUAL
  - IF PROBLEM STILL EXISTS
  - CHECK POSITION OF LOCAL–DIST. SWITCH (FM RADIOS ONLY)
  - IF PROBLEM STILL EXISTS
  - CHECK ALL ELECTRI-CAL ACCESSORIES BY CONNECTING A .5 MFD CAP FROM AC-CESSORY TO GROUND UNTIL THE INTER-FERING ACCESSORY IS ELIMINATED

FENDER

GOOD GROUND NECESSARY

LEAD MUST BE TIGHT

OHMS 1   OHMS 2   OHMS 3

Make these checks with an ohmmeter. (1) If the center pin of the antenna lead shows resistance, replace the antenna lead. (2) If there is any current passing from antenna to fender, look for a shorted antenna. (3) If the antenna shielding conducts any current, replace the antenna. Resistance here should be zero.

8852IG08

20

CLUTCH AND MANUAL TRANSMISSION/ TRANSAXLE

CLUTCH AND MANUAL
TRANSMISSION/TRANSAXLE 20-2

CLUTCH AND MANUAL TRANSMISSION/TRANSAXLE

✳✳ CAUTION

The clutch driven disc may contain asbestos, which has been determined to be a cancer causing agent. Never clean clutch surfaces with compressed air! Avoid inhaling any dust from any clutch surface! When cleaning clutch surfaces, use a commercially available brake cleaning fluid.

To overcome inertia and start the vehicle moving, the automobile engine develops power that is transmitted as a twisting force (torque) from the engine crankshaft to the rear wheels. A smooth and gradual transfer of power and torque is accomplished using a clutch friction unit to engage and disengage the power flow. A transmission is used to vary the gear ratio for the best speed and power, and to provide for vehicle movement under the different conditions of starting, stopping, accelerating, maintaining speed and reversing. The various components necessary to deliver power to the drive wheels are the flywheel, pressure plate, clutch plate, release bearing, control linkages and the transmission.

How the Clutch Works

▶ **See Figure 1**

The clutch is a device to engage and disengage power from the engine, allowing the vehicle to be stopped and started.

A pressure plate or "driving member" is bolted to the engine flywheel and a clutch plate or "driven member" is located between the flywheel and the pressure plate. The clutch plate is splined to the shaft extending from the transmission to the flywheel, commonly called a clutch shaft or input shaft.

When the clutch and pressure plates are locked together by friction, the clutch shaft rotates with the engine crankshaft. Power is transferred from the engine to the transmission, where it is routed through different gear ratios to obtain the best speed and power to start and keep the vehicle moving.

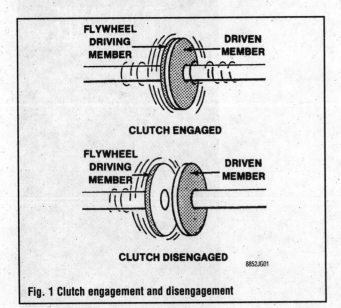

Fig. 1 Clutch engagement and disengagement

THE FLYWHEEL

▶ **See Figure 2**

The flywheel is located at the rear of the engine and is bolted to the crankshaft. It helps absorb power impulses resulting in a smoothly idling engine and provides momentum to carry the engine through its operating

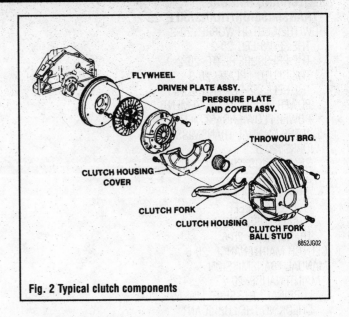

Fig. 2 Typical clutch components

cycle. The rear surface of the flywheel is machined flat and the clutch components are attached to it.

THE PRESSURE PLATE

▶ **See Figures 3, 4, 5 and 6**

The driving member is commonly called the pressure plate. It is bolted to the engine flywheel and its main purpose is to exert pressure against the clutch plate, holding the plate tight against the flywheel, and allowing the power to flow from the engine to the transmission. It must also be capable of interrupting the power flow by releasing the pressure on the clutch plate. This allows the clutch plate to stop rotating while the flywheel and pressure plate continues to rotate. The pressure plate consists of a heavy metal plate, coil springs or a diaphragm spring, release levers (fingers), and a cover.

When coil springs are used, they are evenly spaced around the metal plate and located between the plate and the metal cover. This places an even pressure against the plate, which in turn presses the clutch plate tight against the flywheel. The cover is bolted tightly to the flywheel and the

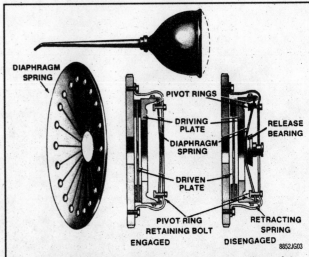

Fig. 3 The operation of a diaphragm spring-type pressure plate can be compared to the effect of the bottom of a can of oil

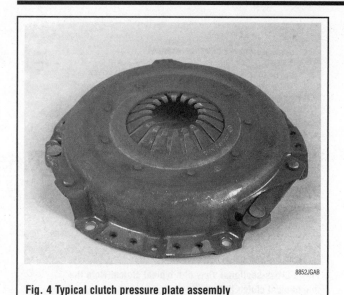

Fig. 4 Typical clutch pressure plate assembly

8852JGAB

Fig. 5 The underside of the pressure plate contains the friction surface which is compressed against the clutch disc

8852JGCD

Fig. 6 The clutch pressure plate assembly is bolted to the flywheel on the back of the engine

TCCS7116

metal plate is movable, due to internal linkages. The coil springs are arranged to exert direct or indirect tension upon the metal plate, depending upon the manufacturers design. Three release levers (fingers) are used on most pressure plates, evenly spaced around the cover, to release the holding pressure of the springs on the clutch plate, allowing it to disengage the power flow.

When a diaphragm spring is used instead of coil springs, the internal linkage is necessarily different to provide an "over-center" action to release the clutch plate from the flywheel. Its operation can be compared to the operation of an oilcan. When depressing the slightly curved metal on the bottom of the can, it would go over-center and give out a loud "clicking" noise; when released, the noise again would be heard and the metal would return to its original position. A click is not heard in the clutch operation, but the action of the diaphragm spring is the same as the oil can.

THE CLUTCH PLATE

▶ **See Figures 7 and 8**

The clutch plate or driven member consists of a round metal plate attached to a splined hub. The outer portion of the round plate is covered with a friction material of molded or woven asbestos and is riveted or

Fig. 7 Typical clutch driven disc plate

8852JGEF

Fig. 8 The clutch disc is installed between the pressure plate assembly and the flywheel

TCCS7118

bonded to the plate. The thickness of the clutch plate and/or facings may be warped to give a softer clutch engagement. Coil springs are often installed in the hub to help provide a cushion against the twisting force of clutch engagement. The splined hub is mated to (and turns) a splined transmission shaft when the clutch is engaged.

THE RELEASE BEARING

The release (throw out) bearing is usually a ball bearing unit, mounted on a sleeve, and attached to the release or throwout lever. Its purpose is to apply pressure to the diaphragm spring or the release levers in the pressure plate. When the clutch pedal is depressed, the pressure of the release bearing or lever actuates the internal linkages of the pressure plate, releasing the clutch plate and interrupting the power flow. The release bearing is not in constant contact with the pressure plate. A linkage adjustment clearance should be maintained.

POWER FLOW DISENGAGEMENT

Mechanical Clutch Activation

▶ See Figure 9

The clutch pedal provides mechanical means for the driver to control the engagement and disengagement of the clutch. The pedal is connected mechanically, to either a cable or rods, which are directly connected to the release bearing lever.

When the clutch pedal is depressed, the linkage moves the release bearing lever. The release lever is attached at the opposite end to a release bearing which straddles the transmission clutch shaft, and presses inward on the pressure plate fingers or the diaphragm spring. This inward pressure acts upon the fingers and internal linkage of the pressure plate and allows the clutch plate to move away from the flywheel, interrupting the flow of power.

Hydraulic Clutch Activation

▶ See Figure 10

Hydraulic clutch activation systems consist of a master and a slave cylinder. When pressure is applied to the clutch pedal (the pedal is depressed), the pushrod contacts the plunger and pushes it up the bore of the master cylinder. During the first $\frac{1}{32}$ in. (0.8mm) of movement, the center valve seal closes the port to the fluid reservoir tank and as the plunger continues to move up the bore of the cylinder, the fluid is forced through the outlet line to the slave cylinder mounted on the clutch housing. As fluid

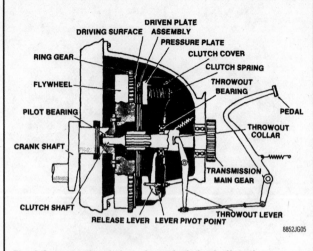

Fig. 9 Cross-sectional view of a typical clutch. Note the mechanical clutch linkage.

is pushed down the pipe from the master cylinder, this in turn forces the piston in the slave cylinder outward. A pushrod is connected to the slave cylinder and rides in the pocket of the clutch fork. As the slave cylinder piston moves rearward the pushrod forces the clutch fork and the release bearing to disengage the pressure plate from the clutch disc. On the return stroke (pedal released), the plunger moves back as a result of the return pressure of the clutch. Fluid returns to the master cylinder and the final movement of the plunger lifts the valve seal off the seat, allowing an unrestricted flow of fluid between the system and the reservoir.

A piston return spring in the slave cylinder preloads the clutch linkage and assures contact of the release bearing with the clutch release fingers at all times. As the driven disc wears, the diaphragm spring fingers move rearward forcing the release bearing, fork and pushrod to move. This movement forces the slave cylinder piston forward in its bore, displacing hydraulic fluid up into the master cylinder reservoir, thereby providing the self-adjusting feature of the hydraulic clutch linkage system.

POWER FLOW ENGAGEMENT

While the clutch pedal is depressed and the power flow interrupted, the transmission can be shifted into any gear. The clutch pedal is slowly

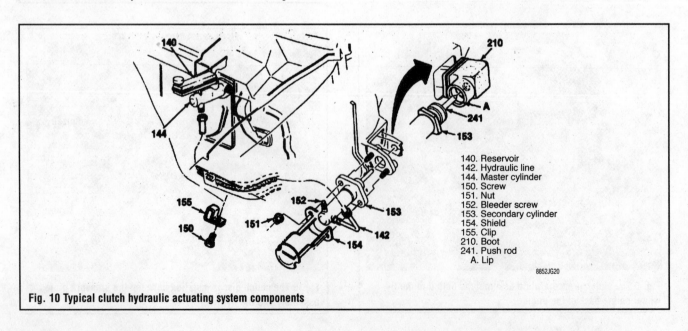

140. Reservoir
142. Hydraulic line
144. Master cylinder
150. Screw
151. Nut
152. Bleeder screw
153. Secondary cylinder
154. Shield
155. Clip
210. Boot
241. Push rod
A. Lip

Fig. 10 Typical clutch hydraulic actuating system components

released to gradually move the clutch plate toward the flywheels under pressure of the pressure plate springs. The friction between the clutch plate and flywheel becomes greater as the pedal is released and the engine speed increased. Once the vehicle is moving, the need for clutch slippage is lessened, and the clutch pedal can be fully released.Coordination between the clutch pedal and accelerator is important to avoid engine stalling, shock to the driveline components and excessive clutch slippage and overheating.

How the Manual Transmission Works

The internal combustion engine creates a twisting motion or torque, which is transferred to the drive wheels. However, the engine cannot develop much torque at low speeds; it will only develop maximum torque at higher speeds. The transmission, with its varied gear ratios, provides a means of providing this low torque to move the vehicle.

The transmission gear ratios allow the engine to be operated most efficiently under a variety of driving and load conditions. Using gear ratios, the need for extremely high engine rpm at high road speeds is avoided.

The modern transmission provides both speed and power through selected gear sizes that are engineered for the best all-around performance. A power (lower) gear ratio starts the vehicle moving and speed gear ratios keep the vehicle moving. By shifting to gears of different ratios, the driver can match engine speed to road conditions.

GEAR RATIOS

▶ **See Figure 11**

To obtain maximum performance and efficiency, gear ratios are engineered to each type of vehicle, dependent upon such items as the size of the engine, the vehicle weight and expected loaded weight, etc.

The gear ratio can be determined by counting the teeth on both gears. For example, if the driving gear has 20 teeth and the driven gear has 40 teeth, the gear ratio is 2 to 1 the driven gear makes one revolution for every two revolutions of the drive gear. If the driving gear has 40 teeth and the driven gear 20 teeth, the gear ratio is 1 to 2 the driven gear revolves twice, while the drive gear revolves once.

The transmissions used today may have four, five or six speeds forward, but all have one speed in reverse. The reverse gear is necessary because the engine rotates only in one direction and cannot be reversed. The reversing procedure must be accomplished inside the transmission.

By comparing gear ratios, you can see which transmission transmits more power to the drive wheels at the same engine rpm. The five-speed

Fig. 11 Example of determining gear ratio. Gear ratio can be found by dividing the number of teeth on the smaller gear into the number of the teeth on the larger gear.

transmission's low or first gear with a ratio of 3.61 to 1 means that for 3.61 revolutions of the input or clutch shaft (coupled to the engine by the clutch), the output shaft of the transmission will rotate once. This provides more power to the drive wheels, compared to the four-speed transmission's low gear of 2.33 to 1.

When the transmission is shifted into the high gear in the four-speed transmission, and fourth gear in the five-speed transmission, the gear ratio is usually 1 to 1 (direct drive). For every rotation of the engine and input shaft, the output shaft is rotating one turn.

Fifth gear in a five-speed transmission is usually an overdrive. This gear is used for higher speed driving where very little load is placed on the engine. This gear ratio provides better economy by lowering the engine RPM to maintain a specific speed. The input shaft rotates only 0.87 of a turn, while the output shaft rotates one revolution, resulting in the output shaft rotating faster than the input shaft.

The overdrive is normally incorporated in the transmission.

SYNCHROMESH TRANSMISSIONS

▶ **See Figure 12**

The power flow illustrated in a typical four-speed is a conventional, spur-geared transmission. To obtain a quiet operation and gear engagement, synchronizing clutches are added to the main-shaft gears. The addition of synchronizers allows the gears to be in constant mesh with the cluster gears (gears that provide a connection between input and output shafts), and the synchronizing clutch mechanism locks the gears together.

The main purpose of the synchronizer is to speed up or slow down the rotation speeds of the shaft and gear, until both are rotating at the same speeds so that both can be locked together without a gear clash.

Since the vehicle is normally standing still when shifted into reverse gear, a synchronizing clutch is ordinarily not used on reverse gear.

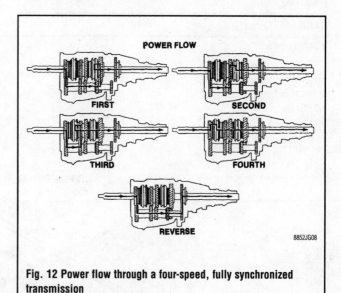

Fig. 12 Power flow through a four-speed, fully synchronized transmission

FIVE & SIX-SPEED TRANSMISSIONS

The power flow through the five-speed transmission can be charted in the same manner as the four-speed transmission.

As a rule, the power flow in high gear is usually straight through the transmission-input shaft to the mainshaft, which would be locked together. When in the reduction gears, the power flow is through the input shaft, to the cluster gear unit, and through the reduction gear to the mainshaft.

TRANSAXLES

▶ See Figures 13 and 14

When the transmission and the drive axle are combined in one unit, it is called a "transaxle." The transaxle is bolted to the engine and has the advantage of being an extremely rigid unit of engine and driveline components. The complete engine transaxle unit may be located at the front of the vehicle (front wheel drive) or at the rear of the vehicle (rear wheel drive).

The power flow through the transmission section of the transaxle is the same as through a conventional transmission.

Clutch Maintenance

▶ See Figure 15

The only maintenance associated with the mechanical clutch actuation is to periodically check the distance between the release bearing and the pressure plate. This clearance is commonly called "clutch pedal free-play" and is the distance the pedal moves before the slack is taken from the linkage and the release bearing begins to move the clutch away from the flywheel.

This distance can be measured by standing a 12-inch ruler on the floor-

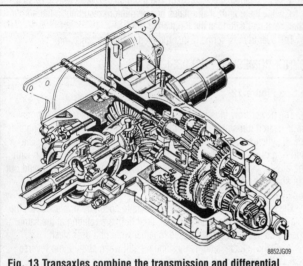
Fig. 13 Transaxles combine the transmission and differential into one unit

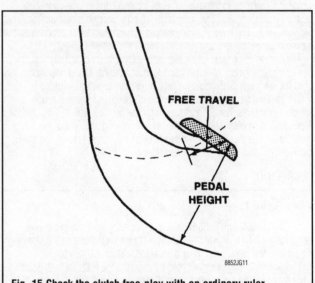
Fig. 15 Check the clutch free-play with an ordinary ruler

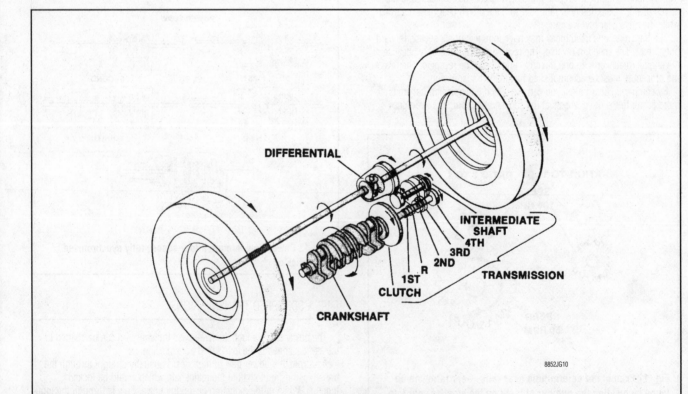
Fig. 14 This simple illustration shows the power flow through a front wheel drive transaxle. Note how the direction of rotation of the engine crankcase and the axle shafts (attached to the wheels) are the same, this is made possible using an intermediate shaft.

board and measuring the height of the pedal in the released position. Take the slack from the clutch linkage (depress the pedal until resistance is felt) and re-measure. The difference between the two measurements is the amount of clutch linkage free-play (measured at the pedal). Generally, the clearance should be approximately ⅞" to 1 inch (20–25mm). This clearance can be maintained by adjustment of the clutch linkage. If not, the clutch and pressure plate should be replaced as a set.

On systems with hydraulically actuated clutch, the fluid level in the master cylinder reservoir should be checked at least every 6 months or whenever underhood service is performed. As with many brake master cylinder reservoirs, you normally check the fluid level through the translucent plastic body of the reservoir. Fill to the line in the reservoir.

➥**Although the level should drop slowly with clutch wear, the need to constantly add large amounts of fluid points to the probability of a leak. If a leak is suspected the system should be thoroughly checked to prevent a hydraulic system failure which could leave you stranded.**

▶ **See Figure 16**

The transmission requires little maintenance, other than checking/changing the lubricant, and lubricating the shift linkage.

Internal problems usually require removal and overhaul of the transmission.

LUBRICATE THE SHIFT LINKAGE

▶ **See Figures 17, 18 and 19**

➥**Many modern transmissions/transaxles utilize linkage which is mounted directly into the top of the transmission housing assembly through a hole in the floor of the vehicle chassis. On these models there is usually no exposed linkage to be lubricated.**

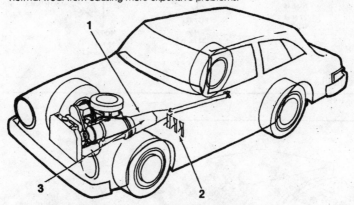

A little preventive maintenance in the clutch and transmission can prevent normal wear from causing more expensive problems.

1. **Check lubricant level ▲**	**3 mos/3000 miles**
Change lubricant ▲	**2 years/24,000 miles**
2. **Check clutch pedal free-play ▲**	**6 mos/6000 miles**
3. **Lubricate shift linkage**	**6 mos/6000 miles**

▲If the vehicle is used for severe service (trailer pulling, constant stop/start driving, off-road operation), cut the maintenance interval in half.

8852JG12

Fig. 16 Clutch and transmission maintenance intervals

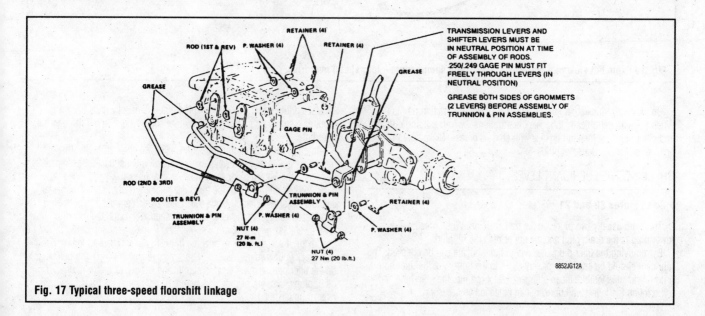

Fig. 17 Typical three-speed floorshift linkage

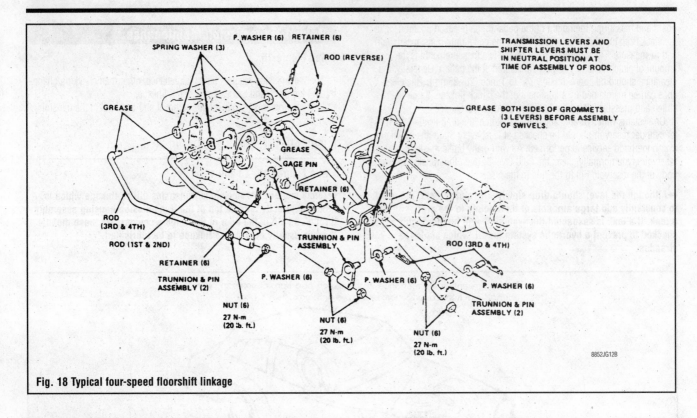

Fig. 18 Typical four-speed floorshift linkage

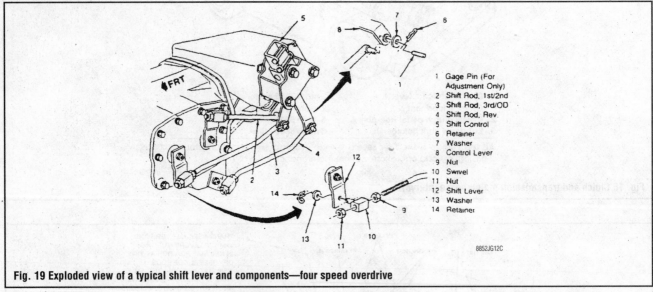

1 Gage Pin (For Adjustment Only)
2 Shift Rod, 1st/2nd
3 Shift Rod, 3rd/OD
4 Shift Rod, Rev.
5 Shift Control
6 Retainer
7 Washer
8 Control Lever
9 Nut
10 Swivel
11 Nut
12 Shift Lever
13 Washer
14 Retainer

Fig. 19 Exploded view of a typical shift lever and components—four speed overdrive

On models with external linkage, check for pivot and friction points. When present, periodically lubricate the trunnions, swivels, sliding surfaces and pivot points of the shift linkage with chassis grease. Make sure that the linkage is free and does not bind.

CHECKING THE LUBRICANT LEVEL

◆ **See Figures 20 and 21**

There are usually two plugs on the transmission. When present, the lower plug is the drain plug and the upper plug the fill plug.

By removing the filler plug, the level of the lubricant can be checked. The lubricant should be level with or very close to the bottom of the filler hole. If no lubricant is visible, insert a finger or bent rod into the filler hole and try to touch the lubricant. Lubricant can be added as necessary.

When adding gear oil, keep in mind that it is usually quite thick and requires a suction gun or squeeze bulb of some type to add it through the filler hole.

Although MOST transmissions/transaxles are checked in this manner, remember that there are always exceptions. Some manuals utilize dipsticks. For years, the Saturn manual transaxle was equipped with a hinged dipstick, located on the top of the transaxle housing (right below the master cylinder). Also, on some Mazda transaxles (which are used in both Ford and Mazda vehicles) fluid is checked and added through the mounting hole for the vehicle speed sensor (which is also found on the top of the transaxle). If you are unsure how the fluid should be checked for your vehicle, check your owner's manual. If you remove a plug which you believe to be the filler plug and the level is significantly above or below it, check for other plugs, sensors or dipsticks before deciding that the transmission is over or under-filled.

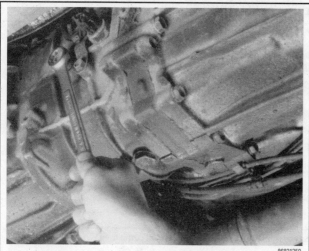

Fig. 20 On most transmissions, use a wrench or socket to remove the filler plug on the side of the case . . .

Fig. 22 To change the transmission fluid loosen the drain plug using a wrench or a ratchet and socket with a short extension

Fig. 21 . . . then check fluid level with a finger through the fill hole and add fluid, as necessary

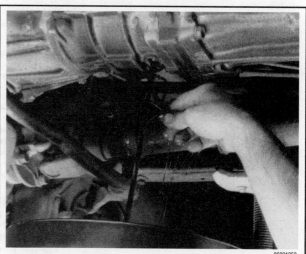

Fig. 23 Quickly withdraw the plug down and to the side, to avoid getting oil on your hands

CHANGING TRANSMISSION LUBRICANT

▶ See Figures 22, 23 and 24

The lubricant is usually changed every two years or 24,000 miles by removing the drain (lower) plug from the transmission case and draining the old lubricant into a catch pan. If you have operated the vehicle under extreme conditions, from towing or off-road driving, to driving in extreme dusty conditions or high water, you will probably want to check and change the fluid more often.

➡**Be sure the fluid is at operating temperature so that it will flow better and remove more impurities.**

The drain plug is sometimes magnetic to attract stray metal particles, keeping them out of the bearings and gear teeth. Be sure to clean the magnet of any metal particles before installing the drain plug.

➡**ALWAYS keep and measure the amount of fluid drained from the transmission. This will help assure that the proper amount of fluid will be added during the refill.**

A few transmissions have no drain plugs. In this case, the lower rear extension housing bolt is removed to drain the transmission. Be sure to place sealant on the bolt threads when installing the bolt.

Fig. 24 Allow the fluid to drain completely into a pan or container, before reinstalling the plug

To fill the transmission, use a lubricant dispenser, suction gun or hand bulb-type syringe through the fill hole, (usually, but NOT always located on the side of the transmission case). On any fill hole that is located in the side of the transmission, overfill slightly and allow the lubricant to find its own level by spilling out of the hole. Keep adding lubricant until the level is constant at the bottom of the filler hole. Install the fill plug and tighten securely. Clean any excess lubrication from the case surface to avoid road dirt buildup.

LUBRICANT RECOMMENDATION

Manufacturers differ in type and grade of lubricant usage; consult your owners manual for the proper lubricant to use in your transmission or transaxle.

TROUBLESHOOTING BASIC CLUTCH AND MANUAL TRANSMISSION PROBLEMS

As you drive your car, you become used to noises, vibrations and the feel of the car in different gears. Any changes in these sensations may indicate the beginning of a problem. It's important to note what gear you are in, at what speeds the problem occurs, noise level and whether it disappears from one gear to another.

Most problems in the clutch and transmission are a job for a mechanic, and usually require removal and service.

Problem	Cause(s)
Excessive clutch noise	**Throwout bearing noises** are more audible at the lower end of pedal travel. The usual causes are: • Riding the clutch • Too little pedal free-play • Lack of bearing lubrication A **bad clutch shaft pilot bearing** will make a high pitched squeal, when the clutch is disengaged and the transmission is in gear or within the first 2" of pedal travel. The bearing must be replaced. **Noise from the clutch linkage** is a clicking or snapping that can be heard or felt as the pedal is moved completely up or down. This usually requires lubrication.① **Transmitted engine noises** are amplified by the clutch housing and heard in the passenger compartment. They are usually the result of insufficient pedal free-play and can be changed by manipulating the clutch pedal.
Clutch slips (the car does not move as it should when the clutch is engaged)	This is usually most noticeable when pulling away from a standing start. A severe test is to start the engine, apply the brakes, shift into high gear and SLOWLY release the clutch pedal. A healthy clutch will stall the engine. If it slips it may be due to: • A worn pressure plate or clutch plate • Oil soaked clutch plate • Insufficient pedal free-play • Bad waste or slave cylinder • Low fluid
Clutch drags or fails to release	The clutch disc and some transmission gears spin briefly after clutch disengagement. Under normal conditions in average temperatures, 3 seconds is maximum spin-time. Failure to release properly can be caused by: • Too light transmission lubricant or low lubricant level • Improperly adjusted clutch linkage • Bad cylinder • Low fluid • Air in line
Low clutch life	Low clutch life is usually a result of poor driving habits or heavy duty use. Riding the clutch, pulling heavy loads, holding the car on a grade with the clutch instead of the brakes and rapid clutch engagement all contribute to low clutch life.
Transmission shifts hard	Common causes of hard shifting are: • Improper lubricant viscosity or lubricant level • Clutch linkage needs adjustment/lubrication①
Transmission leaks lubricant	The general location of a leak can be found by putting a clean newspaper under the transmission overnight. • Lubricant level too high • Cracks in the transmission case • Loose or missing bolts • Drain or fill plug loose or missing • Vent hole plugged
Transmission is noisy in gear	Most problems such as this require the services of a mechanic. Causes include: • Insufficient lubricant • Worn gears (excessive end-play) • Worn bearings • Damaged synchronizers • Chipped gear teeth
Transmission is noisy in Neutral	Noises in Neutral are usually caused by: • Insufficient/incorrect lubricant • Worn reverse idler gear • Worn bearings or gear teeth

① Mechanically operated clutch only

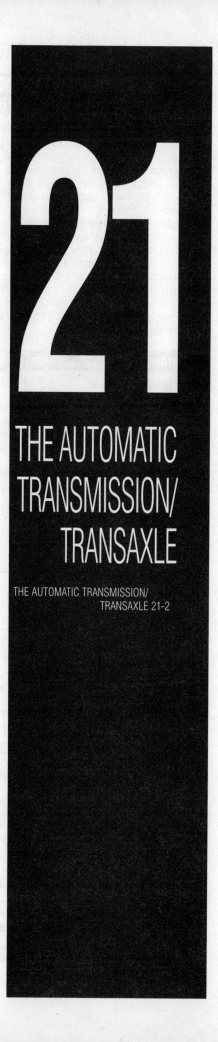

21

THE AUTOMATIC TRANSMISSION/ TRANSAXLE

THE AUTOMATIC TRANSMISSION/TRANSAXLE

The automobile has become so sophisticated and the automatic transmissions so reliable; that automatic transmissions are the most popular option, or are even standard on many models. Over 85% of all new vehicles are ordered with an automatic transmission. All the driver has to do is start the engine, select a gear and operate the accelerator and brakes. It may not be as much fun as shifting gears, but it is far more efficient if you haul heavy loads or pull a trailer.

The automatic transmission anticipates the engines needs and selects gears in response to various inputs (engine vacuum, road speed, throttle position, etc.) to maintain the best application of power. The operations usually performed by the clutch and manual transmission are accomplished automatically, through the use of the fluid coupling, which allows a very slight, controlled slippage between the engine and transmission. Tiny hydraulic valves control the application of different gear ratios on demand by the driver (position of the accelerator pedal), or in a preset response to engine conditions and road speed.

How the Automatic Transmission Works

▶ **See Figures 1, 2 and 3**

The automatic transmission allows engine torque and power to be transmitted to the drive wheels within a narrow range of engine operating speeds. The transmission will allow the engine to turn fast enough to produce plenty of power and torque at very low speeds, while keeping it at a sensible rpm at high vehicle speeds.

The transmission uses a light fluid as the medium for the transmission of power. This fluid also operates the hydraulic control circuits and acts as a lubricant. Because the transmission fluid performs all of these three functions, trouble within the unit can easily travel from one part to another.

The automatic transmission operates on a principle that fluids cannot be compressed, and that when put into motion, will cause a similar reaction

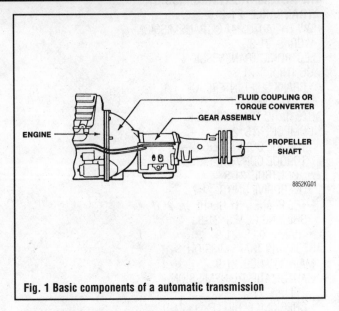

Fig. 1 Basic components of a automatic transmission

upon any resisting force. To understand this law of fluids, think of two fans placed opposite each other. If one fan is turned on, it will begin to turn the opposite fan blades. This principle is applied to the operation of the fluid coupling and torque converter by using driving and driven members in place of fan blades.

Every type of automatic transmission has two sections. The front section contains the fluid coupling or torque converter and takes the place of the driver operated clutch. The rear section contains the valve body assembly and the hydraulically controlled gear units, which take the place of the manually shifted standard transmission.

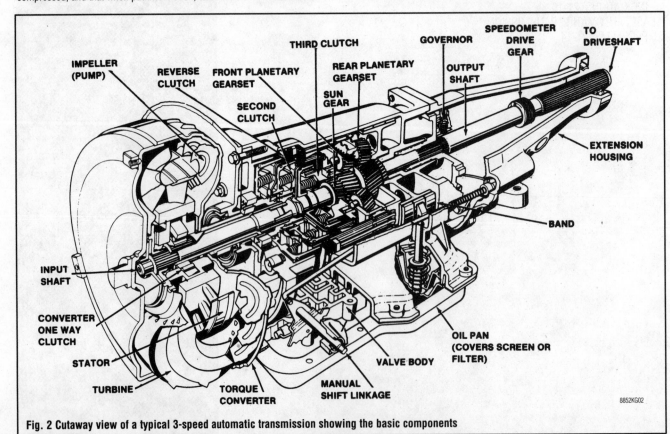

Fig. 2 Cutaway view of a typical 3-speed automatic transmission showing the basic components

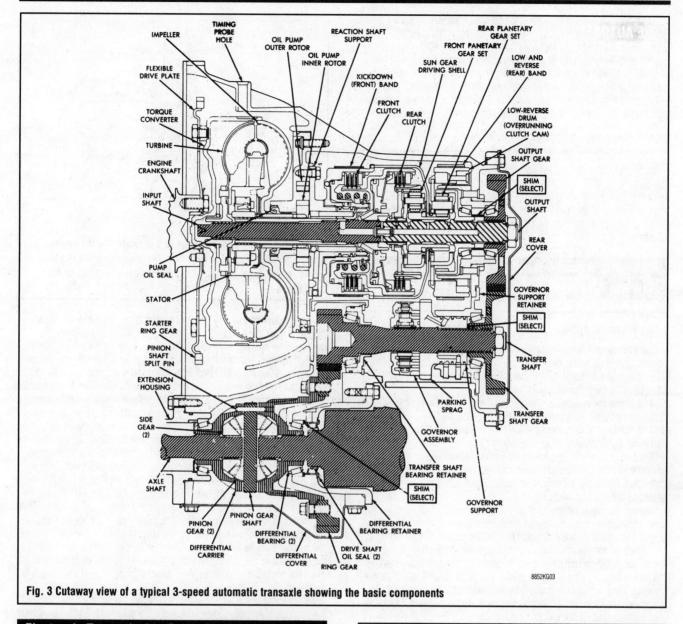

Fig. 3 Cutaway view of a typical 3-speed automatic transaxle showing the basic components

Electronic Transmission Controls

▶ **See Figure 4**

Numourous changes have occurred in transaxles and transmissions in the last decade. The demand for lighter, smaller and more fuel efficient vehicles has resulted in the use of electronics to control both the engine and transmission to achieve the fuel efficient results that are required by law. The transaxle/transmisson assembly is a part of the electronic controls, by sending signals of vehicle speed to an on-board computer. Which in turn relates these signals, along with others from the engine assembly, to determine gear selection for the best performance.

Sensors are used for engine and road speeds, engine load, gear selector lever position, and the kickdown switch operation. In addition, the driving program, set by the factory, is used to send signals to the microcomputer to determine the optimum gear selection, according to a preset program. The shifting is accomplished by solenoid valves in the hydraulic system. The electronics also control the modulated hydraulic pressure during shifting, along with regulating engine torque to provide smooth shifts between gear ratio changes. This type of system can be designed for different driving programs, such as giving the operator the choice of operating the vehicle for either economy or performance.

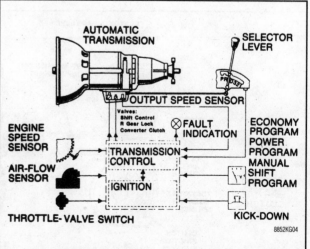

Fig. 4 Electronic controlled transmissions use solenoids for gear selection with microcomputer control.

The transmission's sensors also let the operator of the vehicle know if there are any problems with the system. If the transmission control computer detects a problem it will store a trouble code in memory and it will light or flash a transmission warning lamp (or engine service light) on the dash to alert the operator something is wrong. Using the proper scan tools or techniques a technician can retrieve the code (depending on the manufacturer) in order to help diagnose the trouble. To get a better understanding of engine and transmission trouble codes see the Chilton's Total Car Care book for your car.

BRAKE SHIFT INTERLOCK SYSTEM

As a safety feature on some vehicles the transmission will not allow the operator to shift into drive or start the car until they place their foot onto the brake pedal. This system is usually controlled by a cable from the brake pedal to the transmission or the transmission computer and sensors. On some vehicles the driver will hear a clicking which is the sensor operation.

Automatic Transmission Components

TORQUE CONVERTER

▶ **See Figures 5 and 6**

The front section is called the torque converter. In replacing the traditional clutch, it performs three functions:
- It acts as a hydraulic clutch (fluid coupling), allowing the engine to idle even with the transmission in gear.
- It allows the transmission to shift from gear to gear smoothly, without requiring that the driver close the throttle during the shift.
- It multiplies engine torque making the transmission more responsive and reducing the amount of shifting required.

The torque converter is a metal case that is shaped like a sphere that has been flattened on opposite sides and is bolted to the rear of the engine's crankshaft. Generally, the entire metal case rotates at engine speed and serves as the engine's flywheel.

The case contains three sets of blades. One set is attached directly to the case forming the impeller or pump. Another set is directly connected to the output shaft, and forms the turbine. The third set (stator) is mounted on a hub which, in turn, is mounted on a stationary shaft through a one-way clutch. Rollers are wedged into slots, preventing backward rotation. When the rollers are not in the slots, the stator turns in the same direction as the impeller. The pump, which is driven by the converter hub at engine speed, keeps the torque converter full of transmission fluid at all times. Fluid flows continuously through the unit to provide cooling.

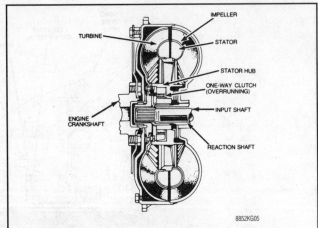

Fig. 5 The torque converter housing is rotated by the engine crankshaft and turns the impeller. The impeller spins the turbine, which gives motion to the turbine (output) shaft to drive the gears

A fluid coupling will only transmit the torque the engine develops; it cannot increase the torque. This is one job of the torque converter. The impeller drive member is driven at engine speed by the engine's crankshaft and pumps fluid, to its center, which is flung outward by centrifugal force as it turns. Since the outer edge of the converter spins faster than the center, the fluid gains speed. Fluid is directed toward the turbine driven member by curved impeller blades, causing the turbine to rotate in the same direction as the impeller. The turbine blades are curved in the opposite direction of the impeller blades.

In flowing through the pump and turbine, the fluid flows in two separate directions. It flows through the turbine blades, and it spins with the engine. The stator, whose blades are stationary when the vehicle is being accelerated at low speeds, converts one type of flow into another. Instead of allowing the fluid to flow straight back into the pump, the stator's curved blades turn the fluid almost 90° toward the direction of rotation of the engine. Thus the fluid does not flow as fast toward the pump, but is already spinning when the pump picks it up. This has the effect of allowing the pump to turn much faster than the turbine. This difference in speed may be compared to the difference in speed between the smaller and larger gears in any gear train. The result is that engine power output is higher, and engine torque is multiplied.

As the speed of the turbine increases, the fluid spins faster and faster in the direction of engine rotation. Therefore, the ability of the stator to redirect

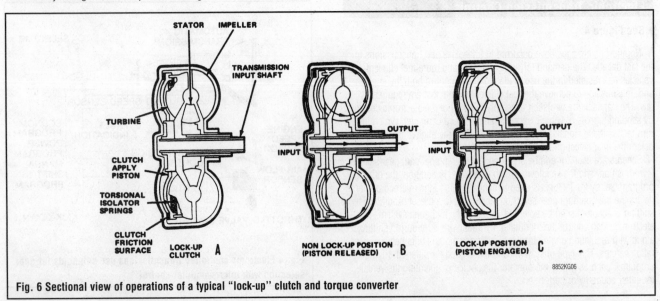

Fig. 6 Sectional view of operations of a typical "lock-up" clutch and torque converter

the fluid flow is reduced. Under cruising conditions, the stator is eventually forced to rotate on its one-way clutch and the torque converter begins to behave almost like a solid shaft, with the pump and turbine speeds being almost equal.

In the late 70's, Chrysler Corporation introduced an automatic transmission, featuring what is called a "lock-up" clutch in the transmission's torque converter. The lock-up is a fully automatic clutch that engages only when the transmission shifts into top gear or when needed based on a predetermined demand factor.

The lock-up clutch is activated by a piston. When engaged, the lock-up clutch gives the benefits of a manual transmission, eliminating torque converter slippage. In the engaged position, engine torque is delivered mechanically, rather than hydrodynamically (through fluid). This gives improved fuel economy and cooler transmission operating temperatures.

In the early 80's, Ford introduced what is known as the Automatic Overdrive Transmission (AOT). Essentially, this transmission uses a lock-up torque converter, by offering an additional refinement. The transmission is a four-speed unit, with fourth gear as an overdrive (0.67:1). Torque is transmitted via a full mechanical lock-up from the engine, completely bypassing the torque converter and eliminating hydraulic slippage.

In third gear (1:1 ratio), engine power follows a "split-torque" path, in which there is a 60% lock-up. Sixty percent of the power is transmitted through solid connections and 40% of the engine power is delivered through the torque converter.

Throughout the 90's, Subaru introduced an Electronic Continuously Variable Transmission (ECVT) and Honda introduced their version (CVT). This transmission uses a metal belt and two variable-diameter pulleys to keep smooth, uninterrupted range of gearing. Size of the pulleys is controlled through the use of hydraulics. This unit produces a miles per gallon closer to a manual transmission, while attaining a smother shift than an automatic transmission.

TORQUE CONVERTER CLUTCH CONTROL

♦ See Figures 7 and 8

Electrical and Vacuum Controls

The torque converter clutch should apply when the engine has reached near normal operating temperature in order to handle the slight extra load and when the vehicle speed is high enough to allow the operation of the clutch to be smooth and the vehicle to be free of engine pulses.

➡When the converter clutch is coupled to the engine, the engine pulses can be felt through the vehicle in the same manner as if equipped with a clutch and standard transmission. Engine condition, engine load and engine speed determines the severity of the pulsation.

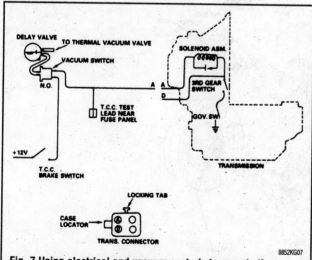

Fig. 7 Using electrical and vacuum controls to operate the torque converter clutch

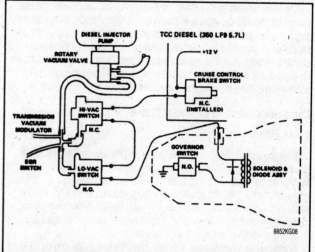

Fig. 8 Typical diesel engine vacuum and electrical schematic for the torque converter clutch

The converter clutch should release when torque multiplication is needed in the converter, when coming to a stop, or when the mechanical connection would affect exhaust emissions during a coasting condition.

The typical electrical control components consist of the brake release switch, the low vacuum switch and the governor switch. Some vehicle models have a thermal vacuum switch, a relay valve and a delay valve. Diesel engines use a high vacuum switch in addition to certain above listed components. These various components control the flow of current to the apply valve solenoid. By controlling the current flow, these components activate or deactivate the solenoid, which in turn engages or disengages the transmission converter clutch, depending upon the driving conditions as mentioned previously. The components have the two basic circuits, electrical and vacuum.

ELECTRICAL CURRENT FLOW

All of the components in the electrical circuit must be closed or grounded before the solenoid can open the hydraulic circuit to engage the converter clutch. The circuit begins at the fuse panel and flows to the brake switch and as long as the brake pedal is not depressed, the current will flow to the low vacuum switch on the gasoline engines and to the high vacuum switch on the diesel engines. These two switches open or close the circuit path to the solenoid, dependent upon the engine or pump vacuum. If the low vacuum switch is closed (high vacuum switch on diesel engines), the current continues to flow to the transmission case connector, into the solenoid and to the governor pressure switch. When the vehicle speed is approximately 35–50 mph (56–80 kph), the governor switch grounds to activate the solenoid. The solenoid, in turn, opens a hydraulic circuit to the converter clutch assembly, engaging the unit.

It should be noted that external vacuum controls include the thermal vacuum valve, the relay valve, the delay valve, the low vacuum switch and a high vacuum switch (used on diesel engines). Keep in mind that all of the electrical or vacuum components may not be used on all engines, at the same time.

VACUUM FLOW

The vacuum relay valve works with the thermal vacuum valve to keep engine vacuum from reaching the low vacuum valve switch at low engine temperatures. This action prevents the clutch from engaging while the engine is still warming up. The delay valve slows the response of the low vacuum switch to changes in engine vacuum. This action prevents the low vacuum switch from causing the converter clutch to engage and disengage too rapidly. The low vacuum switch deactivates the converter clutch when engine vacuum drops to a specific low level during moderate acceleration just before a part-throttle transmission downshift. The low vacuum switch also deactivates the clutch while the vehicle is coasting because it receives no vacuum from its ported vacuum source.

The high vacuum switch, when on diesel engines, deactivates the converter clutch while the vehicle is coasting. The low vacuum switch on the diesel models only deactivates the converter clutch only during moderate acceleration, just prior to a part-throttle downshift. Because the diesel engine's vacuum source is a rotary pump, rather than taken from a carburetor port, diesel models require bath the high and the low vacuum switch to achieve the same results as the low vacuum switch on the gasoline models.

Computer Controlled Converter Clutch

▶ See Figure 9

With the use of microcomputers governing the engine fuel and spark delivery, most manufacturers change the converter clutch electronic control to provide the grounding circuit for the solenoid valve through the microcomputer, rather than the governor pressure switch. Sensors are used in place of the formerly used switches and send signals back to the microcomputer to indicate if the engine is in its proper mode to accept the mechanical lock-up of the converter clutch.

Normally a coolant sensor, a throttle position sensor, an engine vacuum sensor and a vehicle speed sensor are used to signal the microcomputer when the converter clutch can be applied. Should a sensor indicate the

need for the converter clutch to be deactivated, the grounding circuit to the transmission solenoid valve would be interrupted and the converter clutch would be released.

Hydraulic Converter Clutch

Numerous automatic transmissions rely upon hydraulic pressures to sense, determine when and to apply the converter clutch assembly. This type of automatic transmission unit is considered to be a self-contained unit with only the shift linkage, throttle cable or modulator valve being external. Specific valves, located within the valve body or oil pump housing, are caused to be moved when a sequence of events occur within the unit. For example, to engage the converter clutch, most all automatic transmissions require the gear ratio to be in the top gear before the converter clutch control valves can be placed in operation. The governor and throttle pressures must maintain specific fluid pressures at various points within the hydraulic circuits to aid in the engagement or disengagement of the converter clutch. In addition, check valves must properly seal and move to exhaust pressured fluid at the correct time to avoid "shudders" or "chuckles" during the initial application and engagement of the converter clutch.

Centrifugal Torque Converter Clutch

▶ See Figure 10

A torque converter was used that locks up mechanically without the use of electronics or hydraulic pressure. At specific input shaft speeds, brake-like shoes move outward from the rim of the turbine assembly, to engage the converter housing, locking the converter unit mechanically together for a 1:1 ratio. Slight slippage can occur at the low end of the rpm scale, but the greater the rpm, the tighter the lock-up. Again, it must be mentioned, that when the converter has locked-up, the vehicle may respond in the same manner as driving with a clutch and standard transmission. This is considered normal and does not indicate converter clutch or transmission problems. Keep in mind if engines are in need of tune-ups or repairs, the lock-up "shudder" or "chuckle" feeling may be greater.

Mechanical Converter Lock-Up

Another type of converter lock-up is the Ford Motor Company's AOD Automatic Overdrive transmission, which uses a direct drive input shaft splined to the damper assembly of the torque converter cover to the direct clutch, bypassing the torque converter reduction components. A second shaft encloses the direct drive input shaft and is coupled between the converter turbine and the reverse clutch or forward clutch, depending

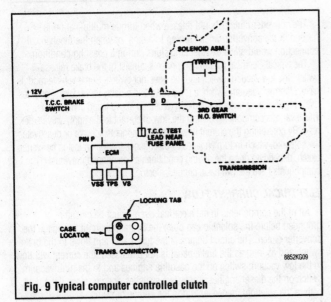

Fig. 9 Typical computer controlled clutch

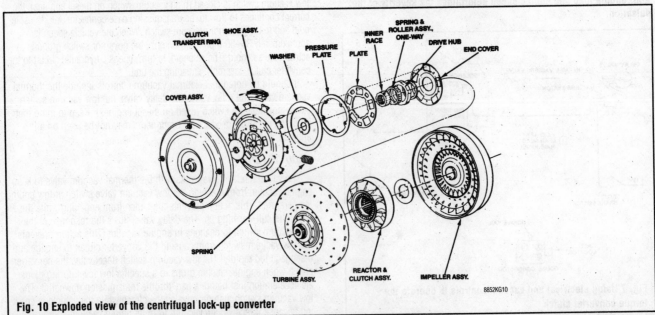

Fig. 10 Exploded view of the centrifugal lock-up converter

upon their applied phase. With this type of unit, when in third gear, the input shaft torque is split, 30% hydraulic and 70% mechanical. When in the overdrive or fourth gear, the input torque is completely mechanical and the transmission is locked mechanically to the engine.

OVERDRIVE UNITS

♦ See Figure 11

When the need for greater fuel economy stirred the world's automakers into action, the automatic transmission/transaxles were among the many vehicle components that were modified to aid in this quest. Internal changes have been made and in some cases, additions of a fourth gear to provide the over direct or overdrive gear ratio. The reasoning for adding the overdrive capability is that an overdrive ratio enables the output speed of the transmission/transaxle to be greater than the input speed, allowing the vehicle to maintain a given road speed with less engine speed. This results in better fuel economy and a slower running engine.

The overdrive unit usually consists of an overdrive planetary gear set, a roller one-way clutch assembly and two friction clutch assemblies, one as an internal clutch pack and the second for a brake clutch pack. The overdrive carrier is splined to the turbine shaft, which in turn, is splined into the converter turbine.

Another type of overdrive assembly is a separation of the overdrive components by having them at various points along the gear train assembly and utilizing them for other gear ranges. Instead of having a brake clutch pack, an overdrive band is used to lock the planetary sun gear. In this type of transmission, the converter cover drives the direct drive shaft clockwise at engine speed, which in turn drives the direct clutch. The direct clutch then drives the planetary carrier assembly at engine speed in a clockwise direction. The pinion gears of the planetary gear assembly "walk around" the stationary reverse sun gear, again in a clockwise rotation. The ring gear and output shafts are therefore driven at a faster speed by the rotation of the planetary pinions. Because the input is 100% mechanical drive, the converter can be classified as a lock-up converter in the overdrive position.

THE PLANETARY GEARBOX

♦ See Figures 12, 13 and 14

The rear section of the transmission is the gearbox, containing the gear train and valve body to shift the gears.

The ability of the torque converter to multiply engine torque is limited, so the unit tends to be more efficient when the turbine is rotating at relatively high speeds. A planetary gearbox is used to carry the power output from the turbine to the driveshaft to make the most efficient use of the converter.

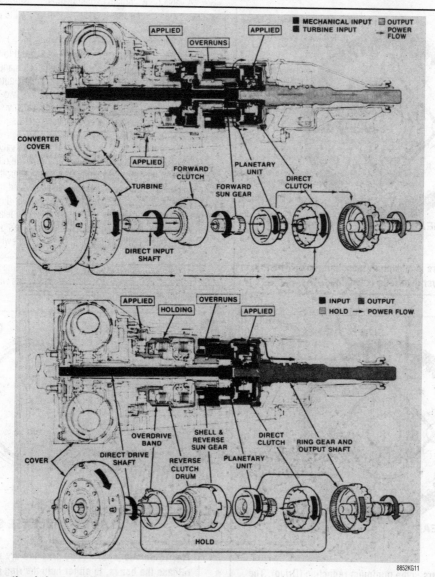

Fig. 11 Exploded and sectional views of direct drive and overdrive power flows

8852KG11

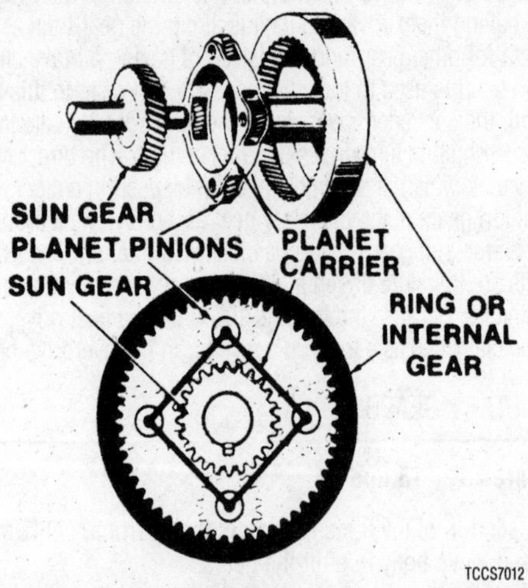

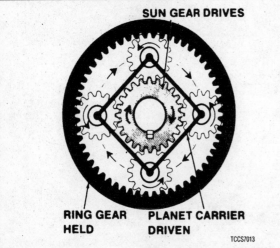

Fig. 12 Planetary gears are similar to manual transmission gears, but are composed of three parts

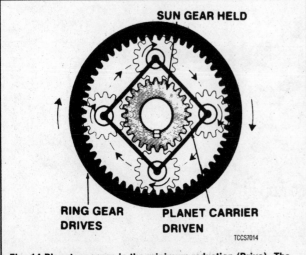

Fig. 13 Planetary gears in maximum reduction (Low). The ring gear is held and a lower gear ratio is obtained.

Fig. 14 Planetary gears in the minimum reduction (Drive). The ring gear is allowed to revolve, providing a higher gear ratio.

Planetary gears function very similarly to conventional transmission gears. Their construction is different in that three elements make up one gear system, and in that the three elements are different from one another. The three elements are:

• An outer gear that is shaped like a hoop, with teeth cut into the inner surface.

• A sun gear mounted on a shaft and located at the very center of the outer gear.

• A set of three planet gears, held by pins in a ring-like planet carrier and meshing with both the sun gear and the outer gear.

Either the outer gear or the sun gear may be held stationary, providing more than one possible torque multiplication factor for each set of gears. If all three gears are forced to rotate at the same speed, the gear set forms, in effect, a solid shaft.

Bands and clutches are used to hold various portions of the gear-sets to the transmission case or to the shaft on which they are mounted.

SHIFTING GEARS

▶ **See Figures 15 and 16**

Shifting is accomplished by changing the portion of each planetary gear set that is held to the transmission case or shaft.

A valve body contains small hydraulic pistons and cylinders. Fluid enters the cylinder under pressure and forces the pistons to move to engage the bands or clutches.

The hydraulic fluid used to operate the valve body comes from the main transmission oil pump. This fluid is channeled to the various pistons through the shift valves. There is generally a manual shift valve that is operated by the transmission selector lever and an automatic shift valve for each automatic upshift the transmission provides. Two-speed automatics have a low-high shift valve; while three-speeds will have a 1-2 shift valve, and a 2-3 shift valve; whereas four-speeds have a 1-2 shift valve, a 2-3 shift valve, and a 3-4 shift valve.

Two pressures effect the operation of these valves. One (governor pressure) is determined by vehicle speed, while the other (modulator pressure) is determined by intake manifold vacuum or throttle position. Governor pressure rises with an increase in vehicle speed, and modulator pressure rises as the throttle is opened wider. By responding to these two pressures, the shift valves cause the upshift points to be delayed with increased throttle opening to make the best use of the engine's power output. If the accelerator is pushed further to the floor the upshift will be delayed longer, (the vehicle will stay in gear).

The transmission modulator also governs line pressure, used to actuate the servos. In this way, the clutches and bands will be actuated with a force matching the torque output of the engine.

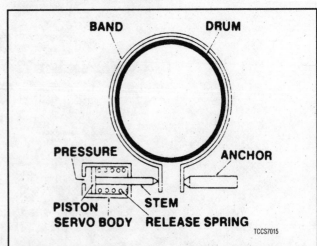

Fig. 15 Servos, operated by pressure are used to apply or release the bands, to either hold the ring gear or allow it to rotate

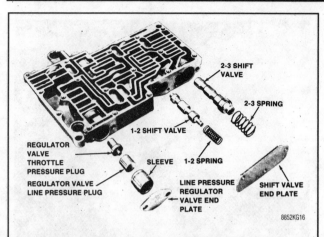

Fig. 16 The valve body, containing the shift valves, is normally located at the bottom of the transmission. The shift valves (there are many more than shown) are operated by hydraulic pressure

Most transmissions also make use of an auxiliary circuit for downshifting. This circuit may be actuated by the throttle linkage or the vacuum line that actuates the modulator or by a cable or solenoid. It applies pressure to a special downshift surface on the shift valve or valves, to shift back to low gear as vehicle speed decreases.

TRANSAXLES

When the transmission and the drive axle are combined in one unit, it is called a "transaxle." The transaxle is bolted to the engine and has the advantage of being an extremely rigid unit of engine and driveline components. The complete engine transaxle unit may be located at the front of the vehicle (front wheel drive) or at the rear of the vehicle (rear wheel drive).

The power flow through the transmission section of the transaxle is the same as through a conventional transmission.

Automatic Transmission Maintenance

AUTOMATIC TRANSMISSION FLUID

Automatic transmission fluids can be broken down into two types, Dexron® III and Ford type F. These fluids are specific to the transmission using them. Don't assume that all Ford vehicles use type F, they don't!

There are the following types of fluids.

• Dexron® III, sometime referred to as multi purpose ATF. This replaces the old Type A, Suffix A, which was recommended by GM, Chrysler and AMC between 1956–1967. It also supercedes Dexron® and Dexron® II fluids. Ford vehicles 1977 and later with the C6 transmission or the Jatco transmission in the Granada and Monarch also use this fluid. Ford refers to this fluid as Mercon®, or on older models as type H or CJ where recommended.

• Type F fluid is recommended by Ford Motor Co. and a few imported manufacturers, and contains certain frictional compounds required for proper operation in these transmissions.

There is not much of a problem here, since the bottles are clearly marked to indicate the type of fluid. If you are in doubt, check your owner's manual. Also, some transmission dipsticks are labeled or stamped with the recommended fluid type.

CHECKING FLUID LEVEL

▶ **See Figures 17, 18, 19 and 20**

Check the transmission fluid level at least every 6000 miles (9654 km) or 6 months, whichever comes first. Under extreme usage the fluid should be checked at shorter intervals or if a problem exists.

In most cases the vehicle should be on a level surface, transmission in Park, and the engine running. The fluid should be at normal operating temperature. If the vehicle has been used to haul a trailer or has been on an extended trip, wait half an hour before checking so a correct reading can be read.

1. Park the vehicle on a level surface, with the parking brake on. Start the engine and allow to idle for about 15 minutes. Move the transmission through the gears and then back to **P**.

2. Remove the dipstick and carefully touch the wet end of the dipstick to see if fluid is cool, warm, or hot. Wipe it clean and then reinsert it firmly. Be sure that it is pushed all the way in. Remove the dipstick again while holding it horizontally.

   a. If fluid is cool (room temperature), the level should be about 1/8–3/8 in. (3–10mm) below the ADD/COLD mark.

   b. If fluid is warm, the level should be close to the **ADD** mark, either above or below.

   c. If fluid is hot, the level should be at the **FULL/HOT** mark.

3. If the level is low, add the appropriate fluid through the dipstick tube. This is easily done with the aid of a funnel. Check the level often as

Fig. 17 Remove the dipstick and wipe clean. Reinsert the dipstick all the way. Remove it again and check the fluid level

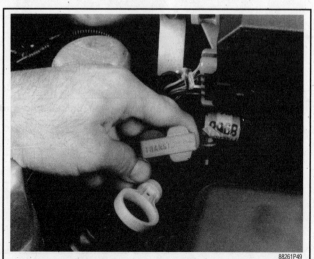

Fig. 18 Some dipsticks are hinged (locking into place to seal the guide/filler tube)

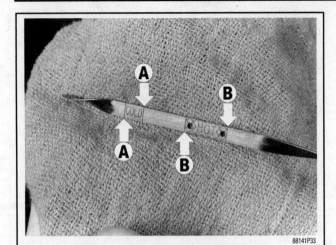

Fig. 19 The fluid level should be between the ADD and FULL marks depending upon transmission temperature. COLD (A) HOT (B) Also, check the appearance of the fluid

Fig. 20 If the level is low, add fluid through the dipstick tube, using a long funnel. Do not mix fluid types and do not overfill.

you are filling the transmission. Be extremely careful not to overfill it. Overfilling may cause slippage, seal damage and overheating. Typically, 1 pint (0.473L) of ATF will raise the fluid level from one notch/line to the other.

➡️If the fluid on the dipstick appears discolored (brown or black), or smells burnt, serious transmission troubles (probably due to overheating) should be suspected. The transmission should be inspected by a qualified technician to locate the cause of the burnt fluid.

Fluid Temperature

▶ See Figure 21

Transmission fluid is designed to last many thousands of miles under normal conditions. However, one of the most important factors affecting the life of the fluid and the transmission is the temperature of the fluid. Overheated fluid forms sludge and particles of carbon that can block the minute passages and lines that circulate the fluid throughout the transmission. This causes the transmission to overheat even more and will lead to eventual failure of the transmission.

TRANSMISSION FLUID INDICATIONS

The appearance and odor of the transmission fluid can give valuable clues to the overall condition of the transmission. Always note the appearance of the fluid when you check the fluid level or change the fluid. Rub a small amount of fluid between your fingers to feel for grit and smell the fluid on the dipstick.

If the fluid appears:	It indicates:
Clear and red colored	• Normal operation
Discolored (extremely dark red or brownish) or smells burned	• Band or clutch pack failure, usually caused by an overheated transmission. Hauling very heavy loads with insufficient power or failure to change the fluid, often result in overheating. Do not confuse this appearance with newer fluids that have a darker red color and a strong odor (though not a burned odor).
Foamy or aerated (light in color and full of bubbles)	• The level is too high (gear train is churning oil) • An internal air leak (air is mixing with the fluid). Have the transmission checked professionally.
Solid residue in the fluid	• Defective bands, clutch pack or bearings. Bits of band material or metal abrasives are clinging to the dipstick. Have the transmission checked professionally.
Varnish coating on the dipstick	• The transmission fluid is overheating

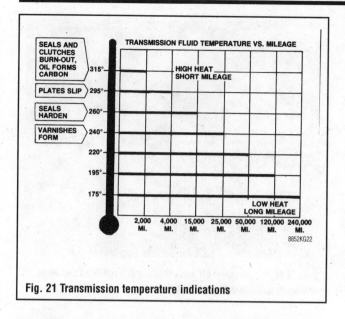

Fig. 21 Transmission temperature indications

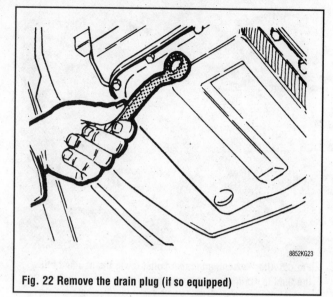

Fig. 22 Remove the drain plug (if so equipped)

Some cars come from the factory with coolers that help with the temperature. The transmission oil flows through the cooler as air flows across the cooler to lower the temperature of the transmission fluid. The coolers can be purchased at any after-market store for most cars. Some cars have warning lights for the transmission that will alert the owner of any maintenance intervals or overheating problems.

Anything that puts a load on the engine can cause the transmission to heat up and speed the deterioration of the fluid. Towing a trailer, idling in traffic and climbing long hills is all hard on a transmission. The accompanying graph illustrates just how much transmission temperature affects the life of transmission components. Fluid that lasts 50,000 miles (80,450 km) at a temperature of 220°F (104°C), will only last half that long if the temperature is consistently 20° higher.

The secret to long transmission life is regular fluid changes and keeping an eye on the condition of the fluid—both temperature and color.

CHECKING FOR LEAKS

If the fluid level is consistently low, suspect a leak. The easiest way is to slip a piece of clean newspaper under the vehicle overnight, but this is not always an accurate indication, since some leaks will occur only when the transmission is operating.

Other leaks can be located by driving the vehicle. Wipe the underside of the transmission clean and drive the vehicle for several miles to bring the fluid temperature to normal. Stop the vehicle, shut **OFF** the engine and look for leakage.

➡**Remember, however, that where the fluid is located may not be the source of the leak. Airflow around the transmission while the vehicle is moving may carry the fluid to some other point.**

CHANGING THE FLUID & FILTER

▶ **See Figures 22 thru 29**

The fluid and filter should be changed about every 24,000 miles (38,616 km) or 2 years, under normal usage. Some transmissions may have a screen that only needs cleaning. If the vehicle is used in severe service (trailer pulling, extreme stop-and-start driving, etc.), you should at least cut the interval in half.

➡**Keep in mind that this is a basic procedure, but manufacturers use many different filter configurations. For instance, Saturn and Mercedes-Benz use external spin-on filters on certain applications. For more detailed procedures written specifically for your make and model, please refer to a Chilton's Total Car Care Manual.**

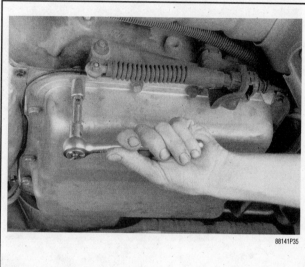

Fig. 23 Remove the pan side bolts

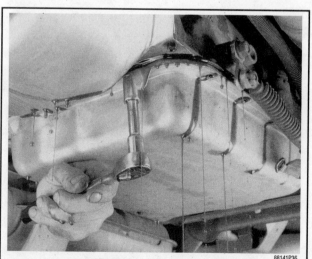

Fig. 24 When removing the front pan bolts, some fluid may start to drain out

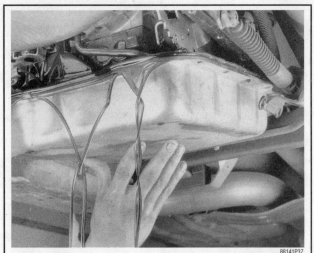

Fig. 25 After loosening the rear bolts, lower the pan and allow the fluid to drain completely

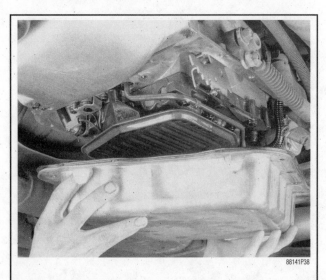

Fig. 26 Remove the rear pan bolts, then remove the oil pan

Fig. 27 Remove and discard the gasket from the fluid pan

Fig. 28 Note that some oil pans contain a magnet as shown to pickup any metal particles in the oil

Fig. 29 Remove the automatic transmission filter and seal

1. Raise and support the vehicle on jackstands. Place an suitable drain pan under the transmission. If equipped, remove the drain plug. Be careful the fluid may be hot.

2. Most late-model vehicles have no drain plug. Remove the oil pan bolts from the sides and front only.

3. Loosen the rear oil pan bolts approximately 4 turns.

4. Lightly tap the oil pan with a rubber mallet or gently pry it downward to allow fluid to drain.

✷✷ WARNING

Do not damage the transmission case or oil pan sealing surfaces.

5. Remove the remaining oil pan bolts, then remove the oil pan and pan gasket.

6. Some internal filters or screens may be held on by screws or bolts, others have an interference fit. Remove the filter and seal.

7. Clean the transmission case and oil pan gasket surfaces with suitable solvent and air dry. Make sure to remove all traces of the old gasket material.

✳✳ WARNING

Be cautious when cleaning transmission case. Cases are usually made of aluminum and are easily scored. Possible leakage could occur if case gets scored.

To install:

8. Install the new seal onto the filter.

9. Position the new filter into the case. Where applicable, install retaining brackets, bolts or nuts.

10. Install the oil pan and new gasket.

11. Install the oil pan bolts and tighten them to specifications. Do not overtighten the bolts.

12. Carefully lower the vehicle.

13. Fill the transmission to proper level with the correct automatic transmission fluid.

14. Check cold fluid level reading for initial fill. Do not overfill the transmission.

15. Follow the fluid level check procedure described earlier.

16. Check the oil pan gasket for leaks.

Servicing the Transmission

Aside from changing the fluid and filter and tightening nuts and bolts, repair or overhaul of the automatic transmission should be left to a trained technician. This is because there are some many special tools needed for inspection (such as hydraulic pressure testers, electronic scan tools for retrieving trouble codes, etc.) and for the repair of the transmissions. Transmissions are heavy and special jacks or hydraulic tables are needed to remove them from the vehicle. In some cases special tools are used to separate the transmission from the engine.

AUTOMATIC TRANSMISSION MAINTENANCE INTERVALS

To keep your automatic transmission as troublefree as possible, it should be maintained at the following intervals.

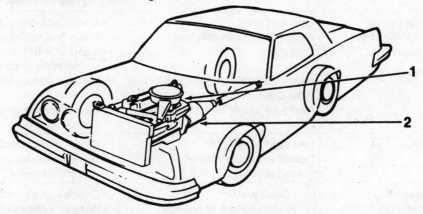

1. **Check fluid level ▲**	**Every 6000 miles/6 months**
Check fluid condition ▲ (color and odor)	
2. **Change fluid ▲**	**Every 24,000 miles/24 months**
Replace filter or clean screen ▲	

▲ If the vehicle is used for severe service (trailer pulling, constant stop/start driving, off-road operation), cut the interval in half.

8852KC24

TROUBLESHOOTING BASIC AUTOMATIC TRANSMISSION PROBLEMS

Given proper maintenance and care, the automatic transmission will provide many miles of trouble-free operation. Most minor problems can be traced to fluid level; maintaining the proper fluid level will avoid these problems. Keeping alert to changes in the operation of the transmission (different shifting patterns, abnormal sounds, fluid leakage) can prevent small problems from becoming large ones. If the problem cannot be traced to loose bolts, fluid level, overheating or clogged filter seek professional service.

Problem	Is Caused By	What to Do
Fluid leakage	• Defective pan gasket • Loose filler tube • Loose extension housing to transmission case • Converter housing area leakage	• Replace gasket or tighten pan bolts • Tighten tube nut • Tighten bolts • Have transmission checked professionally
Fluid flows out the oil filler tube	• High fluid level • Breather vent clogged • Clogged oil filter or screen • Internal fluid leakage	• Check and correct fluid level • Open breather vent • Replace filter or clean screen (change fluid also) • Have transmission checked professionally
Transmission overheats (this is usually accompanied by a strong burned odor to the fluid)	• Low fluid level • Fluid cooler lines clogged • Heavy pulling or hauling with insufficient cooling • Faulty oil pump, internal slippage	• Check and correct fluid level • Drain and refill transmission. If this doesn't cure the problem, have cooler lines cleared or replaced. • Install a transmission oil cooler. • Have transmission checked professionally.
Buzzing or whining noise	• Low fluid level • Defective torque converter, scored gears	• Check and correct fluid level • Have transmission checked professionally
No forward or reverse gears or slippage in one or more gears	• Low fluid level • Defective vacuum or linkage controls, internal clutch or band failure	• Check and correct fluid level • Have unit checked professionally
Delayed or erratic shift	• Low fluid level • Broken vacuum lines • Internal malfunction	• Check and correct fluid level • Repair or replace lines • Have transmission checked professionally

8852KC25

22

DRIVELINE

DRIVESHAFTS AND DRIVE AXLES 22-2

DRIVESHAFTS AND DRIVE AXLES

Driveshafts

▶ See Figures 1 and 2

In a conventional longitudinally mounted front-engine/rear wheel drive vehicle, a driveshaft is used to transfer the torque from the engine, through the transmission output shaft, to the differential in the axle, which in turn transmits torque to the wheels. The driveshaft can be made out of steel or aluminum and can be either solid or hollow (tubular).

A splined slip yoke assembly, either as an integral part of the shaft or utilizing a splined transmission output shaft, permits the driveshaft to move forward and rearward as the axle moves up and down. This provides smooth performance during vehicle operation.

On some four wheel drive vehicles, a front driveshaft connects the power flow from the transfer case to the front drive axle.

The driveshaft uses flexible joints, called Universal joints (U-joints) or Constant Velocity joints (CV-joints) to couple the transmission/transaxle to the drive axle/drive wheels. Refer to the Universal and Constant Velocity joints section for more information.

Front wheel drive vehicles also utilize driveshafts, although they are usually referred to as halfshafts. The halfshafts are usually equipped with CV-joints on each end which allow the wheels to turn as well as move up and down while still smoothly transferring engine power to the wheels. Front wheel drive vehicles typically use a transaxle (a combination TRANSmission and drive AXLE)

Some rear and four wheel drive vehicles use halfshafts. These vehicles will usually have a rigidly mounted differential and an independent suspension with halfshafts linking the differential to the drive wheels. For example, the 1998 Chevrolet Corvette; not only does it use halfshafts to drive the rear wheels, the rigidly mounted transaxle is actually in the rear of the vehicle with a driveshaft connecting the front mounted engine to the transaxle! As another example, the four wheel drive Subaru models; these vehicles use a modified front wheel drive transaxle assembly with an additional power output. A driveshaft couples the front transaxle to the rear differential with four halfshafts driving the front and rear wheels.

Universal and Constant Velocity Joints

▶ See Figures 3, 4, 5, 6 and 7

Because of changes in the angle between the driveshaft or halfshaft and the axle housing or driven wheel, U-joints and CV-joints are used to provide flexibility. The engine is mounted rigidly to the vehicle frame (or subframe), while the driven wheels are free to move up and down in relation to the vehicle frame. The angle between the driveshaft or halfshaft and the axle housing or driven wheels changes constantly as the vehicle responds to various road conditions.

To give flexibility and still transmit power as smoothly as possible, several types of U-joints or CV-joints are used.

The most common type of universal joint is the cross and yoke type. Yokes are used on the ends of the driveshaft with the yoke arms opposite each other. Another yoke is used opposite the driveshaft and when placed together, both yokes engage a center member, or cross, with four arms spaced 90° apart. A bearing cup is used on each arm of the cross to accommodate movement as the driveshaft rotates.

The second type is the ball and trunnion universal, a T-shaped shaft that is enclosed in the body of the joint. The trunnion ends are each equipped with a ball mounted in needle bearings and move freely in grooves in the outer body of the joint, in effect creating a slip-joint. This type of joint is always enclosed.

A conventional universal joint will cause the driveshaft to speed up or slow through each revolution and cause a corresponding change in the

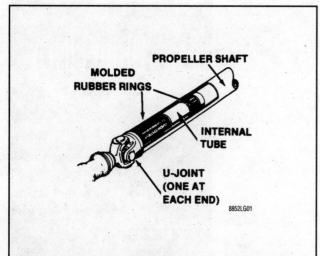

Fig. 1 Cut-away view of a typical solid driveshaft and related components

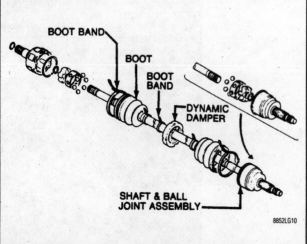

Fig. 2 Exploded view of a typical front wheel drive halfshaft assembly using CV joint components on both ends

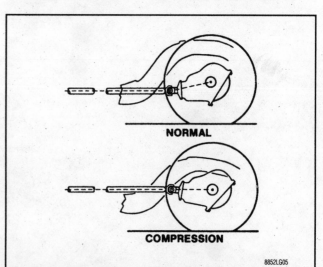

Fig. 3 U-joints are necessary to compensate for changes in the angle between the driveshaft and the drive axle

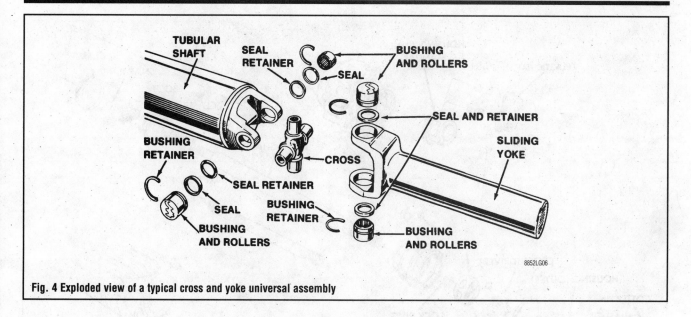

Fig. 4 Exploded view of a typical cross and yoke universal assembly

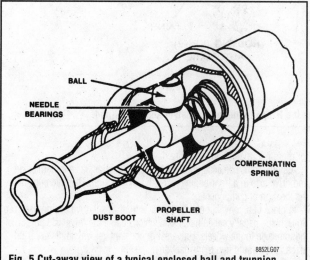

Fig. 5 Cut-away view of a typical enclosed ball and trunnion type U-joint

velocity of the driven shaft. This change in speed causes natural vibrations to occur through the driveline necessitating a third type of universal joint— the double cardan joint. A rolling ball moves in a curved groove, located between two yoke-and-cross universal joints, connected to each other by a coupling yoke. The result is uniform motion as the driveshaft rotates, avoiding the fluctuations in driveshaft speeds.

The CV-joints, which are most commonly associated with front wheel drive vehicles, include the Rzeppa, the double offset, Tri-pod and Birfield joint.

The Rzeppa and double offset are similar in construction. They use a multi-grooved cross which is attached to the shaft. Balls ride in the cross grooves and are retained to the cross by a cage. The entire assembly then slides into an outer housing which has matching grooves for the balls to ride in.

The Tri-pod design is similar to the ball and trunnion design, except it has three needle bearing mounted balls inside the housing space evenly apart (thus its name).

The newest of the CV-joints is called the Birfield. This joint is primarily found on import vehicles although some domestic vehicles are starting to use it as well. This joint is not serviceable and the manufacturers give no pictures or descriptions of its construction.

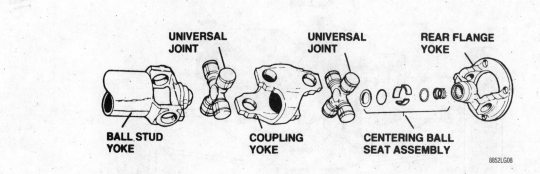

Fig. 6 Exploded view of a typical double cardan U-joint assembly

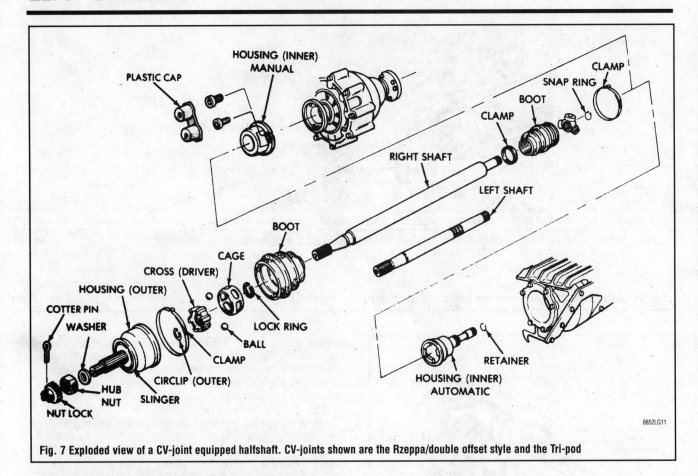

Fig. 7 Exploded view of a CV-joint equipped halfshaft. CV-joints shown are the Rzeppa/double offset style and the Tri-pod

Front wheel Drive

▶ **See Figure 8**

Front wheel drive vehicles are the more common arrangement for most cars and mini-vans these days. These vehicles do not have conventional transmissions, drive axles or driveshafts. Instead, power is transmitted from the engine to a transaxle, or combination of transmission and drive axle, in one unit. Refer to the Automatic or Manual Transmission/Transaxle Section for more information on the transaxle.

A single transaxle accomplishes the same functions as a transmission and drive axle in a front-engine/rear-drive axle design. The difference is in the location of components.

In place of a conventional driveshaft, a front wheel drive design uses two driveshafts, usually called halfshafts, which couple the drive axle portion of the transaxle to the wheels. Universal or constant velocity joints are used just as they would in a rear wheel drive design.

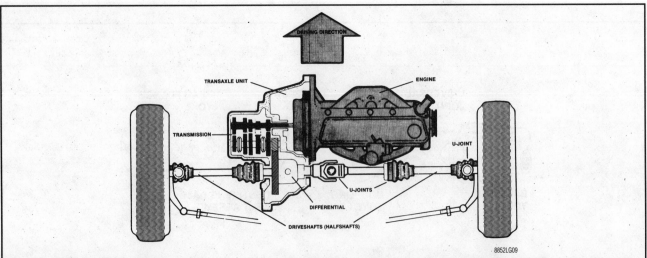

Fig. 8 Example of a typical transverse engine, front wheel drive system. Notice that the components are similar to the rear wheel drive systems, except for location

Rear wheel Drive

▶ **See Figure 9**

Rear wheel drive vehicles are mostly trucks, very large sedans and many sports car and coupe models. The typical rear wheel drive vehicle uses a front mounted engine and transmission assemblies with a driveshaft coupling the transmission to the rear drive axle. The rear axle assembly is usually a solid (or live) axle, although some import and/or performance models have used a rigidly mounted center differential with halfshafts coupling the wheels to the differential.

Some vehicles do not follow this typical example. Such as the older Porsche or Volkswagen vehicles which were rear engine, rear drive. These vehicles use a rear mounted transaxle with halfshafts connected to the drive wheels. Also, some vehicles were produced with a front engine, rear transaxle setup with a driveshaft connecting the engine to the transaxle, and halfshafts linking the transaxle to the drive wheels.

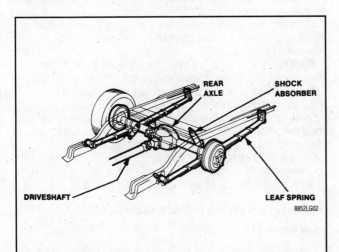

Fig. 9 View of the typical rear wheel drive axle system with leaf springs

Four wheel Drive

▶ **See Figure 10**

When the vehicle is driven by both the front and rear wheels, two complete axle assemblies are used and power from the engine is directed to both drive axles at the same time. A transfer case may be attached to, or mounted near, the rear of the transmission/transaxle and directs the power flow to the rear and/or front axles through two driveshafts. Since the angles between the front and rear driveshafts change constantly, slip joints are used on the shafts to accommodate the changes in distance between axles and transfer case.

Another form of four or All Wheel Drive (AWD) design may use a front mounted engine and modified front wheel drive transaxle assembly with an additional power output. Two halfshafts connect the front wheels to the transaxle. Some models may have a transfer case connected to the transaxle's additional power output. A driveshaft couples the front transaxle or transfer case to the rear differential with two halfshafts driving the rear wheels.

Shifting devices attached to transfer cases disengage the front drive axle when four wheel drive capability is not needed. However, some newer trans-

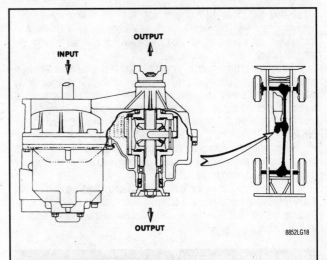

Fig. 10 Typical transmission and transfer case design four wheel drive system. The shaded area represents the power flow.

fer cases are in constant mesh and cannot be totally disengaged. These are known as "full-time" four wheel drive and are just what the name says, four wheel drive operating all the time. This is made possible by a either differential in the transfer case or through the use of a hydraulic viscous coupling.

Jeep® vehicles use a full-time system called Quadra-Trac, which is full-time four wheel drive with a limited slip differential in the transfer case. All you have to do is drive.

VISCOUS COUPLING TRANSFER CASE

Back in the early 80's, American Motors created a full-time four wheel drive system that requires no action by the driver to activate the system, and take advantage of the improved traction and handling of four wheel drive.

Since this time other similar systems have been implemented both in domestic and import vehicles.

The heart of these systems is a transfer case, which distributes the torque between front and rear axles by means of a viscous or fluid coupling. The coupling provides a slip-limiting action and absorbs minor driveline vibrations, giving smoother and quieter operation.

When the front and rear driveshafts turn at the same speed, as they do when the vehicle drives straight down the road, there is no differential action. In a turn or other maneuvers where front and rear wheels must travel slightly different distances, differential action is required because the driveshafts must be able to rotate at slightly different speeds. When this happens, the fluid in the coupling—a liquid silicone—permits normal differential action.

Greater variations in speed between the driveshafts, such as occur when a wheel or pair of wheels encounter reduced traction and tend to spin, bring the viscous coupling's slip-limiting characteristics into action. The action of the viscous coupling is velocity-sensitive, permitting the comparatively slow movements typical of normal differential action but quickly building up resistance and effectively transmitting available torque to the axle with the best traction.

The action of the fluid between the plates in the coupling could be compared to the action of water against a body when wading across a pool. In waist-deep water, a person can walk with comparatively little effort as long as he moves slowly and gently. However, when he tries to hurry, the additional effort that is required is proportionate to the increase in speed one attempts to achieve. Therefore, it is with the viscous coupling. However, instead of water, there is liquid silicone with a viscosity nearly the consistency of honey.

This four wheel drive system is more efficient than other automatic four wheel drive systems because there is no "open" differential (as opposed to a limited-slip differential) between the driveshafts. In the "open" differential system, the loss of traction at one wheel results in no torque being delivered to the other wheels, since it is the nature of the open differential to deliver motion to the "easy" shaft—the one that is slipping. When using a viscous coupling, the loss of traction at one wheel on the rear axle, brings the slip-limiting character of the viscous coupling into action, causing drive torque to be transferred to the front axle.

In addition to the differential function, the viscous coupling also improves braking effectiveness. It acts as a skid deterrent, tending to equalize drive-shaft speeds when the wheels at one end or the other wants to lock and slide.

Drive Axle/Differential

All vehicles will have some type of drive axle/differential assembly incorporated into the driveline. Whether it is front, rear or four wheel drive, differentials are necessary for the smooth application of engine power to the road.

POWERFLOW

▶ **See Figure 11**

The drive axle must transmit power through a 90° angle. The flow of power in conventional front engine/rear wheel drive vehicles moves from the engine to the drive axle in approximately a straight line. However, at the drive axle, the power must be turned at right angles (from the line of the driveshaft) and directed to the drive wheels.

This is accomplished by a pinion drive gear, which turns a circular ring gear. The ring gear is attached to a differential housing, containing a set of smaller gears that are splined to the inner end of each axle shaft. As the housing is rotated, the internal differential gears turn the axle shafts, which are also attached to the drive wheels.

DIFFERENTIAL OPERATION

▶ **See Figure 12**

The differential is an arrangement of gears with two functions: to permit the rear wheels to turn at different speeds when cornering and to divide the power flow between both rear wheels.

The accompanying illustration has been provided to help understand how this occurs. The drive pinion, which is turned by the driveshaft, turns the ring gear (1).

The ring gear, which is attached to the differential case, turns the case (2).

The pinion shaft, located in a bore in the differential case, is at right angles to the axle shafts and turns with the case (3).

The differential pinion (drive) gears are mounted on the pinion shaft and rotate with the shaft (4).

Differential side gears (driven gears) are meshed with the pinion gears and turn with the differential housing and ring gear as a unit (5).

The side gears are splined to the inner ends of the axle shafts and rotate the shafts as the housing turns (6).

When both wheels have equal traction, the pinion gears do not rotate on the pinion shaft, since the input force of the pinion gears is divided equally between the two side gears (7).

When it is necessary to turn a corner, the differential gearing becomes effective and allows the axle shafts to rotate at different speeds (8).

As the inner wheel slows down, the side gear splined to the inner wheel axle shaft also slows. The pinion gears act as balancing levers by maintaining equal tooth loads to both gears, while allowing unequal speeds of rotation at the axle shafts. If the vehicle speed remains constant, and the inner wheel slows down to 90 percent of vehicle speed, the outer wheel will speed up to 110 percent. However, because this system is known as an open differential, if one wheel should become stuck (as in mud or snow), all of the engine power can be transferred to only one wheel.

Limited-Slip and Locking Differential Operation

▶ **See Figure 13**

Limited-slip and locking differentials provide the driving force to the wheel with the best traction before the other wheel begins to spin. This is accomplished through clutch plates, cones or locking pawls.

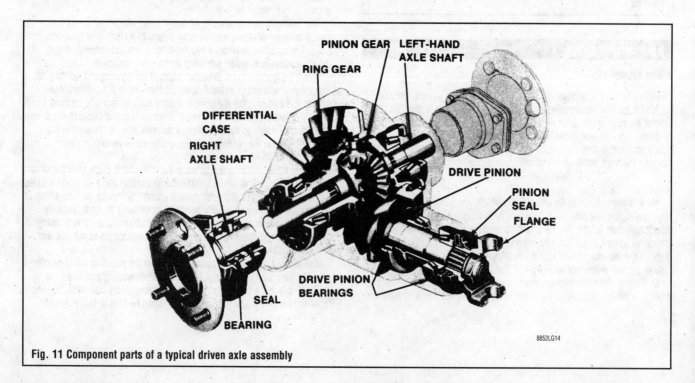

Fig. 11 Component parts of a typical driven axle assembly

8852LG14

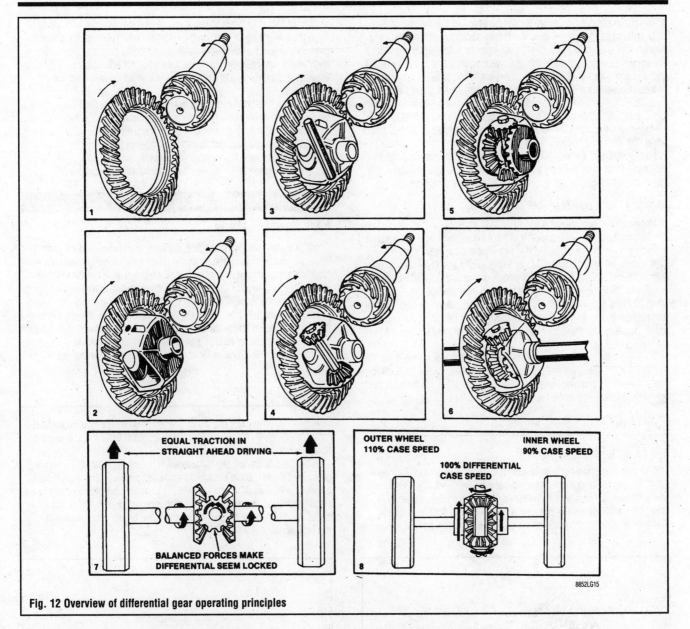

Fig. 12 Overview of differential gear operating principles

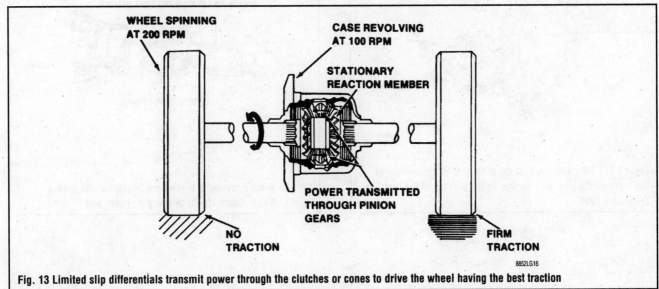

Fig. 13 Limited slip differentials transmit power through the clutches or cones to drive the wheel having the best traction

The clutch plates or cones are located between the side gears and the inner walls of the differential case. When they are squeezed together through spring tension and outward force from the side gears, three reactions occur. Resistance on the side gears causes more torque to be exerted on the clutch packs or clutch cones. Rapid one wheel spin cannot occur, because the side gear is forced to turn at the same speed as the case. So most importantly, with the side gear and the differential case turning at the same speed, the other wheel is forced to rotate in the same direction and at the same speed as the differential case. Thus, driving force is applied to the wheel with the better traction.

Locking differentials work similar the clutch and cone type of limited slip, except that when tire speed differential occurs, the unit will physically lock both axles together and spin them as if they were a solid shaft.

IDENTIFYING A LIMITED-SLIP DRIVE AXLE

Metal tags are normally attached to the axle assembly at the filler plug or to a bolt on the cover. During the life of the vehicle, these tags can become lost and other means must be used to identify the drive axle.

To determine whether a vehicle has a limited-slip or a conventional drive axle by tire movement, raise the rear wheels off the ground. Place the transmission in PARK (automatic) or LOW (manual), and attempt to turn a drive wheel by hand. If the drive axle is a limited-slip type, it will be very difficult (or impossible) to turn the wheel. If the drive axle is the conventional (open) type, the wheel will turn easily, and the opposing wheel will rotate in the reverse direction.

Place the transmission in neutral and again rotate a rear wheel. If the axle is a limited-slip type, the opposite wheel will rotate in the same direction. If the axle is a conventional type, the opposite wheel will rotate in the opposite direction, if it rotates at all.

GEAR RATIO

▶ **See Figure 14**

The drive axle of a vehicle is said to have a certain axle ratio. This number (usually a whole number and a decimal fraction) is actually a comparison of the number of gear teeth on the ring gear and the pinion gear. For example, a 4.11 rear means that theoretically, there are 4.11 teeth on the ring gear for each tooth on the pinion gear or, put another way, the drive-shaft must turn 4.11 times to turn the wheels once. Actually, with a 4.11 ratio, there might be 37 teeth on the ring gear and 9 teeth on the pinion gear. By dividing the number of teeth on the pinion gear into the number of teeth on the ring gear, the numerical axle ratio (4.11) is obtained. This also provides a good method of ascertaining exactly which axle ratio one is dealing with.

Another method of determining gear ratio is to jack up and support the vehicle so that both drive wheels are off the ground. Make a chalk mark on the drive wheel and the driveshaft. Put the transmission in neutral. Turn the wheel one complete turn and count the number of turns that the drive-shaft/halfshaft makes. The number of turns that the driveshaft makes in one complete revolution of the drive wheel approximates the axle ratio.

Driveline Maintenance

▶ **See Figures 15 and 16**

Maintenance includes inspecting the level of and changing the gear lubricant, and lubricating the universal joints if they are equipped with "zerk" or grease fittings. Apply high temperature chassis grease to the U-joints. CV-joints require special grease, which usually comes in a kit along with a new rubber boot.

Most modern universal joints are of the "extended life" design, meaning that they are sealed and require no periodic lubrication. However, it is wise to inspect the joints for hidden grease plugs or fittings, initially.

Also, inspect the driveline for abnormal looseness, whenever the vehicle is serviced.

DRIVE AXLE LUBRICANTS

In general, drive axles use either SAE 80 or 90 weight gear oil for lubrication, meeting API (American Petroleum Institute) GL-4 or GL-5 specifications. This will be stated on the container.

In the case of limited-slip drive axles, it is very important that the proper gear lube be used. Some manufacturers have specific friction modifying additives, which must be used as well. The wrong lubricant can damage the clutch packs and cause grabbing or chattering on turns. If this condition exists, try draining the oil and refilling with the proper gear lube before having it serviced.

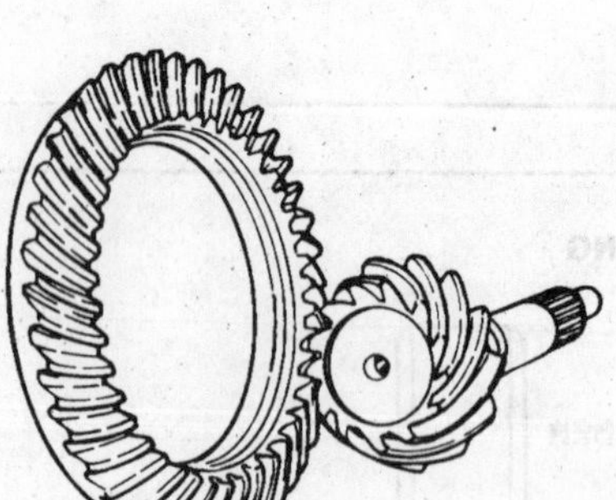

8852LG17

Fig. 14 The numerical ratio of the drive axle is the number of the teeth on the ring gear divided by the number of the teeth on the pinion gear

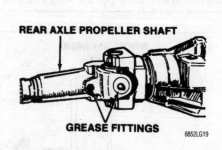

8852LG19

Fig. 15 Some driveshafts U-joint are equipped with grease (zerk) fittings. Lubricate these using a grease gun.

DRIVESHAFT AND REAR AXLE PERIODIC MAINTENANCE

The driveshaft and rear (drive) axle should give trouble-free service if they are maintained at these intervals.

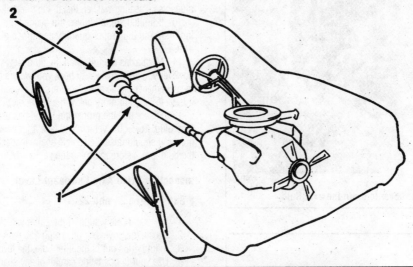

1. **Lubricate universal joints**	**6 months/6000 miles**
2. **Check rear (drive) axle fluid level ▲**	**6 months/6000 miles**
3. **Change rear (drive) axle fluid ▲**	**2 years/24,000 miles**

▲ If the vehicle is used for severe service (trailer pulling, continual stop/start driving, off-road operation) cut the maintenance interval in half.

8852LC20

Fig. 16 Recommended service intervals

Changing Drive Axle Lubricant

▶ **See Figures 17, 18, 19 and 20**

There are two types of drive axle design. One type uses a removable (bolted-on) rear cover (integral carrier) and the other type uses no rear cover (removable carrier).

Most integral carrier axles do not have a drain plug to use when changing lubricant. The rear cover must be unbolted and removed in order to drain the fluid.

Removable carrier axles usually have a drain plug, which allows you to easily drain the fluid. Although if there is no drain plug on the housing, the entire carrier assembly will need to be removed from the housing in order to change the fluid.

An alternative to removing the cover, or carrier is to purchase an inexpensive suction gun that can be used to suck the fluid out through the filler hole, and will make installing new fluid easier.

Before deciding to change the drive axle fluid, examine the unit carefully to determine if a drain plug exists. If there is no drain plug, make sure to have a new gasket, or a tube of silicone sealant for the carrier or cover before draining the fluid.

1. Ensure that you have enough of the proper grade of drive axle lubricant, including any limited slip additives if so required. Also have a new gasket or tube of silicone sealant on hand if removing the carrier or cover is necessary.

2. Raise and safely support both the front and rear of the vehicle. Support the vehicle in a level position to assure a proper reading of the fluid level when refilling the axle later.

3. Gather up a drain pan, some rags and the tools necessary to remove the fill plug, the drain plug (if equipped) and/or the cover/carrier from the axle housing. If the carrier must be removed, you must also remove the drive wheels and any components which retain the axles, as well as the driveshaft and/or halfshafts.

4. Before draining the fluid, always remove the fluid filler plug first. This will ensure that you can refill the axle housing before you render the vehicle inoperable should the fill plug be seized or stripped.

5. If the axle housing is equipped with a drain plug, position the drain pan beneath the housing and remove the plug.

6. If no drain plug exists, consider using a suction gun to pull the fluid from the housing through the filler hole. While this is not as complete a service as a full drain down (as some old fluid will be left in the housing), it may be an easier task than removing the cover or carrier from the vehicle.

85551110

Fig. 17 Integral carrier axles sometimes have only a filler plug. In these cases, and if equipped, remove the rear cover attaching bolts . . .

Fig. 18 . . . then the rear cover to drain the axle fluid

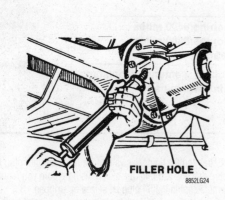

FILLER HOLE

8852LG24

Fig. 19 Also, axle fluid can be removed or installed using a suction gun through the filler hole

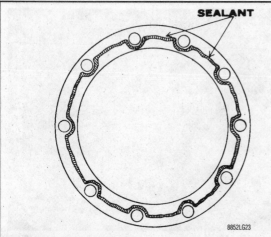

SEALANT

8852LG23

Fig. 20 To form your own gasket, apply the sealant in an ⅛ inch continuous bead as shown. Follow the manufacturers directions for hardening time.

7. If not using a suction gun, position the drain pan beneath the axle housing and remove the cover or carrier and allow the fluid to drain.

8. If removed, thoroughly clean the cover and carrier gasket mating surfaces of any oil, grease or dirt. Install a new gasket or apply silicone sealant the mating surfaces and reinstall the cover or carrier.

9. If equipped, install a new sealing washer to the drain plug. Not all plugs use a sealing washer. Install the drain plug and tighten securely.

10. If limited slip additives are needed, pour them into the axle housing first. Add the proper quantity and grade of lubricant to the drive axle.

11. Most axles are full when the fluid slowly drips from the fill hole, however you should always check you owners manual for any specific level measurements (some manufacturers may recommend the fluid is full when it is ¼–⅝ inch or more below the filler hole).

12. Ensure that the proper fluid level has been achieved and install the filler plug. Lower the vehicle and take it for a test drive. As an extra precaution, you should raise the vehicle again, inspect for leaks and double check the fluid level before returning the vehicle to full-time road use.

Inspecting Drive Axle Lubricant Level

▶ See Figures 21 and 22

1. Raise and safely support the entire vehicle in a level position.
2. Locate the drive axle filler plug and remove it.
3. If fluid drips out of the filler hole, the level is full.
4. Use your finger, being careful of any sharp threads, and feel inside the filler hole for the fluid. If no fluid can be felt, you are probably low, however, some manufacturers have an allowable distance which the fluid level can be below the filler plug. Check you owners manual if unsure.
5. As necessary, add the proper grade of lubricant until a full reading is achieved.
6. Install the filler plug and lower the vehicle.

TRANSFER CASE LUBRICANT

Transfer cases can use either 80W or 90W gear lube, or they may use Automatic Transmission Fluid (ATF) or motor oil. If equipped with a limited slip device in the transfer case, additives may be required. Check with your owners manual to ensure that the proper fluid is used.

✳✳ WARNING

Installing the wrong fluid can cause serious damage to the transfer case unit.

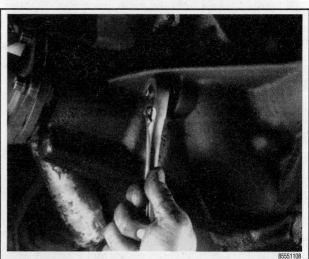

85551108

Fig. 21 To check the drive axle lubricant, loosen the fluid filler plug . . .

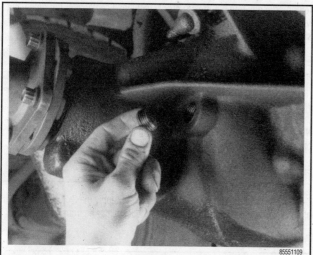

Fig. 22 . . . then remove it. The fluid level should be at, or just below, the filler hole

Changing Transfer Case Lubricant

Most transfer cases have both a filler plug and a drain plug. If no drain plug is available on your case, a suction gun must be used.

1. Ensure that you have enough of the proper grade of transfer case lubricant, including any limited slip additives if so required.
2. Raise and safely support both the front and rear of the vehicle. Support the vehicle in a level position to assure a proper reading of the fluid level when refilling the transfer case later.
3. Gather up a drain pan, some rags and the tools necessary to remove the fill plug and the drain plug (if equipped)
4. Before draining the fluid, always remove the fluid filler plug first. This will ensure that you can refill the transfer case before you render the vehicle inoperable should the fill plug be seized or stripped.
5. If the transfer case is equipped with a drain plug, position the drain pan beneath the case and remove the plug.
6. If no drain plug exists, use a suction gun to pull the fluid from the housing through the filler hole. While this is not as complete a service as a full drain down (as some old fluid will be left in the case), it will ensure that most of the fluid is new.
7. If equipped, install a new sealing washer to the drain plug. Not all plugs use a sealing washer. Install the drain plug and tighten securely.
8. If limited slip additives are needed, pour them into the transfer case first. Add the proper quantity and grade of lubricant to the transfer case.
9. Most cases are full when the fluid slowly drips from the fill hole, however you should always check you owners manual for any specific level measurements (some manufacturers may recommend the fluid is full when it is 1/4–5/8 inch or more below the filler hole).
10. Ensure that the proper fluid level has been achieved and install the filler plug. Lower the vehicle and take it for a test drive. As an extra precaution, you should raise the vehicle again, inspect for leaks and double check the fluid level before returning the vehicle to full-time road use.

Inspecting the Transfer Case Lubricant Level

1. Raise and safely support the entire vehicle in a level position.
2. Locate the transfer case filler plug and remove it.
3. If fluid drips out of the filler hole, the level is full.
4. Use your finger, being careful of any sharp threads, and feel inside the filler hole for the fluid. If no fluid can be felt, you are probably low, however, some manufacturers have an allowable distance which the fluid level can be below the filler plug. Check you owners manual if unsure.
5. As necessary, add the proper grade of lubricant until a full reading is achieved.
6. Install the filler plug and lower the vehicle.

CV-BOOT INSPECTION

▶ **See Figures 23 and 24**

It is vitally important during any service procedures requiring boot handling, that care be taken not to puncture or tear the boot by over tightening clamps, misuse of tool(s) or pinching the boot. Pinching can occur by rotating the CV joints (especially the tripod) beyond normal working angles.

The driveshaft boots are not compatible with oil, gasoline, or cleaning solvents. Care must be taken that the boots never encounter any of these liquids.

➡**The ONLY acceptable cleaning agent for driveshaft boots is soap and water. After washing, the boot must be thoroughly rinsed and dried before reusing.**

Many manufacturers recommend inspecting the CV-boots at every oil change (every 3,000 miles or 4,800 km). However, a good rule of thumb is that, if the vehicle needs to be raised for any procedure, check the CV-boots. Noticeable amounts of grease on areas adjacent to or on the exterior of the CV joint boot is the first indication that a boot is punctured, torn or that a clamp has loosened. When a CV joint is removed for servicing of the joint, the boot should be properly cleaned and inspected for cracks, tears and scuffed areas on the interior surfaces. If any of these conditions exist, boot replacement is recommended.

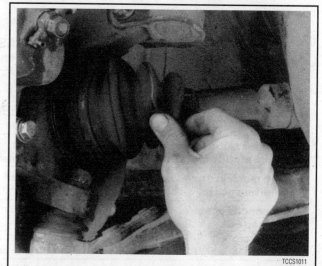

Fig. 23 Inspect CV-Boots periodically for damage

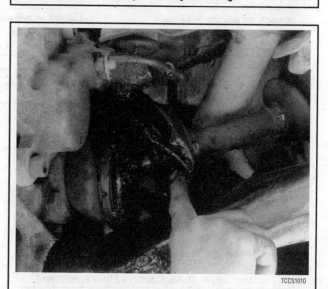

Fig. 24 A torn boot should be replaced immediately

Basic Drive Axle Problems

Drive axle problems frequently give warnings in the form of abnormal noises. Unfortunately, they are often confused with noise produced by other parts.

First, determine when the noise is most noticeable.

- Drive noise: Produced during vehicle acceleration.
- Coast noise: Produced while the vehicle coasts with a closed throttle.
- Float noise: Occurs while maintaining constant vehicle speed on a level road.

Second, make a thorough check to be sure the noises are coming from the drive axle, and not from some other part of the car.

ROAD NOISE

Brick or rough concrete roads produce noises that seem to come from the drive axle. Road noise is usually identical whether driving or coasting. Driving on a different type of road will tell whether the road is the problem.

TIRE NOISE

Tire noises are often mistaken for drive axle problems. Snow treads or unevenly worn tires produce vibrations seeming to originate elsewhere.

Temporarily inflating the tires to 40 psi will significantly alter tire noise, but will have no effect on drive axle noises (which normally cease below about 30 mph).

ENGINE/TRANSMISSION NOISE

Determine at what speed the noise is most pronounced and then stop the vehicle in a quiet place. With the transmission in Neutral, run the engine through speeds corresponding to road speeds where the noise was noticed. Noises produced with the vehicle standing still are coming from the engine or transmission.

FRONT WHEEL BEARINGS

While holding the vehicle speed steady, lightly apply the foot brake; this will often decrease bearing noise, as some of the load is taken from the bearing.

DRIVE AXLE NOISES

Eliminating other possible sources can narrow the cause to the drive axle, which normally produces noise from worn gears or bearings. Gear noises tend to peak in a narrow speed range, while bearing noises will usually vary in pitch with engine speeds.

TROUBLESHOOTING BASIC DRIVESHAFT PROBLEMS

When abnormal vibrations or noises are detected in the driveshaft area, this chart can be used to help diagnose possible causes. Remember that other components such as wheels, tires, rear axle and suspension can also produce similar conditions.

BASIC DRIVESHAFT PROBLEMS

The Problem	Is Caused By	What to Do
Shudder as car accelerates from stop or low speed	• Loose U-joint • Defective center bearing	• Tighten U-joint or have it replaced • Have center bearing replaced
Loud clunk in driveshaft when shifting gears	• Worn U-joints	• Have U-joints replaced
Roughness or vibration at any speed	• Out-of-balance, bent or dented driveshaft • Worn U-joints • U-joint clamp bolts loose	• Have driveshaft serviced • Have U-joints serviced • Tighten U-joint clamp bolts
Squeaking noise at low speeds	• Lack of U-joint lubrication	• Lubricate U-joint; if problem persists, have U-joint serviced
Knock or clicking noise	• U-joint or driveshaft hitting frame tunnel • Worn constant velocity joint	• Correct overloaded condition • Have constant velocity joint replaced

NOISE DIAGNOSIS

The Noise Is	Most Probably Produced By
1. Identical under Drive or Coast	Road surface, tires or front wheel bearings
2. Different depending on road surface	Road surface or tires
3. Lower as the car speed is lowered	Tires
4. Similar with car standing or moving	Engine or transmission
5. A vibration	Unbalanced tires, rear wheel bearing, unbalanced driveshaft or worn U-joint
6. A knock or click about every 2 tire revolutions	Rear wheel bearing
7. Most pronounced on turns	Damaged differential gears
8. A steady low-pitched whirring or scraping, starting at low speeds	Damaged or worn pinion bearing
9. A chattering vibration on turns	Wrong differential lubricant or worn clutch plates (limited slip rear axle)
10. Noticed only in Drive, Coast or Float conditions	Worn ring gear and/or pinion gear

8852LC26

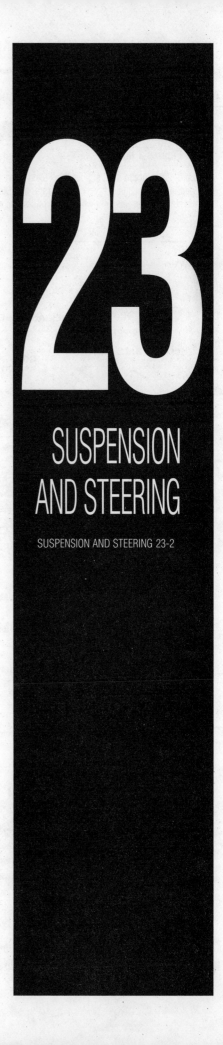

23

SUSPENSION AND STEERING

SUSPENSION AND STEERING

Types of Front Suspensions

▶ **See Figures 1 thru 7**

The most common front suspensions used on vehicles today are the independent (2 unequal length control arms) and McPherson strut suspension systems. (used on front wheel drive and some rear wheel drive vehicles).

INDEPENDENT FRONT SUSPENSION

▶ **See Figures 2 and 3**

This is also called an unequal length A-arm or control arm type, because the upper and lower control arms attached to the frame are of different lengths. This design is typical of American sedans and is designed this way to reduce tire scuffing.

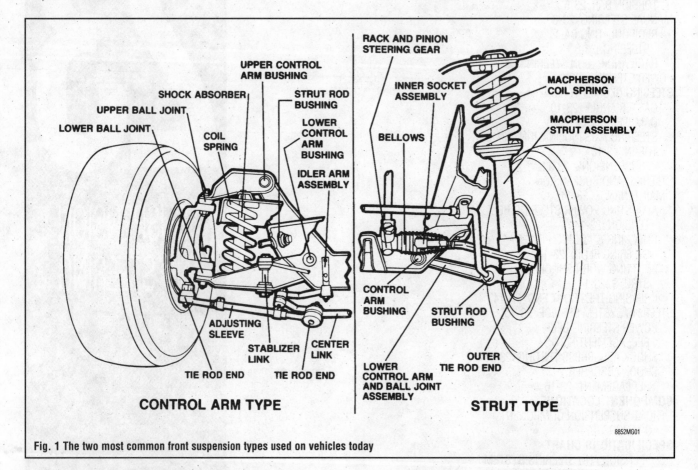

Fig. 1 The two most common front suspension types used on vehicles today

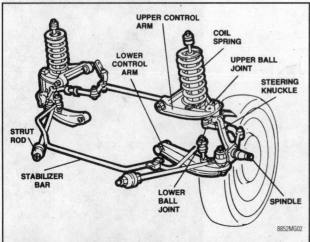

Fig. 2 On this design, the coil spring is mounted on top of the upper control arm with the shock absorber in the center of the coil spring. Only the upper control arm is of A-arm design

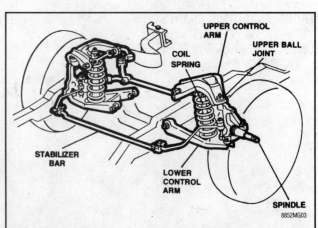

Fig. 3 Typical unequal length A-arm suspension used on rear wheel drive sedans. In this design, the shock absorber and coil spring are positioned between the upper and lower control arms. Note that the control arms (A-arms) are not the same length

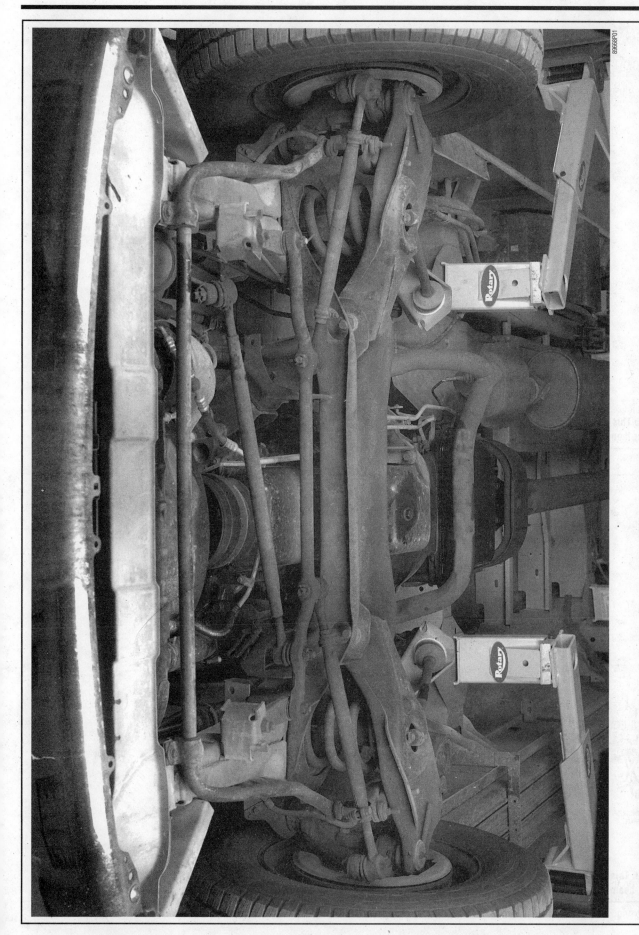

Fig. 4 This independent front truck suspension is very similar to the unequal length A-arm suspension used on rear wheel drive sedans. It functions in the same manner, but the components are of a heavier duty construction to handle the added stress

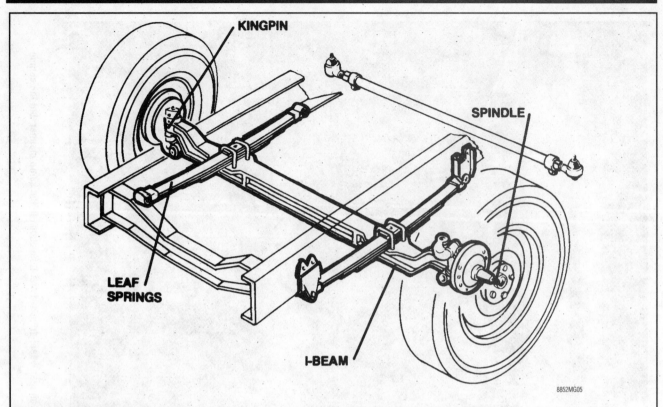

Fig. 5 This straight I-beam front suspension, used mostly in heavy duty trucks, is uncomplicated and meant to handle heavy loads, rather than give a comfortable ride

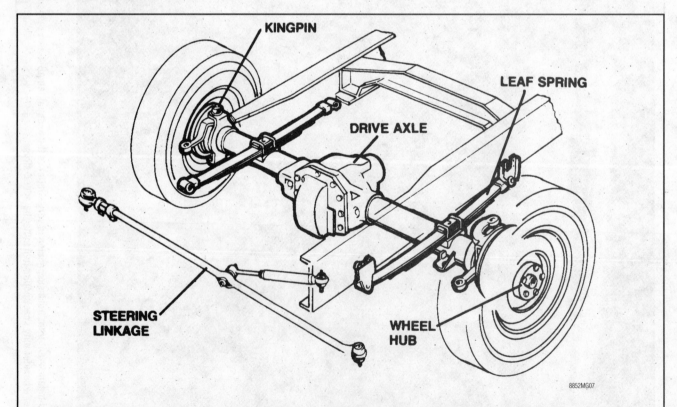

Fig. 6 This four wheel drive suspension is basically the same as an I-beam suspension, except that a front drive axle takes the place of the I-beam.

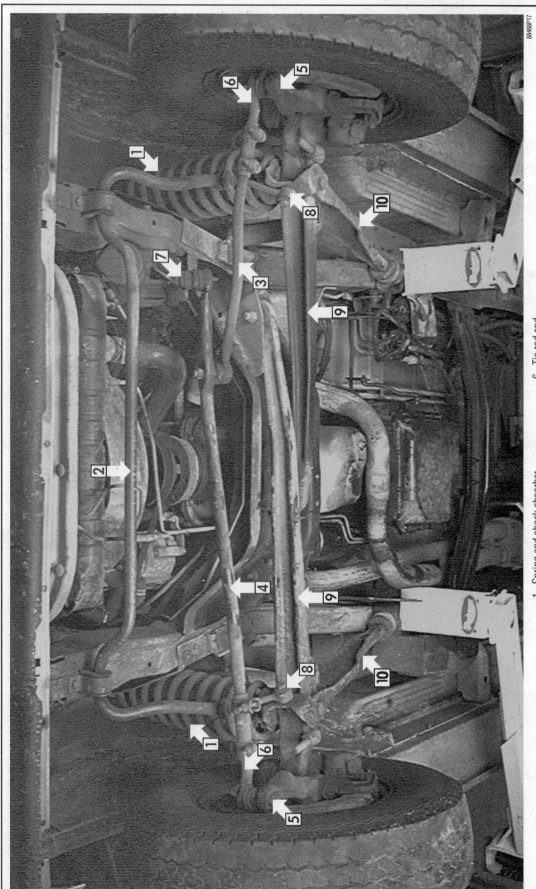

8848P17

1. Spring and shock absorber
2. Stabilizer bar
3. Tie rod
4. Drag link
5. Steering knuckle
6. Tie rod end
7. Pitman arm
8. Stabilizer links
9. I-beam
10. Trailing arm

Fig. 7 The twin I-beam front suspension is used almost exclusively by Ford trucks. The coil spring is mounted between the frame and an I-beam that carries each wheel. The I-beam is pivoted at the other end, and a radius rod serves to locate the fore-and-aft position of each I-beam.

Ball joints are used to attach the outer ends of the control arms to the spindle. This type of front suspension most often uses coil springs between the control arms, though they can be positioned between the control arm and frame or even on top of the upper control arm. Shock absorbers are used to dampen vibrations.

McPHERSON STRUT

▶ **See Figure 8**

McPherson strut front suspension differs considerably from unequal length A-arm suspension. McPherson strut suspension is found most frequently on compact and subcompact cars, both domestic and imported. With this type of suspension, the shock absorber, strut and spindle are a combined unit, which is supported by the coil spring at the upper end and the lower control arm (sometimes called track control arm or transverse link) at the bottom.

Another type of front strut suspension is referred to as a modified McPherson strut suspension, which is the same as the regular McPherson strut unit except the coil spring is mounted separately from the strut, between the lower control arm and the frame.

There is only one ball joint in this design, and it is attached to the lower part of the spindle. Generally, this ball joint is not a load carrying ball joint, but a follower ball joint, which means it is isolated from vehicle weight.

The shock absorber is built into the strut outer casing and, except for the modified McPherson strut, a coil spring sits on a seat welded to this casing. The upper mount of the shock absorber bolts to the vehicle body. On some models, the strut cartridge may be replaced, while on others the entire strut must be replaced. Due to the design of this type of suspension, the only front-end alignment procedure possible is toe-in adjustment, since caster and camber are fixed.

Spring Types

At the core of every suspension system are the springs. Suspension systems utilize three types of springs—coil, leaf (both mono and multi-leaf) and torsion bar. This is the component that maintains proper riding height while absorbing all levels of shock force. If worn out or damaged, other elements of the suspension will shift out of their correct positions, subjecting them to increased wear which they are not designed for. This will severely affect the vehicle's ride and handling.

Larger, heavier vehicles require stiffer springs than a lightweight vehicle. Spring rate is classified as the amount of deflection displayed under a specific load. In reference to the law of physics, a weight or force applied to a spring will compress it proportionally to the force applied. The spring will return to its original position once the force is removed, if not overloaded.

COIL SPRING

▶ **See Figure 9**

The most common springs used today on independent suspensions is the coil spring. The coil spring is nothing more than a steel bar that has been bended into a flexible coil. The spring absorbs shock forces by compressing in and recoiling back to its original spring height. They can be located between control arms, frame and control arms and in most strut assemblies.

Most coil springs fail due to constant overloading, excessive up and down movement or just a general breakdown due to metal fatigue.

LEAF SPRING

▶ **See Figure 10**

Leaf springs are the first type of spring used on vehicle suspensions and are still in use today, however, they are more commonly found on light duty trucks, SUVs, vans and on some passenger vehicles (on the rear only). Two basic types of leaf spring are, mono-leaf and multi-leaf.

Mono-leaf, or single-leaf, springs are thick in the center and taper off at each end, which provide a variable spring rate for good load carrying capability as well as a good ride. Mono-leaf springs are also less noisy while producing less static friction of multi-leaf springs.

Multi-leaf springs are made up of several flat steel leaves bound together and retained with a bolt or clips. The main leaf is the one leaf that is the full length of the spring from the front mounting bushing to the rear mounting shackle. Each leaf bound to the main leaf is gradually shorter which gives the spring a tapered profile. Each leaf added to the spring assembly contributes to its stiffening ability. Because of the curved construction of the leaf spring, it is also referred to as a semi-elliptical spring.

Leaf eye at the rear of the spring leaf is secured to the vehicle frame using a shackle. The spring shackles allow some movement fore and aft in response to the physical forces on acceleration, deceleration and braking.

TORSION BAR

▶ **See Figure 11**

The torsion bar is a coil spring stretched out straight, and used instead of a coil spring to control wheel action. The torsion bars are attached to the chassis at one end and to the upper or lower control arm at the other end. As the control arm moves up or down in response to road surface, it twists the torsion bar, which resists the twisting force and returns the control arm to the normal position.

The outer ends of the control arms are kept an equal distance apart by spindles sometimes called steering knuckles, which are held, in place by ball joints at the top and bottom. Ball joints permit upward and downward motion of the steering knuckle, and the turning motion required for turning corners, while keeping the steering knuckles vertical.

Manual Steering

There are two types of manual steering in general use today. The first is called worm and sector steering, also known as re-circulating ball, while the second is called rack and pinion steering.

RECIRCULATING BALL STEERING

▶ **See Figures 12 and 13**

In this type of steering, the end of the steering input shaft, called the wormshaft, is machined with a continuous spiral groove holding ball bearings. These ball bearings move a ball nut assembly up or down the wormshaft when the steering wheel is turned.

Since the wormshaft is coupled directly to the steering column shaft, turning the steering wheel causes the wormshaft to turn in the same direction. This action moves the ball nut assembly along its length. The balls circulate in one direction for a right-hand turn and in the other direction for a left-hand turn. Teeth on the ball nut assembly then engage teeth on the sector shaft (also called the Pitman shaft since it is connected to the Pitman arm) causing the Pitman or sector shaft to move the Pitman arm,

FRONT SUSPENSION COMPONENT LOCATIONS

1. Lower control arm
2. Ball joint
3. Tie rod end
4. MacPherson strut
5. Halfshaft
6. Inner CV joint
7. Outer CV joint
8. Stabilizer (sway) bar
9. Power steering gear
10. Crossmember

Fig. 8 McPherson strut type front suspensions are used on most of today's passenger vehicles

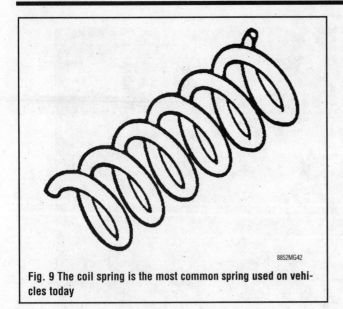

Fig. 9 The coil spring is the most common spring used on vehicles today

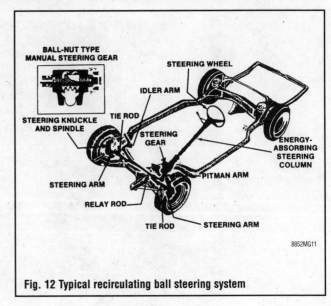

Fig. 12 Typical recirculating ball steering system

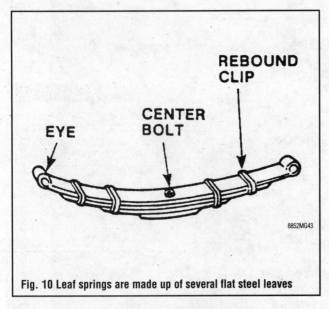

Fig. 10 Leaf springs are made up of several flat steel leaves

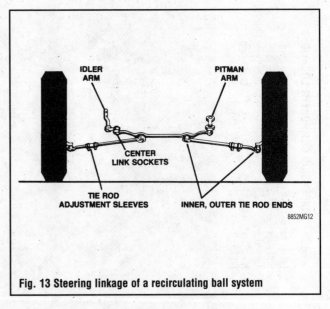

Fig. 13 Steering linkage of a recirculating ball system

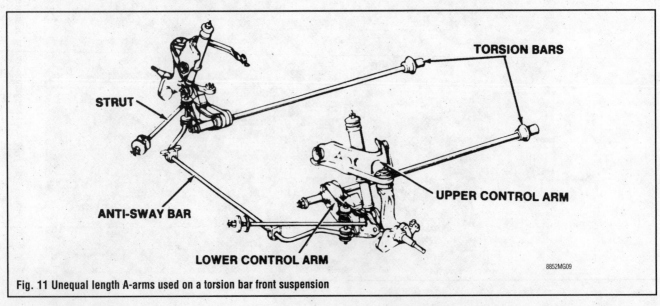

Fig. 11 Unequal length A-arms used on a torsion bar front suspension

thereby converting the rotating force of the steering wheel into the slower, higher torque rotation of the Pitman arm. The Pitman arm in turn transmits the desired directional movement to the front wheels through the steering linkage. Tubes connect the locknut/sleeve unit and allow the balls to constantly re-circulate, distributing wear evenly among them.

RACK AND PINION STEERING

▶ See Figure 14

This steering design uses a steering gear connected to the steering column shaft by a flexible coupling. This gear, similar in design to the pinion gear used in a differential, is cut on an angle and meshed on one side with a steel bar or rack that also has teeth cut in it. This rack is contained in the steering gearbox, which is positioned between the tie rods in the steering linkage. When the steering wheel is turned, the pinion gear operates

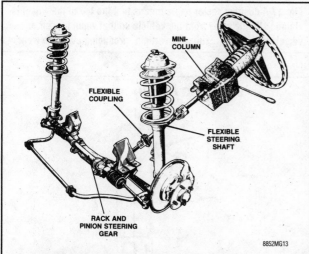

Fig. 14 Typical rack and pinion steering gear, used on most of today's passenger vehicles

directly on the rack, causing it to move from side to side and transmitting motion to the front wheels. This type of steering gear avoids the use of a Pitman arm and is a more direct and precise type of steering, although drivers accustomed to re-circulating ball steering occasionally find its directness disconcerting.

Power Steering

▶ See Figure 15

Power steering units are mechanical steering gear units incorporating a power assist.

Power steering for the recirculating ball type steering system consists of a pump, fluid reservoir, pressure and return hoses and steering gear. The pump, which is driven by an accessory drive belt, consists of an impeller, pressure valve, and fluid reservoir. Pump pressure builds only when the engine is running. The pump impeller turns, picking up hydraulic fluid from the reservoir and feeding it to the steering gear under pressure through the pressure line. The fluid is then returned to the fluid reservoir through the non-pressurized return line.

The power assisted rack and pinion steering system is very similar to that of the recirculating ball system in that its power cylinder and control valve are in the same housing. The power piston is part of the rack while the rack housing is the cylinder. The pinion housing contains the control valve. Rotating the steering wheel moves the control valve, directing pressure to both ends of the steering rack piston. The rack and pinion system uses a pressure hose from the power steering pump to the control valve housing, and a return line to the fluid reservoir.

Steering Geometry

Front wheel alignment (also known as front-end geometry) is the position of the front wheels relative to each other and to the vehicle. Correct alignment must be maintained to provide safe, accurate steering, vehicle stability and minimum tire wear. The factors that determine wheel alignment are interdependent. Therefore, when one of the factors is adjusted, the others must be adjusted to compensate.

Front-end alignment is best checked with sophisticated equipment, such as an alignment rack.

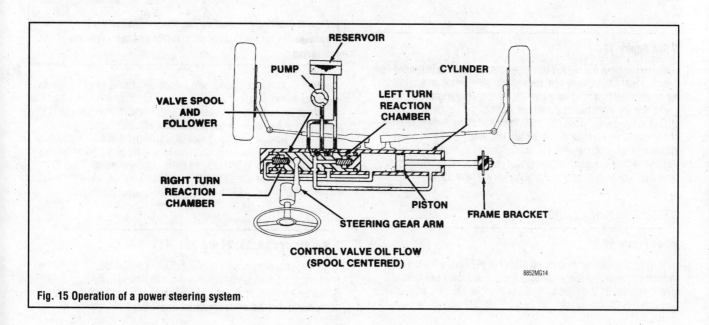

Fig. 15 Operation of a power steering system

CASTER ANGLE

▶ See Figure 16

Caster angle is the number of degrees that a line, drawn through the center of the upper and lower ball joints (or strut and lower ball joint) and viewed from the side, can be tilted forward or backward. Positive caster means that the top of the upper ball joint (or strut) is tilted toward the rear of the vehicle, and negative caster means that it is tilted toward the front. A vehicle with a slightly positive caster setting will have its lower ball joint pivot slightly ahead of the tire's center. This will assist the directional stability of the vehicle by causing a drag at the bottom center of the wheel when it turns, thereby resisting the turn and tending to hold the wheel steady in whatever direction the vehicle is pointed. A vehicle with too much (positive) caster will be hard to steer and shimmy at low speeds. A vehicle with insufficient (negative) caster may tend to be unstable at high speeds and may respond erratically when the brakes are applied.

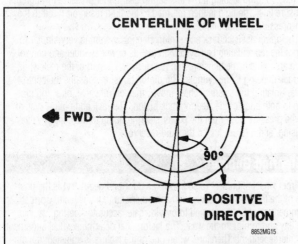

Fig. 16 A positive caster angle will have the lower ball joint pivot slightly ahead of the center of the tire and the strut or upper ball joint tilted toward the rear of the vehicle

CAMBER ANGLE

▶ See Figure 17

Camber angle is the number of degrees that the wheel itself is tilted from a vertical line, when viewed from the front. Positive camber means that the top of the wheel is slanted away from the vehicle, while negative camber means that it is tilted toward the vehicle. Ordinarily, a vehicle will have a slight positive camber when unloaded. Then, when the vehicle is loaded and rolling down the road, the wheels will just about be vertical. If you started with no camber at all, then loading the vehicle would produce a negative camber. Excessive camber (either positive or negative) will produce rapid tire wear, since one side of the tire will be more heavily loaded than the other side.

STEERING AXIS INCLINATION

▶ See Figure 18

Steering axis inclination is the number of degrees that a line drawn through the upper and lower ball joints (or strut and lower ball joint) and viewed from the front is tilted to the left or the right. This, in combination with caster, is responsible for the directional stability and self-centering of

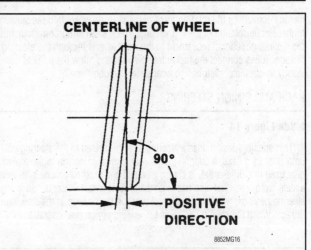

Fig. 17 A positive caster angle means that the top of the wheel is slanted slightly away from the vehicle so that when loaded, the wheels will be approximatley verticle, producing even tire wear

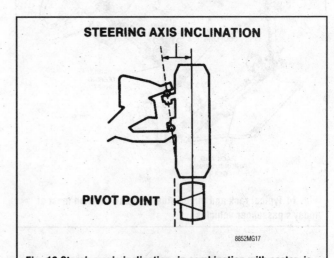

Fig. 18 Steering axis inclination, in combination with caster, is responsible for the directional stability and self-centering of the steering.

the steering. As the steering knuckle swings from lock to lock, the spindle generates an arc, causing the vehicle to be raised when it is turned from the straight-ahead position. The reason the body of the vehicle must rise is straightforward: since the wheel is in contact with the ground, it cannot move down. However, when it is swung away from the straight-ahead position, it must move either up or down (due to the arc generated by the steering knuckle). Not being able to move down, it must move up. Then, the weight of the vehicle acts against this lift, and attempts to return the spindle to the straight-ahead position when the steering wheel is released.

TOE-IN

▶ See Figures 19, 20, 21 and 22

Toe-in is the difference (in inches) between the front and the rear of the front tires. On a vehicle with toe-in, the distance between the front wheels is less at the front than at the rear. Toe-in is normally only a few fractions of an inch, and is necessary to ensure parallel rolling of the front wheels and

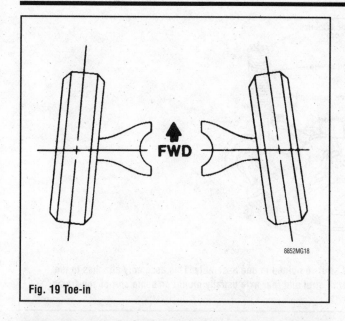

Fig. 19 Toe-in

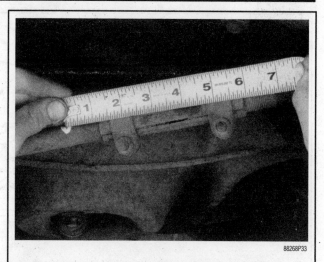

Fig. 22 When you have finished, the adjuster tube should be centered in the threads between the tie rod ends

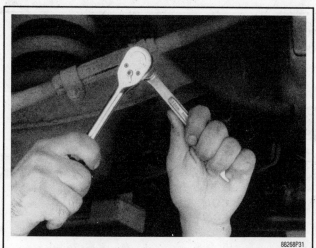

Fig. 20 To adjust Toe-in, first loosen the tie rod adjuster clamp bolts . . .

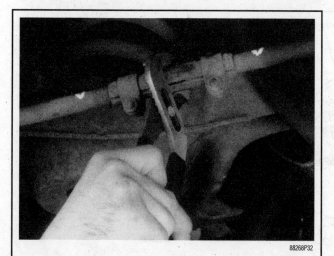

Fig. 21 . . . then turn the adjuster tube assembly as necessary to achieve the required toe-in specification

to prevent excessive tire wear. As the vehicle is driven at increasingly faster speeds, the steering linkage has a tendency to expand slightly, thereby allowing the front wheels to turn out and away from each other. Therefore, initially setting the front wheels so that they are pointing slightly inward (toe-in) allows them to turn straight ahead when the vehicle is underway.

Rear Suspensions

▶ See Figures 23, 24, 25, 26 and 27

There are three basic types of rear suspension: independent, semi-independent and live axle. Each of these suspension systems has their own distinctive variations, but the general principles and component types are relatively similar to that of front suspension systems described earlier in this chapter.

Independent rear suspension systems may be found on both rear, front, and 4-wheel drive vehicles. They utilize control arms which allow one wheel to move separately from the other wheel.

Semi-indepenedent rear suspension systems are often found on front wheel drive vehicles. These systems utilize a cross member, which connects to two trailing arms. Despite the fact that there is a solid connection with the cross member and the trailing arms, the cross member will twist with each up and down movement of the wheels. This twisting

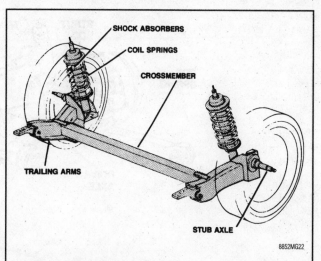

Fig. 23 The semi-independent axle used on many of today's front wheel drive vehicles

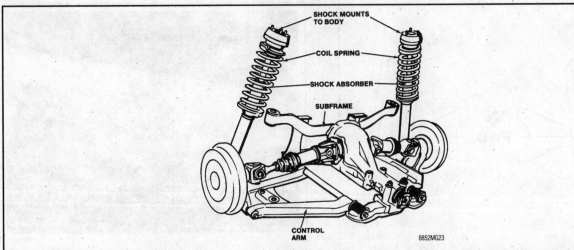

Fig. 24 This is a strut suspension with coil spring, shock absorber and strut combined in one assembly. This assembly attaches to the body and wheel spindle. In this type of suspension the lower control arm, strut and rear axle usually mount on some sort of sub-frame, which is attached to the body of the vehicle

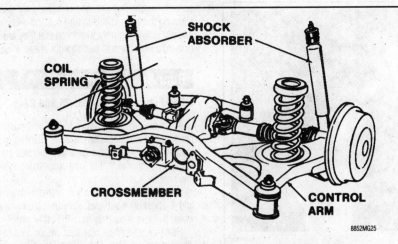

Fig. 25 This is an independent rear suspension used on many sportier vehicles. Coil springs are used between the control arm and the vehicle body, and the control arms pivot on a cross-member and are attached at the other end to a spindle. A shock absorber attached to the spindle or control arm absorbs vibrations

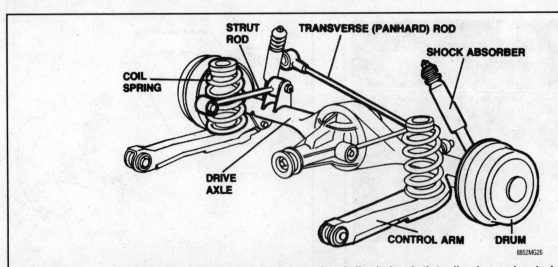

Fig. 26 This is a non-independent rear suspension. It differs from other similar designs in that coil springs replace leaf springs, and strut rods and control arms serve to position the rear axle

1. Rear shock absorber
2. Shock absorber lower mounting bracket
3. Axle housing
4. Leaf springs
5. Spring U-bolts

Fig. 27 This is a basic leaf spring rear suspension with shock absorbers to control vibration as well as up and down axle movement

action provides not only semi-independent movement, but also a stabilizer effect.

Live axle rear suspension systems are usually found on rear and four wheel drive vehicles. These systems consist of leaf or coil springs utilized in conjunction with the live axle, which is the differential axle, wheel bearings, and brakes operating as a unit.

Rear suspensions, in general, can be much simpler than front suspensions since all they have to do is support the rear of the vehicle and provide some sort of suspension control. However, some rear suspensions, especially those found on sports cars, are quite complex.

Steering and Suspension Maintenance

♦ See Figure 28

ADJUSTING POWER STEERING BELT TENSION

➡**For more information on checking, adjusting and replacing V-belts and serpentine belts please refer to the belt section in the chapter on "The Cooling System".**

CHECKING & ADDING POWER STEERING FLUID

♦ See Figure 29

➡**Many power steering fluid dipsticks or fluid reservoirs utilize two ranges for checking the fluid level: "FULL HOT" and "FULL COLD" or some other hot and cold level markings.**

If the system isn't leaking, you shouldn't need to add fluid very often at all. Nonetheless, it's a good idea to periodically check the fluid. Most manufacturers recommend checking the fluid with the engine at operating temperature (hot) and the wheels pointed straight ahead.

To check the fluid, turn the engine **OFF**, then check to see that the fluid level is at the "full hot" mark. Use power steering fluid to top up the reservoir. If the reservoir fluid level is being checked before starting the engine, first thing in the morning for example, the level is checked to the "full cold" mark. Regardless of what temperature the engine is at, if the fluid level is down to the "add" mark, power steering fluid must be added to the system. While you're adding fluid, check the power steering hoses for wear or chafing. Ordinarily, there should be no problem, but it's always a good idea to check.

SPOTTING WORN SHOCKS OR STRUTS

➡**To spot or check for worn shocks/struts, refer to "SHOCK ABSORBER TESTING" later in this section.**

GREASING THE FRONT END

Depending on the age of your car or light truck and the intentions of the manufacturer, there may be as many as a dozen, or as few as zero lubrication fittings on the front end. Typical places to look for grease nipples are the ball joints, control arm pivot points, steering linkage and tie-rod ends.

Lubricate any of these fittings with a small, hand-operated grease gun filled with EP chassis lubricant. If you plan to buy a grease gun to do this, buy a flexible extension to go with it. This will allow you to get at those hard-to-reach fittings.

Pump grease into the fitting until the rubber boot of the joint starts to swell out, indicating that it's full. Be sure to stop pumping before it starts to ooze out around the joint.

Occasionally, these grease nipples will be clogged with dirt. If so, simply unscrew them with a small wrench and clean them out. When you put them back, cover them with a small, plastic grease fitting cap to seal out dirt.

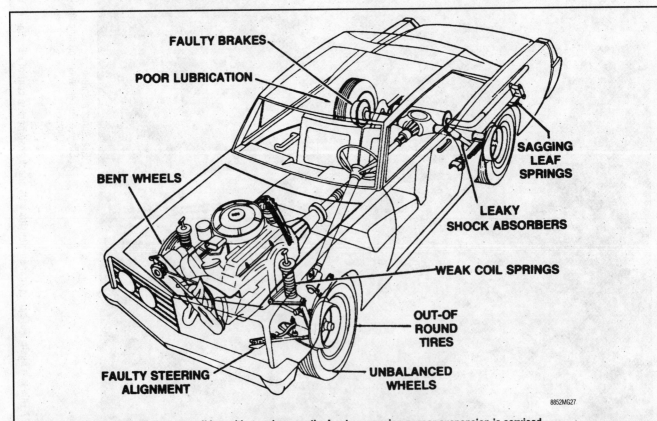

FAULTY BRAKES
POOR LUBRICATION
BENT WHEELS
FAULTY STEERING ALIGNMENT
SAGGING LEAF SPRINGS
LEAKY SHOCK ABSORBERS
WEAK COIL SPRINGS
OUT-OF-ROUND TIRES
UNBALANCED WHEELS

8852MG27

Fig. 28 You should check for these possible problems whenever the front suspension or rear suspension is serviced

SUSPENSION AND STEERING SYSTEM MAINTENANCE INTERVALS

Your car's suspension and steering system will work efficiently if it is maintained at these intervals.

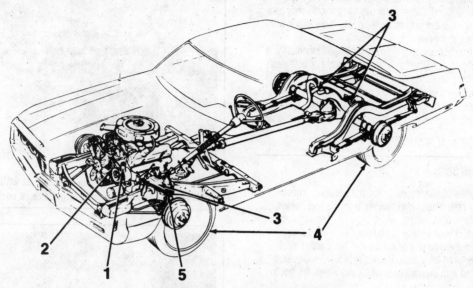

(AS MANY AS 10–12 LOCATIONS)

1. Check/add power steering fluid	Every 3 months or 3000 miles
2. Check/adjust belt tension	Every 3 months or 3000 miles
Replace power steering belt ▲	Every 2 yrs or 24,000 miles
3. Check shock absorbers	Every year or 12,000 miles
4. Check tires for abnormal wear	Every month or 1000 miles
5. Grease front end	Every 3 months or 3000 miles

▲Retighten the belt after 300 miles of use. New belts have a tendency to stretch.

8852MC01

Fig. 29 Remove the pump dipstick and check the fluid level. Depending on if the vehicle was running or not, keep the fluid level at the "full hot" or the "full cold" level.

Steering System Service

POWER STEERING BELT REPLACEMENT

➥**For more information on checking, adjusting and replacing V-belts and serpentine belts please refer to the belt section in the chapter on "The Cooling System."**

SHOCK ABSORBERS TESTING

The purpose of the shock absorber is simply to limit the motion of the spring during compression and rebound cycles. If the vehicle is not equipped with these motion dampers, the up and down motion would multiply until the vehicle was alternately trying to leap off the ground and pound itself into the pavement.

Countrary to popular myth, shock absorbers do not affect the ride height of the vehicle, unless they are pneumatic or air adjustable shocks. However, ride height is mostly controlled by other suspension components such as springs and tires. Worn shock absorbers can affect handling; if the front of the vehicle is rising or falling excessively, the "footprint" of the tires changes on the pavement and steering is affected.

The simplest test of the shock absorber is to simply push down on one corner of the unladen vehicle and release it. Observe the motion of the body as it is released. In most cases, it will come up beyond its original resting position, dip back below it, and settle quickly to rest. This shows that the damper is controlling the spring action. Any tendency toward excessive pitch (up-and-down) motion or failure to return to rest within 1–2 cycles is a sign of poor function within the shock absorber. Oil-filled shocks may have a light film of oil around the seal, resulting from normal breathing and air exchange. This should NOT be taken as a sign of failure, but any sign of thick or running oil definitely indicates failure. Gas filled shocks may also show some film at the shaft; if the gas has leaked out, and the shock will have almost no resistance to motion.

While each shock absorber can be physically replaced individually, it is recommended that they be changed as a pair (both front or both rear) to maintain equal response on both sides of the vehicle. Failure to replace shock absorbers in pairs could result in dangerous vehicle handling situations. Chances are quite good that if one has failed, its mate is also weak.

SHOCK ABSORBER REPLACEMENT

▶ **See Figures 30 thru 38**

There are various types of shock mountings, but generally, shock replacement is an easy task. The only exception to this is McPherson strut suspension cartridge replacement, which requires a spring compressor and some expertise. If your vehicle is equipped with McPherson strut suspension, we recommend you rent or purchase a McPherson strut compressor and be prepared for a complicated procedure. However, if your vehicle is equipped with conventional shock absorbers, it's not too hard a job.

1. Jack up the vehicle and support it with safety stands. Use genuine safety stands, not cinder blocks or pieces of wood.

2. Squirt the shock-mounting studs with some penetrating oil before trying to loosen them. If the vehicle is not too old, there shouldn't be much problem, but on older vehicles, the mounting nuts are generally rusted in place.

3. Remove the shock absorber mounting nuts. This sounds easy, but sometimes it isn't. Many top shock mounts require you to hold the top of the shock with a pair of vise grips, wrench, hex or allen key (depending on

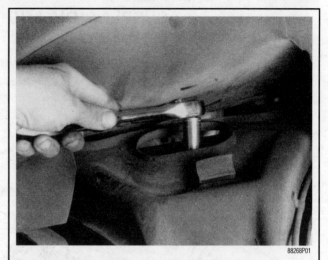

Fig. 31 On front shocks loosen the retainer while holding the shaft (a box wrench is usually better than a socket)

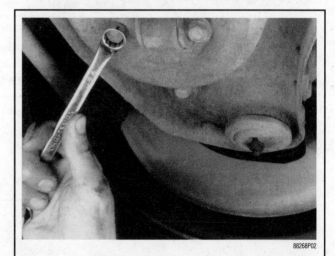

Fig. 32 Once the upper shock retainer is removed, loosen the lower retaining bolts . . .

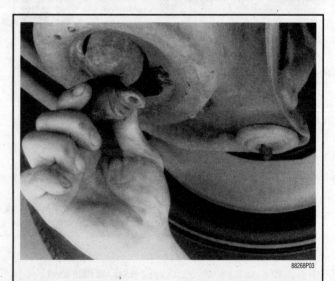

Fig. 33 . . . and carefully lower the shock from the vehicle

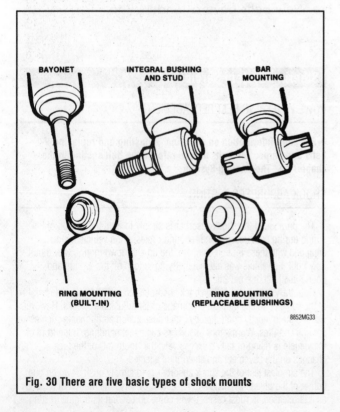

Fig. 30 There are five basic types of shock mounts

BAYONET

INTEGRAL BUSHING AND STUD

BAR MOUNTING

RING MOUNTING (BUILT-IN)

RING MOUNTING (REPLACEABLE BUSHINGS)

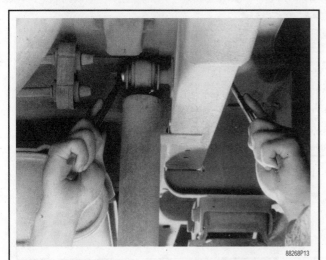

Fig. 34 On the rear shocks, loosen and remove the upper retaining nut . . .

Fig. 37 Lift the shock out of the lower mounting bracket, then . . .

Fig. 35 . . . then remove the lower retainers

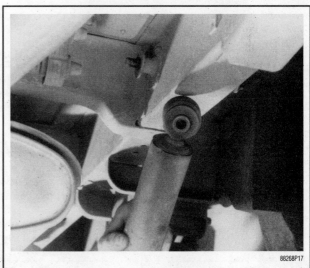

Fig. 38 . . . remove it from the vehicle

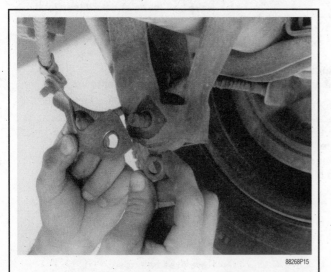

Fig. 36 Often brackets must be removed and repositioned

the type of shock), while you turn the mounting nut. There are other variations on this, depending on the type of shock mounting.

4. Once you have the mounting nuts removed, remove the old shock and install the new one. Note which way the rubber bushings went so the new ones can be reinstalled correctly.

5. Install the new shock using the new hardware. Tighten the mounting bolts and lower the car.

TREAD WEAR PATTERNS

CONDITION	RAPID WEAR AT SHOULDERS	RAPID WEAR AT CENTER	CRACKED TREADS	WEAR ON ONE SIDE	FEATHERED EDGE	BALD SPOTS	SCALLOPED WEAR
EFFECT							
CAUSE	UNDER-INFLATION OR LACK OF ROTATION	OVER-INFLATION OR LACK OF ROTATION	UNDER-INFLATION OR EXCESSIVE SPEED*	EXCESSIVE CAMBER	INCORRECT TOE	UNBALANCED WHEEL OR TIRE DEFECT*	LACK OF ROTATION OF TIRES OR WORN OR OUT-OF-ALIGNMENT SUSPENSION
CORRECTION	ADJUST PRESSURE TO SPECIFICATIONS WHEN TIRES ARE COOL; ROTATE TIRES			ADJUST CAMBER TO SPECIFICATIONS	ADJUST TOE-IN TO SPECIFICATIONS	DYNAMIC OR STATIC BALANCE WHEELS	ROTATE TIRES AND INSPECT SUSPENSION

*HAVE TIRE INSPECTED FOR FURTHER USE.

8852MC03

TROUBLESHOOTING BASIC STEERING AND SUSPENSION PROBLEMS

Most problems in the front end and steering are caused by improperly maintained tires which you can correct yourself, or by incorrect wheel alignment, which requires the services of a professional mechanic. Get in the habit of checking tires frequently; this is usually the first place that problems in the front end or steering will show up.

The Condition	Is Caused By	What to Do
Hard Steering (steering wheel is hard to turn)	• Low or uneven tire pressure • Loose power steering pump drive belt • Low or incorrect power steering fluid • Incorrect front end alignment • Defective power steering pump • Bent or poorly lubricated front end parts	• Inflate tires to correct pressure • Adjust belt • Add fluid as necessary • Have front end alignment checked/adjusted • Have pump checked/repaired • Lubricate and/or have defective parts replaced
Loose Steering (too much play in the steering wheel	• Loose wheel bearings • Loose or worn steering linkage • Faulty shocks • Worn ball joints	• Adjust wheel bearings • Have worn parts serviced • Replace shocks • Have ball joints checked/serviced
Car Veers or Wanders (car pulls to one side with hands off the steering wheel)	• Incorrect tire pressure • Improper front end alignment • Loose wheel bearings • Loose or bent front end components • Faulty shocks	• Inflate tires to correct pressure • Have front end alignment checked/adjusted • Adjust wheel bearings • Have worn components checked/serviced • Replace shocks
Wheel oscillation or vibration transmitted through steering wheel	• Improper tire pressures • Tires out of balance • Loose wheel bearings • Improper front end alignment • Worn or bent front end components	• Inflate tires to correct pressure • Have tires balanced • Adjust wheel bearings • Have front end alignment checked/adjusted • Have front end checked/serviced
Uneven tire wear (see Section 26—Tires)	• Incorrect tire pressure • Front end out of alignment • Tires out of balance	• Inflate tires to correct pressure • Have front end alignment checked/adjusted • Have tires balanced

8852MC02

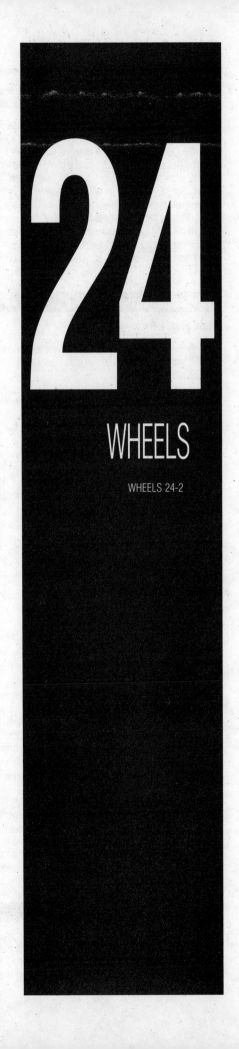

24

WHEELS

WHEELS 24-2

WHEELS

Any discussion of wheels inevitably involves tires. The most common reason for new wheels is for appearance, (custom wheels) or to use larger tires. The failure rate of wheels is small, but custom wheels are extremely popular. The subject of wheels can be complex and technical, but there are a few tips for those shopping around for new wheels.

The correct capacity, rim width, type of wheel, offset, bolt pattern and diameter all must be considered when selecting a replacement or custom wheel. Having the right wheel is just as important as having one that's not defective. At highway speeds, the wheels on an average vehicle will rotate close to 600 times a minute, about 10 times every second. The wrong type or size of wheel can destroy tires and bearings very quickly at that rate.

Wheel Construction

▶ See Figure 1

A wheel is made up of a rim and center member, known as a disc or spider. The rim supports the tire and the spider (disc) connects the vehicle with the rim.

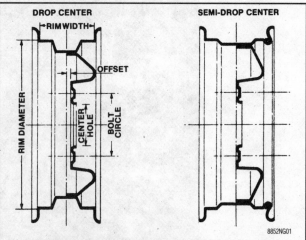

Fig. 1 Two types of wheel construction. The semi-drop center has removable flanges and does not need the severe drop in the center of the rim. These wheels are used on heavy equipment.

Wheels are usually of two types—the Drop Center (DC) and the Semi-Drop Center (SDC). Drop center wheels are used on all cars and light trucks; semi-drop center wheels are usually only used with large multi-ply, heavy-duty tires on over-the-road trucks. The SDC wheel has a removable outer ring that allows easier installation and higher inflation pressure. Above six plys, tires would be extremely rigid in the bead and be very difficult to mount on a single-piece wheel without damaging the bead.

Most passenger vehicle wheels fall into two types. The all-steel wheel is the type found on many vehicles as original equipment from the factory. Custom or "MAG" wheels were named for their resemblance to magnesium racing wheels. True magnesium wheels are too porous to hold the air pressure of a street tire and never should be used on the street. Custom wheels are a cast aluminum alloy, a steel rim with cast aluminum alloy spider or a two-piece steel wheel.

Wheel Capacity

Just as tires have a maximum load capacity and inflation pressure, so do wheels. Any wheels you install should have a greater load capacity and inflation pressure capacity than the tires, or you could have problems. Obviously, the load-carrying capacity of the vehicle is only as strong as the weakest part. If you have selected your tires to carry an anticipated load of, say, 1500 lbs., then the wheel should be capable of carrying at least that, preferably more.

Wheel Dimensions

SIZE

▶ See Figures 2, 3 and 4

Wheel sizes are determined by three measurements—rim diameters, rim width and flange height. A typical wheel size might be 14 x 7J. Rim diameter and rim widths are always expressed in inches, so this wheel is 14 inches in diameter and has a rim width of 7 inches. The letter combination following the rim width indicates the flange height in inches. A J rim has 0.68 inch high flange while a K rim has 0.77 inch high flange. The circumferences on which the centers of the wheel bolt holes are located is the bolt circle. It is usually shown as a double number: 5–5½. The first number indicates the number of holes, and the second, the diameter of the bolt circle.

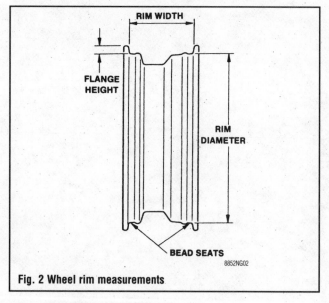

Fig. 2 Wheel rim measurements

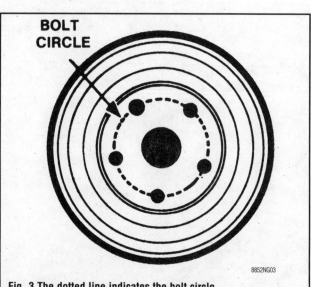

Fig. 3 The dotted line indicates the bolt circle

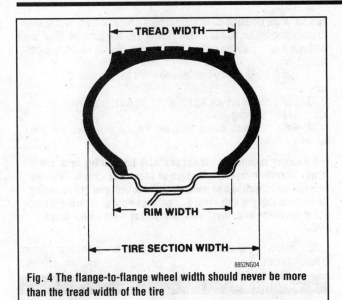

Fig. 4 The flange-to-flange wheel width should never be more than the tread width of the tire

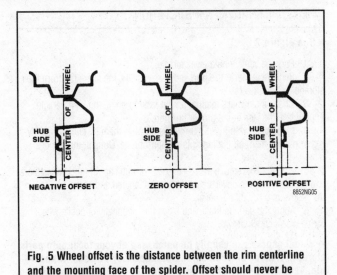

Fig. 5 Wheel offset is the distance between the rim centerline and the mounting face of the spider. Offset should never be increased more than ½ inch (12mm)

The rim width will be dictated by the tire section width and/or the tread width. The general rule is that the flange-to-flange width of the rim should be a minimum of three-quarters of the tire section width. The maximum flange-to-flange wheel width should be equal to the width of the tire tread. Narrow tires on wide rims tend to make the outer edges of the tire curl in toward the center. The result is less tread on the road, increased tire wear and a harsher ride. At high speeds, centrifugal action can pull the tire beads away from the bead seat on the rim.

Wide tires on narrow rims create a poor bead seal and force the tread to assume a convex shape causing abnormal tire wear, reduction of control with a somewhat smoother ride.

The general rule is that the tire and wheel combination is satisfactory if, when the tire is flat, no part of the underside of the vehicle touches the ground. This will prevent a shower of sparks, should a blowout occur.

OFFSET

▶ See Figure 5

Another important dimension to be considered when looking for wheels is offset. Offset is the distance from the mounting face of the wheel spider to the rim centerline. Offset is positive when the mounting face (lug circle) is outboard of the centerline and negative if the lug circle is inboard of the centerline. All wheels are designed for either positive, negative or zero offset, usually for disc brake clearance or for handling characteristics.

Generally, you should not increase the offset more than ½ inch (12mm) or tire width by 1 inch (25mm), or you'll create further problems. Increasing offset ½ inch (12mm) or tire width 1 inch (25mm) will put the entire extra tire width ½ inch (12mm) to the outside, where it may not clear the wheel well. Increasing the offset also has the effect of loading the front wheel bearings past their design limits and can actually "cock" the bearings causing rapid wear or premature failure.

Occasionally, disc brakes cause a mounting problem; some wheels were not designed for use with disc brakes and will not clear the brake caliper or will interfere with the disc. Be sure to check before buying wheels, especially used wheels, that they will fit your vehicle. Be sure that the tires on wider wheels will clear the wheel wells, especially when turned at full lock, and that the tires do not interfere with suspension travel.

Caring for Wheels

TIRE MOUNTING

▶ See Figure 6

Most steel wheels require little care. But, more and more vehicles have been equipped with aluminum and custom wheels. Tires must be mounted carefully to avoid scratching any wheel which is not hidden by a wheel cover. Wheels with steel rims and alloy spiders can be somewhat easier to work with than all-alloy wheels, but many service facilities charge extra to mount tires on custom wheels, or will refuse to work on them at all.

Aluminum and custom wheels are balanced in the same way as steel wheels, but adhesive backed weights are often used instead of the hammered on type. Adhesive weights must be checked more frequently than the others, and, as with mounting tires, many service stations charge extra to dynamically (spin) balance custom wheels, or will not do it at all.

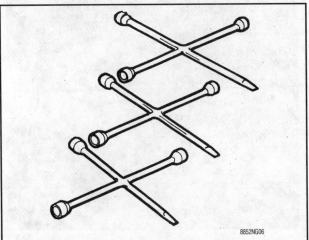

Fig. 6 A cross-wrench works best for wheel removal & installation. However, always check the lug nut torque with a torque wrench

WHEEL/TIRE REMOVAL & INSTALLATION

▶ **See Figure 7**

1. Park the vehicle on a level surface.
2. Remove the jack, tire iron and, if necessary, the spare tire from their storage compartments.
3. Check the owner's manual for the jacking points on your vehicle. Then, place the jack in the proper position.
4. If equipped with lug nut trim caps, remove them by either unscrewing or pulling them off the lug nuts, as appropriate. Consult the owner's manual, if necessary.
5. If equipped, remove the wheel cover or hub cap. In most cases there is a groove along the cover's edge, insert the tapered end of the tire iron in the groove and pry off the cover.
6. Apply the parking brake and block the diagonally opposite wheel with a wheel chock or two.

➥**Wheel chocks can usually be purchased at your local auto parts store, or a block of wood cut into wedges may be used. If possible, keep one or two of the chocks in your tire storage compartment, in case any of the tires has to be removed on the side of the road.**

7. If equipped with an automatic transmission/transaxle, place the selector lever in **P** or Park; with a manual transmission/transaxle, place the shifter in Reverse.
8. With the tires still on the ground, use the tire iron/wrench to break the lug nuts loose.

➥**If a nut is stuck, never use heat to loosen it or damage to the wheel and bearings may occur. If the nuts are seized, one or two heavy hammer blows directly on the end of the bolt usually loosens the rust. Be careful, as continued pounding will likely damage the brake drum, rotor and/or wheel bearings.**

9. Using the jack, raise the vehicle until the tire is clear of the ground. Support the vehicle safely using jackstands.
10. Remove the lug nuts, then remove the tire and wheel assembly.

To install:

11. Make sure the wheel and hub mating surfaces, as well as the wheel lug studs, are clean and free of all foreign material. Always remove rust from the wheel mounting surface and the brake rotor or drum. Failure to do so may cause the lug nuts to loosen in service or may allow the wheel to all but freeze onto the surface making future removal difficult or nearly impossible.

12. Install the tire and wheel assembly and hand-tighten the lug nuts.
13. Using the tire wrench, tighten all the lug nuts, in a criss-cross pattern, until they are snug.
14. Raise the vehicle sufficiently to withdraw the jackstands, then lower the vehicle.

➥**If a torque specification is not available for your lug nuts, use a torque wrench to measure the lugs on your other wheels. Find the average specification and match it on the wheel you are installing. Remember that the nuts must be tightened enough to prevent loosening in service and, most importantly, they must be tightened EVENLY.**

15. Using a torque wrench, tighten the lug nuts in a criss-cross pattern to specifications.

✳✳ WARNING

Do not overtighten the lug nuts! Over-tightening lugs can lead to broken studs, and over-tightening, uneven tightening, or tightening in the wrong sequence can lead to warped brake drums or rotors.

16. If so equipped, install the wheel cover or hub cap. Make sure the valve stem protrudes through the proper opening before tapping the wheel cover into position.
17. If equipped, install the lug nut trim caps by pushing them or screwing them on, as applicable.
18. Remove the jack from under the vehicle. If you have just finished changing a flat, place the jack and tire iron/wrench in their storage compartments.
19. Remove the wheel chock(s).
20. If you have removed a flat or damaged tire, place it in the storage compartment of the vehicle and take it to your local repair station to have it fixed or replaced as soon as possible.

TIGHTENING WHEELS

▶ **See Figures 8 and 9**

➥**Although it is frequently done for speed, wheel lug nuts should not be tightened with an electric or air impact gun. ALWAYS, hand-tighten them with a cross-type wrench, then torque to specifications using a torque wrench.**

Torque specifications for lug nuts should be adhered to and applied evenly in a criss-cross pattern. Over tightening lugs can lead to broken studs. Over-tightening, uneven tightening, or tightening in the wrong sequence can lead to warped brake drums or rotors.

If a torque specification is not available for your lug nuts, you can use a torque wrench to measure the lugs on your other wheels. A beam type wrench with a needle indicator works best for this, but a dial-clicker type can also be used. When measuring with a clicker, dial a torque that you are pretty sure is below the specification , say 50– 60 ft. lbs. (68–81 Nm), and test it on a lug nut. If the wrench clicks without turning the lug, keep increasing the torque by 5 ft. lbs. (7 Nm) increments until the nut begins to turn. Then, check that setting on other lugs. Be sure to properly loosen and retorque the test lug nuts when you are finished so that no lugs are over-tightened.

8852NP01

Fig. 7 Most of today's wheel locks require a uniquely shaped adapter to remove the lock.

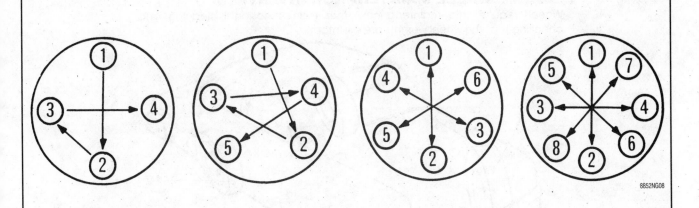

Fig. 8 Most of the common wheel bolt tightening patterns are illustrated. If in doubt, tighten in a criss-cross pattern.

Fig. 9 Always perform the final tightening to specifications with a torque wrench

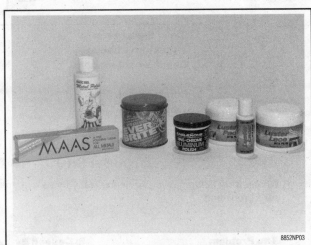

Fig. 10 There are a variety of quality wheel polishes currently available. Always read the label for proper application instructions.

KEEPING YOUR WHEELS CLEAN

▶ See Figures 10 and 11

➡For more information on cleaning of wheels please refer to the "Body Care" chapter.

Oxidation and theft are the main enemies of custom wheels. Oxidation is caused by a chemical reaction between air and water that causes the alloy to pit. Various waxes and cleaners are available to hold the oxidation process to a minimum and keep the wheels looking like new.

❊❊ WARNING

Remember that many aluminum wheels are painted or clearcoated to help prevent corrosion. Use of harsh chemicals or abrasives will remove the coating allowing for oxidation to occur. Also, remember that exposure to dirt, gravel, cinder and road salts will eventually take their toll on even the best coated wheel, but proper care can provide significant protection while beautifying your wheels.

Fig. 11 Using a spray-on wheel cleaner to remove brake dust prior to washing

WHEEL MAINTENANCE INTERVALS

Wheels require little maintenance, other than occasional cleaning and checking that the wheel weights are still intact.

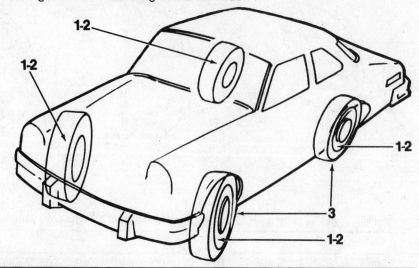

1. Clean the wheels (custom wheels)	As necessary
2. Check wheel weights	Every fuel stop/2 weeks (when you check tire pressure)
3. Rotate wheel/tire See Section 26 "Tires"	Every 6000 miles/6 months

8852NC01

TROUBLESHOOTING BASIC WHEEL PROBLEMS

Wheels very seldom give problems. Many times a suspected wheel problem is actually a problem in the tires or the car's front end.

The Problem	Is Caused By	What to Do
The car's front end vibrates at high speed	• The wheels are out of balance • Wheels are out of alignment	• Have wheels balanced • Have wheel alignment checked/adjusted
Car pulls to either side	• Wheels are out of alignment • Unequal tire pressure • Different size tires or wheels	• Have wheel alignment checked/adjusted • Check/adjust tire pressure • Change tires or wheels to same size
The car's wheel(s) wobbles	• Loose wheel lug nuts • Wheels out of balance • Damaged wheel • Wheels are out of alignment • Worn or damaged ball joint • Excessive play in the steering linkage (usually due to worn parts) • Defective shock absorber	• Tighten wheel lug nuts • Have tires balanced • Raise car and spin the wheel. If the wheel is bent, it should be replaced • Have wheel alignment checked/adjusted • Check ball joints • Have steering linkage checked • Check shock absorbers
Tires wear unevenly or prematurely	• Incorrect wheel size • Wheels are out of balance • Wheels are out of alignment	• Check if wheel and tire size are compatible • Have wheels balanced • Have wheel alignment checked/adjusted

8852NC02

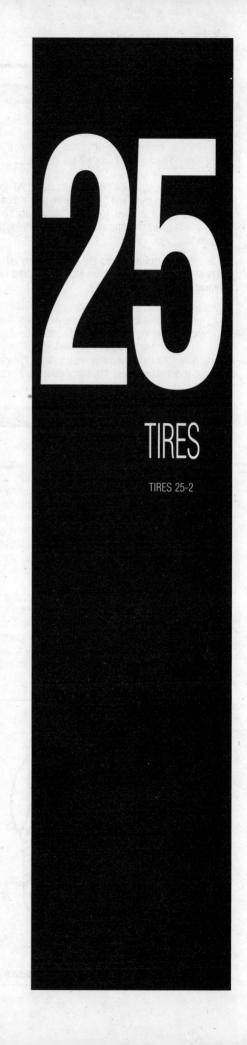

25

TIRES

TIRES 25-2

TIRES

Tires are among the most important and least understood parts of the vehicle. Everything concerned with driving—starting, moving and stopping—involves the tires. Because of their importance to driving ease and safety, learning the basics of tires will pay off in dollar savings and safe driving.

Common sense and good driving habits will afford maximum tire life. Fast starts, sudden stops and hard cornering are hard on tires and will shorten their useful life span. Make sure that you don't overload the vehicle or run with incorrect pressure in the tires. Both of these practices will increase tread wear.

➡**For optimum tire life, keep the tires properly inflated, rotate them every six months or 6,000 miles (9,600 km), and have the wheel alignment checked periodically.**

Inspect your tires frequently. Be especially careful to watch for bubbles in the tread or sidewall, deep cuts or under-inflation. Replace any tires with bubbles in the sidewall. If cuts are so deep that they penetrate to the cords, discard the tire. Any cut in the sidewall of a radial tire renders it unsafe. Also, look for uneven tread wear patterns that may indicate the front end is out of alignment, the tires are out of balance or are improperly inflated.

Tire Construction

▶ **See Figure 1**

Modern tires use a combination of materials to contain pressurized air. The foundation of the tire is the plies (layers of nylon, polyester, fiberglass or steel) just beneath the tread that provides flexibility and strength. Regardless of size, cost or brand, there are only three types of tires—bias, bias-belted, and radial, now the standard on all passenger vehicles.

Bias tires, the old stand-by, are constructed with cords running across the tread (from bead-to-bead) at an angle about 35° to the tread centerline; alternate plies reverse direction. Crisscrossing adds strength to the tire sidewalls and tread. When properly inflated, these tires give a relatively soft, comfortable ride.

Bias-belted tires are similar, but additional belts of fiberglass or rayon encircle the tire under the tread. The belts stabilize the tread, holding it flatter against the road with less squirm (side movement). Belted tires offer a firmer ride, better traction, improved puncture resistance and longer life than bias ply tires. Bias tires are now found mainly on antique vehicles to preserve their original appearance, and in some commercial applications.

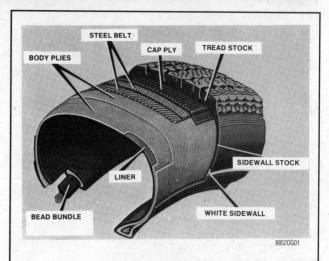

Fig. 1 Various components of a radial tire shown in this cutaway view

Radial tires now rule the road as they are original equipment on virtually every passenger car and light truck. Radials are constructed with steel or fabric carcass plies crossing the tread at approximately a 90° angle, and two or more belts circle the tire under the tread. The sidewalls flex while the tread remains rigid, accounting for the characteristic sidewall bulge of a radial. The tread runs flatter on the road with a better grip and the inherently harsher ride is offset by superior handling and mileage.

Tire Technology

▶ **See Figure 2**

Since 1985, when the 27.5 mpg CAFE (Corporate Average Fuel Economy) standards took effect, there were a lot of changes in tires. Tires are very important in meeting the CAFE standards because they are responsible for 20% of a vehicle's total drag. The reduced rolling resistance of radial tires has made them the standard design. However, even with all the recent tire developments, it has to be a compromise. A tire that handles well sacrifices tread wear; a soft-riding tire sacrifices traction; a tire that reduces rolling resistance and delivers improved fuel economy sacrifices braking stability.

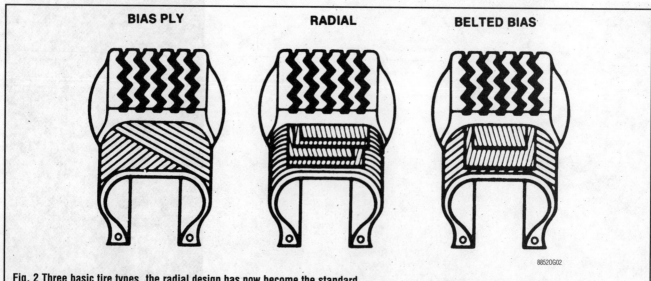

Fig. 2 Three basic tire types, the radial design has now become the standard

ELLIPTIC TIRES

▶ See Figure 3

A variation of the radial tire is the elliptic tire—a polyester cord body within steel belts. It resembles a conventional radial, except that it has a slightly more squatty appearance. The elliptically shaped sidewall forms a curve to the point where the tire meets the wheel rim, allowing up to 50% higher inflation pressures without causing an uncomfortable ride. The higher inflation pressure reduces rolling resistance and can increase fuel economy up to 3 or 4% at highway speeds.

A conventional radial inflated to 35–40 pounds per square inch delivers better gas mileage, but also transmits more road shocks from the tread to the wheel because the sidewall is almost vertical. Lower inflation pressures tend to lessen road shocks because the curved sidewall absorbs much of the vibration. The elliptic tire has extremely thick sidewalls that maintain the curved shape even at high inflation pressures.

The problem with elliptic tires is that they require an entirely new wheel to hold the tire on the rim. A special "low flange rim" required for the elliptic tire will not support a conventional radial, nor will a conventional rim support an elliptic tire.

SPARE TIRES

A conventional wheel and spare tire weigh about 38 pounds, and the jack another 10 pounds, so the auto industry has turned a good deal of attention here toward saving weight by eliminating the conventional spare. There are three alternatives to the spare tire problem.

Temporary Spare

The most prevalent alternative today is the Temporary Spare used on many new vehicles. The Temporary Spare is a special, emergency-only tire that is more compact than the original tire yet retains the outside diameter dimensions. These tires usually run at a much higher inflation pressure

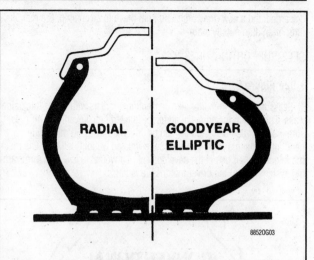

Fig. 3 The elliptic tire uses inflation pressures as much as 50% higher than conventional radials

than the conventional tires. Check the sidewall of the spare or your owners manual for correct inflation pressures. The Temporary Spare is designed to be used only as a device to get the vehicle off the road or to a local service center to have the original tire repaired or replaced.

Space-Saver® Spares

▶ See Figure 4

Now obsolete, the Space-Saver was a special, emergency-only tire that was stored deflated and folded around the wheel when not in use. It was designed to be mounted on the vehicle and inflated only with a special inflation canister that is supplied with the tire. Once used, the canister was

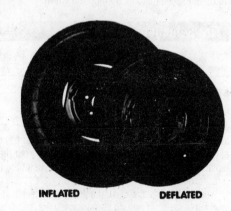

INFLATED   DEFLATED

Several precautions should be followed with Space-Saver tires:

1. The Space-Saver should only be inflated with the special canister provided. Never use an air hose. The canister is good for one use only; a new canister must be obtained for future use.

2. Follow the approved mounting and use instructions.

3. As early as possible, remove the Space-Saver and replace it with a normal tire.

4. The Space-Saver is a load range B tire and should never be inflated past 32 psi.

5. Because of its construction, the Space-Saver tire beads may appear to be improperly seated on the wheel. This is normal. Do not attempt to seat the beads by adding more air.

6. To deflate the tire, remove the valve stem and fold the tire around the rim.

7. No attempt should be made to remove the Space-Saver tire from the rim or to repair the tire.

Fig. 4 Space-saver spares required special handling to preserve their usefulness

discarded and a new one purchased from the auto dealership, tire manufacturer or an auto supply store.

SELF-SUPPORTING TIRES

▶ **See Figure 5**

Self-supporting tires look like conventional radials with super-thick sidewalls. They retain the shape of an under-inflated radial even with no pressure inside. When deflated they can be driven as far as 50 miles with no handling problems. They can also be re-inflated without damage. The main roadblock to their use is the development of a workable low-pressure warning system to alert the driver that the tire is flat.

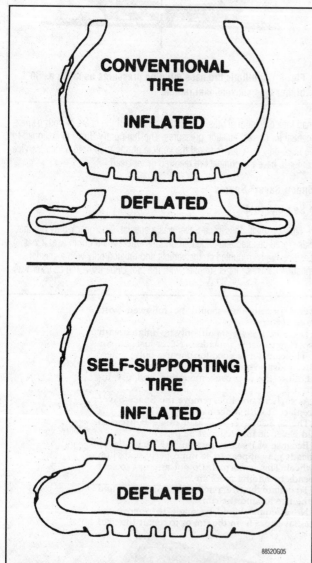

Fig. 5 A conventional and a self-supporting tire. Note the extremely thick sidewalls used on a self-supporting tire.

RUN-FLAT TIRES

▶ **See Figure 6**

For years, tire engineers have been trying to develop a "run flat" tire—one that would allow the vehicle to run a given distance even if

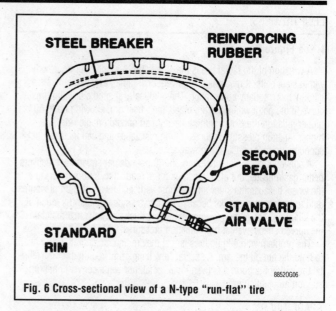

Fig. 6 Cross-sectional view of a N-type "run-flat" tire

the tire loses air pressure due to a puncture. Drawbacks on prototypes developed by major manufacturers have been the need for expensive "tire-within-a-tire" designs, lubricants to cool the tire sidewall due to high temperatures generated when the tire operates at low air pressure, and the need for special wheels to support unconventional tires.

However, tire engineers developed a run-flat tire that uses a simple design, requires a conventional air valve and can be mounted on the wheel with conventional tire changing equipment. It is based on a steel-belted radial tire, but uses reinforced sidewalls for support in a run-flat condition. The tire weighs about 25% more than a conventional tire, but about 15 pounds per vehicle can be saved because the spare and the jack are unnecessary. The deflated tire can run about 100 miles (160 km) at a maximum speed of about 50 mph (80 km/h).

Tire Selection

TIRE DESIGN

▶ **See Figure 7**

For maximum satisfaction, tires should be used in sets of four. Mixing of different types (radial, bias-belted, fiberglass belted) must be avoided. In most cases, the vehicle manufacturer has designated a type of tire on which the vehicle will perform best. Your first choice when replacing tires should be to use the same type of tire that the manufacturer recommends.

When radial tires are used, tire sizes and wheel diameters should be selected to maintain ground clearance and tire load capacity equivalent to the original specified tire. Radial tires should always be used in sets of four.

✳✳ CAUTION

Radial tires should never be used on only the front axle.

When selecting tires, pay attention to the original size as marked on the tire. Most tires are described using an industry size code sometimes referred to as P-Metric. This allows the exact identification of the tire specifications, regardless of the manufacturer. If selecting a different tire size or brand, remember to check the installed tire for any sign of interference with the body or suspension while the vehicle is stopping, turning sharply or heavily loaded.

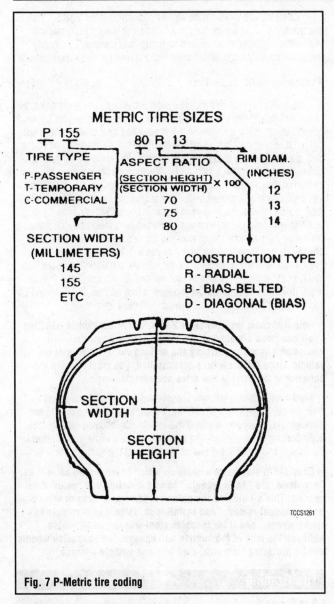

METRIC TIRE SIZES

P 155 80 R 13

TIRE TYPE — ASPECT RATIO — RIM DIAM.
(INCHES)

P-PASSENGER
T-TEMPORARY
C-COMMERCIAL

(SECTION HEIGHT)
————————— x 100
(SECTION WIDTH)

70
75
80

12
13
14

SECTION WIDTH
(MILLIMETERS)
145
155
ETC

CONSTRUCTION TYPE
R - RADIAL
B - BIAS-BELTED
D - DIAGONAL (BIAS)

SECTION WIDTH

SECTION HEIGHT

TCCS1261

Fig. 7 P-Metric tire coding

UNDERSTANDING TIRE SIZES

The P-Metric system is now used as the measurement standard for passenger car tires. The first number in the P-Metric system is the width of the tire in millimeters, measured from sidewall to sidewall. To convert to inches, divide by 25.4 In the example above, the width is 185mm or 7.28 inches.

The second number is the aspect ratio. This is a ratio of sidewall height to width. In the example above, the tire is 7.28 inches wide, multiply that by the aspect ratio to find the height of one sidewall. In this case, 185x0.60=111mm or 7.28 inches x 0.6 = 4.36 inches.

The last number is the diameter of the wheel in inches.

To figure the outside diameter of a tire, take the sidewall height and multiply by two,(remember that the diameter is made up of two sidewalls, the one above the wheel, and the one below the wheel) and add the diameter of the wheel to get your answer.

Example . . . 185/60R14 85H or 185/60HR14

185mm x .60=111mm x 2=222mm + 355.6mm(14 inches)= 577.6mm or 22.74 inches

PLUS SIZING

A popular trend with high performance wheels and tires is "Plus Sizing". This is done to improve both the performance and appearance of the vehicle. By using a larger diameter wheel with a lower profile tire it's possible to properly maintain the overall diameter of the tire, keeping odometer and speedometer changes negligible. By using a tire with a shorter sidewall, you gain quickness in steering response and better lateral stability. The visual appeal is obvious, most wheels look better than the sidewall of the tire, so the more wheel and less sidewall there is, the better it looks.

TIRE PERFORMANCE RATING

♦ **See Figure 8**

Late model vehicles, whether the family sedan or the sleek sports coupe are lighter with considerably better suspensions and handling characteristics than their predecessors. It is only natural that drivers want tires that match the vehicle's capabilities.

The original push for high performance tires started in Europe, where tire manufacturers worked together with auto manufacturers to perfect the handling characteristics of high performance vehicles and where tires are speed-rated for performance.

Many drivers of high performance vehicles are familiar with the European speed ratings, where the speed-rated tire is matched with the speed of the automobile. U.S. tire manufacturers have adopted the European speed rating system. The most common speed ratings are:

- M—for cars speed rated up to 81 mph, (130km/h).
- N—for cars speed rated up to 87 mph, (140km/h).
- P—for cars speed rated up to 93 mph, (150km/h).
- Q—for cars speed rated up to 99 mph, (160km/h).
- R—for cars speed rated up to 106 mph, (170km/h).
- S—for cars speed rated up to 112 mph, (180km/h).
- T—for cars speed rated up to 118 mph, (190km/h).
- U—for cars speed rated up to 124 mph, (200km/h).
- H—for cars speed rated up to 130 mph, (210km/h).
- V (VR)—for cars speed rated up to 149 mph, (240km/h).
- W (ZR)—for cars speed rated up to 168 mph, (270km/h).
- Y (ZR)—for cars speed rated up to 186 mph, (300km/h).
- Z —for cars speed rated 149 mph and over, (240km/h).

Old Speed Rating	New Speed Rating	Maximum Speed (mph)
SR	P	93
	Q	99
	R	106
	S	113
HR	T	116
	H	130
VR	V	Over 130

88520G08

Fig. 8 Old vs. new speed ratings

Current tire speed rating markings include the use of the service description to identify the tire's speed capability (P215/65R15 95V—maximum speed 149 mph). Previous customs included the speed symbol in the size designation only (P215/65VR15) and the speed capability was listed as "above 130 mph."

Any tire with a speed capability above 149 mph (240 km/h) can, at the tire manufacturers option, include a "ZR" in the size designation (P275/40ZR17). If a service description IS NOT included, the tire manufacturer must be consulted for the maximum speed capability (P275/40ZR17—speed capability is > 149 mph). If a service description IS included with the size description, the speed capability is limited by the speed symbol in the service description.

Example . . . (P275/40ZR17 93W— maximum speed 168 mph).

THE CONTACT PATCH

The shape of a tire's contact patch or "footprint" greatly influences its performance and is dependent on its profile or "aspect ratio". Low profile tires (most performance tires) have a short and wide contact patch that is effective in converting the driver's input into very responsive handling, cornering stability and traction, especially on dry roads.

High profile tires (light truck and most passenger tires) have a long and narrow contact patch which helps to provide predictable handling, a smooth ride and especially good traction in snow.

TIRE TYPES

Original Equipment (OE) tires are usually a compromise. The vehicle designer needs to blend handling, noise, ride, and wear to create a "prefect tire" for the average driver. Most people find that their needs may be biased more toward handling or ride than the average driver. When replacing OE tires it is recommended, and in some municipalities required, that the replacement tires are of OE specifications or better. Tires are known by many names and styles. Each type has a slightly different function, as well as different capabilities:

• **Max/Exotic performance tires** are usually technically advanced, combining expensive materials and precision lightweight construction techniques to provide superior handling in wet or dry conditions and have extremely high speed capabilities (Z rated or higher).

• **Ultra high performance tires** are the top level of tires that are available in a wide range of sizes. They are low profile tires designed to give high speed capabilities and quick steering response with outstanding cornering in wet or dry conditions (V or Z speed rating).

• **High performance tires** are a slight upgrade from OE tires in terms of handling. They offer nearly the handling of the ultra high performance tires, but at a significantly lower price (H or lower speed rating).

➡**Ultra high performance and high performance all season tires are derived and usually based on the ultra high/high performance non-all season tire. They are altered in tread pattern to gain in snow traction and the rubber compound is changed to be pliable over a wider temperature range. The snow capabilities of this type of tire is minimal, but is usually enough to get through an inch or two of snow (H to Z speed ratings).**

• **Touring tires** combine the appearance and responsive handling of a performance tire with more of a smooth ride quality and lower noise levels. this type of tire will, typically wear longer than a performance tire (S to V speed ratings).

• **All season (or mud+snow) tires** are aimed mainly at domestic sedans, these tires offer very long tread wear, plush ride, and predictable handling.

• **Snow tires** are specially constructed to grip snowy surfaces. The rubber is specially formulated to stay pliable in the cold and provide better traction on ice. The interlocking tread pattern of the snow tire allows it to bite the snow for additional stop-and-go traction.

• **Competition tires** are the highest performing street legal tire you can purchase. These are special purpose tires that feature a very shallow tread pattern, stiff construction, and high grip tread compounds. Usually these tires are very prone to hydroplaning, and offer practically no treadwear.

Another Word On Snow Tires

If the weather in your area includes strong possibilities for snow or ice, we highly recommend that you consider mounting 4 snow tires on your car, truck or sport utility vehicle every winter. Most snow and ice tires are made of specialized rubber compounds which will maximize the available traction on the cold, slippery surfaces found in winter driving. Most snow tires include specialized tread patterns to channel snow away from the tire (allowing it to find traction on the pavement underneath). Some snow tires use siping (slits cut into the rubber allowing tread to flex outward, increasing the available surface area) to help increase the amount of rubber in contact with the road.

Although snow tires cannot work miracles (and must obey the same laws of physics as other tires) they will provide the best combination of driveability and increased traction that you will find in a foul weather tire. Even if you have a four wheel drive vehicle, snow tires will increase the ability of the vehicle to deal with foul weather. Remember that a four wheel drive may offer certain advantages in foul weather, but it doesn't do you any good if the tires do not provide sufficient traction.

➡**Note that snow tires, whether 2 or 4, will affect vehicle handling in all non-snow situations. The stiffer, heavier snow tires will noticeably change the turning and braking characteristics of the vehicle. Once the snow tires are installed, you must re-learn the behavior of the vehicle and drive accordingly.**

Most manufacturers strongly recommend the use of 4 snow tires on their vehicles for reasons of stability. If snow tires are fitted only to the drive wheels, the opposite end of the vehicle may become very unstable when braking or turning on slippery surfaces. This instability can lead to unpleasant endings if the driver can't counteract the slide in time.

➡**Consider buying extra wheels on which to mount the snow tires. Once done, the "snow wheels" can be installed and removed as needed. This eliminates the potential damage to tires or wheels from seasonal removal and installation. Even if your vehicle has styled wheels, see if inexpensive steel wheels are available. Although the look of the vehicle will change, the expensive wheels will be protected from salt, curb hits and pothole damage.**

Tire Grading

▶ **See Figure 9**

The Uniform Tire Quality Grading System (UTQG) took effect in April, 1979. Under this system the Department of Transportation requires each manufacturer to grade its tires and establish ratings for treadwear, traction, and temperature resistance. These tests are conducted independently by each manufacturer following government guidelines to assign values that represent a comparison between the tested tire and a control tire. While traction and temperature resistance ratings are specific performance levels, the treadwear ratings are assigned by the manufacturers following field testing and are most accurate when comparing tires of the same brand.

TREADWEAR

The treadwear grade is expressed by a number in multiples of 10—a higher number indicating a comparatively longer tread life. The number 100 is assigned as the standard of 30,000 mile (48,300 km) tread life on a test track under controlled conditions, and other numbers represent a percentage up or down from 100. As an example, a grade of 150 represents a tread life 50% greater than 30,000 miles (48,300 km), or 45,000 miles (72,400 km).

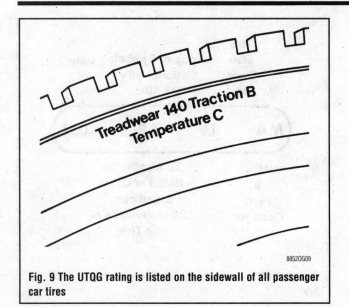

Fig. 9 The UTQG rating is listed on the sidewall of all passenger car tires

TRACTION

The test for traction involves towing a trailer mounted with the test tires over concrete and an asphalt course wetted with a controlled amount of water. As the brakes are slammed on, the tire's coefficient of friction is measured. An "A" grade means that its traction exceeds a predetermined standard on both courses. A "B" grade indicates that it exceeds a lower predetermined standard on both courses. If the tire can't make the "B" grade on either concrete or asphalt, it receives a "C" grade.

In 1997 a new top rating of "AA" was introduced to indicate even greater wet braking traction. However, due to its newness, this grade will probably be applied initially to new tire lines as they are introduced and later to existing lines which excel in wet braking, but had been limited to the previous top grade of "A". Note that traction grades do not indicate wet cornering ability.

➡The UTQG ratings are not required on winter or light truck sized tires.

TEMPERATURE RESISTANCE

The test for temperature resistance is to roll the tire against a large steel wheel at increasing speeds until the tire either is destroyed or achieves a grade of "A", indicating that it can survive a sustained run of 115 mph (185 km/h) at 95°F (35°C). A grade of "B" indicates endurance at 100 mph (160 km/h), and anything less, but still above the federal minimum tire safety standard, receives a grade of "C".

Reading the Tire Sidewall

▸ **See Figures 10, 11, 12 and 13**

The tire sidewall contains just about anything you would want to know about a tire, most of it required by federal law. The UTQG rating is listed on the sidewall indicating treadwear, traction and temperature ratings.

Size—Tire width and diameter are identified on the sidewall as shown in the accompanying illustrations and tire size comparison chart. Up to

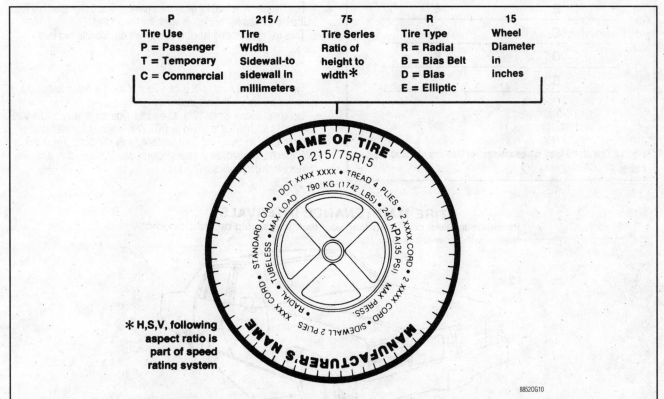

P	215/	75	R	15
Tire Use	**Tire**	**Tire Series**	**Tire Type**	**Wheel**
P = Passenger	**Width**	**Ratio of**	R = Radial	**Diameter**
T = Temporary	Sidewall-to-	height to	B = Bias Belt	in
C = Commercial	sidewall in	width*	D = Bias	inches
	millimeters		E = Elliptic	

NAME OF TIRE
P 215/75R15
DOT XXXX XXXX • TREAD 4 PLIES • 2 XXXX CORD • 2 XXXX CORD • 240 kPA (35 PSI) MAX PRESS. • SIDEWALL 2 PLIES • XXXX CORD • RADIAL • TUBELESS • MAX LOAD 790 KG (1742 LBS) • STANDARD LOAD
MANUFACTURER'S NAME

*H,S,V, following aspect ratio is part of speed rating system

Fig. 10 The side wall of a tire using the metric designations looks similar to this. Although the measurements are in metric, wheel diameter is given in inches. Load and pressure are given in both metric (kg/kPA) and English (lb./psi).

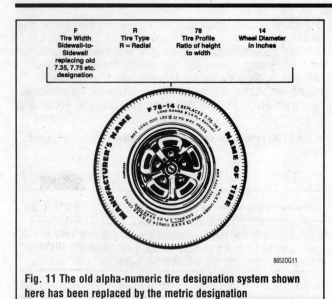

Fig. 11 The old alpha-numeric tire designation system shown here has been replaced by the metric designation

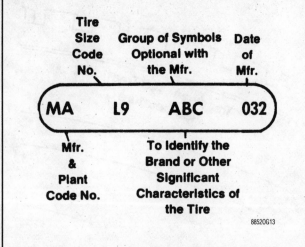

Fig. 13 The DOT code supplies identifying information about the tire

Load Range	Replaces Ply-Rating
A	2
B	4
C	6
D	8
E	10

Fig. 12 The alpha load range ratings replace the old bias ply rating

1978, tires were designated in the alpha-numeric system. To conform to standards, most tire manufacturers have converted to use the metric designation

Maximum pressure and load—This is the maximum load the tire should carry when inflated at its maximum cold inflation pressure. Consult your owners manual or tire dealer for the recommended inflation pressure for your vehicle. Very seldom will the tires be inflated to their maximum pressure.

Load range—The load range in the alpha-numeric designation is a letter indicating the number of plies at which the tire is rated.

Tires using the metric labeling system are divided into two load ranges:

- SL = Standard Load (35 psi max)
- XL= Extra load (41 psi max.)

Type of cord and number of plies—Each of these is dependent on the other and will vary with tire construction.

Dot compliance—Since 1971, all tires are required to carry certain standard coded information, prefixed by DOT. This indicates that the tire conforms to U.S. Department of Transportation safety standards. The coded information also identifies the manufacturer, date of manufacture and other significant characteristics on the tire.

TIRE MAINTENANCE INTERVALS

For maximum wear and safety from your tires, they should be maintained at the following intervals.

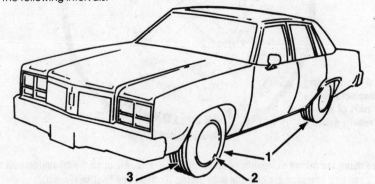

1.	Rotate tires	Every 6 months/6000 miles
2.	Check tire pressure	Every fuel stop/2 weeks
3.	Check tread depth	Every 6 months/6000 miles
	Clean tread of stones, glass, debris	As necessary

Tire Care

Caring for tires is easy and important for safety, but many vehicle owners neglect this important part of vehicle maintenance.

A survey by a major tire manufacturer found that:
- Nine of every 10 vehicles inspected had improperly inflated tires.
- One of every five vehicles inspected had at least one tire with too little tread for safe use.
- One of every 20 tires inspected was in danger of imminent fail-ure.
- Nearly one of every five tires inspected showed unusual tread wear due to alignment, improper inflation or improper balance.

INFLATION & INSPECTION

▶ **See Figures 14 thru 25**

The importance of proper tire inflation cannot be over-emphasized. A tire employs air as part of its structure. It is designed around the supporting strength of the air at a specified pressure. For this reason, improper inflation drastically reduces the tire's ability to perform as intended. A tire will lose some air in day-to-day use; having to add a few pounds of air periodically is not necessarily a sign of a leaking tire.

Two items should be a permanent fixture in every glove compartment: an accurate tire pressure gauge and a tread depth gauge. Check the tire pressure (including the spare) regularly with a pocket type gauge. Too often, the gauge on the end of the air hose at your corner garage is not accurate because it suffers too much abuse. Always check tire pressure when the tires are cold, as pressure increases with temperature. If you must move the vehicle to check the tire inflation, do not drive more than a mile before checking. A cold tire is generally one that has not been driven for more than three hours.

A plate or sticker is normally provided somewhere in the vehicle (door post, hood, tailgate or trunk lid) which shows the proper pressure for the tires.

✳✳ CAUTION

Never exceed the maximum tire pressure embossed on the tire! This is the pressure to be used when the tire is at maximum loading, but it is rarely the correct pressure for everyday driving. Consult the owner's manual or the tire pressure sticker for the correct tire pressure.

Once you've maintained the correct tire pressures for several weeks, you'll be familiar with the vehicle's braking and handling personality.

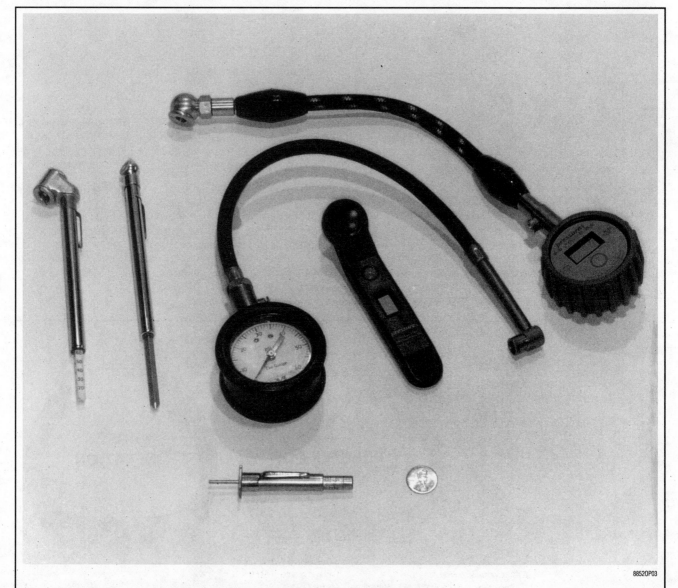

Fig. 14 A variety of high quality pressure gauges are available, get one and use it often

88520P03

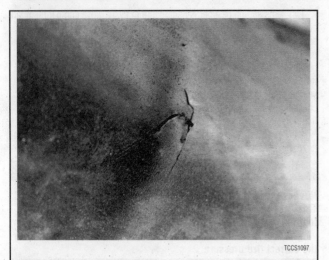

Fig. 15 Tires should be checked frequently for any sign of puncture or damage

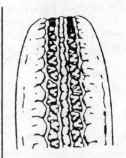
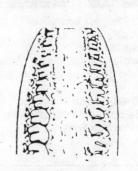

• DRIVE WHEEL HEAVY
  ACCELERATION
• OVERINFLATION

• HARD CORNERING
• UNDERINFLATION
• LACK OF ROTATION

TCCS1262

Fig. 17 Examples of inflation-related tire wear patterns

Fig. 16 Tires with deep cuts, or cuts which show bulging should be replaced immediately

Slight adjustments in tire pressures can fine-tune these characteristics, but never change the cold pressure specification by more than 2 psi (14 kPa). A slightly softer tire pressure will give a softer ride but also yield lower fuel mileage. A slightly harder tire will give crisper dry road handling but can cause skidding on wet surfaces. Unless you're fully attuned to the vehicle, stick to the recommended inflation pressures.

All tires made since 1968 have built-in tread wear indicator bars that show up as ½ inch (13mm) wide smooth bands across the tire when 1/16 inch (1.5mm) of tread remains. The appearance of tread wear indicators means that the tires should be replaced. In fact, many states have laws prohibiting the use of tires with less than this amount of tread.

You can check your own tread depth with an inexpensive gauge or by using a Lincoln head penny. Slip the Lincoln penny (with Lincoln's head upside-down) into several tread grooves. If you can see the top of Lincoln's head in 2 adjacent grooves, the tire has less than 1/16 inch (1.5mm) tread left and should be replaced. You can measure snow tires in the same manner by using the "tails" side of the Lincoln penny. If you can see the top of the Lincoln memorial, it's time to replace the snow tire(s).

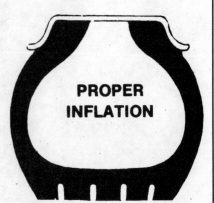

OVERINFLATION UNDERINFLATION PROPER INFLATION

88520G17

Fig. 18 Tire inflation pressure is a major factor in determining how long your tires last and how well they perform

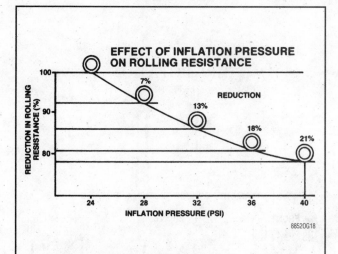

Fig. 19 The rolling resistance of a tire decreases dramatically as the inflation pressure increases

Fig. 22 A plate or sticker is normally provided somewhere in the vehicle (door post, hood, tailgate or trunk lid) which shows the proper pressure for the tires

Fig. 20 Radial tires have a characteristic sidewall bulge; don't try to measure pressure by looking at the tire. Use a quality air pressure gauge

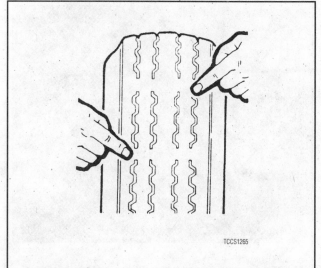

Fig. 23 Tread wear indicators will appear when the tire is worn

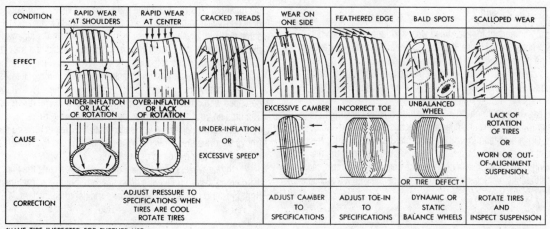

CONDITION	RAPID WEAR AT SHOULDERS	RAPID WEAR AT CENTER	CRACKED TREADS	WEAR ON ONE SIDE	FEATHERED EDGE	BALD SPOTS	SCALLOPED WEAR
EFFECT							
CAUSE	UNDER-INFLATION OR LACK OF ROTATION	OVER-INFLATION OR LACK OF ROTATION	UNDER-INFLATION OR EXCESSIVE SPEED*	EXCESSIVE CAMBER	INCORRECT TOE	UNBALANCED WHEEL OR TIRE DEFECT *	LACK OF ROTATION OF TIRES OR WORN OR OUT-OF-ALIGNMENT SUSPENSION.
CORRECTION	ADJUST PRESSURE TO SPECIFICATIONS WHEN TIRES ARE COOL ROTATE TIRES			ADJUST CAMBER TO SPECIFICATIONS	ADJUST TOE-IN TO SPECIFICATIONS	DYNAMIC OR STATIC BALANCE WHEELS	ROTATE TIRES AND INSPECT SUSPENSION

*HAVE TIRE INSPECTED FOR FURTHER USE.

Fig. 21 Common tire wear patterns and causes

Fig. 24 Accurate tread depth indicators are inexpensive and handy

Fig. 25 A penny works well for a quick check of tread depth

ROTATING THE TIRES

▶ See Figures 26, 27 and 28

Tire rotation is important for even tread wear and long life. When performed at the recommended times, it will ensure that the tires wear evenly and prolong the useful life of the tires. Tires should be rotated at regular intervals. Tires can be rotated conveniently during every other regular oil change, which for most vehicles, would put rotation at about every 5000–7500 mi. (8000–12000 km).

Front and rear, drive and non-drive tires exhibit different wear patterns. Front tires tend to wear in the shoulder area, because of steering and cornering forces. Drive tires tend to wear in the center because of drive traction forces. On front wheel drive vehicles, front tires wear faster then the rear. Personal driving habits and vehicle performance characteristics also cause tires to wear differently. Vehicles are designed to operate with a matched set of tires.

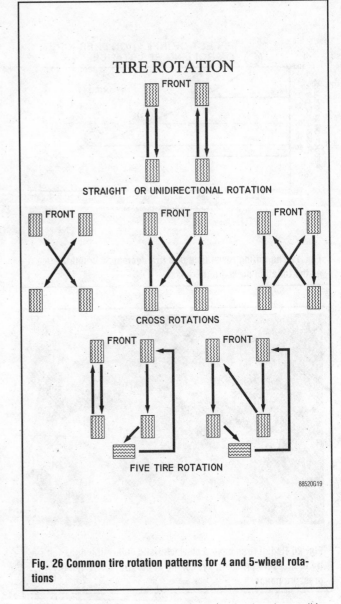

Fig. 26 Common tire rotation patterns for 4 and 5-wheel rotations

When rotating "uni-directional tires," make sure that they always roll in the same direction. This means that a tire used on the left side of the vehicle must not be switched to the right side and vice-versa. Such tires should only be rotated front-to-rear or rear-to-front, while always remaining on the same side of the vehicle. These tires are marked on the sidewall as to the direction of rotation; observe the marks when reinstalling the tire(s).

There are many tire rotation patterns. Any routine pattern is better than no rotation at all. The important factor in a tire rotation pattern is that all tires eventually are placed at all applicable wheel positions. If the vehicle is equipped with a full size spare, it should be included in the rotation pattern. The tires on your vehicle according to the following rules:

• On front wheel drive vehicles, rotate the tires in forward cross pattern (move the drive tires straight to the rear then, cross the rear tires and mount on the front) or a regular cross pattern.

• On rear wheel or four wheel drive vehicles, rotate the tires in a rearward cross pattern (move the drive tires straight to the front then, cross the front tires and mount on the rear) or a regular cross pattern.

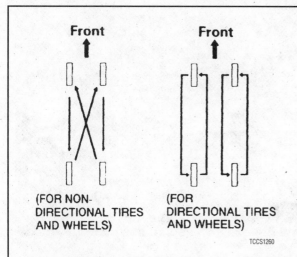

Fig. 27 Compact spare tires must NEVER be used in the rotation pattern

Fig. 28 Uni-directional tires are identifiable by sidewall arrows and/or the word "rotation"

• If the vehicle is equipped with directional wheels or tires, rotate them from the front to back.

• If the vehicle is equipped with non-directional tires that are different size from front to rear, rotate them from the side to side.

Some styled or "Mag" wheels may have different offsets front to rear. In these cases, the rear wheels must not be used up front and vice-versa. Furthermore, if these wheels are equipped with uni-directional tires, they cannot be rotated unless the tire is remounted for the proper direction of rotation.

➡The compact or space-saver® spare is strictly for emergency use. It must never be included in the tire rotation or placed on the vehicle for everyday use.

Some years ago, many manufacturers believed that radials should be treated as directional tires in order to prevent rapid wear and possible handling difficulties. But, over the years most tire and vehicle manufacturers

(even ones that formerly warned against cross-switching radials) began to change their tune. Now most vehicle and tire manufacturers recommend including radials in rotational patterns which switch the direction of tire rotation.

STORING THE TIRES

If they are mounted on wheels, store the tires at proper inflation pressure. All tires should be kept in a cool, dry place. If they are stored in the garage or basement, do not let them stand on a concrete floor; set them on strips of wood, a mat or a large stack of newspaper. Keeping them away from direct moisture is of paramount importance. Tires should not be stored upright, but in a flat position.

When You Have A Flat Tire

▶ **See Figures 29 thru 34**

Safety is the first consideration when you have a flat tire. If a flat tire occurs while driving, DO NOT apply the brakes heavily. Instead, gradually decrease the speed of the vehicle, while holding the steering wheel firmly. Slowly move the vehicle to a safe place on the side of the road. Park on a level spot, turn the ignition **OFF**, set the parking brake, and turn on the hazard flashers. If a front tire goes flat, the flat tire will create a drag that pulls the vehicle toward that side, whereas a flat rear tire acts much like a skid on a slippery road.

The location and instructions of the equipment you need to change a flat tire are found in the owner's manual and may also be found a decal located in the jack storage area.

Pull well off the road onto a level surface and set the parking brake. Switch on the hazard flashers and raise the hood to indicate mechanical trouble to passing motorists. Place automatic transmission vehicles in **P** (park) and manual transmissions in Reverse.

Remove the wheel cover (if equipped). To make the job a little easier, loosen all of the lug nuts a few turns, while the wheel is resting on the ground. If possible, chock the wheel diagonally opposite from the flat tire.

Operate the jack slowly and smoothly according to the directions supplied. Raise the vehicle so that the tire clears the ground. Keep in mind that you may have to raise the vehicle a little more to accommodate the height

Fig. 29 Place the jack at the proper lifting point on your vehicle

Fig. 30 Before jacking the vehicle, block the diagonally opposite wheel with one or, two chocks

Fig. 31 With the vehicle still on the ground, break the lug nuts loose using the wrench end of the tire iron

Fig. 32 After the lug nuts have been loosened, raise the vehicle using the jack until the tire is clear of the ground

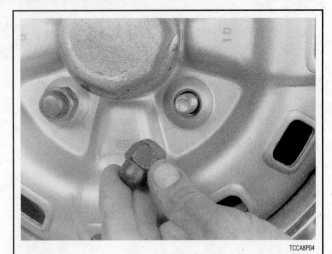

Fig. 33 Remove the lug nuts from the studs (NOTE: some vehicles use lug bolts instead of nuts and studs)

Fig. 34 Remove the wheel and tire assembly from the vehicle

of an inflated tire. But don't over do it and drop the vehicle from the jack! Remove the lug nuts and wheel, and replace it with the spare. Tighten the lug nuts hand-tight.

Lower the vehicle to the ground and fully tighten the lug nuts or bolts in a crisscross pattern. Install the wheel cover (if equipped) and stow the jack and flat tire. Have the flat serviced as soon as possible.

HOW TO READ TIRE WEAR

The way your tires wear is a good indicator of other parts of your car. Abnormal wear patterns are often caused by the need for simple tire maintenance, or for front end alignment.

Tires should be inspected at every opportunity; once a week isn't too often. Learning to read the early warning signs of trouble can prevent wear that shortens tire life or indicates the need for having other parts of the car serviced. Tires should be inspected 3 ways. First, visually examine all 4 tires; second, feel the tread by hand to detect wear such as feathering and third, check all 4 tires with a pocket type pressure gauge.

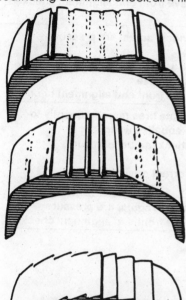

Over Inflation

Excessive wear at the center of the tread indicates that the air pressure in the tire is consistently too high. The tire is riding on the center of the tread and wearing it prematurely. Many times, the "eyeball" method of inflation (pumping the tires up until there is no bulge at the bottom) is at fault; tire inflation pressure should always be checked with a reliable tire gauge. Occasionally, this wear pattern can result from outrageously wide tires on narrow rims. The cure for this is to replace either the tires or the wheels.

Under Inflation

This type of wear usually results from consistent under inflation. When a tire is under inflated, there is too much contact with the road by the outer treads, which wear prematurely. Tire pressure should be checked with a reliable pressure gauge. When this type of wear occurs, and the tire pressure is known to be consistently correct, a bent or worn steering component or the need for wheel alignment could be indicated. Bent steering or idler arms cause incorrect toe-in and abnormal handling characteristics on turns.

Feathering

Feathering is a condition when the edge of each tread rib develops a slightly rounded edge on one side and a sharp edge on the other. By running your hand over the tire, you can usually feel the sharper edges before you'll be able to see them. The most common cause of feathering is incorrect toe-in setting, which can be cured by having it set correctly. Occasionally toe-in will be set correctly and this wear pattern still occurs. This is usually due to deteriorated bushings in the front suspension, causing the wheel alignment to shift as the car moves down the road.

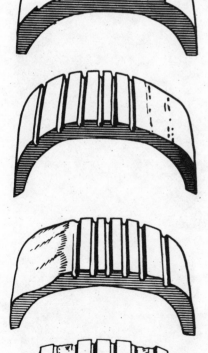

One Side Wear

When an inner or outer rib wears faster than than the rest of the tire, the need for wheel alignment is indicated. There is excessive camber in the front suspension, causing the wheel to lean too much to the inside or outside and putting too much load on one side of the tire. The car may simply need the wheels aligned, but misalignment could be due to sagging springs, worn ball joints, or worn control arm bushings. Because load has a great effect on alignment, be sure the vehicle is loaded the way it's normally driven when you have the wheels aligned; this is particularly important with independent rear suspension cars.

Cupping

Cups or scalloped dips appearing around the edge of the tread on one side or the other, almost always indicate worn (sometimes bent) suspension parts. Adjustment of wheel alignment alone will seldom cure the problem. Any worn component that connects the wheel to the car (ball joint, wheel bearing, shock absorber, springs, bushings, etc.) can cause this condition. Worn components should be replaced with new ones. The worn tire should be balanced and possibly moved to a different location on the car. Occasionally, wheels that are out of balance will wear like this, but wheel imbalance usually shows up as bald spots between the outside edges and center of the tread.

Second-rib Wear

Second-rib wear is normally found only in radial tires, and appears where the steel belts end in relation to the tread. Normally, it can be kept to a minimum by paying careful attention to tire pressure and frequently rotating the tires. Some car and tire manufacturers consider a slight amount of wear at the second rib of a radial tire normal, but that excessive amounts of wear indicate that the tires are too wide for the wheels. Be careful when having oversize tires installed on narrow wheels.

8852OC02

TROUBLESHOOTING BASIC TIRE AND WHEEL PROBLEMS

The most common cause of tire problems is improperly inflated tires. The majority of tire problems can be cured by maintaining the proper inflation pressure, rotating the tires regularly and by correct good driving habits.

Problem	Is Caused by	What to Do
The car's front end vibrates at high speeds and the steering wheel shakes	• Wheels out of balance • Front end needs aligning	• Have wheels balanced • Have front end alignment checked
The car pulls to one side while cruising	• Unequal tire pressure (car will usually pull to the low side) • Mismatched tires • Front end needs aligning	• Check/adjust tire pressure • Be sure tires are of the same type and size • Have front end alignment checked
Abnormal, excessive or uneven tire wear See "How to Read Tire Wear"	• Infrequent tire rotation • Improper tire pressure • Sudden stops/starts or high speed on curves	• Rotate tires more frequently to equalize wear • Check/adjust pressure • Correct driving habits
Tire squeals	• Improper tire pressure • Front end needs aligning	• Check/adjust tire pressure • Have front end alignment checked

88520C04

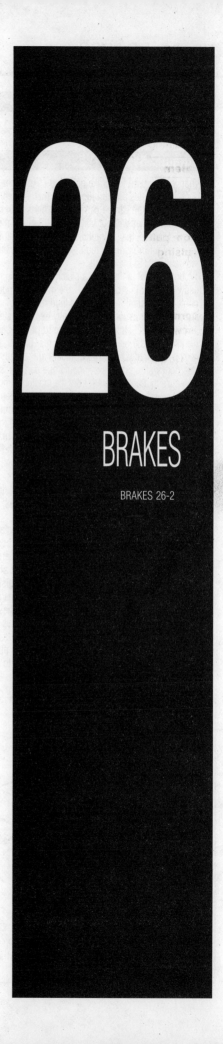

26

BRAKES

BRAKES 26-2

BRAKES

▶ See Figures 1, 2 and 3

Hydraulic System

When you step on the brake pedal, you expect the vehicle to stop. The brake pedal operates a hydraulic system that is used for two reasons. First, fluid under pressure can be carried to all parts of the vehicle by small hoses or metal lines without taking up a lot of room or causing routing problems. Second, the hydraulic fluid offers a great mechanical advantage—little foot pressure is required on the pedal, but a great deal of pressure is generated at the wheels.

The brake pedal is linked to a piston in the brake master cylinder, which is filled with hydraulic brake fluid. The master cylinder consists of a cylinder containing a small piston and a fluid reservoir.

Modern master cylinders are actually two separate cylinders. Such a system is called a dual circuit, because the front cylinder is connected to the front brakes and the rear cylinder to the rear brakes. (Some vehicles are connected diagonally.) The two cylinders are actually separated, allowing for emergency stopping power should one part of the system fail.

The entire hydraulic system from the master cylinder to the wheels is full of hydraulic brake fluid. When the brake pedal is depressed, the pistons in the master cylinder are forced to move, exerting tremendous force on the fluid in the lines. The fluid has nowhere to go, and forces the wheel cylinder pistons (drum brakes) or caliper pistons (disc brakes) to exert pressure on the brake shoes or pads. The friction between the brake shoe and wheel drum or the brake pad and rotor (disc) slows the vehicle and eventually stops it.

Also attached to the brake pedal is a switch that lights the brake lights as the pedal is depressed. The lights stay on until the brake pedal is released and returns to its normal position.

Each wheel cylinder in a drum brake system contains two pistons, one at either end, which push outward in opposite directions. In disc brake systems, the wheel cylinders are part of the caliper (there can be as many as four or as few as one). Whether disc or drum type, all pistons use some type of rubber seal to prevent leakage around the piston, and a rubber dust boot seals the outer ends of the wheel cylinders against dirt and moisture.

When the brake pedal is released, a spring pushes the master cylinder pistons back to their normal positions. Check valves in the master cylinder piston allow fluid to flow toward the wheel cylinders or calipers as the piston returns. Then as the brake shoe return springs pull the brake shoes back to the released position, excess fluid returns to the master cylinder

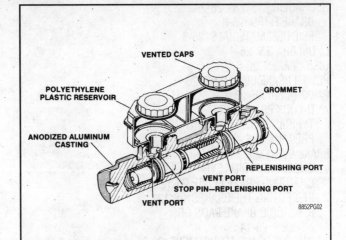

Fig. 2 Typical master cylinder. Since 1967, all master cylinders are of the dual circuit type

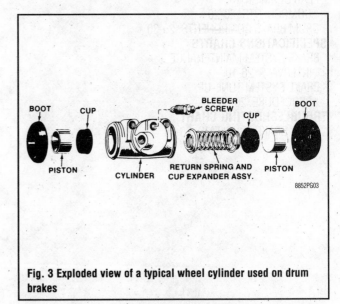

Fig. 3 Exploded view of a typical wheel cylinder used on drum brakes

through compensating ports, which have been uncovered as the pistons move back. Any fluid that has leaked from the system will also be replaced through the compensating ports.

All dual circuit brake systems use a switch to activate a light, warning of brake failure. The switch is located in a valve mounted near the master cylinder. A piston in the valve receives pressure on each end from the front and rear brake circuits. When the pressures are balanced, the piston remains stationary, but when one circuit has a leak, greater pressure during the application of the brakes will force the piston to one side or the other, closing the switch and activating the warning light. The light can also be activated by the ignition switch during engine starting or by the parking brake.

Front disc, rear drum brake systems also have a metering valve to prevent the front disc brakes from engaging before the rear brakes have contacted the drums. This ensures that the front brakes will not normally be used alone to stop the vehicle. A proportioning valve is also used to limit pressure to the rear brakes to prevent rear wheel lock-up during hard braking.

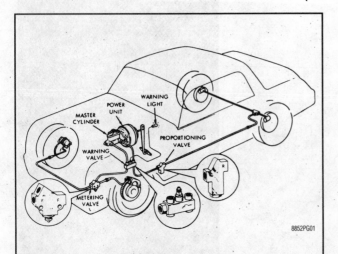

Fig. 1 Typical components found on a front disc/rear drum brake system

BRAKE FLUID

▶ See Figure 4

✳✳ WARNING

Clean, high quality brake fluid is essential to the safe and proper operation of the brake system. You should always buy the highest quality brake fluid that is available. If the brake fluid becomes contaminated, drain and flush the system, then refill the master cylinder with new fluid. Never reuse any brake fluid. Any brake fluid that is removed from the system should be discarded.

At first, vehicles used mechanically actuated brakes. Simple and easy, the system worked okay until vehicles started going more than 10 miles per hour on a regular basis. At this point, the idea for hydraulically actuated brakes came up.

A liquid, for all practical purposes, can't be compressed. So, if you fill a sealed system with liquid and try to compress it, say with a master cylinder, the liquid exerts equal force on all other parts of the system, for instance calipers and wheel cylinders. Get the idea?

Vehicle manufacturers recognized the need for a fluid that resisted high temperatures, had lubricating capabilities, had a low freezing point and resisted corrosion. Almost all vehicles on the road today use brake fluid designated DOT 3 or DOT 4. DOT stands for Department of Transportation. The DOT established the standards by which brake fluid, among other things, is regulated.

Some vehicles have been built using a silicone-based (DOT 5) brake fluid, but these are few and far between. DOT 3 and 4 fluids are petroleum-based liquids. Silicone fluids are, of course, not petroleum-based and are completely incompatible with other types and may cause damage to the rubber seals if added to systems that are not designed for silicone fluid. There are 2 chief advantages to silicone-based brake fluid. For one thing, it has a superior ability to withstand heat. And for another, it does not share the petroleum-based fluid's tendency to absorb moisture. However, petroleum based fluids are perfectly able to withstand the heat generated by just about all modern vehicles. If you maintain the DOT 3 or 4 fluid in your brake system through periodic changes, and keep the system sealed to protect it from dirt or moisture, silicone based fluids are unnecessary.

➡ The best rule of thumb with brake fluid is to use the fluid recommended by your owner's manual. Changing the fluid from DOT 3 to DOT 4 is often allowed, but do not change from DOT 3 or 4 to DOT 5.

Brake fluid is a specialized liquid and should never be mixed with any other type of fluid, such as mineral oil. Also, brake fluid has the ability to absorb moisture from the air, so, it can become contaminated simply by age. Over the years, you'll be removing the master cylinder cap or disconnecting brake lines. During the time that the system is open, the brake fluid will absorb small amounts of moisture, thereby reducing its effectiveness. Brake fluid contaminated with moisture will cause rust in the system as well as losing its ability to stand up to heat.

Therefore, it is recommended by many vehicle manufacturers and most professionals that the brake fluid system be flushed and refilled every 2 years. This is especially true on vehicles with ABS systems.

When adding brake fluid to your vehicle's brake system, use brake fluid that is fresh and kept in a small, sealed container. If your brake fluid jar has been sitting around for a while, get new stuff. It's not expensive and is critical to the performance of the braking system. Don't forget, use only approved DOT 3 or 4 fluid. If you're in doubt about the fluid recommendation for your vehicle, check your owner's manual.

Used fluids such as brake fluid are hazardous wastes and must be disposed of properly. Before draining any fluids, consult with your local authorities; in many areas waste oil, etc. is being accepted as a part of recycling programs. A number of service stations and auto parts stores are also accepting waste fluids for recycling.

Be sure of the recycling center's policies before draining any fluids, as many will not accept different fluids that have been mixed together.

A final note . . . brake fluid should be handled with care. Brake fluid is a nasty and poisonous substance. Keep it out of your eyes and off your skin. Also, remember that it is an excellent paint remover. If you don't care for your personal safety, think of your vehicle; if brake fluid gets on your vehicle's paint, wipe if off immediately and rinse the area with water. It is probably not a bad idea to also clean the area with a gentle household cleaner or car wash detergent.

FRICTION MATERIALS

▶ See Figure 5

Brake shoes and pads are constructed in a similar manner. The pad or shoe is composed of a metal backing plate and a friction lining. The lining is either bonded (glued) to the metal, or riveted. Generally, riveted linings provide superior performance, but good quality bonded linings are perfectly adequate.

Friction materials will vary between manufacturers and type of pad and the material compound may be referred to as: asbestos, organic, semi-metallic, metallic. The difference between these compounds lies in the types and percentages of friction materials used, material binders and performance modifiers.

Fig. 4 When filling the master cylinder, use only clean, fresh fluid specified for your vehicle

Fig. 5 When purchasing brake pads (and shoes) remember that in the end, they are the only things stopping your vehicle

✳✳ CAUTION

Asbestos was used in friction lining compounds for many years because of its ability to withstand heat, but became less popular as health concerns arose. It may still be found in different types of pads and, unless you personally replaced the last set of brakes on your vehicle, for safety reasons you should assume that a compound containing asbestos may have been used.

Generally speaking, organic and non-metallic asbestos compound brakes are quiet, easy on rotors and provide good feel. But this comes at the expense of high temperature operation, so they may not be your best choice for heavy duty use or mountain driving. In most cases, these linings will wear somewhat faster than metallic compound pads, so you will usually replace them more often. But, when using these pads, rotors tend to last longer.

Semi-metallic or metallic compound brake linings will vary in performance based on the metallic contents of the compound. Again, generally speaking, the higher the metallic content, the better the friction material will resist heat. This makes them more appropriate for heavy duty applications, but at the expense of braking performance before the pad reaches operating temperature. The first few applications on a cold morning may not give strong braking. Also, metallics and semi-metallics are more likely to squeal. In most cases, metallic compounds last longer than non-metallic pads, but they tend to cause more wear on the rotors. If you use metallic pads, expect to replace the rotors more often.

When deciding what type of brake lining is right for you, keep in mind that today's modern cars have brake materials which are matched to the expected vehicle's performance capabilities. Changing the material from OEM specification could adversely affect brake feel or responsiveness. Before changing the brake materials, talk to your dealer or parts supplier to help decide what is most appropriate for your application. Remember that heavy use applications such as towing , stop and go driving, driving down mountain roads, and racing may require a change to a higher performance material.

Some more exotic materials are also used in brake linings, among which are Kevlar® and carbon compounds. These materials have the capability of extremely good performance for towing, mountain driving or racing. Wear characteristics can be similar to either the metallic or the non-metallic linings, depending on the product you buy. Most race applications tend to wear like metallic linings, while many of the street applications are more like the non-metallics.

Drum Brakes

♦ See Figures 6 and 7

Drum brakes use two brake shoes mounted on a stationary backing plate on each wheel. These shoes are positioned inside a circular cast iron drum that rotates with the wheel assembly. The shoes are held in place by springs; this allows them to slide toward the drums (when they are applied) while keeping the linings and drums in alignment.

The shoes are actuated by a wheel cylinder that is usually mounted at the top of the backing plate. When the brakes are applied, hydraulic pressure forces the wheel cylinder's two actuating links outward. Since these links bear directly against the top of the brake shoes, the tops of the shoes are then forced outward against the inner side of the drum. This action forces the bottoms of the two shoes to contact the brake drum by rotating the entire assembly slightly (known as servo action). When pressure within the wheel cylinder is relieved, return springs pull the shoes away from the drum.

Modern drum brakes are designed to self-adjust during application when the vehicle is moving in reverse. This motion causes both shoes to rotate very slightly with the drum, rocking an adjusting lever. The self-adjusters are only intended to compensate for normal wear. Although the adjustment is "automatic," there is a definite method to actuate the self-adjuster, which is done during normal driving. Driving the vehicle in reverse and applying the brakes usually activates the automatic adjusters. If the brake pedal was low, you should be able to feel an increase in the height of the brake pedal.

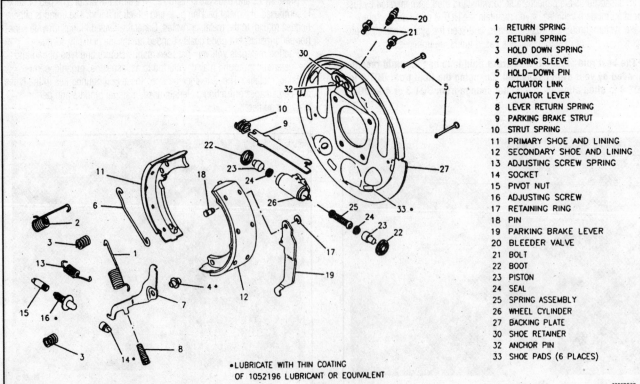

1	RETURN SPRING
2	RETURN SPRING
3	HOLD DOWN SPRING
4	BEARING SLEEVE
5	HOLD-DOWN PIN
6	ACTUATOR LINK
7	ACTUATOR LEVER
8	LEVER RETURN SPRING
9	PARKING BRAKE STRUT
10	STRUT SPRING
11	PRIMARY SHOE AND LINING
12	SECONDARY SHOE AND LINING
13	ADJUSTING SCREW SPRING
14	SOCKET
15	PIVOT NUT
16	ADJUSTING SCREW
17	RETAINING RING
18	PIN
19	PARKING BRAKE LEVER
20	BLEEDER VALVE
21	BOLT
22	BOOT
23	PISTON
24	SEAL
25	SPRING ASSEMBLY
26	WHEEL CYLINDER
27	BACKING PLATE
30	SHOE RETAINER
32	ANCHOR PIN
33	SHOE PADS (6 PLACES)

•LUBRICATE WITH THIN COATING
OF 1052196 LUBRICANT OR EQUIVALENT

8852PG27

Fig. 6 Exploded view of a typical drum brake assembly

REAR DRUM BRAKE COMPONENTS

1. Secondary shoe
2. Adjusting screw assembly
3. Primary shoe
4. Adjuster spring
5. Adjuster lever
6. Hold-down pin

7. Hold-down spring
8. Hold-down assembly
9. Adjuster cable guide
10. Parking brake lever
11. Parking brake link
12. Link spring

13. Primary shoe return spring
14. Anchor pin plate
15. Secondary shoe return spring
16. Adjuster cable

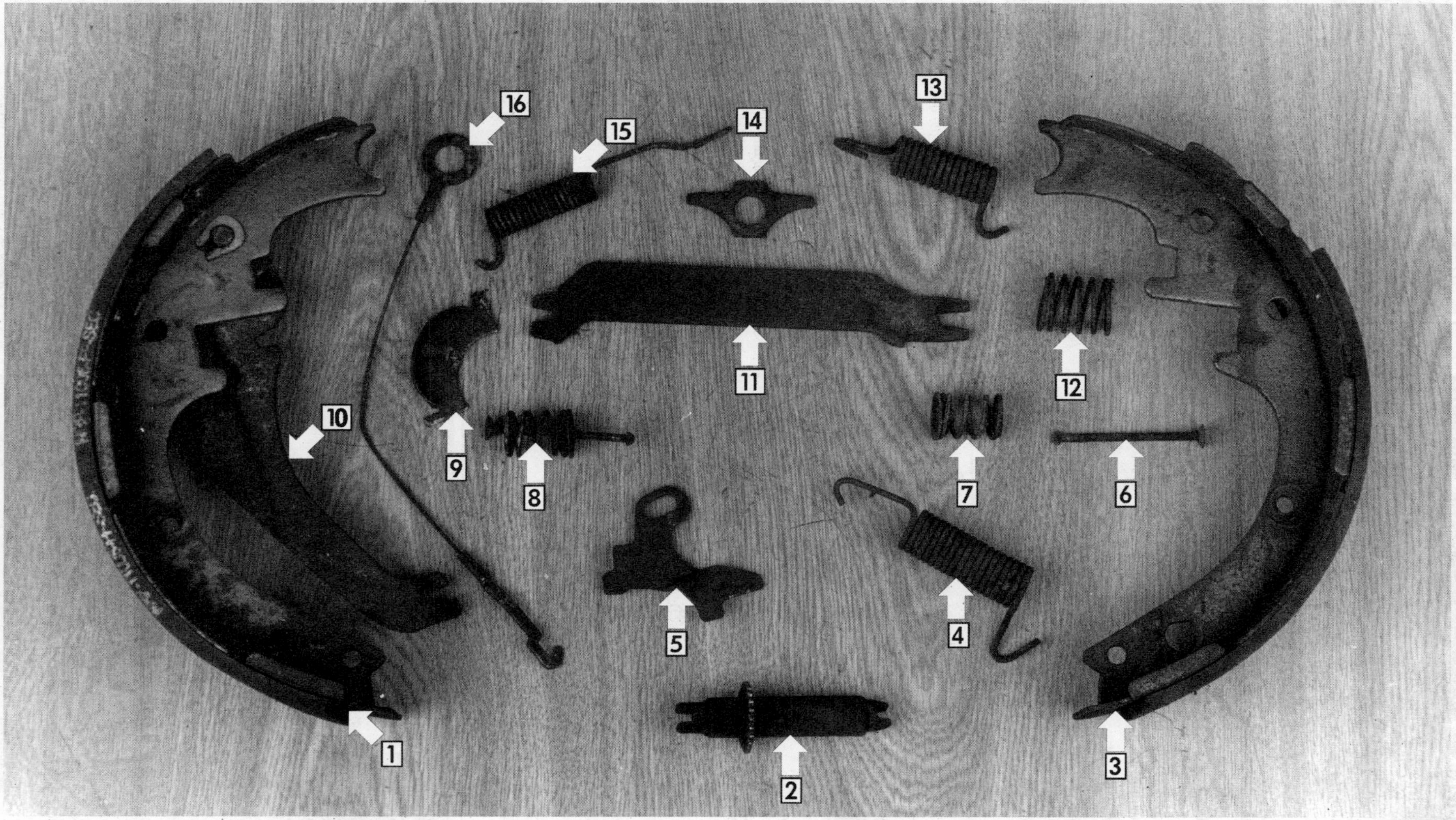

Fig. 7 Common dual return spring drum brake setup component identification

Disc Brakes

♦ See Figures 8, 9 and 10

Instead of the traditional expanding brakes that press outward against a circular drum, disc brake systems utilize a cast iron rotor (disc) with brake pads positioned on either side of it. Braking effect is achieved in a manner similar to the way you would squeeze a spinning disc between your fingers.

The rotor (disc) is a one-piece casting with cooling fins between the two braking surfaces. This enables air to circulate between the braking surfaces making them less sensitive to heat buildup and more resistant to fade. Dirt and water do not affect braking action since contaminants are thrown off by the centrifugal action of the rotor (disc) or scraped off by the pads. In addition, the equal clamping action of the two brake pads tends to ensure uniform, straight-line stops. All disc brakes are inherently self-adjusting.

There are three general types of disc brake:

- A fixed caliper
- A floating caliper
- A sliding caliper

1. Brake caliper	4. Rotor retainer
2. Support bracket	5. Rotor
3. Outboard brake pad	

88239P42

Fig. 10 Typical rear disc brake component identification

The fixed caliper design uses one or two pistons mounted on each side of the rotor (in each side of the caliper). The caliper is mounted rigidly and does not move.

The sliding and floating designs are quite similar. In fact, these two types are often lumped together. In both designs, the pad on the inside of the rotor is moved into contact with the rotor by hydraulic force. The caliper, which is not held in a fixed position, moves slightly, bringing the outside pad into contact with the rotor.

Floating calipers use threaded guide pins and bushings, or sleeves to allow the caliper to slide and apply the brake pads.

There are typically three methods of securing a sliding caliper to its mounting bracket: with a retaining pin, with a key and bolt, or with a wedge and pin. On calipers that use the retaining pin method, you will find pins driven into the slot between the caliper and the caliper mount. On calipers which use the bolt and key method, a key is used between the caliper and the mounting bracket to allow the caliper to slide. The key is held in position by a lock bolt. On calipers which use the pin and wedge method, a wedge, retained by a pin, is used between the caliper and the mounting bracket.

For pad removal purposes, fixed calipers are usually not removed, floating calipers are either removed or flipped (hinged up or down on one pin), and sliding calipers are removed.

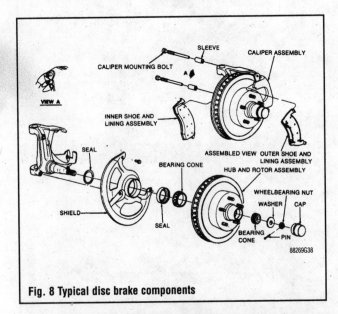

Fig. 8 Typical disc brake components

Power Brake Boosters

♦ See Figure 11

Power brakes operate just as standard brake systems, except in the actuation of the master cylinder pistons. A vacuum diaphragm is located behind the master cylinder and assists the driver in applying the brakes, reducing both the effort and travel he must put into moving the brake pedal.

The vacuum diaphragm housing is connected to the intake manifold by a vacuum hose. A check valve at the point where the hose enters the diaphragm housing ensures that during periods of low manifold vacuum brake assist vacuum will not be lost.

Depressing the brake pedal closes the vacuum source and allows atmospheric pressure to enter on one side of the diaphragm. This causes the master cylinder pistons to move and apply the brakes. When the brake pedal is released, vacuum is applied to both sides of the diaphragm, and return springs return the diaphragm and master cylinder pistons to the released position. If the vacuum fails, the brake pedal rod will butt against the end of the master cylinder—actuating rod and direct mechanical application will occur as the pedal is depressed.

The hydraulic and mechanical problems that apply to conventional brake systems also apply to power brakes.

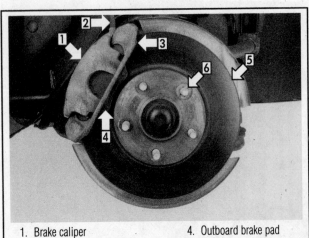

1. Brake caliper	4. Outboard brake pad
2. Brake hose	5. Rotor
3. Support (anchor) plate	6. Rotor retainer

88239P41

Fig. 9 Common front disc brake component identification

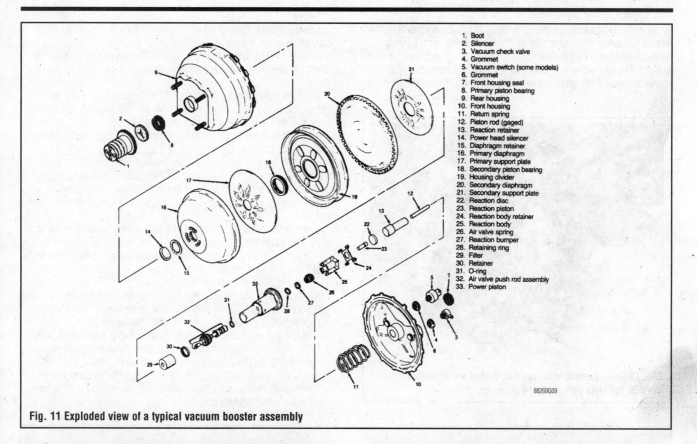

1. Boot
2. Silencer
3. Vacuum check valve
4. Grommet
5. Vacuum switch (some models)
6. Grommet
7. Front housing seal
8. Primary piston bearing
9. Rear housing
10. Front housing
11. Return spring
12. Piston rod (gaged)
13. Reaction retainer
14. Power head silencer
15. Diaphragm retainer
16. Primary diaphragm
17. Primary support plate
18. Secondary piston bearing
19. Housing divider
20. Secondary diaphragm
21. Secondary support plate
22. Reaction disc
23. Reaction piston
24. Reaction body retainer
25. Reaction body
26. Air valve spring
27. Reaction bumper
28. Retaining ring
29. Filter
30. Retainer
31. O-ring
32. Air valve push rod assembly
33. Power piston

Fig. 11 Exploded view of a typical vacuum booster assembly

Parking Brake

▶ **See Figures 12, 13 and 14**

The emergency or parking brake is used simply to hold the vehicle stationary while parked. It has no hydraulic connection and is simply a means of activating the rear (usually) or front (rarely) wheel brakes with a cable attached to a floor-mounted lever or dash-mounted pedal or lever.

Anti-Lock Brakes

▶ **See Figures 15, 16 and 17**

Anti-lock Braking Systems (ABS) are designed to prevent locked-wheel skidding during hard braking or during braking on slippery surfaces. The front wheels of a vehicle cannot apply steering force if they are locked and sliding; the vehicle will continue in its previous direction of travel. The four

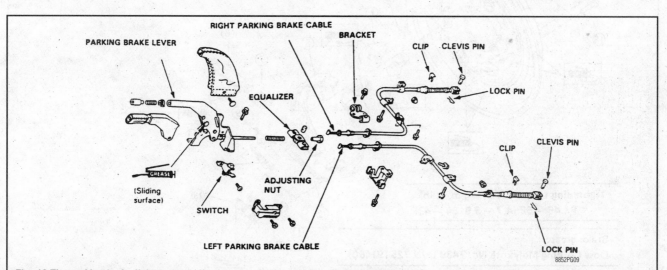

Fig. 12 The parking brake linkage normally operates the rear brakes. Depressing the pedal (not shown) or pulling up on the lever expands the rear brake shoes against the drum.

wheel anti-lock brake systems found on many of today's vehicles hold the wheels just below the point of locking, thereby allowing some steering response and preventing the rear of the vehicle from sliding sideways while braking. The Rear Wheel Anti-Lock (RWAL) systems used primarily on trucks and vans is designed to prevent the rear wheels from locking up dur-

ing severe braking. Especially since these vehicles are often designed to carry heavy loads, the rear brakes can be very touchy when the truck or van is unloaded. RWAL systems usually utilize a load sensing mechanism to adjust the sensitivity of the system to compensate for heavy or no load situations.

There are conditions for which the ABS system provides no benefit. Debris, gravel, snow or sheets of ice render the ABS system ineffective since it relies on an underlying amount of road traction, which is not available when driving on gravel, excessive debris, snow or ice. Hydroplaning is possible when the tires ride on a film of water, losing contact with the paved surface. This renders the vehicle totally uncontrollable until road contact is regained. Extreme steering maneuvers at high speed or cornering beyond the limits of tire adhesion can result in skidding which is independent of vehicle braking. For this reason, the system is named anti-lock rather than anti-skid.

Under normal braking conditions, the ABS system functions in the same manner as a standard brake system. The system is a combination of electrical and hydraulic components, working together to control the flow of brake fluid to the wheels when necessary.

The anti-lock brake system's Electronic Control Unit (ECU) is the electronic brain of the system, receiving and interpreting speed signals from the speed sensors. The ECU will enter anti-lock mode when it senses impending wheel lock at any wheel and immediately control the brake line pressure(s) to the affected wheel(s). The hydraulic actuator assembly is separate from the master cylinder and booster. It contains the wheel circuit valves used to control the brake fluid pressure to each wheel circuit. If the ABS becomes inoperative for any reason, the fail-safe system insures that the normal braking system is operative. The dashboard warning lamp is activated to show that the ABS is disabled.

87979P46

Fig. 13 Some models with rear disc brakes are equipped with a drum in hat style parking brake assembly

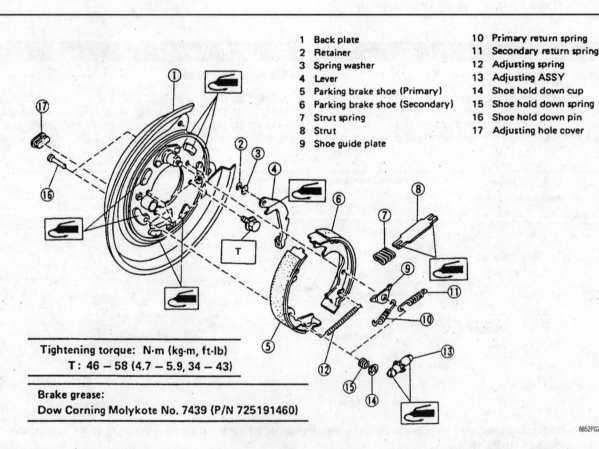

1	Back plate	10	Primary return spring
2	Retainer	11	Secondary return spring
3	Spring washer	12	Adjusting spring
4	Lever	13	Adjusting ASSY
5	Parking brake shoe (Primary)	14	Shoe hold down cup
6	Parking brake shoe (Secondary)	15	Shoe hold down spring
7	Strut spring	16	Shoe hold down pin
8	Strut	17	Adjusting hole cover
9	Shoe guide plate		

Tightening torque: N·m (kg-m, ft-lb)
T : 46 — 58 (4.7 — 5.9, 34 — 43)

Brake grease:
Dow Corning Molykote No. 7439 (P/N 725191460)

8852PG28

Fig. 14 Exploded view of a drum in hat style parking brake assembly—on this type of parking brake, there are brake shoes mounted inside the disc rotor

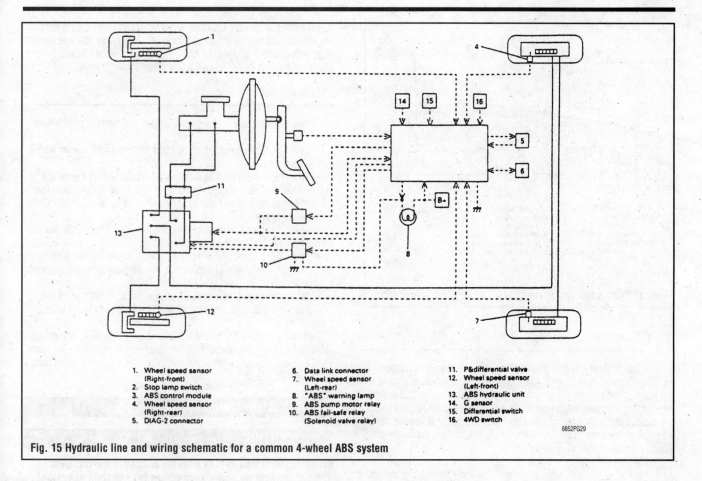

1. Wheel speed sensor
   (Right-front)
2. Stop lamp switch
3. ABS control module
4. Wheel speed sensor
   (Right-rear)
5. DIAG-2 connector

6. Data link connector
7. Wheel speed sensor
   (Left-rear)
8. "ABS" warning lamp
9. ABS pump motor relay
10. ABS fail-safe relay
    (Solenoid valve relay)

11. P&differential valve
12. Wheel speed sensor
    (Left-front)
13. ABS hydraulic unit
14. G sensor
15. Differential switch
16. 4WD switch

8852PG29

Fig. 15 Hydraulic line and wiring schematic for a common 4-wheel ABS system

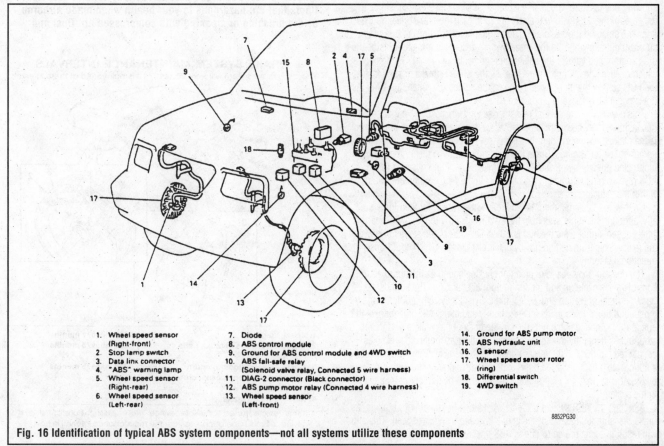

1. Wheel speed sensor
   (Right-front)
2. Stop lamp switch
3. Data link connector
4. "ABS" warning lamp
5. Wheel speed sensor
   (Right-rear)
6. Wheel speed sensor
   (Left-rear)

7. Diode
8. ABS control module
9. Ground for ABS control module and 4WD switch
10. ABS fail-safe relay
    (Solenoid valve relay, Connected 5 wire harness)
11. DIAG-2 connector (Black connector)
12. ABS pump motor relay (Connected 4 wire harness)
13. Wheel speed sensor
    (Left-front)

14. Ground for ABS pump motor
15. ABS hydraulic unit
16. G sensor
17. Wheel speed sensor rotor
    (ring)
18. Differential switch
19. 4WD switch

8852PG30

Fig. 16 Identification of typical ABS system components—not all systems utilize these components

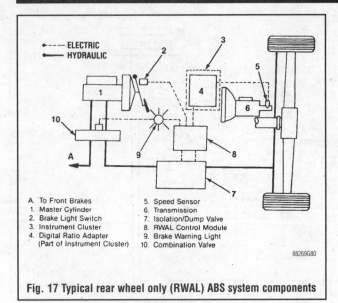

ELECTRIC
HYDRAULIC

A. To Front Brakes
1. Master Cylinder
2. Brake Light Switch
3. Instrument Cluster
4. Digital Ratio Adapter
   (Part of Instrument Cluster)
5. Speed Sensor
6. Transmission
7. Isolation/Dump Valve
8. RWAL Control Module
9. Brake Warning Light
10. Combination Valve

88269G80

Fig. 17 Typical rear wheel only (RWAL) ABS system components

TYPICAL SYSTEM OPERATION

A typical 4-wheel anti-lock brake system uses a 4-sensor, 4-channel system. A speed signal for each wheel is generated by a speed sensor at the wheel. The hydraulic actuator contains 4 control solenoids, one for each wheel brake line. On RWAL systems, there is either one wheel speed sensor mounted at each rear wheel or one sensor mounted in the differential case, which reads the axle speed. The hydraulic actuator controls the brake line(s) feeding the rear wheel brakes.

The system is capable of controlling brake line fluid pressure to any or all of the wheels as the situation demands. When the ECU receives signals showing one or more wheels about to lock, it sends an electrical signal to the solenoid valve(s) within the actuator to release the brake pressure the line. The solenoid moves to a position which holds the present line pressure without allowing it to increase. If wheel deceleration is still outside the pre-programmed values, the solenoid is momentarily moved to a position which releases pressure from the line. As the wheel unlocks or rolls faster, the ECU senses the increase and signals the solenoid to open, allowing the brake pedal to increase line pressure.

This cycling occurs several times per second when ABS is engaged. In this fashion, the wheels are kept just below the point of lock-up and control is maintained. When the hard braking ends, the ECU resets the solenoids to its normal or build mode. Brake line fluid pressures are then increased or modulated directly by pressure on the brake pedal. Fluid released to the ABS reservoirs is returned to the master cylinder by the pump and motor within the actuator.

On 4-wheel systems, the front and rear wheels are controlled individually, although the logic system in the ECU reacts only to the lowest rear wheel speed signal. This method is called Select Low and serves to prevent the rear wheels from getting greatly dissimilar signals which could upset directional stability.

The operator may hear a popping or clicking sound as the pump and/or control valves cycle on and off during normal operation. The sounds are due to normal operation and are not indicative of a system problem. Under most conditions, the sounds are only faintly audible. If ABS is engaged, the operator may notice some pulsation in the body of the vehicle during a hard stop; this is generally due to suspension shudder as the brake pressures are altered rapidly and the forces transfer to the vehicle. There may also be a noticeable pulsation in the brake pedal as the hydraulic fluid is controlled by the ABS system; this is normal and should not be thought of as a defect in the system.

Although the ABS system prevents wheel lock-up under hard braking, as brake pressure increases wheel slip is allowed to increase as well. This slip will result in some tire chirp during ABS operation. The sound should not

be interpreted as lock-up, but rather as an indication of the system holding the wheel(s) just outside the point of lock-up. Additionally, the final few feet of an ABS-engaged stop may be completed with the wheels locked; the electronic controls do not operate below about 3 mph (5 km/h).

PRECAUTIONS

Failure to observe the following precautions may result in system damage:

• Before performing electric arc welding on the vehicle, disconnect the control module and the hydraulic unit connectors.

• When performing painting work on the vehicle, do not expose the control module to temperatures in excess of 185°F (85°C) for longer than 2 hours. The system may be exposed to temperatures up to 200°F (95°C) for less than 15 minutes.

• Never disconnect or connect the control module or hydraulic modulator connectors with the ignition switch ON.

• Never disassemble any component of the Anti-Lock Brake System (ABS) which is designated unserviceable; the component must be replaced as an assembly.

• When filling the master cylinder, always use brake fluid which meets DOT-3 or 4 specifications; petroleum-based fluid will destroy the rubber parts.

• Working on the ABS system requires an extreme amount of mechanical ability, training and special tools. If you are not comfortable have your vehicle repaired by a certified technician or refer to a more advanced publication on this subject.

Brake System Maintenance

❊❊ CAUTION

Breathing asbestos dust is hazardous to your health. Dust and dirt present on brake assemblies may contain asbestos fibers that are hazardous to your health when made airborne by dry brushing or cleaning with compressed air. Dust and

BRAKE SYSTEM MAINTENANCE INTERVALS
Your car's brake system will work efficiently if it is maintained at these intervals.

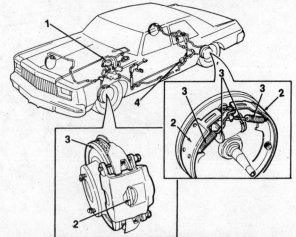

1. Check fluid level ▲	Every 1000 miles/1 month
2. Check conditions of brake pads or shoes ▲	Every 6000 miles/6 months
3. Check wheel cylinders, return springs, calipers, hoses, drums and/or rotors ▲	Every 6000 miles/6 months
4. Adjust parking brake	As necessary

▲ If the vehicle is used for severe service, (trailer pulling, constant stop/start driving, off-road operation, etc.) cut the maintenance interval in half.

8852PC01

dirt should be cleaned using a vacuum cleaner recommended for use with asbestos fibers, and should be disposed of in a manner that prevents dust exposure. If cleaning by vacuuming is not possible, work on brake assemblies should be done in a well-ventilated area using an approved toxic-dust respirator.

CHECKING FLUID LEVEL

▶ See Figures 18, 19, 20, 21 and 22

✳✳ WARNING

Clean, high quality brake fluid is essential to the safe and proper operation of the brake system. You should always buy the highest quality brake fluid that is available. If the brake fluid becomes contaminated, drain and flush the system, then refill the master cylinder with new fluid. Never reuse brake fluid. Any brake fluid that is removed from the system should be discarded.

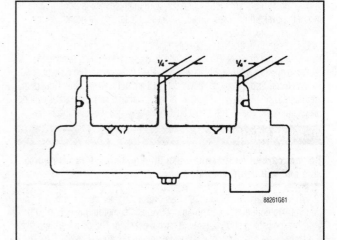

Fig. 20 If there are no markings on the reservoir, keep the fluid approximately ¼ inch (6mm) from the top

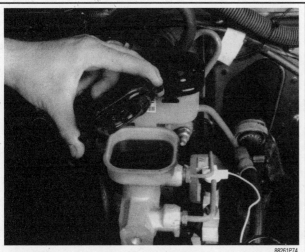

Fig. 18 Some brake master cylinders contain two separate reservoirs . . .

Fig. 21 Some brake master cylinders contain a common reservoir . . .

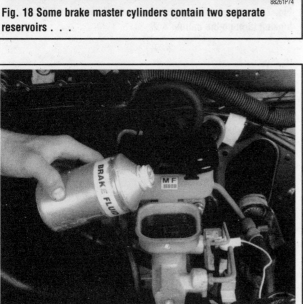

Fig. 19 . . . remove the cover ONLY from the side that requires fluid

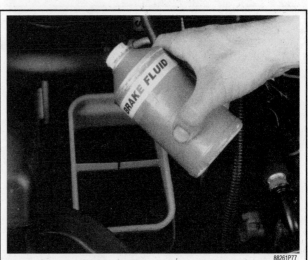

Fig. 22 . . . however the fluid is added in the same manner, clean the cover, remove and pour

The most important item in brake system maintenance is periodic checking of the brake fluid level. Check the level at least once a month, more often if possible.

Before checking the level, carefully wipe off the master cylinder cover to remove any dirt or water that would fall into the reservoir. Then remove the retaining clip (sometimes a bolt) and cap. The fluid level should be kept about ¼ inch (6mm) from the top on cylinders that are not marked. On cylinders that are marked, simply keep the fluid up to the specified line. If the master cylinder needs fluid, add heavy-duty brake fluid meeting DOT 3 or 4 specifications.

✳✳ WARNING

Be very careful not to spill brake fluid on paint. It is very corrosive and will destroy paint.

While a certain amount of fluid loss over a long period is normal, if you find you are continually adding fluid, obviously something is wrong with your brake system, and you should have it checked. The color of the brake fluid can also warn of trouble. The fluid should not appear overly dark or have a "burned" appearance. If it does, something is probably wrong, but this doesn't happen very often.

Brake fluid will deteriorate with age. Buy only as much as you need, and store it in a cool dark place in a tightly capped container.

CHANGING BRAKE FLUID

It is always a good idea, and recommended by many vehicle manufacturers, to completely flush the brake hydraulic system at least every 2 years to prevent brake system failure. Brake fluid looses effectiveness over time due to its tendency to absorb moisture. Brake fluid contaminated with water can lead to rusted brake components, and can vaporize during hard braking. Both of these will lead to brake system failure eventually, so be sure to flush the brake hydraulic system at least every 2 years.

INSPECTING THE BRAKES

Brakes should be inspected every 6000 miles or 6 months. The rate at which the linings wear will be influenced by many variables, among them where and how you drive, whether or not you pull a trailer, etc.

Disc Brakes

▶ See Figures 23, 24, 25, 26 and 27

Inspecting disc brakes is very easy. Normally, all you have to do is remove a wheel and maybe an anti-rattle clip from the caliper. Fortunately,

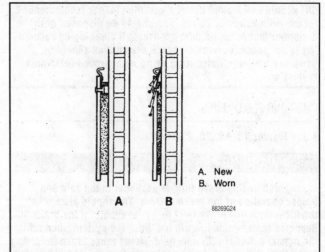
Fig. 24 Another type of wear indicator produces a squeal when wear reaches the replacement point

A. New
B. Worn

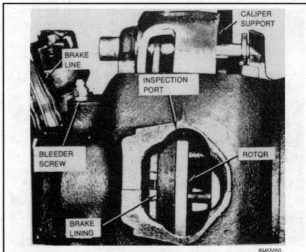
Fig. 25 On most vehicles, brake pad wear can be checked by looking through the caliper hole

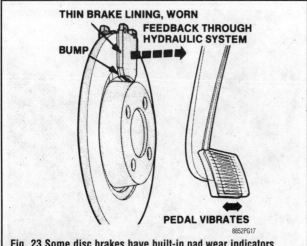
Fig. 23 Some disc brakes have built-in pad wear indicators. When wear reaches the replacement point, the rotor (disc) produces a vibration in the pedal when the brakes are applied.

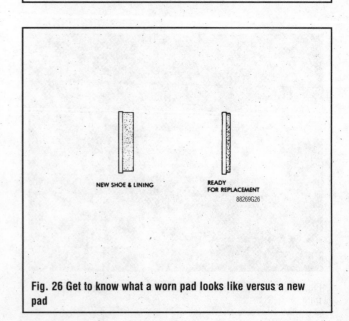
Fig. 26 Get to know what a worn pad looks like versus a new pad

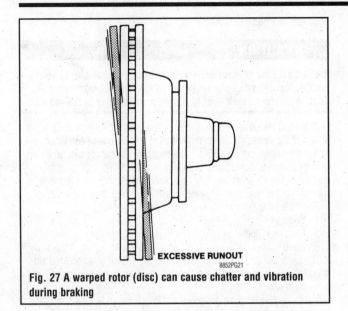

Fig. 27 A warped rotor (disc) can cause chatter and vibration during braking

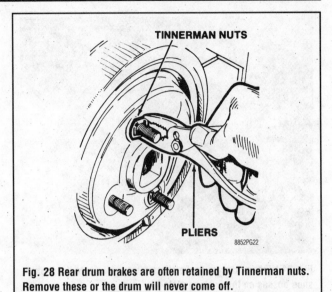

Fig. 28 Rear drum brakes are often retained by Tinnerman nuts. Remove these or the drum will never come off.

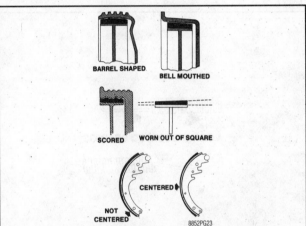

Fig. 29 Improperly worn linings are cause for concern only if braking is unstable and noise is objectionable. Compare the lining and drum wear pattern, the drum being more important, since the drum shapes the wear on the shoe.

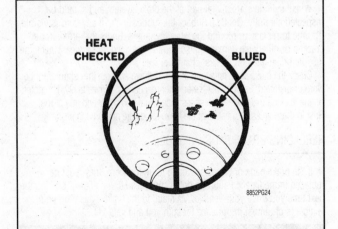

Fig. 30 A "blued" or severely heat-checked drum and "blued", charred or heavily glazed linings are the result of overheating. The brakes should be checked immediately.

few vehicles require that the caliper actually be removed to inspect the pads.

Most late model vehicles have a disc brake wear indicator, which will screech or provide a pedal vibration as the brakes are applied to warn the driver that the pad lining is low.

The pad thickness should be inspected every time that the tires are removed for rotation. The outer pad can be checked by looking in at each end of the caliper, which is the point at which the highest rate of wear occurs. The inner pad can normally be checked by looking down through the inspection hole in the top of the caliper. If the thickness of the pad is worn below the thickness of the backing plate, you should consider replacing the pads. Please refer to a Chilton's Total Car Care manual, or your local inspection requirements for actual specifications.

Inspect the brake rotors (discs) for a wobbly movement of the rotor (disc) from side to side as it rotates. Check the rotor (disc) surface for grooves worn in the surface (very small grooves are OK) and for "bluing" caused by severe overheating. Check around the calipers and brake lines for leaks.

Drum Brakes

▶ See Figures 28, 29, 30, 31 and 32

Rear drums require you to first remove the wheel and then the drum. On primarily new vehicles, speed nuts are used on the wheel studs to retain the drum, these must be removed to take off the brake drum. Once the wheel is removed, the drum should pull straight off, provided the parking brake is not on and the brakes are not too tightly adjusted. On brake drums that are severely worn, you may have to remove the rubber plug from the backing plate and adjust the brakes manually to release the shoes from the drum. Do not pry the drum off. If it's stubborn, apply some penetrating oil to the lugs and then tap lightly with a hammer around the perimeter of the drum. Don't risk breaking any parts. If the drum is too stubborn, leave the job to a pro.

Once the drum is off, clean the shoes and springs with a stiff brush to remove the accumulated brake dust. Grease on the shoes can be removed with alcohol or fine sandpaper.

After cleaning, examine the brake shoes for glazed, oily, loose, cracked or improperly worn linings. Light glazing is common and can be removed with fine sandpaper. Linings that are worn improperly, or below 1/16 inch (1.5mm) above rivet heads (riveted) or brake shoe (bonded) should be replaced. The NHSTA advises states with inspection programs to fail vehicles with brake linings less than 1/32 inch (0.8mm). A good "eyeball" test is to replace the linings when the thickness is the same as or less than the thickness of the metal backing plate of the shoe.

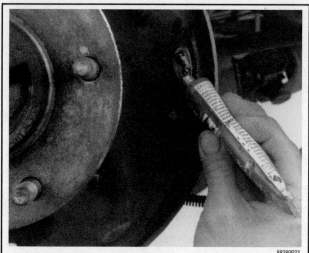

Fig. 31 When replacing brake shoes always lubricate the brake shoe bosses on the backing plate

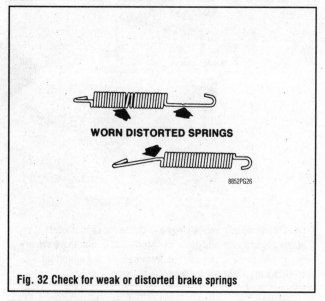

WORN DISTORTED SPRINGS

8852PG26

Fig. 32 Check for weak or distorted brake springs

Wheel cylinders are a vital part of the brake system and should be inspected carefully. Gently pull back the rubber boots; if any fluid is visible, it's time to replace or rebuild the wheel cylinders. Boots that are distorted, cracked or otherwise damaged also point to the need for service. Check the flexible brake lines for cracks, chafing or wear.

Check the brake shoe retracting and hold-down springs; they should not be worn or distorted. Be sure that the adjuster mechanism moves freely. The points on the backing plate where the shoes slide should be shiny and free of rust. Rust in these areas suggests that the brake shoes are not moving properly.

REPLACING BRAKE PADS OR SHOES

If the brake pads or shoes are found to be too worn, they must be replaced immediately. Failure to do so could lead to insufficient braking the next time you drive your vehicle. Maintaining the brake system on your vehicle is of utmost importance for both you and your vehicle.

✳✳ WARNING

Always replace the brake shoes in sets. Replace all four front pads/shoes at a time and all four rear pads/shoes at a time; NEVER replace the pads/shoes on one wheel only.

Disc Brake Pads

✳✳ CAUTION

Brake dust may contain asbestos! Asbestos is harmful to your health. Never use compressed air to clean any brake component. A filtering mask should be worn during any brake repair.

Brake pad replacement should always be performed on both front or rear wheels at the same time. Never replace pads on only one wheel. When servicing any brakes use only OEM or better quality pads and parts. When the caliper is removed some brake pads stay with the caliper, others remain on the caliper mounting bracket. Use new pad mounting hardware (springs, anti-rattle clips, or shims) whenever possible to make for a better repair.

There are three general types of disc brake:
1. Sliding caliper.
2. Floating caliper.
3. Fixed caliper.

The fixed caliper design uses one or two pistons mounted on each side of the rotor (in each side of the caliper). The caliper is mounted rigidly and does not move.

The sliding and floating designs are quite similar. In fact, these two types are often lumped together. In both designs, the pad on the inside of the rotor is moved into contact with the rotor by hydraulic force. The caliper, which is not held in a fixed position, moves slightly, bringing the outside pad into contact with the rotor.

Floating calipers use threaded guide pins and bushings, or sleeves to allow the caliper to slide and apply the brake pads.

There are typically three methods of securing a sliding caliper to its mounting bracket: with a retaining pin, with a key and bolt, or with a wedge and pin. On calipers which use the retaining pin method, you will find pins driven into the slot between the caliper and the caliper mount. On calipers which use the bolt and key method, a key is used between the caliper and the mounting bracket to allow the caliper to slide. The key is held in position by a lockbolt. On calipers which use the pin and wedge method, a wedge, retained by a pin, is used between the caliper and the mounting bracket.

For pad removal purposes, fixed calipers are usually not removed, floating calipers are either removed or flipped (hinged up or down on one pin), and sliding calipers are removed.

SLIDING AND FLOATING CALIPERS

▶ See Figures 33 thru 46

➥**On certain floating calipers it may be possible to remove one of the guide pins and pivot the caliper up or down to gain access to the brake pads. If you decide to do this, be sure that pivoting the caliper will not damage the flexible brake hose.**

1. Open the hood and locate the master brake cylinder fluid reservoir. Clean the area surrounding the reservoir cap, then remove the cap. Remove some of the brake fluid from the reservoir.
2. Loosen the lug nuts on the applicable wheels.
3. If servicing the front brakes, apply the parking brake, block the rear wheels, then raise and safely support the front of the vehicle securely on jackstands.
4. If servicing the rear wheels, block the front wheels, then raise and safely support the rear of the vehicle securely on jackstands.
5. Remove the wheels.
6. Disconnect any electrical brake pad wear sensors.

➥**It is not necessary, and actually discouraged, to detach the brake hose from the caliper during this procedure. If you decide to detach the hose, it will be necessary for you to bleed your brake system.**

7. Remove and suspend the caliper with a piece of wire, cord or strong string. Make sure that it is not placing any stress on the brake hose.
8. For caliper bracket-mounted pads, perform the following:
   a. If present, remove any anti-squeal shims noting their positions.

Fig. 33 Exploded view of typical brake pad mounting on the caliper bracket

CALIPER BRACKET
MOUNTING BOLTS

PAD RETAINERS

WASHERS

CALIPER
BRACKET

OUTER
PAD SHIM B

OUTER
PAD SHIM A

OUTER
BRAKE PAD

INNER PAD SHIM

INNER
BRAKE PAD

89455G06

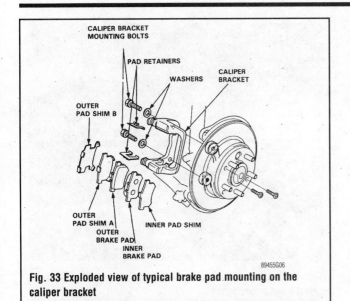

Fig. 36 Using a vacuum pump, or some other method, remove some of the brake fluid from the reservoir

Fig. 34 To remove the brake pads, first clean the brake master cylinder reservoir cap . . .

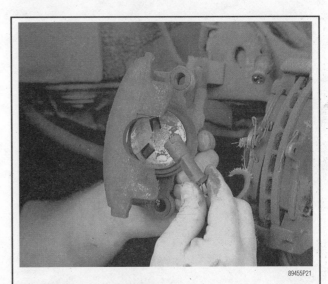

Fig. 37 Remove the disc brake caliper from the rotor

Fig. 35 . . . then remove it

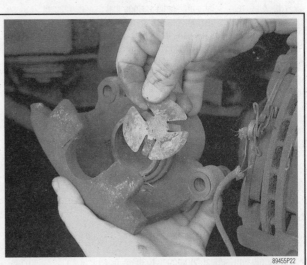

Fig. 38 Be sure to note the positions of any clips or springs on the caliper

Fig. 39 Remove the outboard pad from the mounting bracket . . .

Fig. 40 . . . then remove the inboard pad

Fig. 41 Clean the caliper and mounting bracket with spray brake solvent and a wire brush

Fig. 42 Apply a thin coat of high-temperature brake grease to the sliding surfaces of the bracket and caliper

b. Also, remove any anti-rattle springs that may be present. If these springs don't provide good tension, then replace them.

c. Remove the brake pads from the caliper bracket by lifting the pad out by hand or with a slight tap of a hammer to help.

9. For caliper mounted pads, perform the following:

a. Some outer pads have tabs that are bent over the edge of the caliper, which hold the pads tight in the caliper. Straighten the tabs with pliers before trying to remove the brake pad from the caliper.

b. Then, remove the outer brake pad by a slight tap to the back of the pad with a hammer.

c. Other outer pads use a spring-clip to mount to the caliper. To remove this type of pad, press the pad towards the center of the caliper and slide it off. It maybe helpful to use a small prybar.

d. Remove the inner pad by pulling it out of the piston.

To install:

10. Clean the caliper sliding area using a wire brush and spray brake cleaner.

11. Lubricate the sliding area of the caliper and the pins with high temperature brake grease.

12. Apply anti-squeal compound to the back side of both brake pads. Allow the compound to set-up according to the instructions on the package.

Fig. 43 A large C-clamp can be used to seat the piston in the caliper bore on most calipers without parking brakes

Fig. 44 Install all of the springs and clips in their original positions

Fig. 45 When installing the caliper and pads, make sure not to pinch the sensor wire (if equipped)

13. Unless the caliper is part of the parking brake, install one of the old brake pads against the caliper piston, then use a large C-clamp to press the piston back into its bore.

14. Install any new hardware provided with the new pads.

15. For bracket-mounted pads, perform the following steps:

a. Install the pads onto the caliper bracket. Some pads are marked for position.

b. Make sure that the notches or ears of the brake pads are properly engaged on the bracket.

c. Place the caliper over the pads and onto the caliper mounting bracket.

d. Install the caliper mounting hardware and anti-rattle clips. Tighten the guide pins or lockbolt to the proper specification.

➡️**It is a good idea to use some thread-locking compound (removable type) to the threaded fasteners of the caliper.**

16. For caliper mounted pads, perform the following:

a. Install the inner pad by pushing the retaining fingers of the pad into the piston of the caliper.

b. If the outer pad has a spring-clip, slide the pad over the edge of the caliper into the caliper frame.

c. If you have the bent-tab style outer brake pad, then test fit the pad; it should fit tight. If the tabs do not secure the pad snugly in the caliper,

Fig. 46 Clean the area around the reservoir to prevent contamination

place the pad on a piece of wood and tap the tab with a hammer to adjust it. It may take a few tries to get it right.

d. Place the caliper with the pads onto the rotor and, if equipped, caliper bracket.

e. Install the caliper mounting hardware and anti-rattle clips. Tighten the guide pins or lockbolt to the proper specification.

➡️**It is a good idea to use some thread-locking compound (removable type) on the threaded fasteners of the caliper.**

17. Connect any electrical brake pad wear sensors.

18. Seat the brake pads, otherwise the vehicle may coast out of the work area and into traffic before the brakes become effective. It will take several pumps of the brake pedal to seat the pads against the rotor.

19. If a firm pedal is not achieved, it may be necessary to bleed the brakes.

20. Check the brake fluid level in the reservoir and top off as needed.

21. Install the wheels and snug the lug nuts.

22. Lower the vehicle.

23. Tighten the lug nuts fully.

24. Road test the vehicle.

FIXED CALIPERS

➡️**It is not necessary to remove the caliper to replace the brake pads on a fixed caliper.**

1. Loosen the lug nuts on the applicable wheels.

2. If servicing the front brakes, apply the parking brake, block the rear wheels, then raise and safely support the front of the vehicle securely on jackstands.

3. If servicing the rear wheels, block the front wheels, then raise and safely support the rear of the vehicle securely on jackstands.

4. Remove the wheels.

5. Disconnect any electrical brake pad ware sensors.

6. Remove the pad retaining pins by pulling out the spring-clip or cotter pin, then use a punch and hammer to drive the pin out. Pins without a spring-clip or cotter pin, may be equipped with a spring steel collar on the head of the pin. To remove this style pin, just drive the pin out with a punch and hammer.

7. On calipers with hold-down clips, remove the bolt that holds the clip down.

8. Remove the pads from the caliper with a pair of pliers.

9. To seat the pistons of a fixed caliper, use a piece of wood or a pry-bar with a rag wrapped around the end, then wedge it between the rotor and the piston and slide the piston into its seat.

→It is helpful to replace one pad at a time, to reduce the risk of a piston coming out of its bore, which would lead to its needing to be rebuilt.

10. Lubricate the sliding area of the caliper and the brake pads with high temperature brake grease.

11. Apply anti-squeal compound to the back side of both brake pads. Allow the compound to set-up according to the instructions on the product.

12. Insert the new pads into the caliper.

13. If equipped, install the anti-rattle clip or retaining pin spring-clip or cotter pin. On pins with a spring steel collar, you must knock them in until seated against the shoulder in the caliper.

→It is a good idea to use some thread-locking compound (removable type) to the threaded fasteners of the caliper.

14. Connect any electrical brake pad wear sensors.

15. Seat the brake pads, otherwise the vehicle may coast out of the work area and into traffic before the brakes become effective. It will take several pumps of the brake pedal to seat the pads against the rotor.

→If a firm pedal is not achieved, it may be necessary to bleed the brakes.

16. Check the brake fluid level in the reservoir and top off as needed.
17. Install the wheels and snug the lug nuts.
18. Lower the vehicle.
19. Tighten the lug nuts fully.
20. Road test the vehicle.

Drum Brake Shoes

▶ See Figures 47, 48, 49 and 50

On older cars and trucks, drum brakes were used on all 4 wheels. The only difference between the front and rear brakes is the presence of the parking brake assembly.

There are often a lot of springs, washers and clips involved with drum brakes. Usually these components are contained in brake hardware kits available at your local auto parts store. Purchase the kit and replace these parts whenever you replace the shoes. You should never reuse these parts.

❋❋ CAUTION

Used brake components, especially springs, are worn out from repeated normal use, do not work as well as new parts, and are subject to failure. A worn spring or retainer may break and fall inside the drum causing damage to the shoes, drums and other parts, and possibly even causing the wheel to lock up (a very dangerous situation). Decide for yourself, but considering the risk to you and anyone riding in your vehicle it is cheap insurance to buy a new parts kit.

→It is not a good idea to disassemble the brakes on both sides at the same time. There are a lot of parts involved which must be replaced in a certain way. Work on one side at a time, only. If you become confused as to the particular position of the various brake parts during the brake shoe replacement, refer to the other side. Remember, however, the other side is a mirror image (everything is reversed).

While the brake shoes are off, pull back slightly on the wheel cylinder rubber caps. If any brake fluid leakage is evident, replace the defective wheel cylinder.

There is a tool that is, essentially, a large spring clamp used to make sure that the wheel cylinder pistons do not pop out while the shoes are removed. This occurrence is unlikely, but it's cheap insurance to use the tool.

Speaking of tools, brake work can often be frustrating because of the various springs and cables, which are often difficult to remove and install. Most of the work can be accomplished without the use of special tools, however brake tools are not expensive, can be purchased at most auto parts stores, and reduce the risk of personal injury and component damage. Also, brake tools can make the job a lot easier and quicker.

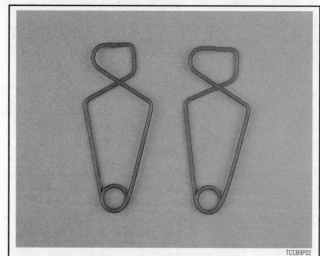

TCCB9P02

Fig. 47 Spring clamp tools, such as those shown, can hold the wheel cylinder pistons in while servicing the shoes

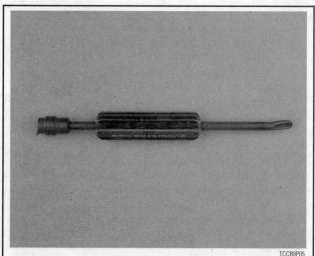

TCCB9P05

Fig. 48 There are several varieties of spring removal and installation tools available, such as this straight one . . .

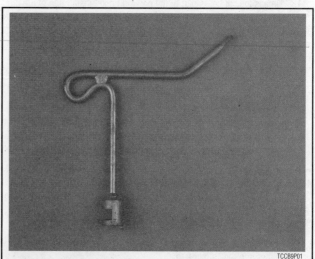

TCCB9P01

Fig. 49 . . . and this curved one—The shape of this tool is designed to provide more leverage during use

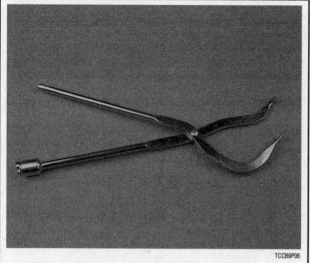

Fig. 50 This spring tool combines three different tools into one

※ CAUTION

Since you'll be working around heavy-duty springs, the use of safety glasses is STRONGLY recommended!

MODELS WITH DUAL RETURN SPRINGS AND STARWHEEL-TYPE ADJUSTER

▶ See Figures 51 thru 79

※ CAUTION

It is always a good idea to wear eye protection when working on brake components, especially drum brakes. Drum brakes often use powerful springs which could cause severe eye injury if they accidentally break.

1. Loosen the lug nuts on the applicable wheels.
2. If servicing the front brakes, apply the parking brake, block the rear wheels, then raise and safely support the front of the vehicle securely on jackstands.

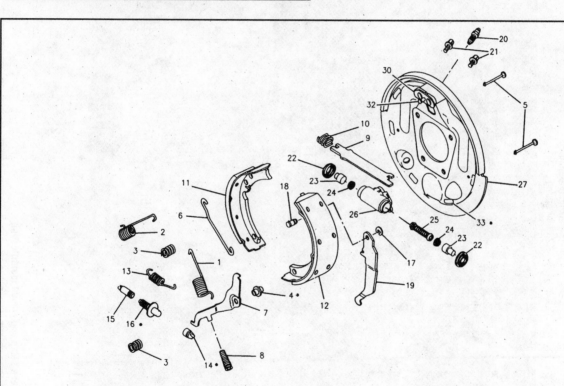

1	RETURN SPRING	11	PRIMARY SHOE AND LINING	21	BOLT
2	RETURN SPRING	12	SECONDARY SHOE AND LINING	22	BOOT
3	HOLD DOWN SPRING	13	ADJUSTING SCREW SPRING	23	PISTON
4	BEARING SLEEVE	14	SOCKET	24	SEAL
5	HOLD-DOWN PIN	15	PIVOT NUT	25	SPRING ASSEMBLY
6	ACTUATOR LINK	16	ADJUSTING SCREW	26	WHEEL CYLINDER
7	ACTUATOR LEVER	17	RETAINING RING	27	BACKING PLATE
8	LEVER RETURN SPRING	18	PIN	30	SHOE RETAINER
9	PARKING BRAKE STRUT	19	PARKING BRAKE LEVER	32	ANCHOR PIN
10	STRUT SPRING	20	BLEEDER VALVE	33	SHOE PADS (6 PLACES)

•LUBRICATE WITH THIN COATING
OF 1052196 LUBRICANT OR EQUIVALENT

87959042

Fig. 51 Exploded view of the most common GM rear drum brake setup

REAR DRUM BRAKE COMPONENTS

1. Secondary shoe
2. Adjusting screw assembly
3. Primary shoe
4. Adjuster spring
5. Adjuster lever
6. Hold-down pin
7. Hold-down spring
8. Hold-down assembly
9. Adjuster cable guide
10. Parking brake lever
11. Parking brake link
12. Link spring
13. Primary shoe return spring
14. Anchor pin plate
15. Secondary shoe return spring
16. Adjuster cable

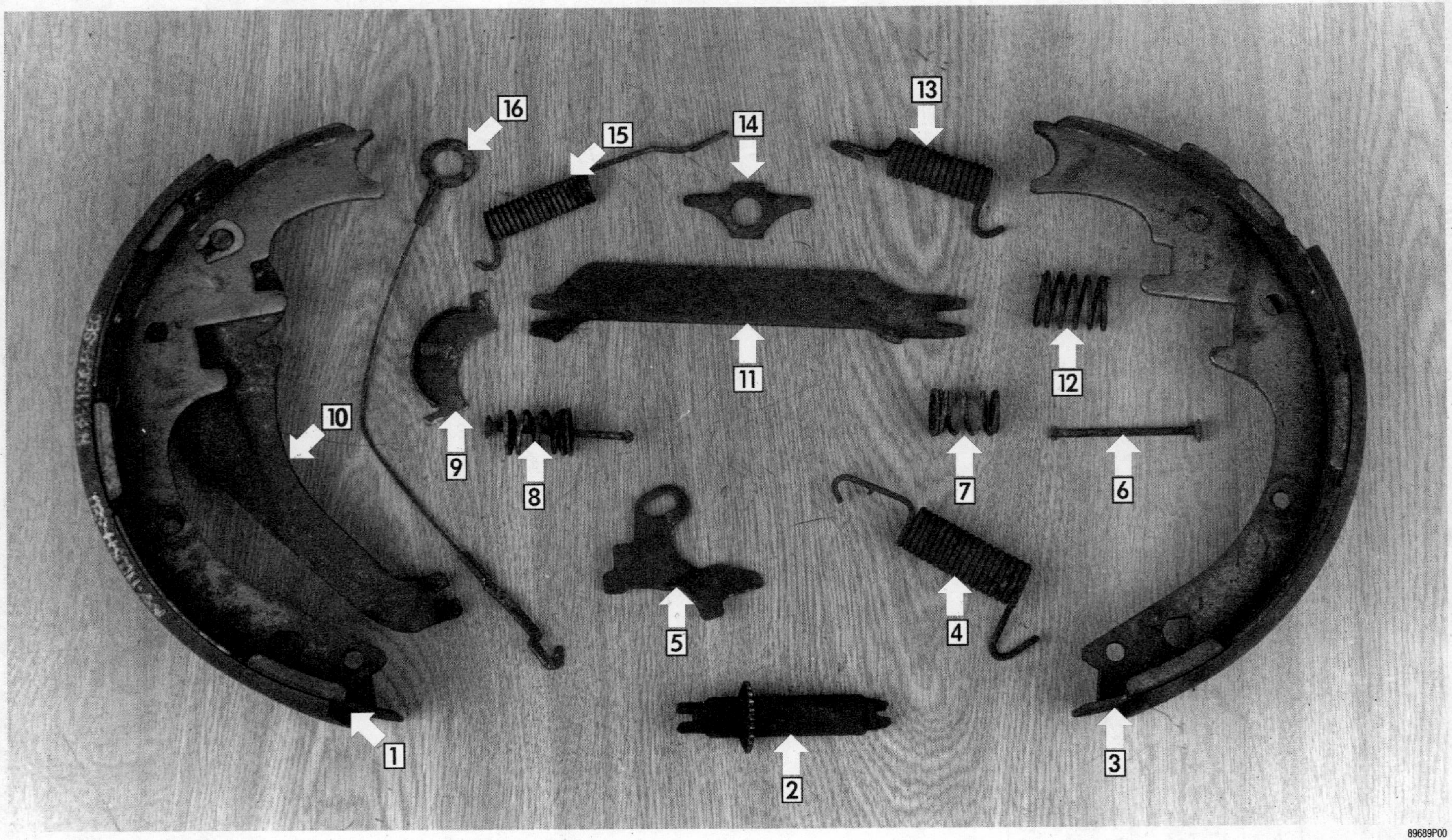

Fig. 52 Typical Ford dual return spring drum brake setup component identification

Fig. 53 Clean the brake shoe assemblies with a liquid cleaning solution, NEVER with compressed air

Fig. 56 Detach the upper return springs first from the anchor bolt, then from the brake shoes . . .

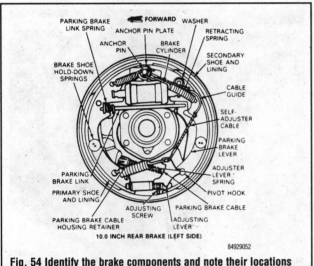

Fig. 54 Identify the brake components and note their locations prior to disassembling the brake assembly

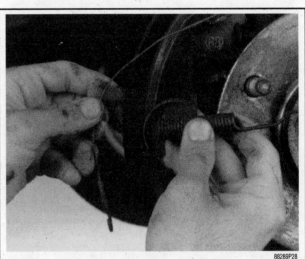

Fig. 57 . . . then remove the adjusting cable from the guide, and the guide from the brake shoe

Fig. 55 A specially-designed brake tool can make disconnecting the upper return springs much easier

Fig. 58 Remove the anchor block plate . . .

Fig. 59 . . . then remove the hold-down springs, retainers and pins from both shoes

3. If servicing the rear brakes, block the front wheels, then raise and safely support the rear of the vehicle securely on jackstands.

4. Remove the wheels.

5. Remove the brake drum.

6. Spray the brake assembly thoroughly with brake parts cleaner and let it dry. Similarly, spray the inside of the drum.

7. Inspect the drum for wear and/or damage. Machine or replace as necessary. When machining, observe the maximum diameter specification. The maximum machining diameter is stamped into the drum. If the drum braking surface shows signs of blue discoloration, overheating is indicated. If the bluing is extensive the drum/hub assembly must be replaced. Extensive bluing indicates a weakening of the metal.

➡ **Note the location of all springs and clips for proper assembly. If you own an instant camera, it may be a good idea to take a picture of your brake assembly with the brake drum removed. This will make reassembly much easier.**

8. Completely retract the adjuster by rotating the starwheel to relieve tension on the lower spring.

9. Remove the starwheel assembly and adjuster lever from between the two brake shoes.

Fig. 60 Lift the brake shoes off of the backing plate . . .

Fig. 62 Another way to remove the shoes for a dual spring setup is to pull the adjuster cable toward the shoe . . .

Fig. 61 . . . then detach the parking brake cable from the lever

Fig. 63 . . . and disconnect the pivot hook from the adjusting lever. Wind the starwheel all the way in

10. Using a brake spring tool, remove the 2 upper return springs.

11. Remove the adjuster cable and cable guide.

12. Remove the anchor block plate.

13. Using a hold-down spring tool or pliers, while holding the back of the spring mounting pin with one hand, press inward on the hold-down spring plate, turn it slightly to align the notches and pin ears, then remove the hold-down spring assembly with your other hand. Remove the other hold-down spring in the same manner.

14. Lift the shoes off the pins and remove the pins from the backing plate.

15. Remove the parking brake link.

16. Pull back on the parking brake cable spring and twist the cable out of the parking brake lever.

17. The parking brake lever is held onto the rear shoe with a horseshoe clip. Spread the clip and remove the lever and washer.

To install:

18. Thoroughly clean and dry the backing plate and starwheel assembly.

19. Lubricate the backing plate bosses, anchor plate surfaces, and starwheel threads and contact points with silicone grease. High-temperature wheel bearing grease or synthetic brake grease also work well for this application.

Fig. 66 Next, using a brake spring removal tool . . .

Fig. 64 Disconnect the adjuster lever return spring from the lever . . .

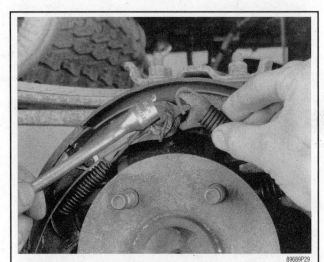

Fig. 67 . . . disconnect the primary brake shoe return spring from the anchor pin

Fig. 65 . . . and remove the spring and the lever

Fig. 68 Repeat the procedure and remove the secondary return spring, adjuster cable and its guide

Fig. 69 Also remove the anchor pin plate

Fig. 72 . . . and release to remove the hold-down spring. Pull the nail out from the backing plate

Fig. 70 Pull the bottoms of the shoes apart and remove the adjuster screw assembly

Fig. 73 Remove the primary (front) brake shoe from the backing plate . . .

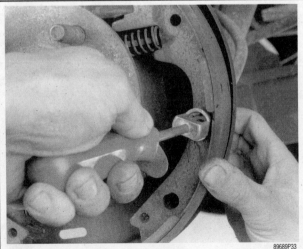

Fig. 71 Press in the hold-down springs while holding in on the nail from behind, then turn the cup 90° . . .

Fig. 74 . . . and the parking brake strut as well

Fig. 75 Remove the secondary shoe hold-down, pull the shoe out then press up on the cable spring . . .

Fig. 76 . . . and disconnect the parking brake cable from its lever by pulling it from the slot

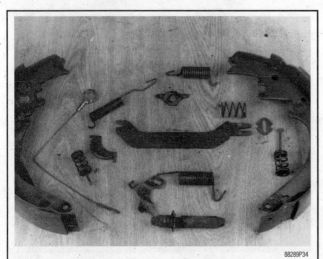

Fig. 77 It's a good idea to arrange all the parts in their approximate installed positions on a clean work surface

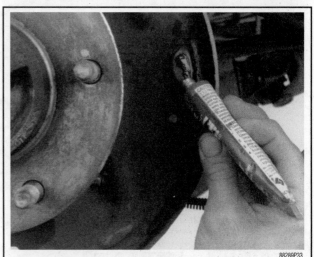

Fig. 78 Thoroughly clean the backing plate, then be sure to lubricate the brake shoe bosses on the backing plate

✲✲ CAUTION

When applying lubricant to the backing plate and other components, do not use so much grease that it may get spread onto the new brake shoes friction material; this can adversely affect the performance of the new brake shoes and, therefore, increase vehicle stopping distance.

20. Insert the parking brake lever pivot stud through the applicable hole in the rear shoe, then install a new wave washer and horseshoe clip. Squeeze the clip ends until the clip cannot be pulled from the lever pivot stud.

21. Connect the parking brake cable to the lever.

22. Position the rear shoe assembly on the backing plate and install the hold-down pin and spring assembly.

23. Install the front shoe and secure it with the hold-down spring assembly.

24. Position the parking brake link and spring between the front shoe and parking brake lever.

25. Position the adjuster cable on the anchor plate pin, install the cable guide and lay the cable across the guide.

✲✲ CAUTION

Be careful! Wear safety glasses during the next few steps, because they involve stretching heavy-duty springs. Getting hurt is very possible, even if you are careful.

26. Make sure that the notch in the upper end of the shoe is engaging the wheel cylinder piston or piston pin.

27. Position the rear shoe return spring into the guide and shoe hole, and, using a brake spring tool, stretch the spring onto the anchor plate pin. Make sure that the cable guide remained in place.

28. Position the front shoe return spring in its hole in the shoe.

29. Make sure that the parking brake link is properly positioned and that the upper end of the shoe will enter the wheel cylinder or engage the wheel cylinder piston.

30. Using the spring tool, stretch the spring into position on the anchor plate pin.

➡If the shoe doesn't properly engage the link or wheel cylinder piston, try again by removing the spring.

31. Position the adjuster lever in its hole in the rear shoe and hook the cable to it.

32. Position the lower spring in its hole in the front shoe. Now comes the hard part. Clamp a pair of locking pliers, like Vise Grips® on the spring

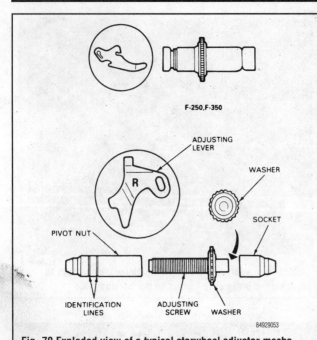

F-250, F-350

ADJUSTING LEVER

WASHER

SOCKET

PIVOT NUT

IDENTIFICATION LINES

ADJUSTING SCREW

WASHER

Fig. 79 Exploded view of a typical starwheel adjuster mechanism—the adjusting levers may be stamped for left side and right side applications

Fig. 80 Remove the brake drum for access to the brake components

and stretch it to engage the hole in the adjuster lever. Make sure that the cable stays in place on the guide.

33. Check that the shoes are evenly positioned on the backing plate.

34. Turn the starwheel to spread the shoes to the point at which the drum can be installed with very slight drag.

35. Install the drum and adjust the starwheel until the drum can't be turned. Then, back off the adjustment until the drum can just be turned without drag.

36. Install the wheels, lower the vehicle and check brake action. A firm pedal should be felt.

37. To activate the adjusters, some vehicles require you to make several quick pulls on the parking brake lever. On most, however, several short back-ups, about 10 ft. (3m) each, should do it.

MODELS WITH A SINGLE UPPER SHOE-TO-SHOE RETURN SPRING—WITH LOWER ANCHOR PLATE

▶ See Figures 80 thru 85

※※ CAUTION

It is always a good idea to wear eye protection when working on brake components, especially drum brakes. Drum brakes often use powerful springs which could cause severe eye injury if they accidentally break. Also, Brake shoes may contain asbestos, which is a known cancer-causing agent. As soon as the drum is removed, generously spray the entire brake assembly with brake parts cleaner. Let it dry before proceeding. It's a good idea to wear a filter mask when doing brake work.

1. Loosen the lug nuts on the applicable wheels.

2. If servicing the front brakes, apply the parking brake, block the rear wheels, then raise and safely support the front of the vehicle securely on jackstands.

3. If servicing the rear brakes, block the front wheels, then raise and safely support the rear of the vehicle securely on jackstands.

4. Remove the wheels.

5. Remove the brake drum.

Spray the brake assembly thoroughly with brake parts cleaner and let it dry. Similarly, spray the inside of the drum.

Fig. 81 Pliers can be used to disengage the hold-down spring retainer by rotating it until aligned with the pin tabs . . .

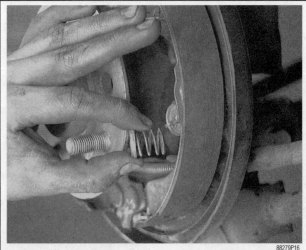

Fig. 82 . . . then remove the retainer, spring and pin from the shoe and backing plate

Inspect the drum for wear and/or damage. Machine or replace as necessary. When machining, observe the maximum diameter specification. The maximum machining diameter is stamped into the drum. If the drum braking surface shows signs of blue discoloration, overheating is indicated. If the bluing is extensive the drum/hub assembly must be replaced. Extensive bluing indicates a weakening of the metal.

➡ **Note the location of all springs and clips for proper assembly. If you own an instant camera, to make installation easier it may be a good idea to take a picture of your brake assembly with the brake drum removed.**

6. Remove the shoe-to-lever spring and remove the adjuster lever.
7. Remove the auto-adjuster assembly.
8. Remove the retainer spring.
9. Using a hold-down spring tool or pliers, while holding the back of the spring mounting pin with one hand, press inward on the hold-down spring plate, turn it slightly to align the notches and pin ears, then remove the hold-down spring assemblies with your other hand.
10. Remove the shoe-to-shoe spring.
11. Remove the brake shoes from the backing plate.

Fig. 83 Use a pair of needlenose pliers, or similar tool, to detach the upper return spring from both shoes . . .

Fig. 84 . . . then remove the brake shoes from the backing plate . . .

Fig. 85 . . . and detach the parking brake cable from the applicable brake shoe

12. Using a flat-tipped tool, pry open the parking brake lever retaining clip. Remove the clip and washer from the pin on the shoe assembly and remove the shoe from the lever assembly.

➡ **On some vehicles, the parking brake actuating lever is permanently attached to the trailing brake shoe assembly. Do not attempt to remove it from the original brake shoe assembly or reuse the original actuating lever on a replacement brake shoe assembly. All replacement brake shoe assemblies for these vehicles must come with the actuating lever as part of the trailing brake shoe assembly.**

To install:
13. Thoroughly clean all parts.
14. On vehicles with the ratcheting upper mounted adjuster, clean and inspect the brake support plate and the automatic adjuster mechanism. Be sure the quadrant (toothed part) of the adjuster is free to rotate throughout its entire tooth contact range and is free to slide the full length of its mounting slot. Check the knurled pin. It should be securely attached to the adjuster mechanism and its teeth should be in good condition. If the adjuster is worn or damaged, replace it. If the adjuster is serviceable, lubricate lightly with high-temperature grease between the strut and the quadrant.

✳✳ CAUTION

The trailing brake shoe assemblies used on the rear brakes of these vehicles are different for the left and right side of the vehicle. Care must be taken to ensure the brake shoes are properly installed in their correct side of the vehicle. Otherwise the brakes will probably malfunction, thereby creating a very dangerous condition. When the trailing shoes are properly installed on their correct side of the vehicle, the park brake actuating lever will be positioned under the brake shoe web.

15. Thoroughly clean and dry the backing plate. Lubricate the backing plate at the brake shoe contact points. Also, lubricate backing plate bosses, anchor pin, and parking brake actuating mechanism with silicone grease. High-temperature wheel bearing grease or synthetic brake grease also work well for this application.
16. Install the parking brake lever assembly on the lever pin. Install the wave washer and a new retaining clip. Use pliers, or the like, to install the retainer on the pin. If removed, connect the parking brake lever to the parking brake cable and verify that the cable is properly routed.
17. Clean and lubricate the adjuster assembly. Make sure the nut-adjuster is drawn all the way to the stop, but the nut must NOT lock firmly at the end of the assembly.

18. Install the brake shoes on the backing plate with the hold-down springs, washers and pins.

19. Install the shoe-to-shoe spring.

20. Install the retainer spring.

21. Install the auto-adjuster assembly and install the adjuster lever and the shoe-to-lever spring.

22. Pre-adjust the shoes so the drum slides on with a light drag and install the brake drum.

23. Adjust the brake shoes, as described in Section 3 of this manual.

24. Install the rear wheels.

25. To activate the adjusters, some vehicles require you to make several quick pulls on the parking brake lever. On most, however, several short back-ups, about 10 ft. (3m) each, should do it.

26. Adjust the parking brake cable.

27. Lower the vehicle and check for proper brake operation.

MODELS WITH A SINGLE UPPER SHOE-TO-SHOE RETURN SPRING—WITH LOWER STARWHEEL-TYPE ADJUSTER

▶ **See Figures 86 thru 98**

1. Loosen the lug nuts on the applicable wheels.

2. If servicing the front brakes, apply the parking brake, block the rear wheels, then raise and safely support the front of the vehicle securely on jackstands.

3. If servicing the rear brakes, block the front wheels, then raise and safely support the rear of the vehicle securely on jackstands.

4. Remove the wheels.

5. Remove the drums.

6. Spray the brake assembly thoroughly with brake parts cleaner and let it dry. Similarly, spray the inside of the drum.

7. Inspect the drum for wear and/or damage. Machine or replace as necessary. When machining, observe the maximum diameter specification. The maximum machining diameter is stamped into the drum. If the drum braking surface shows signs of blue discoloration, overheating is indicated. If the bluing is extensive the drum/hub assembly must be replaced. Extensive bluing indicates a weakening of the metal.

➡**Note the location of all springs and clips for proper assembly. If you own an instant camera, to make installation easier it may be a good idea to take a picture of your brake assembly with the brake drum removed.**

8. Remove the parking brake lever assembly from the backing plate.

9. Remove the adjusting cable assembly from the anchor pin, cable guide and adjusting lever.

Fig. 87 Remove the brake drum from the rear axle

Fig. 88 Remove the parking brake lever retaining nut which is located behind the backing plate

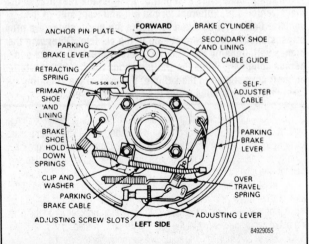
Fig. 86 Identification of the typical components used on drum brakes which use dual return springs and a lower starwheel-type adjuster

Labels in figure 86: ANCHOR PIN PLATE, FORWARD, BRAKE CYLINDER, PARKING BRAKE LEVER, SECONDARY SHOE AND LINING, RETRACTING SPRING, CABLE GUIDE, THIS SIDE OUT, SELF-ADJUSTER CABLE, PRIMARY SHOE AND LINING, BRAKE SHOE HOLD DOWN SPRINGS, PARKING BRAKE LEVER, CLIP AND WASHER, OVER TRAVEL SPRING, PARKING BRAKE CABLE, ADJUSTING SCREW SLOTS, LEFT SIDE, ADJUSTING LEVER

1. Adjusting cable   2. Cable guide
Fig. 89 Disconnect the adjusting cable from the anchor pin, guide and lever

Fig. 90 Slide the parking brake lever out from its mounting

Fig. 93 Disengage the hold-down springs from the retaining clips on the backing plate

Fig. 91 Disconnect the parking brake cable from the lever

Fig. 94 Back off the adjusting screw and remove it from the brake assembly

Fig. 92 Use an appropriate tool to disconnect the return springs from their retaining holes

Fig. 95 Spread the shoes apart and remove them from the backing plate

10. Remove the brake shoe retracting springs.
11. Remove the brake shoe hold-down spring from each shoe.
12. Remove the brake shoes and adjusting screw assembly.
13. Disassemble the adjusting screw assembly.

➡It's a good idea to arrange all the parts in the approximate installed positions as a guide for reassembly.

To install:

14. Clean the ledge pads on the backing plate. Apply a light coat of silicone grease to the ledge pads (where the brake shoes rub the backing plate). High-temperature wheel bearing grease or synthetic brake grease (designed specifically for this) also work well. Also, apply grease to the adjusting screw assembly and the hold-down and retracting spring contacts on the brake shoes.

15. Install the upper retracting spring on the primary and secondary shoes, then position the shoe assembly on the backing plate with the wheel cylinder pistons engaged with the shoes.

16. Install the brake shoe hold-down springs.

17. Install the brake shoe adjustment screw assembly so that the slot in the head of the adjusting screw is toward the primary (leading) shoe, along with the lower retracting spring, adjusting lever spring, adjusting lever assembly and connect the adjusting cable to the adjusting lever. Position the cable in the cable guide and install the cable anchor fitting on the anchor pin.

18. Install the adjusting screw assemblies in the same locations from which they were removed.

❋❋ CAUTION

Interchanging the brake shoe adjusting screws from one side of the vehicle to the other will cause the brake shoes to retract rather than expand each time the automatic adjusting mechanism is operated; this will create an extremely dangerous condition when driving the vehicle. To prevent incorrect installation, the socket end of each adjusting screw is usually stamped with an R or an L to indicate their installation on the right or left side of the vehicle. In some cases, the adjusting pivot nuts can be distinguished by the number of lines machined around the body of the nut. Two lines indicate a nut which should be installed on the right side of the vehicle; one line indicates a nut that must be installed on the left side of the vehicle.

19. Install the parking brake assembly in the anchor pin and secure with the retaining nut behind the backing plate.

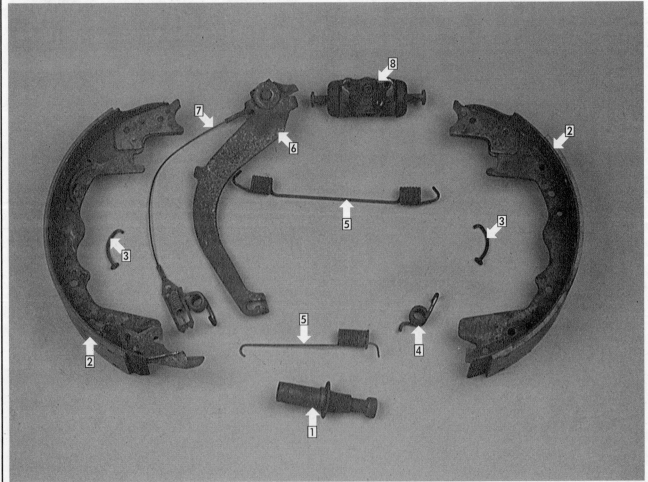

DRUM BRAKE COMPONENTS

1. Adjusting screw
2. Brake shoes
3. Pins
4. Hold-down spring
5. Return springs
6. Parking brake lever
7. Adjusting cable
8. Wheel cylinder

88489P44

Fig. 96 It is a good idea to lay the brake parts out in their positions on a clean work surface as they are removed

Fig. 97 Connecting the lower retracting spring can often be difficult—be careful and have patience

Fig. 98 This is how everything should look after assembly

20. Adjust the brakes before installing the brake drums and wheels. Install the brake drums and wheels.

21. To activate the adjusters, some vehicles require you to make several quick pulls on the parking brake lever. On most, however, several short back-ups, about 10 ft. (3m) each, should do it. .

22. Lower the vehicle and road test the brakes. New brakes may pull to one side or the other before they are seated. Continued pulling or erratic braking should not occur. .

MODELS WITH A SINGLE U-SHAPED RETURN SPRING

▶ See Figures 99 thru 107

❊❊ CAUTION

It is always a good idea to wear eye protection when working on brake components, especially drum brakes. Drum brakes often use powerful springs which could cause severe eye injury if they accidentally break. Also, brake shoes may contain asbestos,

which is a known cancer-causing agent. As soon as the drum is removed, generously spray the entire brake assembly with brake parts cleaner. Let it dry before proceeding. It's a good idea to wear a filter mask when doing brake work.

1. Loosen the lug nuts on the applicable wheels.

2. If servicing the front brakes, apply the parking brake, block the rear wheels, then raise and safely support the front of the vehicle securely on jackstands.

3. If servicing the rear brakes, block the front wheels, then raise and safely support the rear of the vehicle securely on jackstands.

4. Remove the wheels.

5. Remove the brake drum.

6. Spray the brake assembly thoroughly with brake parts cleaner and let it dry. Similarly, spray the inside of the drum.

7. Inspect the drum for wear and/or damage. Machine or replace as necessary. When machining, observe the maximum diameter specification. The maximum machining diameter is stamped into the drum. If the drum braking surface shows signs of blue discoloration, overheating is indicated. If the bluing is extensive the drum/hub assembly must be replaced. Extensive bluing indicates a weakening of the metal.

➥Note the location of all springs and clips for proper assembly. If you own an instant camera, to make installation easier it may be a good idea to take a picture of your brake assembly with the brake drum removed.

8. Remove the return spring clip from the lower anchor block.

9. Squeeze the upper ends of the return spring slightly and remove it from the shoes.

10. Using a hold-down spring tool or pliers, remove the hold-down springs. While holding the back of the spring mounting pin with one hand, press inward on the hold-down spring plate, turn it slightly to align the notches and pin ears, then remove the hold-down spring assemblies with your other hand.

11. Lift the shoes off of the pins, then remove the pins from the backing plate.

12. Remove the shoes and adjuster as an assembly.

13. Pull back on the parking brake cable spring and twist the cable out of the parking brake lever.

14. The parking brake lever is held onto the rear shoe with a horseshoe clip. Spread the clip and detach the lever and washer from the shoe.

To install:

15. Thoroughly clean and dry the backing plate assembly.

16. Lubricate the backing plate bosses, anchor plate surfaces, and all contact points with silicone grease. High-temperature wheel bearing grease or synthetic brake grease (designed specifically for this) also work well.

17. Lubricate the parking brake lever pivot stud, then insert the pivot stud through the applicable hole in the rear shoe, then install a new wave washer and horseshoe clip. Squeeze the clip ends until the clip cannot be pulled from the lever pivot stud.

18. Connect the parking brake cable to the lever.

19. Position the front and rear shoe assemblies and adjuster on the backing plate, then install the hold-down pin and spring assemblies.

20. Position the return spring in the shoes, rotate it down into position on the anchor block, and install the retaining clip.

21. Turn the strut adjusting screw to spread the shoes to the point at which the drum can just be installed without drag.

22. Install the drum.

23. Adjust the brake shoes, as described in Section 3 of this manual.

24. Install the wheels, lower the vehicle and check brake action. A firm pedal should be felt.

25. To activate the adjusters, some vehicles require you to make several quick pulls on the parking brake lever. On most, however, several short back-ups, about 10 ft. (3m) each, should do it.

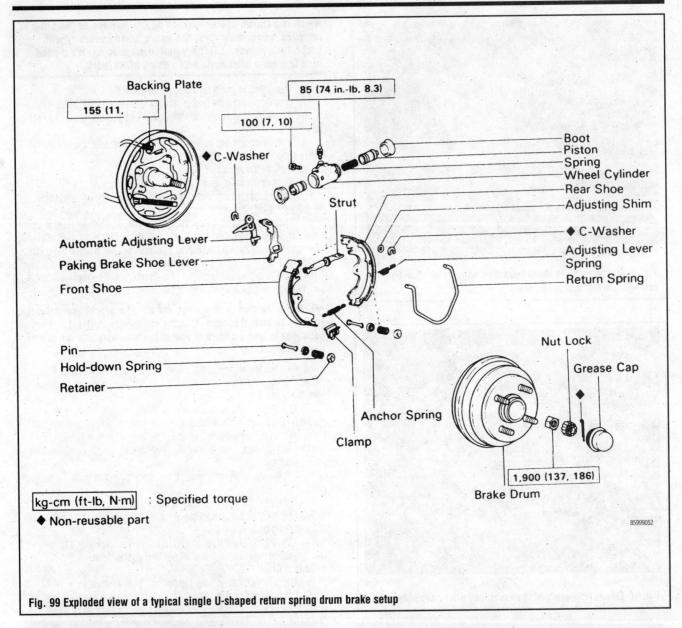

155 (11,

Backing Plate

85 (74 in.-lb, 8.3)

100 (7, 10)

◆ C-Washer

Boot
Piston
Spring
Wheel Cylinder
Rear Shoe
Adjusting Shim

◆ C-Washer

Strut

Automatic Adjusting Lever

Paking Brake Shoe Lever

Front Shoe

Adjusting Lever
Spring

Return Spring

Pin

Hold-down Spring

Retainer

Nut Lock

Grease Cap

Anchor Spring

Clamp

1,900 (137, 186)

Brake Drum

kg-cm (ft-lb, N·m) : Specified torque

◆ Non-reusable part

85999052

Fig. 99 Exploded view of a typical single U-shaped return spring drum brake setup

85999055

Fig. 100 Before removing any parts, make a note of their positions

85999056

Fig. 101 Depress and rotate the hold-down spring retainer . . .

Fig. 102 . . . then remove the spring, retainer and pin from the backing plate and shoes

Fig. 103 Remove the return spring from both brake shoes . . .

Fig. 104 . . . then separate the shoes from the backing plate

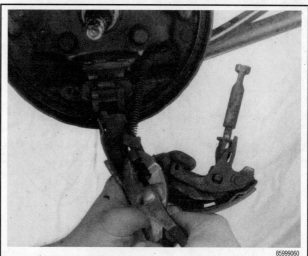

Fig. 105 A large pair of pliers can be used to disconnect the parking brake cable from the lever

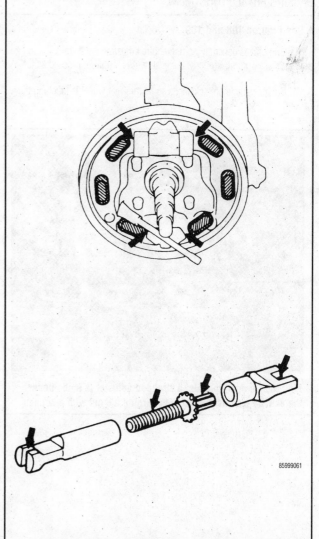

Fig. 106 Before brake shoe installation, clean the backing plate and adjuster mechanism, then apply high temperature grease at these points (arrows)

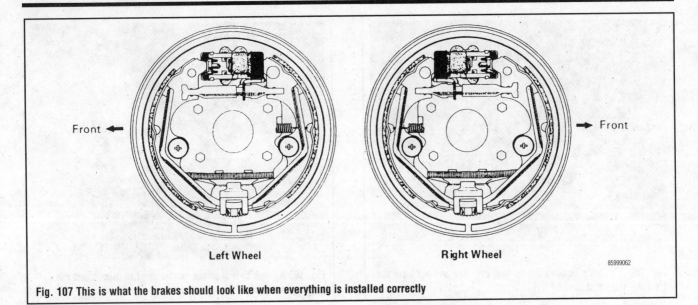

Fig. 107 This is what the brakes should look like when everything is installed correctly

PARKING BRAKE ADJUSTMENT

▶ **See Figures 108 and 109**

Parking brakes generally do not require adjustment if the automatic adjusters are working properly. If adjustment is required, proceed as follows:

1. Put the vehicle on jackstands so neither rear wheel is touching the ground.

2. Engage the parking brake about halfway.

3. Loosen the locknut on the equalizer yoke located under the vehicle, and then turn the adjusting nut until drag can be felt on both rear wheels.

4. Release the brake and check for free rotation of the rear wheels.

On systems where a floor-mounted hand-lever is used, the adjustment is usually contained under the rubber boot that covers the base of the lever. Tighten each of the adjusting nuts on these systems until an equal, slight torque is required to turn each rear drum.

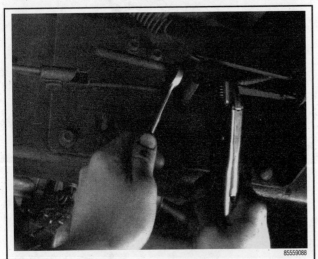

Fig. 108 On most models, a threaded adjuster is found under the vehicle—adjust the cable by turning the nut with a wrench

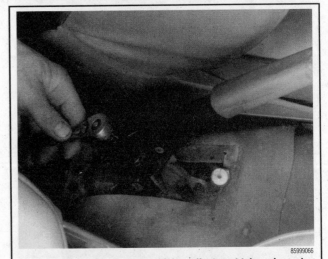

Fig. 109 However, on some vehicles adjustment takes place at the hand lever (if equipped)

BRAKE SYSTEM TUNE-UP PROCEDURE

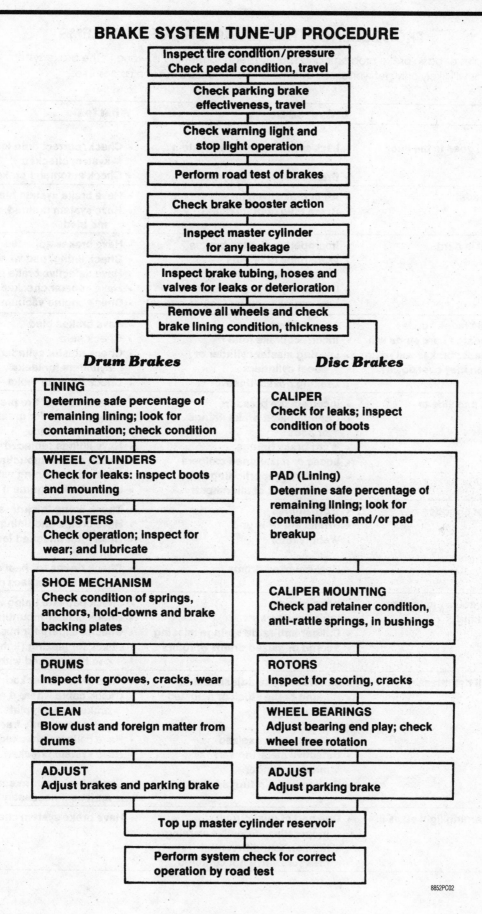

Inspect tire condition/pressure
Check pedal condition, travel

Check parking brake
effectiveness, travel

Check warning light and
stop light operation

Perform road test of brakes

Check brake booster action

Inspect master cylinder
for any leakage

Inspect brake tubing, hoses and
valves for leaks or deterioration

Remove all wheels and check
brake lining condition, thickness

Drum Brakes

LINING
Determine safe percentage of
remaining lining; look for
contamination; check condition

WHEEL CYLINDERS
Check for leaks: inspect boots
and mounting

ADJUSTERS
Check operation; inspect for
wear; and lubricate

SHOE MECHANISM
Check condition of springs,
anchors, hold-downs and brake
backing plates

DRUMS
Inspect for grooves, cracks, wear

CLEAN
Blow dust and foreign matter from
drums

ADJUST
Adjust brakes and parking brake

Disc Brakes

CALIPER
Check for leaks; inspect
condition of boots

PAD (Lining)
Determine safe percentage of
remaining lining; look for
contamination and/or pad
breakup

CALIPER MOUNTING
Check pad retainer condition,
anti-rattle springs, in bushings

ROTORS
Inspect for scoring, cracks

WHEEL BEARINGS
Adjust bearing end play; check
wheel free rotation

ADJUST
Adjust parking brake

Top up master cylinder reservoir

Perform system check for correct
operation by road test

8852PC02

TROUBLESHOOTING BASIC BRAKE PROBLEMS

These are examples of basic brake problems and usually mean something is wrong in the brake system. Left alone, any of these problems will likely only get worse, so have the brakes checked as soon as possible.

The Problem	Is Caused By	What to Do
The brake pedal goes to the floor	• Leak somewhere in the system • Brakes out of adjustment	• Check/correct fluid level; have system checked • Check automatic brake adjusters
Spongy brake pedal	• Air in brake system • Brake fluid contaminated	• Have brake system bled • Have system drained, refilled and bled
The brake pedal is hard	• Improperly adjusted brakes • Worn pads or linings • Kinked brake lines • Defective power brake booster • Low engine vacuum (power brakes)	• Have brakes adjusted • Check lining/pad wear • Have defective brake line replaced • Have booster checked • Check engine vacuum
The brake pedal "fades" under pressure (repeated hard stops will cause brake fade; brakes will return to normal when they cool down)	• Air in system • Incorrect brake fluid • Leaking master cylinder or wheel cylinders • Leaking hoses/lines	• Have brakes bled • Check fluid • Check master cylinder and wheel cylinders for leaks • Check lines for leaks
The car pulls to one side or brakes grab	• Incorrect tire pressure • Contaminated brake linings or pads • Worn brake linings • Loose or misaligned calipers • Defective proportioning valve • Front end out of alignment	• Check/correct tire pressure • Check linings for grease; if greasy, replace • Have linings replaced • Check caliper mountings • Have proportioning valve checked • Have wheel alignment checked
Brakes chatter or shudder	• Worn linings • Drums out-of-round • Wobbly rotor • Heat checked drums	• Check lining thickness • Have drums and linings ground • Have rotor checked for excessive wobble • Check drums for heat checking; if necessary, replace drums
Brakes produce noise (squealing, scraping, clicking)	• Worn linings • Loose calipers • Caliper anti-rattle springs missing • Scored or glazed drums or rotors	• Check pad and lining wear • Check caliper mountings • Check calipers for missing parts • Check for glazing (light glazing can be removed with sandpaper)
Brakes drag (will not release)	• Incorrect brake adjustment • Parking brake stuck or adjusted too tight • Caliper pistons seized • Defective metering valve or master cylinder • Broken brake return springs	• Have brakes checked • Check cable where it enters the brake backing plate. In winter, water frequently freezes here • Have calipers checked • Have system checked • Check brake return springs, replace if necessary
Brake system warning light stays lit	• One part of dual circuit inoperative, defective warning light switch, differential pressure valve not centered	• Have brake system checked

8852PC03

27

TRAILER TOWING

TRAILER TOWING 27-2

TRAILER TOWING

Towing a trailer is not the nerve-wracking experience many people imagine, but proper equipment is necessary. Is your vehicle powerful enough to pull your trailer? Is your vehicle properly equipped for towing?

Your vehicle was primarily designed to carry passengers and cargo. It is important to remember that towing a trailer will place additional loads on your vehicle's engine, drivetrain, steering, braking and other systems. However, if you decide to tow a trailer, using the prior equipment is a must.

Local laws may require specific equipment such as trailer brakes or fender mounted mirrors. Check your local laws.

Trailer Weight

The weight of the trailer is the most important factor. A good weight-to-horse-power ratio is about 35:1—35 pounds (16kg) of gross cargo weight (GCW) for every horsepower your engine develops. Multiply the engines rated horsepower by 35 and subtract the weight of the vehicle, passengers and luggage. The result is the approximate ideal maximum weight you should tow, although a numerically higher axle ratio can help compensate for heavier weight.

➡It is always a good idea to check your owner's manual for specific towing recommendations from the manufacturer. This will avoid overloading your vehicle and prevent potential damage to the drivetrain.

Hitch (Tongue) Weight

▶ See Figures 1 and 2

Calculate the hitch weight in order to select a proper hitch. The weight of the hitch is usually 9–11% of the trailer gross weight and should be measured with the trailer loaded. Hitches fall into various categories: those that mount on

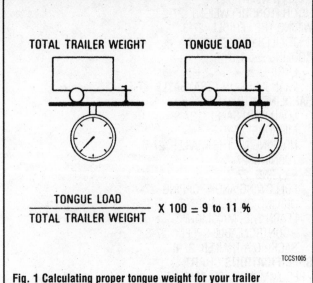

$$\frac{\text{TONGUE LOAD}}{\text{TOTAL TRAILER WEIGHT}} \quad \text{X } 100 = 9 \text{ to } 11 \text{ \%}$$

TCCS1005

Fig. 1 Calculating proper tongue weight for your trailer

the frame and rear bumper, the bolt-on or the weld-on type used for larger trailers. Axle mounted or clamp-on bumper hitches should never be used.

Installation of a bolt-on hitch is easy. When the hitch is installed, the tongue should be level and parallel to the road, and in the exact center of the vehicle.

Check the gross weight rating of your trailer. Tongue weight is usually figured as 10% of gross trailer weight. Therefore, a trailer with a maximum gross

1. Electrical connector
2. Receiver
3. Weight distributing hitch assembly
4. Trailer ball
5. Sway control ball
6. Weight distributing bars
7. Sway control

Fig. 2 Typical hitch components. A class four, weight distributing hitch is shown

weight of 2000 lbs. (908 kg) will have a maximum tongue weight of 200 lbs. (90 kg)—Class I trailers fall into this category. Class II trailers are those with a gross weight rating of 2000–3000 lbs.(908–1362 kg), while Class III trailers fall into the 3500–6000 lbs. (1,590–2,724 kg) category. Class IV trailers are those over 6000 lbs. (2,724 kg) and are for use with fifth wheel trucks, only.

If you're installing a load-distributing hitch, the vehicle will "squat" front and rear when the trailer is coupled. You will have to get the hitch ball at the height where the vehicle will be when fully loaded. Add the average "squat" to the distance from the ground to the top of the coupler to get the ball height.

To determine the average "squat," multiply the hitch weight by two-thirds. Load this weight into the front seat (use approximate weight of people) and measure how much the vehicle squats from the unloaded height both front and rear. Average the front and rear figures.

Load distributing hitches generally use equalizer bars and chain links to level the tow vehicle after the trailer is hooked up.

With the trailer directly behind the vehicle, measure the vehicle height front and rear. Hook up the trailer and adjust the chain links so that it levels the vehicle and provides approximately the same vehicle height, front and rear, with maybe ½ inch (13mm) difference.

For larger trailers or if you are towing with a short vehicle, a sway control may be necessary. The sway control connects between the hitch and the tongue of the trailer. It dampens the swaying motion of the trailer and helps keep the trailer under control. While testing the rig, you should be able to let go of the wheel and feel no fishtailing.

Wiring the Vehicle

▶ See Figures 3, 4, 5, 6 and 7

Wiring the vehicle for towing is fairly easy. There are a number of good wiring kits available and these should be used, rather than trying to design your own.

All trailers will need brake lights and turn signals as well as tail lights and side marker lights. Most areas require extra marker lights for over-wide trailers. Also, most areas have recently required back-up lights for trailers, and most trailer manufacturers have been building trailers with back-up lights for several years.

Additionally, some Class I, most Class II and just about all Class III trailers will have electric brakes. Add to this number an accessories wire, to operate trailer internal equipment or to charge the trailer's battery, and you can have as many as seven wires in the harness.

Determine the equipment on your trailer and buy the wiring kit necessary. The kit will contain all the wires needed, plus a plug adapter set which includes the female plug, mounted on the bumper or hitch, and the male plug, wired into, or plugged into the trailer harness.

Several popular kits are on the market that don't require cutting into your factory wires at all. Instead, they tee into a junction point in the rear of the vehicle. When installing the kit, follow the manufacturer's instructions. The color coding of the wires is usually standard throughout the industry.

If you own vehicle with separate turn signals, the wiring problem is slightly more complicated. Some domestic vehicles, and most imported vehicles, have separate turn signals.

The most practical way around this is to use a commercially available isolation unit, which takes separate brake and turn signal impulses and combines them into a common output to the trailer, allowing use of the standard harness.

Otherwise, the wiring is the same as for conventional vehicles, except that you tap into the isolation unit.

One final point—the best kits are those with a spring loaded cover on the vehicle mounted socket. This cover prevents dirt and moisture from corroding the terminals. Never let the vehicle socket hang loosely; always mount it securely to the bumper or hitch.

You should also use a variable load or heavy-duty flasher to take care of heavier demands on your turn signals.

➡**Most trailer wiring connectors follow an SAE standard for wire color and position. However, there are some exceptions. When wiring a trailer use the standard to avoid potential electrical damage and to make hooking up to different trailers easier.**

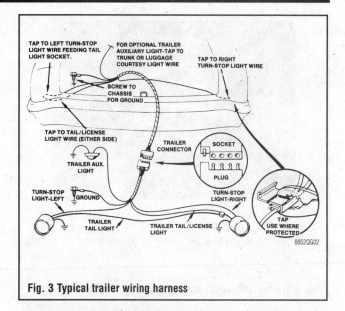

Fig. 3 Typical trailer wiring harness

Fig. 4 Electrical connectors, such as this 7-wire connector, must be mounted solidly to the rear of the tow vehicle

1. Ground (white)
2. Tail, license and running lights (green)
3. Stop and LH turn (red)
4. Stop and RH turn (brown)

Fig. 5 Typical color codes and positions for a 4-wire connector

1. Ground (white)
2. Electric brakes (blue)
3. Tail, license and running lights (green)
4. Trailer battery (black)
5. Stop and LH turn (red)
6. Stop and RH turn (brown)
7. Auxiliary circuit (yellow)

8852QP03

Fig. 6 Typical color codes and positions for a 7-wire connector

8852QP01

Fig. 8 Electric brake controllers should be mounted level and within easy reach of the driver

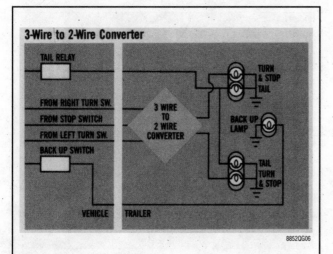

8852QG06

Fig. 7 Isolation unit is used to convert vehicles with separate turn signals

TRAILER BRAKES

▶ **See Figure 8**

Two types of trailer brake systems are currently in use—Hydraulic (Surge) Brakes and Electric Brakes.

Hydraulic braking is performed by the installation of a controller and master cylinder mounted on the tongue of the trailer. The system operates much like the drum brakes on your vehicle. The push of the trailer on the tow vehicle during deceleration synchronizes the trailer brakes with the tow vehicle braking action. As the trailer pushes against the tow vehicle during a stop, the actuator pushes a piston in the master cylinder and supplies hydraulic pressure to the wheel cylinder. The wheel cylinder expands the brake pads against the drums and slows the trailer.

Electric brakes are a popular option on trailers because of their reliability and simplicity of operation. Most states require electric brakes to be installed on trailers of a certain weight rating, or on trailers which have multiple axles.

The electric brake system is actuated by a controller mounted under the dashboard. As the tow vehicle's brakes are applied, a signal from the brake light switch is sent to activate the controller. Simultaneously, the pendulum weight inside the controller moves forward, changing the resistance inside

the controller and activating the trailer brake magnets. The natural G-force of deceleration move the pendulum in direct proportion to the amount of braking applied by the driver.

Back at the wheels, an electromagnet pivots on an arm with a cam that is attached between the brake shoes. When the magnet is energized, it attempts to follow the rotation of the brake drum. This causes the cam to rotate, actuating the primary brake shoe. The movement of the primary shoe causes the secondary shoe to activate, thus stopping the trailer.

If you own or plan on towing a trailer with electric brakes ensure your vehicle is properly equipped with the appropriate electric brake controller.

Cooling

ENGINE

A frequent hazard of towing is engine overheating, due to increased load. To aid cooling, most manufacturers include a heavy-duty cooling system as part of the trailer package. It usually consists of a larger capacity radiator, heavy-duty water pump and coolant recovery system. A/C equipped vehicles also use a clutch-type fan, which uses a heat sensor, allowing the fan to free-wheel, or push air, depending on engine temperature.

Cooling System

One of the most common, if not THE most common, problems associated with trailer towing is engine overheating. Cleaning and flushing the cooling system is good preventative maintenance. Ensure all cooling system components are functioning properly. If your vehicle is not equipped with a factory towing package, installation of aftermarket high capacity radiators, high flow water pumps and auxiliary electric cooling fans will all help keeping your vehicle running cool.

Oil Cooler

Aftermarket engine oil coolers are helpful for prolonging engine oil life and reducing overall engine temperatures. Both of these factors increase engine life. While not absolutely necessary in towing a Class I trailer, all vehicles towing Class II trailers and above should be equipped with an engine oil cooler. Engine oil cooler systems usually consist of an adapter, screwed on in place of the oil filter, a remote filter mounting and a multi-tube, finned heat exchanger, which is mounted in front of the radiator or air conditioning condenser.

TRANSMISSION / TRANSAXLE

▶ **See Figures 9 and 10**

In recent years, the automatic has become the recommended transmission for trailer towing. The overall reliability and power of the automatic makes pulling easier than having to ride the clutch and lug the rig to get moving.

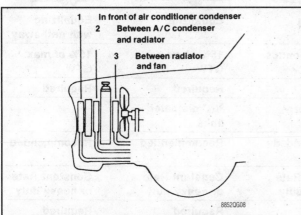

1. In front of air conditioner condenser
2. Between A/C condenser and radiator
3. Between radiator and fan

8852QG08

Fig. 9 The location of the transmission cooler is important. Position 1 provides 100% of capacity; Position 2, 75%, and Position 3 gives 60%, when installed in series with the original cooler. Alternate mounting locations should be chosen where the maximum, coldest air flow will pass over the cooler.

On the negative side, the automatic transmission is far more complicated than a manual, and overheating is responsible for the majority of automatic transmission failures. Under normal service, fluid is designed to last about 50,000 miles (80,450 km) at operating temperatures of 195°F (90°C). As the temperature of the fluid increases, the life of the fluid decreases rapidly—a 20°F (-7°C) temperature rise will halve the life of the fluid:

- At 212°F (100°C), fluid life is 25,000 miles (40,200 km)
- At 235°F (113°C), fluid life is 12,500 miles (20,100 km)
- At 255°F (124°C), fluid life is 6,250 miles (10,000 km)
- At 275°F (135°C), fluid life is 3,000 miles (4,800 km)

Installation of an oil cooler will protect against high heat and premature transmission failure. A 20° drop in transmission fluid temperature will approximately double the fluid life; most coolers will reduce temperatures by 30° or more.

➡ **A transaxle cooler can, sometimes, cause slow or harsh shifting in the cold weather, until the fluid has a chance to come up to normal operating temperature. Some coolers can be purchased with or retrofitted with a temperature bypass valve which will allow fluid flow through the cooler only when the fluid has reached above a certain operating temperature.**

To select a cooler:

1. Estimate the combined weight of the vehicle and the load pulled or carried.
2. Select a cooler of equal capacity.
3. Determine the mounting location. Be sure that cooling is adequate and that the cooler will fit.
4. If you are planning a by-pass installation, select a cooler two sizes larger.

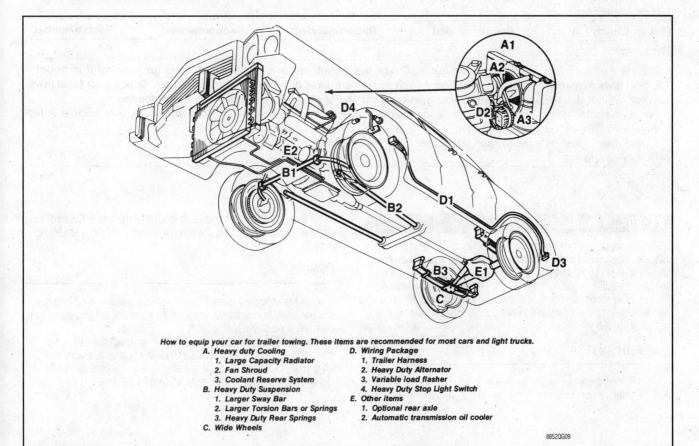

How to equip your car for trailer towing. These items are recommended for most cars and light trucks.

A. Heavy duty Cooling
  1. Large Capacity Radiator
  2. Fan Shroud
  3. Coolant Reserve System
B. Heavy Duty Suspension
  1. Larger Sway Bar
  2. Larger Torsion Bars or Springs
  3. Heavy Duty Rear Springs
C. Wide Wheels

D. Wiring Package
  1. Trailer Harness
  2. Heavy Duty Alternator
  3. Variable load flasher
  4. Heavy Duty Stop Light Switch
E. Other items
  1. Optional rear axle
  2. Automatic transmission oil cooler

8852QG09

Fig. 10 Pulling a trailer requires a variety of special equipment.

RECOMMENDED EQUIPMENT CHECKLIST*

Equipment	Class I Trailers Under 2,000 pounds	Class II Trailers 2,000–3,500 pounds	Class III Trailers 3,500–5,000 pounds	Class IV Trailers 5,000 pounds and up
Hitch	Frame or Equalizing	Equalizing	Equalizing	Equalizing with anti-sway
Tongue Load Limit**	Up to 200 pounds	200–350 pounds	15% of max. GTW	15% of max. GTW
Trailer Brakes	Not Required	Required	Required	Required
Safety Chain	3/16" diameter links	¼" diameter links	5/16" diameter links	—
Fender Mounted Mirrors	Useful, but not necessary	Recommended	Recommended	Recommended
Turn Signal Flasher	Standard	Constant Rate or heavy duty	Constant Rate or heavy duty	Constant Rate or heavy duty
Coolant Recovery System	Recommended	Required	Required	Required
Transmission Oil Cooler	Recommended	Recommended	Recommended	Recommended
Engine Oil Cooler	Recommended	Recommended	Recommended	Recommended
Air Adjustable Shock Absorbers	Recommended	Recommended	Recommended	Recommended
Flex or Clutch Fan	Recommended	Recommended	Recommended	Recommended
Tires	***	***	***	***

NOTE: The information in this chart is a guide. Check the manufacturer's recommendations for your car if in doubt.
 * Local laws may require specific equipment such as trailer brakes or fender-mounted mirrors. Check your local laws.
   Hitch weight is usually 10–15% of trailer gross weight and should be measured with trailer loaded.
*** Most manufacturers do not recommend towing trailers of over 1,000 pounds with compacts. Some intermediates cannot tow Class III trailers.
*** Check manufacturer's recommendations for your specific car/trailer combination.
—Does not apply

8852QC01

Handling a Trailer

Towing a trailer with ease and safety requires a certain amount of experience. The handling and braking characteristics of any tow vehicle may be radically changed by the added weight of a trailer. It's a good idea to learn the "feel" of a trailer by practicing turning, stopping and backing in an open area (an empty parking lot is a good place). Make mental notes of space requirements and trailer response and follow these common sense tips to help avoid accidents.

LOAD WITH SAFETY

When loaded, the trailer should be heavier at the front; this will transfer most of the weight to the rear of the tow vehicle. Approximately 60% of the gross trailer weight should be forward of the axle. If the load is centered, or toward the rear, it will cause the trailer to sway, sometimes violently.

MIRRORS

Large rear view mirrors are essential, especially when towing long trailers. The ability to view obstacles behind the trailer and see passing traffic is extremely important to towing safely.

If you find that the mirrors on your vehicle are insufficient, there are many different types of add on mirrors available to provide a better view while you are towing. Follow the manufacturer's instructions for installation and be sure the mirrors are properly adjusted for the driver.

HOOKING UP THE TRAILER

1. Park the tow vehicle and trailer on level ground in the normal towing position.

2. Block the trailer wheels.

3. If the trailer has never been towed before, use the following procedure to adjust the ball height.

    a. Level the trailer using the tongue jack.

    b. Measure the height to the inside top of the coupler socket on the trailer. Also measure the height to the bottom of the bumper at all four corners of the tow vehicle.

    c. Measure the height to the top of the ball on the tow vehicle.

    d. Adjust the height of the ball equal to the height of the coupler socket, plus and additional 0.031 in. (0.78 mm) higher for each 100 lbs (45 kg) of tongue weight.

4. Lower the weight of the hitch onto the ball, making sure the lock mechanism grasps the ball securely.

5. Measure the height to the bottom of the bumper at all four corners of the tow vehicle. The vehicle should squat somewhat, but should be approximately level.

➡ **If the tow vehicle squats unequally, a weight distributing hitch may be necessary to tow the trailer.**

6. Connect the safety chains from the trailer to the tow vehicle is a criss-cross fashion. This will prevent trailer sway if the trailer should become disconnected from the two vehicle.

7. Connect the breakaway cable and plug in the electrical connector. Ensure each is connected securely.

8. Test the trailer lights and electric brakes for proper operation prior to taking the trailer out on the road.

TURNING

▶ **See Figure 11**

Be sure to signal all turns well in advance. Remember that the trailer wheels will be closer to the inside of a turn than the vehicle wheels.

The arc of the turn is greater with a trailer; you cannot turn as tightly. Starting a turn near the center of the street will place you on the far right side of the new street when the turn is complete. Starting the turn at the outside portion of the road will complete the turn near the center of the new street. This means that you have to drive slightly "deeper" into the turn, or beyond your normal turning point.

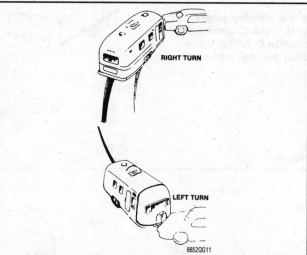

Fig. 11 Notice the track of the trailer wheels compared to the vehicle wheels

PASSING

▶ **See Figures 12 and 13**

Never pass on a hill or curve. Leave enough room before starting to pass; acceleration is considerably slower with the added weight. Remember to allow for extra length when pulling back in after passing.

You may notice when a large truck or bus passes you, that the displaced air pushes the trailer to the right and then affects the front of the trailer. Don't hit the brakes or make any sudden maneuvers; this will only make it worse. Slow a little and the trailer will straighten itself out.

FOLLOWING AND STOPPING

It takes longer to stop with a trailer. Allow at least twice your normal stopping distance and try to anticipate all stops. Avoid panic stops, which cause the trailer to "jackknife" or try to catch up with the vehicle. Taking your foot off the brakes will usually cure this condition. Remember that everything must be done slowly, especially starting and stopping.

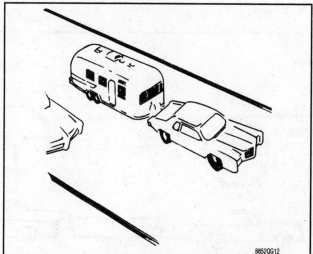

Fig. 12 Allow extra room for the length of the trailer when passing

Fig. 13 When being passed by a large truck or bus, slow down a little to counteract sway.

DRIVING ON HILLS

On down grades, use lower gears and let engine compression slow the vehicle and trailer. Overuse of the brakes will only result in overheating and loss of effectiveness.

When going up long hills, you can reduce the chance of overheating by using a lower gear. The engine will turn faster, causing the fan to push more air. Should overheating occur, pull off the road, turn off all accessories except the heater and run the engine at fast idle until the temperature returns to normal. Check for leaks, broken drive belts, cracked hoses, etc., but never open the radiator cap.

LEARN THE "MAXIMUM CONTROLLABLE SPEED"

Every rig has a maximum speed, above which, it is out of control. Above this speed, many external factors can cause sudden, violent and uncontrolled trailer sway. Gusts of wind, passing vehicles, rough road surface; crosswinds and sudden maneuvers can all have disastrous consequences when driving above the rig's maximum controllable speed.

BACKING A TRAILER

▶ **See Figure 14**

One of the worst experiences for a new trailer owner is backing a trailer. It can be a source of annoyance and frustration until you learn the trick to it.

There is no substitute for experience and one of the best places to practice is an empty parking lot. Practice backing between two trash cans, gradually decreasing the space between them.

Every driver has his own technique, but above all, go slowly. The trick is to turn the vehicle steering wheel in the opposite direction that you want the trailer to go.

An easy way to remember this is to put your right hand on the bottom of the steering wheel. To move the trailer left, turn your hand to the left; to move the trailer right, turn your hand right. Once the trailer is moving in the right direction, turn the wheels back in the opposite direction, so that the vehicle will "follow" the trailer through the turn. If you find the trailer is not going where you want it, pull forward, straighten the rig and try again.

Be patient. Turn the steering wheel a little at a time to start out. It's easier to begin backing with the vehicle and trailer in a straight line. This minimizes the corrections required, although, with practice, this becomes less important.

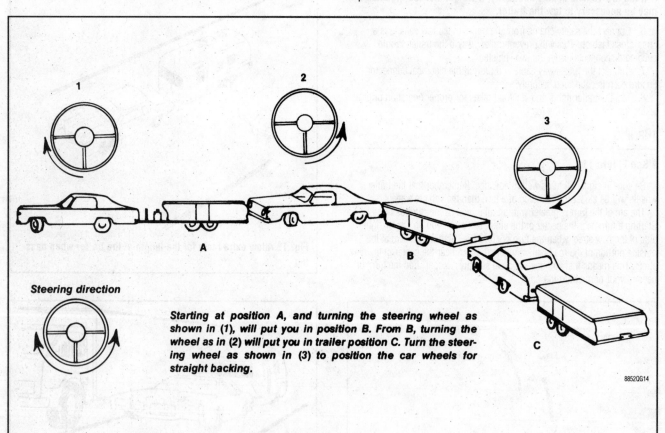

Steering direction

Starting at position A, and turning the steering wheel as shown in (1), will put you in position B. From B, turning the wheel as in (2) will put you in trailer position C. Turn the steering wheel as shown in (3) to position the car wheels for straight backing.

8852QG14

Fig. 14 Backing up a trailer can be mastered by following these simple directions

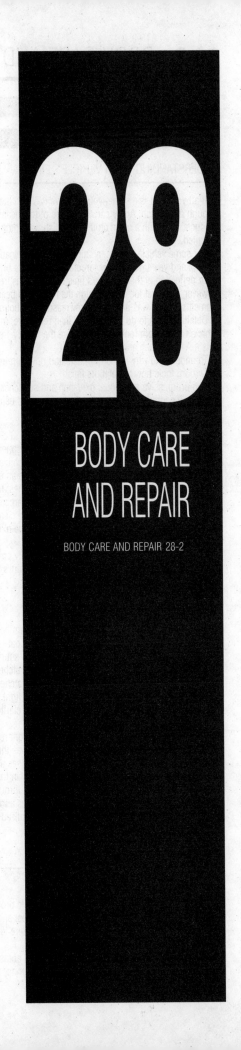

28

BODY CARE
AND REPAIR

BODY CARE AND REPAIR

Exterior Detailing

UNDERSTANDING YOUR VEHICLE'S FINISH

If all you want is a shine, you can have it. Wash the vehicle or run it through a car wash. Apply car wax or one of the cleaner/wax combination products. Buff with a clean cloth. The finish will shine—but it won't be "detailed."

For some vehicle owners, a shine is enough, because, as the miles and months and years go by, they forget the mirror-like brilliance and vibrant color perfection of their vehicle's finish when it was fresh from the factory. However, that "wet look," as though the finish had been applied only moments before, was probably a key reason they bought the vehicle!

Detailing aims to do nothing less than recapture, insofar as possible, a vehicle's showroom look: And to restore the factory-fresh "wet look" to its finish. A mere wash and wax won't do it.

To understand why not is to understand how to refresh and restore its showroom look: how to detail its finish.

Two progressive afflictions, oxidation and scratches, first dim, then dull, and finally degrade a vehicle's finish, as described below.

Oxidation

Oxidation is a chemical reaction between atmospheric pollutants and the paint's pigments. The oxidation of conventional vehicle paint (and, to a lesser extent, the newer clearcoat finishes) creates an ever-growing layer of scum on the paint's surface. In conventional finishes, the scum is "dead paint": the oxidized top color layer of paint. In clearcoat finishes, what's oxidized is the see-through protective top layer of the clearcoat. Unless the finish is regularly detailed and the scum removed, the oxidation layer thickens and builds and dulls the paint.

Waxing does not remove the oxidation. It merely covers it up. No amount of waxing alone can recapture oxidized paint's original color or vibrancy. Only detailing can.

Scratches

Look closely at your vehicle's finish. Better, examine it with a magnifying glass. The finish—whether conventional or clearcoat—is cross-hatched by a myriad tiny scratches. Wear and tear from many sources—from car wash brushes to wind friction— cause vehicle paint scratches. Whether in conventional paint or in the top layer of clearcoat, scratches have the same effect: they opaque the paint, bending (refracting) light rays from their normal straight paths. The result is ever-diminishing clarity. (Pro-detailers call clarity "DOI"—Distinction of Image.)

Waxing does not remove or correct a finish's light refracting hairline scratches; however, detailing can. Detailing removes the oxidation, the finish's "dead paint." Doing so, it uncovers and exposes a fresh, original color layer once covered and obscured by oxidation; or, in the case of clearcoat, removes what amounts to a film that blurs its see-through clarity. Detailing also removes or fills in the light-bending scratches and, with oxidation removed and scratches filled in, protects the revitalized finish from further oxidation or scratching.

DETAILING PRODUCTS

♦ **See Figures 1, 2, 3, 4 and 5**

You can pick and choose from dozens of vehicle products formulated to remove the oxidized paint layer, fill in the scratches, and protect the revitalized paint or clearcoat from further degradation. Here is how finish detailing products are generally classified:

• Oxidation removers (in order, from the most abrasive to the least abrasive): rubbing compounds, polishing compounds, cleaners, and polishes.

• Scratch removers: polish and glaze.
• Scratch fillers: glaze and sealer.
• Finish protectors: wax.

If, reading various product labels, you're confused as to what is a "cleaner" and what is a "polish," to say nothing of "compounds," you aren't alone. Even their makers only hazily differentiate between "cleaners" and "polishes."

There is, however, a critical difference between the four types of oxidation-removers. The critical difference is their degree of abrasives. Whatever their type, most oxidation removers contain grit, a sandlike abrasive that acts much like sandpaper to remove surface imperfections. Oxidation is a surface imperfection.

Polishes, Cleaners and Compounds

In detailing your vehicle's finish, start with the least abrasive, a polish. (So fine are some grits used in the polishes and cleaners especially formulated for clearcoat finishes, which cannot tolerate abrasion, that they produce a paste that is not abrasive in the usual sense.) If polish doesn't

Fig. 1 Polish, glaze, and pre-cleaner products are usually meant for a multi-step process

Fig. 2 Polishes and waxes come in both paste and liquid forms. Some are intended for machine application and others for hand application, read the label.

remove the oxidation, progress to a slightly more abrasive oxidation remover, a cleaner. If you are absolutely convinced that something even more abrasive is needed to remove badly oxidized finish, usually found on long neglected paint jobs, use the even more abrasive product, a polishing compound— but use it with great care and with minimum application pressure SO as not to cut right through the finish and down to base metal. Rubbing compounds are 50 abrasive ("aggressive," in detailing lingo) that they should probably only be used by pro-detailers and paint shop experts. Improper use of such products puts your paint job at risk.

Glazes

Often a watery, sometimes transparent liquid, glaze has two primary jobs: to fill in tiny scratches and, buffed, to produce a brilliant shine. Glaze is applied with a clean, non-abrasive 100% cotton cloth and allowed to dry. The glaze dries as a haze, which is buffed to a lustrous shine. Buffed semi-wet, either by hand or machine, glaze often produces an ultimate shine—a shine which, almost immediately, must be protected by wax. If left unwaxed, glaze and its benefits are quickly dissipated by sunlight.

Sealers

Sealers perform and are applied much like glaze. The chief difference between a sealer and a glaze is the visible effect on the finish. Glaze gives the finish a higher luster than does sealer. However, sealers generally do a better job of enhancing a finish's depth of color and reflective clarity (DOI). Like glaze, most sealers lose their effect unless protected by wax.

Wax

▶ **See Figures 6 and 7**

Wax, in vehicle detailing, has four important functions:
1. It protects the newly exposed fresh paint or clear-coat layer.
2. It protects the scratch-filling glaze or sealer.
3. It produces a brilliant, mirror-like shine.
4. It weather and waterproofs the finish.

What about combination products which claim to do two, even three, things in one step? Among combination products are cleaner/waxes, sealer/waxes, polish/waxes, and wash/waxes. Most combinations are easy and quick to apply, but the combinations seldom if ever do either job as well as do single-purpose products. Exceptions may he some sealer/glazes and some cleaner/polishes. Both partners in these combinations do essentially the same job.

If it's simply a shine you want, the combinations may deliver it, and in considerably less time than the sequential application of two to four single-purpose detailing products. However, if you want your vehicle's finish to be

Fig. 3 Protectants should do more than apply a sheen, check each product for its ultraviolet protection

Fig. 4 Tire and wheel cleaners and protectants should be applied first, always start your detailing with the dirtiest parts

Fig. 5 A good commercial glass product should make the windows almost "invisible". Glass coating products on the right are just a few of the magical chemicals currently available.

Fig. 6 Among the handiest tools for detailing is an inexpensive spray bottle. Filled, a pint-size bottle weighs only a little more than a pound.

8852RP02

Fig. 7 Don't overlook the tires. Tire protectant gives your vehicle, "the complete detailing look".

the best it can be, detailing's ultimate promise, stick with single-purpose products.

Before you begin detailing the finish, you need to know whether your vehicle has a conventional finish or the newer clear-coated finish. Abrasive polishes and cleaners, as previously noted, must never be used on clearcoat finish. Abrasives can permanently scratch the clearcoat, destroying its see-through clarity.

If you are unsure whether your vehicle's finish is conventional or clearcoat, ask the dealer from whom you bought the vehicle. A quick test of the finish may also help you to decide: With a non-abrasive cloth, apply wax or a mild polish to a few inches of finish in some out-of-sight place. Rub firmly but gently. If finish color comes off on the cloth, the vehicle probably has a conventional finish. If no paint shows on the cloth, the finish is probably clearcoat.

One last decision remains before you set to work. Should you randomly select various finish-detailing products, such as cleaner, polish, glaze, and wax? Or should you use a step-by-step, product-by-product detailing "system" as formulated and tested by the various product makers? While finish restorative systems invariably use only a particular maker's products, these maker-recommended products—and their step-by-step application—all but guarantee superlative results. The systems take the guesswork out of product selection and help you avoid finish-damaging mistakes.

❊❊ WARNING

If you are in doubt about whether your paint job is conventional or clearcoat, treat it and detail it as though it were clearcoat finish. Use only products whose labels specify that they may be used on clearcoat finish.

DETAILING THE EXTERIOR

Washing

Three basic rules about washing:
1. Do not wash and detail your vehicle in the sun.
2. In extremely cold weather, do your washing and detailing indoors (preferably in a heated place).
3. Work only on a cool vehicle (hand-test the vehicle's surface temperature before you begin).

While car wash products will remove most oil and grease stains, road tar—which may smudge a vehicle's lower parts—may need special effort and special products. Stubborn, dried tar and grease can be removed with special tar removers, but they also remove car wax. Specially formulated tar cleaners are available from most local automotive supply retailers.

Steps:
4. With hose's nozzle adjusted to medium spray, thoroughly wet vehicle's finish, washing off loose grit, dirt, and pollutants.
5. Soak towels thoroughly in sudsy car wash solution. Use minimum application pressure. The sudsy solution acts as a lubricant between your wash cloth and the vehicle's finish. The aim is to loosen surface dirt and pollutants, float them off the finish, and hold them in suspension within the solution. Floating them off prevents them from scratching the finish. Dunk the cloth frequently in your bucket of wash water to get rid of suspended, potentially abrasive particles. Work with a clean, sopping wet cloth, heavy with solution. While application in a circular motion is easier, and for most detailers more natural, a forward-backward motion is better because it does not leave circular swirl marks in the finish.
6. Some pro-detailers wash the dirtiest parts—wheels, wheel wells, and lower body area—first. Others start at the roof, then move to the hood and the trunk lid, doing wheels and fender wells last.
7. Pay particular attention to hard-to-reach places: areas behind the bumpers, hood edges (you may have to raise the hood to reach them), wheel wells, wheel spokes, front and taillight assemblies.
8. Rinse well with a medium spray from the hose, flooding areas to float particles off.
9. Dry with clean, non-abrasive cotton cloths, preferably terry towels, or with a soft chamois or sponge.

Quick-dry tip: Drive around the block. Air and wind will get rid of excess rinse water, especially in hard to dry places as the radiator grills, vents, and emblems. But don't drive so far as to dry the finish. Some moisture must remain to prevent spotting during final towel-drying.

As you dry, be sure not to let any water droplets remain, because they'll leave spots in the finish. Don't neglect to dry bumpers, wheels, and chrome. If any dirt comes off on your drying cloth, you didn't wash the finish well enough.

Removing Oxidation

If the finish is heavily oxidized, use a good cleaner; use a polish if the finish is only moderately or marginally oxidized. Whatever the product, make sure its label specifies it's to be used:
1. For your vehicle's type of finish (conventional or clearcoat, or both) and . . .
2. For the way you want to apply it (manually or by buffing machine, or both).

There are many cleaners available for either conventional or clearcoat finishes. Read labels carefully to determine what is appropriate for your vehicle's finish.

Polishes, cleaners, sealers, and glazes, when manually applied, are allowed to dry only up to the point of being "nearly dry"—then they are wiped and buffed. Allowing any of these products to dry completely before rubbing them off and buffing the finish risks the possibility of abrasive "chalking"; that is, the tiny particles of hard, dried product can, themselves, become abrasives.

Steps:
3. Apply cleaner or polish to a 1-foot-square area with a clean, non-abrasive, 100% cotton cloth. (Experienced detailers usually work on somewhat larger areas.)
4. Use the preferred back-and-forth motion if you can; use a circular motion if you must. Apply only enough cleaner or polish, and buff with only enough pressure, to remove oxidation. Stop frequently to observe results. When oxidation is removed from a conventional finish, the newly exposed color layer shows deep, original color; a clearcoat finish relieved of oxidation has renewed, see-through clarity. Guidelines for buffing conventional finishes and clearcoat finishes appear below:
   a. **CONVENTIONAL FINISH** Since you're working directly on pigmented paint, expect some color to come off on your rag. You are working to remove only the oxidized, dead paint, and to expose a fresh layer; when deep-toned, fresh paint shows, stop. You want to remove as little paint as possible. Removing more than necessary will only thin the pigment layer, not improve its color.

b. **CLEARCOAT FINISH** To remove the oxidized top layer of clearcoat, follow the procedure given for conventional paint—but be aware that clearcoat can be tricky. Because you aren't working on color pigment, but rather on the finish's transparent protective paint, no color shows on your cloth. You must therefore stop more frequently to observe results. When the clarity of the clearcoat has been restored and the deep-toned color underlying the clearcoat shows through, stop. Further application of cleaner or polish will needlessly remove good clearcoat, reducing the clearcoat's protective thickness.

✳✳ WARNING

Before you use any product on clear-coat finish, carefully read the product's label. Use no product unless its label specifies that it is safe to use on clearcoat. Old cloths from your household rag bag may be good enough for dusting the furniture, but not for cleaning and polishing your vehicle's finish. Use only clean, soft, 100% cotton cloths, preferably pre-washed with a fabric softener. Anything else risks scratching your vehicle's finish—especially clearcoat finish.

5. When a small area has been cleaned and buffed, move to an adjacent small area. Doing one small area at a time reduces the chances of the product thoroughly drying and abrasively "chalking." Typically, pro detailers clean and polish one-half of the hood at a time.

6. Work carefully around insignias, headlights, taillights, moldings, crevice areas, and the "opening" edges of doors and trunk—places where cleaner or polish, if allowed to dry thoroughly, will be tedious to remove.

7. Hand-buff to a high gloss.

Glazing/Sealing

Closely inspect the cleaned, oxidation-free finish and note where hairline scratches are most severe. Glaze and/or sealer fills in minute scratches and is buffed to a high shine. The finish's ultimate shine depends on the shine you buff into the glaze or sealer, not on the shine of its final wax protective coating. Glazes buff to a high luster; sealers generally do not buff to as high a luster, but they produce deeper-toned color.

If you use glaze, use a single-purpose product; if you choose to use a sealer, use a combination product, such as a glaze/sealer. Single-purpose sealers have other finish corrective uses not discussed in this book.

Steps:

1. Apply successively to small finish areas with a clean, non-abrasive 100% cotton cloth. (Some detailers prefer cheesecloth available at your local automotive parts retailer.)

2. Allow to semi-dry to a haze. Buff to a high gloss.

3. If you can't achieve a high gloss, reapply glaze or sealer/glaze and buff again.

Waxing

▶ **See Figures 8 and 9**

Waxing after application of glaze or sealer is essential to protect the glaze from dissipation by sunlight and to achieve ultimate depth of color in conventional finishes and ultimate clarity in clearcoat finishes.

There are a few exceptions to this wax-after-glazing rule. Some glazes do not require wax protection; however, these glazes must be reapplied frequently—too frequently to suit most driveway detailers. Most glazes of this type are used to super-shine show cars or vehicles being entered in a concours competition (in which vehicles are judged on their excellence of appearance).

For a long-lasting wax job the best choice is Carnauba. The wax, derived from the Brazilian Carnauba palm, is nature's hardest wax, providing hard, long-lasting finish protection. Carnauba also has the highest melting point of any natural wax. It remains protective even at temperatures of 200°F (94°C). During summer's hottest days, in the hottest regions (as the Southwest), a black vehicle left in the sun can reach such elevated temperatures.

➡ **Waxing is seldom a one-step operation. Far better to apply a thin coat of wax initially, then buff it, then apply a second thin coat. The**

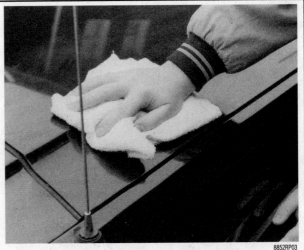

Fig. 8 Buff the finish with a clean non-abrasive cloth using a straight back-forth motion

Fig. 9 Water should bead up like this on a well-waxed finish

first merely gets into the "pores" of the finish; the second fully overcoats the finish.

Choose a Carnauba paste wax over a Carnauba liquid wax. The paste contains a slightly greater percentage of Carnauba. Spray-on waxes contain considerably less Carnauba because the formula must be thinned to spray. With the paste, it is also easier to apply the wax in a very thin layer, which gives best results and which buffs easiest to a super shine. Two thin wax applications with buffing in between is usually the best approach for long-lasting results. Properly applied, Carnauba wax may continue to protect your finish, depending on climate and other conditions, for as long as 3–6 months—and sometimes longer. The hood and the roof—body areas that receive lots of sun—may need waxing more frequently.

Steps:

1. Apply successively to small areas of the finish (best: areas of about 1 square foot) with a damp 100% cotton cloth. A terry cloth towel that has been laundered in fabric softener is the best applicator.

2. With back-forth motion (or circular motion, if you must), apply a thin, even layer of wax.

3. Buff with a clean terry cloth towel. Repeat until the finish is completely waxed and buffed to a brilliant shine.

Cleanup

▶ **See Figure 10**

Wherever cleaner or wax has hardened in crevices (on door edges and the like), remove it with a cotton swab or a used, soft-bristled toothbrush. Also recommended: a soft paintbrush, its bristles trimmed to about a 2-inch (50mm) length, which can get into the smallest places— such as insignias and where molding meets the body's sheet metal.

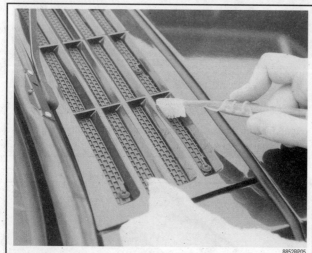

8852RP05

Fig. 10 A soft-bristled toothbrush is an excellent tool for getting wax out of hard to reach places

POLISHING CHROME (BUMPERS, MOLDING, TRIM)

A good chrome polish renews and shines most chrome. Once chrome has been cleaned and shined, apply the same Carnauba wax used on the finish. Waxing a vehicle's chrome is as important as waxing its finish. Wax preserves chrome's brilliance and prevents rusting. Most chrome is cleaned and polished with a dual-purpose chrome cleaner/polish. Where chrome is pitted or rusting, a two-step chemical cleaning treatment often works best. Chrome-plated plastics—as grilles and trim on some late models frequently are—are best cleaned and protected by products specially designed for chromed plastics.

Clean and polish body chrome—chromed molding and stripping— before glazing the finish (just after you apply cleaner or polish) to prevent chrome cleaner from streaking the glaze. When you wax the finish, wax body chrome, too. Non-body chromed parts, like bumpers, can be cleaned, polished, and waxed later.

Steps:

1. With a soft cloth, apply chrome cleaner/polish to a small area of chrome. Let it dry, then rub and buff with a clean cloth.

2. Inspect the cleaned area. Remove any road tar with tar remover. If there are pits or scratches in the chrome, soak a toothbrush in cleaner and scour them clean. Rusty places may require two or three applications of cleaner and gentle use of steel wool (00 or 000).

3. Be careful not to get chrome cleaner on the finish, or in the crevices of chromed fittings (for example, headlight and taillight assemblies). Most chrome polish, once dry, is hard to remove from crevices, rubber, and plastic components (such as taillight lenses). Removing the cleaner from unwanted places is time-consuming and tedious, even using a clean toothbrush or cotton swab. Shorten the cleanup time by nor getting the cleaner where you don't want it.

4. When the chrome is clean and shined, wax it.

DETAILING VINYL BUMPERS AND OTHER EXTERIOR VINYL PARTS

Vinyl or plastic bumpers, after washing, should be cleaned with a vinyl cleaner/polish. Clean black vinyl or rubber bumpers with any good vinyl cleaner. There are products available that are specially designed for cleaning and restoring black vinyl and rubber bumpers and trim.

Do not attempt to wax vinyl bumpers or other components unless they are non-textured and painted. Should wax get on textured or non-painted surface, clean the surface with soap and water, scrubbing with a soft brush. Wax removing solvents are also available to remove stubborn residue.

DETAILING WHEELS AND TIRES

Wheels and tires are "show parts." In detailing wheels, especially, consult your owner's manual for any special manufacturer's instructions. Clearcoated or painted wheels can be scratched or permanently damaged by abrasive cleaners or polishes. Wheels made of magnesium ("Mag") or aluminum clean and shine best and safest with special products.

It works best to detail one wheel at a time and to detail the tire/whitewall areas first.

Detailing Tires

Steps:

1. Clean whitewalls with a whitewall cleaner or with wetted household steel wool and soap pads (or with both). Black curb scuffs are often difficult to erase. First apply a whitewall cleaner; then, if necessary, use the steel wool and soap pads. Rinse, and observe your progress. Repeat the process as needed.

2. If your whitewalls are splotched with scuff-caused intrusions of black or white into adjacent tire areas, touch out the intrusion places with touch-up paint.

3. When the touch-up is thoroughly dry, use a tire brush and an all-purpose cleaner to clean the tire to the tread line.

4. Let the tire dry.

5. Apply a protectant to all visible black tire areas. Protectant brings out and renews the tire's deep black color. Most protectants work best when you leave them on for several hours (or, even better, overnight) before wiping off any residue. Never paint a tire's rubber, except for small area "touch outs" (step #2, above).

Detailing Wheels

Steps:

1. Rewash wheels. Then apply an all-purpose cleaner, as for tires, above. Wheels and their wheel wells are often the dirtiest parts of your vehicle (other than a non-detailed engine compartment). Wheels pick up road tar, grease, and black brake dust.

2. With a soft cloth apply a good wheel cleaner. You can use one of the specialty wheel cleaners designed for the type of wheels you have (Mag, aluminum, or painted), or you can use one of the cleaners that work safely and efficiently on most kinds of wheels.

3. Whatever cleaner you use, use it gently. Wheels are surprisingly scratchable, especially if clear-coated. If your wheels are clear-coated, use only wheel cleaners specified for clearcoat. Work the cleaner into wheel recesses using a toothbrush or cotton swab.

4. Spoked wheels and wheels with intricate designs take some extra doing—generally with a toothbrush, swabs, and a non-abrasive cloth soaked in cleaner or soap suds. And, yes, your fingers, too, which can reach into places many cleaning aids can't (many vehicle enthusiasts even detail the back of the wheel). It's a labor-intensive job, but the good news is that once done right, spoked, finned, and other designer wheels are easier to clean the next time around.

5. Rinse with a hose or bucket(s) of water and let dry.

6. Wax with the same wax you used on the finish.

DETAILING EXTERIOR GLASS: WINDOWS, MIRRORS, & WINDSHIELD

Dirty windows make a detailed vehicle look. . . well, undetailed. Besides, they obscure your vision. Although you washed the windows and windshield when you washed the vehicle, they probably need close-up detailing to rid them of bugs, decals (they're "no-no's" on a well-detailed vehicle), and the last vestige of grime. Many car care product makers make good glass cleaners. Also, household glass-cleaning products work well, as does a simple mix of ammonia and water (8 ounces of household ammonia to 2 gallons of water).

✖✖ CAUTION

Use extreme care in handling and working with inflammable products (as petroleum-based engine cleaners, spray-on products (which can be harmful if sprayed or blown into your face or eyes). and products that are potentially harmful if inhaled (such as ammonia or ammonia-based products).

➡**If your vehicle's windows and windshield are glass, any glass cleaner is safe to use. However, if they are plastic, you should use a plastic cleaner formulated for plastic convertible windows.**

Steps:
1. With a soft cloth, an applicator, a squeegee, or a squirt bottle, wet no more than half the windshield.
2. Rub dry, giving special attention where it's seldom given: windshield (and window) corners and edges.
3. If bugs or road tar remains, remove with gentle use of very fine steel wool (00 or 000).
4. Reapply window cleaner. Again rub dry.
5. Inspect in sunlight. Some streaking will probably remain. Detailing aims to clean glass totally. If that is your aim, too, repeat the cleaning cycle until the glass is spotless.

DETAILING'S DETAILS

♦ **See Figure 11**

Here's a quick checklist of detailing's details:
• Antennas. Use a good chrome cleaner. Polish, then wax. If antennas are clear-coated, treat as clearcoat finish.
• Gas fill port and cap. They were spotless when you bought the vehicle; detail them to showroom condition.
• Chromed tailpipes. Use 00 or 000 steel wool to rid them of rust; then use chrome polish. Tailpipe heat makes waxing a waste of time.

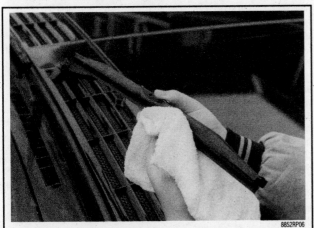
8852RP06

Fig. 11 Neglected wiper rubber can permanently scratch windshields. Wash the wipers with car wash solution and water to rid it of abrasive particles or slippery wax. If wipers are worn or frayed, replace them.

• Plastic taillight and headlight lenses. An all-purpose cleaner and soft-bristled toothbrush (an old toothbrush, not a new one) routes grime and road film from crevices without scratching scratch-prone lenses. After cleaning, apply a plastic polish.
• Radiator grille. If your vehicle has an exposed one, go over it grille piece by grille piece, topside as well as bottom, with an all-purpose cleaner. If chromed, follow with chrome polish. Finally, apply wax. Leave no recess undetailed.
• Windshield/rear window wipers. Choose a cleaner appropriate to the finish or material and give wiper arms a thorough cleaning; then wax. While protectant is used on other vehicle rubber, it should not be used on wiper blades because it will affect their wiping efficiency.

Your vehicle's initial bumper-to-bumper detailing, described here step-by-step, admittedly takes time, effort, and energy. But the upkeep—keeping it detailed—is relatively easy. And, if detailing is done regularly— perhaps three to four times a year—requires relatively little time. Some things get easier once done right; detailing is one of them.

A MASTER DETAILER DISCUSSES CLEARCOAT FINISHES

Clearcoat: New High-Tech Finish

Today, on many makes and models of vehicles, there is a whole new system of finishes, high-tech vehicle paints which differ fundamentally from their predecessors in construction and in the way they must be cared for and detailed.

In simplest terms, the final, top layer of finish on all vehicles of the past, and still on some today, is a pigmented paint. Detailing these conventional finishes, you work directly on the vehicle's color—the paint layer that gives a vehicle its color. Using polish or cleaner, color actually comes off on your polishing cloth or buffing pad if the paint, aging, is oxidized. But this does not happen if your vehicle is clear-coated.

On vehicles with a clearcoat finish, the paint's color layer lies protected by a clear, colorless, usually urethane or polyurethane final finish. The urethanes are part of a new family of high-tech vehicle finishes.

The urethanes and polyurethanes—often called the 'clearcoat' because they comprise the clear, see through final top finish overlying the pigmented paint layers—are more forgiving than conventional finishes, yet, oddly, they need more care.

Faults in the clearcoat finish can be more easily corrected than in such pigmented finishes as enamel, acrylic, lacquer, or other conventional vehicle paints. Scuffs or scratches in these pigmented paint layers are difficult to correct. For one reason, a scratch or deep scuff actually penetrates, and likely mars or even discolors, the finish's pigmented color layers, since the paint's color layers are the finish's top layers.

In the clearcoat, many scuffs—minor scratches, for example—never reach the paint layers. And while in the clearcoat they may be visible, they are usually not nearly as obvious as would he damage to the finish's color layers.

Still, the clearcoat is vulnerable not only to casual damage, but to environmental damage and degradation. The clearcoat, to maintain its luster and impregnability, demands more frequent washing: once a week, certainly.

An example of casual damage is the scuffing and scratching that happens when somebody uses his or her vehicle as a shelf for a shopping bag. Slide the bag off the clearcoat, and you leave a scuff mark. With clear-coating, a scuff mark like that is relatively easier to repair than when the damage is in the top, color layer of conventional paint.

Protecting Clearcoat From Environmental Damage

Environmental damage is a clear and present danger to the clearcoat. And even more so than for conventional finishes. If you live in an area where there's a lot of traffic or you commute long distances, carbon black from other vehicle exhausts builds up on the clear-coat. Live or drive near an airport and there's fallout from jet fuel. In industrial zones of the Eastern and Northeastern states, and moving farther south every year, is industrial pollution, including acid rain. Acid fog is common in Southern California.

So, in the industrial north, is acid snow. Include, too, early morning's acid mist. Every form of precipitation carries the threat of acid fallout and clearcoat damage.

What happens is this: If your vehicle isn't frequently washed, it becomes coated with acid fallout. A light rain, a morning mist, fog, or dew mixes with the acid particles, putting them into solution. Now your vehicle s finish is wetted with an acid solution. All that's needed for catalytic activity—an increase in finish-destroying chemical action—is heat. It doesn't take much sunlight to supply it. And you have all the ingredients for acid-burning the finish. It probably won't happen in one day, or two. Or even a week. But the damaging process, unless you frequently wash your vehicle, goes on day after day: more acid fallout, an ever stronger acid solution, more catalytic action spurred, day after day, by the sun's heat and light.

Only washing the vehicle to rid it of acid fallout breaks this potentially damaging cycle. That's why it's so important, especially with the clearcoats, to wash your vehicle frequently.

Washing Your Vehicle's Clearcoat

The key to washing a vehicle to rid it of acid build up is to use the right techniques, the right products, and the right tools.

Two things are basic: (1) you don't ever want to wash your vehicle in sunlight, and (2) you don't ever want to wash a hot vehicle.

Before you use a wash product on a sun-warmed hot vehicle, rinse it with cool, clear water. Rinsing washes away the heaviest concentrations of atmospheric pollutants. And, just as important, pre-rinsing cools the finish. Neglect the pre-rinse, and you aid and abet chemical activity. The reason is basic: the chemical activity of many car wash solutions, among them the detergents, is accelerated by a vehicle's body heat. A chemical reaction is produced which can either streak or burn the finish, especially if it's a clearcoat. Before you use a wash product, rinse the vehicle with a flood of cool water. Rinsing quick-cools a hot vehicle. Also, a clean water pre-rinse also gets rid of possibly abrasive materials.

Basic Clearcoat Systems

Understanding your vehicle's clearcoat is a first step toward properly caring for—and detailing—it.

Currently, there are four basic clearcoat 'systems,' although the technology is changing rapidly. There are urethane, polyurethane, polyester, and fluorine high-tech clearcoat systems. All are pretty much built up, layer by layer, in the same way: you've got a primer coat (the first coat on the vehicle's bare metal skin), then one color coat or several (this is the 'base coat,' which is often surprisingly thin), and lastly, the far thicker final clearcoat.

The color coat can be quite thin in clearcoat finishes because all it does is introduce the color. When, in conventional finishes, the color is contained in the final paint layer, the color layer is quite thick because it serves both as the color-carrying layer and as the final, protective top coat. Today's clearcoat is probably twice as thick as the combined thickness of the primer and colored base coats. It's not unusual for the clearcoat to have three times the thickness of the color (pigment) coat—and sometimes more.

Clearcoat: A See-Through Solar Window

Consider the clearcoat as a kind of window. As viewed through the clearcoat 'window,' the base coat is dull. What illuminates and lusterizes it are properties in the clearcoat—among them screening agents which screen out ultraviolet rays, which, in conventional vehicle finishes, bleach and fade the color layer. The clear-coat's ultraviolet screening agents also protect the color coat from fading. Conventional finishes have no such protection. So, what you have in the clearcoat is not just a window, but a 'solar window.'

You've got to keep that solar window clean to maintain, in the color finish, what the industry calls 'DOI,'—Distinction of Image. In essence, DOI is the deep gloss you are trying to maintain in your vehicle's finish.

To test for this reflective depth of image, hold a newspaper over the finish. If you can read it from its reflection in the finish, you have depth and clarity in the finish. The same thing happens when, polishing or waxing the clearcoat, you look into the finish for a reflection of yourself. Detailing or clearcoat flaws show up when your reflected image is wavy or imperfect.

In detailing, you aim to achieve a 'slippery wet look' in the finish. One example is the wet look of those faddish vehicles painted with 'neon' colors. The dazzle colors you see are the result of looking through the finish's clearcoat window. For most vehicles, however, the wet look achieved by the clearcoat is harder to describe precisely—even though it's one of the beauties you get with a clearcoat finish.

Abrasives: Clearcoat's Kiss Of Death

But you can destroy that look if you use the wrong products in detailing the clearcoat. The clearcoat is not designed to have anything—let me repeat and emphasize, anything—used on it which is abrasive. Anything abrasive used on the clearcoat can scuff and scar its surface. Abrasives are the kiss of death to a clearcoat finish.

Now, when I emphasize no abrasives, I'm talking about products used by the do-it-yourself detailer. Paint shops, in repairing clearcoats and when finishing a newly repainted/clear-coated vehicle or repair, do use 'abrasive' products and techniques. Commonly used by pro-detailers is ultra-fine wet sanding paper, with an almost non-abrasive 1500–2000 grit rating. Wet-sanding enhances the clearcoat finish by removing sags, dust, and other flaws. Flaws removed, the new clearcoat finish is allowed to dry anywhere from 72 hours to 30 days, and then, when cured and dry, is cleaned with a non-abrasive cleaner and then polished. Finally, the clearcoat is waxed.

Certainly the skilled weekend detailer can wet sand a clearcoat when virtually everything else has failed to restore its original, 'new vehicle' look. But you need skill and a 'feel' for the clearcoat to do it without further surface damage.

Choosing The Right Wash Product

Now, in washing the clearcoat—and, in fact any automotive paint finish—you should use a wash product specifically formulated for vehicle finishes.

I know, dishwashing detergents have been recommended for vehicle washing. On the basis of overwhelming evidence, I totally disagree. Dishwashing detergent is formulated to wash dishes—specifically, to remove grease. That same formulation is going to remove the wax from the vehicle's finish and also any protective silicones. Silicones are contained in many vehicle polishes and in some car waxes. Use dishwashing detergent and you remove them—which means, at the very least, that every time the vehicle is washed with detergent you have to reapply polish and wax.

The same de-waxing occurs when you put your vehicle through some commercial or coin-op washes: the detergents generally used, because these wash places' main goal is to turn out clean vehicles, are strong enough to remove most of a finish's waxes and silicones.

Saying this, I have to again concede that some professional detailers use all-purpose cleaners and dishwashing detergents. They do so for the very reason the do-it-yourself detailer should seldom, if ever, use them. The professional detailer wants to strip all the wax from the finish. This enables him, starting from scratch, to better polish and wax the vehicle. Eliminated by using those products is one of the chores he'd normally have to do—remove the wax.

Unless, after washing the vehicle, you intend to polish (glaze) and wax it, you don't want to remove the wax. You don't because the wax's purpose isn't simply to 'shine' a vehicle's finish. Wax forms a protective barrier and also a slipperiness which tends to deflect street debris, such as stones, which might otherwise chip the finish. It also resists scuffing, caused, for example, by somebody rubbing against the vehicle in a parking lot. The wax, being slippery, reduces possible abrasive damage. The analogy is the difference between a waxed kitchen floor and one that's unwaxed. Drag something across an unwaxed floor and you leave scratches. Drag something across your vehicle's unwaxed finish and it scratches.

If you've waxed the vehicle, you certainly don't want to undo what you've done by washing it with an aggressive, all-purpose cleaner. If a wash solution degreases the finish or body parts, you can be sure it will also 'de-wax' the finish.

To wash clearcoats, use any of a number of products specially formulated for clearcoat washing. Almost all are liquids, not powders. Powders may not completely dissolve in your wash water. The tiny, undissolved granules have the potential to become abrasives.

Defining The Just-Right Clearcoat Wash Product

The proper and ideal slippery, soapy solution for frictionless dirt removal from an automotive finish, including clearcoat, can be defined by a number of characteristics:

- High-foaming—inherent cleaning action
- High lubricity—slipperiness, like a lubricant
- Free-rinsing—a solution which, in itself, leaves no residue
- pH balance—a product with an acid-alkaline balance which is slightly alkaline to counter the acidic nature of a finish's collected fallout pollutants

What commonly available wash products fit these criteria? There are several available (check labels carefully). The choice comes down to personal preference.

Clearcoats must also be critically washed in a specific way. The 'tools' you use should be just as critically designed for clearcoat washing. Among these tools are natural fiber body brushes, synthetic-wool washing mitts, sponges, and terry cloth towels.

Washing Clearcoat Finish

Whatever washing tools you use, the basic washing techniques for clearcoat are the same. First, you hose and clean-water flush the finish to remove any loose dirt or pollutants. Then you wash the finish with a free-rinsing wash solution.

The first step—flushing with water—purges the surface of anything loose that can be quickly and easily removed.

If any dirt remains, it's got to be removed with a minimum of friction. What is likely holding dirt on the clearcoat finish is surface tension. To remove stubborn dirt or other stick-to-surface materials—bird and tree droppings being the most common—you've got to disturb the surface tension without creating friction enough to scratch the clearcoat.

Ideally, what you want your wash solution—your wash water—to do is 'free-rinse,' that is, to dislodge and rinse all pollutants, including abrasives, from the clearcoat and hold them in frictionless, non-abrasive suspension within the wash water. What does it is a soapy, slippery wash solution that meets the criteria for an ideal clearcoat wash product.

Keep these same criteria in mind when choosing your washing 'tool.' A sponge is not a free-rinsing tool, because grit and dirt can get caught in the sponge's pores. You're going to trap dirt and grit in the sponge, even if you wash with a soapy solution that has high lubricity and is high-foaming, two of the more important criteria of a clearcoat wash solution.

The ideal tool for washing clearcoat finishes is a natural fiber body brush. This usually imported, bleached pig's hair brush is super soft. Commonly, the hair is set into a mahogany block with epoxy cement.

Natural fiber body brushes (they're designed for vehicle washing) are user-friendly tools for washing clear-coats. Using them, you need exert only minimal pressure. That means less friction on the clearcoat—and less washing effort, too.

The brush has a nap that's about 3 inches (76mm) deep. You use only the tips of the brush's super-fine hairs— just the first ½ to ¾ inch of the nap. You use very little pressure. All you want to do is loosen the dirt's surface tension and get the dirt into the carrier solution—your soapy wash water or finish shampoo. If you can't find a body brush, then use the second-choice 'ideal' clearcoat washing tool: a synthetic wool mitt.

One caution: Not all car wash brushes are the hog hair—China bristle natural fiber kind I'm describing. Some, with coarser hair, may be too aggressive—too abrasive—for clearcoat finishes.

You may have to settle for something less than the ideal clearcoat washing tool. A terry cloth towel, perhaps, or even a sponge. If you keep them forever lubricated in your wash water to make sure they are clean, and if you use them carefully and with minimum pressure, they'll generally do a satisfactory job on clearcoat finishes.

Clearcoat Polishes and Cleaners

❊❊ WARNING

The use of abrasive compounds on clearcoat can be fatal to the finish.

Polish. A lot of detailing pros use the words 'polish' and 'glaze' interchangeably. As if they are the same things. Generally, they are not. A polish is a polish. A glaze is a glaze. And a cleaner is a cleaner. Whatever the product, use the least 'aggressive'—the least abrasive. A more abrasive product generally gets the polishing job done faster. But an overly aggressive polishing/cleaning product also risks scratching, and in fact removing, some of the finish—such as the clearcoat.

A polish is a minimally abrasive cleaner and lusterizer. A cleaner, more aggressive than a polish, contains chemical cleaning agents. Even more abrasive—often very abrasive—are compounding products. Compounds are sometimes the preferred products for treating heavily oxidized conventional finishes. Using a compound—called 'compounding'—you are apt to remove paint as well as oxidation. Today, the cleaners—far less abrasive than compounds—are usually all you need to work with on even the most oxidized conventional finishes.

While compounds can be used—and still often are—on conventional paints, their use on clearcoat finishes risks major damage. The minute particles of pumice, which give the compounds their cutting action, cut little holes in the clearcoat. The result: 'swirl' marks which are difficult, and sometimes impossible, to remove from the clearcoat.

'Swirls' are residual evidences of abrasive polishing. There should, of course, be no evidences in a finish that it has been polished—just an even, unbroken, reflective shine. Hand-polish swirls are irregular, non-reflective blotches in the finish's polished surface. Machine-polish swirls—evidence of machine buffing— tend to be circular blotches. Swirl marks are the nemesis of detailers, whether pros or weekenders.

If you get swirl marks when you buff a finish by hand, it means there are abrasive particles in the product you're using. Or, perhaps, some abrasives in whatever you're using to apply the product—a rough towel, for example. Or a foam sponge applicator that's not clean and has some grit or hardened cleaner in its pores. In short, there are only two ways that swirls develop when cleaning, polishing or buffing a clearcoat finish: (1) the product you're using, whether hand- or machine-applied, is too abrasive; (2) the polishing tool is abrasive.

In machine polishing, the problem is often a wool buffing pad. Wool buffing pads are, by their very nature, abrasive. Wool buffing pads are an anachronism in today's era of high-tech vehicle finishes, as clearcoat. They are plainly out of date, although wool buffing pads are still being used on conventional finishes. But not on clearcoats. There's no question about it: in machine buffing, wool buffer pads are the number one swirl-maker.

Today's preferred and widely used machine polishing pads for clearcoat are made of synthetic foam. They all but eliminate swirl marks, and they can be used on both conventional and clearcoat finishes.

How Do You Know If It's Clear-Coated?

One vexing question: How do you know, in this era of fast-changing technology, whether your vehicle has a conventional or clearcoat finish?

It isn't always easy to tell. One test is to gently rub an out-of-sight place on the finish with a mild cleaner. If color comes off on your cloth, you can be fairly sure it's conventional finish. If no color comes off, you can be almost as sure it's clear-coated.

Still, there's only one sure-sale rule-of-thumb: When in doubt, treat it as a clearcoat finish. Obviously, if your vehicle is clear-coated, it needs special handling and special care.

DETAILING A SCRATCHED OR NICKED WINDSHIELD

Most windshield scratches or nicks defy do-it-yourself fixing. And, in fact, fixing at all. Pro-detailers and windshield glass specialists have a "rule of thumbnail": if, rubbing a thumbnail across the scratch, you can feel the scratch, it's probably too deep to fix.

A tiny surface scratch can sometimes be rubbed or buffed out with very fine powdered pumice or with jeweler's rouge (both are available from glass shops). Make a heavy paste using water and pumice (or jeweler's rouge). Spread the paste on and around the scratch. If machine buffing, use a non-abrasive foam buffing pad on a low-speed orbital buffer. Use very gentle pressure while buffing. You may have to re-apply the paste and rebuff several times to buff out the scratch.

Rubbing out the scratch manually involves the same water and pumice/rouge technique, only you use a very soft, non-abrasive cotton cloth as your rubbing tool.

While deeper scratches can sometimes be removed by machine buffing, the result is seldom satisfactory. Although you may rid the windshield of the scratch, deep buffing causes a concave place where the scratch was. Result: Vision through the former scratch area is distorted. Far better to keep the scratch than to cause windshield—and vision—distortion.

On the market are a number of "fixit" kits for reducing the visibility of windshield nicks, rock pocks, and scratches. Generally, the results are not very satisfactory. The patch places are often as obvious as the windshield damage they "correct. In most cases, it's not detailing that an injured windshield needs, but replacement.

Aside from detailing the windshield for visibility and cleanliness, a number of products are available to (I) help keep it clean and clear; (2) reduce fogging or steaming; and (3) disperse rain, snow, ice and sleet. Rain-X, originally named Repcon and developed for the U.S. Air Force to keep jet fighter windshields rain-free, is a wipe-on liquid that quick-dries to coat the windshield with an optically clear, transparent polymer (plastic) coating, which disperses rain, snow, ice and sleet. Used on windshields, it largely eliminates the "vision tunnels" produced by wipers. In fact, it is often not necessary to operate wipers on a windshield treated with Rain-X. The film causes an aerodynamic runoff of rainwater and snow, clearing the windshield without any, or only infrequent, wiper assist—thus its claim to being "the invisible windshield wiper."

Applied to rear and side windows, and on rear-view mirrors, Rain-X provides greater visibility in rainy or snowy weather. It is also effective on many convertible and off-road vehicle plastic windows. The product is not, however, a defogger. Its useful life varies, depending in part on a vehicle's speed and use. If you commute several hours daily at superhighway speeds, Rain-X may have to be reapplied every few weeks.

Snow skiers have long used anti-fog, chemically impregnated cloths to keep their goggles clean. Larger versions of the anti-fog cloths work well on windshields. You should be able to find them at local ski shops. There are also interior window defogging formulas available.

While there are many useful glass cleaners available, from household glass cleaners to auto-specialized pre-moistened towelettes for quick-cleaning windshields, what cleans them about as well as most commercial products is ammonia and water. The mix: 1 part ammonia to 4 parts water.

To rid windshields of stubborn grime, stains, and bugs, many pro-detailers use super-fine 0000 (be sure it's 4-0) steel wool. The same super-fine, non-scratch grade of steel wool is also frequently used by pro-detailers to polish windshields, especially those streaked by hard-water residues.

The nemesis of interior glass and, in fact, all interior surfaces is vinyl vapor residue: the oily vapor given off by vinyl (upholstery, vinyl dashes, other interior vinyls), especially as vinyl grows older, when exposed to sunlight. The hotter the weather—and the hotter a vehicle's interior—the greater the vaporization of the vinyl. Not all vinyls vaporize as readily as others; nor do all give off equal amounts of vapor.

Most people seeing a vinyl-vapor-smudged windshield or windows assume the driver is a smoker. Maybe, but vinyl vapor leaves a far more bothersome residue on glass—and on the vehicle's entire interior— than any dozen packs of cigarettes. In sunbelt states, especially in summer with the windows shut, vinyl residue can come close to coating interior glass in a single day. Not only is the residue vehicle-disfiguring, it is dangerous, limiting visibility.

To remove vinyl residue, use any good household or automotive window cleaner, an ammonia-water solution, or all-purpose cleaner.

THE ADVENT OF "NO-WAX" CLEARCOAT FINISHES

The newest technological advancement in clearcoat finishes is a fluorine-type clearcoat that needs little or no waxing. Currently available on Nissan Motor Corporation's Infiniti luxury automobile, "no-wax" clear-coats are likely to be available on other vehicles and from other manufacturers in the future.

The fluorine-type clearcoat finish requires special detailing, especially to correct damage to the clearcoat, and should be treated exactly per the manufacturer's instructions in the owner's manual. Polishing and waxing in the usual detailing sense are not appropriate for these high-tech finishes.

For the Infiniti, the manufacturer outlines particular procedures and brand-name products for buffing out fine scratches in the clearcoat finish and for wet-sanding finish damage that remains after buffing. Because no-wax/minimum-wax finishes are so different from conventional finishes and from most other clear-coat finishes that have been available to date, it is likely that each manufacturer that produces such a finish in the future will also include very specific product and procedure recommendations for its individual formulation of no-wax clearcoat.

BUFFERS—WHICH ONE FOR YOU?

▶ **See Figure 12**

Some of the finest, most lustrous, most flawless polishing and waxing jobs, on some of the world's most expensive and exotic auto exteriors, are done by pro detailers who advertise, "All work done by hand."

These pros never use a "buffer"—either an orbital or rotary buffing machine. Nor, in fact, do they go looking for customers or need to. Owners of the exotic vehicles they detail solely by hand often willingly wait weeks for a detailing appointment. Just as willingly, these vehicle owners pay handsomely for the hours of hand labor, expertise, and skill for which these top-echelon detailers are locally—and sometimes regionally—renowned.

Some other pro-detailers, equally skilled and equally capable of producing show car exteriors, regularly use machine buffers to help speed (and, some claim, make better) their buffing jobs. The difference? The time spent, thus the charge, for equally top-quality exterior detailing.

Where the strictly by hand detailer may spend 4–6 hours, and sometimes more than a day, detailing a vehicle's exterior, the buffer-using detailer may accomplish much the same results in 2–4 hours. The manual detailer may charge $100–$300, and more, for the same job the buffer-wielding detailer turns out for $75–$125.

Nonetheless, some owners of exotic vehicles absolutely will not permit a buffer anywhere near their paint jobs, no matter how skilled and practiced the buffer operator. They know something many do-it-yourself detailers may not: some types of buffing machines, notably the rotary kind, are unforgiving. A momentary lapse of the operator's attention can allow the buffer, because it is powerful, to cut—"burn"—right through a paint job. And, in the case of clear-coated vehicles, right through the clearcoat and down to, even through, the color layer of paint. By contrast, other types of buffing machines—orbital buffers—are far less apt to do damage, even in the hands of a weekend detailer.

While pro-detailers may endlessly argue whether or not the weekend detailer should attempt to speed exterior detailing with a buffer, there is only one super-safe decision: if you have never before used a buffer, or lack real buffer skill, don't hone your skill on your vehicle's fragile and expensive paint job. Do exterior detailing by hand. If you want eventually to speed the job with a buffer, learn and practice buffer skills on another paint surface.

Still, knowing about buffers and how to use them are important first steps toward deciding, for yourself, whether you will eventually do some detailing with an assist from a buffer.

First, some facts:

1. Almost all makers of professional detailing polishes and waxes offer three choices of products: those designed to be applied only by hand, those designed to be applied only by machine, and those which can be applied either by hand or by machine. Polishes, glazes, and waxes formulated for machine application are almost universally in liquid form.

2. Some of the top producers of detail products, who make both manual and machine polishes and waxes, recognize at least one type of buffing machine—the orbital buffer—as a relatively safe tool even in unskilled hands. Orbital buffing machines get their name from the fact that their rotation describes an ellipse, or orbit, rather than a circle, as do rotary buffers. (Even so, many experts concede that the orbital is not capable of the same exacting paint-finish work as the rotary buffer.)

Fig. 12 The wool polishing/buffing pad (right) is still often favored for polishing conventional finishes (non-clearcoat). The foam pad (left) is favored by pro detailers for clearcoat and other high tech finishes (and can be used on conventional paint).

One type of orbital buffing/polishing machine is called a "random orbital" buffer. Its random elliptical orbits simulate the eccentric circular motion of hand polishing. Another type of buffing machine, although it's more commonly employed in sanding, is a "dual action" (DA) buffer. It can be switched from orbital rotation to straight line operation. Some weekend detailers use an electric drill fitted with a buffing pad, although most experts don't recommend it because it is difficult to control.

3. Although wool, synthetic wool, and terry cloth buffing pads (called "bonnets") have long been used as the buffer's applicator of polishes and waxes, preferred today by many pro-detailers, and certainly when working on many clearcoat vehicle finishes, is the new foam buffing/polishing pad.

On clearcoat finish, especially, wool buffing pads are notorious for leaving swirl marks—the circular pattern of the buffer's action. Wool is also abrasive. The new foam pads, properly used, are virtually non-abrasive. So are the best of terry cloth buffing pads, although to a lesser degree.

4. Buffer speed is critical to achieving a brilliant finish without finish damage. Do-it-yourself detailers should use low buffer speeds—in the order of 1200–1750 rpm. Buffers operated at higher speed (1750–3000 rpm) require professional skill.

There are two buffer types, with basic differences. Their detailing uses are discussed below.

Orbital Buffers

▶ **See Figure 13**

Orbital buffers are suited for the application of non-abrasive products to improve gloss without leaving buffer swirl marks. The results are similar to those created by hand buffing, it's just easier. Do not expect to remove paint defects or oxidization with an orbital buffer, but it is ideally suited to an operator with limited skill who might easily burn (damage or cut through) paint with a rotary buffer.

Rotary Buffers

The buffing machines used by pros for all types of automotive paint finishes are rotary, available in a range of speeds. The correct buffing speed is determined by the type of vehicle paint being worked on:

• Low-speed buffers (1200–1750 rpm) are most effective on the newer, high-tech paint finishes which are more reactive to excessive heat buildup and static electricity.

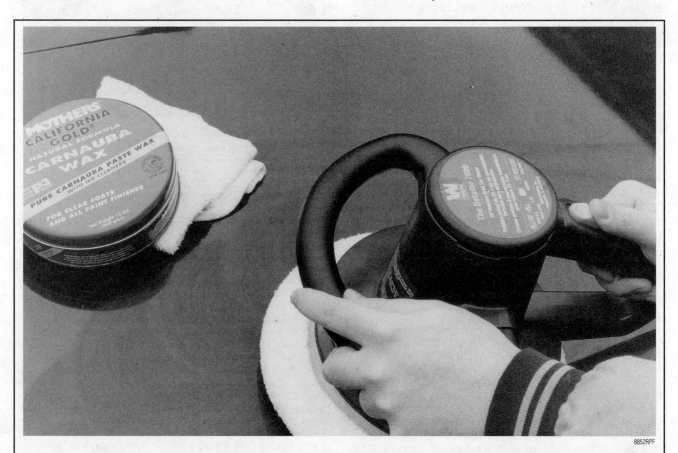

Fig. 13 The orbital buffer is an excellent tool for the "weekend waxer". It is much lighter and easier to handle than a professional buffer.

• High-speed buffers (1750–3000 rpm) are ideal for use on conventional acrylic lacquer and acrylic enamel auto finishes. High-speed buffers require a greater level of operator skill.

Variable speed machines—which can operate effectively at both high and low rpms—are also available. While high-quality "variables" do an effective job, low-quality "variables" often lose their speed when pressure is put on them.

Buffing machines can often be inexpensively rented for a few hours. Pads cannot be rented; you'll have to buy fresh ones.

HOW TO USE BUFFING MACHINES

▶ **See Figures 14, 15, 16 and 17**

Basic rules and techniques:

1. Use only polishes, waxes, and other buffing products specifically designed—and designated—"for machine buffing." Almost all are liquids, not pastes or waxes.

2. Use only buffing pads or bonnets recommended for the buffing products you use. There are two types of conventional wool buffing pads: cutting pads, used with slightly abrasive polishes to remove oxidation and scratches, and finishing pads, used with non-abrasive wax, to remove swirl marks left by the cutting pad and to create a final mirror-like finish.

3. If you buff with several different products, use a separate buffing pad for each. Change or clean pads frequently to avoid abrasive buildup of the buffing product.

4. Buff only a small area of the finish at a time—an area about 2 feet x 2 feet.

5. Never buff a vehicle's finish with the buffing pad alone (dry). Always buff using a buffing product.

6. Buffing products are usually applied (squirted from a squeeze bottle) directly on the small surface to be buffed, rather than on the pad or bonnet. (However, some buffing products are applied to both the pad and the surface of the finish.) If the label instructs you to apply the product directly on the finish, don't make a puddle. Squirt the product in a continuous line pattern to cover the area.

7. With the machine turned off, use the buffer's pad to manually spread the buffing product evenly over the area you plan to buff.

8. Before you turn the machine on, be sure you have a firm and controlling grasp. Most buffing machines are equipped with a side grasp or handle. In effect, the operator's hands are working at right angles to one another for better control. Even so, buffers are not lightweight. (Buffers offered by one maker weigh from 7–8¼ pounds.) If the buffer feels too heavy, an indication that you may not have the strength or skill to control it, play it safe—don't attempt machine buffing. Buff the finish manually instead.

9. Buff only on a clean, cool surface. The friction of buffing causes heat buildup, which must be avoided. If, after a couple of passes, the surface you're buffing feels warm or hot to the touch, stop. Turn off the machine and let the surface cool. Or, in some cases, depending on the product you're using, you can quick-cool the surface with a damp cloth. Usually, two to four passes complete most buffing jobs.

10. Never let your eyes or attention wander from what you're doing. To do so risks "burning" through the finish. Burning can happen in a split second. To avoid distractions, such as the buffer's electric cord hanging up on a vehicle part or scraping over the finish, drape the cord over your shoulder, keeping it away from the vehicle's finish.

11. Hold the buffer so that the pad is flat (parallel) to the surface you're buffing. As you buff, you can tip the pad slightly in the direction you're buffing: tip it to the right when moving the buffer to the right, and tip it left when moving the buffer left. Tipping the pad slightly gives better buffing control. But never tip it so much that you're buffing with the pad's edge. Edge buffing can easily burn through the finish.

12. Keep the buffer moving at all times. Move the buffer in short, straight, even, and overlapping strokes. Exert minimum pressure to achieve the results you want (removal of oxidation on conventionally painted surfaces, if you're using a cleaner/polish; luster and shine, if you're using a final wax).

13. Do not, ever, buff over "ridges"—such "ridge lines" as the edges of fenders, head and taillights, hood "ridges," or the like. Running a buffing pad over ridges, where finish is thinnest, risks instant burning. Instead, spread whatever liquid product you're using up to, but on either side of a ridge. Buff up to the ridge, never over or right on it. Very gently, very carefully, "feather" (tilt, with virtually no pressure) the pad so as merely to brush the ridge. That is buffing enough on such thin-painted, vulnerable ridge areas.

14. Clean buffer pads frequently. Wool pads (used on conventional finishes only) can be rid of wax or other product buildup with a special pad-cleaning tool called a spur. It's available at most auto supply stores. Or you can use a dull screwdriver, although, unlike the spur, it can damage a wool or terry cloth bonnet. To clean a bonnet, grasp the machine firmly, perhaps resting it on your knee. Turn the buffer on and as the pad spins, apply the spur (or screwdriver) to the pad. Buildup will be dislodged. Dislodged, too, whether you're buffing or cleaning the bonnet, will be product splatter. If you buff, expect splatter. Wear old clothes and, as do some pros, protective glasses or goggles. Wool and terry cloth bonnets may also shed. Splatter or bonnet shed—or whatever—that falls on the buffed finish can be removed with a clean, soft, non-abrasive 100% cotton cloth.

15. Static electricity sometimes causes excessive buildup of buffing products on bonnets and pads. Some pros, before starting to buff, ground

Fig. 14 When wax or polish builds up an the bonnet, use a spur to clean the excess wax or polish

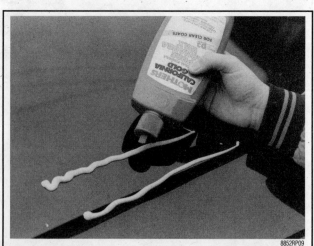

Fig. 15 Squirt parallel lines, covering the polishing area. Some products say "use sparingly" — use considerably less than shown here.

Fig. 16 With the buffer OFF, use the pad to spread the liquid over the area you intend to polish. To spread evenly, hold the pad flat to the surface and move it back and forth.

Fig. 17 A foam pad polishes wax and also removes and swirls left by a wool pad. Always use a foam pad on clearcoat and other high-tech finishes.

the vehicle to prevent the buildup of static electricity. A simple grounding wire is clamped to any bare metal chassis member and run to the nearest bare metal water pipe, or to a metal grounding stake.

16. Besides avoiding ridge lines, work carefully around places—and appendages—where the whirling bonnet or pad can get caught. Or, worse, tear off vehicle parts, such as windshield wipers (front and back), antennas, fuel doors, or retractable headlight covers. If possible, remove such vulnerable parts as wipers and antennas before buffing.

17. Frequently evaluate the results of your buffing. Check the surface under full sunlight, and from various angles. If working indoors, use a shop trouble light to reveal swirl marks or flaws. Excellent for in-garage or shop inspection is a 300-watt quartz halogen light, available at hardware and home supply centers. Fluorescent lights generally fail to fully reveal swirl marks and faint scratches. A foam buffing pad can be used to remove any swirls a wool pad may leave behind.

18. You can begin buffing the finish almost anywhere. Some detailers prefer to start with the roof. Since it is usually flat, there's little chance of burn-through. Others begin at one side of the hood, working from windshield to front, then doing the hood's other half. For the right-handed, it's

generally easier working to the right, all the way around the vehicle. Lefties usually find it easier to buff in the opposite direction. "Leading" with one's strongest hand gives most buffer-users more confidence and control.

Both confidence and control increase with practice. The more you buff, the easier—and quicker—the buffing. No doubt about it, buffing shortcuts exterior detailing and often achieves a mirror-finish that's arduous to achieve manually.

3-HOUR DETAILING: INSIDE AND OUT

▶ **See Figures 18, 19, 20, 21 and 22**

Automotive purists may spend 20 hours or more over a couple of weekends detailing their vehicles, inside and out. If you don't have 20 hours or two weekends to spend and are satisfied with a "good," but not "super best," detail job, you can do the required detailing in about 3 hours' time.

To detail your vehicle inside and out and under the hood in so short a time assumes that:

1. Your vehicle's finish is in average shape, and not excessively oxidized or faded.

2. You don't have a convertible or vinyl top, which adds 30 minutes to the total time.

3. You're willing to skip such niceties as a repainting underhood components.

4. You prepare for the quickie detailing by having in hand, before you start, all the products and tools you'll need for the job.

5. You have average car care skills and are willing to apply them efficiently and stick steadfastly to the job once begun.

6. You're willing to take necessary shortcuts—for example, taking the vehicle to a self service car wash to do the dirty work, and applying one-step products rather than the more professional two-step products—to "beat the clock" and finish in the allotted 3 hours.

✳ WARNING

Never attempt to detail your vehicle's exterior finish in sunlight. That's our my advice, as well as virtually every detailing product label. The reason is simple: direct sunlight dries solutions before you have a chance to properly use them, causing spots and streaking.

Fig. 18 Start with the wheels and tires, probably the dirtiest part of your vehicle . . .

Fig. 19 . . . Next move on to the engine compartment. Be careful not to get engine degreaser on the vehicles painted surface.

Fig. 20 Washing your vehicle at a self-service coin-op saves time.

Fig. 21 Don't forget to pressure wash rubber mats

Fig. 22 Drying the vehicle after a quick wash at a self-service bay is a 5- to 10-minute chore with a chamois.

Procedures and Time Allotments for 3-Hour Detailing

➡ **Steps 1, 2, and 3 are done at a self-service coin-op car wash.**

1. Exterior: Wash and dry including wheels/tires and wheel wells (30 minutes)— Wash the exterior yourself at a self-service wash bay. (A commercial car wash could save you time and energy in this initial step, but a self-service place has added quick-detail advantages, outlined below.)

2. Underhood: Degrease and wash (20 minutes)— Detail underhood areas at an engine detailing bay of a self-service car wash. (You save time here because most self-service coin-op places have everything on the premises: washing and engine degreasing bays, and vacuum machines for vacuuming the interior.)

❋❋ WARNING

Do not direct water spray toward electrical components. Protect electrical components from water by using plastic bags and spraying terminals with silicone spray.

3. Interior: Vacuum carpets, upholstery, and floor mats (10 minutes)— While you're at the self-service place, vacuum the interior, including carpets, fabric upholstery, and floor mats. If mats are vinyl or rubber, wash them.

➡ **Steps 4 through 9 can be done at your home or at any other suitable place.**

4. Exterior Finish: Clean, wax, and buff (45 minutes)— Now that the vehicle is washed, clean it (to rid paint/clearcoat of oxidation) and wax it with a hand-applied one-step cleaner/wax. Hand-buff to a brilliant shine.

5. Exterior Chrome: Clean, wax, and polish trim, bumpers, etc. (15 minutes)— Clean and brighten exterior chrome with any good chrome/metal polish; then wax and polish trim and bumpers. If bumpers are painted, or plastic, clean and wax.

6. Upholstery: Clean and condition fabric, vinyl, leather, velour, etc. (30 minutes)— Shampoo fabric upholstery; clean and condition vinyl or leather. Upholstery vacuuming was done previously, at self-service vacuum bay.

7. Interior Trim: Clean and brighten dashboard, instrument panels, door/window/windshield moldings, etc. (10 minutes)— Clean; then apply protectant to dashboard, instrument panels, shift console, window/windshield molding, in-car electronics, etc. Most interior trim can be cleaned/renewed with a rub-on/rub-off protectant.

8. Interior Glass: Clean windows, windshield, and other interior glass (10 minutes)— Clean windows and windshield with any good household/automotive glass cleaner or with weak ammonia/water solution.

9. Carpets and Seat Belts: Shampoo carpeting; wash seat belting (10 minutes)— Shampoo, rinse carpeting; wash seat belting. Use any good carpet shampoo or neutral soap and water.

Windshield and Fixed Glass

REMOVAL & INSTALLATION

If your windshield, or other fixed window, is cracked or chipped, you may decide to replace it with a new one yourself. However, there are two main reasons why replacement windshields and other window glass should be installed only by a professional automotive glass technician: safety and cost.

The most important reason a professional should install automotive glass is for safety. The glass in the vehicle, especially the windshield, is designed with safety in mind in case of a collision. The windshield is specially manufactured from two panes of specially-tempered glass with a thin layer of transparent plastic between them. This construction allows the glass to "give" in the event that a part of your body hits the windshield during the collision, and prevents the glass from shattering, which could cause lacerations, blinding and other harm to passengers of the vehicle. The other fixed windows are designed to be tempered so that if they break during a collision, they shatter in such a way that there are no large pointed glass pieces. The professional automotive glass technician knows how to install the glass in a vehicle so that it will function optimally during a collision. Without the proper experience, knowledge and tools, installing a piece of automotive glass yourself could lead to additional harm if an accident should ever occur.

Cost is also a factor when deciding to install automotive glass yourself. Performing this could cost you much more than a professional may charge for the same job. Since the windshield is designed to break under stress, an often life saving characteristic, windshields tend to break VERY easily when an inexperienced person attempts to install one. Do-it-yourselfers buying two, three or even four windshields from a salvage yard because they have broken them during installation are common stories. Also, since the automotive glass is designed to prevent the outside elements from entering your vehicle, improper installation can lead to water and air leaks. Annoying whining noises at highway speeds from air leaks or inside body panel rusting from water leaks can add to your stress level and subtract from your wallet. After buying two or three windshields, installing them and ending up with a leak that produces a noise while driving and water damage during rainstorms, the cost of having a professional do it correctly the first time may be much more alluring. We here at Chilton, therefore, advise that you have a professional automotive glass technician service any broken glass on your vehicle.

WINDSHIELD CHIP REPAIR

♦ **See Figures 23 thru 37**

➥Check with your state and local authorities on the laws for state safety inspection. Some states or municipalities may not allow chip repair as a viable option for correcting stone damage to your windshield.

Although severely cracked or damaged windshields must be replaced, there is something that you can do to prolong or even prevent the need for replacement of a chipped windshield. There are many companies which offer windshield chip repair products, such as Loctite's® Bullseye™ windshield repair kit. These kits usually consist of a syringe, pedestal and a sealing adhesive. The syringe is mounted on the pedestal and is used to create a vacuum which pulls the plastic layer against the glass. This helps make the chip transparent. The adhesive is then injected which seals the chip and helps to prevent further stress cracks from developing. Refer to the sequence of photos to get a general idea of what windshield chip repair involves.

➥Always follow the specific manufacturer's instructions.

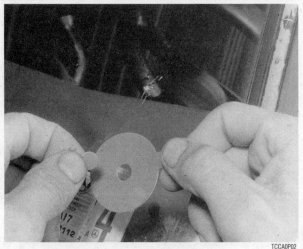

Fig. 25 Remove the center from the adhesive disc and peel off the backing from one side of the disc . . .

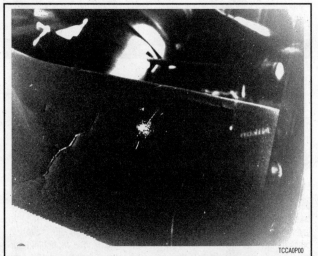

Fig. 23 Small chips on your windshield can be fixed with an aftermarket repair kit, such as the one from Loctite®

Fig. 26 . . . then press it on the windshield so that the chip is centered in the hole

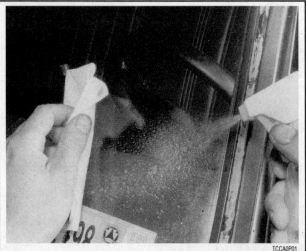

Fig. 24 To repair a chip, clean the windshield with glass cleaner and dry it completely

Fig. 27 Be sure that the tab points upward on the windshield

Fig. 28 Peel the backing off the exposed side of the adhesive disc . . .

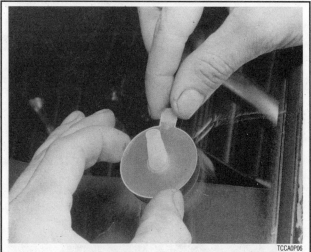

Fig. 29 . . . then position the plastic pedestal on the adhesive disc, ensuring that the tabs are aligned

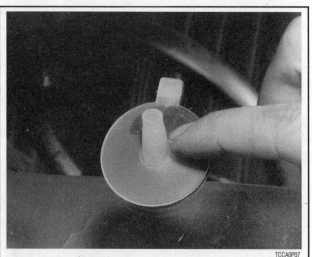

Fig. 30 Press the pedestal firmly on the adhesive disc to create an adequate seal . . .

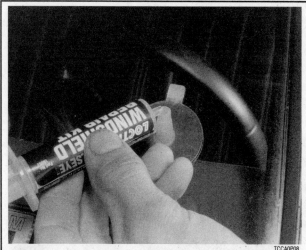

Fig. 31 . . . then install the applicator syringe nipple in the pedestal's hole

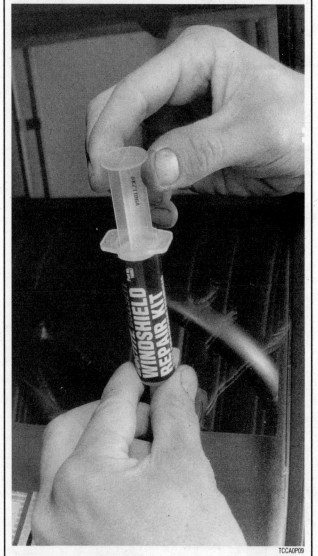

Fig. 32 Hold the syringe with one hand while pulling the plunger back with the other hand

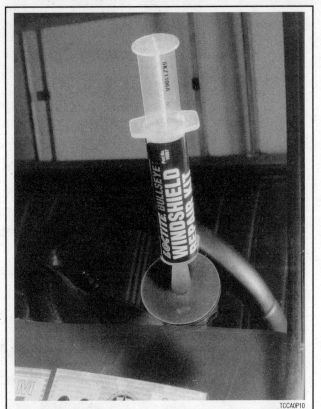

Fig. 33 After applying the solution, allow the entire assembly to sit until it has set completely

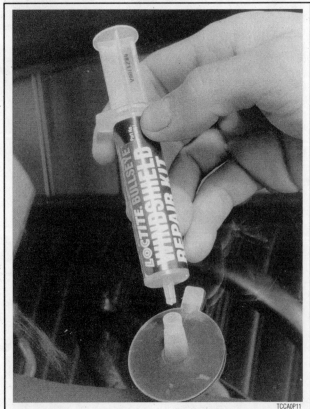

Fig. 34 After the solution has set, remove the syringe from the pedestal . . .

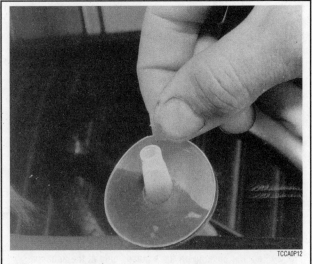

Fig. 35 . . . then peel the pedestal off of the adhesive disc . . .

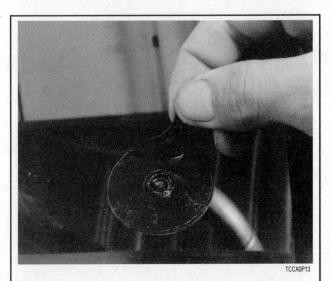

Fig. 36 . . . and peel the adhesive disc off of the windshield

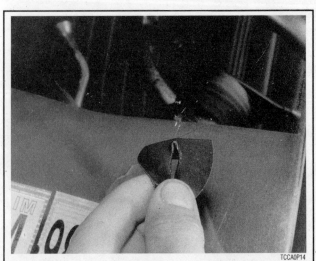

Fig. 37 The chip will still be slightly visible, but it should be filled with the hardened solution

Rust, Undercoating and Rust proofing

RUST

About the only technical information the average backyard mechanic needs to know about rust is that, it is an electrochemical process that works from the inside out. It works on ferrous metals (iron and steel) from the inside out due to exposure of unprotected surfaces to air and moisture. The possibility of rust exists practically nationwide-anywhere humidity, industrial pollution or chemical salts are present, rust can form. In coastal areas, the problem is high humidity and salt air; in snowy areas, the problem is chemical salt (de-icer) used to keep the roads clear; and in industrial areas, sulfur dioxide is present in the air from industrial pollution and is changed to sulfuric acid when it rains. The rusting process is accelerated by high temperatures, especially in snowy areas, when vehicles are driven over slushy roads and then left overnight in a heated garage.

Automotive styling also can be a contributor to rust formation. Spot welding of panels creates small pockets that trap moisture and form environments for rust formation. Fortunately, auto manufacturers have been working hard to increase the corrosion protection of their products. Galvanized sheet metal enjoys much wider use, along with the increased use of plastic and various rust-retardant coatings. Manufacturers are also changing designs to eliminate areas in the body where rust-forming moisture can collect.

RUSTPROOFING

Current trends in metal preparation and new vehicle corrosion warranties, (typically up to 100,000 miles) have eliminated aftermarket rustproofing. In fact adding rustproofing to your new vehicle may void its corrosion warranty. However, there are a few steps that you can take to help assure a rust free body.

First, keep a garden hose handy for your vehicle in winter. Use it a few times on nice days during the winter for underneath areas, and it will pay big dividends when spring arrives. Spraying under the fenders and other areas which even carwashes don't reach will help remove road salt, dirt and other buildups that help breed rust. Adjust the nozzle to a high-force spray. An old brush will help break up residue, permitting it to be washed away more easily.

It's a somewhat messy job, but it will be worth it in the end because a vehicle's rust often starts in those hidden areas.

At the same time, wash grime off the doorsills and, more importantly, the under portions of the doors and the tailgate if you have a station wagon or truck. Applying a coat of wax to those areas at least once before and once during winter will help fend off rust.

When applying the wax to the under parts of the doors, you will note small drain holes. These holes often are plugged with undercoating or dirt.

Make sure they are cleaned out to prevent water build-up inside the doors. A small punch or penknife will do the job.

Water from the high-pressure sprays in carwashes sometimes can get into the housings for parking and taillights, so take a close look, and if they contain water merely loosen the retaining screws and the water should run out.

UNDERCOATING

Undercoating should not be mistaken for rustproofing. Undercoating is a black, tar-like substance that is applied to the underside of the vehicle.

Contrary to what most people think, the primary purpose of undercoating is not to prevent rust, but to deaden noise that might, otherwise be transmitted to the vehicle's interior. Undercoating simply cannot get into the crevices and seams where moisture tends to collect, and in fact may clog up drainage holes and ventilation passages.

Since vehicles are quiet these days anyway, dealers are very willing to promote undercoating as a rust preventative. Undercoating will of course, prevent some rust, but only if applied when the vehicle is brand-new. In any case, undercoating doesn't provide the protection that a good rustproofing does. If you do decide to undercoat your vehicle and it's not brand-new, you have a big clean-up job ahead of you. It's a good idea to have the underside of the vehicle professionally steam-cleaned and save yourself a lot of work. Spraying undercoat on dirty or rusty parts is only going to make things worse, since the undercoat will trap any rust-causing agents.

DRAIN HOLES

Rusty rocker panels are a common problem on nearly every vehicle, but they can be prevented by simply drilling some holes in your rocker panels to let the water out, or by keeping the ones that are already there clean and unclogged. Most vehicles these days have a series of holes in the rocker panels to prevent moisture collection there, but they frequently become clogged. Just use a small screwdriver or penknife to keep them clean.

Repairing Minor Body Damage

Unless your vehicle just rolled off the showroom floor, chances are it has a few minor scratches or dings in it somewhere, or a small rust spot you've been meaning to fix. You just haven't been able to decide whether you can really do the job. Well, if the damage is anything like that presented here, the answer is yes. There are a number of auto body repair kits that contain everything you need to repair minor scratches, dents and rust spots.

If you're unsure of your ability, start with a small scratch. Once you've mastered small scratches and dings, you can work your way up to the more complicated repairs. When doing rust repairs, remember that unless all the rust is removed, it's going to come back in a year or less. Just sanding the rust down and applying some paint won't work.

REPAIRING MINOR SURFACE RUST OR SCRATCHES

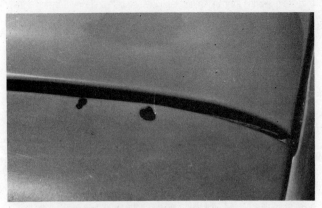

1. Just about everybody has a minor rust spot or scratches on their car. Spots such as these can be easily repaired in an hour or two. You'll need some sandpaper, masking tape, primer and a can of touch-up paint.

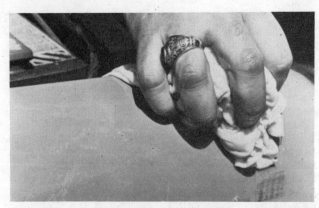

2. The first step is to wash the area down to remove all traces of dirt and road grime. If the car has been frequently waxed, you should wipe it with thinner or some other wax remover so that the paint will stick.

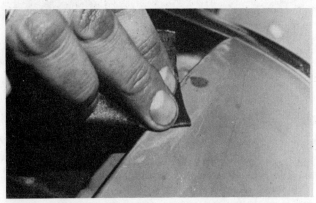

3. Small rust spots and scratches like these will only require light hand sanding. For a job like this, you can start with about grade 320 sandpaper and then use a 400 grit for the final sanding.

4. Once you've sanded the area with 320 paper, wet a piece of 400 paper and sand it lightly. Wet sanding will feather the edges of the surrounding paint into the area to be painted. For large areas, you could use a sanding block, but it's not really necessary for a small job like this.

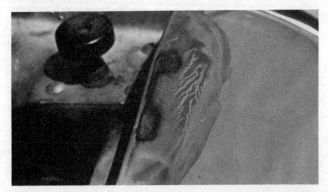

5. The area should look like this once you're finished sanding. Wipe off any water and run the palm of your hand over the sanded area with your eyes closed. You shouldn't be able to feel any bumps or ridges anywhere. Make sure you have sanded a couple of inches back in each direction so you'll get good paint adhesion.

6. Once you have the area sanded to your satisfaction, mask the surrounding area with masking tape and newspaper. Be sure to cover any chrome or trim that might get sprayed. You'll have to mask far enough back from the damaged area to allow for overspray. If you mask right around the sanded spots, you'll end up with a series of lines marking the painted area.

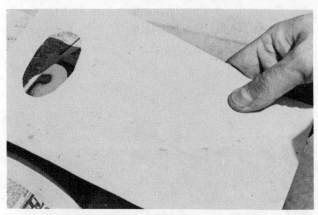

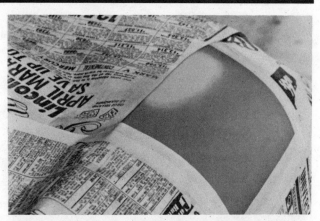

7. You can avoid a lot of excess overspray by cutting a hole in a piece of cardboard that approximately matches the area you are going to paint. Hold the cardboard steady over the area as you spray the primer on. If you haven't painted before, it's a good idea to practice on something before you try painting your car. Don't hold the paint can in one spot. Keep it moving and you'll avoid runs and sags.

8. The primered area should look like this when you have finished. It's better to spray several light coats than one heavy coat. Let the primer dry for several minutes between coats. Make sure you've covered all the bare metal.

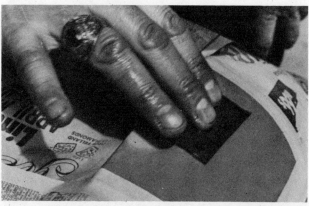

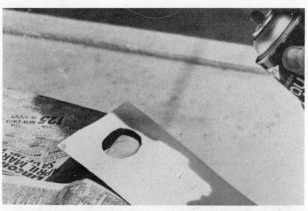

9. After the primer has dried, sand the area with wet 400 paper, Wash it off and let it dry. Your final coat goes on next, so make sure the area is clean and dry.

10. Spray the touch-up paint on using the cardboard again. Make the first coat a very light coat (known as a fog coat). Remember to keep the paint can moving smoothly at about 8–12 inches from the surface.

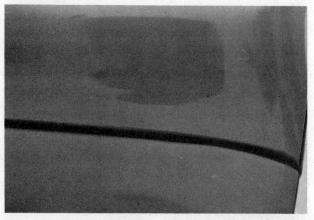

11. Once you've finished painting, let the paint dry for about 15 minutes before you remove the masking tape and newspaper.

12. Let the paint dry for several days before you rub it out lightly with rubbing compound, and the finished job should be indistinguishable from the rest of the car. Don't rub hard or you'll cut through the paint.

REPAIRING MINOR DENTS AND DEEP SCRATCHES

1. This dent (arrow) is typical of a deep scratch or minor dent. If deep enough, the dent or scratch can be pulled out or hammered out from behind. In this case no straightening was necessary.

2. Using an 80-grit grinding disc on an electric drill, grind the paint from the surrounding area down to bare metal. This will provide a rough surface for the body filler to grab.

3. The area should look like this when you're finished grinding.

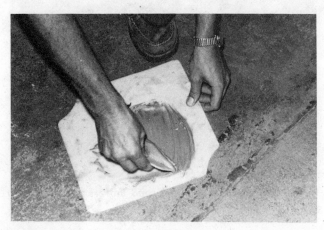

4. Mix the body filler and cream hardener according to the directions.

5. Spread the body filler evenly over the entire area. Be sure to cover the area completely.

6. Let the body filler dry until surface can just be scratched with your fingernail.

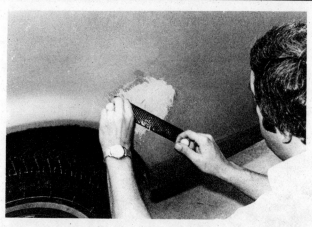

7. Knock the high spots from the body filler with a body file.

8. Check frequently with the palm of your hand for high and low spots. If you wind up with low spots, you may have to apply another layer of filler.

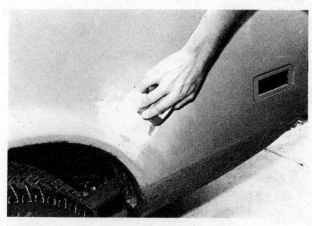

9. Block sand the entire area with 320 grit paper.

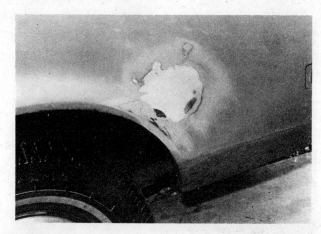

10. When you're finished, the repair should look like this. Note the sand marks extending 2–3 inches out from the repaired area.

11. Prime the entire area with automotive primer.

12. The finished repair ready for the final paint coat. Note that the primer has covered the sanding marks (see Step 10). A repair of this size should be spotpainted with good results.

REPAIRING RUST HOLES WITH FIBERGLASS

1. Rust areas such as this are common and are easily fixed.

2. Grind away all traces of rust with a 24-grit grinding disc. Be sure to grind back 3–4 inches from the edge of the hole down to bare metal.

3. Be sure all rust is removed from the edges of the metal. The edges must be ground back to un-rusted metal.

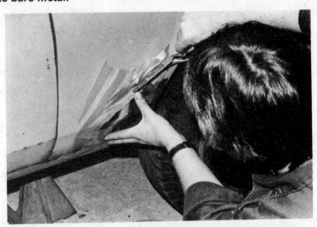

4. If you are going to use release film, cut a piece about 2" larger than the area you have sanded. Place the film over the repair and mark the sanded area on the film. Avoid any unnecessary wrinkling of the film.

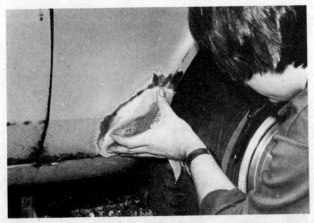

5. Cut two pieces of fiberglass matte. One piece should be about 1" smaller than the sanded area and the second piece should be 1" smaller than the first. Use sharp scissors to avoid loose ends.

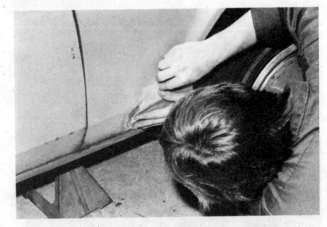

6. Check the dimensions of the release film and cloth by holding them up to the repair area.

7. Mix enough repair jelly and cream hardener in the mixing tray to saturate the fiberglass material or fill the repair area. Follow the directions on the container.

8. Lay the release sheet on a flat surface and spread an even layer of filler large enough to cover the repair. Lay the smaller piece of fiberglass cloth in the center of the sheet and spread another layer of repair jelly over the fiberglass cloth. Repeat the operation for the larger piece of cloth. If the fiberglass cloth is not used, spread the repair jelly on the release film, concentrated in the middle of the repair.

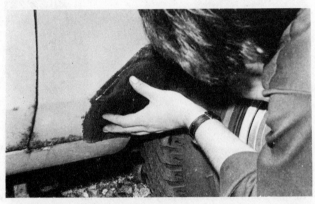

9. Place the repair material over the repair area, with the release film facing outward.

10. Use a spreader and work from the center outward smoothing the material, following the body contours. Be sure to remove all air bubbles.

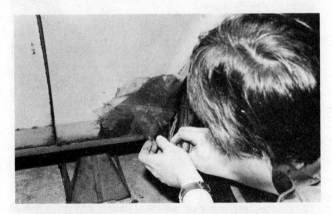

11. Wait until the repair has dried tack-free and peel off the release sheet. The ideal working temperature is 65–90° F. Cooler or warmer temperatures or high humidity may require additional curing time.

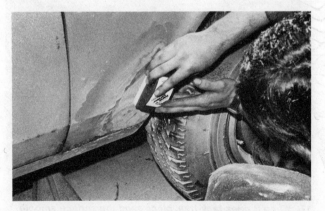

12. Sand and feather-edge the entire area. The initial sanding can be done with a sanding disc on an electric drill if care is used. Finish the sanding with a block sander.

13. When the area is sanded smooth, mix some topcoat and hardener and apply it directly with a spreader. This will give a smooth finish and prevent the glass matte from showing through the paint.

14. Block sand the topcoat with finishing sandpaper.

15. To finish this repair, grind out the surface rust along the top edge of the rocker panel.

16. Mix some more repair jelly and cream hardener and apply it directly over the surface.

17. When it dries tack-free, block sand the surface smooth.

18. If necessary, mask off adjacent panels and spray the entire repair with primer. You are now ready for a color coat.

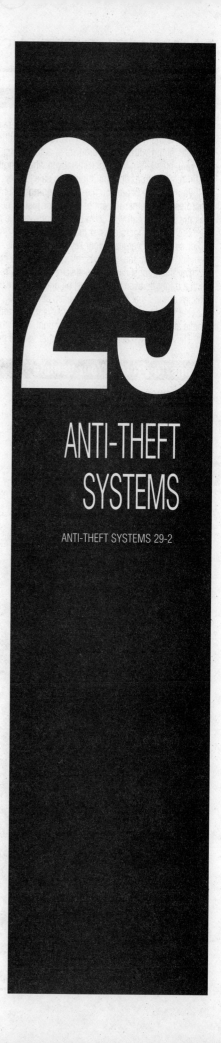

29

ANTI-THEFT SYSTEMS

ANTI-THEFT SYSTEMS

Every 32 seconds, a vehicle is stolen somewhere in the United States. Automotive theft is big business—more than a million vehicles were stolen last year, along with untold numbers of auto stereos, batteries, tires, wheels, and valuables left in vehicle trunks. Even whole engines disappear in what is still referred to as "the midnight auto sale."

If your vehicle is next on the list, it's going to set you back a bundle, regardless of whether the entire vehicle or just some part of it vanishes one dark night. What can you do to protect your vehicle and everything in it from the sticky fingers of your local vehicle thief?

For starters, never leave your keys in your vehicle. Don't leave the doors unlocked either, or the windows rolled down even a crack. Contrary to what you may think, most car thieves are amateurs. They're not interested in a vehicle that might be even the slightest bit difficult to steal. There are plenty of vehicles around that present no problem at all: 80% of all the vehicles stolen last year were unlocked; 40% had the keys in the ignition. So if you lock the vehicle and keep the windows rolled up tight, most amateurs won't bother you. They'll simply keep looking for another vehicle that's easier to steal.

Steps To Protect Your Vehicle

▶ **See Figures 1, 2, 3, 4 and 5**

Besides never leaving the keys in the vehicle and rolling the windows up tight, there are a couple of other simple things you can do to protect your vehicle and all its parts. One of the simplest things you can do on older vehicles is replace the standard interior door lock knob with the tapered kind. They're almost impossible to pull up with a coat hanger and will deter most amateurs. Many vehicles these days don't have different locks for the ignition, doors, and trunk, if your vehicle doesn't, it's a good idea to have

them installed. That way, a thief who gets your door key won't have your ignition key. On the subject of keys, if you keep a spare key for your vehicle (and you should), keep it in your wallet, not in the vehicle or under the hood. If a professional thief is interested in stealing your vehicle, he'll know where to find the key, so don't hide it on the vehicle somewhere.

Fig. 1 Custom wheels can be secured with wheel locks

Fig. 2 Clover shaped pattern on McGard® type locks make it impossible to pick . . .

Fig. 3 . . . a special adapter is required to remove these special lug nuts

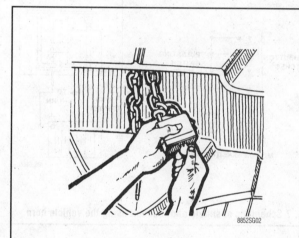

Fig. 4 Lock the hood with case-hardened chain and lock or hood pins

Fig. 5 Locking gas cap keeps gas in and other things out.

Locking gas caps, hood locks, and wheel locks are cheap insurance. Locking gas caps are easy to install, and the only sure way to keep that expensive gas in your tank where it belongs and to keep other things from finding their way into your tank. They can be forced open, of course, but most thieves aren't about to take the time.

If you have custom wheels, either factory-installed or aftermarket items, wheel locks are the best thing you can do for them. Simply take the old lug nuts off, and screw the new ones on. Custom wheels are high on car thieves "most wanted" list, but generally, the sight of wheel locks will deter the average thief.

Most late model vehicles are equipped with an interior hood release, for earlier models hood locks are recommended. Hood locks are an excellent way to keep what's under the hood where it's supposed to be. There are two basic types of hood locks, one uses a strap or length of heavy chain and limits the distance the hood can be opened until the lock is released. The other type is just like a trunk lock with a key, and requires that you cut a hole in the hood to install the locks (usually one on each side of the hood).

Insurance

Auto theft coverage is usually included with the Comprehensive portion of your policy, as is the theft of components or contents. You may find that the insurer has specifically exempted some items (such as Cellular Phones) unless they are installed in the dash or are factory equipment.

Check your individual policy for fine print, such as:

• Is there a deductible for contents or for the vehicle itself? The higher the deductible (the amount you pay), the lower the premium.

• Does the policy cover cell phones, stereos, and CD players if not installed in the dash or as factory equipment?

• Does the policy cover items stolen along with the vehicle, or only from the vehicle?

• If your vehicle or contents of the vehicle are stolen, be prepared to provide the police with a list of what was stolen, along with any identifying marks.

How Anti-Theft Systems Work

With the widespread and increasing rate of auto theft, automotive anti-theft systems have come into general use. Many auto manufacturers now offer anti-theft or alarm systems as optional equipment. In addition, there are literally dozens of after-market suppliers who manufacture these systems.

Most systems can be installed with hand tools in a few hours, but more complicated systems are best left to professionals.

There are two basic types of automotive anti-theft systems—alarm systems and movement inhibitors.

ALARM SYSTEMS

▶ **See Figure 6**

There are two basic types of burglar alarm systems for automobiles—those which actuate the vehicle horn, and those which set off an auxiliary siren or bell. Regardless of which type it is, each one can be broken down into its separate components: the trigger, trigger control and the alarm itself.

Trigger Mechanisms

The trigger mechanism is the device used to activate the alarm. In most cases, the trigger consists of a switch or switches, and a drop relay. A drop relay is a relay that, once activated, will not recycle until reset manually; therefore, the alarm will not stop functioning even if the trigger switch is deactivated.

Motion sensitive switches such as mercury switches, pendulum switches, etc. are excellent means of detecting tampering. The switch may be mounted anywhere in the vehicle, and its sensitivity adjusted to the desired level. The disadvantage of a motion-sensitive switch is the accuracy with which it must be adjusted. The switch must respond to the opening of a door, the hood or trunk, but not to such things as parking on an incline,

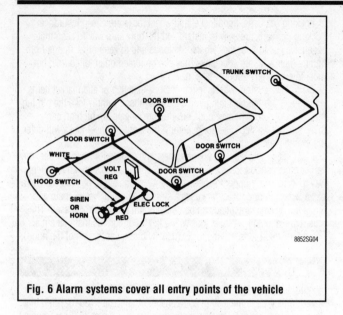

Fig. 6 Alarm systems cover all entry points of the vehicle

being bumped by a pedestrian, or traffic passing by. Once the proper sensitivity is determined, it is a good idea to include a timer in the trigger circuit, to shut the alarm off after a certain period if it is accidentally triggered.

Pushbutton switches (such as interior light doorjamb switches) mounted on all doors and the hood and trunk may be used to trigger an alarm. These spring-loaded, normally closed switches may be positioned adjacent to the existing switches on the doorjambs and on the hood and trunk latch plates. A combination system of motion sensitive and pushbutton switches will provide excellent protection. Mercury switches used to activate hood and trunk lights may be used as triggers, in lieu of pushbutton switches, on the hood and trunk.

Trigger Control Switches

The trigger control switch acts as an on-off switch for the alarm system. It must be arranged in such a manner so that the owner may enter the vehicle without triggering the alarm, but a thief must be unable to detect or disarm it.

The simplest type of control switch is a toggle switch mounted outside the vehicle in an inconspicuous place. Inside the fender well or under the rocker panel are two typical places that this type of switch is mounted. The only drawbacks to this type of switch are that the switch and wiring must be waterproofed, and that someone may find the switch and deactivate the alarm.

The most popular type of switch is the locking type that may be mounted anywhere on the outside of the vehicle. These switches use cylindrical "pickproof" locks, and provide excellent protection, in addition to acting as a visual deterrent.

Alarms

◆ See Figures 7 and 8

An alarm may be devised as an integral part of the electrical system to set off the horn, or the warning system may contain its own alarm. To connect an alarm system utilizing the vehicle horn, proceed as follows: Locate the terminal on the horn relay that will sound the horn when it is bridged to

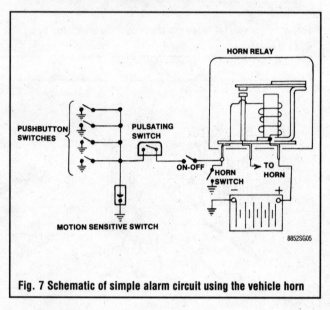

Fig. 7 Schematic of simple alarm circuit using the vehicle horn

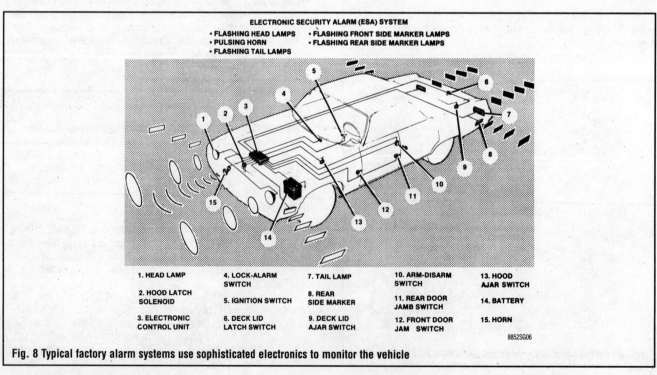

Fig. 8 Typical factory alarm systems use sophisticated electronics to monitor the vehicle

ground. Connect one lead from the on-off switch to this terminal. Connect the other lead from the on-off switch to a pulsating (flasher-type) terminal. Connect the open terminal of the pulsating switch to the trigger mechanism. Now firmly ground the trigger mechanism.

Non-integral, self-contained alarm systems may be connected to the accessory position in the fuse box. The alarm itself (siren, bell, buzzer, etc.) must be loud enough to attract attention at a reasonable distance, and should be positioned somewhere where full advantage can be taken of its capabilities (such as behind the grill). A drop relay and/or a timer should be installed somewhere in the circuit. The drop relay will keep the alarm activated, even after the trigger is deactivated, unless all current is removed from the alarm circuit. The timer is used to deactivate the alarm a certain period after the trigger is deactivated, to prevent the alarm running down the battery, and to prevent disturbing the peace after accidental triggering.

One of the best things you can do after you install one of these alarm systems is to mount the "protected by alarm" sticker that comes with the system. A casual thief seeing this sticker isn't going to stick around to see if it's telling the truth or not.

MOVEMENT INHIBITORS

Mechanical

▶ See Figures 9 and 10

The most common systems available inhibit the movement of the brake pedal and/or the steering wheel. Of these, the most prevalent (best known by its trade name—The Club®) utilizes a long steel bar that hooks and locks onto the steering wheel, and prevents it from turning beyond a certain point by wedging against interior components. A similar system is a locking, telescoping steel bar, with a hook at each end. In use, one hook is positioned around a steering wheel spoke and the other around the brake pedal arm. The steel shaft is then telescoped down and locked into position, preventing movement of the brake pedal and limiting movement of the steering wheel.

Both of these devices have the advantage of being easily visible from outside the vehicle, thereby acting as a visual deterrent. Their main disadvantage is that they are somewhat awkward and must be removed and installed each time that vehicle is moved.

Because they are relatively easy to steel and have a high "street" value, airbags are fast becoming the accessory of choice for car thieves. It has been estimated that as much as 10% of all vehicle theft claims last year were for airbags. Shield type devices are available to adjust to fit most steering wheels, one-, two-, and three-spoke. These are used in conjunction with a Club® type device. These devices also serve another important

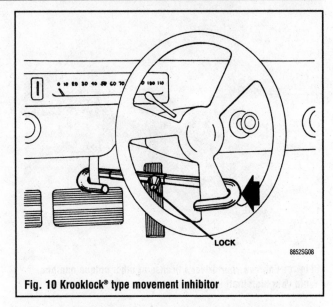

Fig. 10 Krooklock® type movement inhibitor

purpose, although the Club® type devices are usually hardened steel which makes them difficult to cut, steering wheels left unprotected cut like butter. These shields cover and protect the steering wheel from being cut and the Club® type device removed.

Electronic

Electronic vehicle immobilizers are relatively new on the market . They are available with different levels of protection—a one level interrupt version that interrupts either the ignition or the starter; a two level system that may incorporate the visual deterrence of "The Club"® type device with the one level version; a three level version which will interrupt the ignition, starter and the fuel system; and a four level version which uses "The Club"® device with the three level interrupt unit.

TRACKING SYSTEMS

A system has been developed to track a stolen vehicle. Services are available through dealers and some private installation shops which will install an aftermarket tracking device to your car or truck. If you report that your vehicle has been stolen, a signal from a police radio tower activates the transmitter in your vehicle. The hidden transmitter in your vehicle then broadcasts a silent, coded signal. The police tracking computer receives the signal that identifies your vehicle and leads them to it.

Accessories and Theft

IDENTIFY YOUR EQUIPMENT

▶ See Figure 11

Once the stereo is stolen, it's not lost and gone, forever, if you take certain precautions. Many stolen sets are recovered, but the tragedy is that the owner cannot positively identify the set, or the police cannot trace the owner through the serial number because the owner did not send in the warranty card. The "That's my set! I recognize that little nick on the front," line just doesn't work unless you report the identifying features beforehand. In a move to ease stolen stereo identification, the FCC, since the late 70's, has required manufacturers to engrave the serial number or other unique identifying number on the chassis of the set.

Police are encouraging people to engrave an identifying number on the stereo, or other component and will often supply the engraver free of charge. Your social security number should not be used for this purpose, because the social security office in Washington will not release the name and address of the social security number's owner—not even to the police.

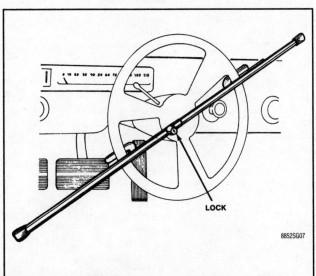

Fig. 9 Typical Club® type steering wheel wedge bar installed

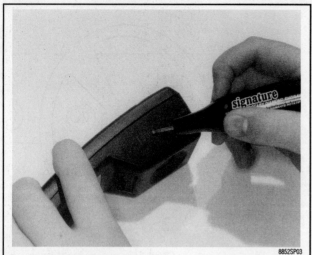

Fig. 11 Engrave your driver's license or other unique number onto your high theft items

Use your driver's license number, your name and address, or some other number that can be easily and officially traced to you and no one else.

There are also national computer registration programs, which for a set one-time fee provide an identifying number (guaranteed yours and yours alone) and a complete kit for engraving it. The number is registered with the computer service. Police can easily trace the number to you through a toll-free telephone number to the computer service. No matter what number you use, be sure you have a copy of it, and be sure you can prove the number is used only by you. It is also a good idea to register it with the local police.

SAFETY PRECAUTIONS

Most thieves work fast. Once inside a vehicle, prying at the stereo with a stout screwdriver usually frees it in seconds. A couple of snips with the side cutters and the thief is on his way. Because speed is of the essence, anything that will slow a thief down may be a deterrent. Alarms and mounting brackets are sometimes useful, but alarms can be disabled in seconds (by a professional) and locking mounting brackets are generally pried loose with a stout crowbar, tearing up your dash in the process. Locking barrels over the mounting nuts offer approximately the same resistance, are dealt with in the same crude manner, and gain the same net result. The truth is if you leave your rig in plain sight regularly, you're inviting trouble.

To sum the whole thing up:

1. Don't park in the bad parts of town and leave your radio in the vehicle.

2. When you do park on the streets or in a lot for short periods, try to park under a light.

3. When you are going to be gone for a while, remove the set and stow it out of sight. If you don't remove it, AT LEAST cover it with something.

4. Many local law enforcement agencies provide a number etching service. A number (driver's license, or other number) is etched onto your set and logged in police files. It won't keep the set from being stolen, but it may aid recovery.

30

BUYING AND OWNING A VEHICLE

BUYING AND OWNING A
VEHICLE 30-2

BUYING AND OWNING A VEHICLE

For most people, next to a house, their vehicle represents the single, largest purchase they will make. While you wouldn't think of buying a house that wasn't "just right" for what you need, many people blunder into the showroom and drive a new vehicle home that night because "it was cute," "the color was right," or a hundred other reasons, many supplied by the salesman. Some estimates put the number of buyers who even bother to take a test drive at less than four out of five.

Buying a New Vehicle

Naturally, everyone is influenced somewhat by brand loyalty, advertising, or reputation, but the obvious point is to buy what you really need. Once you have decided that you want or need another vehicle, set down some basic limits—subcompact or intermediate, room for four people, type of engine, etc. Then start shopping around for what fits your needs.

Some factors to consider are:

Weight—If maximum fuel economy is your goal, weight of the vehicle is the single most important factor. Roughly, each 500-lb gain in weight over 2,000 lbs. will cost you 2–5 mpg. On the other hand, the fuel economy penalty for heavier vehicles is less if most of your driving is at sustained highway speeds.

Body Style—This will largely be determined by your needs and the way you use a car or truck. Generally, the smallest vehicle that fits your needs will be most economical.

Engines—All other factors being equal, smaller engines are considered more economical to operate, but this can be deceiving. One of the biggest mistakes new vehicle buyers make is to under power their vehicle. This is particularly true with intermediate and larger size vehicles. In fact, compared to weight, engine size is not a significant factor in fuel economy at highway speeds.

Ease of Service—If you plan to maintain the vehicle yourself, look for easy accessibility of parts frequently replaced (plugs, filters, lube fittings, etc.). Even if you don't want to get your hands dirty, easy accessibility will lower your mechanic's bill.

OPTIONS

If you're looking for a "loaded" popular model, you may be lucky enough to find just the vehicle you want already on a dealer's lot. Otherwise, don't count on it.

After you've finally narrowed your choices down to about three models, how do you decide which vehicle is going to give you the most for your

WHAT SIZE CAR IS BEST FOR YOU?

Size	Advantages	Disadvantages
Subcompact	Cost least Best gas mileage Easiest to handle Simpler engines Cheapest to run, maintain	Stiff ride Very limited space All options not available
Compact	Costs a little more Good gas mileage Good for commuting Easy to handle Cheap to run, maintain	Somewhat stiff ride Limited space Options somewhat limited
Intermediate	Good room and comfort Fairly easy to handle Good choice of engines, options Fairly cheap to run, maintain	Costs quite a bit more Lower gas mileage Not as good for big families, heavy loads as full size
Full size	Most comfortable Widest choice of engines, options Best long-trip car Best for heavy loads	Costs most to buy, run, maintain Hardest to handle Lowest gas mileage

8852TC01

money? Start by looking at the sticker prices of all three, and paying close attention to exactly what equipment each includes. "Standard equipment" is a flexible term, and there is a lot of difference in its meaning from one vehicle maker to another. What one vehicle maker offers as standard equipment may be considered an accessory by others.

Beyond the essential parts needed to make the vehicle run, the more equipment you get for the same money, the better off you are. The cost of options can add up fast, though. They can drive up the price of your vehicle by the thousands before you know it.

Performance-related parts are things like sport suspension, Anti-lock disc brakes, and overdrive transmission, which no one will know you have, but will make all the difference in the way your vehicle handles and performs. In addition, they can help you achieve the maximum degree of economy.

Sport suspension and Anti-lock disc brakes may be either standard or optional equipment. In addition, both are options you really might like to have.

Overdrive transmission is great to have if you do a lot of highway driving. It saves gas and reduces wear and tear on your vehicle. If you plan to use your vehicle for quick jaunts around town, you won't see the difference. Look at it as one of those things that are nice to have if the vehicle maker throws it in free.

Air conditioning is almost never considered standard equipment. Where you live plays an important part in your decision as to whether you need it or not. In addition, remember that the performance and the fuel economy of your vehicle are probably going to suffer, but you will be comfortable.

Style/trim accessories have no real function, and are usually described in glowing terms like "deluxe custom interior, custom wheel covers," "sport package," etc. If you're really shopping for a bargain, forget about these. There are many kits available for the do-it-yourselfer to customize the vehicle nicely without the expense of the factory doing it for you.

BEST TIME TO BUY

Usually the best time to buy a new vehicle is toward the end of the month. Many dealerships run monthly sales incentive programs, and many salesmen have quotas to meet each month. Depending on circumstances, the salesman may be willing to take slightly less commission to sell a vehicle somewhere between what you want to pay and what the sales manager will accept.

Time of year also is important to new vehicle sales. New vehicles are in short supply shortly after the fall introductions, so prices are slightly higher then. The winter months are traditionally slow for new vehicle sales, and sometimes you can find a good deal then.

TRADE INS

If you plan to trade in your old vehicle, don't discuss this until you have arrived at a price for your new vehicle. This avoids a lot of confusion about what the vehicle is costing and how much trade you're allowed.

All vehicle dealers subscribe to one of several used vehicle valuation books that list the average wholesale and retail value for a vehicle depending on condition. If the dealer can't make money on selling you a new vehicle, he may try to get your "cherry" used vehicle at rock-bottom trade in.

A good rule of thumb is to accept a dealer's trade-in offer if it is within $500 of the price your vehicle commands in the local papers. The aggravation and cost of selling your vehicle is worth that much at least. If the dealer can't come closer than $500, sell it yourself.

It is almost impossible to tell how much your vehicle will depreciate or what it will be worth several years after you have owned it. Determining your vehicle's trade-in value are such factors as gasoline availability vs. your vehicle's fuel economy, frequency of repairs, general public acceptance (popularity), and whether it is an Import or Domestic made.

EPA MILEAGE ESTIMATES

♦ **See Figure 1**

How realistic are the EPA mileage estimates? There is no question that fuel economy in a particular vehicle will vary widely, depending on the driver. Complicating the estimate is the fact that vehicles are even more variable than drivers are.

There has been considerable criticism of the EPA fuel consumption figures as being too optimistic. The EPA procedure is useful as a simplified representation of the wide variation in conditions that affect customer fuel consumption. In addition to the driving cycle itself, the EPA procedure establishes many standard test conditions for variables such as type of fuel, ambient temperature, and "soaktime" (elapsed time since vehicle was last operated, which affects warm-up conditions). Though the specifications are meant to be representative, each introduces into the measurement of fuel consumption a variable that tends to make it higher or lower than customer usage indicates.

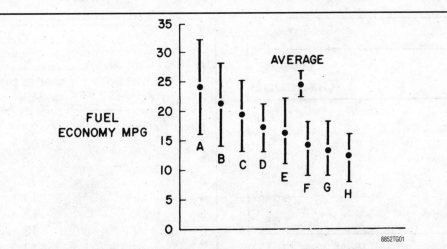

Fig. 1 This chart shows results of tests, published by the Society of Automotive Engineers, that measured the real world fuel economy of eight different kinds of vehicles (identified A–H). Drivers of these vehicles recorded their fuel mileage for three successive tank fillings. The range of fuel economy indicated by the highs and lows is compared to the EPA estimates, shown by the dots.

As an example, look at the dynamometer tests. The vehicle is run in a stationary position on large rollers that allow the wheels to spin simulating road speed. Tire rolling resistance is affected by vehicle weight distribution and tire pressure, among other factors. Only one pair of tires (front or rear) is cradled on the dynamometer rollers. Because of this, front-wheel-drive vehicles can experience higher losses due to tire rolling resistance than rear-wheel-drive vehicles. Tire pressure also influences rolling resistance and the EPA specifies an artificially high tire pressure to increase durability during the tests.

Other factors contributing small biases toward the final EPA economy number include road surface, state of road repair, wind, weather conditions, altitude, engine accessory loads, and customer maintenance. All will affect the actual in-use fuel economy.

Fuel economy labels are meant to be useful in comparing relative economy of vehicles and in estimating the actual fuel consumption experienced in use. Obviously, the in-use fuel economy obtained by any given driver/vehicle combination is subject to many variables and cannot be determined exactly.

MAKING THE DEAL

▶ **See Figures 2 and 3**

Now that you have your choice narrowed down, it's time to shop for the best deal. A dealer has to make between $300–$500 on each vehicle to stay in business. However, that doesn't mean that the sticker price on the window reflects this profit margin—it's probably much more. You can easily figure the approximate cost of the vehicle to the dealer by looking in any of several publications available on newsstands.

Depending on the model of vehicle you're considering, figure what it cost the dealer. If this hypothetical vehicle were an intermediate, it would cost the dealer about $10,140 (sticker price minus about 18% of sticker price). To this, you have to add dealer preparation, transportation, taxes, and tags. A good deal on a vehicle is this bottom line plus the dealer profit of $300–500.

Arriving at what you consider a fair price is relatively easy. However, that doesn't mean the dealer or salesman has to sell the vehicle at that price. Get the salesman to put his best offer in writing, then go to different dealers and try to bargain for a lower price. Remember, too, that no price a salesman quotes is binding until the sales manager accepts it.

Fig. 3 Always check the sticker carefully before making an offer on a new vehicle

Buying a Previously Owned Vehicle

▶ **See Figure 4**

With new vehicle prices skyrocketing, many vehicle buyers are turning to used vehicles. The old saw that you're only buying someone else's trouble is not true today. Approximately 13–14 million used vehicles are sold every year in the United States by dealers, private sellers, and renting/leasing agencies, totaling more than $21 billion. Almost 75% of all passenger vehicles purchased for private use are previously owned.

Obviously, many buyers are convinced that a quality used vehicle is a bargain. The Hertz Corporation annually publishes its compilation of vehicle operating costs, and their figures show a used vehicle can be a bargain. The figures in the accompanying chart are rounded off to the nearest cent per mile.

People sell or trade vehicles for all kinds of reasons, and if you're willing to compromise a little on the vehicle of your dreams, you may get a good buy. First, decide what kind of vehicle you want and start looking for it, either privately or on new or used car lots.

Size	Dealer Discount
Subcompact	13%
Compact	14%
Intermediate	18%
Full-Size	20%
Luxury	22%
Specialty	15%

8852TG02

Fig. 2 Discounts vary across the types of vehicles available.

Age of Car when Purchased (in Years)	Ownership/Operating Cost	
	Cents per Mile	Percent Saved
New	28	—
1	25	10
2	20	30
3	15	48
4	14	51
5	13	52
6	13	53
7	13	53

8852TG03

Fig. 4 There are significant savings in purchasing a previously owned vehicle

Vehicles on used car lots are easier to find, but they frequently cost more than those offered for sale privately in newspapers. The reason is simple—the dealer has to make money over what he paid for the vehicle to stay in business. While private vehicles may be less expensive, they require considerably more legwork to track down and weed out the clunkers. You are also strictly on your own when buying a used vehicle from a private party. True, you don't have to deal with a used car salesman who's a pro. However, there's no law requiring honesty from private citizens selling used vehicles, either.

Once you've located a promising vehicle, how can you lessen the chances that you're buying someone else's trouble? Start by following these shopping rules:

1. Never shop for used vehicles at night. The glare of bright lights makes it easy to overlook body imperfections.

2. Take along a small pocket magnet. Casually try the magnet in locations all along the fenders. Anywhere the magnet doesn't stick—beware. The fender has been filled with plastic.

3. Ask to see the title. Many states identify vehicles that were bought out of state with a code, and the codes are usually explained somewhere on the title. Vehicles on a lot were frequently bought at an auction. Occasionally, a used-car dealer may get an exceptional vehicle at auction, but for the most part, the auction is a dumping ground for vehicles that other dealers took in trade and were not worth reselling. Generally, you should beware of a vehicle that was bought out of state or at an auction.

4. If the vehicle is on a lot, ask for the name and address of the former owner from the title and try to contact the owner. No reputable dealer will refuse the information. If he does, walk away.

5. Write down the year, model, and serial number before you buy any used vehicle. Then dial 1-800-424-9393, the toll-free number of the National Highway Traffic Safety Administration (NHTSA) and ask the clerk if the vehicle has ever been included on any manufacturer's recall list. If so, make sure the needed repairs were made.

USED VEHICLE INSPECTION CHECKLIST

▶ See Figures 5, 6 and 7

In addition to making sure everything works (wipers, radio, clock, gauges, heater, defroster, lights, turn signals, etc.), carefully evaluate these areas on any used vehicle you are considering buying. The number preceding each paragraph corresponds to the numbers in the accompanying drawing.

1. **Mileage (1)**—Average mileage is about 12,000 miles (19,300km) per year. The numbers should be straight across the odometer.

2. **Paint (2)**—Check around tailpipe, molding, and windows for overspray indicating the vehicle has been repainted.

3. **Body damage (3)**—Check where the body panels meet; severe misalignment indicates crash work. Sight down the contours of the body panels; ripples indicate bodywork. Check overall condition of moldings, bumpers, and grille.

4. **Leaks (4)**—Look under the vehicle. There are no normal "leaks," other than water from the A/C condenser.

5. **Tires (5)**—Check the tire pressure. A common used-vehicle trick is to pump the tire pressure up to make the vehicle easier to roll. Check the tread wear. Uneven wear is a clue that the front end needs alignment.

6. **Rust (6)**—Check all around the vehicle (fenders, doors, rocker panels, rain gutters, window moldings, wheelwells, under floor-mats) for signs of rust. Any rust at all will be a problem. There is no inexpensive way to stop the spread of rust. The only sure way is to replace the rusted part.

7. **Shocks (7)**—Check the shock absorbers by bouncing each corner of the vehicle. Good shocks will not bounce more than twice after you let go.

8. **Interior (8)**—Check the entire interior. You're looking for an interior condition that doesn't agree with the overall condition of the vehicle. Reasonable wear is expected, but be suspicious of new seatcovers on sagging seats, new pedal pads, and worn armrests. These indicate an attempt to cover up hard use. Pull back the carpets and look for evidence of water leaks or flooding.

Look for evidences of a leak or rust in the trunk. New welds indicate recent crash work. Look for missing door handles, control knobs, and other miscellaneous pieces of hardware. Check for proper operation of all lights and signals. Look for scratches and cracks in all glass.

9. **Hoses, belts (9)**—Check all belts and hoses for wear or weak spots.

10. **Battery terminals (10)**—Low electrolyte level, corroded terminals, and/or cracked case indicate a lack of maintenance.

11. **Radiator/coolant (11)**—Look for corrosion or rust around the radiator, signifying a leak. Rust in the coolant indicates a lack of maintenance.

12. **Air filter (12)**—A dirty air filter usually means a lack of preventive maintenance.

13. **Ignition wires (13)**—Check the ignition wires for cracks, burned spots, or wear. Worn wires will have to be replaced.

14. **Oil level (14)**—If the oil level is low, chances are even that the engine uses oil. Beware of water in the oil (cracked block), excessively thick oil (used to quiet a noisy engine), or thin dirty oil with a distinct gasoline smell (internal problems in the engine).

Fig. 5 Inspect the area around the wheel wells on used vehciles for rust and corrosion

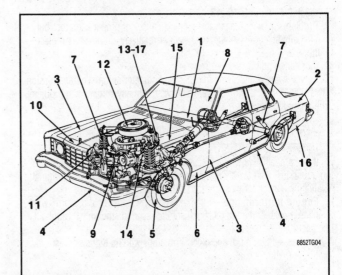

Fig. 6 Used vehicle checklist, refer to text for more information

8852TP05

Fig. 7 An old inspection sticker on a vehicle can be the sign of big problems

15. **Automatic transmission (15)**—Pull the automatic transmission dipstick out when the engine is running. The level should read "Full," and the fluid should be clear and bright red. Dark brown or black fluid, or fluid that has a distinct burnt odor, signals a transmission in need of repair or overhaul.

16. **Exhaust (16)**—Check the color of the exhaust smoke. Blue smoke indicates worn rings; black smoke can indicate burnt valves or that a tune-up is needed.

17. **Spark plugs (17)**—Remove one of the spark plugs (the most accessible will do). An engine in good condition will show plugs with a light tan or gray-firing tip.

Once you have checked the vehicle out thoroughly and taken careful note of any problems as outlined above, you can come to a reliable initial evaluation of the condition of the vehicle and the care it has received. Below is a guide to help you. If your inspection turns up problems in two of the areas below, or in only one of them but a problem shows up in your road test, proceed with caution. That vehicle is in less than excellent condition.

Illustration numbers **1–8**:
Problems in more than two areas indicate a lack of maintenance, and you should beware.

Illustration numbers **9–13**:
Problems in any of these areas indicate a lack of proper care, too, but can usually be corrected with a tune-up or relatively simple parts replacement.

Illustration numbers **14–17**:
Be very wary of problems in either the engine or automatic transmission. These can mean major expense. Walk away from any vehicle with problems in both areas.

ROAD TEST AND MECHANIC'S OPINION

If you are satisfied with the apparent condition of the vehicle, take it out on a road test. The results of the road test should agree with your original evaluation. Check for these things on the road:

Engine performance—Should be peppy whether cold or warm, with plenty of power and good pickup. It should respond smoothly through all the gears.

Brakes—Should provide quick, firm stops with no signs of noise, pulling, or fading pedal.

Steering—Should provide sure control with no binding, harshness, or looseness and no shimmy in the wheel. Noise or vibration from the steering wheel when turning the vehicle means trouble.

Clutch, manual transmission—Should give quick, smooth response with easy shifting. The clutch pedal should have about 1–1 ½" play before it disengages the clutch. Start engine, set parking brake, put in first gear and slowly release the clutch pedal. Engine should stall when pedal is one-half to three-quarters of the way up.

Automatic transmission— Should shift rapidly and smoothly, with no hesitation and no noise.

Differential—No noise or thumps.

Driveshaft, universal joints—Vibration and shimmy could mean driveshaft problems. Clicking sound at low speeds means worn U-joints.

Suspension—Hit bumps going slow and fast. A vehicle that bounces has weak shocks. Shimmying may be due to driveshaft problems.

Frame—Wet the tires and drive in a straight line on concrete. Tracks should show two straight lines, not four.

After inspecting the vehicle yourself, or if you are not sure how to, it is usually a good idea to take a vehicle to your local trusted mechanic for his or her opinion. It won't take a mechanic more than an hour to check the vehicle over for any problems that may need addressing. Then you can decide for yourself whether or not to purchase the vehicle upon yours and the mechanics opinions.

Leasing a New Vehicle

Leasing which was once the tool of business people who could write off their monthly lease payments as a business expense has attracted the interest of private vehicle buyers. High sticker prices have put many new vehicle models beyond the reach of ordinary consumers. In addition, the tax deduction is gone for both sales tax and interest paid on consumer loans.

In many cases leasing is cheaper than buying. For those who keep a vehicle for three or four years, leasing is even more competitive than financing because depreciation makes a new vehicle very expensive to own in its early years. A typical new vehicle may depreciate almost 50% in its first year and as much as 75% over four years.

The cheapest way to own a vehicle is to buy it and keep it to a ripe old age. If a vehicle is kept for ten years, the percent of depreciation will be much lower per year than a four-year loan. Although maintenance costs will increase, as the vehicle grows older, it should not surpass the higher depreciation that occurs when buying a new vehicle every few years.

Unfortunately, keeping a vehicle for ten years does not seem to be the American way. People's needs and wants changing often, along with manufacturers improvements are just a few reasons why people get a new vehicle every few years.

HOW TO DETERMINE PAYMENTS

To figure your monthly lease payment, the leasing company first determines what the vehicle is expected to be worth at the end of the lease period, or the vehicle's "residual value". The Lease Company subtracts the residual value from the purchase price of the vehicle, and builds the monthly lease payments on the remainder. For example, you lease a $13,000 automobile for four years. If the leasing company estimates that the vehicle will be worth $5,000 at the end of the lease, it must arrange a lease payment schedule to recover the $8,000 difference, along with interest and tax. The lessee might also have the option to purchase the vehicle at the end of the lease period for the residual value or purchase option. It would be to the customers advantage to use a leasing company that works with all makes and models due to their unbiased opinions in comparing different makes and models.

TYPES OF LEASES

The most common type of lease is the "closed-end lease". You pay a fixed price for a fixed number of months. At the end of the lease you return the vehicle and walk away. You owe nothing, unless you have damaged the vehicle or have driven more than the agreed mileage.

A second type of lease is called the "open-end lease". At the end of an open-end lease, you can buy the vehicle for an amount established by the leasing company at the time you sign the contract. If you don't wish to buy the vehicle at the end of the lease, you can ask the leasing company to sell it. If the vehicle sells for more than the price originally established by the leasing company, you either owe nothing or get a refund, depending on how the lease was written. If the vehicle sells for less than the original estimate, you pay the difference between the estimated and actual price of the vehicle.

In most cases, the Consumer Leasing Act of 1976 limits this end-of-lease payment to three times the monthly payment. The leasing company can collect more only if the vehicle suffered excessive use or damage, or if the leasing company wins a lawsuit seeking a higher amount.

Because you the consumer assume some of the risk of depreciation with an open-end lease, the monthly payments are usually lower than with a closed-end lease. Nevertheless, that risk of depreciation is no small matter.

Whether you sign an open- or a closed-end lease, you will be responsible for the following expenses, some of which are negotiable:

Security deposit — Most leasing companies require a security deposit equal to one or two months' payments. In most cases, you get the deposit back (usually without interest) at the end of the lease. Providing the vehicle is in reasonable condition.

Advance payment —You'll probably have to pay the first monthly payment in advance. Some companies require two or more payments up front.

Title and registration — the vehicle must have a title and registration: most leasing companies will pass these charges on to you. The costs differ from state to state.

Monthly payments — The leasing company calculates your monthly payments based on the estimated value of the vehicle at the end of the lease, the company's borrowing costs, overhead expenses, sales tax, and their profit. Most leases run for 36 or 48 months. Monthly payments on a four year lease are usually 10–15 percent lower than payments on a three year lease.

Sometimes companies offer to cut your payments if you trade in your current vehicle. Don't do it if you can aboid it! Sell your vehicle privately. Remember that to stay in business they must pay you less than your vehicle is worth (so they can sell it for what it is worth or more and make a profit).

Insurance— You'll also have to have insurance on the vehicle. Most leasing companies set minimum limits that are higher that those normally required.

Some leasing companies even offer insurance. While buying insurance from the leasing company might seem convenient, it's wise to shop around and compare prices from several different insurance companies.

Maintenance and repairs— The customer is responsible for the vehicle's maintenance and repairs. In some cases for an additional monthly fee, the leasing companies will cover all or part of maintenance. The Consumer Leasing Act requires companies to disclose any warranties provided by the vehicle manufacturers and to tell you if any additional warranties are available.

In some states, you also have protection under state lemon laws, which cover new vehicles that turn out to be nightmares. According to most state laws, a vehicle is a lemon if it has been taken in for repair of the same problem four times without success during the first 12,000 miles (19,00km) or one year (this varies, state-to-state), whichever comes first, or if the vehicle has been out of service at least 30 days. If you have a lemon, the prescribed remedy is a new vehicle or your money back.

Forty-three states have passed lemon laws, but in only 16 states and the District of Columbia do such laws apply to leased vehicles. Those states are: California, Delaware, Florida, Indiana, Maine, Maryland, Minnesota, Mississippi, Missouri, New York, North Carolina, Oregon, Tennessee, Virginia, Washington, and Wisconsin.

Disposition charge — You are not responsible for the sale of your vehicle after you return it to the leasing company, however some companies include a disposition charge to cover the costs of preparing the vehicle for resale. This bill includes expenses for detailing, tune-up, and final maintenance. It usually comes to about $150 but can be as high as $250.

Purchasing Options —This option gives you the right of first refusal to buy the vehicle at a set price at the end of the lease. For a closed-end lease, you must have the option to buy in writing. For an open-end lease, the option to buy is usually part of the contract.

Mileage charge —Most leases allow you to drive only a certain stated number of miles, usually about 10,000–12,000 miles (16,000–19,000km) per year. If you drive more, you'll have to pay a mileage charge usually specified in the lease. Most of the leasing companies charge 15 cents per mile, but some charge as much as 25 cents per mile.

Wear and tear — When you return the vehicle you will have to pay for any damage, missing equipment, or excessive wear and tear. The Consumer Leasing Act requires the leasing company to define unreasonable damage, but the language is often vague. If the lease is unclear, ask for a detailed description of the damage you're responsible for.

Early termination —The Consumer Leasing Act requires the company to tell you under what conditions you can get out of the lease early and what the penalties will be, but it does not limit the penalty. The sooner you break a lease, the stiffer the penalties could be.

In the beginning of the lease, the vehicle depreciates more than the amount covered by your monthly payments; quitting early means that the leasing company will consider you "upside-down" on the lease. Therefore, it levies an early termination fee to make up for the shortfall in your payments. Early termination fees usually range from three to six months worth of but can run much higher. Check with you leasing company about simple interest leasing, this could be the safest type of auto leasing.

HOW TO SHOP FOR A LEASE

You can lease from a dealer who sells the make you want, or you can choose from most any make and model by shopping at an independent leasing company. Carefully compare both the total price and terms of each lease; make sure you are comparing apples to apples.

Monthly vehicle payments for identical vehicles can vary from one leasing company to the next, since the companies' costs may vary — one may have bought the vehicle for a lower price, for example, or another may have arranged more favorable financing. Most companies finance their vehicles through banks or financial institutions just like you do.

Be cautious of ads for super-low monthly rates. Some leasing companies advertise suspiciously low monthly payments, but then demand a "capital cost reduction" payment in order to get that lower monthly rate. In this case, they are having you buy down the lease without realizing it. Since avoiding up-front expenses is one of the main advantages of leasing, it doesn't make sense to pay the equivalent of a down payment.

ACCIDENT COVERAGE

When you lease a vehicle, you're required to carry automobile insurance. Most people assume that their insurance will cover the cost of the vehicle if it is stolen or totaled in an accident before the lease expires. To the surprise of many unhappy leaseholders, this isn't always the case.

Many leasing companies consider a stolen or totaled vehicle as "early termination". Then they slap lease holders with penalty fees in excess of the amount paid by their insurance companies. A recent report cited a New York businessman, who leased a Jeep Cherokee worth about $18,000. Eight days after he drove it off the lot, the vehicle was stolen. His insurance company reimbursed the leasing company for the cost of the vehicle, but he later received a bill for more than $7,000. This is where a simple interest lease would have been a good idea.

Before signing anything, examine every line of the lease and compare all the different aspects, not just price.

Warranties

▶ **See Figures 8, 9, 10, 11 and 12**

There are several different types of warranties that apply to today's vehicles. In the following section, you will learn what the vehicle owner must do to maintain warranty coverage as well as some suggestions for resolving a warranty dispute if one should arise.

The days of the 12 month / 12,000 mile (19,000km) warranty for cars and light trucks appear to be over. The ever-increasing complexities of vehicles, better materials, high tech electronics, and on-board computers have improved the quality and durability of today's vehicles. Manufacturer competition for customers has led to longer and more specialized warranty coverage. This is also the case on many smaller cars and trucks, not just expensive luxury models.

Typical warranty coverage may provide:
- Basic or 'Whole Vehicle' Coverage
- Powertrain Coverage
- Anti-Corrosion Coverage
- Safety Restraint System Coverage
- Emission System Warranty Coverage
- Emission Defects Coverage
- Emission Performance Coverage

Related Topics:
- IM 240 Programs
- Obtaining Warranty Information

BASIC COVERAGE

Basic warranty, sometimes referred to as "Whole Vehicle Coverage", covers just about everything on the vehicle, except for the items which have their own coverage under some other part of the vehicle's warranty plan. This used to be the 12 month /12 ,000 mile (19,000km) coverage plan, but is now usually 24, 36 or even 50 months or thousand miles. It often includes the powertrain coverage. When the basic warranty ends, the specific powertrain warranty coverage begins. If your power window stops working, power steering pump fails or the ignition switch breaks, this basic coverage is the warranty that covers you.

The basic warranty is generally the shortest warranty on the vehicle. Parts and labor are usually covered by this plan. This warranty, (and any

Fig. 9 Check your warranty and owners manuals for basic and extended coverages on your model

others that do not start upon the expiration of a preceding warranty), begin on the delivery date of the vehicle to the customer. In the case of vehicles such as dealer demonstrators, the warranty begins on the vehicle's actual 'inservice' date. The buyer of a used vehicle is entitled to any remaining warranty coverage when the vehicle is purchased. Any authorized dealer can perform warranty repairs, but if you have your vehicle outside the country in which you bought it, you may have to pay for the repairs and submit the receipt for reimbursement in your own country. If you need to have warranty work performed by someone other than an authorized dealer, be sure to obtain the failed part(s) and keep all receipts. You will need these things, and possibly a letter that explains the circumstances in order to request reimbursement from an authorized dealer.

Towing to the nearest authorized dealer may be covered if the vehicle cannot be driven due to the failure of a covered part. Vehicle owners may be responsible for taxes on warranty work in some states.

Other items to discuss about basic warranty are tires and batteries. Tires that fail are generally replaced by the tire manufacturer, not the vehicle manufacturer. Batteries that fail are most often covered by the vehicle's manufacturer. These items are replaced on a pro-rated basis. During the first part of the warranty period, replacement is often free of charge. As more time passes the items fall into a pro-rated coverage plan, where the vehicle manufacturer and the owner share the replacement costs.

You may also have some implied warranties, such as an implied warranty of merchantability that the car or light truck is reasonably fit for the purpose for which it was sold, or an implied warranty of fitness for a particular purpose that the car or light truck is suitable for your special purposes. If the vehicle is to be covered as to whether it is fit for special purposes, these may have to be disclosed to the manufacturer (not merely to the dealer) prior to purchase.

These implied warranties are limited, to the extent allowed by law, to the period covered by the written warranties, or to the applicable period provided by state law, whichever period is shorter. Vehicles used primarily for business or commercial purposes may not be covered by these implied warranties, and are completely disclaimed to the extent allowed by law.

Some states do not allow limitations on how long an implied warranty lasts, so the above limitations may not apply to you.

In order to keep warranties in effect, the vehicle owner may have to meet certain obligations. Some maintenance may need to be performed as specified for the vehicle. If the failure of a warranted part can be attributed to improper maintenance or lack of maintenance, the warranty claim may be

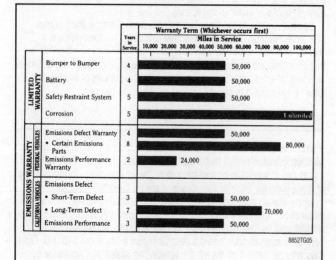

		Years in Service	Warranty Term (Whichever occurs first) Miles in Service
			10,000 20,000 30,000 40,000 50,000 60,000 70,000 80,000 90,000 100,000
LIMITED WARRANTY	Bumper to Bumper	4	50,000
	Battery	4	50,000
	Safety Restraint System	5	50,000
	Corrosion	5	Unlimited
EMISSIONS WARRANTY — FEDERAL VEHICLES	Emissions Defect Warranty	4	50,000
	• Certain Emissions Parts	8	80,000
	Emissions Performance Warranty	2	24,000
EMISSIONS WARRANTY — CALIFORNIA VEHICLES	Emissions Defect		
	• Short-Term Defect	3	50,000
	• Long-Term Defect	7	70,000
	Emissions Performance	3	50,000

Fig. 8 Typical warranty summary bar graph

Abbreviations: R = Replace I = Inspect. Correct or replace if necessary.

MAINTENANCE OPERATION		3.75	7.5	11.25	15	18.75	22.5	26.25	30	33.75	37.5	41.25	45	48.75	52.5	56.25	60
Perform at number of miles,	Miles x 1,000	(6)	(12)	(18)	(24)	(30)	(36)	(42)	(48)	(54)	(60)	(66)	(72)	(78)	(84)	(90)	(96)
kilometers or months, whichever comes first.	(km x 1,000) Months	3	6	9	12	15	18	21	24	27	30	33	36	39	42	45	48
Emission control system maintenance																	
Drive belts									I*								I*
Air cleaner filter	See NOTE (1)								[R]								[R]
Positive crankcase ventilation (P.C.V.) filter (KA24E engine only)	See NOTE (3)								[R]								[R]
Air induction valve filter (KA24E engine only)	See NOTE (2)																
Vapor lines									I*								I*
Fuel lines									I*								I*
Fuel filter	See NOTE (3)*																R
Engine coolant	See NOTE (4)																R*
Engine oil		R	R	R	R	R	R	R	R	R	R	R	R	R	R	R	R
Engine oil filter (Use Nissan PREMIUM type or equivalent.)		R	R	R	R	R	R	R	R	R	R	R	R	R	R	R	R
Spark plugs									[R]								[R]
Timing belt (VG30E engine only)																	[R]
Chassis and body maintenance																	
Brake lines & cables					I				I				I				I
Brake pads, discs, drums & linings			I		I		I		I		I		I		I		I
Manual and automatic transmission, transfer & differential gear oil (exc. L.S.D.)	See NOTE (5)				I				I								I
Limited-slip differential (L.S.D.) gear oil	See NOTE (5)								R								R
Steering gear (box) & linkage, (steering damper 4x2), axle & suspension parts				I		I		I		I		I		I		I	
Drive shaft boots & propeller shaft (4x2)			I		I		I		I		I		I		I		I
Steering linkage ball joints & front suspension ball joints			I		I		I		I		I		I		I		I
Front wheel bearing grease (4x2)									I								I
Front wheel bearing grease & free-running hub grease (4x2)	See NOTE (6)				I				R				I				R
Exhaust system			I		I		I		I		I		I		I		I

NOTE:
(1) If operating mainly in dusty conditions, more frequent maintenance may be required.
(2) If operating mainly in dusty conditions, replace every 30,000 miles (48,000 km).
(3) If vehicle is operated under extremely adverse weather conditions or in areas where ambient temperatures are either extremely low or extremely high, the filters might become clogged. In such an event, replace them immediately.
(4) After 60,000 miles (96,000 km) or 48 months, replace every 30,000 miles (48,000 km) or 24 months.
(5) If towing a trailer, using a camper or a car-top carrier, or driving on rough or muddy roads, change (not just inspect) oil at every 30,000 miles (48,000 km) or 24 months except for L.S.D. Change L.S.D. gear oil every 15,000 miles (24,000 km) or 12 months.
(6) If operating frequently in water, replace grease every 3,750 miles (6,000 km) or 3 months.
(7) Maintenance items and intervals with "*" are recommended by NISSAN for reliable vehicle operation. The owner need not perform such maintenance in order to maintain the emission warranty or manufacturer recall liability. Other maintenance items and intervals are required.

8852TG06

Fig. 10 Typical maintenance schedule for severe service

Abbreviations: R = Replace I = Inspect. Correct or replace if necessary.

MAINTENANCE OPERATION		7.5	15	22.5	30	37.5	45	52.5	60
Perform at number of miles, kilometers or months, whichever comes first.	Miles x 1,000	(12)	(24)	(36)	(48)	(60)	(72)	(84)	(96)
	(km x 1,000) Months	6	12	18	24	30	36	42	48
Emission control system maintenance									
Drive belts					I*				I*
Air cleaner filter					[R]				[R]
Positive crankcase ventilation (P.C.V.) filter (KA24E engine only)	See NOTE (1)				[R]				[R]
Vapor lines					I*				I*
Fuel lines					I*				I*
Fuel filter	See NOTE (1)*								
Engine coolant	See NOTE (2)								R*
Engine oil		R	R	R	R	R	R	R	R
Engine oil filter (Use Nissan PREMIUM type or equivalent.)		R		R		R		R	
Spark plugs					[R]				[R]
Timing belt (VG30E engine only)									[R]
Chassis and body maintenance									
Brake lines & cables			I		I		I		I
Brake pads, discs, drums & linings			I		I		I		I
Manual and automatic transmission, transfer & differential gear oil (exc. L.S.D.)		I			I		I		I
Limited-slip differential (L.S.D.) gear oil			I		R				R
Steering gear (box) & linkage, (steering damper 4x2), axle & suspension parts					I				I
Drive shaft boots (4x2)			I		I		I		I
Steering linkage ball joints & front suspension ball joints									I
Front wheel bearing grease (4x2)					I				I
Front wheel bearing grease & free-running hub grease (4x2)			I		R		I		R
Exhaust system			I		I		I		I

NOTE:
(1) If vehicle is operated under extremely adverse weather conditions or in areas where ambient temperatures are either extremely low or extremely high, the filters might become clogged. In such an event, replace them immediately.
(2) After 60,000 miles (96,000 km) or 48 months, replace every 30,000 miles (48,000 km) or 24 months.
(3) Maintenance items and intervals with "*" are recommended by NISSAN for reliable vehicle operation. The owner need not perform such maintenance in order to maintain the emission warranty or manufacturer recall liability. Other maintenance items and intervals are required.

8852TG07

Fig. 11 Typical maintenance schedule for normal service

8852TP06

Fig. 12 Even tire manufactures offer a warranty on their products

denied. Damages caused by using improper or contaminated fuel, oil, or other lubricants are not covered. Any tampering involving the odometer or Vehicle Identification Number (VIN) may result in denial of all warranty coverage to the vehicle.

However, it should be stated that the vehicle does not need to be serviced by a dealer or have factory parts installed. An example would be that you do not need to use the vehicle manufacturer's oil filter. You can buy an aftermarket oil filter and change the oil yourself. Quality replacement parts that meet manufacturer's specification must be used. You are strongly advised to keep all service records and parts receipts so that proper maintenance can be verified. The manufacturer cannot deny warranty coverage solely on the lack of service records, but it is much more difficult to obtain any type of warranty work if a lack of maintenance is suspected and the owner has no way to show that the maintenance has actually been performed. If you purchase a used vehicle, try to obtain all service records from the previous owner.

Any damage from modifications, abuse, racing, collisions and other similar misuse or mishaps are not covered by warranties and may void existing warranties. Glass breakage is for the most part not covered, unless a defect can be shown.

Traditionally, maintenance items such as spark plugs, belts, hoses, adjustments, and filters were replaced at the owner's expense. Some vehicles now have such items included at no charge or a reduced charge during the warranty period. In any case, as mentioned before, these items should be replaced at the proper intervals.

Also, remember these additional points of interest. In general, warranties do not cover consequential damages; such as loss of time, loss of the use of the vehicle, or lost wages. However, some states do not allow the exclusion of consequential damages, so the above exclusions may not apply to you.

Additionally, manufacturers sometimes offer special programs that will cover some or all of the expense of certain repairs beyond the warranty period. Review your own warranty information to see if your vehicle manufacturer has this type of program, or call your dealer to find out if such a program is in effect.

EXTENDED WARRANTIES

An extended warranty is a coverage offered by vehicle manufacture for purchase on all new models. Extended warranties can be sold to you by the dealership from the manufacture, or through an aftermarket company for them. Some dealerships may offer an extended warranty on a vehicle that is used, but not normally. The warranty is an overextension of the basic warranty on your vehicle. Most components on the extended warranty are ones that should not break for long periods of time such as the engine and transmission.

There are many types of extended warranties sold these days. If your vehicle has a normal warranty of 3 years or 36,000 miles whichever comes first and you are planning on keeping the vehicle for a long time, then you may want to purchase one. All extended warranties are sold to the customer at a cost over and above the price of the vehicle. The higher the warranty year span, the higher the price. A few manufactures will even reimburse you for the price of the warranty if it was never used.

There are usually several year/mileage span extended warranties offered to you such as:

- 5 years or 60,000 miles
- 6 years or 75,000 miles
- 6 years or 100, 000 miles

So when purchasing an extended warranty, look at your particular situation to decide which one is best for you. Do you plan on owning the vehicle for a long period of time? Will the vehicle be used for extended highway travel? Will you be leasing the vehicle and returning it in a few years? All these questions and more should help decide if an extended warranty is best for you.

➡**Many experts agree that extended warranties should not be necessary on makes or models with excellent reputations for reliability. But, you have to look at your own situation. Remember that extended warranties are like insurance policies. You may not ever need them, but if you do you'll be glad to have one (and if you don't have one and find that you need it, you would probably be sorry).**

POWERTRAIN COVERAGE

The powertrain warranty generally covers major parts of the engine, transmission, and final drive unit. Examples of covered parts would be engine cylinder head, block and gaskets; any engine mechanical parts like valves and pistons; transmission parts and components that transmit the power from the engine to the wheels. There may be exceptions on some plans, an example is that the clutch and flywheel are usually not covered on a manual transmission.

ANTI-CORROSION COVERAGE

Anti-corrosion warranties differ quite a bit from manufacturer to manufacturer, but they generally cover rust-through of outer-body sheet metal panels. In a few cases, other sheet metal is covered, but this is not a common practice at this time. Only factory sheet metal is covered. Damage caused to factory sheet metal because non-factory parts were used is not covered. Any collision damage must be properly repaired with factory parts to keep the warranty valid. Non-factory bodies, such as the utility bodies commonly seen on trucks, are not covered by the vehicle manufacturer. In some cases, outer body surface rust is covered if it is the result of a defect in factory-supplied material and workmanship. Surface rust caused by a scratch, for example, is not covered.

Some manufacturers also cover paint damage due to industrial fallout when no defect is involved. This is a type of `goodwill' policy that typically would last no longer than 12 months or 12 thousand miles (19,000km), whichever comes first.

Also, in regards to anti-corrosion warranties, be aware that having the vehicle rust proofed is NOT advised, until after checking your specific warranty. Rust proofing applied by a trained professional can extend your vehicle's life. However, incorrect procedures can damage the vehicle. For that reason, anything that disturbs the factory integrity of the bodywork and/or paint may void a warranty.

The length of the anti-corrosion warranties will usually vary, with the outer-body coverage being the longest, and any other coverage, if applicable, being shorter in duration.

SAFETY RESTRAINT COVERAGE

This warranty covers items such as seat belts and airbags against defects in factory-supplied materials and workmanship. Some manufacturers offer it, check your own warranty information to see if your vehicle has this type of coverage. This warranty is generally longer in duration than the basic warranty on the entire vehicle; one example would be 3/36 coverage on the basic warranty and 5/50 coverage on the restraint system(s).

EMISSION SYSTEM COVERAGE

There are two types of emission system warranties we will discuss. Both are required by U.S. law, and have changed somewhat through the years.

In addition to the usual warranty stipulations, you must be sure that leaded fuel is never used in a vehicle designed to run on unleaded fuel, damages resulting from this would not be covered.

Emissions Defect Coverage

We will discuss this coverage as it applies to passenger cars and light trucks. There are essentially two versions of this warranty, the Federal version and the California version. The Federal version, from 1981 through 1994 covered a period of five years or fifty thousand miles, whichever came first.

The Federal version, beginning in 1995, has a coverage period of 2 years or 24, 000 miles (38,000km), whichever comes first. Some manufacturers may extend this coverage for a longer period. All parts and labor needed to bring the vehicle into compliance should be covered. In summary, the warranty states that the vehicle:

- is designed, built, and equipped to conform, at the time of sale, with the emissions regulations of the Environmental Protection Agency (EPA), and
- is free from defects in factory-supplied materials and workmanship that could cause it to fail to conform to applicable EPA regulations

Here is a sample listing of covered parts:
- Air/Fuel Feedback Control System and Sensors
- Altitude Compensation System
- Catalytic Converter
- Intercooler Assembly-Engine Charger
- Cold Start Enrichment System
- Cold Start Fuel Injector (1)
- Deceleration Controls
- Ignition Distributor
- Electronic Ignition System
- Exhaust Pipe (from exhaust manifold to catalyst)
- Electronic Engine Control Sensors and Switches
- Exhaust Gas Recirculation (EGR) Valve, Spacer, Plate, and related parts
- Exhaust Heat Control Valve
- Exhaust Manifold(s)
- Fuel Filler Cap and Neck Restrictor
- Fuel Injection System
- Fuel Injector Supply Manifold
- Fuel Sensor (1)
- Fuel Tank (gasoline powered vehicles)
- Fuel Tank Pressure Control Valve (1)

- Fuel Vapor Storage Canister, Liquid Separator, and associated Controls
- Ignition Coil and/or Control Module
- Intake Manifold
- Malfunction Indicator Light (MIL)
- PCV System and Oil Filler Cap
- Secondary Air Injection System and related parts
- Spark Control Components
- Spark Plugs and Ignition Wires
- Supercharger Assembly
- Synchronizer Assembly
- Throttle Air Control Bypass Valve
- Throttle Body Assembly
- Turbocharger Assembly
- Three-Way Catalyst (TWC) Air Control Valve
- Volume Air Flow Sensor

(1) Flex-Fuel vehicle only

Remember that this list is a sample. Due to differences in vehicle and engine design, the covered components on your vehicle may vary somewhat from those listed. Items such as related hoses, clamps and gaskets are also covered. Items that require periodic replacement, as shown on the vehicle maintenance schedule, are typically covered only until the end of the first maintenance interval for the specific item in question.

Additionally, there are a few other major emissions components that may be covered by the Emissions Defect Warranty for a longer period, such as eight years/80,000 miles (129,000km) for the 1995 and later Federal version of the warranty. A sample list of these items is as follows:
- Catalytic Converter
- Engine Control Module
- On-Board Diagnostic Device

For California cars and light trucks from 1981 through 1989, the Emissions Defect Warranty provided coverage for five years or 50,000 miles (80,000km), whichever came first. From 1990 through 1997, Emissions Defect Warranty remains in effect for five years or 50,000 miles (80,000km), whichever comes first. Vehicles that are equipped with California certified emissions systems in other areas that have adopted California emissions standards AND California warranty regulations are also covered under the California version of the warranty.

The covered parts are essentially the same as those shown in the proceeding sample lists. This is the short-term Emissions Defect Warranty. The California regulations also require a long-term Emissions Defect Warranty. From 1990 and later, the long-term warranty lasts for seven years or 70,000 miles (112,000km), whichever comes first. Here is a sample list of the covered components:
- Catalytic Converter
- Ignition Distributor
- Exhaust Manifold(s)
- Fuel Injection Rail Assembly
- Fuel Injector
- Fuel Injector Supply Manifold
- Fuel Sensor(1)
- Fuel Tank
- Idle Air Control Valve
- Injector Driver Module
- Intake Manifold
- Intercooler
- Powertrain Control Module(PCM)
- Supercharger
- Synchronizer Assembly
- Throttle Body Assembly
- Transducer Assembly

- Turbocharger Assembly
- Three-Way Catalyst (TWC) Air Control Valve
- Volume Air Flow Sensor

(1) Flex-Fuel vehicle only

Again, keep in mind that this is a sample listing. Check the warranty information for your own vehicle to see which specific items are eligible for coverage.

Emissions Performance Coverage

This warranty applies to vehicles that are registered in areas that require periodic emissions testing. The warranty states that the manufacturer will adjust or repair the vehicle's emission system and/or related parts so that it will pass the emissions test. From 1981 through 1994, Federal vehicles were covered for five years or 50,000 miles (80,000km), whichever came first, except for `primary' emissions parts, which were covered for 2 years or 24,000 miles (38,000km). Primary emissions parts are defined as those, which were not in general use prior to the 1968 model year, and have been added to vehicles for the primary purpose of reducing emissions. This stipulation does not really reduce the number of covered parts by too many; keep in mind that vehicles made before 1968 had very little in the way of emission control devices. Until 1989, California vehicles had the same coverage period. Beginning in 1995, Federal vehicles are covered for 2 years or 24,000 miles (38,000km), whichever comes first. California vehicles, from 1990 through 1995 have a coverage term of three years or 50,000 miles (80,000km), whichever comes first. All of the usual warranty stipulations apply.

There are two other important points in regard to this warranty. In order to make a claim under this warranty, you must be subject to a real penalty, such as a fine or denial of the use of the vehicle because the vehicle failed the emissions test. Also, a vehicle certified for use at sea level will not qualify under this warranty if it fails an emissions test intended for high altitude certified vehicles. The reason for this is that the high altitude emissions standards are more stringent.

To actually make a warranty claim under this warranty, take the vehicle to an authorized dealer or other factory-authorized shop. Take the paperwork that shows that the vehicle failed the emissions test, and tell them that you are seeking a repair under the Emissions Performance Warranty. Having the vehicle's warranty information on hand may also be helpful. The manufacturer has thirty days, or the period specified by your Inspection/Maintenance Program, whichever is shorter, to fix the vehicle or deny the claim. Written notification must be given if the claim is denied, and you should have a written record of the date when the vehicle was presented for repair.

If there are problems involved in getting the vehicle evaluated or repaired, you may agree to extend the deadline, and if there are problems beyond the control of the manufacturer or dealer, the deadline may be automatically extended. Should a deadline be missed for reasons other than these, you are entitled to have the repairs made at the shop of your choice, at the manufacturer's expense.

IM 240 Programs

The topic of emissions testing must also include a few words about IM 240 programs. The abbreviation stands for Inspection/Maintenance 240 Seconds.

Some states require this type of emissions testing. It was mandated to begin on January 1, 1995, but there have been delays in some cases, and earlier program starting dates in others.

There are two types of IM 240 tests, Basic and Enhanced. Factors such as population and pollution levels in a given area are used to determine which test will be utilized. Major metropolitan areas would be more apt to require the Enhanced test, while lightly populated rural areas may not use any type of 1M240 testing at all.

The Basic test is similar to some current IM programs. The Enhanced test, which takes 240 seconds to perform, is designed to provide a more accurate picture of a vehicle's emissions during an actual operating cycle, not just at idle. This is done by testing the vehicle on a chassis dynamometer. Emissions are constantly monitored as the vehicle idles, accelerates, cruises at two different road speeds, and decelerates.

A vehicle that fails the Enhanced test will not be eligible for a waiver until a minimum of $450.00 has been spent to bring the vehicle into compliance. Any repairs performed under warranty do not count towards the minimum. The Basic test has much lower minimum repair limits; generally around $75.00 for pre-1981 vehicles or about $200.00 for 1981 and later models. The requirements and cost vary from state to state, and sometimes even county to county.

WARRANTY DISPUTES

If a warranty issue is not resolved to your satisfaction, there are some steps you can take to try to resolve the problem. The first is always to discuss the complaint with the salespeople or service manager of the dealership where you purchased the vehicle. If no solution is reached, speak with the general manager or the owner of the dealership. In most cases, the general manager or owner does not want an unhappy customer, and should help find a solution or compromise. In cases where coverage is denied, it is a good idea to ask for the reason (in writing) why the claim was denied, and who denied it. Also, find out to whom you can appeal the decision . If the dealership can't help, contact the district or zone office. These are generally listed at the end of the vehicle's warranty information. The zone office may have you try a different dealership repair shop. Remember, the person working on your vehicle may be less knowledgeable about your vehicle's problem than someone at a different location.

If the previous steps weren't satisfactory, you may need to use the customer arbitration board, which serves as an impartial third party in cases of disputes that can't be resolved through the process described above. Always keep all receipts for service, even those performed for no charge. These receipts help prove dates and the number of times you've taken your vehicle for service. Invoking a "lemon law" or taking legal action is usually not necessary. Honest and complete communication of what you feel the problem is and what you expect to be done about it is the best approach. Detailed receipts will help you obtain the best service from the dealership or any other repair shop.

In the case of disputes which involve the Federal or California emissions warranties, you may contact the EPA or the California Air Resources Board (CARB) if you follow the manufacturer's claim procedure through, but you feel that their final decision is unfair. You may write to:

Warranty Complaint
Field Operations and Support Division (6406J)
U.S. Environmental Protection Agency
401 M Street SW
Washington, D.C. 20460
or for emission related information you can contact:
California Air Resources Board
9528 Telstar Avenue
El Monte, CA 91731

Costs of Owning a Vehicle

The costs of owning a vehicle can be broken down into two categories—variable and fixed. Variable costs include fuel, oil, maintenance, and tires and are directly related to the number and type of miles driven. The cost of repairs is also included in this category.

Fixed costs include insurance, license and registration, taxes, and depreciation. Though these may vary from vehicle to vehicle or place to place, these costs are established by business conditions beyond control of the vehicle owner and have less to do with how or when the vehicle is driven.

VARIABLE COSTS

▶ **See Figure 13**

Fuel and Oil—The best way to determine your fuel and oil operating costs is to develop your own figures. As an example, see the accompanying table.

Oil consumption, though not a major expense also varies, and it should be figured in the same way. Remember to add the cost of every oil change. For example, a typical motorist may have the oil changed every 6,000 miles (9,600km), less often if his vehicle is a recent model. One or two quarts of oil may be added between changes. Simply add what you spend on oil during the year, divide the total by the number of miles driven, and add this amount to your variable costs. Generally, the cost of oil represents approximately 3% of the cost per mile for gasoline.

While the most accurate figures are obtained by keeping a record each time you buy gas or oil, it may be sufficient to make the test several times during the year.

Maintenance—Expenses for tune-ups, maintenance, and service items depend largely on the age of the vehicle. The newer it is, the smaller these expenses probably will be. However, even a vehicle under warranty requires regular checkups and service. Money "saved" by neglecting needed service and repairs will usually show up in the form of increased depreciation. This can be prevented by following a regular maintenance schedule.

The only way to determine accurately the cost of maintenance is to keep a record of all expenditures. It's a good idea to keep a small notebook in the glove compartment for this purpose.

Tires—If the vehicle is driven with reasonable care and the wheels are kept properly aligned, tire wear will be kept to a minimum. On the other hand, over or under inflation, high speeds, hard cornering, rapid acceleration, and quick stops all contribute to fast tire wear and increased costs of vehicle operation.

FIXED COSTS

▶ **See Figure 14**

Insurance—There is nothing uniform about insurance premiums. The costs depend on the amount of coverage, where you live, and the purpose for which the vehicle is used. To determine insurance costs, simply add the premiums of all policies you carry that are directly related to vehicle operation, such as property damage and liability, comprehensive and collision.

			odometer reading:
Tank filled			8850
Buy gas	9.7 gallons cost	$ 9.89	9008
Buy gas	9.9 gallons cost	$10.10	9168
Buy gas	10.7 gallons cost	$10.92	9343
TOTAL:	30.3 gallons cost	$30.91	

Miles driven: $9343 - 8850 = 493$
Miles per gallon: $493 \div 30.3 = 16.3$
Cost of gas per mile: $\$19.68 \div 493 = 6.27¢$

8852TG08

Fig. 13 Keeping accurate records will help you estimate you fuel costs

FIGURE YOUR CAR COSTS

Fixed Costs	Yearly Totals
Depreciation (divide by number of years of ownership)	_____
Insurance	_____
Taxes	_____
Licenses and registration	_____
TOTAL FIXED COSTS	_____
Variable Costs	
Gas and oil per mile	_____
Number of miles driven	_____
Cost per year (multiply miles driven by gas and oil per mile)	_____
Maintenance	_____
Tires	_____
Other costs (car wash, repairs, accessories, etc.)	_____
TOTAL VARIABLE COSTS	_____
TOTAL DRIVING COSTS PER YEAR	_____
COST PER MILE (divide yearly total by total miles driven)	_____

8852TG09

Fig. 14 Use this table to calculate your vehicle costs

License, Registration Fees and Taxes—These payments are usually due once a year. No two states use exactly the same schedules. Determine what you spend for license and registration and add the total to your fixed costs. Taxes, such as property or use taxes, should be treated in the same way. Sales or excise taxes, which are paid only when the vehicle is bought, should be considered a part of the total purchase price and not included in calculating annual operating costs.

Depreciation—Depreciation is the largest single expense in owning a vehicle. It is the difference between what you paid for it and what you would get in a trade-in or resale. Depreciation also is the most difficult cost to determine. Vehicles depreciate at different rates, depending on their appearance, mileage on the odometer, and the demand for your particular model at the time you want to dispose of it.

Due to economic conditions and fuel availability, the depreciation of specific makes and models will vary considerably. One figure the average motorist might use to estimate depreciation is the difference between the current market price of his used One figure the average motorist vehicle and the price of a comparable might use to estimate depreciation is the difference between the current market price of a comparable new one with the same optional equipment.

Insurance

▶ **See Figure 15**

There are nearly 132,000,000 motorists driving over 90,000,000 insured vehicles on the nation's highways. Millions of other vehicles are not insured simply because owners cannot afford it.

Vehicle insurance is a $15 billion business that is essentially a game of chance. Insurance companies collect premiums from the people they insure, betting on the chance that they will not have to pay off for bodily injury or property damage claims. It's a risky business with a small profit margin (less than 5%) and the cost that you pay (your premium) is determined by the degree of risk.

HOW YOUR RATE IS DETERMINED

The business of insuring vehicles is based on statistics and probabilities. There are seven factors taken into consideration by an insurer.

Geographic Environment—Rates are based on the geographic area in which you live. Statistics have shown that most accidents occur within

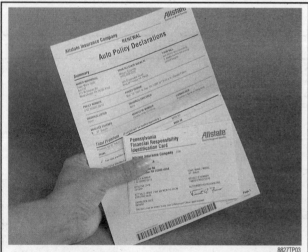

Fig. 15 Every vehicle driven on the road should be insured for financial security

25 miles (40km) of your residence. No matter where an insured person has an accident, if he is at fault or if a claim is paid, it is statistically recorded in the area in which he resides. The territories are rated high or low depending on the experience of the company with drivers living in the territory. If your territory has a high accident record, high medical costs, or high repair costs, your insurance will probably cost more.

Who Uses the Vehicle—The age of the persons driving the vehicle will affect the amount of the premium. Drivers under the age of 24 are involved in 25% of all accidents and are therefore higher risks. The statistics also reveal that male drivers are involved in accidents more than female drivers are and that married males under 30 and married females under 25 are less likely to be involved in an accident than their single counterparts.

How the Vehicle is Used—You will usually be charged a higher premium if you drive your vehicle more than 10 miles (16km) to work, less if it is used for pleasure purposes only. Vehicles not driven to and from work are usually subject to lower premiums.

Driving Record—Statistics prove that the drivers who have had accidents previously or who have been convicted of serious traffic violations are more likely to be involved in an accident than drivers with clean records. Many companies surcharge traffic violations and "at-fault" accidents within the last three years.

Type of Vehicle—The make, model, and engine size are prime rate-determining factors. Studies by the Insurance Institute for Highway Safety show that:
- Within each size group, 2-door models have more injury claims than 4-door models.
- Sports and specialty vehicles have the highest injury claims.
- Subcompacts have the highest percentage of collision claims.

Among vehicles of the same size, sports and specialty models have larger collision claims than other models, and 2-door models frequently have larger claims than 4-door models.

Cost of each claim—Vehicle repair charges, hospital bills, and financial awards vary greatly from area to area. Inflation in the costs of body parts, hospital costs, and repair costs, result in higher premiums.

Discounts—Most companies will offer discounts to young drivers who have successfully completed a driver education course, owners of compact vehicles, and families with more than one vehicle (on the theory that each vehicle is driven less).

TYPES OF VEHICLE INSURANCE

Vehicle insurance protects you against three kinds of risks:
1. In case someone is hurt in a vehicle accident in which you are involved (liability).
2. In case, you destroy someone else's property (property damage).
3. In case your vehicle is stolen or damaged (collision or comprehensive).

Liability insurance

Until 1970, insurance policies protected you; in the event, someone was hurt in an accident through "bodily injury" liability and "medical payments" insurance. If the accident was judged your fault, the bodily injury portion of your policy covered the medical payments of those you injured. Your medical payments insurance covered the medical bills of yourself and any passengers in your vehicle. If the accident was the other person's fault, you collected from his insurance policy under the same arrangement. This system is known as "faultbased," since it involves a question of who was at fault and often resulted in interminable court cases.

Since 1971, 26 states have adopted what has come to be known as "no-fault" insurance. This means that anyone involved in an accident submits claims to, and collects from, their own insurance company, regardless of who is at fault. On the surface, this seems a smooth and equitable way of handling things. However, there is a hitch. In some states, under certain circumstances, even if you are covered under a no-fault policy, persons who are badly injured in accidents can take you to court and sue for additional amounts. In order to sue, damages must exceed a "threshold" amount, which varies from state to state, but it can be as low as $400.

For maximum protection, although you may have no-fault, you need "Bodily Injury Liability."

Property Damage Insurance

As the name implies, this part of the policy covers damages caused to other people's property by your vehicle. It usually covers you if you are driving your own vehicle, someone else's vehicle (with his or her permission), or if someone else is driving your vehicle with your permission

Comprehensive and Collision Insurance

Comprehensive insurance covers damage to your vehicle that results from anything other than a collision. Collision insurance pays the bills if your vehicle is damaged in an accident with another vehicle or if you damage your vehicle, backing into a telephone pole for example.

Both Comprehensive and Collision are sold on a deductible basis. This means that for any claim that you submit, you must pay the deductible amount yourself, before the insurance takes over.

READING THE FINE PRINT

Most auto insurance policies follow a regular form, with each part setting down specific information and conditions.

Declarations—Includes information about the person taking out the policy, the amount of the policy, the kind of coverage, cost, the date and time coverage begins and the date the policy expires.

Insuring agreements—states what the policy will cover.

Exclusions state what the policy will not pay for, sometimes referred to as the "fine print." Some typical exclusions are:
* Intentional damage to your own automobile.
* Damages caused when your automobile is being used as a public or delivery vehicle unless the declarations portion of your policy states that it will be used for this purpose.
* Damages caused while your automobile is being driven by employees of a garage, parking lot or auto sales agency.

Conditions give the policy rules and your duties in case of a loss, such as:
* Report a loss to the company as soon as possible.
* Use reasonable care to prevent further damage to your vehicle.
* Cooperate with the company in settling claims.
* File proper proof of loss.
* Forward all documents concerning suits under your policy to your company.

Endorsements cover changes which must be made in your insurance policy. When this happens, changes are typed on a form called an endorsement, signed by a company official, and attached to your policy.

TYPICAL COVERAGE

Some of the typical coverage afforded by insurance is described below.

Liability covers damages that are the result of negligence on your part. $10,000/$20,000/ $5,000 means that if you have an accident that is your fault, you are covered for $10,000 for any one person you injure, $20,000 for more than one person, and $5,000 for property damage. Bodily injury liability is the $ 10,000/ $20,000 portion of the policy. Property damage liability is the $5,000 portion of the 10/20/5.

You may decide that you need more than just the basic amounts of liability insurance, and higher limits are available. Higher liability coverage will protect you from losing any assets you may have, such as savings accounts or property, should you lose a lawsuit and the person you injured is awarded a sum higher than that covered by no fault.

Personal injury protection or PIP (known as "no-fault") pays for reasonable medical expense and loss of income or earning capacity. PIP is usually available with deductibles, and your premiums will be lower if you choose one of these deductibles.

Physical damage coverage includes those coverage available to a vehicle owner for damages to his vehicle, such as comprehensive, collision, fire, lightning, combined additional coverage, theft, towing, and labor costs.

Collision coverage protects you from losses when your own vehicle is damaged in an accident. Carrying collision insurance is usually voluntary. However, you will be required to reject it in writing.

Basic property protection is a less expensive form of collision that pays for full damages to your vehicle if an accident is not your fault.

Broad form collision is full collision coverage. It pays for all damages to your vehicle if an accident is not your fault and for damages above, a deductible if the accident is your fault.

Comprehensive coverage protects your vehicle from losses other than those caused by collision. Common losses such as fire, theft, windstorm, hail, flood, vandalism and glass breakage, malicious mischief, or riot are covered under comprehensive.

Fire, theft, and combined additional coverage is an alternative to comprehensive coverage and usually covers the same as comprehensive except for glass breakage. It applies to "named perils" which are specifically listed in your insurance policy.

Towing and labor costs pays a stated amount for towing and labor costs in an emergency.

Medical payments insurance pays for medical, surgical, or dental expenses. It will pay up to the limits you have chosen regardless of fault.

Uninsured motorist coverage pays if you are hit by an uninsured motorist and your loss of income and medical bills are more than the $5,000 paid under the personal injury protection portion of your no-fault policy.

Your vehicle insurance shopping should include a scrutiny of all discounts and rate structures available.

SHAVING INSURANCE COSTS

◆ See Figure 16

Auto insurance rates take a big bite of the family budget, especially when young drivers are involved. Here are a few suggestions on how to save money on your policy.

First, you might consider buying collision and comprehensive coverage with higher deductibles. Collision coverage can be reduced about 17% when the deductible is changed from $100–$200. Going from $50–$100, deductible for comprehensive could work out to a 20% saving. Carefully evaluate the need for collision and the amount of deductible, but don't skimp on bodily injury or property damage liability.

Another possibility is to drop collision insurance entirely on an older vehicle, because regardless of how much coverage you carry, the insurance company will pay only up to the vehicle's "book value." For example, if your vehicle requires $1,000 in repairs but its book value is only $500, the insurance company is required only to pay $500.

Investigate special discounts offered by some companies in some states. They may be available for young drivers who have successfully completed driver education courses. There also are special discounts for those with good driving records, for college students attending a school more than 100 miles (160km) from home, for women over 30, and for families with two or more vehicles.

RATE COMPARISON WORKSHEET

COMPANY NAMES: _____ _____ _____

Type of Coverage	Amount of Coverage	Annual Rates	Annual Rates	Annual Rates
Liability	$_____	$_____	$_____	$_____
Medical payments	_____	_____	_____	_____
Property damage	_____	_____	_____	_____
Uninsured motorist	_____	_____	_____	_____
Collision	_____ (Deductible)	_____	_____	_____
Comprehensive	_____ (Deductible)	_____	_____	_____
Other	_____	_____	_____	_____
	_____	_____	_____	_____
TOTAL		$_____	$_____	$_____

8852TG10

Fig. 16 When comparing insurance cost obtain estimates from at least three different companies

The lowest premium should not be your only goal. You should consider that you want to get the satisfaction you're entitled to when you make a claim and that your claims will neither increase your premium in the future nor be grounds for canceling your policy. If you stay with your present company and have an accident, your company will consider your previous record. If you are getting good service from your present company, making a switch may not be to your advantage in the end.

31

HOW TO DEAL WITH MOTOR VEHICLE EMERGENCIES

HOW TO DEAL WITH MOTOR VEHICLE EMERGENCIES

▶ **See Figure 1**

At one time or another, most drivers encounter some sort of emergency involving a malfunction of their vehicle or a situation requiring emergency driving techniques. If these emergencies are not handled properly, the result can be accident, injury or even death.

In an emergency, panic is the real enemy. Emergency plans, like the ones described here, can help prevent panic and possibly save lives. Following are some of the most common emergencies and how they can be handled, so that accident prevention, along with pedestrian and motorist safety, are the prime concerns.

Fig. 1 By now we shouldn't even have to say it, BEER IS FOR AFTER driving NOT BEFORE!

Stopping on the Highway

Many emergencies require stopping on the highway. Stopping on a highway for any reason is dangerous, so if you must stop, observe the following precautions:

• If the highway has paved shoulders, signal your intention to pull off the highway, pull off at near traffic speed, then slow down. If the shoulder is unpaved, signal a right turn and slow down to a safe speed before pulling off the paved roadway.

• In dusk, darkness, or bad weather, leave your low-beam headlights on and turn on your interior lights and your four-way flasher.

• If you have to stop in a risky location (such as over the crest of a hill or on a curve), get everyone out of the vehicle and well away from traffic.

• Place a flare or other warning device just behind the vehicle and another at least 300 feet (91m) farther back. Retrieve them before you drive away.

• If you need help, raise the hood and tie a white cloth to the antenna or left door handle.

➡**The hazard (emergency) lights on many vehicles will not operate when the brakes are applied. Once you are off the road (or if stranded on the road), you should shut off the engine, put the vehicle in PARK, apply the parking brake, and take your foot off the brake pedal.**

Throttle Sticking

You're driving along a street or highway and for some reason, you must slow down. You reduce the foot pressure on the accelerator but the accelerator pedal does not respond and the vehicle does not slow down. On the other hand, for some reason, the accelerator pedal is suddenly depressed to the floor, and the vehicle lurches forward, although you've taken your foot off the accelerator. What can you do?

If this situation occurs on the open highway and you have a lot of distance between you and other traffic, you can first lightly tap the accelerator pedal a few times to see if it will spring back to its normal position. If this fails, try to pull the pedal up with the toe of your shoe, or have a front seat passenger reach down and do it. Don't reach down yourself because that would divert your attention from the road.

If you must slow or stop rapidly, turn your ignition to **OFF** and apply the brakes. However, be sure you turn the key to **OFF**, not **LOCK**. On most vehicles, you can't turn the steering wheel when the key is in the lock position. If you have power steering and power brakes, turning off the ignition will require increased physical effort to steer and brake the vehicle as the vehicle slows. As the vehicle slows down, steer it off the roadway, if possible.

➡**Off means any key position that will turn off the engine but not lock the steering. Ignition systems on vehicles vary. Make sure you know which position will cut the engine without locking the steering.**

After you stop the vehicle, look for the source of trouble. The accelerator pedal may be binding on the floor mat or the rug in your vehicle, and you can easily free the pedal by moving the rug or mat. If the problem is not in the passenger compartment, look in your engine compartment and check the accelerator linkage. Some of the parts may be stuck or binding and a little oil (from the dipstick used to check your oil) may solve the problem.

If you can't locate and remedy the problem (for example, it may be caused by a broken or missing accelerator return spring or by a broken motor mount), don't drive the vehicle. Get help so the problem can be corrected.

If you think you've corrected the problem, make certain before driving the vehicle. Apply the emergency (or parking) brake firmly, put the gear selector in Park or Neutral, and start the vehicle. Exercise the accelerator pedal a few times to make sure it returns to its normal position after you remove your foot from the pedal. Then put the vehicle in gear and try revving the engine a few times before releasing the parking brake and proceeding on your way.

Brake Failure

Newer vehicles have a split braking system designed to reduce the possibility of total brake failure (loss of brakes on all four wheels). They have a warning light on the instrument panel which lights up when your brakes are failing due to such problems as loss of pressure in the braking system. When the brake failure light comes on, slow, pull off the road, and don't proceed until you have the problems corrected or determine that you can drive safely to the nearest service facility. Because of the split braking system, the chances are that you will have some braking power left when the brake failure light comes on, but you may have to apply more force to the brake pedal and will need a greater distance to stop. If half of the braking system remains, proceed cautiously to the nearest service station or garage.

However, if you have a complete brake failure, what can you do to stop? There are several things you can try, but you must act rapidly.

• First, get off the highway onto the shoulder or other clear area, if possible.

• Try pumping your brakes rapidly to bring up your brake pressure.

• If pumping doesn't work, put the gear selector in a lower range (DI, 2, or equivalent in vehicles with automatic transaxles/transmissions or shift to a lower gear in vehicles with manual transaxles/transmissions) to give some braking power from the engine, and apply the emergency or parking brake with increased force.

• If none of the above works and you are in danger of crashing into someone or something, or of going down an embankment, there is one more thing you can try—but only as a last resort. Turn the ignition **OFF** and move the gear selector to low. This may damage your transaxle/transmission, but it may help you to stop in a real emergency.

If your brakes fail on a hill or mountain grade and the above remedies do not work, look for something to sideswipe—a snow bank, a guard rail, dirt mounds on the side of the road, or anything that will slow you down.

Driving with Anti-lock Brake Systems (ABS)

When used properly, an Anti-lock Brake System (ABS) is a safe and effective braking system. ABS allows the driver to maintain directional stability, control over steering, and in some situations, to reduce stopping distances during emergency braking situations, particularly on wet and slippery road surfaces. To gain this safety advantage, drivers must learn how to operate their ABS correctly.

An anti-lock braking system works with the regular brakes on your vehicle. Your vehicle will always have its foundation braking system, even if ABS were to fail. ABS simply keeps the foundation brakes from locking up. Only the foundation brakes are needed in most stops. ABS activates only in slippery conditions or during panic stops when a driver slams on the brakes, thus causing them to lock up. In vehicles not equipped with ABS, the driver can manually pump the brakes to prevent wheel lockup. In vehicles equipped with ABS, the driver's foot should remain firmly on the brake pedal, allowing the system to automatically pump the brakes.

When your brakes lock up on wet and slippery roads or during a panic stop, you lose steering control and your vehicle can spin. ABS prevents wheel lockup so that your vehicle stays in a straight line. If your vehicle has ABS control on all four wheels, you also keep steering control. If you have steering control, it is possible to avoid a crash by steering around hazards if a complete stop cannot be accomplished in time.

AVERAGE STOPPING DISTANCES

Two factors are involved with stopping the vehicle: 1) Driver reaction time, and 2) Vehicle braking efficiency. Vehicle weight and velocity are also important considerations in total braking. Here are how the above-named factors enter into overall braking:

Miles Per Hour	20	30	40	50	60	70	80	90
Driver Reaction Time (in feet)[1]	21	31	41	51	62	72	82	92
Braking Distance (in feet)[2]	17	39	70	109	156	213	278	360
Total	38	70	111	160	218	285	360	452

[1] Before a driver's mind and body react to the need for vehicle braking, the vehicle travels this far.
[2] Even excellent brakes require time to "take ahold," and this means the vehicle will travel further when the brakes are first applied than it will when maximum braking is achieved.

Weight/Speed Relationship:
• If weight is doubled—stopping power must be doubled.
• If speed is doubled—stopping power must be increased four times.
• If weight and speed are doubled—stopping power must be increased 8 times.

Coefficient of Friction/Temperature/Fade Relationship:

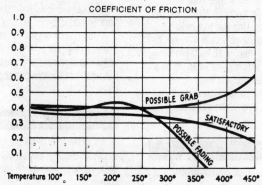

Differently formulated brake lining materials react differently in identical braking/temperature situations, as indicated above. Note that linings with a "cold" coefficient of friction of approximately D.4 behave almost the same up to a temperature of approximately 250°F (121.11°C), thereinafter each lining takes on a different operating characteristic. Only the highest grade linings should be used in every application.

8852UC01

Most newer models offer ABS as either standard or optional equipment. There are different ways to find out whether your vehicle has an anti-lock brake system:

• Read the owner's manual.

• Check your instrument panel for an amber ABS indicator light after you turn on the ignition.

• When you buy, lease or rent, ask your dealer or rental car company.

In many vehicles, drivers may experience a rapid pulsation of the brake pedal—almost as if the brakes are pushing back at you. Sometimes the pedal could suddenly drop. Also, the valves in the ABS controller may make a noise that sounds like grinding or buzzing. In some vehicles you may feel a slight vibration—this means the ABS brakes are working. In other vehicles, you can't even tell when ABS is working. It is important NOT to take your foot off the brake pedal when you hear noise or feel pulsation, but instead continue to apply firm pressure.

If you normally pump the brakes, you shouldn't do so if you have ABS. Just hold your foot firmly on the brake pedal and ignore the sounds or pedal pulsing you may experience. And remember that you can still steer.

What ABS does is similar to a person pumping the brakes. It automatically changes the pressure in your vehicle's brake lines to maintain maximum brake performance just short of locking up the wheels. ABS does this very rapidly with electronics.

ABS systems are all very similar in the way they control brake pressure, but some systems are designed to prevent only the rear wheels from locking up. These rear-wheel-only systems are found on some older pickups and sport utility vehicles. Rear wheel ABS keeps your vehicle from spinning out of control, but you will not have steering control if the front wheels lock up. All other ABS systems—including those for cars and minivans—are designed to keep all four wheels from locking up. If you own a pickup or sport utility vehicle, you can check your owner's manual to see what type of ABS you have.

ABS is designed to help the driver maintain control of the vehicle during emergency braking situations, not make the vehicle stop more quickly. ABS will shorten stopping distances on wet or slippery roads and many systems will shorten distances on dry roads. On very soft surfaces, such as loose gravel or unpacked snow, an ABS system may actually lengthen stopping distances. In wet or slippery conditions, you should still make sure you drive carefully, always keep a safe distance behind the vehicle in front of you, and maintain a speed consistent with the road conditions.

Read your owner's manual for more details on the complete operation and benefits of ABS. The anti-lock brake system is speed sensitive, and the brake system will not activate at very slow speeds. One way to familiarize yourself with the operation of ABS is to test drive the vehicle at a speed above which the ABS activates (usually above 10 mph or 16 km/h) in an unobstructed parking lot and stand on the brakes. This is easier to do on a wet and slippery road surface. The anti-lock system should prevent the wheels from skidding. Pulsation may be felt in the brake pedal and you will hear a clicking sound. Avoid pumping the brake, even if the brake pedal is pulsating.

Loss of Steering

Loss of steering can occur suddenly and without warning. Something in the steering mechanism or its related components may break, fall off, or jam, leaving the driver with no control of the vehicle's direction.

In such situations, there is little you can do except to apply the brakes to come to a stop as quickly as possible. While applying the brakes, some warning to other motorists and pedestrians may be possible by turning on your emergency flashers, using your headlights, blowing your horn, and using hand signals.

To those accustomed to power steering or power brakes, a malfunction in the system providing the power may lead the driver to think his brakes or steering have failed. If your vehicle is equipped with these power features, and if you suddenly find that steering is more difficult, or the brakes will not respond when you touch the brake pedal, you can still steer and brake. It takes considerably more effort, but it can be done. Proceed with caution until your vehicle is repaired.

Fires

UNDER THE HOOD OR UNDER THE DASHBOARD

Fires are generally caused by a fault in the electrical system or by leakage in the fuel system, which may cause raw gas to leak onto a hot engine. When such a fire develops, pull off the roadway just as soon as it is safe to do so. Turn off the ignition, and get out of the vehicle in a safe manner.

Every vehicle should have a fire extinguisher for emergencies. If you don't have an extinguisher, fires in the engine compartment can sometimes be put out by throwing dirt on them. You can also try smothering the fire by using a heavy cloth. Be careful when raising the hood to get at such a fire—use a rag to protect your hand when releasing the hood latch and turn your head aside as the hood is released to prevent facial burns from flashing flames.

✳✳ CAUTION

Consider the severity of the fire and the risk involved before trying to put it out. If the fire is a major one or is a fuel-fed fire, stand clear of the vehicle and wait for the fire department.

If you don't have a fire extinguisher and there is a passenger with you, have him flag down a passing motorist (especially a truck) who may have a fire extinguisher.

If the fire occurs while you're driving in a city or town, ask a passerby to summon the fire department.

Finally, don't attempt to drive the vehicle until the cause of the blaze is determined and the problem corrected, including any damage caused by the fire itself.

IN THE REAR OF THE VEHICLE

Fires in the rear of the vehicle are potentially the most hazardous since most vehicles have their gas tanks in the rear. The biggest danger here is explosion of the gas tank.

If you notice smoke or flames coming from the rear of your vehicle, immediately pull off the road to a safe spot. Get all passengers out of the vehicle and remain at a great distance from it. Warn motorists and passersby of the danger, and have someone call the nearest fire department.

Loss of Oil Pressure

A sudden loss of oil pressure, if not promptly corrected, can result in extensive damage to your vehicle's engine as well as a highway breakdown. Most vehicles have an oil pressure light on the instrument panel. This light comes on as soon as you turn on the ignition. Shortly after the engine starts, this light should go out. If the light doesn't go out when the engine is running, or if it comes on while you're driving, you have trouble. You may not have enough oil in your engine, or your oil pump may be bad and not pumping oil through the engine.

If the oil light comes on and stays lit, the first thing to do after pulling off the road is turn off the ignition and check your oil. If the oil level is at or below the "ADD" or "MIN" mark on the dipstick, add oil before driving the vehicle any farther. A spare can of oil carried in your trunk is ideal for just such an emergency. If this was the problem, the oil light should go out when you restart the vehicle.

It is not advisable to operate the engine with the oil light ON. If there are no abnormal engine noises and if your oil check shows you have enough oil, in an emergency you may cautiously drive, with the oil light ON, a few miles to the nearest service facility but no farther. Get a mechanic to check the vehicle, because something else is wrong. Do this only as a last resort, and if possible have the vehicle towed to the service facility.

Windshield Wiper Failure

Windshield wipers may fail when you need them most. To lower the odds of your wipers failing, periodically check them. Make sure you have good blades and that they are properly adjusted to conform to the shape of the windshield.

If you have the disappearing type wipers, periodically check the opening to the front of your windshield. Do this more frequently in the fall and winter. Remove leaves, twigs, snow or ice from the wiper recesses and from around the wiper motor shaft and wiper arms. Such obstructions can place a strain on your wiper motor and result in wiper failure.

If you have a failure on the highway (loose wiper, motor ceases to turn wipers, blade flies off), get off the highway (open the window and stick your head out to see, if necessary) and see if you can correct the problem. Some obstruction may be hampering wiper movement, or it may be possible to push a loose wiper arm on the spindle more firmly.

If you find that you can't fix the wipers yourself, wait until the rain or snowstorm has let up, then proceed with caution to the nearest service facility. If it's impractical to wait, you'll have to get help.

Hood Pop-up

Failure of hood latch (both primary and secondary) or improper closure of hood and subsequent failure of the secondary latch can result in the hood popping open while you are driving. When the hood opens in this fashion, it will block your view of the road in front of you.

A federal safety standard, which became effective in January 1969, requires that a front opening hood, which in any open position partially or completely obstructs a driver's forward view through the windshield, be provided with a second latch position on the hood latch system or with a second hood latch system. Despite this, hood latch failure can occur and you should know what to do if your hood suddenly pops open while driving.

The first thing to remember is don't panic and don't panic stop. If you apply your brakes suddenly and hard, you may be inviting a rear end collision. Instead, ease the vehicle to the right or left (depending on the lane of traffic you're in and the room you have on either side) and use your limited view from the left window for forward steering reference (you may have to stick your head out the window to look). Also, glance in your rear view mirror to see how much room you have between you and the vehicle behind you. Remove your foot from the accelerator and apply your brakes slowly. Turn on your emergency flashers and give a hand signal to indicate that you are going to stop. After you've signaled drivers to the rear, pull off the road (to the left or the right depending on the type highway and lane you're driving in) and try to remedy your problem.

If, for some reason, you cannot get the vehicle off the highway (for example, if you're driving on a bridge or have a guardrail to the right,), do not leave your vehicle. After traffic has cleared behind you, proceed with caution to the nearest point at which you can safely exit the highway.

✵ CAUTION

A frequent cause of hood popup is the failure to close the hood properly after checking the oil, radiator or battery. Get accustomed to the sound made by your hood when it is closed firmly. Thereafter, if you fail to hear the customary "THUNK" when you or an attendant closes your hood, check the hood before proceeding.

Submersion in Water

Emergencies of this nature are very rare and unpredictable, and speedy and proper reactions by the driver and passengers are critical to survival. If your vehicle goes through a bridge railing, over an embankment into a deep body of water, or is surrounded by flooding waters, the following tips may help you survive:

• Vehicles with their windows and doors closed will float for a few minutes. Don't try to open a door to get out because the water pressure will hold it shut.

• Windows can be rolled down easily, so open the window (windows in case of passengers) and use the opening as an escape route.

• If you have power windows, open them immediately before they short out. If they do short out and won't open, your only recourse is to try to break them out with a heavy hard object. The tempered glass used in modern vehicles is hard to break.

• If you can't open or break a window and must open a door, remember that vehicles with engines in the front will sink nose first. This will push some air to the rear of the vehicle near the roof, helping to equalize the pressure and making it easier to open a door.

Loss of Lug Nuts on the Wheels

If you notice a wobble in a wheel or hear a rattling noise coming from a wheel, especially at low speeds, the problem may be loose lug nuts or a lug nut that has come off the wheel stud and is rattling inside the hub cap or wheel cover. This problem is often caused by improper tightening of the nuts when a tire is replaced, or by faulty lug bolt threads that will not retain the lug nuts tightly.

Take care of such a problem immediately before you lose a wheel. Pull off the road, display warning devices, remove the hub caps or wheel covers, and check the tightness of all the lug nuts. Tighten all the nuts that may be loose. If all the lug nuts are tight, the sound could be caused by a faulty or burned-out bearing. Drive cautiously to the nearest service facility for repairs.

If you've already lost more than one nut from a wheel, borrow one nut (no more) from another wheel so that you can tighten the wheels adequately. Then, at your first opportunity, replace all the missing lug nuts.

If two or more of the wheel studs are too badly stripped to permit tightening of the nuts, leave the vehicle beside the road and get help. Have all faulty lug nuts or lugs replaced as necessary.

Exhaust System Failures

There's nothing you can do about a blown muffler or broken tailpipe when you're out on the highway except to get the problem taken care of as soon as you can.

Sometimes a hanger holding your muffler or tailpipe in position can break due to rust and corrosion. The muffler or tailpipe may separate and drag along the pavement. You may be able to hear the dragging noise. You'll also hear the loud engine noise caused by a damaged muffler. When this happens, pull off the road and examine your tailpipe and muffler. Often a temporary fix can be made by pushing the muffler/tailpipe in place or raising it and holding it in place with a piece of wire or a coat hanger.

✴✴ CAUTION

Wait for the exhaust system to cool down. You can be severely burned if you grasp a muffler or tailpipe while it is hot. Until the exhaust system is repaired, drive with a side window at least partially open to prevent carbon monoxide accumulation in the passenger compartment.

Flat Tires and Blowouts

▶ See Figure 2

A blowout will be sudden. You'll feel it in the wheel and you may hear it. You may feel a part of the vehicle dip. Control of the vehicle may be difficult. A flat tire will also be felt in the handling of the vehicle and steering may become unnatural, but this is more gradual than a blowout.

If you have a flat tire or a blowout on the highway, get a firm grip on the wheel and apply your brakes gently to slow. Pull off the road to a safe spot where you have enough room to park and get out of the vehicle without danger to yourself and without causing a traffic hazard for other motorists. Don't slam on the brakes. Sudden braking may throw your vehicle into a spin or out of control.

If you can't pull off the road where you are, drive to a spot where you can pull off and change the tire safely. Do this even if you have to drive on a flat or blown-out tire—but drive slowly and put on your emergency flashers.

Don't try to change a tire on uneven or hilly ground. It's better to risk ruining a tire or wheel by driving on a flat tire than to risk having a jack slip when you're changing a tire on uneven ground.

Tire sealants are available for application prior to having a flat. These sealants will seal most small tread punctures, allowing you to get the vehicle to a repair center.

Another type of sealant, one popular brand of which is called "Fix-A-Flat®," can be used to seal and inflate tires after a small tread puncture occurs. The vehicle should then be taken to have the tire permanently repaired.

➡ **Tire sealants are intended for treating tread punctures only; they are not effective against sidewall damage.**

Fig. 2 The tire sealant on the left is added prior to a puncture to prevent flats; the sealant on the right is added after a puncture to repair flats

Driving on Flooded Roads or in Heavy Rain

▶ See Figures 3 and 4

Driving under these conditions can result in several major problems, including engine drown-out, brake failure, loss of vehicle control, and hydroplaning, which results in loss of steering control (water builds up between the tires and the road, causing the vehicle to "float" on a layer of water).

Every year people drown trying to drive across flooded roads. Before crossing a flooded road, know the depth of the water or don't cross it. If you drive through a deep puddle, especially if your vehicle is moving fast, water can be thrown up into your engine compartment and cause your vehicle to stall out due to moisture on your spark plug wires, coil, or distributor. A vehicle moving in the other direction can cause the same problem if it's moving too fast and throws a lot of water (or road slush in case of a snow-storm) onto your vehicle. If you encounter deep puddles or high water along the highway, drive through slowly.

Fig. 3 Don't drive through large puddles too fast, you could hit a hidden pothole or lose control of the vehicle

Fig. 4 Remember that heavy rain and flooded roadways will reduce available traction

If your vehicle stalls out, try to coast to the side of the road and wait for the engine to dry out. If you know the parts of your electrical system, the drying out process can be quickened by taking a dry rag and wiping the plugs, wires, and coil, and by drying the inside of the distributor cap.

If your vehicle stalls in the middle of a puddle and you can't move it, and if you're near a stream that is overflowing onto the highway, be alert to the possibility of a flash flood. For your own safety, you may have to leave the vehicle where it is and seek shelter until the water recedes.

After moving through water, your brakes may have lost their stopping power. Apply your brakes lightly while driving to dry out the linings and other components.

Driving on Snow and Ice

♦ **See Figures 5 and 6**

Driving safely on snow and ice requires caution, alertness, and skill. Adhering to the following tips will help.

START GENTLY

• Install all season tires or, preferably, snow tires, on all four wheels, before the first snowfall and add chains when the going is difficult. On

8852UG01

Fig. 5 Winter driving requires special care to maintain traction and avoid accidents

8852UP02

Fig. 6 Winter chemicals can improve driveability and visibility for your vehicle

loosely packed snow, snow tires increase traction 50% and the tire chains quadruple traction.

➡ In areas where snow is anticipated, snow tires are recommended for all four wheels, whether the vehicle be Front Wheel Drive (FWD), Rear Wheel Drive (RWD) or All Wheel Drive (AWD).

• Start with an easy foot on the accelerator—start out in second gear on manual transaxle/transmission vehicles, or in LOW on automatic transaxle/transmission vehicles. Don't spin the wheels. Traction is greatest just before the wheels spin.

• If the wheels start to spin, try rocking the vehicle forward and backward. If you dig yourself a pocket, use sand or traction mats to get out. Do not stand behind the wheel while performing this maneuver, as the driven tires will often send out debris. Keep the front wheels pointed straight ahead when possible.

• Once underway, keep going. When approaching a hill, keep far enough behind the vehicle ahead so you will not have to slow or stop. A little extra speed at the bottom of the hill will give extra momentum to help carry you over the top. If the wheels start to spin, release the accelerator slightly.

• During snow and ice conditions, leave yourself an "out" when you park. On a downhill slope, leave ample space in front of your vehicle so you can pull out without backing. Avoid parking on an upgrade unless there is ample room to back out.

TURN GRADUALLY

• Icy surfaces make steering difficult. Slow down before reaching curves. It may be necessary to creep around curves to avoid sideway skids. When entering a curve, turn the steering wheel gradually and no further than necessary. On icy curves, traction may sometimes be improved by using the shoulder.

• If the rear of the vehicle starts skidding, release the accelerator and steer the front of the vehicle in the direction of the skid. As soon as the vehicle starts to straighten out, straighten the front wheels. Don't oversteer.

• On a winter day when the road surface is clear, watch for icy patches in shaded areas, beneath overpasses, and on bridges. These can easily cause a skid if you are going too fast.

STOP GENTLY

Experience has shown that stopping on glare ice and hard-packed snow can take up to ten times the braking distance on a dry road. However, a vehicle equipped with studded tires on the drive wheels alone can reduce stopping distance under these conditions by 30% at 32°F (0°C). In other words, a normal stopping distance of 200 feet (61m) on glare ice would be reduced to 140 feet (43m) .

➡ Studded tires are illegal in many states. Be sure to check with your local authorities before installing studded tires.

Be especially wary on days when the temperature rises to 32°F (0°C). At that temperature, stopping distances on ice are twice as great as at 0° F. Sleet, which is treacherous and slick, also forms at 32°F (0°C).

• Follow other vehicles at greater distances to compensate for longer stopping distances.

• Pump the brakes when stopping. This gives maximum steering control while the brakes are off, and maximum braking while the brakes are applied.

• Reduce speed to a minimum when going over the crest of a hill, and starting down. Put the vehicle in second gear (manual) or low range (automatic) and pump the brakes to keep the speed down. On manual transaxle/transmission equipped vehicles, avoid the use of low gear, as this tends to make the rear wheels skid.

• Keep the tires properly inflated. To avoid swerving while braking, the tire pressures on each axle must be equal.

• Drive defensively. Slow on slippery roads and at intersections. Increase the following distance between you and the vehicle in front of you. Other vehicles may not have the advantage of studded tires and won't stop as quickly as a vehicle that does. Avoid the abrupt use of brakes, acceleration or steering on turns and sharp curves, and watch out for wind gusts. Never jam on the brakes—pump them to avoid locking wheels, which can cause a skid.

IF A SKID STARTS

The most important thing to do when your car starts to lose traction and enters a skid is to keep driving! Just because your car isn't going the way you initially expected it to go, this is no time to give up on the situation. With a little thought, training and practice, a skid can be corrected for and reduced in severity.

The best way of correcting for a skid is not to get into one in the first place. Keep your speeds controlled and within the realm of traction. If you sense that your vehicle is starting to skid, utilize the following techniques:

1. Don't panic! "Keep your cool" and remain focused. Many situations are only made worse by sudden, panic induced reactions.

2. Ease up on the accelerator and, if equipped with a manual transaxle/transmission, press in the clutch. Sometimes this is the only thing that you need to do, and the vehicle will stop skidding. Do not "saw" at the wheel and do not jam on the brakes! Hitting the brakes hard at this time is about the worst thing you could do!

➡ If the vehicle skid is preceded by a tire blowout, it is especially critical not to jam on the brakes; doing so could result in further loss of control. For additional information, refer to Flat Tires and Blowouts, earlier in this section.

3. If the vehicle continues to skid, gently turn the wheels in the direction the car is skidding. Hopefully, the tires will regain traction and allow you to steer the car back into a direction of safety. Make all your steering motions gently with the wheel. If you slash at the wheel, you will not help the tires do their job.

4. If you have a four wheel drive vehicle, a gentle application of the accelerator pedal can help the vehicle regain stability. This is only true if the vehicle is presently in four wheel drive mode and, if applicable, you let the clutch back out with the vehicle in gear. This is a technique best left to people who have practiced this manuever. Find a big parking lot to try this out the next time it rains.

5. In the worse case, the vehicle may start to spin. Even then, don't panic! There is an old saying that goes, "In a spin, both feet in." This means to press in the clutch (if applicable) and apply the brakes as hard as you can. This will lock up the tires and allow the vehicle to slide to a stop, while still going in the direction it was going. If the wheels aren't locked up, the vehicle can go all over the place as the tries grip and let go in an unpredictable fashion. If the vehicle is equipped with an Antilock Brake System (ABS), be prepared to steer the vehicle, since the ABS will try to keep the wheels from locking.

6. Once you have regained control of the vehicle, be ready to head for safety, since you may have slid out of your lane. You haven't stopped driving yet! Once you have composed yourself, relax and allow the excitement to pass.

These techniques can be practiced in a large parking lot during rainy or snowy conditions. With a slippery surface, the speeds to start the car slipping will be lower and you can practice in a safer, more controlled manner. After a while, you will become comfortable driving and better equipped to keep yourself out of trouble.

First Aid Supplies For Your Vehicle

♦ **See Figures 7 and 8**

Many of the little problems that can disable a vehicle along the roadway can be taken care of by the driver if he has some simple tool or some little thing like a piece of tape or wire. You don't have to be a mechanic to fix many of the little things that can go wrong. Your vehicle's fan belt may become loose because the bolt holding the alternator in position became loose; this would be reflected by the warning light on your dashboard indicating that the alternator is not charging. A wire may become disconnected, a tailpipe hanger may break, and so on. The following is a list of some of the things you can carry in your trunk or glove compartment that you may find useful from time to time:

NECESSARY ITEMS

Glove Compartment

• The names, addresses, and telephone number of someone to call in an emergency

8852UG02

Fig. 7 You should keep a variety of emergency equipment in your vehicle

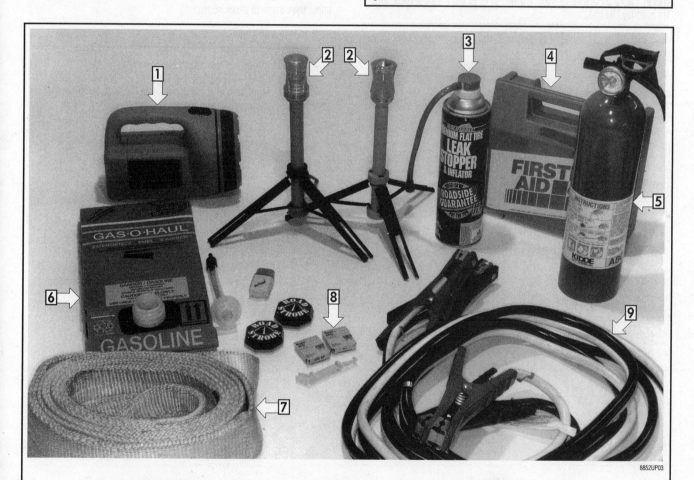

8852UP03

1. Lantern (or flashlight)	4. First aid kit	7. Tow strap
2. Flares and stands	5. Fire extinguisher	8. Fuses and fuse puller
3. Tire sealant	6. Folding fuel container	9. Jumper cables

Fig. 8 A variety of emergency items should always be kept in your vehicle

- Spare fuses for the electrical system
- A good flashlight with reliable batteries
- An ice scraper for winter driving
- A pocket knife

Trunk

- Spare tire (with enough air in it)
- Can of tire sealant
- Fire extinguisher
- First aid kit
- Jack and lug wrench for changing tires
- Flares or reflective day/night devices

VERY USEFUL ITEMS

- An empty can to carry gasoline (if you run out of gas) and a plastic jug of water (if your engine boils over and you lose your coolant)

❉❉ CAUTION

Never carry gasoline in your trunk—this is very dangerous and frequently illegal.

- Pliers—useful for tightening clamps, small nuts that may work loose, and twisting wires
- Screwdrivers—several sizes, including a Phillips head
- Adjustable wrench or small set of open-end wrenches—to tighten nuts and bolts that may have worked loose
- Electrical and duct tape—to repair broken or frayed wires and to temporarily stop small leaks in a hose until you can get to a service facility
- Wire—to temporarily hold a muffler or tailpipe in place if one of the hangers breaks or falls off
- Rags—to dry up your distributor or wet wires if your engine is drowned out in heavy rain or high water
- Battery jumper cables—to get your vehicle started if your battery is weak, especially in the winter

➡**Refer to the "Electrical System/Battery and Cables" section for details on how to use jumper cables.**

- Piece of sandpaper—useful for cleaning dirty battery terminals when the vehicle won't start
- Bottle of engine oil—nice to have when the oil light comes on and you're far from a service station

OTHER USEFUL ITEMS

- Air compressor (cigarette lighter plug-in type)—to use when one of your tires has developed a slow leak and you'd rather drive to a service station to have it changed than do it yourself
- Plastic sheets—for changing a tire in the rain or if you have to get under the vehicle to check something

FOR WINTER DRIVING

- Tire chains—even if you don't have snow tires
- A small shovel—to help you get out of ruts and snow banks
- A small bag of sand or traction mats—to throw under the wheels for better traction if you are stuck in ice or snow

32

WAYS TO SAVE FUEL

WAYS TO SAVE FUEL 32-2

WAYS TO SAVE FUEL

Fuel Economy

There are over 136,000,000 passenger cars registered in the United States, traveling an average of 12,000–18,000 miles (19,000–29,000km) per year. In total, private vehicles consume close to 90 billion gallons of gasoline each year, which is about ⅔ of the oil imported by the United States every year.

The federal government's goal is to reduce gasoline consumption progressively each year. Varieties of methods are either implemented or under serious consideration, all of them affecting your driving and the vehicles you drive. In addition to "down-sizing," the industry is using and investigating alternative engines, alternate fuels, smaller and lighter vehicles, and streamlining, to name a few, in an effort to meet the federally mandated Corporate Average Fuel Economy (CAFE) standards.

CAFE is not the same as mpg. Miles per gallon refers to the miles that any given vehicle will travel on a single gallon of fuel. The CAFE figure is a measure of average fuel consumption of a manufacturer's entire fleet. To determine the CAFE number, the manufacturer uses the EPA miles-per-gallon rating for each model in its line. Each manufacturer is assigned an EPA mileage figure based on a weighted (55/45) average of city and highway fuel economy numbers. This number will be somewhat higher than the official EPA rating because the EPA is only publishing city ratings now. Then a fleet, or corporate, average is computed. The mileage of each model contributes to the corporate average in proportion to the number of units sold of that model.

Consider a hypothetical case. A vehicle getting 20 mpg and a vehicle getting 40 mpg would average 30 mpg, using the mile-per-gallon formula. However, the CAFE formula is different. Let's assume that each vehicle is actually driven 100 miles (160km). The 20-mpg-vehicle would use 5 gallons of fuel to travel 100 miles (160km) and the 40-mpg-vehicle would use 2.5 gallons of fuel to go the same distance. Add the 5 and 2.5 gallons for a total of 7.5 gallons of fuel consumed by the two vehicles to travel a total of 200 miles (320km). Divide the 200 miles by 7.5 gallons and you arrive at a "fleet" average of 26.67 mpg, not 30 mpg, as you would get if you simply averaged the two vehicles' mpg ratings.

Using the CAFE method, not only are the gas mileage figures of each vehicle taken into account, but also the sales mix of each particular model. It is obvious that it takes more than one high-mileage vehicle to offset the sale of one low-mileage vehicle.

This brings us to the diesel. The fuel efficiency of the diesel is another way some manufacturers see to meet the CAFE requirements set down by the federal government. The stakes in the CAFE game are not small, either. If the manufacturer does not achieve the required CAFE figure, there are provisions that they could be fined $5 per vehicle for every one-tenth mile the manufacturer falls short.

Further federal regulation could possibly be avoided if just one gallon of gasoline per week could be saved for every automobile. This would amount to 8% of the government's goal of 10% reduction in fuel consumption.

There are three areas where the motorist can save on fuel—proper maintenance, efficient driving habits, and intelligent purchase of a vehicle.

Care and Maintenance

▶ **See Figures 1 thru 7**

Proper care and maintenance of your vehicle(s) will save you money and conserve gas. Tune-ups and a regular maintenance program like the one in this book can save up to 20% in fuel.

Tests by the Champion Spark Plug Company showed a tune-up, on vehicles judged to be in need of one, increased fuel economy by over 11%. The same tests also revealed that of the vehicles checked, ¾ had maintenance deficiencies that adversely affected fuel economy, emissions or performance.

A regular maintenance program should at least include:

1. Change the oil and filter as recommended. Dirty oil is thick and causes extra friction between the moving parts; cutting efficiency and increasing wear. Use a "Energy Conserving" type motor oil.

2. Radial tires have been standard equipment on most vehicles since the middle 80's. However, be sure the tires are properly inflated. Under-inflated tires can cost as much as 1 mpg. Better mileage can be achieved by over-inflating the tires (never exceed the maximum inflation pressure on the side of the tire), but the tires will wear faster and the ride will be rougher.

3. Replace spark plugs at regularly scheduled intervals. New plugs alone can increase fuel economy by 3%.

4. Be sure the plugs are the correct type and properly gapped.

5. Be sure the ignition timing is set to specifications.

6. If your vehicle does not have electronic ignition, check the points, rotor, and cap in your distributor as specified.

7. Replace the air filter regularly. A dirty air filter enriches the air/fuel mixture and can increase fuel consumption as much as 10%. Tests show one third of all vehicles have air filters in need of replacement.

8. Replace the fuel filter at least as often as recommended.

9. On carbureted vehicles, be sure the idle speed and carburetor fuel mixture is set to specifications.

10. On carbureted vehicles, check the automatic choke. A sticking or malfunctioning choke wastes gas.

Fig. 1 Change the engine oil regularly, as dirty oil causes extra friction between moving parts

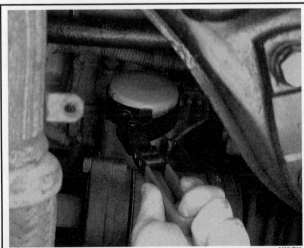

Fig. 2 Whenever you change the oil, you should also replace the filter, because the old filter holds about a quart of dirty oil

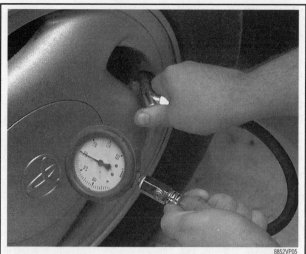

Fig. 3 Check your tire pressure often. If the tires are underinflated, they can lower gas mileage substantially

Fig. 6 Replacing a faulty thermostat can increase your fuel economy

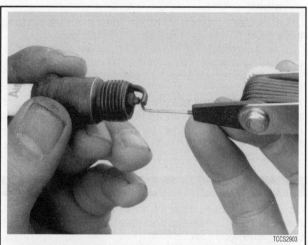

Fig. 4 Installing new spark plugs at the proper intervals will help your vehicle run more efficiently. Make sure the plugs are properly gapped

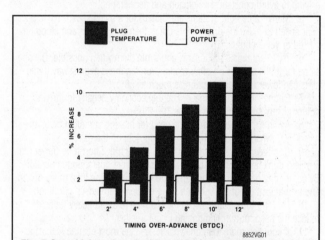

Fig. 7 On vehicles where ignition timing can be adjusted, it's important that it be set to specifications. Advancing the timing past specifications leads to a rapid rise in plug temperature with little appreciable gain in power output.

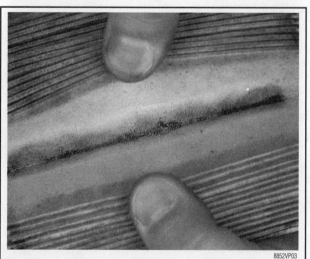

Fig. 5 This air filter element is dirty and in need of replacement. A new filter element will consume less gas

11. Replace the PCV valve at regular intervals.

12. Service the cooling system at regular recommended intervals.

13. Be sure the thermostat is operating properly. A thermostat that is stuck open delays engine warm-up, and a cold engine uses twice as much fuel as a warm engine.

14. Be sure the drive or serpentine belts (especially the fan belt) are in good condition and properly adjusted.

15. Be sure the battery is fully charged for fast starts.

16. Use the recommended viscosity motor oil to reduce friction. Use "Energy Conserving" type motor oil.

17. Use the recommended viscosity fluids in the drive axle and transmission.

18. Be sure the wheels are properly balanced.

19. Be sure the front end is correctly aligned. A misaligned front end actually has wheels going in different directions creating additional drag.

20. Correctly adjust the wheel bearings. Wheel bearings adjusted too tight increase rolling resistance.

21. Install a flex-type fan if you don't have a clutch fan. Flex fans push more air at low speeds when more cooling is needed. At high speeds, the blades flatten out for less resistance.

22. Check the radiator cap for a cracked or worn gasket. If the cap doesn't seal properly, the cooling system will not function properly.

23. Check the spark plug wires for cracks and burned or broken insulation. Cracked wires decrease fuel efficiency by failing to deliver full voltage to the spark plugs.

Driving Habits

Getting the best gas mileage depends not only on how the vehicle is maintained, but also on how it is driven. By planning and driving by intention rather than instinct, gasoline mileage can increase as much as 20%. Here are some fuel-saving driving tips to follow:

1. Avoid extended warm-ups. As soon as your vehicle is driveable, accelerate gently and slowly until the vehicle is fully warmed.

2. Avoid unnecessary idling. One minute of idling uses more gas than it takes to restart the engine. Prolonged idling uses gas at the rate of about ½ gallon per hour.

3. Avoid sudden stops and starts. Hard acceleration uses up to one third more gas. Achieve your desired speed with a steady foot on the accelerator and try coasting to stop.

4. Drive at a steady pace. Plan your route to avoid stop-and-start conditions and heavy traffic. Be aware of the traffic around you and adjust your driving to avoid constant acceleration and deceleration.

5. Many traffic light systems are "timed" for a given speed. Try to pace your speed to make the green lights rather than going faster and stopping for red or yellow lights.

6. Try to anticipate traffic jams and avoid them when possible. Despite stops for traffic signals on other roads, avoiding those expressway traffic jams can lower fuel consumption as much as 50%.

7. Choose your road surface. The fuel economy penalty for driving on soft or poorly surfaced roads can be 10—30%.

8. Avoid excessive braking. The need for braking can often be eliminated by downshifting or simply taking your foot off the gas.

9. Combine several short trips into a single trip. Short trips (fewer than 5 miles) don't let the engine reach its most efficient operating temperature. By combining numerous short trips, you can save on the total miles driven and take advantage of the vehicle's more efficient warmed-up condition.

10. On long trips, start early in the morning to avoid heavy traffic and to reduce the need for air conditioning in hot weather.

11. If you own more than one vehicle, use the most economical, especially for commuting or stop-and-go driving.

12. Use the transmission properly. If your vehicle has a manual transmission, shift gears as soon as the engine can run smoothly in the next gear. Low gear at 20 mph gives only about two-thirds the mileage as high gear at the same speed. In second gear, it's four-fifths the mileage you'd get in high. With an automatic transmission, lifting your foot slightly off the accelerator will make the transmission shift sooner.

13. When approaching hills, don't wait until the vehicle begins to "lug" before shifting gears. Don't accelerate once you have started up the hill, because speed increase is slight and gas consumption is high. You can minimize the speed loss by gradually increasing speed as you approach a hill.

14. If you can, take advantage of good weather, and avoid bad weather driving. Rain or snow can reduce gas mileage as much as 2 mpg. A strong headwind can mean a 10% loss in fuel economy.

15. Summer temperatures above 70°F (21°C) are better for fuel economy than winter temperatures. There is an approximate 85% difference in economy between 70°F (21°C) and 20°F (-7°C).

16. If equipped, use the cruise control. A cruise control can gain 1–2 mpg by maintaining a steady, preset speed over any kind of terrain.

17. The best fuel economy is obtained at moderate speeds. More fuel is consumed below 35 mph than at 45 mph, and generally, you'll lose 1 mpg for every 5 mpg over 50.

18. Use the A/C at highway speeds. Although the weight and operation of the air conditioner reduce economy, tests have shown that wind drag at 55 mph with the windows open can consume more fuel that using the air conditioner with the windows shut. The least efficient time to use the air conditioner is at lower speeds. Turn off the air conditioning, at lower speeds, and use the vents when the outside temperature is in the comfort range.

19. Don't carry unnecessary equipment in the trunk. Weight is the largest single factor in fuel usage, and every extra hundred pounds in cargo costs about 1% in fuel economy.

20. Don't load cargo on a roof rack. This just creates frontal area, increases air resistance, and lowers your mpg.

21. Learn to drive by instruments. Reading the tachometer (if equipped) can keep the engine in the optimum 1000–3000 rpm operating range. A vacuum gauge indicates the highest engine vacuum (best mileage).

22. Relax while driving. Find a comfortable driving position; fidgeting in the seat leads to constant speed changes and decreases gas mileage.

23. Avoid buying super-wide tread tires. They only create extra rolling resistance. Stick to the manufacturer's recommendations.

24. If you drive a manual transmission vehicle, start in second when going downhill.

25. On a 4-barrel carburetor engine, learn how to move the gas pedal to avoid activating the secondary circuit, except in an emergency.

26. Avoid using large mud-flaps or oversize rear view mirrors unless necessary. They only create extra drag (air resistance).

27. Don't drive fast until the engine has fully warmed to normal operating temperature.

28. In winter, clean accumulated snow and ice from the trunk, hood, and roof before driving. Carrying heavy, wet snow uses fuel.

29. Keep accurate records. Over a period, you can check your fuel economy; a sudden drop in miles per gallon may mean it's time for a tune-up or other maintenance.

Buying a Vehicle

Fuel consumption is the biggest contributor to operating cost, and it should be a primary consideration when buying a vehicle. Some things to remember about options and fuel economy are:

How you will use the vehicle—Your driving needs may be adequately served by a compact instead of a full-size vehicle.

Engines—Smaller engines generally require less gas than larger V8's, but an under-powered vehicle will use more gas than one with sufficient power.

Transmissions—If used properly, a manual transmission can provide up to 8% better mileage than an automatic, in city driving. At highway speeds, the difference is negligible.

Axle ratios—Numerically higher axle ratios give more power, but numerically lower ratios save gas at highway speeds because the engine doesn't have to rotate as many times.

Weight—The lighter the vehicle, the less gas it will use. On an average vehicle, every extra hundred pounds will cost about 1% in fuel economy.

Tires—Radial tires can deliver as much as ½ mpg over bias or bias-belted tires.

Cruise control—If you do a lot of highway driving, a cruise control can gain 1–2 mpg.

Fuel Injection—Fuel injection is generally more efficient than a carburetor because it meters fuel more precisely.

33

GLOSSARY

GLOSSARY 33-2

GLOSSARY

Understanding your mechanic is as important as understanding your car. Just about everyone drives a car, but many drivers have difficulty understanding automotive terminology. Talking the language of cars makes it easier to effectively communicate with professional mechanics. It isn't necessary (or recommended) that you diagnose the problem, but it will save time, and you money, if you can accurately describe what is happening. It will also help you to know why your car does what it is doing, and what repairs were made.

ABS: Anti-lock braking system. An electro-mechanical braking system which is designed to minimize or prevent wheel lock-up during braking.

ACCELERATOR PUMP: A small pump located in the carburetor that feeds fuel into the air/fuel mixture during acceleration.

ADVANCE: Setting the ignition timing so that spark occurs earlier before the piston reaches top dead center (TDC).

AFTER TOP DEAD CENTER (ATDC): The point after the piston reaches the top of its travel on the compression stroke.

AIR BAG: Device on the inside of the car designed to inflate on impact of crash, protecting the occupants of the car.

AIR CLEANER: An assembly consisting of a housing, filter and any connecting ductwork. The filter element is made up of a porous paper, sometimes with a wire mesh screening, and is designed to prevent airborne particles from entering the engine through the carburetor or throttle body.

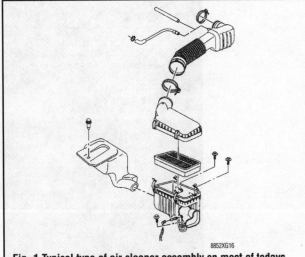

Fig. 1 Typical type of air cleaner assembly on most of todays vehicles

AIR INJECTION: One method of reducing harmful exhaust emissions by injecting air into each of the exhaust ports of an engine. The fresh air entering the hot exhaust manifold causes any remaining fuel to be burned before it can exit the tailpipe.

AIR PUMP: An emission control device that supplies fresh air to the exhaust manifold to aid in more completely burning exhaust gases.

AIR/FUEL RATIO: The ratio of air-to-gasoline by weight in the fuel mixture drawn into the engine.

ALIGNMENT RACK: A special drive-on vehicle lift apparatus/measuring device used to adjust a vehicle's toe, caster and camber angles.

ALL WHEEL DRIVE: Term used to describe a full time four wheel drive system or any other vehicle drive system that continuously delivers power to all four wheels. This system is found primarily on station wagon vehicles and SUVs not utilized for significant off road use.

ALTERNATING CURRENT (AC): Electric current that flows first in one direction, then in the opposite direction, continually reversing flow.

ALTERNATOR: A device which produces AC (alternating current) which is converted to DC (direct current) to charge the car battery.

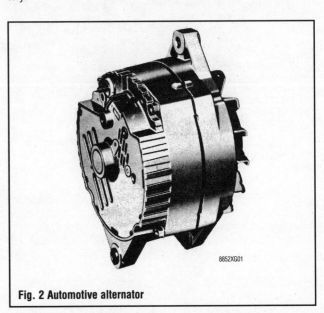

Fig. 2 Automotive alternator

AMMETER: An instrument, calibrated in amperes, used to measure the flow of an electrical current in a circuit. Ammeters are always connected in series with the circuit being tested.

AMP/HR. RATING (BATTERY): Measurement of the ability of a battery to deliver a stated amount of current for a stated period of time. The higher the amp/hr. rating, the better the battery.

AMPERE: The rate of flow of electrical current present when one volt of electrical pressure is applied against one ohm of electrical resistance.

ANALOG COMPUTER: Any microprocessor that uses similar (analogous) electrical signals to make its calculations.

ANTIFREEZE: A substance (ethylene or propylene glycol) added to the coolant to prevent freezing in cold weather.

ANTI-LOCK BRAKING SYSTEM: A supplementary system to the base hydraulic system that prevents sustained lock-up of the wheels during braking as well as automatically controlling wheel slip.

ANTI-ROLL BAR: See stabilizer bar.

ARMATURE: A laminated, soft iron core wrapped by a wire that converts electrical energy to mechanical energy as in a motor or relay. When rotated in a magnetic field, it changes mechanical energy into electrical energy as in a generator.

ATDC: After Top Dead Center.

ATF: Automatic transmission fluid.

ATMOSPHERIC PRESSURE: The pressure on the Earth's surface caused by the weight of the air in the atmosphere. At sea level, this pressure is 14.7 psi at 32°F (101 kPa at 0°C).

ATOMIZATION: The breaking down of a liquid into a fine mist that can be suspended in air.

AWD: All wheel drive.

AXIAL PLAY: Movement parallel to a shaft or bearing bore.

AXLE CAPACITY: The maximum load-carrying capacity of the axle itself, as specified by the manufacturer. This is usually a higher number than the GAWR.

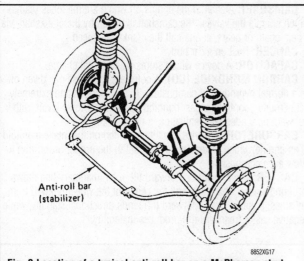

Fig. 3 Location of a typical anti-roll bar on a McPherson strut suspension

AXLE RATIO: This is a number (3.07:1, 4.56:1, for example) expressing the ratio between driveshaft revolutions and wheel revolutions. A low numerical ratio allows the engine to work easier because it doesn't have to turn as fast. A high numerical ratio means that the engine has to turn more rpm's to move the wheels through the same number of turns.

BACKFIRE: The sudden combustion of gases in the intake or exhaust system that results in a loud explosion.

BACKLASH: The clearance or play between two parts, such as meshed gears.

BACKPRESSURE: Restrictions in the exhaust system that slow the exit of exhaust gases from the combustion chamber.

BAKELITE®: A heat resistant, plastic insulator material commonly used in printed circuit boards and transistorized components.

BALL BEARING: A bearing made up of hardened inner and outer races between which hardened steel balls roll.

BALL JOINT: A ball and matching socket connecting suspension components (steering knuckle to lower control arms). It permits rotating movement in any direction between the components that are joined.

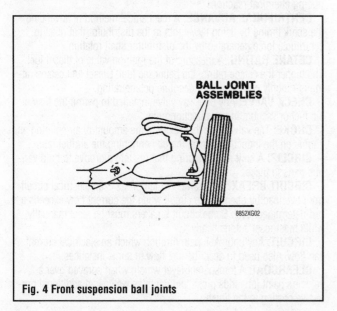

Fig. 4 Front suspension ball joints

BALLAST RESISTOR: A resistor in the primary ignition circuit that lowers voltage after the engine is started to reduce wear on ignition components.

BATTERY: A direct current electrical storage unit, consisting of the basic active materials of lead and sulphuric acid, which converts chemical energy into electrical energy. Used to provide current for the operation of the starter as well as other equipment, such as the radio, lighting, etc.

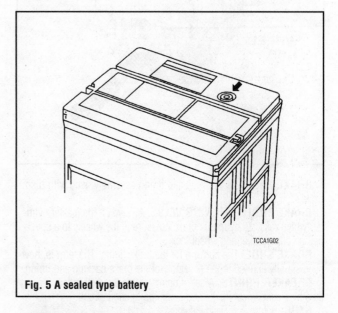

Fig. 5 A sealed type battery

BEAD: The portion of a tire that holds it on the rim.

BEARING: A friction reducing, supportive device usually located between a stationary part and a moving part.

BEFORE TOP DEAD CENTER (BTDC): The point just before the piston reaches the top of its travel on the compression stroke.

BELTED TIRE: Tire construction similar to bias-ply tires, but using two or more layers of reinforced belts between body plies and the tread.

BEZEL: Piece of metal surrounding radio, headlights, gauges or similar components; sometimes used to hold the glass face of a gauge in the dash.

BIAS-PLY TIRE: Tire construction, using body ply reinforcing cords which run at alternating angles to the center line of the tread.

BI-METAL TEMPERATURE SENSOR: Any sensor or switch made of two dissimilar types of metal that bend when heated or cooled due to the different expansion rates of the alloys. These types of sensors usually function as an on/off switch.

BLOCK: See Engine Block.

BLOW-BY: Combustion gases, composed of water vapor and unburned fuel, that leak past the piston rings into the crankcase during normal engine operation. These gases are removed by the PCV system to prevent the buildup of harmful acids in the crankcase.

BOOK TIME: See Labor Time.

BOOK VALUE: The average value of a car, widely used to determine trade-in and resale value.

BORE: Diameter of a cylinder.

BRAKE CALIPER: The housing that fits over the brake disc. The caliper holds the brake pads, which are pressed against the discs by the caliper pistons when the brake pedal is depressed.

BRAKE FADE: Loss of braking power, usually caused by excessive heat after repeated brake applications.

BRAKE HORSEPOWER: Usable horsepower of an engine measured at the crankshaft.

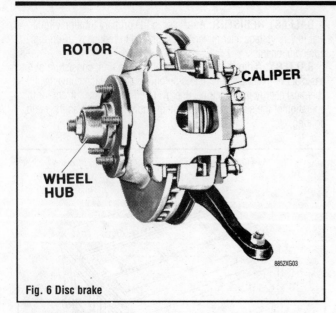

Fig. 6 Disc brake

BRAKE PAD: A brake shoe and lining assembly used with disc brakes.

BRAKE PROPORTIONING VALVE: A valve on the master cylinder which restricts hydraulic brake pressure to the wheels to a specified amount, preventing wheel lock-up.

BRAKE SHOE: The backing for the brake lining. The term is, however, usually applied to the assembly of the brake backing and lining.

BREAKER POINTS: A set of points inside the distributor, operated by a cam, which make and break the ignition circuit.

BTDC: Before Top Dead Center.

BUSHING: A liner, usually removable, for a bearing; an anti-friction liner used in place of a bearing.

CALIFORNIA ENGINE: An engine certified by the EPA for use in California only; conforms to more stringent emission regulations than Federal engine.

CALIPER: A hydraulically activated device in a disc brake system, which is mounted straddling the brake rotor (disc). The caliper contains at least one piston and two brake pads. Hydraulic pressure on the piston(s) forces the pads against the rotor.

CAMBER: One of the factors of wheel alignment. Viewed from the front of the car, it is the inward or outward tilt of the wheel. The top of the tire will lean outward (positive camber) or inward (negative camber).

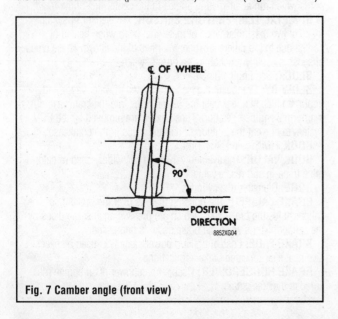

Fig. 7 Camber angle (front view)

CAMSHAFT: A shaft in the engine on which are the lobes (cams) which operate the valves. The camshaft is driven by the crankshaft, via a belt, chain or gears, at one half the crankshaft speed.

CANCER: Rust on a car body.

CAPACITOR: A device which stores an electrical charge.

CARBON MONOXIDE (CO): A colorless, odorless gas given off as a normal byproduct of combustion. It is poisonous and extremely dangerous in confined areas, building up slowly to toxic levels without warning if adequate ventilation is not available.

CARBURETOR: A device, usually mounted on the intake manifold of an engine, which mixes the air and fuel in the proper proportion to allow even combustion.

CASTER: The forward or rearward tilt of an imaginary line drawn through the upper ball joint and the center of the wheel. Viewed from the sides, positive caster (forward tilt) lends directional stability, while negative caster (rearward tilt) produces instability.

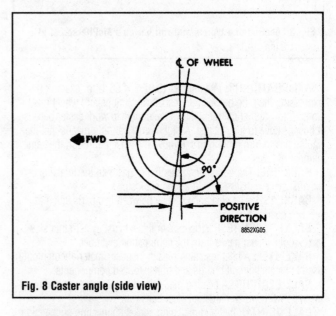

Fig. 8 Caster angle (side view)

CATALYTIC CONVERTER: A device installed in the exhaust system, like a muffler, that converts harmful byproducts of combustion into carbon dioxide and water vapor by means of a heat-producing chemical reaction.

CENTRIFUGAL ADVANCE: A mechanical method of advancing the spark timing by using flyweights in the distributor that react to centrifugal force generated by the distributor shaft rotation.

CETANE RATING: A measure of the ignition value of diesel fuel. The higher the cetane rating, the better the fuel. Diesel fuel cetane rating is roughly comparable to gasoline octane rating.

CHECK VALVE: Any one-way valve installed to permit the flow of air, fuel or vacuum in one direction only.

CHOKE: The valve/plate that restricts the amount of air entering an engine on the induction stroke, thereby enriching the air:fuel ratio.

CIRCLIP: A split steel snapring that fits into a groove to hold various parts in place.

CIRCUIT BREAKER: A switch which protects an electrical circuit from overload by opening the circuit when the current flow exceeds a pre-determined level. Some circuit breakers must be reset manually, while most reset automatically.

CIRCUIT: Any unbroken path through which an electrical current can flow. Also used to describe fuel flow in some instances.

CLEARCOAT: A transparent layer which, when sprayed over a vehicle's paint job, adds gloss and depth as well as an additional protective coating to the finish.

CLUTCH: Part of the power train used to connect/disconnect power to the rear wheels.

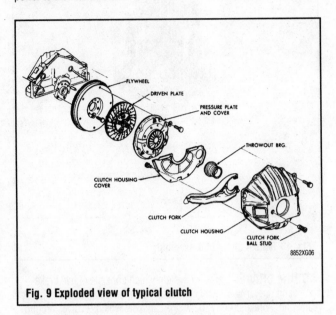

Fig. 9 Exploded view of typical clutch

COIL: Part of the ignition system that boosts the relatively low voltage supplied by the car's electrical system to the high voltage required to fire the spark plugs.

COMBINATION MANIFOLD: An assembly which includes both the intake and exhaust manifolds in one casting.

COMBINATION VALVE: A device used in some fuel systems that routes fuel vapors to a charcoal storage canister instead of venting them into the atmosphere. The valve relieves fuel tank pressure and allows fresh air into the tank as the fuel level drops to prevent a vapor lock situation.

COMBUSTION CHAMBER: The part of the engine in the cylinder head where combustion takes place.

COMPRESSION CHECK: A test involving removing each spark plug and inserting a gauge. When the engine is cranked, the gauge will record a pressure reading in the individual cylinder. General operating condition can be determined from a compression check.

COMPRESSION RATIO: The ratio of the volume between the piston and cylinder head when the piston is at the bottom of its stroke (bottom dead center) and when the piston is at the top of its stroke (top dead center).

CONDENSER: 1. An electrical device which acts to store an electrical charge, preventing voltage surges. 2. A radiator-like device in the air conditioning system in which refrigerant gas condenses into a liquid, giving off heat.

CONDUCTOR: Any material through which an electrical current can be transmitted easily.

CONNECTING ROD: The connecting link between the crankshaft and piston.

CONSTANT VELOCITY JOINT: Type of universal joint in a half-shaft assembly in which the output shaft turns at a constant angular velocity without variation, provided that the speed of the input shaft is constant.

CONTINUITY: Continuous or complete circuit. Can be checked with an ohmmeter.

CONTROL ARM: The upper or lower suspension components which are mounted on the frame and support the ball joints and steering knuckles.

CONVENTIONAL IGNITION: Ignition system which uses breaker points.

COOLANT: Mixture of water and anti-freeze circulated through the engine to carry off heat produced by the engine.

COUNTERSHAFT: An intermediate shaft which is rotated by a mainshaft and transmits, in turn, that rotation to a working part.

CRANKCASE: The lower part of an engine in which the crankshaft and related parts operate.

CRANKSHAFT: Engine component (connected to pistons by connecting rods) which converts the reciprocating (up and down) motion of pistons to rotary motion used to turn the driveshaft.

CURB WEIGHT: The weight of a vehicle without passengers or payload, but including all fluids (oil, gas, coolant, etc.) and other equipment specified as standard.

CV-JOINT: Constant velocity joint.

CYLINDER BLOCK: See engine block.

CYLINDER HEAD: The detachable portion of the engine, usually fastened to the top of the cylinder block and containing all or most of the combustion chambers. On overhead valve engines, it contains the valves and their operating parts. On overhead cam engines, it contains the camshaft as well.

CYLINDER: In an engine, the round hole in the engine block in which the piston(s) ride.

DEAD CENTER: The extreme top or bottom of the piston stroke.

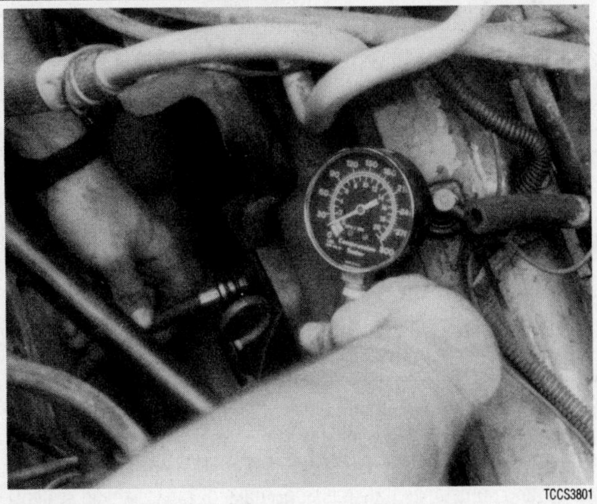

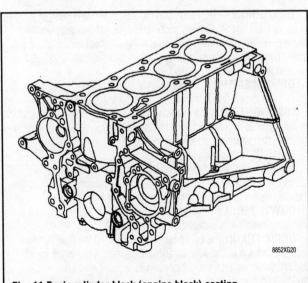

Fig. 10 Performing a compression check using a compression gauge

Fig. 11 Basic cylinder block (engine block) casting

DETERGENT: An additive in engine oil to improve its operating characteristics.

DETONATION: An unwanted explosion of the air/fuel mixture in the combustion chamber caused by excess heat and compression, advanced timing, or an overly lean mixture. Also referred to as "ping".

DEXRON®: A brand of automatic transmission fluid.

DIAPHRAGM: A thin, flexible wall separating two cavities, such as in a vacuum advance unit.

DIESELING: The engine continues to run after the car is shut off; caused by fuel continuing to be burned in the combustion chamber.

DIFFERENTIAL: A geared assembly which allows the transmission of motion between drive axles, giving one axle the ability to rotate faster than the other, as in cornering.

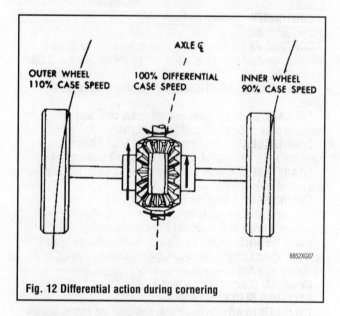

Fig. 12 Differential action during cornering

DIGITAL VOLT OHMMETER: An electronic diagnostic tool used to measure voltage, ohms and amps as well as several other functions, with the readings displayed on a digital screen in tenths, hundredths and thousandths.

DIODE: An electrical device that will allow current to flow in one direction only.

DIRECT CURRENT (DC): Electrical current that flows in one direction only.

DISC BRAKE: A hydraulic braking assembly consisting of a brake disc, or rotor, mounted on an axleshaft, and a caliper assembly containing, usually two brake pads which are activated by hydraulic pressure. The pads are forced against the sides of the disc, creating friction which slows the vehicle.

DISPLACEMENT: The total volume of air that is displaced by all pistons as the engine turns through one complete revolution.

DISTRIBUTOR: A mechanically driven device on an engine which is responsible for electrically firing the spark plug at a pre-determined point of the piston stroke.

DOHC: Double overhead camshaft.

DOUBLE OVERHEAD CAMSHAFT: The engine utilizes two camshafts mounted in one cylinder head. One camshaft operates the exhaust valves, while the other operates the intake valves.

DOWEL PIN: A pin, inserted in mating holes in two different parts allowing those parts to maintain a fixed relationship.

DRIVE TRAIN: The components that transmit the flow of power from the engine to the wheels. The components include the clutch, transmission, driveshafts (or axle shafts in front wheel drive), U-joints and differential.

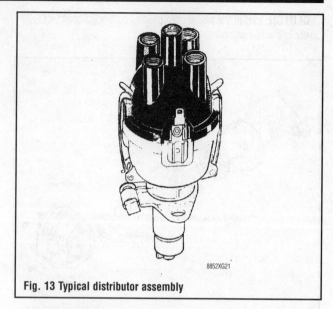

Fig. 13 Typical distributor assembly

DRUM BRAKE: A braking system which consists of two brake shoes and one or two wheel cylinders, mounted on a fixed backing plate, and a brake drum, mounted on an axle, which revolves around the assembly.

DRY CHARGED BATTERY: Battery to which electrolyte is added when the battery is placed in service.

DVOM: Digital volt ohmmeter

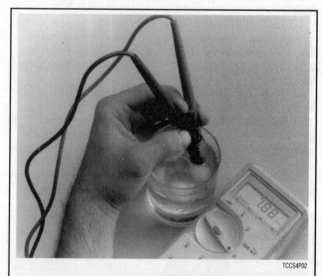

Fig. 14 Performing a resistance check using a DVOM

DWELL: The rate, measured in degrees of shaft rotation, at which an electrical circuit cycles on and off.

EBCM: See Electronic Control Unit (ECU).

ECM: See Electronic Control Unit (ECU).

ECU: Electronic control unit.

ELECTRODE: Conductor (positive or negative) of electric current.

ELECTROLYTE: A solution of water and sulfuric acid used to activate the battery. Electrolyte is extremely corrosive.

ELECTRONIC CONTROL UNIT: A digital computer that controls engine (and sometimes transmission, brake or other vehicle system) functions based on data received from various sensors. Examples used by some manufacturers include Electronic Brake Control Module

(EBCM), Engine Control Module (ECM), Powertrain Control Module (PCM) or Vehicle Control Module (VCM).

ELECTRONIC IGNITION: A system in which the timing and firing of the spark plugs is controlled by an electronic control unit, usually called a module. These systems have no points or condenser.

ENAMEL: Type of paint that dries to a smooth, glossy finish.

END-PLAY: The measured amount of axial movement in a shaft.

ENGINE: The primary motor or power apparatus of a vehicle, which converts liquid or gas fuel into mechanical energy.

ENGINE BLOCK: The basic engine casting containing the cylinders, the crankshaft main bearings, as well as machined surfaces for the mounting of other components such as the cylinder head, oil pan, transmission, etc..

EP LUBRICANT: EP (extreme pressure) lubricants are specially formulated for use with gears involving heavy loads (transmissions, differentials, etc.).

ETHYL: A substance added to gasoline to improve its resistance to knock, by slowing down the rate of combustion.

ETHYLENE GLYCOL: The base substance of antifreeze.

EXHAUST MANIFOLD: A set of cast passages or pipes which conduct exhaust gases from the engine.

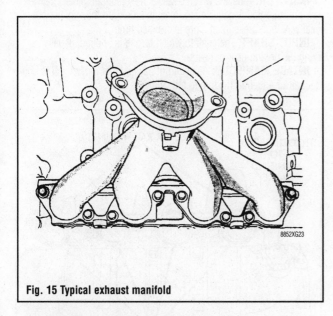

Fig. 15 Typical exhaust manifold

FAST IDLE: The speed of the engine when the choke is on. Fast idle speeds engine warm-up.

FEDERAL ENGINE: An engine certified by the EPA for use in any of the 49 states (except California).

FEELER GAUGE: A blade, usually metal, of precisely predetermined thickness, used to measure the clearance between two parts.

FILAMENT: The part of a bulb that glows; the filament creates high resistance to current flow and actually glows from the resulting heat.

FINAL DRIVE: See axle ratio.

FIRING ORDER: The order in which combustion occurs in the cylinders of an engine. Also the order in which spark is distributed to the plugs by the distributor.

FLAME FRONT: The term used to describe certain aspects of the fuel explosion in the cylinders. The flame front should move in a controlled pattern across the cylinder, rather than simply exploding immediately.

FLAT ENGINE: Engine design in which the pistons are horizontally opposed. Porsche, Subaru and some old VWs are common examples of flat engines.

FLAT RATE: A dealership term referring to the amount of money paid to a technician for a repair or diagnostic service based on that particular service versus dealership's labor time (NOT based on the actual time the technician spent on the job).

FLAT SPOT: A point during acceleration when the engine seems to lose power for an instant.

FLOODING: The presence of too much fuel in the intake manifold and combustion chamber which prevents the air/fuel mixture from firing, thereby causing a no-start situation.

FLYWHEEL: A heavy disc of metal attached to the rear of the crankshaft. It smoothes the firing impulses of the engine and keeps the crankshaft turning during periods when no firing takes place. The starter also engages the flywheel to start the engine.

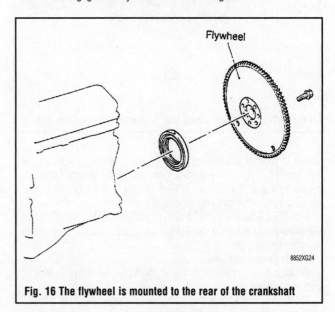

Fig. 16 The flywheel is mounted to the rear of the crankshaft

FOOT POUND (ft. lbs. or sometimes, ft. lb.): The amount of energy or work needed to raise an item weighing one pound, a distance of one foot.

FREEZE PLUG: A plug in the engine block which will be pushed out if the coolant freezes. Sometimes called expansion plugs, they protect the block from cracking should the coolant freeze.

FRONT END ALIGNMENT: A service to set caster, camber and toe-in to the correct specifications. This will ensure that the car steers and handles properly and that the tires wear properly.

FRONTAL AREA: The total frontal area of a vehicle exposed to air flow.

FUEL FILTER: A component of the fuel system containing a porous paper element used to prevent any impurities from entering the engine through the fuel system. It usually takes the form of a canister-like housing, mounted in-line with the fuel hose, located anywhere on a vehicle between the fuel tank and engine.

FUEL INJECTION: A system replacing the carburetor that sprays fuel into the cylinder through nozzles. The amount of fuel can be more precisely controlled with fuel injection.

FULL FLOATING AXLE: An axle in which the axle housing extends through the wheel giving bearing support on the outside of the housing. The front axle of a four-wheel drive vehicle is usually a full floating axle, as are the rear axles of many larger (ton and over) pick-ups and vans.

FULL-TIME FOUR-WHEEL DRIVE: A four-wheel drive system that continuously delivers power to all four wheels. A differential between the front and rear driveshafts permits variations in axle speeds to control gear wind-up without damage.

FUSE: A protective device in a circuit which prevents circuit overload by breaking the circuit when a specific amperage is present. The

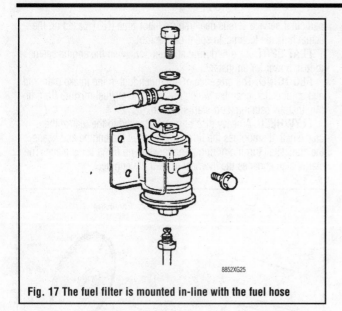

Fig. 17 The fuel filter is mounted in-line with the fuel hose

device is constructed around a strip or wire of a lower amperage rating than the circuit it is designed to protect. When an amperage higher than that stamped on the fuse is present in the circuit, the strip or wire melts, opening the circuit.

FUSIBLE LINK: A piece of wire in a wiring harness that performs the same job as a fuse. If overloaded, the fusible link will melt and interrupt the circuit.

FWD: Front wheel drive.

GAWR: (Gross axle weight rating) the total maximum weight an axle is designed to carry.

GCW: (Gross combined weight) total combined weight of a tow vehicle and trailer.

GEAR RATIO: A ratio expressing the number of turns a smaller gear will make to turn a larger gear through one revolution. The ratio is found by dividing the number of teeth on the smaller gear into the number of teeth on the larger gear.

GEARBOX: Transmission

GEL COAT: A thin coat of plastic resin covering fiberglass body panels.

GENERATOR: A device which produces direct current (DC) necessary to charge the battery.

GVWR: (Gross vehicle weight rating) total maximum weight a vehicle is designed to carry including the weight of the vehicle, passengers, equipment, gas, oil, etc.

HALOGEN: A special type of lamp known for its quality of brilliant white light. Originally used for fog lights and driving lights.

HEADER TANK: An expansion tank for the radiator coolant. It can be located remotely or built into the radiator.

HEAT RANGE: A term used to describe the ability of a spark plug to carry away heat. Plugs with longer nosed insulators take longer to carry heat off effectively.

HEAT RISER: A flapper in the exhaust manifold that is closed when the engine is cold, causing hot exhaust gases to heat the intake manifold providing better cold engine operation. A thermostatic spring opens the flapper when the engine warms up.

HEMI: A name given an engine using hemispherical combustion chambers.

HORSEPOWER: A measurement of the amount of work; one horsepower is the amount of work necessary to lift 33,000 lbs. one foot in one minute. Brake horsepower (bhp) is the horsepower delivered by an engine on a dynamometer. Net horsepower is the power remaining (measured at the flywheel of the engine) that can be used to

turn the wheels after power is consumed through friction and running the engine accessories (water pump, alternator, air pump, fan etc.)

HUB: The center part of a wheel or gear.

HYDROCARBON (HC): Any chemical compound made up of hydrogen and carbon. A major pollutant formed by the engine as a by-product of combustion.

HYDROMETER: An instrument used to measure the specific gravity of a solution.

HYDROPLANING: A phenomenon of driving when water builds up under the tire tread, causing it to lose contact with the road. Slowing down will usually restore normal tire contact with the road.

IDLE MIXTURE: The mixture of air and fuel (usually about 14:1) being fed to the cylinders. The idle mixture screw(s) are sometimes adjusted as part of a tune-up.

IDLER ARM: Component of the steering linkage which is a geometric duplicate of the steering gear arm. It supports the right side of the center steering link.

INCH POUND (inch lbs.; sometimes in. lb. or in. lbs.): One twelfth of a foot pound.

INDUCTION: A means of transferring electrical energy in the form of a magnetic field. Principle used in the ignition coil to increase voltage.

INJECTOR: A device which receives metered fuel under relatively low pressure and is activated to inject the fuel into the engine under relatively high pressure at a predetermined time.

INPUT SHAFT: The shaft to which torque is applied, usually carrying the driving gear or gears.

INTAKE MANIFOLD: A casting of passages or pipes used to conduct air or a fuel/air mixture to the cylinders.

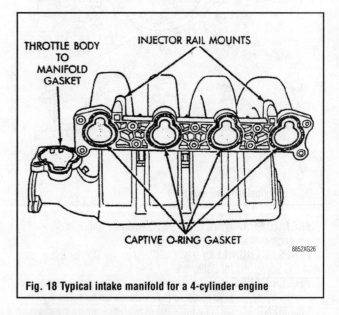

Fig. 18 Typical intake manifold for a 4-cylinder engine

JOURNAL: The bearing surface within which a shaft operates.

JUMPER CABLES: Two heavy duty wires with large alligator clips used to provide power from a charged battery to a discharged battery mounted in a vehicle.

JUMPSTART: Utilizing the sufficiently charged battery of one vehicle to start the engine of another vehicle with a discharged battery by the use of jumper cables.

KEY: A small block usually fitted in a notch between a shaft and a hub to prevent slippage of the two parts.

KNOCK: Noise which results from the spontaneous ignition of a portion of the air-fuel mixture in the engine cylinder caused by overly advanced ignition timing or use of incorrectly low octane fuel for that engine.

KNOCK SENSOR: An input device that responds to spark knock, caused by over advanced ignition timing.

LABOR TIME: A specific amount of time required to perform a certain repair or diagnostic service as defined by a vehicle or after-market manufacturer .

LACQUER: A quick-drying automotive paint.

LIMITED SLIP: A type of differential which transfers driving force to the wheel with the best traction.

LITHIUM-BASE GREASE: Chassis and wheel bearing grease using lithium as a base. Not compatible with sodium-base grease.

LOAD RANGE: Indicates the number of plies at which a tire is rated. Load range B equals four-ply rating; C equals six-ply rating; and, D equals an eight-ply rating.

LOCKING HUBS: Accessories used on part-time four-wheel drive systems that allow the front wheels to be disengaged from the drive train when four-wheel drive is not being used. When four-wheel drive is desired, the hubs are engaged, locking the wheels to the drive train.

LOCK RING: See Circlip or Snapring

MANIFOLD VACUUM: Low pressure in an engine intake manifold formed just below the throttle plates. Manifold vacuum is highest at idle and drops under acceleration.

MANIFOLD: A casting of passages or set of pipes which connect the cylinders to an inlet or outlet source.

MASTER CYLINDER: The primary fluid pressurizing device in a hydraulic system. In automotive use, it is found in brake and hydraulic clutch systems and is pedal activated, either directly or, in a power brake system, through the power booster.

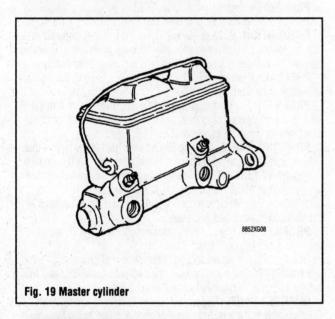

Fig. 19 Master cylinder

McPHERSON STRUT: A suspension component combining a shock absorber and spring in one unit.

MISFIRE: Condition occurring when the fuel mixture in a cylinder fails to ignite, causing the engine to run roughly.

MODULE: Electronic control unit, amplifier or igniter of solid state or integrated design which controls the current flow in the ignition primary circuit based on input from the pick-up coil. When the module opens the primary circuit, high secondary voltage is induced in the coil.

MULTI-WEIGHT: Type of oil that provides adequate lubrication at both high and low temperatures.

needed to move one amp through a resistance of one ohm.

NEEDLE BEARING: A bearing which consists of a number (usually a large number) of long, thin rollers.

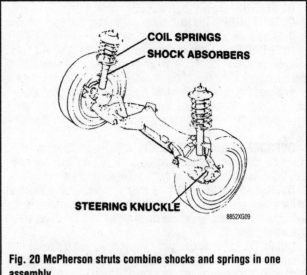

Fig. 20 McPherson struts combine shocks and springs in one assembly

NITROGEN OXIDE (NOx): One of the three basic pollutants found in the exhaust emission of an internal combustion engine. The amount of NOx usually varies in an inverse proportion to the amount of HC and CO.

OCTANE RATING: A number, indicating the quality of gasoline based on its ability to resist knock. The higher the number, the better the quality. Higher compression engines require higher octane gas.

OEM: Original Equipment Manufactured. OEM equipment is that furnished standard by the manufacturer.

OFFSET: The distance between the vertical center of the wheel and the mounting surface at the lugs. Offset is positive if the center is outside the lug circle; negative offset puts the center line inside the lug circle.

OHM: The unit used to measure the resistance of conductor-to-electrical flow. One ohm is the amount of resistance that limits current flow to one ampere in a circuit with one volt of pressure.

OHMMETER: An instrument used for measuring the resistance, in ohms, in an electrical circuit.

OSCILLOSCOPE: A piece of test equipment that shows electric impulses as a pattern on a screen. Engine performance can be analyzed by interpreting these patterns.

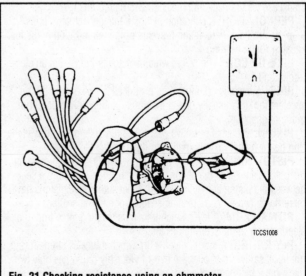

Fig. 21 Checking resistance using an ohmmeter

O2 SENSOR: See oxygen sensor.

OUTPUT SHAFT: The shaft which transmits torque from a device, such as a transmission.

OVERDRIVE: (1.) A device attached to or incorporated in a transmission that allows the engine to turn less than one full revolution for every complete revolution of the wheels. The net effect is to reduce engine rpm, thereby using less fuel. A typical overdrive gear ratio would be .87:1, instead of the normal 1:1 in high gear. (2.) A gear assembly which produces more shaft revolutions than that transmitted to it.

OVERHEAD CAMSHAFT (OHC): An engine configuration in which the camshaft is mounted on top of the cylinder head and operates the valve either directly or by means of rocker arms.

OVERHEAD VALVE (OHV): An engine configuration in which all of the valves are located in the cylinder head and the camshaft is located in the cylinder block. The camshaft operates the valves via lifters and pushrods.

OVERSTEER: The tendency of some vehicles, when steering into a turn, to over-respond or steer more than required, which could result in excessive slip of the rear wheels. Opposite of understeer.

OXIDES OF NITROGEN: See nitrogen oxide (NOx).

OXYGEN SENSOR: Used with a feedback system to sense the presence of oxygen in the exhaust gas and signal the computer which can use the voltage signal to determine engine operating efficiency and adjust the air/fuel ratio.

PARTS WASHER: A basin or tub, usually with a built-in pump mechanism and hose used for circulating chemical solvent for the purpose of cleaning greasy, oily and dirty components.

PART-TIME FOUR WHEEL DRIVE: A system that is normally in the two wheel drive mode and only runs in four-wheel drive when the system is manually engaged because more traction is desired. Two or four wheel drive is normally selected by a lever to engage the front axle, but if locking hubs are used, these must also be manually engaged in the Lock position. Otherwise, the front axle will not drive the front wheels.

PASSIVE RESTRAINT: Safety systems such as air bags or automatic seat belts which operate with no action required on the part of the driver or passenger. Mandated by Federal regulations on all vehicles sold in the U.S. after 1990.

PAYLOAD: The weight the vehicle is capable of carrying in addition to its own weight. Payload includes weight of the driver, passengers and cargo, but not coolant, fuel, lubricant, spare tire, etc.

PCM: Powertrain control module.

PCV VALVE: A valve usually located in the rocker cover that vents crankcase vapors back into the engine to be reburned.

PERCOLATION: A condition in which the fuel actually "boils," due to excessive heat. Percolation prevents proper atomization of the fuel causing rough running.

PICK-UP COIL: The coil in which voltage is induced in an electronic ignition.

PING: A metallic rattling sound produced by the engine during acceleration. It is usually due to incorrect ignition timing or a poor grade of gasoline.

PINION: The smaller of two gears. The rear axle pinion drives the ring gear which transmits motion to the axle shafts.

PISTON RING: An open-ended ring which fits into a groove on the outer diameter of the piston. Its chief function is to form a seal between the piston and cylinder wall. Most automotive pistons have three rings: two for compression sealing; one for oil sealing.

PITMAN ARM: A lever which transmits steering force from the steering gear to the steering linkage.

PLY RATING: A. rating given a tire which indicates strength (but not necessarily actual plies). A two-ply/four-ply rating has only two plies, but the strength of a four-ply tire.

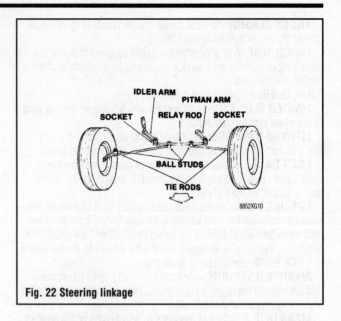

Fig. 22 Steering linkage

POLARITY: Indication (positive or negative) of the two poles of a battery.

POWER-TO-WEIGHT RATIO: Ratio of horsepower to weight of car.

POWERTRAIN: See Drivetrain.

PCM: See Electronic Control Unit (ECU).

Ppm: Parts per million; unit used to measure exhaust emissions.

PREIGNITION: Early ignition of fuel in the cylinder, sometimes due to glowing carbon deposits in the combustion chamber. Preignition can be damaging since combustion takes place prematurely.

PRELOAD: A predetermined load placed on a bearing during assembly or by adjustment.

PRESS FIT: The mating of two parts under pressure, due to the inner diameter of one being smaller than the outer diameter of the other, or vice versa; an interference fit.

PRESSURE PLATE: A spring-loaded plate (part of the clutch) that transmits power to the driven (friction) plate when the clutch is engaged.

PRIMARY CIRCUIT: The low voltage side of the ignition system which consists of the ignition switch, ballast resistor or resistance wire, bypass, coil, electronic control unit and pick-up coil as well as the connecting wires and harnesses.

PROFILE: Term used for tire measurement (tire series), which is the ratio of tire height to tread width.

Psi: Pounds per square inch; a measurement of pressure.

PUSHROD: A steel rod between the hydraulic valve lifter and the valve rocker arm in overhead valve (OHV) engines.

QUARTER PANEL: General term used to refer to a rear fender. Quarter panel is the area from the rear door opening to the tail light area and from rear wheelwell to the base of the trunk and roof-line.

RACE: The surface on the inner or outer ring of a bearing on which the balls, needles or rollers move.

RACK AND PINION: A type of automotive steering system using a pinion gear attached to the end of the steering shaft. The pinion meshes with a long rack attached to the steering linkage.

RADIAL TIRE: Tire design which uses body cords running at right angles to the center line of the tire. Two or more belts are used to give tread strength. Radials can be identified by their characteristic sidewall bulge.

RADIATOR: Part of the cooling system for a water-cooled engine, mounted in the front of the vehicle and connected to the engine with rubber hoses. Through the radiator, excess combustion heat is dissipated into the atmosphere through forced convection using a water and glycol based mixture that circulates through, and cools, the engine.

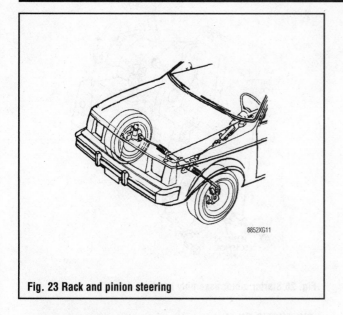

Fig. 23 Rack and pinion steering

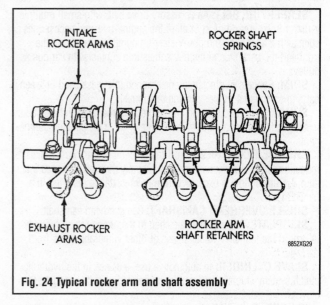

Fig. 24 Typical rocker arm and shaft assembly

REAR MAIN OIL SEAL: A synthetic or rope-type seal that prevents oil from leaking out of the engine past the rear main crankshaft bearing.

RECIRCULATING BALL: Type of steering system in which recirculating steel balls occupy the area between the nut and worm wheel, causing a reduction in friction.

RECTIFIER: A device (used primarily in alternators) that permits electrical current to flow in one direction only.

REFRIGERANT 12 (R-12) or 134 (R-134): The generic name of the refrigerant used in automotive air conditioning systems.

REGULATOR: A device which maintains the amperage and/or voltage levels of a circuit at predetermined values.

RELAY: A switch which automatically opens and/or closes a circuit.

RELUCTOR: A wheel that rotates inside the distributor and triggers the release of voltage in an electronic ignition.

RESIN: A liquid plastic used in body work.

RESISTANCE: The opposition to the flow of current through a circuit or electrical device, and is measured in ohms. Resistance is equal to the voltage divided by the amperage.

RESISTOR SPARK PLUG: A spark plug using a resistor to shorten the spark duration. This suppresses radio interference and lengthens plug life.

RESISTOR: A device, usually made of wire, which offers a preset amount of resistance in an electrical circuit.

RETARD: Set the ignition timing so that spark occurs later (fewer degrees before TDC).

RING GEAR: The name given to a ring-shaped gear attached to a differential case, or affixed to a flywheel or as part of a planetary gear set.

ROCKER ARM: A lever which rotates around a shaft pushing down (opening) the valve with an end when the other end is pushed up by the pushrod. Spring pressure will later close the valve.

ROCKER PANEL: The body panel below the doors between the wheel opening.

ROLLER BEARING: A bearing made up of hardened inner and outer races between which hardened steel rollers move.

ROTOR: (1.) The disc-shaped part of a disc brake assembly, upon which the brake pads bear; also called, brake disc. (2.) The device mounted atop the distributor shaft, which passes current to the distributor cap tower contacts.

ROTARY ENGINE: See Wankel engine.

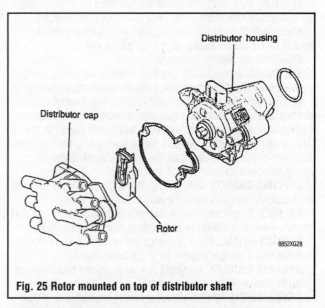

Fig. 25 Rotor mounted on top of distributor shaft

RPM: Revolutions per minute (usually indicates engine speed).

RUN-ON: Condition when the engine continues to run, even when the key is turned off. See dieseling.

SEALED BEAM: A automotive headlight. The lens, reflector and filament from a single unit.

SEATBELT INTERLOCK: A system whereby the car cannot be started unless the seatbelt is buckled.

SECONDARY CIRCUIT: The high voltage side of the ignition system, usually above 20,000 volts. The secondary includes the ignition coil, coil wire, distributor cap and rotor, spark plug wires and spark plugs.

SEMI-FLOATING AXLE: In this design, a wheel is attached to the axle shaft, which takes both drive and cornering loads. Almost all solid axle passenger cars and light trucks use this design.

SENDING UNIT: A mechanical, electrical, hydraulic or electromagnetic device which transmits information to a gauge.

SENSOR: Any device designed to measure engine operating conditions or ambient pressures and temperatures. Usually electronic in nature and designed to send a voltage signal to an on-board computer, some sensors may operate as a simple on/off switch or they may provide a variable voltage signal (like a potentiometer) as conditions or measured parameters change.

SERPENTINE BELT: An accessory drive belt, with small multiple v-ribs, routed around most or all of the engine-powered accessories such as the alternator and power steering pump. Usually both the front and the back side of the belt comes into contact with various pulleys.

SHIM: Spacers of precise, predetermined thickness used between parts to establish a proper working relationship.

SHIMMY: Vibration (sometimes violent) in the front end caused by misaligned front end, out of balance tires or worn suspension components.

SHORT CIRCUIT: An electrical malfunction where current takes the path of least resistance to ground (usually through damaged insulation). Current flow is excessive from low resistance resulting in a blown fuse.

SINGLE OVERHEAD CAMSHAFT: See overhead camshaft.

SKIDPLATE: A metal plate attached to the underside of the body to protect the fuel tank, transfer case or other vulnerable parts from damage.

SLAVE CYLINDER: In automotive use, a device in the hydraulic clutch system which is activated by hydraulic force, disengaging the clutch.

SLUDGE: Thick, black deposits in engine formed from dirt, oil, water, etc. It is usually formed in engines when oil changes are neglected.

SNAP RING: A circular retaining clip used inside or outside a shaft or part to secure a shaft, such as a floating wrist pin.

SOHC: Single overhead camshaft.

SOLENOID: An electrically operated, magnetic switching device.

SPARK PLUG: A device screwed into the combustion chamber of a spark ignition engine. The basic construction is a conductive core inside of a ceramic insulator, mounted in an outer conductive base. An electrical charge from the spark plug wire travels along the conductive core and jumps a preset air gap to a grounding point or points at the end of the conductive base. The resultant spark ignites the fuel/air mixture in the combustion chamber.

SPECIFIC GRAVITY (BATTERY): The relative weight of liquid (battery electrolyte) as compared to the weight of an equal volume of water.

SPLINES: Ridges machined or cast onto the outer diameter of a shaft or inner diameter of a bore to enable parts to mate without rotation.

SPONGY PEDAL: A soft or spongy feeling when the brake pedal is depressed. It is usually due to air in the brake lines.

SPRUNG WEIGHT: The weight of a car supported by the springs.

SRS: Supplemental restraint system

STABILIZER (SWAY) BAR: A bar linking both sides of the suspension. It resists sway on turns by taking some of added load from one wheel and putting it on the other.

STARTER: A high-torque electric motor used for the purpose of starting the engine, typically through a high ratio geared drive connected to the flywheel ring gear.

STEERING GEOMETRY: Combination of various angles of suspension components (caster, camber, toe-in); roughly equivalent to front end alignment.

STRAIGHT WEIGHT: Term designating motor oil as suitable for use within a narrow range of temperatures. Outside the narrow temperature range its flow characteristics will not adequately lubricate.

STROKE: The distance the piston travels from bottom dead center to top dead center.

SUPERCHARGER: An air pump driven mechanically by the engine through belts, chains, shafts or gears from the crankshaft. Two general types of supercharger are the positive displacement and centrifugal type, which pump air in direct relationship to the speed of the engine.

SUPPLEMENTAL RESTRAINT SYSTEM: See air bag.

SYNCHROMESH: A manual transmission that is equipped with devices (synchronizers) that match the gear speeds so that the transmission can be downshifted without clashing gears.

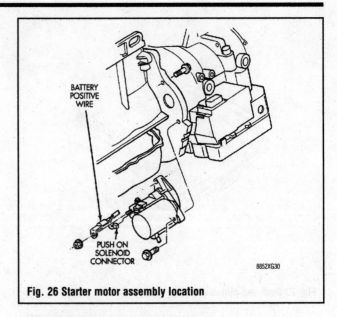

Fig. 26 Starter motor assembly location

SYNTHETIC OIL: Non-petroleum based oil.

TACHOMETER: A device used to measure the rotary speed of an engine, shaft, gear, etc., usually in rotations per minute.

TDC: Top dead center. The exact top of the piston's stroke.

THERMOSTAT: A valve, located in the cooling system of an engine, which is closed when cold and opens gradually in response to engine heating, controlling the temperature of the coolant and rate of coolant flow.

THROW-OUT BEARING: As the clutch pedal is depressed, the throwout bearing moves against the spring fingers of the pressure plate, forcing the pressure plate to disengage from the driven disc.

TIE ROD: A rod connecting the steering arms. Tie rods have threaded ends that are used to adjust toe-in.

TIMING BELT: A square-toothed, reinforced rubber belt that is driven by the crankshaft and operates the camshaft.

TIMING CHAIN: A roller chain that is driven by the crankshaft and operates the camshaft.

TIRE ROTATION: Moving the tires from one position to another to make the tires wear evenly.

TOE-IN (OUT): A term comparing the extreme front and rear of the front tires. Closer together at the front is toe-in; farther apart at the front is toe-out.

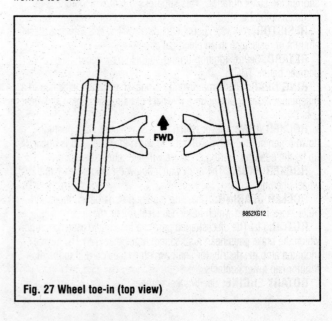

Fig. 27 Wheel toe-in (top view)

TOP DEAD CENTER (TDC): The point at which the piston reaches the top of its travel on the compression stroke.

TORQUE CONVERTER: A turbine used to transmit power from a driving member to a driven member via hydraulic action, providing changes in drive ratio and torque. In automotive use, it links the driveplate at the rear of the engine to the automatic transmission.

TORQUE: Measurement of turning or twisting force, expressed as foot-pounds or inch-pounds.

TORSION BAR SUSPENSION: Long rods of spring steel which take the place of springs. One end of the bar is anchored and the other arm (attached to the suspension) is free to twist. The bars' resistance to twisting causes springing action.

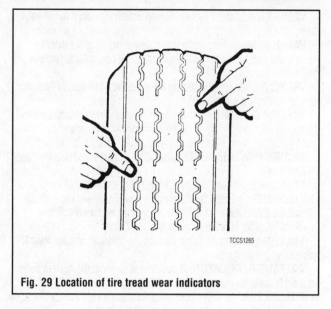

Fig. 29 Location of tire tread wear indicators

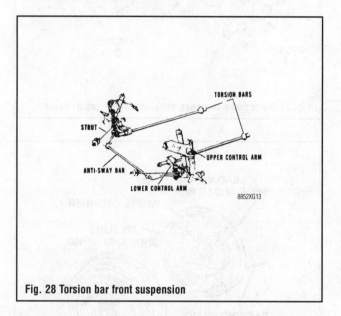

Fig. 28 Torsion bar front suspension

TRACK: Distance between the centers of the tires where they contact the ground.

TRACTION CONTROL: A control system that prevents the spinning of a vehicle's drive wheels when excess power is applied.

TRANSAXLE: A single housing containing the transmission and differential. Transaxles are usually found on front engine/front wheel drive or rear engine/rear wheel drive cars.

TRANSDUCER: A device used to change a force into an electrical signal.

TRANSFER CASE: A gearbox driven from the transmission that delivers power to both front and rear driveshafts in a four-wheel drive system. Transfer cases usually have a high and low range set of gears, used depending on how much pulling power is needed.

TRANSISTOR: A semi-conductor component which can be actuated by a small voltage to perform an electrical switching function.

TREAD WEAR INDICATOR: Bars molded into the tire at right angles to the tread that appear as horizontal bars when 1/16th in. of tread remains.

TREAD WEAR PATTERN: The pattern of wear on tires which can be "read" to diagnose problems in the front suspension.

TUNE-UP: A regular maintenance function, usually associated with the replacement and adjustment of parts and components in the electrical and fuel systems of a vehicle for the purpose of attaining optimum performance.

TURBOCHARGER: An exhaust driven pump which compresses intake air and forces it into the combustion chambers at higher than atmospheric pressures. The increased air pressure allows more fuel to be burned and results in increased horsepower being produced.

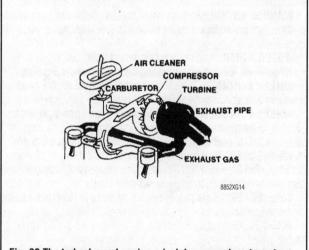

Fig. 30 The turbocharged engine principle uses exhaust gas to spin the turbocharger, increasing maximum engine power output

U-JOINT (UNIVERSAL JOINT): A flexible coupling in the drive train that allows the driveshafts or axle shafts to operate at different angles and still transmit rotary power.

UNDERSTEER: The tendency of a car to continue straight ahead while negotiating a turn.

UNIT BODY: Design in which the car body acts as the frame.

UNLEADED FUEL: Fuel which contains no lead (a common gasoline additive). The presence of lead in fuel will destroy the functioning elements of a catalytic converter, making it useless.

UNSPRUNG WEIGHT: The weight of car components not supported by the springs (wheels, tires, brakes, rear axle, control arms, etc.).

VACUUM ADVANCE: A device which advances the ignition timing in response to increased engine vacuum.

VACUUM GAUGE: An instrument used to measure the presence of vacuum in a chamber.

VALVE CLEARANCE: The measured gap between the end of the valve stem and the rocker arm, cam lobe or follower that activates the valve.

VALVE GUIDES: The guide through which the stem of the valve passes. The guide is designed to keep the valve in proper alignment.

VALVE LASH (clearance): The operating clearance in the valve train.

VALVE TRAIN: The system that operates intake and exhaust valves, consisting of camshaft, valves and springs, lifters, pushrods and rocker arms.

VALVE: A device which control the pressure, direction of flow or rate of flow of a liquid or gas.

VAPOR LOCK: Boiling of the fuel in the fuel lines due to excess heat. This will interfere with the flow of fuel in the lines and can completely stop the flow. Vapor lock normally only occurs in hot weather.

VARNISH: Term applied to the residue formed when gasoline gets old and stale.

VCM: See Electronic Control Unit (ECU).

VISCOSITY: The ability of a fluid to flow. The lower the viscosity rating, the easier the fluid will flow. 10 weight motor oil will flow much easier than 40 weight motor oil.

VOLT: Unit used to measure the force or pressure of electricity. It is defined as the pressure

VOLTAGE REGULATOR: A device that controls the current output of the alternator or generator.

VOLTMETER: An instrument used for measuring electrical force in units called volts. Voltmeters are always connected parallel with the circuit being tested.

WANKEL ENGINE: An engine which uses no pistons. In place of pistons, triangular-shaped rotors revolve in specially shaped housings.

WATER PUMP: A belt driven component of the cooling system that mounts on the engine, circulating the coolant under pressure.

WHEEL ALIGNMENT: Inclusive term to describe the front end geometry (caster, camber, toe-in/out).

WHEEL CYLINDER: Found in the automotive drum brake assembly, it is a device, actuated by hydraulic pressure, which, through internal pistons, pushes the brake shoes outward against the drums.

WHEEL WEIGHT: Small weights attached to the wheel to balance the wheel and tire assembly. Out-of-balance tires quickly wear out and also give erratic handling when installed on the front.

WHEELBASE: Distance between the center of front wheels and the center of rear wheels.

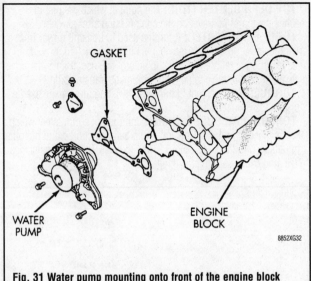

Fig. 31 Water pump mounting onto front of the engine block

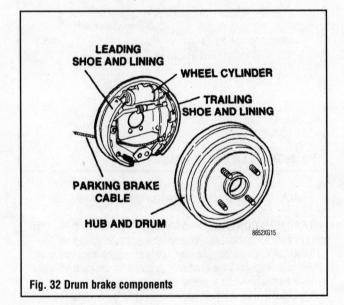

Fig. 32 Drum brake components

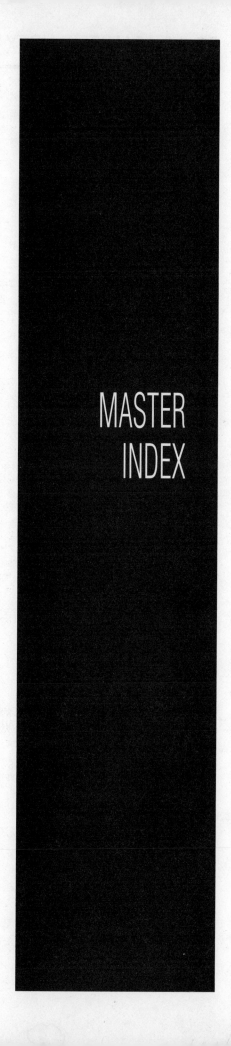

MASTER INDEX